FOOTPRINTS
INTO NEWPORT TOWNSHIP

REVEALING A HIDDEN HISTORY OF LIVES LIVED

Based on Settlers' Handwritten Diaries, Personal Letters, and Documents

Frederick Edmund[11] Hurd

Copyright © 2021 Frederick Edmund[11] Hurd

All rights reserved. All content, photographs, including those otherwise indicated, etc., contain source evidence that are copyrighted and/or trademarked by the respective organizations unless otherwise specified. Care has been taken to trace and ensure all pictures and prose subject to copyright ownership material used in this book has been noted; however, if any omission has occurred the publisher and author would welcome any information enabling them to rectify any references or credits in subsequent editions.

This book or parts thereof may not be reproduced in any form, stored, or introduced into a retrieval system, or transmitted in any form or by any means (electronic, mechanical, photocopying, recording or otherwise), without written permission of the copyright holder.
For information: hurdsfs@gmail.com

Front cover image: "Piste des Chevreuils" ("Deer trail" across the Eaton River), an original watercolour painting by Newport artist Denis Palmer

Cover script, front and back: Frederick and Sandra Hurd

Copy editing and layout: Jim Fraser

Published and printed in Canada

People, places, or incidents mentioned and/or information provided herein reflect solely the author's research drawn from original documents: military documents, diaries, letters, journals, magazines, the internet, and other related material serving to further collaborate the story and drive the narrative. The people in the story were and are real; the businesses established over many time periods are real; the events, stories within the story and locales reflect the periods in which they occurred.

This book was written, edited, and published by the author. The publisher assumes no responsibility for damages, direct or indirect, from publication of the included works. The work is included as provided by the author, views expressed are those of the author and any errors, omissions or otherwise are the author's responsibility.

ISBN: 978-1-7774594-0-6

Dedication

Dedicated to the memory of the adventurers, settlers, and the subsequent families of Newport, and to my father, Captain Edmund[10] Lionel Hurd. This book of "lives lived" has been made possible simply because Lionel had retained, kept intact and verified the authenticity of the hundreds of documents, letters, diaries and Heard/Hurd family histories that our ancestors cared enough about to preserve in writing. This allowed me the opportunity to share their past along with other family connections and tell their story for future generations to cherish.

Edmund[10] Lionel Hurd
(photo by Wendy K. Hurd, granddaughter)

This is their story.

Acknowledgements

A lesson I learned while on this book-writing journey is that writing a book of this nature requires a tremendous amount of research and help from family and friends. My heartfelt thanks go out to every single person who has contributed material that has enhanced the overall content to make the story both credible and entertaining. I gratefully acknowledge input from other authors from whom I sought counsel. These were people who have written and successfully taken their own manuscripts to publication and who have readily shared their own writing experiences.

First and foremost, I want to thank my wife, Sandra, my soulmate, best friend, mentor, and wordsmith editor for her ever-enduring patience with me during a long process of research, verifications, fact-checking, and document scanning throughout this process. Her many valid contributions were important in keeping me on track. My life and work have been enriched by her love, her skill sets and her continuous support. Sandra's ancestors were/are also woven into this history in the settling of both Eaton and Newport townships. I am deeply indebted to Sandra for her perseverance and understanding during the long days of research and writing when I was ensconced in the basement of our house for hours on end, oblivious to all things around me. To Sandra, my deepest appreciation for her steadfast support through the many edits and multiple discussions that took place throughout the writing process, an exercise in pure love, I am sure. If I had any thoughts that this might be a good book, then Sandra's work and input has made it a "great book."

Special thanks also to Carol Rand, who reviewed the manuscript based on her love of history and specifically her passion for Newport Township and surrounding region. Many of Carol's questions, that perhaps a reader might also ask, stimulated more research which has enhanced the readability of the material and captured the essence of the story. Carol also graciously shared her family genealogy on both sides of her family as well as her grandmother's diaries which provided an intimate peek into lives lived in the 1920s right through to the 1960s. Carol also has a vested interest in the contents because she is also a descendant of the first settler in Newport Township, Colonel Edmund[5] Heard, as well as a descendant of Randboro's founders.

My appreciation to the many people who have contributed to the stories, photographs and historical material collected by their own families over many years – people such as but not limited to Nina Rowell and Nellie A. Parsons, who compiled historical journals of memories and their own personal thoughts from which the writer could draw. These were personal diaries and vignettes that brought life to a story.

A special thanks to the late Ruth (Burns) Morrow (Mrs. Kenneth Morrow, 1910-1996) who authored *Island Brook: Then and Now*, the history surrounding Island Brook. Ruth was a contributor to the community, an educator, an historian and a staunch supporter of Newport. Thanks to Geraldine (Morrow) Macaulay for her 1995 rewrite of this booklet, from which much material was drawn.

Thanks to Nina (Parsons) Rowell for her story of "Knicky Knocky," for bringing real live history to enhance the story of "lives lived" in Newport. Also, for Nina's participation in compiling the booklet *A Treasury of Historical Articles*, featuring articles written by her mother, Mrs. George Parsons (Nellie A. Parsons) over many years and published in the *Sherbrooke Daily Record*.

The late Edith (Morrison) Rand complied copious daily notes in her diaries from 1922 to 1968. Edith's work was invaluable in telling this story simply because her recording of everyday facts allowed connections to be made with other families and verified timelines of their lives and events. I am grateful to have been able to draw from Edith's diaries. She took time from her busy life to recall her personal memories and stories of her own ancestry and to document them.

My thanks to our first readers, Carol Rand, Linda Ranta and Ilah Batley, for their excellent and valuable feedback, suggestions and comments.

This book could not have been written were it not for the efforts of the following:

- Jim Fraser for copy editing and layout. There are insufficient words to describe the appreciation for Jim's work, a partner in the cause of accurate history. Jim's diligence was superb in ensuring every entry was accurate. Coupled with his tenacity, patience, support and encouragement, his skills were instrumental in dealing with a novice author who was trying to write and deliver a book.

- Winston Fraser for his tips, guidance, and sharing his own publishing experiences with novices in this field.

- Eric French for his family memories and the French families' genealogy that his cousin Linda (French) Oliveras generously put together.

- Carolyn (Grapes) Graham for her extensive genealogy on the Graham and Jones families of Parker Hill and Randboro.

- Ilah Westgate for her extensive material on the Westgate and Painter family connections and her continual encouragement.

- Robert Burns who provided his family connections along with supportive material on Island Brook and environs and for the many hours of telephone collaboration and encouragement.

- Donna (Morrow) and Thead Hodge, Lydia Statton, Robert Tetreault, Bert Drouin and Rodney Hillman for their contribution both of family history as well as many other tidbits of information that have given the book additional value in its scope.

- The Hurd families: my father Lionel; brother Jim Hurd; cousins John, Judy (Hurd) (Jolliffe) Bernard, Peter Hurd, Elizabeth (Hurd) Richardson; Malcolm Hurd; Gillian (Hurd) Anderson; and Mary-Hurd Lawson of Baltimore, Md. who shared a one-year diary of lives lived compiled by her great-grandfather, Edmund Haskell Hurd in 1875, with a multitude of letters written between the families then living in Canada and the U.S.A.

- Florence (Bowker) McVetty in her compilation on the Bowker family history from the early 1600s to the current families still living in Newport who are carrying on the tradition. Florence headed up a committee dedicated to organizing the Sawyerville School Reunion in 1994 that compiled historical information, some of which helped bridge some gaps in this story line. The committee encompassed many of the people who can claim they are indeed direct descendants of original settlers and a part of this book. Thanks to Bert Drouin for providing the Bowker family material that Florence Bowker had compiled.

- The McCallum family for sharing excerpts from the memoirs of Ernest C. McCallum who took time to write about his early life in Randboro, enhancing the story line and giving a reader a glimpse into real history.

- Shirley Loveland and her second cousin Raymond Loveland, who shared the early history of the Loveland family in Newport.

- Malcolm Burns, President of the Newport Homecoming committee, 1996, and his committee for assembling a pictorial tribute to the history of Newport Homecoming (1801-1996) from which so many pictures were drawn.

- Edward W. Hanson is also a Heard/Hurd descendant from Edmund[1] Heard's younger son, Nathaniel. We were able to contact Ed in London, England, where he currently lives. Ed received his B.A. at Salem State College, Salem, Mass. cum laude in 1973, majoring in history. He received his M.A. at Tufts University in Massachusetts; his 1986 thesis was titled "*John Heard of Ipswich, Massachusetts: An Analysis of Family Contribution Toward Individual Development.*" During this time in Boston, Ed began and compiled an extensive Heard/Hurd genealogy, the family of his paternal grandmother. His thesis covers the period from 1600, tracks the immigration of a family from Great Britain to the New England colonies, as well as the family branch that immigrated to Lower Canada in 1793. Ed completed his Ph.D. at Boston College, Massachusetts, in 1992, also in American history. He has very graciously sent me his Heard/Hurd Genealogy. His work does not pretend to be a complete genealogy; however, it is a most comprehensive accounting of over 4,000 direct descendants. It attempts to trace all descendants of our immigrant ancestors through both male and female lines rather than just following the male descent. As such it is a more accurate indication of the true spreading-out of a family. This was important in writing any story associated with Newport since many of the female descendants married other settlers whose names are as much a part of the Heard/Hurd and Newport "story" as any other. It also serves to make the narrative more understandable. It also includes a partial emigration of the same ancestors from the New England Colonies into Lower Canada before Confederation, specifically to settle Newport beginning in 1793. From his extensive work, I have been able to follow a chronological sequence of materials that greatly enhanced the mechanics of the book. Ed's genealogical endeavours consumed a great deal of time, travel and money and he has expressed his generous desire that *"the products of this work be shared and made available for our extended family to cherish for the foreseeable future generations."*

I am thankful to the many ancestors who kept the hundreds of documents, historical letters and personal letters written throughout each era of over 300 years, along with newspaper clippings, that have made it possible to tell the personal stories of how our ancestors lived their lives. While historical facts can be researched through articles, biographies and archives, the real flavour and culture of any given era only comes from the people who lived it. The material that the author has written reflects on the many people who have inspired and encouraged my efforts. To them and their families I offer my sincere thanks.

I was encouraged by the support of our many Probus friends; in particular, the late Marv McCabe, a friend and avid historian in Gravenhurst, who was my mentor and who encouraged me to stick with it. When I first talked about the many artifacts, documents and personal letters we had, he reacted with "It sounds like a book."

Without the valuable information I was able to garner from other published books, unpublished journals and articles, and their authors, this book would not have the verifications necessary to ensure its validity in an historical sense.

Table of Contents

Dedication 5

Acknowledgements 6

Table of Contents 9

Introduction 11

Prologue 15

    PART ONE   Settling the Waste Lands of Lower Canada 21

Chapter 1   Creation of a Borderline 25

Chapter 2   Exploration 33

Chapter 3   Early Settlers 43

Chapter 4   Survival 47

Chapter 5   Back in Time 63

Chapter 6   Migration from the South 79

Chapter 7   Invaders from the South 103

Chapter 8   Settling In 107

Chapter 9   Progress and Family Connections 141

Chapter 10   Expansion and New Connections 175

    PART TWO   The Diaries and the Letters 199

Chapter 11   Growth in Newport 201

Chapter 12   Families We Knew 239

Chapter 13   Uncertain Times 263

Chapter 14   A Changing World 291

Chapter 15   The Winds of War 323

Chapter 16   Post-war Newport 345

Chapter 17   The Idyllic Years 359

Chapter 18   Reflections 373

Epilogue 387

Appendix: Genealogy Charts 391

Reference Materials 403

Introduction

Footprints into Newport was compiled and written by Frederick Edmund[11] Hurd, a direct-line descendant of Colonel Edmund[5] Heard and Captain Josiah[4] Sawyer, the first settlers of Newport Township, Compton County, Quebec. It is intended as a tribute to the "lives lived" by our ancestors . . . a story that brings the "dash" to life . . . the "dash" that represents real lives but sits quietly on the tombstones between the dates. The settlers developed survival tools based on the only natural resources available to them: water, virgin forest wood and abundant wildlife. This story captures their innovative, resourceful spirit and the resilience demonstrated with each generation's own determination to survive.

When my father, Captain Edmund[10] Hurd, died, I inherited numerous boxes of historical material and artifacts. At the time, my career led me to simply put them into safe storage for "another time." During subsequent years, I would lift a box lid, again become overwhelmed with the box's contents, and replace the lid. After exploring the contents more thoroughly one day, I recognized the historical value inherent, not only for our own family but for others as well. Those connected in some way to Newport and the surrounding townships could likely be curious about these important pieces of the past. It appears that a thirst continues for the history of the Quebec's Eastern Townships. This is not just a story about history or genealogy . . . it is about the connection people have with places that hold special meaning. I also recognized that my own family could likely follow a similar path of putting off dealing with these papers for "another time." Eventually these boxes might simply disappear – a "hidden history" would be possibly lost forever. I am neither a writer nor an historian, but the need to document this insight into the lives of these early settlers for future generations was compelling. I am uncomfortable with the term "author" simply because this compilation in book form is derived from such a variety of sources (facts, stories, letters, diaries) that it should be likened to a quilt. In describing Newport, like a quilt made up of parallel lines, this story of one township reflects the unfolding of all the other Eastern Townships during their developing years.

My earliest motivation was when I started to write a letter to my granddaughter to share my story of growing up on the farm in Newport. I felt it also important to share with her the stories my father and grandparents had told me about their lives when they were growing up. I soon realized I had so much more to tell when I began looking through my grandmother's and then her ancestors' letters, diaries, and documents. This was going to be more than just a letter; it would be a book. As the story began to unfold, I felt I was living with them in their times, like finding an old friend you had not seen since childhood, and I knew then I would need to preserve and share this story not only with my granddaughter, but also with a broader group of potential readers.

Another key motivation was that this material is comprised of handwritten documents, letters, diaries, artifacts and military information carried down by generations from as early as 1634 in the New England Colonies, and carried into the settling of Newport, Lower Canada, from as early as 1793 to the late 1950s. Based on the breadth of information available to me and upon discovering that some of this material is indeed "hidden history," I believed it also important to preserve a small segment of English history for at least one of Quebec's Eastern Townships.

My intent was to create and weave the various document contents into a story in book form that would demonstrate a more intimate understanding of what these early settlers and their subsequent descendants' lives were all about. The story follows several families whose association became intermingled, either through business dealings, civic duties, marriage or in other general activities occurring throughout many decades of residence in Newport Township. The concept of "lives lived" in Newport, Lower Canada, was born. And so, the story began with a background of circumstances that were to change the course of history.

An original book titled *Newport first Records* containing 76 pages of handwritten records, from 1791 to 1814, provided an excellent start. This information allowed insight into how these early settlers conducted their decision-making processes in the business of road building, lot allocations, common lands set aside for church, first school subscriptions, first cemetery allocation and the first mill location. Also identified were subscriptions taken by the settlers to provide labour or produce to trade and/or in-kind for the process of building these entities.

Examining the original *Surveyors Field Book of 1799* and transcribing each 200-acre lot onto a current map of Newport allowed an accurate view of the lot locations. Newport Township, circa 1799, consisted of 100 square miles, containing 308 lots, in 11 ranges. Two men, Col. Edmund[5] Heard and Asa Waters, paid for the survey and were the authorizing signatories. Edmund, as "Leader" of one group of "Associates," was assigned one-quarter of the township for himself, his family, and his group of Associates. This enabled me to identify where exactly each family settled from 1794 to 1810.

***

To sort hundreds of documents relating to settling Newport Township was immense. Documents related to travel to the Judicial Court in Three Rivers (known today as Trois-Rivières), and many other legal formalities in the running of the township are included. These various military and business documents allowed me to weave together their story of simple survival in a harsh land while they simultaneously stood ready to defend their families and their new land in a military sense.

The next huge task was to sort hundreds of personal letters dating from 1794 to 1945, depicting their dreams, sorrows, marriages, children, sicknesses, and their lives in general. Diaries from 1875 to 1945 depict many years of interaction between the settling and subsequent families of Newport. From these letters and diaries, I have been able to determine sequences of events, timelines and how the people of Newport associated and worked within their communities, progressing through each generation within various time frames, beginning in 1793 and ending in the mid-1950s.

Many published books about the region have been referenced and positioned, when needed, to drive the narrative, with these references providing verification. Included are excerpts from unpublished journals written by local people, as well as stories drawn from their diaries and carried down by generations. Many Newporter's who preserved historical family background information provided additional details relating to their own families' stories, incorporating another trove of evidence. Many others have provided invaluable anecdotes, quotes and stories that add both humour and validity.

During the summer of 2019, my wife, Sandra, and I visited many towns in the original New England Colonies referenced in the various documents and personal letters. We wanted to experience the culture of these towns and the landscape where these ancestors had lived and worked. We visited historical sites and gathered information on the Heards of Ipswich, Mass., so we could provide a chapter carrying the story back in time to understand their origins in the New England Colonies. We arranged for a private tour of the Heard House Museum in Ipswich, and garnered further details of their lifestyles for inclusion in the book. I devoted a chapter to their lives and the lives of others during the time frame of 1634-1793, the period of immigrating and settling the New England Colonies prior to when a branch of these settlers began to move north into Lower Canada. Although the source of these documents is history that has been preserved by the Heard families, many other names we recognize within the story of Newport are also prevalent as originating from the Ipswich region, as well as from many towns in the New England states located between Boston and Newport. I am extremely thankful to the many descendants who shared their family histories to be incorporated into this story.

We toured the roads and many regions of New Hampshire, Vermont, and Massachusetts to get a sense for the topography that our Newport ancestors would have experienced, weaving through the mountains and riverbeds during their many early travels, back and forth by horse and ox carts. We travelled through the former "Republic of Indian Stream," an expanse comprised of the Connecticut and Francis lakes, now known as Pittsburg, N.H. This region was a common travel route for our ancestors. We arrived in Chartierville, Que., drove through the same woods as our ancestors had plied their ox carts to arrive at theirs, and arrived at my own ancestral homestead in the original community of Maple Leaf.

Another compelling reason for my interest in telling the story is that I grew up in the original house in Newport Township, built in 1793 by Col. Edmund[5] Heard and his family. The house and farmland were occupied for over 200 years on a continuous basis by the Heard/Hurd families, me included. It is hard to believe I was able to sit in the living room of the original homestead built by Col. Edmund Heard in 1794-95, drafting the manuscript for this book. This whole experience is reflected within different time frames in the book. The house is now designated as a Quebec

Heritage site. It was on this farm that I spent my young years growing up with my father, Capt. Edmund[10] Lionel Hurd, a direct descendant of both Col. Edmund[5] Heard and Capt. Josiah[4] Sawyer. The house as it stands today is a testament to the determination of the new United Empire Loyalist (UEL) settlement, people seeking refuge from the Patriots in the New England states immediately south of Newport.

Maple Leaf Cemetery, also a first in Newport, is located on today's Route 210, a mile east of Randboro and adjacent to the original farm settled by our ancestors.

During our week in Newport, we visited many of the descendants associated with these first settlers. With family and friends still living there, we travelled every road in Newport. Stories were told, pictures taken, and historical sites visited, including one of the last remaining covered bridges. We learned about "ships knees," a term associated with building covered bridges. This piqued our curiosity as to how and why the building of ships and bridges were related. This is explained later in the book.

The author, in his ancestral home, drafting the manuscript, 2019 (photo by Sandra Hurd)

In telling this story, I have concentrated on six known original and extended settler families. All have connections with the Heard/Hurd families, based on the historical manuscripts. This book reveals who they were, where they came from, why they chose this land despite vast obstacles, and their struggles to survive while settling the "waste lands of the Crown."

To provide a structure, I blended Ed Hanson's professional and comprehensive genealogy package of the Heard/Hurd family, which includes the Sawyer, Rand, Planche, French and Bowker families and their descendants, as well as many other settlers.

***

Today, a visitor to the Newport region or a current resident may see things differently than the author remembers them from growing up there, but it is still the same place, with stories connected to every single home. The quaint storybook towns of Randboro, Island Brook, and St. Mathias remain pieces of the past, romantic in their old age, even charming in their changes, new buildings replacing old; except nothing is made up, everything is real, and all of it represents our history.

If there is a message in this story, it is to our grandchildren and great-grandchildren: to value history and embrace it as their own. We not only learn from it, but it is also part of our DNA – it is who we are.

A typical abandoned heritage home, this one on the original settler's route near the Quebec–New Hampshire border in the former Republic of Indian Stream (photo by Sandra Hurd)

***

It is my hope that some readers may discover something of their past that perhaps will be special to them individually. It is like going home to a place we came from, even if we did not live there; our ancestors left an indelible footprint wherever they settled.[24]

I have mentioned "we" several times; my wife, Sandra, has worked with me throughout this journey. She also is a direct descendant of the Heard "Leader and Associate" pioneers who settled Newport in 1793.

Weaving the information found in these documents into a story format was much more complicated than I would have imagined or even anticipated. Once started, however, I felt compelled to learn more and document much of it.

A heartfelt "thank you" goes to so many of the descendants who have shared countless previously unpublished stories that exist within their families, as well as their own genealogy – all shared to enhance this book and its anthology component. Many of these donors are recognized as the story unfolds.

Author's notes:
- *Text and photographs (except where noted) are based on the Ancestral Heard/Hurd Collection that contains the Newport first Records, military documents, Heard/Hurd genealogy documents, letters, personal dairies, photos, and other Heard/Hurd manuscripts.*
- *Much of the general dialogue has originated from a combination of the above Heard/Hurd Collection, as well as unpublished submissions of diaries and documentation from existing descendants of Newport families. The authors imagination, where necessary, was used to drive the narrative.*
- *Monotype Corsiva font has been used when applying the direct words quoted from the documents and letters found in the Ancestral Heard/Hurd Collection.*
- *Book titles, author's notes and/or comments are in Italics.*
- *References are listed at the end of this book.*
- *A selection of family genealogy charts and family connections are also listed at the end of the book.*
- *The story has been limited as much as possible to Newport Township and its people. Because the townships were so interconnected, there will be overlaps spilling into adjacent regions.*
- *To help differentiate the many family members with the same first names from one generation to the next I am using a numbering system. For example, Capt. Josiah^4 Sawyer and his wife Susanna had a son Josiah^5 and a daughter Susanna^5, all of whom I identify accordingly. During my research I found improper references to an event, using a name that one might assume to be a certain generation; but in fact was from a generation beyond, or sometimes even two.*

Prologue

They came on a dream. In the spring of 1793, two entrepreneurial men, Colonel Edmund[5] Heard and Captain Josiah[4] Sawyer, embarked on a journey to explore the "waste lands of Lower Canada," leaving behind the unsettled and hostile environment for them and their families that existed in New England in the newly formed United States of America. They were to begin an adventurous journey from Massachusetts to a "land of promise," finding both refuge and the beginnings of a new life in a new land. With only a compass for their guide, an axe in their hands and a rifle for protection, they headed out into the vast, nearly unbroken wilderness that extended from the original New England Colonies of British America north to the outpost of Montreal. From there, these two adventurers would follow a "spotted" trail to Quebec City to apply for land grants – for land not yet witnessed with their own eyes.

They travelled on horseback through the broad expanse of virgin forest, known as the Green Mountains, between them and their destination, experiencing stunning vistas over hills and valleys, unscarred and as perfect as when formed by the great Creator. Their only company were the songs of birds, the drumming partridge, the stag's call, the cougar's screech and all the varied sounds of its teeming avenues. The distant loon's cry, the sudden noise of the startled ducks escaping from the intruder, the splash of the fish "lunging" and rising to the surface: all captivated the senses of the horses and their riders as they plied their industrious way through the wilderness during those early eventful days.

***

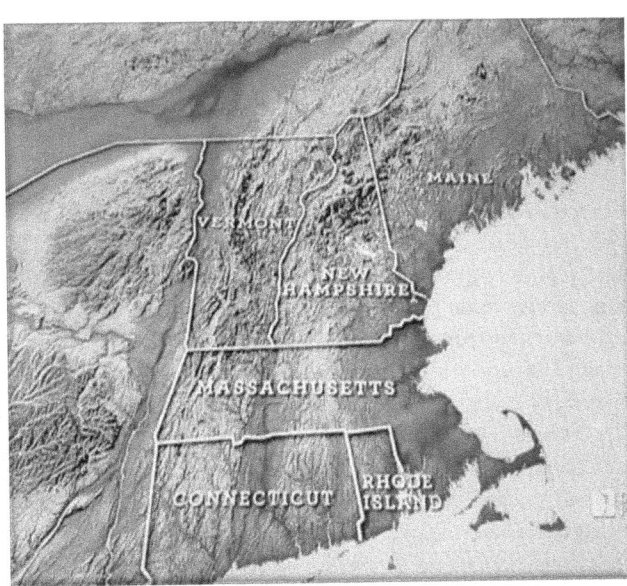

The New England Colonies (unknown Internet source)

If one passes through the current states of New Hampshire and Vermont, the small communities that still exist, like Beecher Falls, Derby Line, Norton, Pittsburg, Canaan, Colebrook, Lancaster, and West Stewartstown, all clustered about Quebec's southeastern corner, one might develop a deeper appreciation of the hardships endured by these early settlers as they travelled through these regions seeking a new life in a new country.

When the War of Independence started and the British began losing colonies to the "Patriots," the British concentrated their efforts on Upper Canada and Lower Canada and essentially initiated the same methodology for land grants as was used in settling the New England Colonies. In this same way, they began to attract those loyal to the Crown to move north to the "waste lands of Lower Canada."

In his book *History of Compton County*, compiled and printed in 1896, Leonard S. Channell writes, "Since the British had already lost 13 Colonies, they were not about to lose their most Northern lands that they had fought for and won from the French."[16] These land grants would oblige the military men and their Associates to defend the British interest in these new lands called Upper Canada and Lower Canada. Under the hand and seal of Robert Shore Milnes, Baronet, Lieutenant Governor, a warrant would be issued for the survey of a tract of land bounded north by Bury, east by Ditton, south by Auckland and west by Eaton.

***

Discover a fascinating "hidden history" of "lives lived," a documented history that was safeguarded and preserved by our ancestors. Many had suffered great losses from the political transitions experienced while living in the New England Colonies. Their homesteads and records had been burned, some even chased by bounty hunters. They were prepared to defend their loyalties, their families, and their lands, with their undying penchant in upholding the order of law. They would find themselves keeping the records of their activities in these new lands, during an ever-growing environment of governmental uncertainties with mounting pressures from the French to the north, the First Nations taking sides, and the U.S. Patriots to the south.

These small settlements and communities within and surrounding Newport Township still retain traces of their first United Empire Loyalist, Scottish and Irish settlers. Travel with the author through this journey in just one of the Eastern Townships of Quebec and you will discover a unique culture with some well-kept secrets.

This is a story of capturing the human side of subduing the forest, harnessing the streams, and battling the brutal winters, giving a reader a valuable inside portrait of an intriguing piece of Canadian history. The story of a small number of families that settled in Newport Township, beginning in 1793, will help to deepen our understanding of how they lived and worked to survive in these small settlements, which over time burgeoned into thriving communities. These were and are the people who were engaged from the beginning of the settlement, who demonstrated an unbroken line of family connections to the present day. Each of them individually, their subsequent families, and ancestors have left their indelible footprint on these small farming communities in the current Municipality of Newport.

They have many stories to tell, surrounding a long history of settlement and culture. The key industries were lumber, grist, clapboard and shingle mills, initiated by these early settlers, expanded, and operated in different parts of the North and South branches of the Eaton River (commonly known as simply North River and South River). A large section of the east-end of Newport is still well-timbered even today. The story begins in the southwest in the late 1790s and moves later into the northwest section, settled primarily during the 1800s and 1900s, with fertile farms and progressive farmers. This is the real story of the common men and women, the pioneers who laid the foundation for our modern world.

The following is a partial excerpt from a 76-page Minute Book (from the hidden history records) titled *"Newport first Records 1800, Province of Lower Canada"*:

> *And whereas the Executive Council of the said Province having duly & maturely considered the said petition have thereof in part approved & have adjudges it to be reasonable & advisable that one quarter of the said tract or parcel of land so situate as aforesaid should be granted unto the said Edmund Heard & his said Associates & his and their heirs and assigns forever upon the terms & conditions prescribed by His Majesty's Royal Instructions in this behalf. Now therefore having taken the premises into consideration by this Warrant of Survey, I do empower & require you at the proper costs & charges of the said Edmund Heard & his Associates to make a faithful & exact Survey of the said tract or parcel of land described as above set forth to be hereafter known and distinguished by the name of the Township of Newport, and to subdivide the said Township into lots of Two Hundred Acres each & in the execution of this Warrant. I do require you & command you to lay out the said Township of Newport conformably to his Majesty's Royal Instructions in this behalf that is to say of the dimensions of Ten Miles Square as nearly as circumstances shall admit provided the said Township of Newport be not intersected by nor be situate upon any Navigable River or Water & of the dimensions of Nine Miles in front by Twelve Miles in Depth of the said Township.*
>
> *Given under my Hand & Seal at Arms at the Castle of St. Louis in the City of Quebec in the said Province of Lower Canada the 25th Day of September in the year of our Lord One Thousand Eight Hundred & in the Fortieth Year of His Majesty's Reign.*
> *By His Excellency's Command* [20] *(Ancestral Heard/Hurd Collection)*

The undertaking for the warrant to survey the township was initiated by Col. Edmund[5] Heard and Asa Waters at his home in Vermont, by notification on September 28, 1798, and was probably the first public meeting of any kind held on behalf of the newly forming Eastern Townships of Lower Canada. On March 8, 1799, the survey was arranged and paid for by Col. Edmund[5] Heard and Asa Waters. The undertaking was authorized on March 9, to commence on March 10, 1799, as evidenced by their signatories in a handwritten surveyor *"Field Book for the Township of Newport in the Province of Lower Canada, made 8th March 1799."*[20]

***

Amongst the artifacts in the Ancestral Heard/Hurd Collection was a book inscribed inside the front cover "Edmund Heard Property." From the book titled *The Massachusetts Justice: Being a Collection of the Laws of the Commonwealth of Massachusetts*, Edmund would draw the guidelines for all settlements, both to deal with any legal digressions and to guide with the establishment of laws. Clearly this was an indication of organized business-minded people with ethics and values as well as a strong interest in the value of laws. As leader, Edmund had later acquired this Second Edition, issued in 1802, with the reference on the back page stating: "The Laws of the United States of America, from the establishment of the Federal Government to the end of the Sixth Congress, which terminated with the Presidency of Mr. Adams, with the Constitution, Amendments, Treaties etc. in their proper places."

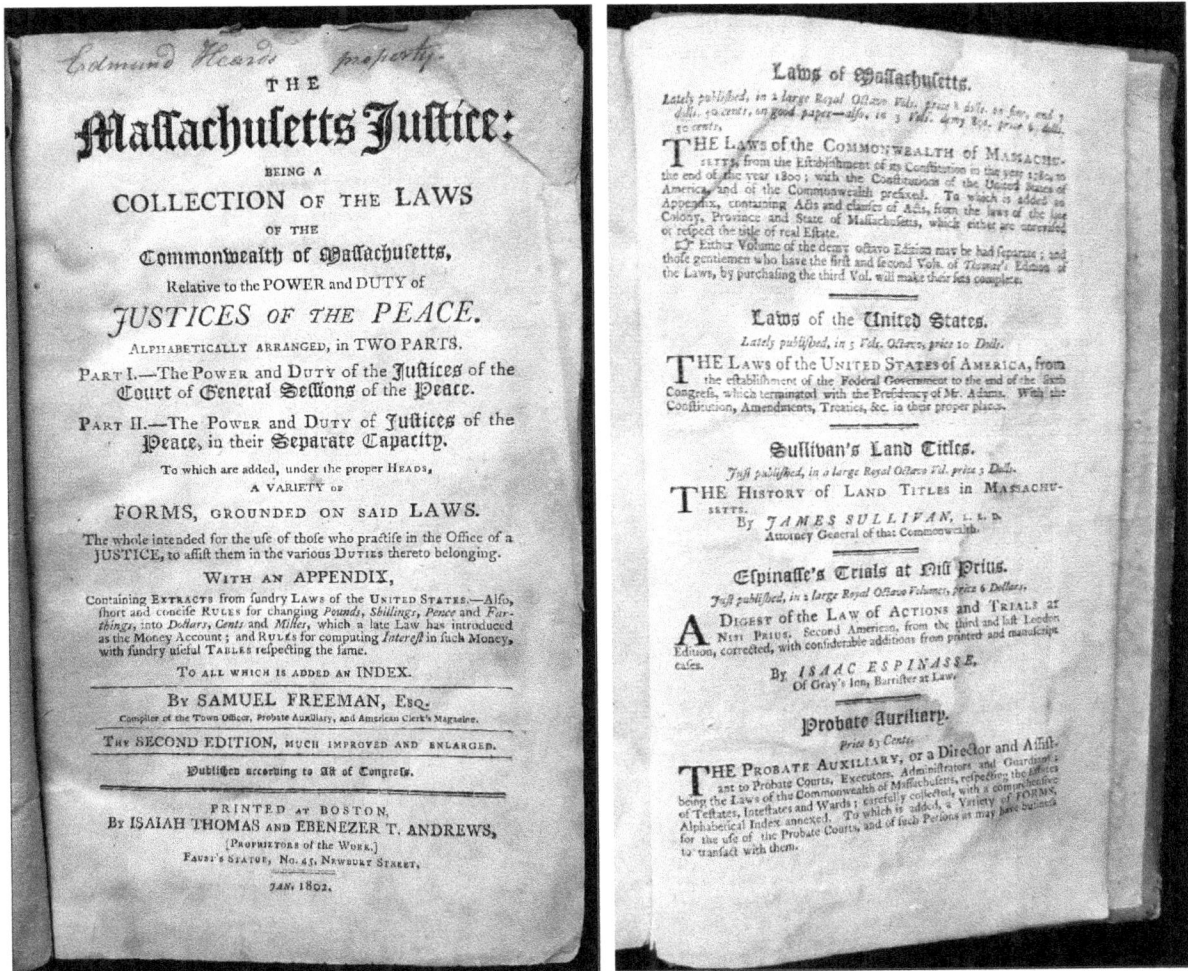

The Massachusetts Justice, front and back pages

[Although settlement started in 1793], The municipality of the Township of Newport was founded in 1801. In spite of strong opposition, it merged with Cookshire-Eaton on January 1, 2003, but regained its autonomy on January 1, 2006. However, the Quebec department of municipal affairs and regions categorically refused to allow it to use the term "township" in its name, so it became the Municipality of Newport. The sectors that make up the municipality include Island Brook, Lawrence, Randboro and Saint-Mathias-de-Bonneterre. The St. Lawrence Anglican Church, built in 1940, reminds us of the colonial period. Residents mainly work in agriculture and forestry, with some working in neighbouring villages. It's worth noting that the municipality of Newport is the region's last and only municipality to have preserved its original surface area of 10 miles by 10 miles [containing 61,600 acres]. *(www.easterntownships.org/towns-and-villages/56/newport)*

***

Author's note: I have included the map below to give the reader a better understanding of Lower Canada in 1792. Note that all the townships are indicated in English. One can clearly see the earlier French-speaking settler "Seigneuries of 1733" that surrounded the "Eastern Townships" of the period. The townships of 1792 came under the umbrella of Buckinghamshire County, the name used in all pre-Confederation military communication. A reader may wish to refer to this map for the various locations referenced in the book's contents.[3]

The portion of Quebec that lies south of the St. Lawrence River and was unconceded at the time of the British Conquest of New France in 1760 is classed as the Eastern Townships. During the French era, and for at least 10 years subsequent, it was a vast wilderness covered with forest untrodden by any but First Nations peoples. The British Government maintained French laws but did not adopt the French system of settlement. They preferred their own colonial system, and this unconceded part of the province was laid out in the same manner as the lands in Upper Canada.[16]

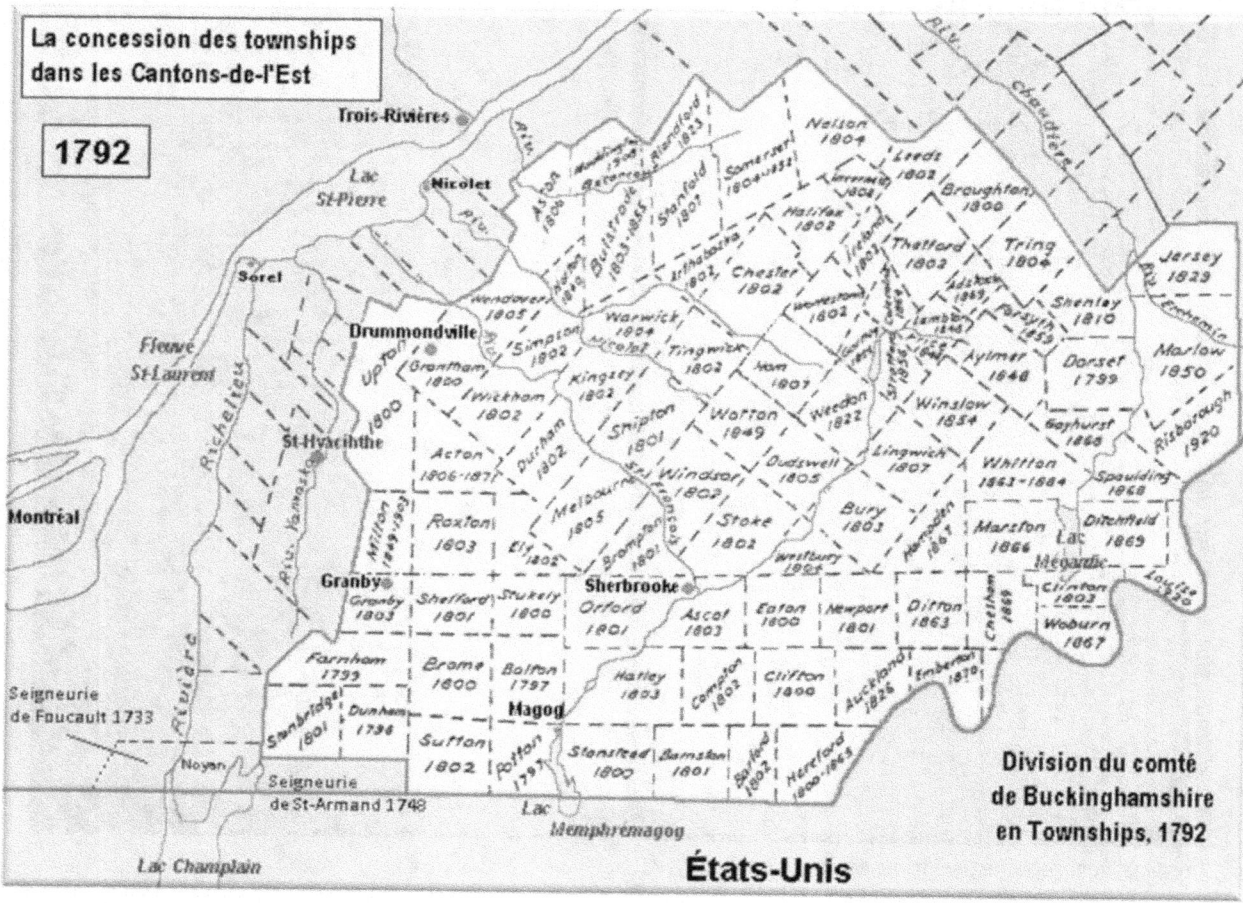

The division of the County of Buckinghamshire into townships, 1792 (Eastern Townships Roots Facebook page)

Field Book for the Township of Newport in the Province of Lower Canada
The first official survey by Christopher S. Bailey of Leamington, Vt.
Beginning March 10, 1799

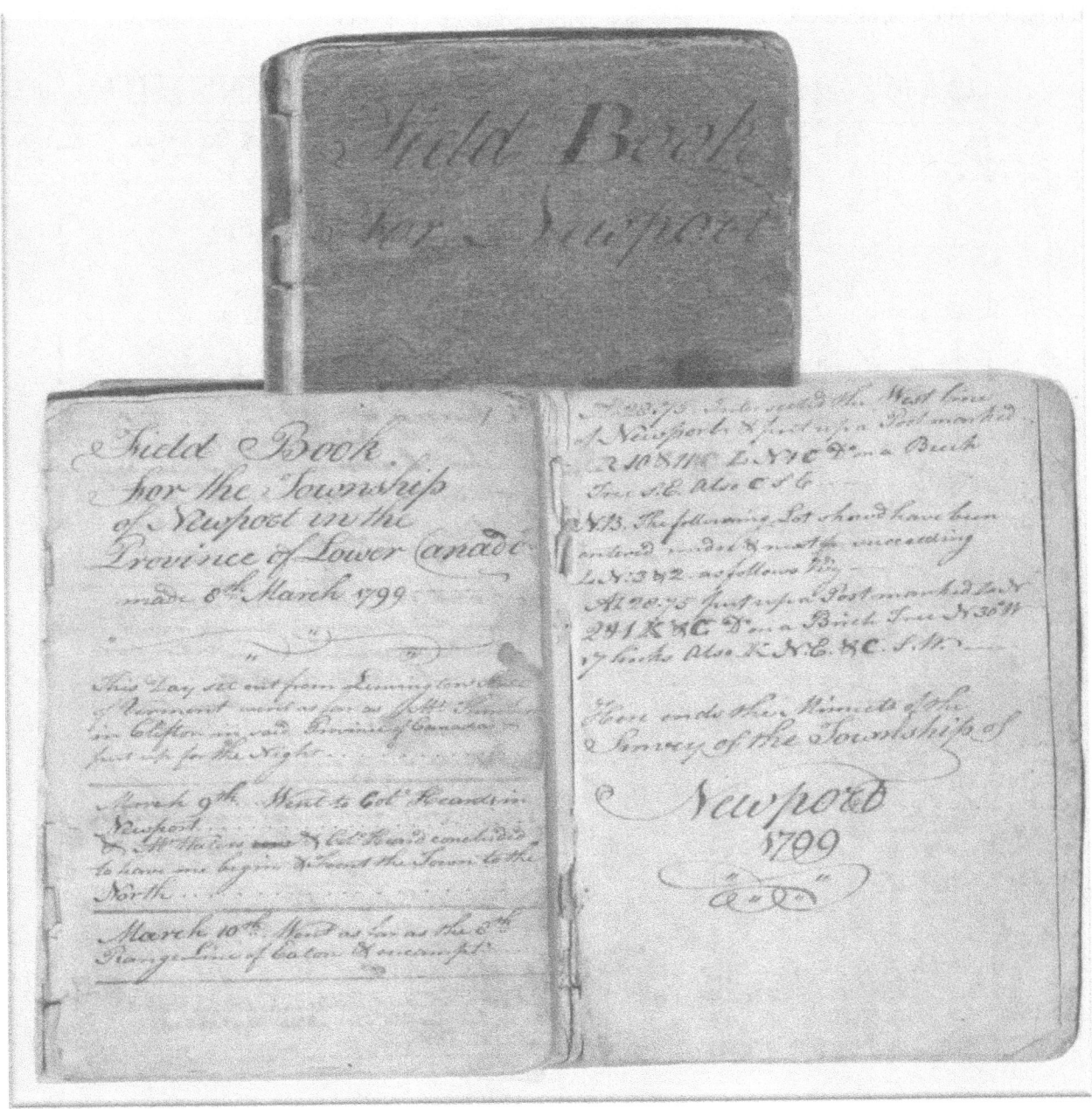

Field Book for Newport showing the cover, first and last pages of the surveyor's handwritten string-bound booklet

A current map of the "Municipality of Newport" shows the original survey lots overlaid on the map as the land grants were identified and distributed from 1793 through to 1810. Newport Township consists of 100 square miles. This map shows 308 lots, each of 200 acres, across 11 ranges. Lot reference numbers have been applied to the edges of this map to provide the reader with a general idea of where the original settlers and their descendants were living during different eras, as described in the various chapters throughout this book.[28]

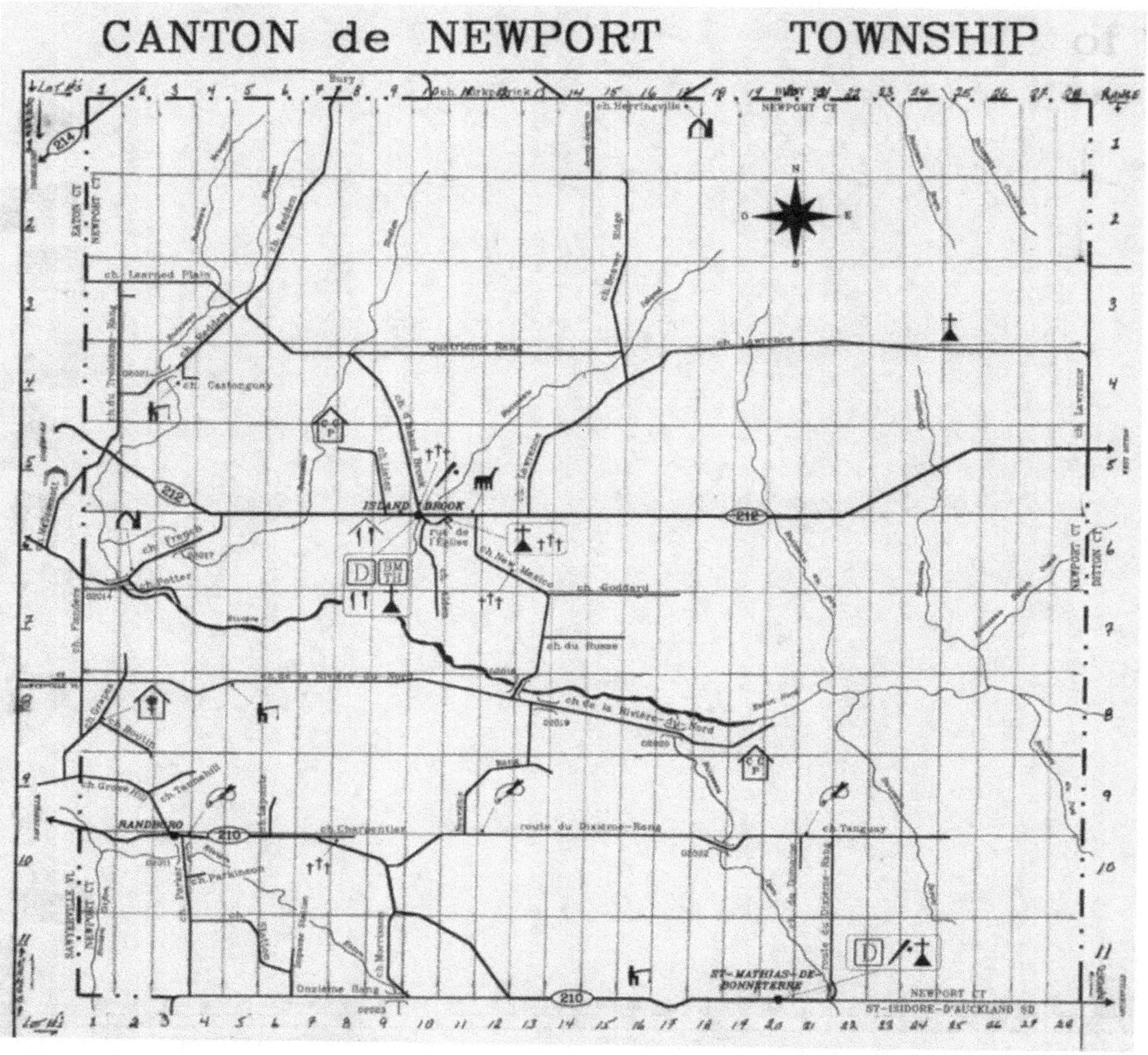

Map of Newport Township with lot and range references, 1995 (original map by Rene Roy)

***

Sign paintings by Newport artist Denis Palmer

Route 212 Island Brook

Lawrence Colony

Auckland corner

Route 210 Randboro

PART ONE
Settling the Waste Lands of Lower Canada
The Documents and Records

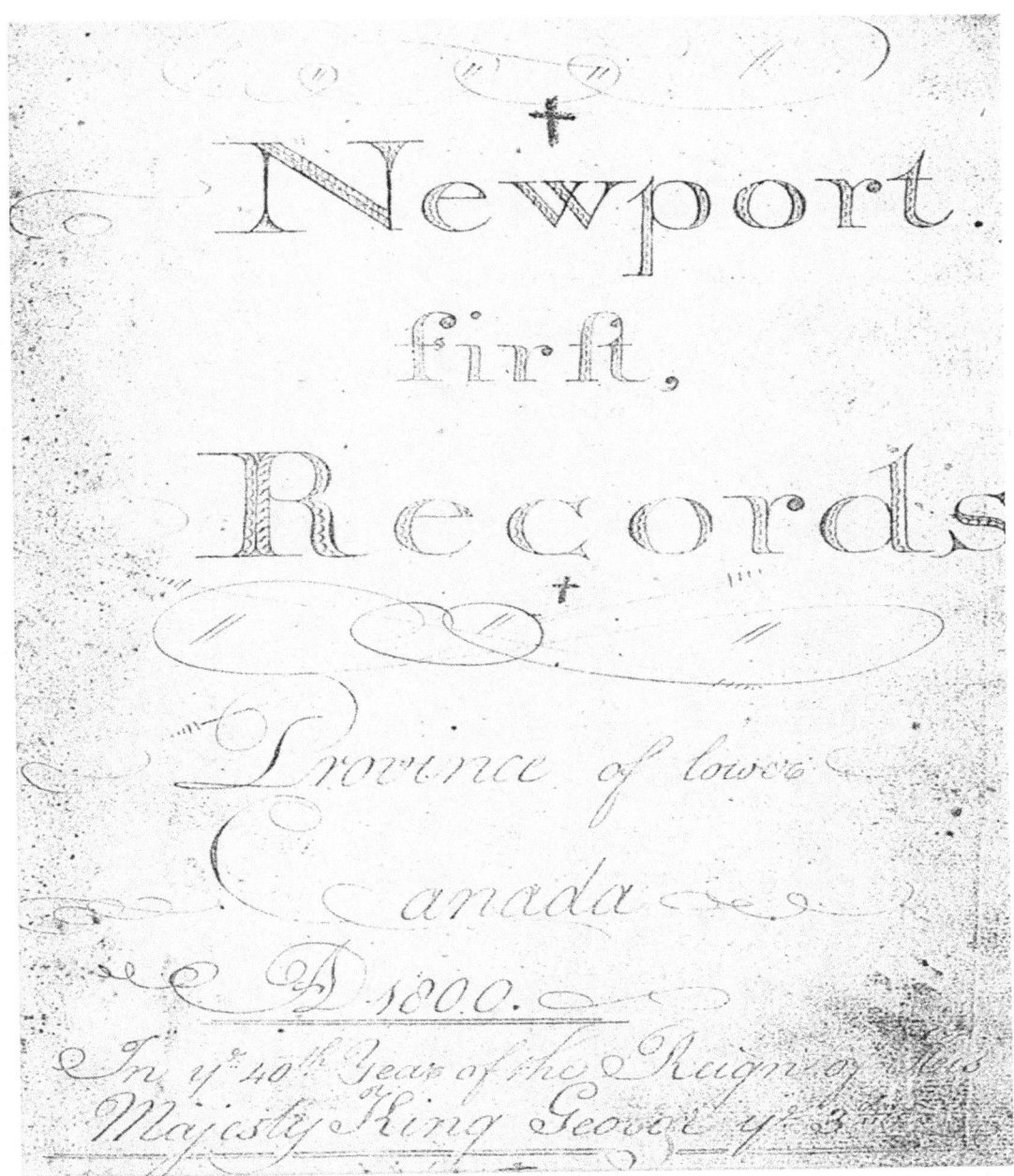

Front cover of *Newport first Records* book, 1800. Note the old-style "long s" in "first."

Historical Facts

In the Year of our Lord 1791, Alured Clark, then Governor of the Province of lower Canada, Isued a Proclamation for Granting the waste Lands of Crown, in Townships of Ten Miles square, to Aplicants, in free & common socage. In consequence thereof, Stephen Williams of Danby in the State of Vermont, petitioned for a Township by the name of Newport to be granted to himself & 40 Associates, the prayer of which was approved of. But the said Stephen Williams, neglected to come forward, as was expected: But Edmund Heard, one of the Associates did in the Year 1793. in company with Josiah Sawyer, set out from Missishoiue Bay on Lake Champlain, with Provisions, Tools, &c. thro' the Woods, Ninety Miles from any Inhabitants to the Westward, & after travelling & exploring the Woods, Thirty One Days, arrived on a Hill now called Pleasant

Page 1 (note the tiny "1" in the top right-hand corner) of *Newport first Records* book, 1800

Hill, in the said Township of Newport, where he & the said Sawyer began to make improvements; distant 25 Miles from any Inhabitants to the South, & 70 from the French settlements to the North. In the Year 1794. Sawyer moved his Family on, & in 1795. said Heard moved his Family on the Township; & finding the said Williams did not come forward, the s[d] Edmund Heard, on the 24th Day of June 1797 Petitioned the Government that the said Township, might be granted him & his Associates, & accordingly on the 22d of March 1800. an Order of Council, passed in his favour. Viz. as recorded on next page

Page 2 (note the tiny "2" in the top left-hand corner) of *Newport first Records* book, 1800

Chapter 1   Creation of a Borderline (1750–1792)

Quebec's Eastern Townships, a tourist and former administrative region, is located in southeastern Quebec, south of the former "seigneuries" that bordered the St. Lawrence River. It is bordered on the east by the state of Maine, on the west by the Richelieu River, and on the south by the states of New York, Vermont, and New Hampshire.

The region was originally comprised of "counties" that were divided into townships following the traditional method of land grants used for the original New England and New York colonies.

In the early 1990s, Quebec was reorganized into "regional county municipalities," better known by the French acronym MRC. The bulk of the Eastern Townships then became the "Estrie Region."

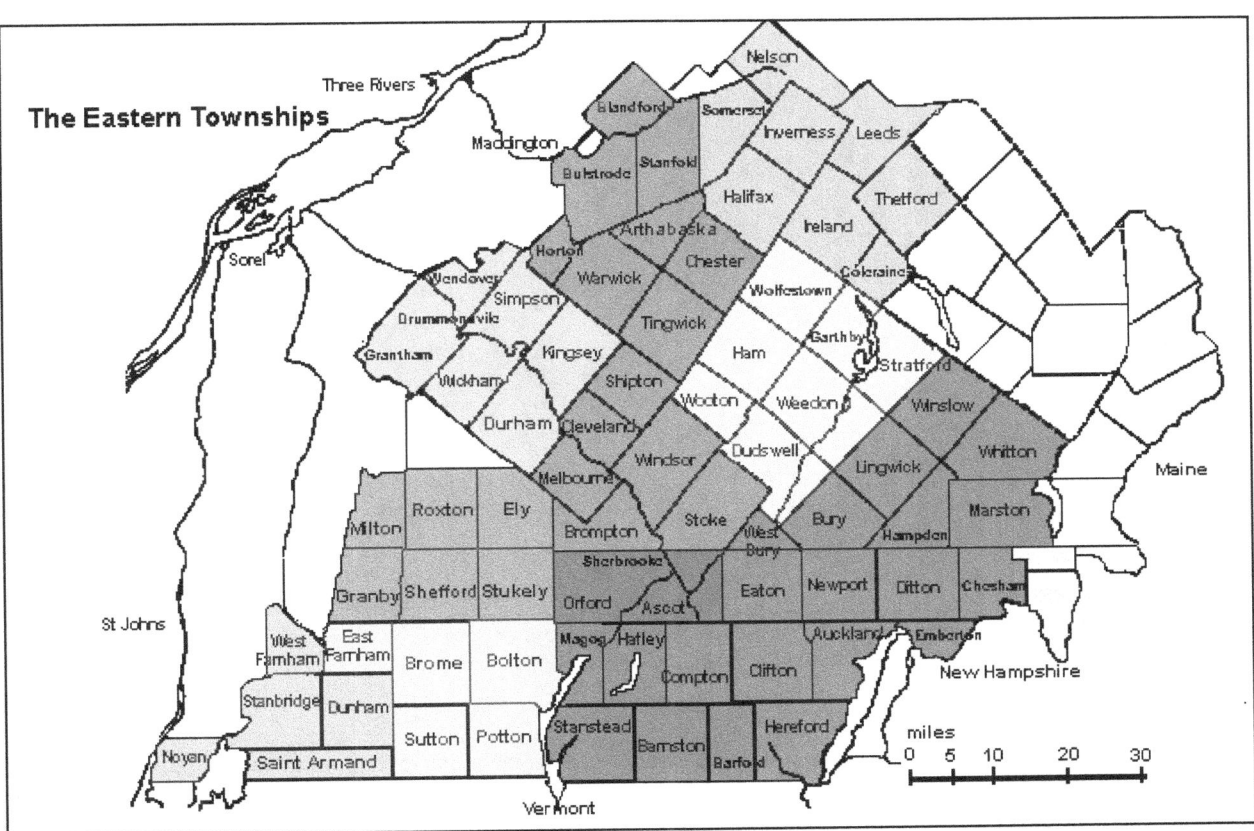

The Eastern Townships in 1871 (unknown Internet source)

The following two passages are reproduced from the United Empire Loyalist website:

> United Empire Loyalists (or simply "Loyalists") is an honorific which was first given by the 1st Lord Dorchester, the Governor of Quebec, and Governor-General of the Canadas, to American Loyalists who resettled in British North America during or after the American Revolution.

> At the time, *Canadian* or *Canadien* was used to refer to the indigenous *First Nations* groups and the French settlers inhabiting the Province of Quebec. They settled primarily in Nova Scotia and Lower Canada (including the Eastern Townships and Montreal). The influx of Loyalist settlers resulted in the creation of several new Colonies. In 1784, New Brunswick was partitioned from the Colony of Nova Scotia after significant Loyalist resettlement around the Bay of Fundy. In 1791, the influx of Loyalist refugees also resulted in the Province of Quebec's division into Lower Canada (present-day Quebec), and Upper Canada (present-day Ontario). *(United Empire Loyalist website, www.uelac.org)*

The Crown gave settlers land grants of one 200-acre lot per person to encourage their resettlement, as it "wanted to develop the frontier of Upper Canada." This resettlement added many English-language residents to the Canadian population. Thus began new waves of immigration that established a predominantly English-speaking population in the future of Canada, from the east toward the west.

The start of exploration and exploitation of the New World for the economic gain of the Old World began in the early 1600s and continued through to the 1700s. The French were the first to penetrate the interior forested lands as explorers and fur traders. The French came for the furs and to save the souls of the Indigenous peoples; the British came first for the fur trade, later for the lumber. As they interacted, the First Nations peoples, French and British began to clash during this period. The region was part of New France until the 1763 Treaty of Paris, which granted the region to Great Britain. Britain, with the world's most powerful navy, was expanding outwards and colonizing large parts of the world, including the future Canada and United States.

***

United Empire Loyalists seeking land grants in Lower Canada and Upper Canada in 1783 (Wikipedia; original drawing by Henry Moses)

These new Colonies were established essentially to feed their wealth back into the coffers of the British Crown. Upper Canada and Lower Canada were formed at this time, with a loosely formed "border" between the British New England Colonies to the south and the "Crown waste lands" immediately north of this border. The Royal Proclamation of 1763 established a British system of laws, government, and property to encourage British subjects to colonize. Officials hoped for settlers from the Colonies. While farmers failed to move here, merchants and traders did come to Quebec. From 1760 to the late 1770s about 100 Protestant English-speaking males arrived, the majority of whom were merchants.[1]

***

The earliest inhabitants of this Lower Canada region were the Abenaki Indians; their name means "dawn land people . . . easterners." They were a loosely organized confederation of Algonquin tribes, relatively peaceful people split off from their northern and western relatives by the intrusion of the Iroquois nation. This can be observed by the different Abenaki origin names for towns, lakes, and rivers. Names such as Massawippi, Missiskouy (Missisquoi), Odanack, Amonoosic, Umbagog and Mooselookmeguntic were translated as they sounded. The Abenaki had been warring with the Iroquois for a long time before the white man came to North America, and Samuel de Champlain allied himself with the Algonquin. The Abenaki allied themselves with the French during the Seven Years' War to fight the British. The Abenaki were essentially sandwiched to the north and west by the Iroquois on the south shore of the St. Lawrence River, and to the east by the Connecticut River and Halls Stream. From their several villages along the St. Lawrence, they travelled inland to hunt and fish in the region, a territory that stretched from the Richelieu River on the west to the Chaudière on the east, and as far south as the northern parts of Vermont, New Hampshire, and Maine. "The Abenaki hunters would spend three or four months at temporary encampments in the region, where they hired themselves out to the whites or to other Indians who engaged in the fur trade. Furs were traded for guns, powder, ball shot, traps, axes, camp kettles and woolen blankets."[25] It was known that the Abenaki Indians followed a path from the Connecticut Lakes to the St. Francis River and that this pathway passed through the townships of Newport and Eaton, following the Eaton River to the St. Francis River.[25]

"The last of that group in our area were the Sharbees. I remember Long Tom and seeing their cabin on the Bowker Road back in the late forties/early fifties . . . so much has been lost. Up the "Nugent Hill" there were the remains of Abenaki houses that were still visible in the late 1950s." *(Eric G. R. French)*

The Connecticut River, however, was reputedly prone to ambush by the Iroquois, and this route continued to be dangerous during the 1700s for the white man travelling from the New England Colonies to Upper Canada. The area surrounding Canaan, Vt., was also the summer hunting and fishing grounds of the Iroquois and was travelled with a degree of acute awareness. This was one reason they travelled through Lake Champlain during the mid-1700s.[2]

In 1752, townships were surveyed along the Connecticut River and stockades were erected by the British at Coos, but of little avail and these were finally abandoned by the late 1700s.[17]

The hostilities were indeed real for a long period of time. All along the route from Massachusetts to Lower Canada, the Iroquois would descend upon frontier towns, killing and capturing many. Among their captives were two young children, a boy and a girl from different families. The boy, Samuel, who was the eldest of the two, remembered that his family name was "Gill." After the cessation of hostilities for the time being, the surviving friends of the children sought to reclaim them, but their captives had become their protectors. Now attached to the little ones, they refused to give them up. An appeal was made to the legal authorities in hope of recovering them by force. The children suddenly went missing and were kept in hiding until the search parties were obliged to abandon the search as hopeless and return without them. They were left to grow up among their captors, however, after they grew up, they were brought to St. Francis Village (Sherbrooke) and married into the Abenakis tribe by a Catholic Priest. In 1866, there were recorded 952 descendants of Samuel Gill. Many of their descendants rejoined the non-Indigenous cultures of French and English settlers and married into some of the Newport and Eaton families.[17, 24]

***

Edmund[10] Lionel Hurd, on a trip to the region in 1990 with a group of United Empire Loyalists, related this quote as follows: "In 1759, the Rogers Rangers around the region of the Indian Stream and wilderness regions of the three Connecticut Lakes were set upon by a band of Iroquois Indians. In the skirmishes that followed, there were many casualties on both sides."[8]

In common with all others of the British North American settlements, there was a military background established. After Robert Rogers and his famous Rogers' Rangers destroyed the Abenaki village of Saint Francis in October 1759, they began their withdrawal while being pursued by parties of both Indians and the French. During this period, it is recorded that a skirmish took place at Kingsey Falls (near Richmond) and near Big Forks, the junction of the St. Francis and Magog rivers (now Sherbrooke) where the Indians were severely defeated by Rogers and his men.[2]

The first 100 years, from 1700 to 1800, saw the beginning of settlements and economic growth in both Lower Canada and Upper Canada. The southern New England Colonies began their desire for independence in the "New World;" more expressly to end exploitation and taxation by the Old World. With the notion of independence from Britain gaining ground in the New England Colonies, people found that they were caught between loyalty to the "Old World" and this notion of separation into states that history shows would ultimately become the United States of America. In 1765 the British Parliament imposed taxation on the Thirteen Colonies, the future United States, while allowing them no representation in the British Parliament. The Thirteen Colonies strenuously objected, which led to confrontations. The Tea Act of 1773 was the last straw and they rebelled. They took up arms and fought a war against the British known as "The American Revolution" and won, gaining their independence from Britain in 1783.

Meanwhile, north of the Colonies, the new political system installed in 1774 divided Quebec into Upper Canada (Ontario) and Lower Canada (Quebec), affording a semblance of self-rule with British-appointed governors in charge. Those long-established in the growing British Colonies shared with the revolution's refugees and newcomers from the British Isles a deep respect for British political values and an abhorrence of the ideals and aspirations upon which the American Revolution had been based. They were determined to remain separate from the newly forming United States. A border was loosely drawn, and American fishermen were granted inland rights, much to the disgust of the Loyalists.[26]

The Quebec Act legislation, passed by the British Parliament in 1774 for governing Canada, then called the Province of Quebec, continued French civil law in the province, admitting Roman Catholics to full citizenship. This Act also permitted the Catholic Church to retain the same privileges it had when the region belonged to France.

The Quebec Act withheld a Representative Assembly, providing instead for government of the Province by an appointed Governor and Council. It also extended the Province's boundaries to include land between the Appalachian Mountains and the Mississippi River north of Ohio. The Act was designed largely to win the loyalty of the French in the Province and may have been influential in keeping them from joining in the American Revolution. The Act, however, infuriated the Colonies to the south because it added to Quebec land that these Colonies had previously claimed. They

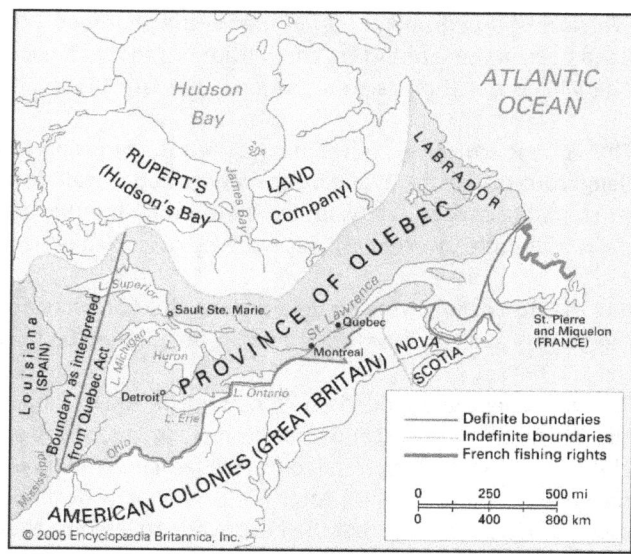

The Province of Quebec, 1774 (britannica.com)

considered the Quebec Act as one of the "Intolerable Acts" adopted by Great Britain in 1774. The Declaration of Independence meant that the Quebec Act, when it denounced Great Britain "for abolishing the free system of English Laws in a neighbouring Province, established an arbitrary government and enlarged its boundaries." This triggered the War of Independence, i.e., the first American civil war. With the added grievance of excessive taxation by the British, the Patriots wanted separation from British rule altogether to form their own independent states.[29]

The Declaration of Independence was drawn up containing the wording for the new Constitution of Governance, completed on July 2, 1776. The document was approved by Congress on July 4, 1776, hence that calendar date became known as Independence Day for the newly formed United States of America. They were, however, still not entirely free of the British for some time, with many skirmishes and legal battles yet to be consummated. Many of these differences of opinions were cumulated with the Boston Tea Party of 1777.[49]

During and after the American Revolution of 1775-1783, supporters of the King of England began to flee the New England Colonies to settle in both Upper Canada and Lower Canada. Life in the New England Colonies had become dangerous for people of their political leanings. During the 1780s, Loyalists migrated from the northern colonies of Vermont, New York, New Hampshire, and Maine during and at the close of the American Revolutionary War. By this time, settlements had been established in the Connecticut River valley as far north as West Stewartstown, N.H., a village known then as Brakeroot Corners. Brakeroot became the point from which many of these first families entered Lower Canada due to its proximity to Lower Canada.[25]

The American Revolution was essentially America's first civil war. The new "United States" was born out of a deep distrust of government. The (American) Patriots won their personal liberties with their blood, so they value their personal liberties above all else, creating a very individualistic society dedicated to "life, liberty and the pursuit of happiness" with individual rights taking precedence. It is their distrust of government and dedication to personal liberties that drives almost every aspect of their lives, the essence of which continues to this day. About a third of the American colonists wanted nothing to do with what John Adams, Thomas Jefferson and others were selling. With every British military defeat, those loyal to the Crown left or were driven out.[49]

Due to its location, the region now known as the Eastern Townships of Quebec, positioned just north of the borders of Vermont, New Hampshire, and western Maine, became an area of keen interest. The story speaks to a time of early settlement circa 1780, in Lower Canada, when immigrants were on the move from the then New England Colonies. They were following the trails through the western side of Vermont along Lake Champlain and the Richelieu River, or on the more eastern side of Vermont through Canaan and Kilbourne Mills into East Hereford, finally arriving in Clifton, Eaton, and Newport townships. Others came along the Connecticut River through the Connecticut Lakes in New Hampshire, arriving in Auckland, Ditton, and Newport townships. Still others from Maine travelled through Woburn and the Megantic Mountains, arriving in Ditton, Newport and Bury townships.

In 1783, the Treaty of Paris ended the American Revolution and gave the disputed territory to the United States. The treaty stipulated that the U.S.-Canada boundary line would follow the "northwesternmost head of the Connecticut River." Unfortunately, there were three tributaries that qualified for this description. Due to the treaty's ambiguity and lack of accurate description, both the United States and Lower Canada (then a colony of Great Britain) claimed that the forested land was theirs. Since both countries ruled over the territory's citizens, both U.S. and Great Britain imposed taxes. Both sides sent in tax collectors and debt-collecting sheriffs. The double taxation infuriated the population who, in revolt and anger, established the Republic of Indian Stream to free the people from the heavy tax burden. The republic was formed to put an end to the issue until the United States and Great Britain could reach a settlement on the boundary line. The Republic of Indian Stream was no laughing matter – its less than 300 residents committed to draft a constitution, printed their own stamps, established a 41-man militia, and elected a local government. The unrecognized territory received so much attention that it was the subject of diplomatic discussions between British ambassadors and American President Andrew Jackson, and even appeared in the 1830 Census as "Indian Stream Territory, or so-called."

This era (1785-1842) depicts the uncertainties of international boundaries, loose law enforcement, rampant land speculation along with public and private events, all lubricated with whiskey and rum. In the period from 1785, when trappers built the first cabins along the Connecticut River in what is now Pittsburg, N.H., the border between Lower Canada and New Hampshire was loosely controlled until 1842 when the Webster-Ashburton Treaty finally established the border as we know it today.

The Republic of Indian Stream was an unrecognized constitutional republic along the border section that divides the current province of Quebec from the U.S. state of New Hampshire. The people who had first settled there had acquired grants from two different land companies until after the war of 1812. It remained a contested area from 1832 until 1840 when this region agreed to pledge allegiance to the United States and established that the border to the western side of the state would be Halls Stream. Ultimately, both land grant companies merged and reconciled all land claims.

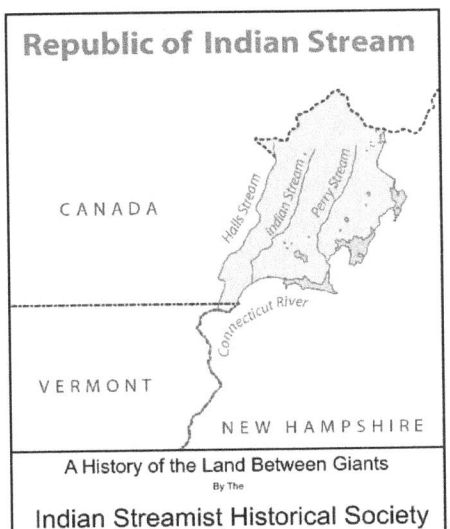

Location of Republic of Indian Stream
(Indian Streamist Historical Society)

The Republic encompassed approximately 282 square miles, the northern reaches of which are now the state of New Hampshire, including the three Connecticut Lakes and Lake Francis. The Connecticut River separates New Hampshire and Vermont. The Republic of Indian Stream arose out of a common theme in territorial disputes – vague legislation. The region was bounded south by the main branch of the Connecticut River.

A tolerably large settlement had been formed on Indian Stream and Connecticut River by persons from the New England Colonies, who claimed to have commenced their settlement in 1792. The settlement at this time consisted of about 20 families who had made extensive improvements and were respectively settled. They claimed to have settled under the auspices and by virtue of a proclamation of Sir Alured Clarke, at that time lieutenant-governor of Lower Canada. Naturally, these settlers believed this part of land was Canada.[16]

The community prospered because of a treaty with Philip, Chief of the St. Francis tribe of the Abenaki First Nation. Under this treaty, the Chief was guaranteed a perpetual supply of clothing and provisions, and that the right of his people to fish and hunt in their former territory would not be interfered with.

To protect this colony that held a deed still in existence bearing the signatures of Philip and other Indigenous people, Indian Stream settlers under the leadership of Luther Parker in 1832 established an entirely separate government which they called the "Indian Stream Republic" and elected their own officials under a private Constitution.

> In 1796, the Native American chief, King Phillip, had placed his mark on a paper deeding his land to three New Hampshire wheeler-dealers. The stalwart northern frontiersman of the Indian Stream Republic adopted their own constitution and declared their independence from both Great Britain and the United States. Debtors, adventurers, farmers, and woodsmen moved in and in 1832 the inhabitants proclaimed their settlement the Indian Stream Republic, with a constitution guaranteeing the right to religious freedom, life, liberty, property, and happiness. Cruel and unusual punishment was initiated, and the "necessities of life" were banned (including books) that were exempt from attachment for non-payment of taxes. The republic's golden age ended in 1835, when the state of New Hampshire sent in the militia, and in 1840 the territory was incorporated as the town of Pittsburg, N.H. *(Republic of Indian Stream website)*

This border conflict is a fascinating account of how a few ornery, cussed farmers and woodsmen put together their own nation against a backdrop of raw politics, greed, and international controversy. Things got chaotic in 1835 when a British sheriff and magistrate arrested a resident of the Republic of Indian Stream for hardware store debt, prompting a posse of "Streamers" to revolt. The posse shot up the judge's house, leading to a diplomatic emergency that forced Great Britain to forfeit its claim to sovereignty over the region, giving Indian Stream to New Hampshire – and New Hampshire alone – once and for all. *(Republic of Indian Stream website)*

The entire area was renamed Pittsburg, N.H. Some settlers who thought they had settled in Lower Canada simply moved north when the militia marched in. These settlers essentially moved into the townships of Ditton, Auckland, Chesham, and northwest to Newport and Eaton. It was through this region that Colonel Edmund[5] Heard, and his Associates plied their oxen and heavily laden ox carts with all their worldly possessions on the long trail from Ipswich, Mass. They would have travelled through Lancaster, N.H., taking one of two routes: either through three of the Connecticut Lakes or through West Stewartstown and down Halls Stream.

Under the terms of the Constitutional Act of 1791, the Eastern Townships (known as Lower Canada before Confederation) were opened to settlement and a land rush followed. The Constitutional Act divided Quebec into Upper Canada and Lower Canada. Most English speakers located in Upper Canada, leaving fewer than 10,000 Anglos in Lower Canada.[1]

From 1791 to 1812, Americans came in larger numbers as land restrictions were lifted and a more British system of land holding was established since a parliamentary system had been established in each of Upper Canada and Lower Canada. Due to American migration, the English-speaking population in Lower Canada grew to 30,000. American immigration changed the nature of Lower Canada's English population from being urban, mercantile, British and Church of England to a much more diverse rural, agricultural American-style Methodist population. The government recognized and supported the Church of England with promises to erect a church and rectory in every township and provide funds to support the clergy.[29]

It is no exaggeration to say the United Empire Loyalists changed Canadian history. Before 1783, the clearest observers saw no future for Canada but that of a French colony under the British Crown. What rendered the thought void was the unexpected influx of refugees of the Revolution to the immediate south. The effect of this immigration was to create two new English-speaking provinces, New Brunswick and Upper Canada, and to strengthen the English element in two other provinces, Lower Canada and Nova Scotia, so that ultimately the French population in Canada was outnumbered by the English population surrounding it. This fact serves to explain a great deal in later Canadian history. Before 1783, the continuance of Canada in the British Empire was by no means assured; after 1783 the imperial tie was well-knit.[49]

On February 7, 1792, following the Constitutional Act of Lower Canada in 1791, Governor Alured Clarke awarded the land southeast of the Saint Lawrence River to Loyalists for settlement, the region now known as the Eastern Townships. Stephen Williams of Danby, Vt., was the first to petition for the Township of Newport to be granted to him and 40 Associates[4]. Later in 1792, a Royal Proclamation further divided the land into townships, where the

British system of landholding was established. Through the Leader and Associate System, both Upper Canada and Lower Canada granted part of each township to a wealthy "Leader" who may be joined by "Associates."[31]

When the American Revolution ended, Sir Frederick Haldimand, Governor of Quebec, expected these first families to move westward with the rest of the Loyalists. Because not all wanted to move west, Haldimand cut off the rations the government had been providing. (Each of the settler families were to have been given certain tools, seeds, and food to last for the first year.) They resisted efforts to be moved by force and were finally permitted to stay by Lieutenant Governor Henry Hamilton after Haldimand's return to England. During this standoff, many of the first groups of settlers (Associates) were denied the rations they had anticipated. This greatly increased the anxiety for their families' chances of survival in this harsh land.[3]

There were two waves of settlers from the New England Colonies just prior to and during the War of Independence and then again in the following years after the full reality set in, i.e., the creation of the United States of America. The first wave consisted of true Loyalists who were forced to flee either during the war or directly afterwards. The greater portion of these settled in Upper Canada; however, an estimated 1,000 settled in Lower Canada.[29]

Land Grant Obligations circa 1750-77 and on to the 1790s:

A practice in the New England states and along the East Coast of America was to grant significant land masses to military men of significance who had served the British in the Colonization of America. In most cases these military men had contacts in the Old World who identified and arranged for many families of good standing, usually of some wealth, to settle in the New World. They would travel to the Americas and become "associates" of these military men who held land grants. Associates would settle in a portion of the holdings, thereby beginning a new community. The caveat was an inference that they be loyal to the British Crown; if not, they may lose their land. This was how the British gained the loyalty of the people and essentially coerced them to defend their governance.

The military officers were paid an annual stipend and were expected at any time to be prepared for the call to duty. It was because of this stipend that officers were considered wealthy compared to those not connected to the military.[3]

At this time, timber in both Upper Canada and Lower Canada began to be diverted. It had been shipped to Britain, but now was being sent south of the border to build cities in the newly formed United States. Simultaneously, Loyalists remaining in the old New England Colonies were under siege and their lands taken.

This brings us to a story of courage, resourcefulness and tenacity that was demonstrated by our early pioneer families in their search for stability during these early tumultuous times. They went north from their settlements in what is now Massachusetts, with all their possessions, some travelling with yokes of ox carts, some by horse, many walking the entire distance. They persevered in rain-soaked clothing, through mosquitoes and swamps, skirting mountainous areas, and experienced drownings, injuries, illnesses, and birthing. Without stamina, perseverance, and the settlers' drive to go north and start over, Canada would not be what it is today.

Much of our heritage today stems from Col. Edmund[5] Heard and Captain Josiah[4] Sawyer, from whom many current Eastern Townships residents are direct descendants. We begin with the story of these two men and their families who came from the New England Colonies and settled in Lower Canada before Confederation, specifically in Newport and Eaton townships.

We could start with asking what the following names have in common: Alden, Allen, Anderson, Annabel, Austin, Aulis, Arnott, Baker, Bailey, Beecher, Benjamin, Bennett, Bernard, Berwick, Beaman, Blair, Bliss, Bowker, Boyd, Brown, Brazenal, Burnham, Burns, Buck, Buchanan, Byrnes, Cable, Chaddock, Chadsey, Christie, Charest, Clout, Clark, Cooper, Curtis, Davis, Dawson, Darker, Drouin, Dorman, Dougherty, Dunsmore, Elias, Ellis, Ewing, Farnsworth, Fraser, French, Flaws, Gates, Gill, Grover, Graham, Goodenough, Harvey, Herrick, Herring, Hodge, Holbrook, Hornby, Hudson, Hunt, Hurd, Jones, Kerr, Lafleur, Lapointe, Lavalier, Lawrence, Learned, Leavitt, Le Bourveau, Leggett, Lepitre, Lindsay, Lister, Laberee, Loveland, Lyon, Manning, Maynard, Metcalf, McCurdy, McCallum, McNaughton, McKeage, Mitchell, Millar, McVetty, Morrow, Morrison, Morgan, Munn, Nourse, Painter, Parker, Parsons, Prince,

Planche, Paquet, Rand, Ranta, Reynolds, Reeves, Riddell, Rowell, Kerr, Todd, Sawyer, Sample, Seale, Stevenson, Spaulding, Speck, Statton, Stickney, Sturdivant, Sunbury, Swail, Stone, Simpson, Squires, Tessier, Thayer, Trueman, Thompson, Todd, Trembley, Tetreault, Theroux, Ward, Westgate, Wheeler, Wilford, Willard, Williams, Worthing, Woods. These are the family names of some of the over 4,000 descendants of the Newport Township settlers.

Those of us who were born and lived in this region, no matter the era or for how short a time, would recognize these names. As the story progresses, the author will try to link many of these names to our earliest ancestors who settled in Newport. Some of these links will have originated from adjacent townships through business, personal association, and marriages; however, the author will focus only on those who ultimately settled and lived in Newport Township. This is us . . . this is our ancestry . . . this is who we are.

Genealogy charts of the Heard/Hurd families and their marriage connections within Newport Township are included in family charts at the end of the book. These are prepared so the reader may refer to the various generations as they unfold in each era. The children who married and continued to live in Newport and who were connected to other families within the communities of Newport are the only ones chronicled here. In some cases, if an individual returns to Newport, then their "lives lived" are referred to again.

***

Chapter 2   Exploration (1700–1800)

Much of the heritage of Newport Township and Eaton Township stems from Colonel Edmund[5] Heard and Captain Josiah[4] Sawyer, from whom the author and many of us who have lived there are direct descendants. This book represents a piece of Canadian history that captures the human side of subduing the forest, harnessing the streams, battling the brutal winters, and exercising the basic skills of simple survival. These two men came from the New England Colonies to explore the possibility of seeking homesteads to settle in Lower Canada in 1793, long before Confederation.

Edmund and Josiah had first met in Lancaster, Mass., the town Josiah's great-great-uncle had founded. These were and are the people who were engaged from the beginning of the New England Colonies settlements and demonstrate an unbroken line to the present day.

Col. Edmund[5] Heard, from Boston, and his wife Sarah (Willington), from Worcester, Mass., were "warned out" of Sutton, Mass., on August 19, 1766. They had three children: Sarah, Edmund[6], and Luke.[6] The family had resided in Worcester in 1768, later living in Lancaster, Mass., where Sarah died in 1770. In June 1772 Edmund married Elizabeth Andrews. As his second family, they had two children, Samuel[6] and Hannah.[5]

> *Author's note: "Warned out" was the terminology used at the time, meaning they had many warnings to alter their thinking or they would be sent an official warning – in this case, get out!*

Up to the outbreak of the American Revolution, Edmund was a man of some note in Worcester. At a town meeting in 1772 he was chosen one of the reeves of the town. His hopes of preferment were dashed by his position on the burning questions then growing out of the Colonies' relationship with the mother country. In 1774, the Tories of Worcester drew up a remonstrance against the actions of the "Patriots" which was overwhelmingly rejected by the voters. The protest was condemned as *"a piece of low cunning to deceive the publick"* and its signatories were pronounced *"unworthy of holding any Town office of profit or honor until they had made satisfaction for their offence."*[37]

> *[Published in] Worcester, October 19, 1775:*
>
> *To Ephraim Curtis Goaler*
>
> *Whereas the conduct of Edmund Heard of Worcester hath given the friend of the Constitutional Rights of the people of America just grounds to suspect that the said Edmund Heard hath been unfriendly to the American interest in our present public dispute with Great Britain and as we have examined into the matter are of opinion that the said Edmund Heard ought to be under confinement for the present. You are therefore hereby desired to take him and keep him under your custody so that he may be forthcoming when called for, or, you have orders from us or other lawful authority for his liberation.*
>
> *Committee of the Correspondents for Worcester.*[5]
>
> *[Signed] Wm Young, Joshua Bigelow, David Bigelow.*

Edmund[5] had distinguished himself, with several other persons, in protesting in the public newspapers against those measures which led to the Revolution against the British. He and his family suffered greatly by the publication of his name in printed handbills, distributed around the country, cautioning all persons against dealing with *"your petitioner or afford him or his family any assistance or support until he should sign the solemn League and Covenant so called"* … which he absolutely refused to do. Finding himself in this deplorable situation, in the spring of 1775 Edmund[5] formed a plan to escape with his family into Canada and join the Royal Cause.[5]

At the commencement of those troubles, Edmund[5] had failed in his attempt to make his escape into Lower Canada. He was captured at Crown Point, a now-historic site on the west side of Lake Champlain. The goods he had collected to assist in a military retreat and his personal effects were seized and distributed among the rebel forces while he

The prison at Crown Point on Lake Champlain where Col. Edmund[5] Heard was incarcerated (Wikipedia)

was held prisoner until he was sent back to Worcester. He was kept in close confinement; because of that he never had an opportunity to rejoin the British Forces.[3]

Edmund was eventually released and had been discreetly silent as to his political views on the issues of the Revolution; however, as the outcome of the war was becoming evident, his actions against the rebellion began to be noticed and he quickly moved his family to Lancaster, Mass.[3]

Having become established in Lancaster, Edmund[5] was initiated into the Masons on October 9, 1777, in St. Andrew's Lodge. He became a charter member of Trinity Lodge and was chosen master in 1778, holding that office for 10 years. "It was due to his early appreciation of the institution and its principals that Trinity Lodge was founded at all; and it was due to his energy and executive ability, his clear judgment and his well-balanced mind that Trinity had so prosperous a start while he was connected to it. He was the one who did well in every task he assumed and carried to success every undertaking."[37]

The next year Edmund was elected town clerk of Lancaster, an office he held for three successive years. He was also active in the business affairs of the town during those years, serving on committees and filling positions at the request of his fellow citizens. It was during this time, where he had been acting for British interests in the colonies, that he began to again look north for his future.[4]

It was for this reason that Edmund[5] suffered embarrassment and had filed his petition of grievance and loss to the British Crown when applying as an Associate for the land grants of Newport Township. "He had literally left all of his property and possessions in Lancaster; his peers had suspected that he had gone to Lower Canada but had no concrete evidence that he had. They did know that his son Edmund[6] eventually sold his holdings in Lancaster and assumed that Edmund[5] probably died in Lower Canada." He was a businessman who "combined in himself the qualities of a dreamer and a builder" and who was to embark on an adventure in an effort to clear his name.[37]

Edmund had served in Shay's Rebellion in 1787, commissioned by Governor John Hancock as lieutenant colonel in Ebenezer Crafts' first regiment of cavalry in Worcester County, in the Seventh Division of the Militia, Commonwealth

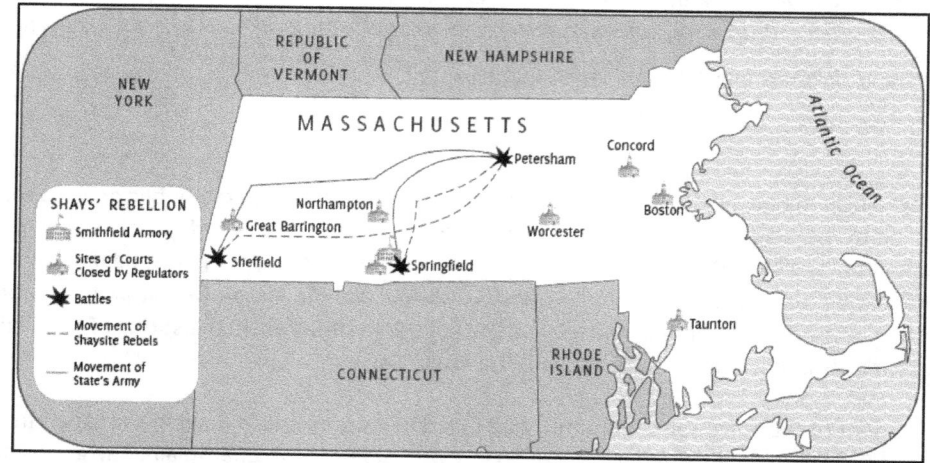

Shay's Rebellion (Gordon Harris, "Shay's Rebellion," historicipswich.org; map by Dolmarva Design)

of Massachusetts. This militia was established to suppress the disturbance in the northwest part of Worcester County. By 1791, Britain's myopic handling of the war's aftermath bred resentments and misunderstandings that were growing on all sides.[4,31]

"Essex County furnished 500 men, including 25 from Ipswich. Col. Nathaniel Wade commanded one of the regiments and Robert Farley served as aide-de-camp to the commander, General Benjamin Lincoln. A march was made to Worcester and Springfield in weather of great severity." From February 2 to 4, General Lincoln continued west from Worcester with 3,000 men through a blinding snowstorm to the rebels' camp at Petersham, where they had raided local merchants for supplies. Many of the rebellion's leaders fled into Vermont and New Hampshire and were never brought to justice. (Script excerpt from Thomas Franklin Waters, *Ipswich in the Massachusetts Bay Colony*)

Relations between Edmund and his Trinity brethren had been strained for some time due to his views on the Revolution as a consequence of his connections with the "Whigs," expressly the British. Reports began to emerge of more serious issues which compelled the Lodge to take decisive action in dismissing his standing with the Lodge. In a letter to "Brother Heard," the Lodge stated that he "had worked in a clandestine and undue manner and that unless he evidenced to this Lodge the falsity of the assertions taken against him, that he be expelled from the Lodge."[37]

This charge resulted in a dark stain upon Edmund's Masonic record and an embarrassment on his character, which he was clearly defending against his "Patriot" Masonic brethren. He was viewed as a man of considerable ability and ambition, having taken part in the public affairs of any community in which he lived. It was unfortunate that his Masonic good name and reputation should be enveloped in such a cloud of mystery -- the last view of the man who probably held the office of Master longer than any other "Brother" connected with the Lodge's history.[37]

Edmund[5] was a man of great courage and unyielding principal, qualities that got him into trouble with the American Patriots. He was resourceful in trying to get his family and children to safety; even splitting allegiances within his own family, to those who sought the safety of being settled against those who sought adventure to the unknown. He essentially escaped to Canada. For many of his business associates in Trinity Lodge, who knew he had gone to Canada, his fate, however, continued to remain a mystery.[37]

Meanwhile, his eldest son, Edmund[6], had signed up with the regiment under the command of Capt. Ezra[4] Sawyer (Josiah[4] Sawyer's older brother). He was promoted to first sergeant on August 14, 1792. The certificate was signed by the commanding officer at that time – his own father, Col. Edmund[5] Heard.[3]

Warrant issued by Captain Erza[4] Sawyer, 1792

On September 11, 1792, a warrant was issued in the name of the Commonwealth of Massachusetts by Capt. Ezra[4] Sawyer to Sgt. Edmund[6] Heard Jr. to advise all non-commissioned officers and privates of his company to assemble at his house in Worcester at 7 a.m. on September 26 to await further orders. (This was considered a "warning" that something was up.) This order was acknowledged by Edmund6 Jr. that he had made the warning to those agreeable to assemble. Some may not have been agreeable to assemble because it could put their families in danger.[3]

There were two types of persecution to which the Loyalists were subjected; that which was perpetrated by "lawless mobs" and that which was carried out "constitutionally." Mobs broke down doors with broadaxes, destroyed the

"Tory Refugees on Their Way to Canada," 1783 (illustration by Howard Pyle, from *Colonies and Nation* by Woodrow Wilson)

furniture, stole the money, and scattered the books and papers. Once all the wine in the cellars was drank, they proceeded to dismantle the roof and walls. The owners barely escaped with their lives. These same mobs attacked the British troops in Boston. A favourite pastime was to tar and feather "obnoxious Tories." This consisted of stripping the victim naked, smearing them with a coat of tar and feathers and parading them around in carts for the contemplation of their neighbours. Once the Declaration of Independence was initiated, a new order was inaugurated. Evidence of loyalty to the British became tantamount to treason to the State, and Loyalists laid themselves open to all the penalties of treason. The Tory who refused to take the Oath of Allegiance became an outlaw, hence the "bounty hunters." It is not difficult to understand how the great majority of avowed Tories came to take refuge within the British lines, to enlist under the British Flag, and, when the Revolution had proven successful, to leave their homes forever and begin life anew amid other surroundings. The persecution to which they were subjected left them no alternative. This 1783 image of a nameless traveller is evidence of the courage and buoyancy of heart with which the UELs faced the tolls and privations of life in their new homes. Not drooping like poor fugitives, they came, in exodus to our Canadian wilds, full of heart and hope, with heads erect, and fearless eyes victorious in defeat.[49]

The post-Revolutionary War years were a time of cautionary and discrete notifications passed between those supportive of the revolution and those who remained loyal to the Crown. Sergeant Edmund[6] Heard would become the second Heard who found himself associated with the wrong side, also needing to look north for a future for himself and his family.

Edmund[5] had another younger son, Luke[6], at that time living in Portland, Me., who was also of the mindset to move to Canada. He wrote several letters to his father, suggesting his plans to join him and his brothers in Canada. They and others became United Empire Loyalists, and many moved north to Lower Canada, thus escaping the Green Mountain Boys and other such militia groups of the Patriots who were confiscating their properties. At that time, the Green Mountain Boys operated clandestine operations on behalf of the Patriots but separate from the "Militia" – in today's world, we might refer to them as contracted "Special Ops."

Luke Heard's sister, Sarah, had married in Shrewsbury, Mass., and chose to stay in the New England Colonies to raise her two sons and a daughter. Families even at this time were choosing different sides to bank on for their future.[4]

Earlier in 1792, their father Edmund[5] Heard had seen the proclamation of General Clarke offering land grants in Canada and took the opportunity to add his name as an Associate with Steven Williams, who had already made claim to a township called Newport.

***

The youngest of 20 children, Josiah[4] Sawyer, born in 1757, was adopted by his mother's brother, Joseph Wilder of Leominster, Mass. (Joseph was in favour of but not in sympathy with the Rebellion of 1775-83.) Josiah's father and grandfather were soldiers among the Minutemen who were to drive Pitcairn's soldiers back to Boston. Josiah[4], at age 16, upon seeing the eight slain men as they lay that day in the church in Lexington, decided against Joseph Wilder's objections to join his family in the service upon which they had embarked "their lives, their fortunes, and their shared honor."[23]

Because Josiah[4] was only 18 in 1775, he began his service as a body servant to his brother, Ezra[4], who was an officer. Soon after, however, because of his height (over six feet tall) and the reorganization of the army under a new commander in chief, he was commissioned as an ensign. He distinguished himself as an officer in the first two battles – Brookland Harlem Heights and White Plains – that raged between loose borders controlled by the British. At this time, however, he contracted "camp-fever" and was sent back to Lancaster, a mere shadow of a man. During his recovery under the care of Dr. John Green from Concord, N.H., he courted the doctor's sister, Susanna Green, and ultimately married her.[23]

During this time Josiah[4] had also learned of land grants in Canada – a township of 100 square miles to any man who would settle 15 men. He took care to ensure everyone knew he was not a refugee who would come to Canada to escape fighting against American Independence, but rather a free citizen of the Republic that he and his family had helped to found. And so, he came to Lower Canada by choice to "found" a town, as his great-uncle had done earlier when he founded Lancaster. Josiah[4] became the first settler in the Township of Eaton.[23]

And so, it came to be that Col. Edmund[5] Heard and Captain Josiah[4] Sawyer, both having learned of the opportunity to obtain land grants in Lower Canada, and each with their own reasons, teamed up to explore this opportunity. These two men were about to change the face of history in a part of Lower Canada now known as part of the Eastern Townships of Quebec, more specifically Newport Township and Eaton Township. These were our ancestors, people with an unshaken confidence and an unquenchable thirst for adventure. Both men had extensive military backgrounds that would benefit them in acquiring the land grants, and that would serve them well in establishing themselves as leaders of their communities.

Because Stephen Williams had neglected to come forward to claim Newport Township, for which he had petitioned earlier, Col. Edmund[5] Heard, one of the original 40 Associates, in the company of Capt. Josiah[4] Sawyer, set out from Missisquoi Bay on Lake Champlain to meet with the land agent at Quebec City. Equipped with provisions and tools, they travelled on horseback through the woods via the trail marked by a simple slash on the bark of the trees ("spotting" was the terminology used at the time), 90 miles from any inhabitants on the westward side, they arrived at the settlement of Quebec City. Edmund[5] was promised 1200 acres of land as an Associate in Newport Township, part of the township that Stephen Williams had previously petitioned. Documents showed that on August 1, 1796, in Vermont, Steven Williams had authorized that Edmund[5] Heard may be appointed Leader in his name for Newport.[20]

Josiah Sawyer had also been promised 1200 acres as an Associate, in the newly formed Eaton Township. Both men would subsequently petition as "Associate Leaders" in their respective townships. The requirement was a minimum of 15 and as many as 40 Associates, with equal opportunity to acquire several lots as agreed upon by their peers.[25]

Edmund Heard was not necessarily a devout man but was a leader who possessed a strong faith in his country and would defend it as best he could. His family background was both military and business. He was the eldest in a family of five children. His background had led him on a path of organized habits in both family upbringing and embracing the British laws that governed the New England Colonies of the early 1700s. He was 50 years of age when he embarked on this journey of exploration in 1793 that would result in moving his family and others to a new life in a new land.

Josiah Sawyer had an adventurist spirit, but he also had a penchant for opportunity. He too had a military family background, but he was not about to choose sides on the winds of independence. He made it known that he was travelling as an adventurer and in no part as a refugee from the Colonies. He was just 35 when he embarked on a journey that would "found" a town and change his life.

Both men had had enough of war. One was facing the loss of everything he had worked for, and perhaps more importantly for him, his integrity and his honour. They would need to travel to Quebec City from their hometowns in Massachusetts. There would be two or three routes to choose from: (1) Follow the Connecticut River north through New Hampshire, connecting to some Indigenous peoples' paths using an old Indigenous peoples' road through a northern and westerly route of rivers, paths, and swamps towards Nicolet to find the path on the south shore of the St. Lawrence River beyond Montreal. This eastern route would take them through the northern tip of

New Hampshire into the southern tip of Newport. (2) They could connect to the Arnold Trail from Maine, leading to Quebec City, a trail blazed by Benedict Arnold in his aborted attack on Quebec City in 1775. (3) Alternatively, they could choose the more westerly route through New Hampshire and Vermont, connecting to Lake Champlain and Missisquoi Bay. This route would take them westward towards Lake Champlain and down the Richelieu River to the south shore of the St. Lawrence River.[25]

Each of these routes posed significant risks. They ran through the hunting grounds of the Algonquin Nation of Iroquois, as well as a subtribe of the Abenaki called the Coosuck Indians, predominant in the northern region now known as Vermont, Massachusetts, and New Hampshire. The Iroquois occupied a tract around the Montreal area which meant they would need to travel in a northerly route from Lake Champlain but to the east.[17]

The Vermont route also would take them directly through a similarly hostile territory of Iroquois. The New Hampshire route between the navigable headwaters of Otter Creek, which enters those of the Black River discharging into the Connecticut River and ultimately the Connecticut Lakes, were also often frequented by these hostile parties. The route through New Hampshire to Lower Canada, down Halls Stream (also known as Indian Stream), became known as the "Indian Road" leading through to Quebec City.[17]

Edmund[5] and Josiah[4], along with their travelling party, embarked on an adventure of risk and purpose. Both men were risk-takers and perhaps the most entrepreneurial of their time. The preliminary steps to obtain a land grant would be to acquire several individuals intending to become settlers and organizing themselves into a company called "Associates." They, along with their other Associates, were to travel many times from the southern New England Colonies to claim and settle this new northern land. Regardless of the route, they travelled through paths, some bushed out, some a simple slash on a tree showing the way, through swamps, across rivers and lakes, and through sometimes hostile First Nations territories. As time was of the essence, they needed to convince not only their own families but the many other families to embark on this journey with them. They would bring their families from a life of relative civilization to one of extreme hardships from nature's uncertainties and the land itself, as well as hostilities from their southern neighbours.

These Associates would also need to understand that only one man is to act as their Leader in all matters of business with the government. Normally a vote would be undertaken to make that decision; however, since they were able to demonstrate they were both of good and able character, then the promise of these grants would be sufficient to carry them forward, each as "Leaders" on their path to settlement. To qualify for these grants, they had to make decisions quickly. These early grants were large tracts of land they would be responsible for, essentially setting up the basics of a society. The Leader was to bear all expenses incurred in managing the township, and bear responsibility to open roads both to and within the territory. He would be responsible for dividing these lots to accommodate road systems that would connect to other township roads.

These Leaders would also be responsible for all the planning and record-keeping to develop their respective communities. They would need to start by recording who was owed labour for road building, who was paid in coin, who was paid in produce and who was paid in kind. Bridges had to be built and land allocated for the eventual erection of churches, schools, and meeting houses, all of which had to be recorded. Simultaneously, they had their own land to clear, families to feed and house, and barns to build. One might wonder what their thinking would have been after learning of the responsibilities they would have to bear as Leaders, as they returned on their horses through the wilderness from Quebec City. All they had was a promise of lands not yet even seen or explored.

The Leaders were entrepreneurial businessmen in the sense that they also needed to create ways to sell produce, timber, grain, etc. Collectively, they would have to arrange for their produce to be taken to the closest market, typically many miles away via primitive roadways, bypassing unrelenting water passages, and then by boat to their destinations. Winter took its toll on these families, as did childbirth, disease, accidents, and the protection of their food stores from wild animals that also strived to survive. They lived on honour and trust, as they were contemplating a huge economic effort predicated on a simple promise of their lands. They would see seven years pass before the land would be officially theirs.

These tours of explorations were usually made on foot, though sometimes horses made the trip somewhat faster. Considering much of their travel was in dense bush, they would often have to walk, leading their horse. Many explorations were done alone, but for safety reasons, more often they were done with others who were also looking for settlement opportunity. These explorers had to be prepared with enough provisions of whatever they might need to survive. The need for axes, guns, ammunition, along with the indispensable camp kettle and foodstuffs were burdened by all in the party.[17]

Fire was indispensable, both for cooking and as a safeguard against the approaches of wild animals such as cougars, bears, moose, and wolves. The men always carried fire material, consisting of flint, lead and "spunk," and a single lead ball mould in their pockets. The mould would be heated in the campfire to remake the lead balls they retrieved from the animals they shot.[17]

Col. Edmund[5] Heard carried an unusual gun, date-stamped 1787. The rifle was a weapon issued to Loyalists soldiers, a sign of and confirming his British allegiance. These original "Wehrs" weapons were first brought into the American Colonies by early German settlers circa 1728.[3]

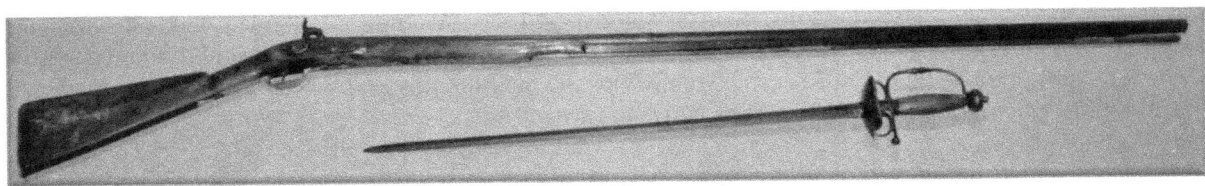

Col. Edmund[5] Heard's Wehrs rifle (gunmaker's script initials are illegible); sword crafted by Jacob Heard in 1752

"Of necessity, to suit the dense forests and tremendous distances of Colonial America, the large-caliber sturdy German rifle soon underwent modification. Originally a flintlock, it was converted to percussion. The caliber was reduced, permitting the hunters and trappers to carry a larger number of smaller lead balls. The barrel was made lighter to avoid fatigue and was lengthened to 61 inches long for greater accuracy and longer power combustion."[29]

These rifles had long been the weapon of choice and marksmanship in Germany, so it was natural that, among these settlers of artisans and craftsmen connected with arms manufacturing, they would prove useful in early America. The rifles were essentially modified as percussion weapons, the direct progenitor of the Kentucky rifle. Edmund[5] also carried a sword (then called a "rapier") made in 1752 by another ancestor, Jacob Hurd. Jacob and his sons, Nathaniel and Benjamin, were silversmiths circa 1702-1781 in the Boston area.[15]

Author's note: The gun, lead balls, cast iron single mould, carrying pouch, powder horn, sword, and a compass are all part of the Ancestral Heard/Hurd Collection.

Edmund and Josiah spent many nights in a first-world virgin forest of immense trees, with only "Mother Earth" for a bed, a widespread canopy of heaven for shelter, perhaps wind sighing, trees rustling, night owls screeching or wolves howling in the distance for a lullaby. The campfire was depended upon to keep away imagined, or otherwise, denizens of the forest. In addition to the fatigue of the journey, they suffered excessive annoyance from the swarms of spring blackflies, mosquitoes, and moose-flies. It is said, "when fully grown, these moose-flies can exceed a honeybee in size and has a sting so acute that horses will rear and become quite unmanageable when bitten by them." They were at their peak for about one month during the last two weeks of June and the first two weeks of July. Many nights were spent creating a smudge fire of "touch wood" taken from the trunks of trees growing in damp soils or, if available, pieces of cedar bark firmly tied together so that when lit they smoked. Travelling by day, the men were nearly blinded by these swarms of insects which seemed to follow them every step of the way.[17]

In the summer of 1793, Edmund and Josiah had built the first cabin and slashed the first 10 acres of land in Newport Township, Compton County. On a very early map of the Eastern Townships there appears a path called the "American Road." This road is shown as a slightly curving line from the upper reaches of the Connecticut River in the general direction of Quebec City. It is presumed that this path was named thus because it was generally the trail followed by our ancestors as they journeyed to Quebec City to make application for their land grants and as they progressed back and forth into the year 1800.[25]

Returning to Lancaster, Mass., Edmund and Josiah told of the wonderful richness of their newly discovered country and opened the way for the venturesome pioneers who were destined to overcome all difficulties to make a home in this new country known as Lower Canada.

Travelling from Massachusetts in 1793, via Missisquoi Bay on Lake Champlain, after exploring for 31 days through the woods with four oxen, two carts, tools, and provisions, Edmund and Josiah arrived on a hill they referred to as "Pleasant Hill." The area is now known as "Chemin Lapointe, Lot No. 6, Range 9," one mile east of what is now Randboro. They liked what they saw and decided this was where they would like to settle.[31]

Contrary to popular belief, these pioneer adventurers did not force anyone from the land. When they arrived, they found themselves completely isolated, "separated by 25 miles between their settlement and the U.S. border, and by 70 miles from the French to the North."[8]

When Josiah and Edmund slashed the first 10 acres in Newport Township, they both thought the area was in Eaton Township. When they returned the following spring of 1794, Josiah discovered his mistake and continued westward to where he now knew to be Eaton Township. That spring, he built the township's first log house, on the banks of the Eaton River where he later built the first mill, named Sawyers Mill.[16]

Josiah did not spend any length of time at Pleasant Hill, taking steps instead to secure the grant for the Township of Eaton. He had now made two or three trips to obtain a Charter for a large portion of Eaton Township, Lower Canada. He petitioned on behalf of his Associates for an equal amount of 1200 acres for each of them in the Township of Eaton, immediately west of Newport.[16]

As a young man, Josiah had met with an accident which bent his nose to one side. One time during his travels, when seeking a specific house, he stopped at a cabin for directions. The lady who answered the door graciously provided those directions, and later noted in her diary: "It would be impossible for him to follow his nose, because if he did, he would probably soon be back at her house."[23]

Edmund[5] was delighted to find himself in Newport in the summer of 1793, the very place he had applied for as an Associate of Steven Williams. This was where he and Josiah had built their first cabin and now his first crop was to be raised on this Newport land.

In 1794, Josiah returned with four men and their families to secure his claim in Eaton Township and to settle the land. Abner Powers and his wife were the first of the group to arrive. "Considering herself to be very plain," and the "first woman in the Township," she laughingly stated that for once she "was the prettiest lady in the Township."[23]

Josiah's wife, Susanna, had remained in New Hampshire for several months after the birth of their daughter, Polly, in late 1792. In the spring of 1794, she mounted her horse with the baby cradled in her arms to join Josiah on his second trip to Eaton to share with the toil of making a new home. The earliest trail used by the pioneers to reach Newport and Eaton townships was a bridle path north from Hereford to Sawyerville. The Hereford Trail left the Connecticut River and followed Hall Stream as far as present-day East Hereford; from where it followed the west branch around the west end of Lindsay Pond, through Clifton and on into Sawyerville.[25]

Josiah settled in and began building a home and a sawmill on the Eaton River at Sawyerville (in the early days called Sawyers Mills). Capt. Josiah Sawyer became one of the first settlers in the Township of Eaton and thus the town was named in his honour. Josiah had expected that the main road to and from Portland, Me., would pass through the town; however, it was to be located elsewhere much to the perceived injury of the town at the time.[25]

This story is not about military conquests and wars . . . we know much about them. It is about the families of Newport Township, the people themselves, their dreams, their hardships, anxieties, their losses, and how they "lived their lives" – the need to simply survive. It is also about the brave women and children who were uprooted to follow their men in carving out a future for their families, and who themselves made huge sacrifices to be a significant part of this new world. It is also about the passion, and happiness, and their lives as they lived them – about the freedom and the entrepreneurial spirit of sharing that drove these families to success. Stories such as this, powered by ancestry, make one feel that, as their descendants, we too are truly part of the history of Canada.

Historical plaque in Maple Leaf Cemetery (photo by Sandra Hurd)

The plaque pictured above is located at Maple Leaf Cemetery, in the area where Col. Edmund Heard and Capt. Josiah Sawyer built their first cabin, which they called "Pleasant Hill." It reads: "In 1793, Col. Edmund Heard and Capt. Josiah Sawyer came from Missisquoi Bay to this site, where they slashed the first acres of land in Newport Township (Compton County). This cemetery was donated in 1802 by William Heard."

This story is a salute to the sturdy pioneers and settlers who were our ancestors; and an appreciation of our inheritance of today . . . This is our culture . . . This is our heritage . . . This is who we are.

It has been said that "to understand the present, we must know the past." In the strenuous issue of daily life today, we are prone to forget things past, and so we lose much of our heritage to posterity and much of our interest in historic values. It is the author's intent to rekindle the memories of the past and bring forward some of the values exhibited by our ancestors as examples of the courage, determination and family sacrifices that have contributed to where we all are today.

***

Chapter 3   Early Settlers (1793–1800)

During the next 10 years, the Eastern Townships rapidly advanced towards settlement. Under the supervision of Joseph Bouchette, Esq., Surveyor General of Lower Canada, the townships were surveyed, named, and laid out for settlement. In Compton County, the townships of Compton, Eaton, Clifton, Newport, Auckland, Hereford, Westbury, Marston and Clinton were surveyed, while those of Bury, Lingwick and Ditton were partially surveyed.[16]

One of the conditions for the land grants assigned to the Leaders and their Associates was that these lands would be surveyed at their own expense. Edmund[5] Heard and Asa Waters arranged for and authorized the survey of Newport Township to be started and completed by the surveyor Christopher S. Bailey, of Leamington, Vt., who commenced the task on March 10, 1799. The detailed minutes are recorded and contained in the surveyor's *Field Book for Newport*. A current map of Newport with the original lots scribed as per the survey book is shown at the front of the book.[6, 38]

A surveying prerequisite stated that the breadth of each lot may be one-third the length, and that the length would not extend beyond any riverbank, but rather back into the mainland. This method would guarantee the township and its settlers would each have a convenient share of what accommodation the river may afford along its entire length. As logs were harvested, the river provided a means of transporting those logs not needed for immediate building use downriver to mills that had been built at falls or sites with a dam. Josiah Sawyer located the first lumber mill on the South Branch of the Eaton River at Sawyerville in Eaton Township, just west of the Newport Township line. He later built a gristmill on the opposite side of the rapids from the sawmill site.

Because there was no official government at the time and as part of the mandate for settling these "Crown waste lands," the Leader was to provide meticulous records of every transaction that took place during this time. Records had to be kept of every meeting, every vote, and all details of any transaction to render an accounting of who owed what, what was owed to whom, as steps were taken towards the building of roads, bridges and developing lands for commercial uses. Because the new government was slow in maturing, first when Upper Canada and Lower Canada were formed, and then following the British American Land Act (BALA), Edmund and his Associates kept these records hidden. This uncertainty continued from 1815 to 1867 (prior to Confederation), while the government was still unstable and so these records were simply kept in safekeeping.[20]

These settlers had experienced the War of Independence in the former New England Colonies where many of their buildings, records and possessions had been ransacked, burned, and destroyed. These events reinforced the notion of keeping these records in safekeeping. They had lost all records and deeds, etc. in the New England Colonies and were not about to risk losing them again.[17]

Edmund[5], when acting as Leader on behalf of the Associates, had to show his authority to act on their behalf to the effect that he was of responsible character. This was accomplished by presenting a petition for a certain tract of land that was to be made available, such as that Edmund was promised in Newport. To acquire land grants or purchase a tract of land from a source, an agent would first have to procure a certificate of reliability. Likewise, this agent would require assurances that those granting the land were equally reliable. This formality evolved due to the large number of people who left the Colonies south of the border and became squatters in Lower Canada. Those who had proven their loyalty to the British Crown through their military activities and had experienced embarrassments and losses in the American Revolution would be compensated for their losses by being issued land grants in Lower Canada. If requested, regress for these grievances could be compensated by cash or land.[3]

Standard procedure during this early stage of settlement was that the Loyalist settlers might draw lots for their lands. The lot numbers were written on paper and placed in a hat, then drawn by the waiting land buyers, one by one. They could not have their own choice of lands; they must take what came to them and make the best of it. In granting this land, every seventh lot was called a Clergy Reserve. The settlers were obliged to undertake a commitment to use these lots for churches, cemeteries, schools or meeting houses. In general, these were men of large families and limited means. These New England Colonies men were mostly of that energetic, self-reliant, and independent nature that gave assurances of success in any enterprise they might undertake.[24]

Arrangements between Agents, Leaders and Associates were mostly personal between the parties who shared equally before an actual "Settlement" was made. The normality for these land grants was 100 acres for every household head and 50 acres to every other person in the household. However, at this early stage, there were special circumstances whereby the Crown had the power to regain possession of the whole or part of the land if the land was required for military purposes. This was one of the reasons that ex-military patriots and supporters of the British colonies received specific regions according to their rank, often resulting in the acquisition of larger tracts of land – usually 200 acres. Exceptions to the rules were common and often made for Associates, particularly if they had sons, who were considered desirable acquisitions to the overall community. During the process of land acquisition, extra inducements were made whereby a larger proportion of land may be considered. Actual land "deeds" would not become available for some time. This process was slow to materialize and happened only after the lands were surveyed and registered in Quebec City.[24]

The instincts of these early settlers were keenly sharpened by the sheer nature of the dangers surrounding them. When Edmund Heard, Josiah Sawyer, and their Associates first arrived, they had to make provision for their own protection; not only from the Indians passing through the region, but also from their neighbours (sometimes relatives) from south of the border. Some of these early settlers were considered criminals and deserters by the Patriots of the newly formed United States, and therefore tracked down by bounty hunters for a fee and returned to the States for prosecution.[3]

The deer, moose, bears, rabbits and other animals of the forests provided an abundant source of tasty and nutritious wild meats. But before taking a shot, the settlers had to be relatively assured there was no enemy or bounty hunter lurking nearby who would be attracted by the report of a rifle.[17]

The settlers' log cabins were fortified to withstand the possible attacks of musket shots. In the spring when the land was to be ploughed and seed planted, a family member would need to be stationed nearby to give warning. Even when they went outside to work, the very woodpiles surrounding their cabins could be places where enemies might lurk, ready to ambush. And so, they carried their muskets with them wherever they went. At this time there were approximately 1000 pioneer settlers scattered in exceedingly small communities in this region of Lower Canada.[17]

These continued attacks by both bounty hunters and the Iroquois effectively aroused a united strength by which the conquest of Canada was finally implemented and ended scenes of massacre and devastation.[17]

Men such as Edmund[5], former residents of the revolting Colonies, having declared their allegiance to the British, would have been treated harshly if captured, so they were encouraged to disappear into the woods. Some were not as fortunate and were taken prisoner and returned south, while others were able to escape within Canada. In many cases women and children had been told by messengers to leave their homes and go to areas where they would be picked up eventually to join their husbands and fathers in British-held territory. At this time, borders were very loosely identified; many thought they were in Canada but were to find out that they were not.

While living in the Colonies, the Loyalists were not only fleeing persecution from their neighbours; vast acres of farmland had been destroyed, making it impossible to provide food for their families. Some of these women had been imprisoned and questioned about their husbands' activities and had also suffered physically. Many of these early settlers shared in the hardship and roles they now found themselves in: orphans, widows, handicapped, sick, young and old. One can only imagine the loneliness and isolation our ancestors would have experienced, virtually in survival mode in the middle of miles and miles of virgin forest timber.[29]

The first few years for Edmund, Josiah, their families, and the other early settlers could be called years of bare subsistence. Potatoes, corn, beans and grain were planted as soon as they had cleared some land among the trees. Every daylight hour was used; a permanent log cabin had to be built before their first winter. These first cabins were rudimentary and small, lacking windows or a floor. Stools cut from round logs became chairs. Logs flattened and legs inserted in holes made with an auger became tables. The cabin usually had only one room. The bedstead was made of "crotchet" stakes, consisting of the Y-shaped branch parts of a tree, driven into the ground. Round poles were laid into the "crotch" of the stakes to form the frame. Then, elm bark and softwood tree boughs were strung across, supporting a bed of straw if they had any. Sometimes this was topped with a bedding of grouse, partridge or goose feathers. Lights were created by placing some bear grease or beaver grease in a saucer in which a cotton rag was inserted, the upper end being lit. This type of living was not exceptional, it was what the settlers had to put up with during these early days. It reflects the typical hardships for hundreds of settlers who first came to the Eastern Townships, Newport being just one of them.[16]

As they waited for their first crops to be harvested, all members of the family had to find necessary food from what nature might provide them in the forest and streams. The forest was their larder; often they would have to reach high to hook something to bring it down for picking. This is probably where the term "by hook or by crook" originated, i.e., "I will get it!" Wild carrots and certain mushrooms were plentiful. Fortunately, wild game was also plentiful, there was an abundance of fish in the streams, and edible berries, plants, and nuts in the surrounding woodland.

However, as their gardens flourished, this brought its own challenges. As the settlers arrived and for a long time afterwards, their gardens also became a larder for the wild animals. Bears, very curious creatures, found these settlements of great interest, for here was a very convenient food supply. The bears were dangerous and destructive in their behavior, and the settlers found themselves defending both themselves and their gardens. Fruit of any kind on branches or stalks, such as raspberries, would be eaten and trampled. Wolves were the most feared; they ran in packs and would raise havoc around the settlements by taking down sheep or even a large cow by simply nipping their hind leg tendons. Domestic cattle and oxen did not kick back like deer would have, and thus became easy prey, requiring the settlers to tie them close to the barn or keep them indoors.

Foxes searched out the chickens, turkeys and geese, along with their eggs, making easy pickings. Rodents of all kinds continuously made a hit on their grains, while deer fed off their grasses and hay. Racoons, skunks and porcupines were abundant: "coons" made a play for any foodstuffs drying in the sun; skunks made nests under porches, and porcupines chewed on freshly cut stairs and barnwood. Rabbits attacked the gardens for any root vegetables. Birds roosted on the clotheslines, dirtying the hung laundry; hawks flew low to catch the young chicks out scratching in the yards. The fight for survival was equal for both humans and wildlife. Fish were perhaps the only wild foodstuff that did not fight back.

While their diet was nourishing, the settlers missed the bread and other grain foods that had played a big part of their previous diet. The story is told that "the wife of one settler dreamed one night that there was a loaf of bread in front of her. Unable to resist the temptation, she bit into the loaf only to discover that she had bitten her husband's shoulder. It is said that the husband left the following morning, travelled thirty miles to the nearest settlement on the Connecticut River, and returned with a sack of flour on his back so the family could again eat bread."[25]

Edmund[5] was a strong, resourceful man, who took charge and engaged all his Associates in the daily running of the Newport colony. His forte was arranging and organizing for the surveying process, road building, "building bees" for house- and barn-building and keeping the legalities in order – all evident in the record-keeping the author has drawn upon.[20]

Oxen were prized by early settlers as their first mode of power to operate their farms. Stoic, sturdy and strong, they required little care. Edmund[5] was experienced in using oxen. He was resourceful; amongst other things he was experienced in making "ox-yokes" and axe handles, cutting and stacking hay, and building fences out of split cedar logs inserted into pre-split posts.

Cutting and burning the trees not only gave the settlers more land to cultivate and more lumber to build with, but it became their first cash crop. Burning the root systems, where possible, gave the settlers ash, which in turn could be reduced to lye for making soap and potash for fertilizer. These could be sold to a ready market both in Canada and abroad.

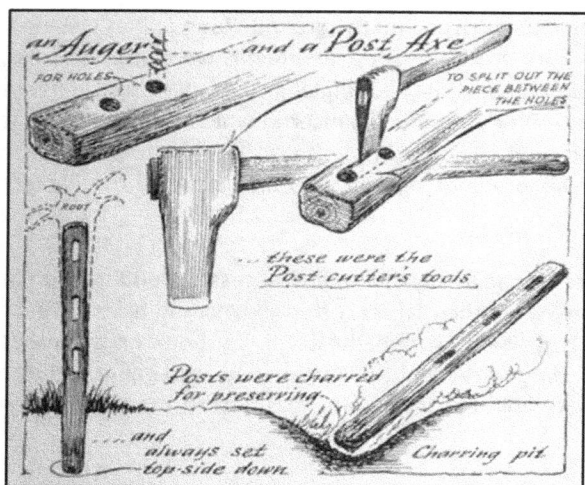
Auger and post axe – tools used to build a fence (pinterest.ca)

Our ancestors had another cash crop opportunity from the furs and hides obtained from the many wild animals in the forest, some of which were continuously attacking their own livestock. Traplines were set along streams and riverbanks during the winter when their furs were at their prime. Deer and moose, in addition to the meat supplied, furnished skins that could be made into fine leather. There were bears, wolves and foxes; otters, beavers, martens and muskrats; some wildcats; hares and squirrels. Game birds were abundant in both the forest and rivers. There were wild ducks and partridges (a species of grouse) and others of the feathered race. In the first few years, passenger pigeons were so plentiful that large flocks would darken the sky. These birds were shot, cleaned, salted, and sold on the Montreal markets by the barrelful.[25]

A bibliographical note on the United Empire Loyalists (UEL) website provides important insight:

It is astonishing how little documentary evidence that Loyalists left behind them with regard to their migration. Of the Loyalists who settled in Upper Canada and Lower Canada there is hardly one who left behind him a written account of his experiences. Many of them were illiterate and those who were literate were so occupied with carving a home for themselves out of a wilderness that they had neither time nor inclination for literary labours.[49]

We are fortunate that Colonel Edmund[5] Heard and his Associates who settled in Newport appeared to be quite educated and had encouraged their children in this regard. The source of much information about early Newport is contained in a document titled *Newport first Records*. This document relates to the settling, organization, land grants and governing aspects of the new Township during the period from 1791 to 1814.[20]

***

Chapter 4   Survival (1793–1814)

Except for Josiah Sawyer nearby in Eaton Township, Edmund[5] Heard was alone in Newport Township for a period of time while he explored the territory. The terms of the settlement for Newport Township, which measured 10 miles x 10 miles (100 square miles), were created with the express provision that settlers populate the land.[28]

The first cabin Edmund built was eight feet square, with log walls, a bark roof, and a floor of packed earth. It was to serve more as a shelter until he would bring his family to the site. The logs were hewn by axe and notched at the corners to create solid walls that would support a roof heavily laden with snow. The large spruce logs had provided him with pitch oozing from the bark, which he had used as glue to stick moss, small branch sticks and clay to fill between the cracks.

The land in the immediate region where Edmund had built his cabin was relatively flat with rolling hills bearing forests of tall spruce, pine, maple, black birch, elm and white ash. During this time alone, Edmund travelled with his horse Jess along the South Branch of the Eaton River, noting where tall softwoods permeated the landscape and groves of cedar were prevalent on the lowlands. In one area he noted the river flowed tightly around some bends between high rock formations, causing a rushing force of waterfalls. Further upriver he noted the openings of meadows, where he would stop to allow Jess to feed on the sweet meadow grasses.

Edmund noted the availability of gravel in large mounds by the curvatures of the river. The eddies in the gravel offered up an abundance of both speckled and rainbow trout. Clearly this would be a great source of available food. It was here that he came upon "as fine a bush as I ever saw, Beech and Maple and a rich undergrowth of rotted leaves from centuries of composting, a perfect site for settlement."[3]

Edmund immediately knew these were beech trees, noted for their leaves hanging on until spring. The leaves remain because the stem base does not form the cork layer next to the branch. The fresh new leaves push off the old leaves in the spring. In the fall, the leaves turn bronze but soon weather to a light tan colour. They get tissue-thin before the winter is over. Our early settlers recognized that these leaves were perfect to stuff their mattresses with, and so treasured finding a beech grove. Beech can grow up to 100 feet tall with a diameter of over six feet, even larger in old-growth forests. Edmund also knew that any settler families would source these groves out for beech nuts, which were a good source of protein.

A mature tree will not produce nuts until it is at least 40 years old. Even then, the beech nuts may only appear every two to eight years. Edmund also knew that these trees attracted black bears that would climb these immense trees for the nuts. It was a long-awaited treat for the bears, therefore when one entered a beech grove that is shedding beech nuts, one needed to be wary.

Edmund travelled with his gun and compass in hand. He took a route from the river in a more northerly direction to find tall hardwoods groves of maple, birch and beech on the higher lands to the north and east as well.

Later Edmund explored the lands to the northwest, coming upon the North Branch of the Eaton River. Following the river downstream through similar meadows, he found an abundance of tall softwoods and cedar. He came to a convergence of yet another river, the two now creating a larger river heading further west. It was at this junction that he suspected that this converging river might be the very same one that would lead him back to his cabin. Indeed, he followed the river upstream, coming upon Josiah Sawyer's camp. Edmund continued his travels until he again came to familiar territory and concluded that Newport offered two rivers, both flowing from east to west. This discovery further encouraged his vision that this was an ideal location to bring settlers.

Edmund found that deer were also as plentiful, as were the fish in the river. When he needed meat, he would stalk a deer, carefully removing the lead ball from the flesh to keep for another time; it was important to conserve any musket shot he had, as he would have to travel many miles to find someone who might have a supply. He carried a supply of these lead balls in a leather pouch along with his powder horn and always with his gun, which he carefully guarded as his life depended on it. Because there was a spring near his cabin, he would take only the choice part of the animal and only enough to last him a few days, travel back to his cabin and hide the meat under a log in the spring-fed brook of cold water to keep it fresh. As he would never leave any animal residue near his cabin, he would leave the rest for the wild animals to eat.

The forest held secrets available only to the bobcats that would shriek in the night, the wolves that stalked the deer, the rabbits trying to outfox the foxes, and the ever-present black bears feeding on berries in the meadows. Because he was a military man, Edmund took notes of the landscape, including the many beaver dams throughout the township. He made note of the countless springs emitting a steady flow of cold drinkable water, all flowing down to the rivers. These streams were loaded with speckled trout in spawning season. Edmund also noticed much bigger fish moving upstream: hundreds of Atlantic salmon, migrating upriver to the smaller streams to spawn. As the land rose to a higher level, he came to another place where he could look over acres and acres of solid woodlands, both to the east and to the west.

Edmund became an avid explorer, a woodsman living off the land from an abundance of ready foods, swimming in crystal clear waters, examining the possibilities before him and thinking of his families and the life of opportunity that lay before him. He stayed in Newport that first winter, having gathered dry driftwood from the river to use as firewood. He had also cut a sizable woodpile earlier in the spring for this very purpose. He added a lean-to shed on the end of the cabin for his horse, Jess, and also a small connecting door from the cabin to the lean-to so heat could be shared on especially cold nights and days.

That first winter, with no hay to feed Jess, Edmund would ride her down to the meadows each day to forage grasses found in secluded spots under cedar trees protected from heavy snows. Free-flowing water from the springs was always available under the brook ice. With the ice frozen on the river, he would guide Jess onto the river ice so she could reach up to feed on the overflowing hay hanging down under the snow off the riverbank. Simple survival requires skill, ingenuity, resourcefulness, and bravery. By the end of the following summer, Edmund had a vision for where he would propose settling the lands. He was satisfied that this was the land where he wanted to secure his resting place, where he would build on his future and invite his family and others to join him.

Upon receiving the promise of 1200 acres from Stephen Williams, the agent of the Township, Colonel Edmund[5] began an opening in the lower southwest part of the township. Before a new house could be built for the family, they had to protect their only investment for survival from the onslaught of winter. The first shanty or log cabin that Edmund had erected the previous year close to Pleasant Hill for this very purpose would protect them for the summer while they built a new homestead. In the spring of 1795, they moved into a new house near his cabin at Pleasant Hill with his second wife, Elizabeth, their son Samuel[6] and daughter Hannah, becoming the first settlers in Newport Township.[20]

To conserve space, Edmund[5] and his youngest son Samuel[6] had removed all the wooden handles from the tools they brought from the New England Colonies. They remade handles for their axes, chisels, saws, spokeshaves and other metal tools in Newport. Along with an axe, the spokeshave was perhaps one of the tools most used in construction for shaving down boards and fashioning handles, door hinges, latches and wooden pegs.

A wooden mallet was another important tool, used for tapping logs and wooden joint pins into place. To construct a mallet, they would select a variety of smaller logs, both hardwood and softwood and cut them into several sizes of round blocks. They would auger a two-inch hole in the middle of the block, use the spokeshave to fashion a handle, then pound the handle into the block. A variety of mallets of various sizes were used for different purposes.

Bounty hunters from the newly independent United States were very active in hunting down British Loyalists escapees. Edmund and his family needed a secure space to hide out if there was any suggestion of a bounty hunter in the region.

Early in the spring of 1795, the Edmund[5] Heard family commenced building a stone foundation and upper-level barn that was to accomplish two key purposes. The building was constructed to look like an ordinary barn, placed directly on the hidden stone foundation. They needed to provide shelter for the oxen as well as the other farm livestock they

Hand-hewn spruce 10 x 10 support post in the original Heard home (photo by Sandra Hurd)

would retrieve from the Colonies in the fall. It also had to provide a place to store food for both the family and their livestock. The livestock would provide supplementary heat for the family, as they were all to be housed together in the stone basement. This was to be their accommodation for the following winter.

The basement itself was deliberately concealed by a large trap door under the hay chute. An air chute, built to look like a beam, extended up from the cellar to the upper floor for ventilation. There were two reasons for their deliberate choice of location for this first "house-barn," hidden away from the original log cabin Edmund had built earlier. First, the empty cabin nearby could possibly serve as a decoy to any bounty hunters; and second, the spring water was abundant and flowed naturally down to the homestead location, serving both the family and their livestock.

The settlers used pole logs for the roof, laying them from the ridge pole to the eaves, arranging the larger ends alternatively to allow the natural tapering to fill in for a tight fit. Where the logs rested on the eaves, they were then caulked with small pieces of wood, hammered tightly in place using a wooden mallet, to create a solid fit. This method served to strengthen the roof poles and also prevented rodents from entering.

Spaces were cut out for doors and windows; the very sturdy doors were built of smaller wood logs, hinged using curled wood knurs or roots carved out in such a way as to allow for wooden pins to be inserted. The roof was covered with hemlock bark they had harvested in the spring when it peeled off readily.

The original cellar is still in place today, on the original Lot 7B, 10th Range, generally known as the "Luke Hurd farm." This first house-barn on the property might have looked much like the beginnings of a barn in the photograph below, in that it was constructed over a cellar base and positioned on the side of a sloping bank. This slope allowed for a door to the outside to move the livestock in and out. Perhaps a corral may have been constructed at the north end of the barn on the slope which would have allowed the livestock water access to the free-flowing brook, running from two springs above. Note the stumpage that was evident everywhere at that time; our ancestors were not interested in keeping trees around the buildings that could otherwise be used for building purposes.

Cleared land leaving stumps around every building, normal for the times (Hélène Landry, Fonds Jean-François Pelletier, Bibliothèque et Archives nationales du Québec (BAnQ))

The rather low log building above the cellar was used in their second year for storage of food for the livestock and served as habitation until a suitable house (1796) was constructed. The original house also on this property was the first built in the township, sometime around 1796-97.[31]

Author's note: Once the sawmills in the area became active, circa 1840-60, these old log houses and barns began to be retrofitted with mill-sawn lumber and planking. The beams, however, were still hand-hewn and pegged for many years to come, and it was not uncommon to rebuild over the previously dug cellars. The barn now on the Heard/Hurd homestead has been rebuilt over the original cellar and was increased in size to what is today.

In 1793, Edmund[5] had received a payout from his eldest son, Edmund[6], now living in Holden, Mass., who had returned to him a debt in the amount of 37 pounds 7 shillings, clearing his debt. With this payment and some additional funds, Edmund[5] paid off his remaining debt to David Baldwin Jr. in February 1794 for the years 1793-95 when he was constructing his new home and securing the livestock the family would need to survive and grow. Now debt free, he and his family could carry on with their new life in this new venture. All commissioned men in the military received a stipend from their local governments and were therefore considered good risks for debt by merchants of the time.[3]

Edmund[5] and his second family had, in good faith, made considerable improvements where he resided, not doubting that his work would be acceptable to the wishes and views of the British government. This was a family that had and continued to persevere through the most difficult struggles, against constant enemies: the harsh winters, short summers, endless forests and the loneliness of living in a vast landscape with none of the amenities we would consider the norm today. His children, Sarah, Edmund[6], and Luke, were now in their mid-twenties. Sarah lived in Shrewsbury; Edmund[6] had previously lived in Lancaster but was now in Holden, Mass.; and Luke lived in Portland, Me., during this time. That now left Samuel and Hannah, who were only 19 and 17 respectively, to work with their parents to settle the new land.[2, 9]

His eldest son, Edmund[6], had been appointed first sergeant in Captain Ezra Sawyer's company of cavalry in 1792 at Lancaster, Mass. The certificate had been signed by his father, Col. Edmund[5] Heard.[19]

On June 24, 1797, Edmund[5] petitioned the Government of Lower Canada to confirm their rights to the land, along with each of their Associates, and a similar quantity of land without prejudice to their former petitions north of and adjoining those lands already ordered to their petitioners and their Associates. In many cases the elder sons were of an age to join the company of Associates and draw land for themselves.[20]

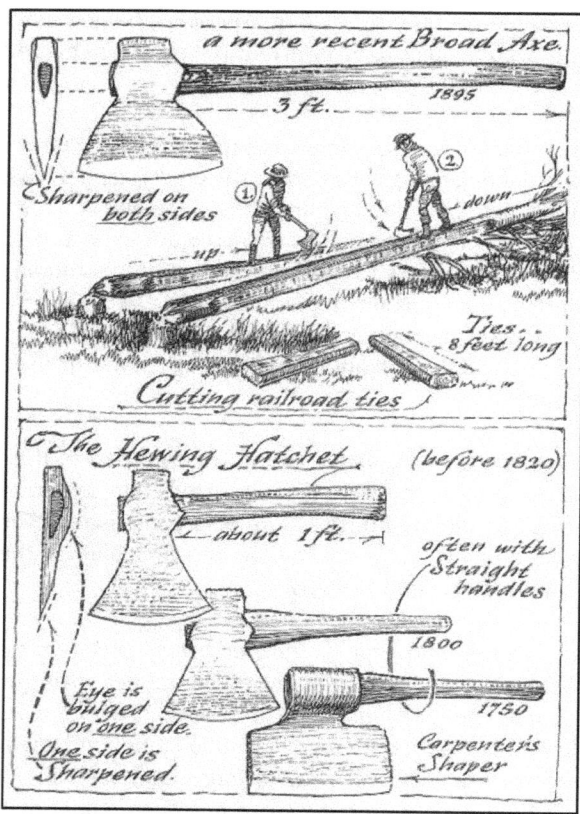

Illustration of early tools carried by every settler (pinterest.ca)

Samuel[6] Heard, youngest son of Col. Edmund[5], born at Worcester, Mass. in 1773, married Miriam Gibbs at Berlin, Mass., in July 1797. Once married, they moved together back to Newport to be with his father and sister Hannah in 1797 but settled on their own Lot 6 on the 11th Range, overlooking his father's farm on Lot 7 in the 10th Range. Miriam and Samuel had eight children – five sons and three daughters – all born in Newport: Henry Herschel (born 1799), Elizabeth Andrews (born 1803), Samuel (born 1805), Robert Powers (born 1807), Alexander (born 1808, died at age 21), and their youngest, daughter Miriam Gibbs (born 1815). Two of their children died in infancy: Hannah (born 1810) and George Augustus (born 1812).[4]

Author's note: The author identifies the lots, even though the official land survey had not yet been completed, so the reader may check the map provided to have a sense where they would have been living.[28]

Samuel and Miriam, with Edmund's assistance, began to build their new home in 1797. Virgin spruce was in abundance in Newport and became a preferred building material for two reasons: it has good strength, yet it is a soft wood and has a straight grain, meaning one can rip-cut it into boards. After cutting down the trees they would be stored crisscrossed in piles to dry. The following spring the bark would peel off easily and they were much lighter to carry and move around to a building site. Also, the pitch was generally dried out, making the logs easier to cut and split. They used a series of axes (some commonly known as a broad axe and an adze) they had brought with them to accomplish this task. Once they had built their log buildings, they cut out the doors and windows, framing them with spruce that was either split or rip-sawn with hand saws into boards. Because their time was important, they generally cut off the ends of the logs on the building corners only after the roof had been built. For door hinges, Samuel selected curved root ends and carved them into large hinges; when fastened to the door they acted as a brace to hold the wide boards together.

When they built their hearth fireplace, they added a low stone shelf about four feet in length along each side. On any cold morning, the small children would sit on this stone-style bench, called the "hob," as soon as they were dressed, there to stay until the room became considerably less chilly.

***

Early in their first year Elizabeth and Miriam planted carrots, potatoes, onions, peas, beans, and radishes. Elizabeth brought some rhubarb roots and other root starts from their garden in Massachusetts to plant in their new garden.

Samuel built a larder on stilts, out of reach from most animals, and not far from the cabin. This small building was equipped with a horizontal bark-free log acting as a spit. The log rested on two carved holders. Four holes were drilled in one end so that he could put a peg in to turn the log, the other hole with a peg to hold it in place. The log could be turned using a simple long peg that he used to crank an animal carcass up through a trap door to hang for curing. After the carcass cured, Samuel cut up the meat for winter use. Once the meat was frozen, it was laid in large barrels. The larder was the perfect place in which to store meat and vegetables, the latter put in sand buckets in the fall and lifted up in the same way. He made a removable ladder to climb up to open the door.

***

William[5] Heard, born in Ipswich in 1755, was Col. Edmund[5] Heard's brother. He and his first wife, Betsey Dix of Holden, Mass., had six children, all born in Holden. However, Betsey died in 1794, leaving him with six young children, two sons and four daughters, ranging in age from a 10-year-old son to a 1-year-old daughter. William and Betsy's children were Thomas (1784-1863), Eunice (1785-1866), William[2] (1788-1850), Betsey (1789-1869), Nancy (1791-1855) and Sally (1793-1877).[4]

William married his second wife, Thirza Williams, in 1797. They resided at Northumberland and Stewartstown, N.H., for a year before they immigrated with his six children to Newport, Lower Canada.[4]

William[5] was in the militia of Minute Men, a company in Col. Doolittle's regiment in which he remained until 1775. The other first settlers in Newport were joined by William and his wife Thirza when he was appointed an Associate under Col. Heard's group. They were granted Lot 8 of Range 10, and lots 10, 11 and 12 in the 7th Range of Newport Township in 1798. Together they raised William's six children and their own nine children on their homestead, which would become known as the Maple Leaf community.[4]

Statira Heard, daughter of William[5] and Thirza Heard

The six children from William's first marriage, as they became teenagers, travelled back to the newly formed New England states to be married. The four eldest continued to live long lives there. Their two youngest daughters, Nancy and Sally, were both married in Newport, later moved and raised their families in Melbourne, Lower Canada.

William and Thirza's nine children were all born at their new homestead in Newport: Wilder (1798); Zilpha (1801); Edmund (1805); twin daughters Anna and Fanny (1805); Chester (1807); Jeremiah ("Jerry") E. (1809); Statira (1812); and Lois (1814). Jerry later moved to Barnston, Lower Canada, when his children were very young, to raise his family on a farm there.[4]

Thirza mentioned in her conversation with Samuel[7] Heard some years later, "*in the first year we had settled, in 1798, we were so short of the necessities of what would keep body and soul together that for three weeks all we had that was eatable was the milk of a three-year-old cow; no bread but some greens herbs that grew in the forest which I gathered and boiled and with a little salt made this food palatable.*"[10]

William's nine children from his second marriage all married and stayed in Canada, raising their families in various places, except for their second-youngest, Statira (1812-1892), who grew up in Newport but moved with her husband to Wisconsin. The photo of Statira on the previous page is the only known picture of any of William's family.

Much later, Edmund[6] Heard's daughter, Lucy, moved to Melbourne, Lower Canada, when she married her husband George Gibson of Melbourne. Her aunts, Nancy and Sally (William and his first wife Betsey's daughters), were still living in Melbourne with their husbands when Lucy joined them in their communities.[4]

William was a military man but known as a yeoman and tanner of leather, and his presence in the community was welcomed by his talents in curing hides and making leather items such as boots, shoes, and leggings for the settlers. He also dabbled in making a few horse collars and saddles that were used by those travelling back and forth to the New England states.

The settlers raised large families because this would be their future. They learned to live on their harvests and gained comfort from their faith. Like all pioneers before them, they became a closely knit and strong, interdependent people, deeply rooted to the land. Ingenuity was key to survival, and together as a group this community was able to survive this wilderness. The winter season defined these settler's mettle more than the other three seasons combined. As there were no real roads between the settlements, all the settlers would, as Samuel[6] did, blaze a trail between the homesteads. At first walking paths, these trails later became single horse paths. In later times some of these were bushed out and became the roads as we might know them today.

> *Author's note: What is being described with regards to their day-to-day survival and how they went about building their homesteads and first crops, whether it is in the names of Heards, or anyone else, the story not only represents what they did but is an example of what **all** the first settlers had to do in order to survive.*

Edmund[5] and his wife Elizabeth; their daughter Hannah; their son Samuel[6] with his wife Miriam; Edmund's brother William[5] and his six children with his second wife, Thirza – all had their first Christmas together in Edmund's house in December 1798. Edmund enjoyed a feeling of family togetherness once more for the first time in many years as they sat around the fireplace. The fireplace filled every need and was the centre of all household activity. Before the advent of old-fashioned "sulphur" matches, particular care was exercised to keep a fire. At bedtime live coals were covered with ashes to keep them through the night and used to kindle the morning fire. From this practice came the word "curfew" from the French "couvre le feu." If the coals should all die out, someone usually had to get on a horse and head to a neighbour's house to borrow some live coals, not something one would want to do at the best of times, especially in the dead of winter. The only alternative would be to strike a spark with flint and steel; a spark falling into a "tinderbox' on some partly scorched bit of linen and gently blown with one's breath into a tiny flickering flame of pine shaving.[18]

And so, they all sat around the hearth fireplace, the young girls sitting on the "settle," drawn up to one side of the fireplace, while the boys and older folks gathered around on wooden chairs and perhaps a couple of rocking chairs for Elizabeth and Thirza. The fireplace was not only for cooking but was also the source of heat for the house. It was also the gathering place for the families to just sit and tell their stories of the day, while a pot of beans might be heating at the back for anybody to eat as the day progressed. The settle was a long bench with room for four children; it had a high back and boards running down to the floor. These back boards kept off the draft toward the fireplace, not only from one's back but from one's feet as well. The high back also reflected the heat from the fireplace. Edmund and William had become adept at whittling and fashioning farm tools and household items, and whittling was a common evening occupation while the family sat together. Native woods were plentiful and of considerable variety, the most-used being white pine, ash, hickory, birch, maple, and cherry. Maple would make the best teeth for a hand rake, ash was used for bows and ax handles, and pine was easily worked into a long-handled spoon for stirring the beans.[18]

For this Christmas, they had a dressed a large turkey which they cooked on a spit in the fireplace. The spit was an iron rod hung on small hooks on the andirons and was turned from time to time with a crank. A large baking pan was used to catch the drippings, which were used to make gravy. This Christmas they were able to exchange gifts, wrapped in homemade pillowcases – flour bags stitched, coloured and embroidered by Miriam and Thirza. Inside each package were homemade socks, mittens, scarves, and hats – all made from wool yarn that Miriam had brought with her from the New England Colonies. Edmund, William and Samuel had found time to hand-whittle some toys for the children. William's children must have been so excited to receive these gifts, perhaps their first. With the previous loss of their mother Betsey, their lives had been in limbo and had changed forever.[31]

Their wives, Elizabeth, Thirza and Miriam, and daughter Hannah were forced to bear their part of the self-denials and deprivations which were invariably the lot of the early settler. Both their strength of mind and their physical energies were often tasked to the utmost in caring for their families and others of their community.

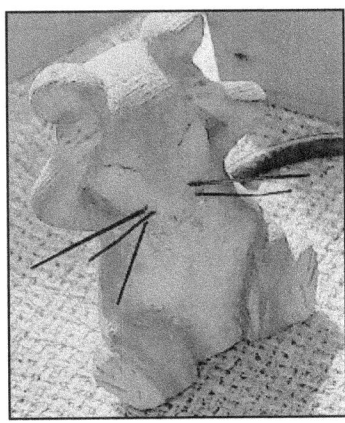

A hand-carved toy typical of the era (unknown Internet source)

Unfortunately, within the following two years, both Edmund's wife, Elizabeth, and their daughter, Hannah, moved back to New England; Elizabeth because of the extreme living conditions and Hannah for the opportunity to marry. Imagine what life must have been like at nighttime . . . many homes with only a dirt floor . . . no lights, wild animals lurking, the sounds of screeching bobcats and even panthers.[4]

There was little time devoted to education in the first decade of settlement. Most teaching took place in the home and was based on general survival for everyone including the children. They learned from life itself and sufficient to read and write for basic requirements. The first settlers worshipped in their homes. Some settlers buried their dead at their farms until community cemeteries were designated. When tragedy struck, with beloved sisters dying in childbirth, there was little time to grieve. They were taught the simplicities of life including reading the Bible, which provided a source of strength as well as literature.

Candle-making was an essential annual chore in all settlement-era households. Taper candles were the primary source of lighting for their homes. These home-made candles did not burn well; they emitted an odour and the light produced was dim and flickering. However, that is all they had to work with. Since they were made from tallow or animal fats, the event usually coincided with the autumn butchering of barnyard animals for meat. Tallow was made from the fat of all barnyard animals, but fat from sheep or cattle was preferred. Pig tallow had a very bad smell and would be used only as a last resort, depending on what animals they had as surplus and/or were not breeding. While butchering in the fall was predominantly men's work, the painstaking task of making candles fell to the women. Since the average household needed several hundred candles a year, this was a large job that took significant investment in time and labour.[42]

Elizabeth, Miriam, Thirza and the other wives of the community made their candles in these first early years by the dripping method. Strands of cotton twine were twisted together to create a wick. The wicks were attached to a stick and then dipped repeatedly until the candles attained the proper size. Homemade candles, prepared in the autumn, chased away the dark of the long winter's night in Newport Township these first years, but beyond that provided little comfort.

Coarse flour and homemade yeast, the ingredients for their bread of daily life, were still tasty and provided the main source of nourishment. Since the settlement began, the outdoor bread oven was an essential feature for most families. Built on loam close to the house or in the summer kitchen, it was covered with sheets of bark or untrimmed planks to protect it from the weather. Stone was mixed with lime and water to create a kind of hut, which was surrounded with stone, providing a flat surface in which the loaves were placed for baking. The fire pit was the "bake oven," heating both the stones above and those surrounding the pit. Once the wood was burned to ash, it would be removed, and the bread slid in the cavity on a paddle for baking. The bread usually had a black bottom, due to ash remaining on the hearth, and so the "upper crust" was the favoured part of the loaf. The "moccasin" loaf of bread weighed six pounds. The head of the house traced a cross, with the blade of a knife, on top of the loaf as an indication of thanks to God for their daily bread.[24]

***

Entered into the *Newport first Records*:

That on the 24th day of June 1797, Edmund Heard petitioned the Government that Newport Township might be granted to him and his associates accordingly, on the 22nd of March 1800, an order of Council parsed on his favour and as follows. And whereas the Executive Council of the said Province, having duly & maturely considered the said petition, have thereof in part approved & have adjudged it to be reasonable & advisable that one Quarter of the said tract or parcel of Land so situate as aforesaid should be granted unto the said Edmund Heard & his said Associates & his and their heirs and assigns forever upon the terms and conditions prescribed by His Majesty's Royal Instructions in this behalf.

Now therefore having taken the premises into consideration by this Warrant of Survey's, I do empower & require you at the proper costs & charges of the said Edmund Heard & his Associates to make a faithful & exact Survey of the said tract or parcel of land described as above, set forth by the name of the Township of Newport and to subdivide the said Township into Lots of Two Hundred acres each & in the execution of this warrant.

Further that you make & reserve appropriation of Lands within the same for the support of the Protestant Clergy within the said Province, that ids to say, one seventh of the Township. Further that the lots be laid out so that the breath of each lot may be one third of the length and the length may not extend along the bank of any river, so that the Grantees may each have a convenient share of what accommodation the said River may afford for navigation or otherwise. [20]

The survey was completed in the fall of 1799 and recorded as indicated in the image below.[20]

1799 land survey *(Newport first Records)*

And so, it came to be that the first settler families in the Township of Newport, circa 1793-99, consisted of Col. Edmund[5] Heard Sr., his son Samuel[6], Edmund's brother William[5] Heard Sr., Langley Willard, Nathanial Beaman Jr., Peter Trueman, John Squires, William Hudson, his son Elisha Hudson Jr., and Caleb Stirdivant, and their respective families. This first grant to Edmund[5] and his Associates consisted of 55 lots, each lot containing 200 acres. A total of 33 lots were granted by Agreement to his Associates along with a total of 22 lots granted to Edmund[5] and other Heard family members.

For later census-taking, it was important that a record be kept identifying exactly which lot they were clearing for their homestead as part of the Agreement. The columns on the right of the document show the year that their homesteads were built and the lots they settled on. This was one of the regulations put in place to ensure speculators were not just acquiring land lots with no intention of settling on them. They were a sturdy group of 10 families, already fifth-generation settlers in North America, determined to make the grade in Lower Canada as did their fathers before them in the New England Colonies. In order to ascertain their specific lots, the survey needed to be completed. The number of Associates increased to 24 in the land survey of Newport Township completed in late 1799.[20]

At this time, Col. Edmund[5] Heard's son Edmund[6], now living with his family in Holden, Mass., had committed to his father his family's desire to move to Canada if the land grants were to materialize, and so the lots assigned to him would have been speculative. His father, Col. Edmund[5], was most anxious for him to make his decision to move as soon as would be possible since he had already identified his homestead on Lot 2.

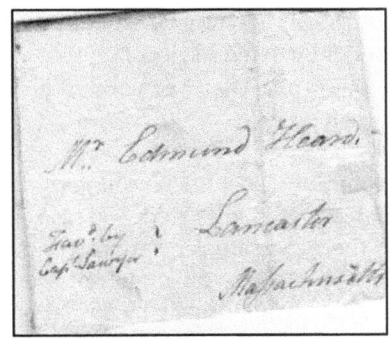

Letter from Col. Edmund[5] Heard to his son Edmund[6]. Note the reference *"Trav. by Capt. Sawyer"*

Edmund[5] became anxious by September 1799, as he had expected his son's appearance by now. He wrote a letter to him asking if he had changed his mind about coming to Canada. He mentioned that his brother, *"Samuel had a fine son and they were looking forward to seeing him and that Samuel, now a Captain in the Reserve Militia for Newport, was out surveying for roads in the woods otherwise he would have written as well, signing off as being in good health, your affectionate father."*[10]

In most cases during these early times, letters were hand-delivered from person to person to those travelling through to the Colonies as there was no mail service within Lower Canada. Mail could be handled, however, within the New England Colonies, and once across the border was deliverable through their mail service. This letter from Edmund was to be taken to John[6] Sage French by Samuel Heard. His father, John[5] and his two eldest sons, Luther[1] and Levi[1] French were Associates with Capt. Josiah[4] Sawyer in Eaton Township. They were supposed to meet halfway at a predetermined spot in the woods, however, *"Samuel could not find Mr. French."* The letter was to have been taken to Josiah Sawyer who was planning another trip to the U.S., where he would mail the letter. [21]

Postage was paid by the recipient, not the sender, and was charged by the number of pages. Paper was scarce, so letters were written covering one side of the page, then turned over to write across their own writing, carefully writing along the edges sideways as well. They would then fold the letter so that a space was left for the address in the centre of the folded sides. Many times, the letter would have writing on the corner leaves of the fold as well.[21] The address would be very simple; like "Edmund Heard, Newport, Canady." (Note the spelling of "Canada" they used at that time in many of their letters.)

The men in these first families generally spent the summer preparing to bring their families north to begin settlement on the lots they had blazed out. They would build a cabin or barn-like dwelling to provide essential shelter for the families and livestock through their first winter. They would then travel back to their respective areas in New England in the winter to fetch their families and their belongings, including additional tools that had been left in safekeeping with relatives. Travel in the winter was much easier than dealing with mud-soaked passages in the spring or summer; the loaded sleds glided over the snow-packed trails.

As recorded in the *Newport first Records*: *"Further that you report whether there is any & what quantity of lands contained within the said Township fit for the production of Hemp & Flax or either of them. [Dated] Sept 25, 1800."*[20]

From the first group of 10 Associates in 1793 to 1797, the group grew by another eight for a total of 18 by 1802. On November 22, 1802, there were 18 participants, resulting in 22 polls, both from Newport and Eaton in a subscription for an undertaking, proportionate to their holdings, in the building of a road to Nicolet.

The total cost of the undertaking was calculated at $50.03, a large sum of money for this time, calculated at $0.055 per ten acres of land held. Samuel Heard was Presiding Clerk at the meeting held at the home of Asa Waters.[20] Among those who signed were some of these new subscribers who signed to work or pay proportionately. They were: *"Solomon Bowker, John Bowker, John Harvey, Rudolphus Harvey, Jeffrey Maynard, David Metcalf and Nathanial Beaman Jr."*

Given under the Hand and Seal at Arms at the Castle of St. Louis in the City of Quebec, by his Excellency's Command:

"Accordingly, on the 12th Day of March 1801, the warrant was returned done by Christopher S Bailey & Deputy Surveyor & signed Samuel Holland Surveyors general of said Province. The cost of the whole survey was (in lieu of) Lbs. currency. And on this day of July, following a Patent parsed the great seal in favour of the said Edmund Heard & his Associates, eleven in number." They were *"Edmund Heard, Samuel Heard, Longley Willard, Edmund Heard Jr., Nathanial Beaman Jr., Peter Trueman, John Squires, William Heard Sr., William Hudson, Elisha, Hudson Jr., and Caleb Stirdivant."*

This community had organized themselves into a body which met regularly for the transaction of any business affecting the interests of the settlement. The settlement was already eight years old when a local committee *"to form some necessary Regulations for the Inhabitants"* and *"keeping and maintaining Good Order"* had been organized in September 1799; it was probably the first local government in all the Eastern Townships.[20]

A meeting of the Newport Township Associates was held in Sutton, Mass., on September 28, 1799, at the house of Asa Waters, a non-resident of Newport. Asa was chosen as moderator, Edmund[5] was voted in as clerk and his son, Samuel[5] Heard, William Hudson and John Lebourveau as a committee to form the necessary regulations for the inhabitants of Newport Township. This first meeting was followed by several meetings, all of which were documented in *"Newport firſt Records of 1800."* The citizens voted to tax themselves in kind, usually by day labour or wheat, to make and improve roads, bridges, a cemetery, and a schoolhouse.[20]

By March 2, 1800, an order of Council passed in his favour and as Leader, granted Edmund[5] and his first 10 Associates one-quarter of the Township of Newport.[31]

Typical notation in the *Newport first Records* Minute Book, here the minutes of the September 1799 meeting with votes for moderator, clerk and committee members

Thus, the lands bounded on the west by the line of Newport, on the south by the line of Auckland, and on the north and east by vacant Crown lands, were granted under the terms and conditions prescribed by His Majesty's Royal Instructions.[4, 7]

Author's note: The properties essentially ran both sides of today's Route 210 to the line bordering on the Township of Auckland, and the south side of today's Route 212 from the line of Newport to Lot 14. This information can be confirmed through Land Grants in Lower Canada, Public Archives of Canada, Public Records Division, microfilm reel C-2532, p. 51121.[7]

Edmund[5] was granted an additional eight lots (1600 acres) in the southwest quarter of the territory for his immediate family members as acknowledgment for his grievance plea and in lieu of his hardship and loss of property in the amount of £500 incurred in the New England Colonies by being loyal to the Crown.

This additional grant put the total number of lots granted at 63: The Associates received 33 lots for a total of 6,600 acres; the Heard families received 30 lots for a total of 6,000 acres. Together these grants accounted for 12,600 acres of the 61,600 acres of the township. An additional caveat of the Agreement called for the granting to the Agent, five acres of every 100 acres granted. This was to be in lieu of personal expenses in the administering and managing of the new settlement.[20, 28]

From these grants, a proportionate number of the lots were to be set aside as expropriation exchange for "common lands" for towns, public access, roads, churches, schools, and other municipal grounds as may be required from time to time. This explains why some lots were left vacant. As Leader, Col. Edmund[5] Heard had full authority to divide these lots or parts of them if public access was deemed necessary on or through a subscribed lot. These other lots or parts of them could be given out in exchange for incursions (such as a road) through an assigned lot.

Every settler was required to clear a road the width of 20 feet in front of his lot and the full width of the lot. In this way all lots were connected, forming a "common ground" road on which all persons may travel between lots to a connective road. The Agreement also called for the reserve of a proportional allotment within the framework for the support of the Protestant clergy and specified Public Lands that may serve the overall community. The Agreement was formalized on March 12, 1801, in Chateau St. Louis in Quebec City. A part of the Agreement was that every settler who was issued land grants was also provided with a year's worth of rations and clothing provided by the British through the military in exchange for settling and developing the lands. In some cases, they were provided tools and seed, which had to be paid back once the land was cleared and producing. In most cases this excess was used as barter for other materials the settlers needed and therefore the "barter system" of trade was initiated.[20, 31]

Edmund[5] secured the book *The Massachusetts Justice: Being a Collection of the Laws of the Commonwealth of Massachusetts*, published in 1802, that he referenced to establish and discharge the means of rule in early Newport.[30] (See image on page 17.) The way in which the records were kept up to 1814 indicated that indeed the first settlers of Newport were an order-loving and efficient class of people. The townspeople of this new settlement created a municipal council whose records still exist. Not knowing any other system of government, the settlers based their system on the British/New England form of municipal government. As the community grew, this township probably held the first public municipal meetings of any in the Eastern Townships. This book of governing laws resides with the Ancestral Heard/Hurd Collection.[30]

***

The first Bowker family and Heard family connection:[4] *(also: Florence (Bowker) McVetty)*

> *Author's note: The Bowker family roots originated in England circa the late 1500s. Edmund John[1] Bowker, born in 1610, was an adventurer and as a young man had immigrated to Massachusetts where he married Ellen Smyth of Dorchester in 1646. They were a hardy and industrious family, their ancestors moving many times throughout the various generations while living in the New England Colonies. Several generations later two of their descendants found themselves engaged in the opening up a new territory in the "waste lands" of Lower Canada.*

Solomon[7] and Johnathon[7] (John) Bowker, two sons of Gideon[6] and Hannah (Fletcher) Bowker, born in Chesterfield, N. H., in 1781 and 1783 respectively, had moved with the family first to Guilford, Vt., in 1785, and later to Lunenburg, Vt. The two eldest boys, at ages 18 and 16, looking for adventure, then immigrated to Newport in 1799, as applicants for land grants joining Col. Edmund[5] Heard and Associates in opening Newport Township. Solomon was appointed to a committee with David Metcalf *"to manage the affairs of the Inhabitants of Newport or the calling of an emergency."*[20]

These Bowker boys would soon find themselves working to build a road to Nicolet with other land grant Associates of Col. Edmund[5] Heard, and under the direction of Samuel Heard, "Road Surveyor."[20]

There appears to be no record of these first Bowker young men staying in Newport after 1815. They had applied for land grants and received the certificates required while they worked in building their future in Newport.

> *Author's note: I speculate they may well have stayed longer; however, the reason for no further reference was simply because the records abruptly stopped, with the last entry by David Metcalf in 1816.*

There was a period when many of these early settlers and entrepreneurs left these new settlements because of the extreme difficulties for them and – more importantly – their families. The challenges included the weather, the social isolation, and especially the lack of suitable marriage partners.

The Bowker boys built a cabin on Lot 3 of Range 6 to live in while they cleared the lot and worked on the roads with the other Associates. This is evidenced in both the subscriptions they took on and the proportionate levies recorded in the Minute Book. Later in the story, there is mention of a proposal to build a bye road connecting the North River, where their cabin was located, to the Maple Leaf cemetery and community.

John[6] Lyon, born in 1740 in Dedham, Mass., had moved to Lunenburg, Vt., in 1799. John had served in the French and Indian Wars, his commission signed by George Washington. He and his wife had only one child, John,[7] born in 1770. When John's family had moved from Dedham to Guilford, they had met the Bowker family.[32]

In 1804 John[7] Lyon married Lucy Bowker, the first daughter of Gideon[6] and Hannah Bowker. They had two sons, Eliphalet and Orra, who were also destined to find their way to Newport.[32]

These families all become freeholders: the lands were granted and considered paid in full in lieu of painful losses and hardships incurred in their escape as British Loyalists from the New England states. They owned their land outright for an unlimited duration and were eligible to dispose of it or create heirs to their holdings as they wished. There were other inhabitants who moved with the Loyalists who did not necessarily own their land but worked for and/or rented or squatted on lands not yet claimed.

Women played a hugely important role in the success of the settlements. They not only risked their lives in childbirth but were the chief caregivers for both the men and children. There were no medical facilities or even doctors during this time of settlement. In many instances, delicate and tenderly reared women were called upon to give up the enjoyments of social life they enjoyed in the New England Colonies. With young and growing children around them, they followed their husbands to the comfortless homes provided for them in the wilderness. Many of these immigrant women were not enamored with this desolate life in the wilderness, some returning and abandoning their husbands, but most satisfied themselves with writing copious letters to their extended families left behind. The younger generation growing up with these hardships had no other experience and so embraced their lives with great enthusiasm.

Notification of Land Grant of 1801 favouring Edmund[5] Heard and Associates

Edmund[5] wrote another letter to his son Edmund[6] in 1801, "*to tell you that I have received the grant of a quarter of the Township of Newport and that you have received a portion of land. I want to see you as quickly as you can conveniently come to Newport as there are some important matters to settle respecting your grant which ought to be finalized soon.*"[10]

Edmund[5] was concerned that the lots he had assigned to his son Edmund[6] might come under scrutiny and be dismissed as "speculation" unless inhabited soon: "*I suggest that you keep this information to yourself till we meet.*" He also told Edmund[6] that his sister "*Hannah is not at home at the moment, but they are all well.*" He sent his love to his wife Elizabeth and signed off because he was being hurried by Mr. Waters. This letter was signed "*your father Edmund.*"[10]

Note: *The document shown confirms the land grant after receiving the Survey for the Township of Newport.*

Edmund[5] noted that the soil in these townships was fertile, as could be plainly seen from the majestic trees and luxuriant shrubbery that covered the landscape. The woods were filled with game and excellent fish abounded in the streams and lakes. Springs producing excellent potable water were abundant throughout Newport, the lands lying directly southwest of the Megantic Mountains. Yet with all this abundance available to help our settlers survive, those who ventured on this journey knew that for years they would be subjected to the most laborious toil and hardships. All sorts of men and women joined in the forward march to the new country, each with his/her own idea of what they wanted to do. Describing pioneer life, a period writer of the day stated that "Danger seems only to sharpen the spirit of adventure and attract rather than repel immigration." And so, they came; it is claimed "into Canada with a Bible under one arm and an axe in the other hand."[17]

Our lakes and rivers were inevitably chosen as strategic travel points. These lakes and rivers throughout the townships were the chief means of travel for the Indigenous peoples and ultimately for the pioneers, while the forests were being cleared for settlement.

When the time came to bring the families up from New England, a road which had been surveyed and marked would have been bushed out along the front lot lines. In those years, winter was the preferred time to travel; they used large sleds that would glide over the frozen ground – much easier than summer travel. The mother and younger children occupied the front part of the sled, leaving the back part for bedding provisions, cooking utensils, bits of furniture, and any other articles deemed absolute necessities. Bibles were treasured possessions for their daily use in newly built homes in an unending forest. They served again for records of births, marriages, deaths and often incidents of importance.[24.] The men and boys followed on foot to save weight on the sleds. Since the rivers and lakes were frozen, winter travel shortened the voyage considerably.

Another trip was usually planned for the men and older boys in the summer months to bring livestock and other equipment to the settlement; provisions to last for one year also had to be transported. This meant building rafts, forging across turbulent rivers under extreme conditions of hardship and loss of lives.

Once settled, Edmund,[5] Samuel,[6] William[5] and their Associate families cleared as much land as possible and planted their stock of seeds as soon as the soil was prepared. It would not be until the second or third year that there might be enough grain produced to provide bread for the family. Any crop failure or depredations by bears or other wild animals could spell disaster for a family, causing them to travel as much as 30, 40 or 50 miles to obtain additional provisions and usually at great hardship.

Oxen were the unheralded contributors to early settlement development. The oxen plodded along at a uniform rate of about two miles per hour. This was a good speed for the early roads; any speedier could jolt the occupants off the ox cart or wagon. There were many occasions when Edmund's son Samuel, who was in charge of the road surveying and subsequent road building, would get stuck hub-deep in a quagmire, necessitating "hand-spikes" (crowbars) to extricate the ox cart. Any splendor of attire in those days soon vanished.

Oxen were favoured by these early settlers because they offered many advantages over horses. First, oxen were far cheaper to purchase. They could survive on a diet of wild grasses, foliage and "beaver hay" (a course grass growing wild in marshlands). Beaver were abundant as were their swampy meadows. Horses are far more discriminating, requiring domestic grasses and grain in the form of oats or barley. Thus, in these early times horses were used more for individual travel on horseback, affordable only for some.

Virgin forest trees were huge by today's standards. This provided a distinct advantage when travelling because there was little underbrush and the hot sun was blocked out by huge canopies. Felling these great trees, however, required skill. It took two men, one on each end of a large crosscut saw pulling and pushing through a girth of four to six feet or more. A skill in notching the tree in order to land it in precisely the right spot also took an experienced cutter. It was equally important to direct these huge trees so that they did not get "hung up" on another tree, making it virtually impossible to move. Many of our ancestors were killed or severely injured in felling these large trees. It was not uncommon for many of these early families to suddenly find themselves without a husband or father – or perhaps worse, crippled and a liability in a time of critical survival. In many cases injuries that might be crippling did not deter these men from work. They would simply continue doing things that needed to be done, both at home and for the community at large. They were able to help with jobs that required enormous amounts of time, which they now had. Children found themselves growing up quickly to share in the survival of their families. It was for this reason that a sense of community spirit was necessary and the strong bonds that existed between these early families extended forward to later generations, becoming a strong a part of the culture that continues to exist today.

Scattered through the southwestern quarter of Newport, amongst acres of silent forest, were the farm settlements consisting of log huts and barns. Fields were laboriously ploughed between stumps and more stumps . . . endless acres of stumps. One might see smoke rising out of this wilderness. Once a settler family had cut down the trees on the land they acquired, they had to wait at least seven years before the huge, ugly stumps were sufficiently rotted to be pulled out of the earth. Whenever possible, they would burn the roots to create potash, an excellent form of fertilizer. Potash was made from hardwood ashes such as elm and maple.

Pearl ash was a powerful alkaline derived from wood ashes, used for making soap and other products. The ashes were put into "leaches" holding about six bushels each and wet down with hot water; the leached lye would drain into a trough below. This process was continued until the ashes were depleted of lye. The lye was then put through a process of being boiled down to salts, much like sap being converted to maple sugar. The salts were then dried and further "scorched," which turned them brown. Next, the salts were put into an oven and the fire kept alive while a man continually stirred the salts until they turned chalk-like. When cool, pearl ash was put into barrels for market and used in place of soda or baking powder.[16]

The women added pearl ash to a cleaning solution they made up, with salt as the abrasive, rosemary as the insecticide, and vinegar as the antibacterial. This was the only cleaning material they had, and it had to be used sparingly. They used lye in the outhouses to break down waste and lessen the pungent odour that sometimes permeated the area.[35]

During these first years in Lower Canada, the Heard family's only income, other than a military stipend, was derived from the sale of both potash and pearl ash. At that time, these products were in great demand in England. However, in order to conduct business, Edmund, William, and Samuel had to make the arduous journey as far as Nicolet, more than 100 miles distant, to sell their product. These and other products from the community would have to be taken by ox team to the St. Francis River, downriver from the falls at East Angus, then by flatboat to Brompton Falls where the load would be portaged around the rapids then reloaded for the final leg of the trip to Nicolet. From Nicolet these products were again transported by boat, crossing the St. Lawrence River to Three Rivers on the North Shore for shipment overseas.

Edmund[5] and one or more of his Associates travelled in a heavy cart drawn by a pair of oxen over newly formed roads, and when they could find it, over corduroy sections, and mud . . . always mud. These loads could weigh well over 300 pounds and the trip was one of extreme hardship; jolting along mile after mile, having to cut fallen trees and brush away from the road which in many areas along the way was not much more than a trail. Accompanying Edmund[5] on many of these travels were Road Committee Associates Nathanial Beaman and William Hudson, so they could officially mark where these roads were to be further improved or altered. Samuel Heard then would follow these markings and establish the necessary surveying process to establish documentation which he would then file in the Minute Book, as Clerk of Newport Township.[20]

In the wintertime, a good road was kept open for ice travel on the St. Francis River, while in the summer carrying the goods to Nicolet and returning with supplies and crossing by means of boats was a nasty business.[16]

For the inhabitants to access their needs, several roads were built in Newport. In 1802 there was a general movement towards cutting a road to Nicolet. The Minutes show that they assisted in building a road from the house of John Ward, in Ascot, to Nicolet. The amount contributed was 12½ days of work each, for four men, amounting to $50. This was when the citizens voted to tax themselves by subscription proportionate to their land holdings. Payment was usually by their own day labour to make and improve roads, bridges, a cemetery and a schoolhouse, and was duly recorded.[20]

In 1803 they raised $107 to improve and alter the road to the Connecticut River, passing through Clifton. *"The inhabitants of the Township of Newport being desirous of opening a more convenient road than that now travelled to the Connecticut River, and to alter or amend in order to open a more safe, expeditious and free communication, between us and the inhabitants of Connecticut, for the better conveyance of produce of this country and carrying on a more free and advantageous trade between the merchants of that country as we are now labour under considerable difficulty of obtaining the necessary goods from our own markets."* Payments might be made sometimes in money, but generally in labour and in wheat. Money was a rare commodity in those days. One bushel of wheat equaled one dollar and was generally the commodity for exchange. Edmund[5] was also the first Township settler who chose to grow wheat that he had to take all the way to Canaan, Vt. to have ground into flour.[4, 10]

Ingenuity was often called for in the procurement and cooking of provisions. You could grow it, you could shoot it, or fish for it. Deer, moose and fish were the most prevalent in Newport and provided much to supplement domestic fare, part eaten at the time and part dried for storage. Wheat from the fields went to a mill for grinding, paid for by a portion of the flour. At this time the settlers had to travel many miles, usually on horseback, with the bags of grain strapped to the horse. The closest gristmill was Kilbourne Mills, later known as Norton Mills, on the border of East Hereford Township and Vermont. The trip could take sometimes days from Grove Hill, through East Clifton and on to the Vermont border. The settlers butchered their usually small excess of beef, pork, sheep and poultry. Most families kept a small flock of chickens, ducks, geese and turkeys. Samuel's wife Miriam wrote: *"I have some ducks and am to have turkeys and geese this summer. I lost several of my best fowls, not by the hawk, but a horrid beast of the same nature as our polecat, called here a scunck, who comes like a thief in the night and invades the perch, leaving headless mementos of his barbarity and blood thirsty propensities."* [10]

***

John Lebourveau had come from Vermont into Eaton Township in 1799 where he worked for Josiah Sawyer helping to build his sawmill. Some people in Vermont had thought they were in Lower Canada before the state decided to join the Union. Thus, many felt they had no choice but to move north after 1791, and John was no exception. He was a capable man, ambitious, and worked with an eye to the future. Not far away in Newport Township lived Sally Stratton; soon to fall in love.[24]

After two years of courtship John and Sally decided to marry, but there was no minister to perform the ceremony. They made their way on one horse to New Hampshire some 40 miles through virgin forest, marked by a simple slash, a "spotted trail" across brooks and rivers and on trails used by other pioneers travelling back and forth between the two countries. Their marriage ceremony had no flowers, no bridal gown, and no stylish attire. Many of the marriages at that time were held in New Hampshire and Vermont (and it appears that sometimes records of these marriages were not kept, perhaps because the marrying couple lived in Canada). Sally mothered nine children, all of whom participated in building the agricultural and industrial heritage of the region.[24]

Because the author is striving to confine the story to the settlers of Newport Township, the heritage of John Lebourveau or Capt. Josiah[4] Sawyer will not be pursued or expanded. While Josiah was a part of the first exploration of Newport Township as already referenced, he settled in the adjacent Township of Eaton. Both John and Josiah and their Associates weaved themselves into businesses that surrounded the two townships, as did many others who settled in Bury and Auckland (East Clifton) townships. Josiah and his wife Susanna raised seven children in Eaton Township. Many of these settlers moved back and forth between the townships, as did John and Josiah's sons and daughters and their descendants, many of whom married people associated with the Township of Newport. The author will blend in these families that migrated between the two townships as the story unfolds.

> *Author's note: As mentioned in the Introduction, I am using a numbering system in order to separate the many people with the same names, sons, wives, and daughters so that a reader has some guidance as to a particular generation where these names keep popping up. For example, Capt. Josiah[4] and Susanna had a son Josiah[5] and a daughter Susanna[5], which I identify accordingly. During my research I have found improper references to an event, using a name that one might assume to be one generation; yet was in fact from a generation beyond, or sometimes even two.*

Stories such as this, powered by ancestry, make one feel that we are really part of the history of Canada. These were our ancestors, people with unshaken confidence and an unquenchable thirst for adventure. They and their stories are handed down as a heritage from generation to generation, much like the First Nations. This country, through our ancestor's sacrifices, was made ours.

> *Author's note: Col. Edmund[5] Heard was determined to leave an account of who his people were and why they mattered. They established a community so in that sense they were successful as the first settlers in Newport before the war of 1812-14.*

***

Chapter 5   Back in Time (1600–1790)

Now that we have introduced the earliest settlers of Newport, perhaps we should take a step back in time to explore their origins and what inspired and motivated them. We know they came from the New England Colonies, and so one might wonder what their lives were like prior to immigrating to Lower Canada. This is a journey where we may garner a snapshot of how they arrived at where they were and even learn a bit of how their own ancestors lived.

One of the initial reasons some people immigrated to the New England Colonies from the "Old World" was because the younger sons did not inherit titles and estates in either England, Scotland or Ireland. Some were freeing themselves of tyranny, others fled for religious reasons. Many joined to become a band of Pilgrims and sailed away to try their luck in a new land. They opted to brave the seas that divided the old from the new worlds. They believed that across those seas there lay a new world of opportunity. Perhaps this sounds familiar enough to substantiate that indeed "history repeats itself."

Women would always play a crucial role in the success of any family's well-being during this and many eras of settlement, and yet, they were the most vulnerable. They showed tremendous strength in these tumultuous times; running the household, birthing, and raising children (on average five per family); responsive in illnesses and many times having to run not only the household but family businesses as well. Many men and women died on these voyages, or once landed in the new land became ill and died. Without one or the other's support, families could not exist; both men and women remarried, sometimes several times, for this very reason. This was also a necessity so that their families had a chance of survival. Because of the many wars, strife and illnesses of the time, women insisted that their first-born sons be named after the father (namesake), the reason for so many of the same names that were carried forward through these three centuries, the 1600s, 1700s and 1800s. They did this because they wanted their sons "to respect their father for all his days by bearing his name and carrying it forward."

This chapter will identify the first of our Newport ancestral generations who landed in the New World and, through their stories, bring our ancestors alive. Newbury, Newburyport, Ipswich, Lancaster, Gloucester, Salem, Worcester, and Lexington became the stomping grounds of our many ancestors. Battles at Lexington and Concord, where the first shot of the American Revolution was heard around the world, began a battle that ended at Boston's Bunker Hill. This is who we are and where we came from.[49]

Several hundred colonists had sailed from England in 1630 in a fleet of 11 ships. They investigated the region of Salem and Cape Ann, then continued sailing south to where some buildings had already been prepared for them at a place newly named Charlestown.[14]

That winter they lost a few hundred colonists from malnutrition and disease. They also experienced their first "nor'easter," which cost them some fingers and toes, as well as houses destroyed by the fires they kept burning, day and night. During the handing out of the last handful of grain, the supply ship *Lyon* entered Boston Harbor, its holds empty of any food.

The Heard family:

The family name "Heard" can be traced at the Herald Office in London, England, as far back as the eleventh century, spelled at that time "Herde." Many of our ancestor's surnames have been spelled differently and for different reasons: some to escape persecution, others simply because of the lack of education and writing skills – the name was spelled as it might sound, scribed and recorded by someone who could write. The Heards emigrated from Wiltshire, England, during the troubles in the reign of Charles I. Some went to Ireland and some to the New World, meaning the New England Colonies and subsequently, Canada. These men, women and children showed great courage and determination to succeed in a new land of economic opportunity. They were immensely resourceful and relentless in the development of this new land.[4]

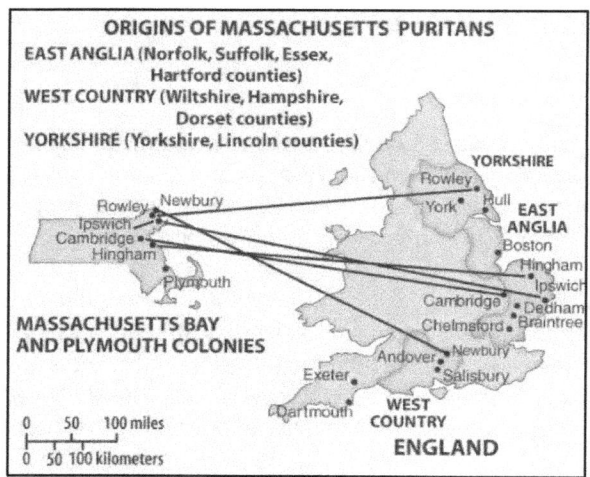

The English origins of the Great Migration (illustration by Abraham Hammatt)

Edmund Heard of Claxton, County Norfolk, England, the first known ancestor of the Heard family, died in 1626. His wife, whose name is unknown, predeceased him. He was a linen weaver and held property both in Claxton and the nearby parishes of Shillington, Rockland and Ashby. His will, dated November 20, 1626, and proved December 4, 1626, requested that he be buried in the Claxton churchyard near his wife. He mentioned "Sister Agnes Bussy," widow; and appointed John Hunn of Claxton, yeoman, and Christopher Tollis of Neatshead, yeoman, to be executors. "To my eldest son, Luke[1] Heard," he left £60, to be paid when he reached the age of 21, plus the "best loom in my shop, six pieces of pewter, a spit, a brass posnet and my little table in the parlor, or six and fifty shillings in money for said loom."[4]

A file letter stated that "We Irish Heards are the descendants of two brothers who had a third, an elder brother, supposed to have gone to America at the date referred to and the Courts have decided that the Irish Heards cannot inherit this money because there may be descendants of the elder brother to be found." The amount of money involved in this case was £80,000 sterling.[4]

In the 19th century there were many spurious claims to cases in the Court of Chancery, raised to get Americans to invest in "proving" their rights to English Estates. This may have been one such fraud, or there may be some element of truth to the story which has not yet been discovered. However, the assumption they had emigrated to the Americas was indeed correct.[4]

Four brothers, named Edmund[1], Luke[1], John and James, immigrated to the New England Colonies, landing at Dover, N.H., in 1632-33. James Heard died without a family; Edmund[1] was appointed his administrator. Edmund[1] Heard had married Joanna Wells on November 28, 1649, at St. Michael's Church in Norwich, England, and they settled in Maine. Edmund died there in 1693.[4]

In the New World the name has since been variously spelled "Heard," "Herde," "Hurd" and "Hird." It is unfortunate that one uniform mode of spelling had not been adopted. Likely not all were educated, and if they were able to write at all, they might have written phonetic versions.

Luke[1] Heard, of Claxton County, son of Edmund Heard Sr., was born in Norfolk, England, probably between 1605 and 1608 (as he was not yet 21 in 1626). He married Sarah Riddellsdale, who was born in Suffolk, England, and died at Boxford, Mass., in June 1704. Luke[1] came to the Massachusetts Bay Colony about 1636, settling first at Newbury. Like his father, he was a linen weaver by trade, and he took his freeman's oath at Boston on September 6, 1639. Later he moved to Salisbury, Mass., where he was listed among 68 settlers who received land in the first division in 1640. He sold his land there, with the house and planting lot, to George Brown of Salisbury, and moved to Ipswich, Mass. He was a constable there in 1643.[4]

The first French/Heard connection:

Thomas[2] French Jr. was born in 1608 at Astington in the Stour Valley of Suffolk, England. It appears that his father, Thomas[1] French Sr., son of Jacob French and Susan French, born in October 1584 in Assington, was in some working relationship – perhaps as a tenant farmer – with Brampton Gordon, a local landowner and friend of the Winthrop family. His wife, Susan (Riddlesdale) French, was a daughter of John Riddlesdale and Dorcas Riddlesdale of Assington. Susan was a cousin of Sarah Riddlesdale, who married Luke Heard, so this was perhaps the first French/Heard connection. *(Roger K. Lancey, great-great-grandson of Charles Ward Bailey French)*

It is easy to see how, when John Winthrop formed the Massachusetts Bay Company, the young Thomas[2] French may have seen this as a great adventure, and so was on board the "Arabella" when she sailed from Southampton with the first group of the so-called "godly" people under John Winthrop in 1630, on their way to found Boston and set up the company. Thomas[1] French Sr., his wife and daughters also sailed to Boston in 1635. Young Thomas[2] French was in good standing with John Winthrop, and went on to help found Ipswich, a few miles north of Boston. The name Ipswich is taken from the most populous town in Suffolk. *(Roger K. Lancey)*

Departure of a Puritan family for New England, 1856 (Charles West Cope)

Thirteen men aboard a shallop sailed into the Bay of Agawam and took up residence there.

The settlement was known by its original Indigenous name, Agawam, before the colonists changed it to Ipswich. There is no record of any native resistance to the colonization, either at Charlestown or at Agawam, even though estimates of the earlier populations run into the thousands. Agawam was incorporated on August 5, 1634, as Ipswich.[14]

The name "Ipswich" was taken "in acknowledgment of the great honor and kindness done to our people who brought shipping there." In 1633, the region of Ipswich was settled by the largest contingent to arrive from the same village: 15 men and women from Assington, Suffolk, England, where the Rev. Nathaniel Rogers, who would become a minister in Ipswich, had been the minister just prior to his emigration to the New World. This group included Thomas French Jr. and his father, Thomas French Sr., John Proctor, Mark Quilter and John Wyatt. Thomas French Sr., a tailor, took the freeman's oath at Boston and relocated to Ipswich on January 27, 1639. Thomas French Sr. died on November 5, 1639, in Ipswich. His wife Susan died on August 10, 1658.[14]

"Little Venice," Ipswich, Mass., circa 1890 (historicipswich.org; photo by George Dexter)

Thomas[1] and Susan French's oldest son, Thomas[2] French, had married Mary Scudmore in Gloucester, England.

> Thomas French was a leader in the revolt against Governor Andros for which Ipswich is known as the "Birthplace of American Independence." Warrants for their arrest were issued, and the first was against the Constable Thomas French, John Appleton Moderator and town clerk John Andrews, the "Disaffected & evil Disposed persons within ye said Town as yet unknown on ye 23rd day of August last past, being met & assembled together at Ipswich aforesaid; who Did in a most factious & Seditious & Contemptuous manner then & there vote & agree that they were not willing nor would not Choose a Commissioner as by a Warrant From his Majesty's Treasurer & Receiver General in pursuance of ye laws of this his Majesty's Dominion to ye Constable & Selectmen of ye said Town."[14]

Luke[1] Heard died at Ipswich at age 39, shortly before September 28, 1647. He left explicit instructions that his children were to be taught to read and write, and that at the age of 13, "be put forth in apprenticeship of a trade." He left two sons: John[2], born at Salisbury, Mass., in 1644 and Edmund[2], born at Ipswich, Mass., in 1646.[4] Luke's widow Sarah married Sgt. Joseph Bixby, raising nine children in addition to Luke and Sarah's two children.[4]

The plague of 1616–18 and again in the early 1630s, perhaps smallpox brought from abroad, had apparently devastated the once-populous Indigenous tribes. It is estimated that 75 to 95 percent of the tribes that lived along the coastline died, just before these particular settlers arrived. The fields stood vacant. The colonists encountered but few natives.[14]

The Sawyer family:

The earliest known Sawyers go back to Sir Edwin Sawyer who was knighted for distinguished service to the Crown of England. A succession of Sawyers, "Admirals of the white and blue sea soldiers, prior to the arrival and as subsequent Sawyer settlers in the New England Colonies, are said to be entitled to claim the arms and honors of Sir Edwin, as well as Sir Robert Sawyer another conspicuous member of the family in England."[4, 23]

Sir Robert Sawyer was an attorney general under Charles II and defended the bishops against James II. He supported the revolution which placed William and Mary of Orange on the English Throne in 1689. Robert's only daughter married the Earl of Carnarvon, who subsequently inherited Highclere Castle in Hampshire in 1901.[23]

> *Author's note: This information was taken from a speech by the Rev. R. A. Sawyer in tribute to Capt. Josiah[4] Sawyer at the unveiling of his monument in Sawyerville, Que., in 1901. Highclere Castle, the magnificent home in Newbury, England, gave rise to "Downton Abbey" and had a formidable story of its own.*[4, 23]

In 1636, Thomas[1] and his brother William[1] Sawyer came to America, landing at Rowley, Mass. (near Salem), also a part of the New England Colonies. William, although settled in Ipswich, Mass., had also founded the town of Lancaster, Mass. Thomas Sawyer's sons Ephriam[2] and Ephriam[3] Jr. were both officers in the Massachusetts contingent that fought in the French and Indian Wars, including the assault that culminated in the deaths of generals Wolfe and Montcalm and the capture of the great fortress of Quebec by the British in 1759.[23]

The Bowker family:

Edmund John[1] Bowker was born in 1610 in England and immigrated to Massachusetts where he married Ellen Smyth at Dorchester, Mass., in 1646. They raised a son, John[2] B., born in Marlborough, Mass., in 1650. Edmund died in Sudbury, Middlesex County, Mass., in 1666. His estate consisted of "40 acres be it more or less of wilderness land and a small house, a chain, axe horns, two axes, two horses and some other small tools including a plow." *(Florence (Bowker) McVetty, Bowker family history)*

John[2] Bowker married Mary Howe in 1678. Their son, John[3] B., born in Marlborough in 1679, married Ruth Howe, a daughter of his mother's brother. John[2] B. was a caulker and died leaving a small dwelling house and barn with about five acres of land and about eight acres of salt marsh, about five acres near the church, and a pew in the meetinghouse. *(Florence (Bowker) McVetty)*

These original English colonists were a very pious group and somewhat strict as to who was worthy enough to join them. Ipswich prospered, and by 1700 it had a population of 1,800 citizens. It was the seat of the local courts, carried on significant trade, and at the time of the American Revolution ranked with Boston and Salem as one of the most important towns in the colony. Clothing industries, shoemaking, lacemaking and machine knitting later became the town's economic success.[14] The wealth of the town's legal history should not go unmentioned. Ipswich is the birthplace of American Independence; the caliber of the people is in part a measure of the quality of the culture. But some 10 years before Ipswich came to be . . . and just three years after they stepped off the boat . . . the people of Plymouth recognized the importance of the legal process, and jury trials in particular, by enacting an ordinance in 1623 that all criminals' facts, and also all matters of trespass and debts between man and man should be tried by the verdict of 12 honest men to be impaneled by authority in form of a jury upon their oaths.[14]

Not long after the land lying in the Bay of Agawam was sold to John Winthrop Jr. for £20 in 1641, the General Court established what is now called the Ipswich District Court as one of four original courts in the Commonwealth. The publication *Body of Liberties*, containing over 100 laws and reputed to be the "first American law book," was accepted by the people in 1641. It supplanted the existing code: the word of "God" and not English common law would now be the measure of justice. The Massachusetts Constitution of 1780 was the template developed only two years earlier. A critical work had emerged from Ipswich which served as the foundation when crafting the federal Constitution of the new United States of America. As the birthplace of American Independence, it should be no surprise that so many notable lawyers and judges came from Ipswich.[14]

These pioneers would become farmers, fishermen, shipbuilders or traders. The tidal Ipswich River provided water power for mills, and salt marshes supplied hay for livestock. A cottage industry in lace-making developed. But in 1687, Ipswich residents, led by Rev. John Wise, protested a tax imposed by the governor, Sir Edmund Andros. As Englishmen, they argued that taxation without representation was unacceptable. Citizens were jailed, but then Andros was recalled to England in 1689, and the new British sovereigns, William and Mary, issued colonists another Charter. These continuous taxation issues initiated much unrest, creating a rebellious mood within the general populace. This is another reason the town calls itself the "Birthplace of American Independence."[13]

***

John[1] Heard remained in Dover and was a very prominent man in the early history of New Hampshire. He created a "safe house" – essentially a stockade within the perimeter of the settlement – as part of Dover's defence system. In the event of an attack by Indigenous warriors, residents would shelter in the safe house, called "Heards First." John was officially dubbed "captain" of this safe house and thus became "Captain of Heards First." He raised a family of 15 children. He died on January 17, 1687; his wife Dorcus died on November 30, 1706.[4]

The descendants of John and Dorcus today number in the thousands and are scattered throughout the United States and Canada as well as several countries overseas. The Heard descendants form a true cross-section of North American society with a common link to their 17th-century artisan ancestor; from senators to truckers, merchants, bankers, gardeners, engineers, actors, farmers, teachers and lawyers, the list goes on.[4]

The impressive geographical characteristics of Franconia Notch must have inspired explorers and settlers throughout the region. Flume Gorge and Lost River Gorge, which snakes through boulder caves and potholes in Dixville Notch, and impressive features like Cathedral Spires and Table Rock would have been both obstacles and awe-inspiring sights for our ancestors as they plied their ox carts through these areas looking for lands to settle. Merely a day's travel between the capitals of Massachusetts and New Hampshire, their taverns prospered as the overnight stop of the Eastern Stage Line (1763-1839).

Twenty years after English sea captains sailed up the Piscataquis River to explore the New Hampshire region, Europeans established the first white settlements at Odiorne Point and Dover in 1623. Others followed in nearly a century of allegiance to the English Crown. When the Colonists would have no more, New Hampshire declared independence from England, and in 1776 became the first colony to adopt a Provisional Constitutional Government.[14] This perhaps explains the opening for the border dispute between Canada and the newly formed New England states that would take place surrounding the Republic of Indian Stream.

Edmund[2] Heard, born in Ipswich in 1646, married Elizabeth Warner in 1672. They had six children: three daughters and three sons. Elizabeth Warner's father gave them the use of the northeast end of his house and provided that, after he died, it would be theirs if they paid £10 each to her brother William and her sister Susanna. They later built a new house on the estate. Their children were all born in Ipswich: Elizabeth in 1674, Sarah in 1676, Abigail in 1679, Edmund[3] in 1681, Nathaniel in 1685 and Daniel in 1695.[4]

Author's note: Please note Daniel as a "person of interest" in later ancestral Heard decendants of Edmund[2] who had business interests that affected both Ipswich and other entities, described later in this chapter.

Edmund[2] Heard was one of "ten of the young generation who took the covenant" on January 18, 1674, to become members of the church. Later that year, on November 18, 1674, he purchased a commonage in Ipswich from Henry Archer for £20 in malt (Ipswich Deeds, 3:330) and another lot in the common field for £15 from John[2] French on September 14, 1677 (Ibid., 4:110). Ipswich has a street, Heard Lane, named in honour of the Heard families of Ipswich who contributed so much to the growth of the town. This was the first Heard connection with the first family of

Frenches. It is likely that John[2] French was divesting his holdings to take an opportunity to move his family, joining his brother Thomas[2] who was contemplating moving his family to Connecticut.[4]

Sketch of Market Square, Ipswich, circa 1800 (Ipswich Historical Commission)

The Ipswich town meeting appointed Edmund[2] as one of the surveyors of highways in 1696-97 and 1699-1700; as a tithing man, 1697-98 and 1703-04; and as a sealer of leather, every year from 1699-1700 through 1709-10. He was a cordwainer or shoemaker by trade, and this undoubtedly led to his appointment as a sealer of leather, a public office held by his descendants throughout the century.[4] Edmund subscribed eight shillings toward the new meetinghouse bell on February 29, 1699, or 1700, and in 1700 was assigned a seat in the new meetinghouse. The matter of seating accommodation was frequently before the town, with constant pressure for special privileges. The question of greater and less dignity, carrying with it the question of higher or lower seat, became so sharp and vexing that, in 1663, the delicate and unenviable task of "seating the congregation" was laid upon the selectmen. This method of public seating carried forward well into the 1800s.[4, 14.]

Great clipper ships of the 19th century bypassed Ipswich in favor of the deep-water seaports at Salem, Newburyport, Quincy, and Boston. The town remained primarily a fishing and farming community, its residents living in older homes they could not afford to replace, leaving Ipswich with a considerable inventory of early architecture. In 1822, a stocking manufacturing machine that had been smuggled out of England arrived at Ipswich, violating a British ban on exporting such technology. However, the entrepreneurial spirit prevailed and the community further developed as a mill town.[14]

***

Ephriam[3] Jr. Sawyer married Dolly Wilder; she bore him 20 children of whom 13 lived to maturity. Josiah[4] was likely the youngest.[23]

In 1759 Ephraim[2] Sawyer the older had conducted British Major-General Jeffery Amherst through Lake Champlain, where he succeeded in taking Fort Ticonderoga from the French. On Lake Champlain, the boats of Amherst's expedition ran into severe thunderstorms of great violence and gale-force winds that drove them to shelter in what is known today as Sawyer Bay on the southwest coast of Grand Isle. This incident introduced Ephraim[2] to the spot which, 25 years later, would become his refuge from the loss of his Massachusetts fortunes. He bore all expenses throughout the Revolution, serving Congress, without pay, and supported many soldiers of his regiment when the funds of Congress failed. In the end he brought all his family, including his sons' daughters and sons-in-law, to Grande Isle, virtually exiting the town of Lancaster for good. Ephraim[2] Sawyer had now engaged himself in the lumber industry.[4, 23]

***

Edmund[3] Heard, (lineage: Edmund[2], Luke[1]) was born at Ipswich, Mass., in 1681, and died there at age 64. He was married five times and had five children, losing each of his wives in childbirth. He first married Annah Todd in November 1706, she died at Ipswich, aged 26. Their son, Edmund, died three months later. Anna and their son were both buried in the Old North Burying Ground in Ipswich. Deaths of this nature were not uncommon in these early settlements due to a lack of medical services, which would not become generally available until later generations.[4]

Edmund[3] married his second wife, Deborah Osgood of Andover, Mass., in November 1713. She is said to have been the daughter of Capt. Christopher Osgood, who moved from Ipswich to Andover and whose Ipswich homestead was

Ipswich Old North Burying Grounds, one of the oldest burying grounds in North America (historicipswich.org)

where the five Heard children were born. Edmund³ and Deborah had four children: Abigail in 1714, Deborah in 1716, Edmund⁴ in 1720, and Thomas in 1722. Thomas died in May 1726. Deborah died at Ipswich, aged 37, and was also buried in the Old North Burying Ground.⁴

Edmund's son-in-law (Abigail's husband) Daniel Hodgkins was lost at sea in 1753 and so Daniel Heard, her cousin, was appointed guardian of the young children. The story as told traditionally among their descendants was that Abigail was much impressed by a dream she had: *"It seemed as if she were upon a most desolate island, vainly endeavoring to dry what at that time worn as socks and nippers. She wandered about completely covered with a sense of desolation. Such was the depth of her depression, that she went to her neighbour's the next day, thinking that some expression would dispel the shadow; but it proved indeed a foreboding. Her husband had indeed perished in the seas."* On the day of her death there was a snowstorm so severe the windows and doors were covered. At her burial, the bier was carried over the roof of the one-storey house that had been completely transfigured into a hill of snow.⁴, ¹⁰

Edmund³ married his third wife, Rebecca Knowlton, in 1724 but she died in 1728. He married his fourth wife, Martha Kimball, in 1729; she also died in childbirth, in 1730. Apparently undaunted, he married his fifth wife, Elizabeth Caldwell, a widow of John Caldwell, who had been slain by the Indians on the coast of Maine. Many women died in childbirth during these early times. So that other members of a family might survive, it was not uncommon for remarriages during these precarious times in our history.⁴

In about 1770, William³ Heard (son of Edmund²) and his brother James moved from Vinalhaven, Me., to South Thomaston, Me., settling at Ash Point, near where Nathaniel Crockett lived. William³, besides farming, soon commenced and carried on with the manufacture of salt. The need for salt was huge. There was no other way of preserving flesh or fish. When the settlers killed their pigs and cattle in November of each year, all the meat had to be salted to preserve it for winter consumption. Venison was treated in the same way. Poultry was different in that it was eaten soon after it was dressed.

Salterns were located in the marshland next to the seashore. Feeder ponds were set just in from the shoreline, into which the sea water could flow at high tide. Salt pans were built-in shallow basins, divided into 20-foot squares by mud banks six inches high and just wide enough for a man to walk on. Water from the feeder ponds was bailed into these pans with wooden scoops to a depth of about three inches. When the water evaporated, the salt remained. The water was moved through a sequence of pans, achieving an increasingly higher concentration of salt. The process usually began in late April and lasted about four months. The hotter the weather the more salt was produced. Another method, using large cast iron pots or kettles, was sometimes used to finish the process further inland.

The American Revolution was just beginning and marauding British Tories made it their mission to burn all that was combustible around him, including his saltworks. "British privateers were one such raiding party that also entered his house, inquired where the men were, would not believe the answer; said they must be hidden or had fled with the money, threatened the women, and set fire to the house. They finally put out the fire they had kindled and departed, having obtained no information or prospect of plunder;" (Cyrus Eaton, History of Thomaston, Rockland, and South Thomaston, Maine).

Author's note: This was the beginning of the political division that began to occur within families. Obviously, William was not enamored with the British burning down his livelihood and threatening his family on the premise of law. He would clearly become subject to Patriot sympathies and begin to distance himself from both British taxation and governance. This is not unlike the divisions that are appearing today in the United States during the 2020 election issues.

William[3] Heard went on to purchase 200 acres of land in Thomaston from General Henry Knox of Revolutionary War fame (that part of Owls Head now known as Ash Point) for $149.82 in January 1800 (Knox Co. Deeds 9:173). He bought an additional 100 acres in Ash Point from Gen. Knox in October 1801 for $400 (ibid., 10:213), and 91 acres more for $100 on the same date (ibid.). William[3] served on the Committee of Safety from South Thomaston in 1779.[4] Much of this land had been given to Gen. Knox for his service during the Revolution (1775-1783), but as it had already been settled there was much transferring of land back and forth. William Heard bought additional property from Israel Thorndike and Daniel Sears of Boston in September 1807: Ash Point Island (nine acres), Fisherman's Island (five acres), Birch Island (four acres) and Oak Island (one-half acre) for £104. (ibid. 17:51). William's descendants have been extensively traced by Charles S. Candage of Hallowell, Me., is his book *Descendants of William Heard and Abigail Crockett of Ash Point, Maine, 1746-1987*. Mr. Candage has contributed significantly to the William Heard genealogy on this project over several years.[4]

Edmund[4] Heard, Jr. "purchased by right of redemption all the estate of my honored father, (Edmund[3] Heard), being deceased, and part of the same belonging to my brothers Nathaniel and Daniel."[4]

***

Meanwhile, two generations later, the direct line of the Thomas[2] French family had moved to Enfield, Conn., circa 1678. (John Winthrop Jr. was the first Governor of Connecticut, so one sees the connection.) *(Roger K. Lancey, French family descendant)*

> *Author's note: Sometime during this period, a John[4] French, perhaps a grandson of Thomas[2], residing in Enfield, married Rachael Bush. The author has been unable to make a definitive connection between the John French and Thomas French families other than to state that they were in the same locales during the same time frames. There is sufficient documentation to suggest that it was their son, John[5] French, who was born in Enfield in 1739.*

The family remained United Empire Loyalists following the inauguration of George Washington as President in 1789. John[4] French would make the move to claim lands with his sons, Luther[1], Levi[1] and John[5] Sage, in Lower Canada circa 1796. *(Roger K. Lancey)*

***

Around the same time, John[3] Bowker and Ruth had moved to Newton, Mass., where they raised their son Josiah[4] B., who was born there in 1707. Josiah was 26 when he met and married Hazadiah Eager in 1733. John[3] was granted permission to build a gallery "over the stairs on the southeast corner of the meeting house in Newton." He was surveyor of highways and a sealer of leather. *(Florence (Bowker) McVetty, Bowker family history)*

In examining records from this period, the author noted discrepancies in birthdates in certain documents. This greatly complicated genealogical research, and in some cases assumptions were made that individuals with different birthdates were from different families. Some of the discrepancies can be explained by the calendar used: some birthdates were recorded using the "Old Style" calendar; others using the "New Style" calendar. The "British Calendar Act of 1750" came into effect on September 3, 1752. Eleven days were added, so September 3, Old Style, became September 14, New Style. Also, the first day of the year was changed from March 25, Old Style, to January 1, New Style. In summary, for any date between January 1 and March 25, Old Style, we add one year and 11 days, and for any date after March 25, Old Style, we merely add 11 days.[15]

> *Author's note: Confusing? Yes, indeed . . . but it explains the discrepancies that many genealogists and families have struggled with. Not unlike the author, when examining the records at Ipswich regarding the birth dates of Edmund's children (above), they differed from those recorded by historian and genealogist Ed Hansen. By using this formula, the records matched perfectly.*

And so, Josiah[4] and Hazadiah Bowker moved their family to Worcester, Mass., where their son Antipas[5] was born in 1733. It was not uncommon for families to move from town to town during this era. Because many new immigrants were arriving from "the other side of the pond," many established residents found themselves in search of work. As well, opportunities were opening up in the western parts of the Colonies as people moved inland from the coastal regions. Josiah[4] served the town of Worcester as surveyor, fence viewer and tithingman. *(Florence (Bowker) McVetty)*

***

Edmund[4] Heard (lineage: Edmund[2], Edmund[3], Luke[1]) was born at Ipswich in August 1720, and died at Holden, Mass., at age 49. He married Priscilla Haskell, who was born at Gloucester in 1718 and died there at age 65. Through her mother, Martha, Priscilla was a descendant of Isaac Allerton of Mayflower fame. (Verification of this documentation can be found in the Cape Cod series, vols. 1 and 2.) They had nine children: Edmund[5] (born 1743), Priscilla (born 1744 and died young), a second Priscilla (born 1746), Mark (born 1748), Thomas (born 1749), Martha (born 1753), William[5] (born 1755), Jeremiah (born 1758 and died young) and Eunice (born 1759).[4] Thomas was a Minuteman under the command of Capt. Isaac Davis, who marched from Holden to Concord, Mass., on the alarm of April 19, 1775. Thomas also served in several other companies, including Colonel John Greaton's regiment, when he was reported killed by Indians at the Battle of Stillwater, N.Y., in July 1777.

Two of Edmund[4] and Priscilla's sons, Edmund[5] and William[5] Heard, would not have known they were to embark on an adventurous journey to found a settlement, a new colony, in a new land called Lower Canada, and would be joined by the next generation of Sawyer, Bowker, Lyon, and French families soon to follow.

In the meetinghouse, built in 1749, Edmund[4] became the purchaser of the pew on the westerly corner of the gallery. He was appointed as a tithing man for the town in 1752 and served as one of the sealers of leather from 1753 through 1761, when he suddenly died. The following bequests were made: "to my son, Thomas, the northwest part of the farm in Holden at the age of 21; to my son, William,[5] the easterly part of the farm; to my son, Mark, one-piece northeast of the farm and one piece southwest of it; to my wife Priscilla, Executrix, all my personal Estate and movable affects and Negros, together with 9 acres of land lying in the Town of Ipswich, which had been given to her by her father."[4]

William[4] Heard, born in Ipswich in 1718, married Mary Newmarch in 1741. They raised two sons and two daughters there. William was a potter by trade and served in the French and Indian Wars.[4]

Most of the fourth generation of Heard families were ensconced in the community of Ipswich and surrounding communities: holding properties and engaging in settlement activities. They were staunch defenders of their rights, their families, faiths and their new country, and the continued support of their mother country. Many served during the French and Indian Wars of 1755 and the campaign of 1758. They also served in the Quebec Expedition of 1759 and the Montreal Expedition of 1760.[4]

Battle of the Plains of Abraham, 1759 (britishbattles.com)

The Battle of the Plains of Abraham (September 13, 1759) was a pivotal moment in the Seven Years' War and in the history of Canada. A British invasion force led by General James Wolfe defeated French troops under the Marquis de Montcalm, leading to the surrender of Quebec to the British.[1]

What started in 1775 as the Revolutionary War (a.k.a. the American Revolution) became commonly known as the American War of Independence when Great Britain's 13 New England Colonies, south of Lower Canada, declared their independence as the United States of America. During this 1775-83 conflict, colonists were caught between loyalty to the Old World and independence from their overseas masters.

During that period, our ancestors had been living in Massachusetts, one of the 13 British New England Colonies. Newbury and Newburyport, Ipswich, Lancaster, Gloucester, Salem, Worcester and Lexington, all in Massachusetts, were the stomping grounds of our many ancestors. Battles at Lexington and Concord, where the first shot of the American Revolution was heard around the world, were the beginning of battles that ended at Boston's Bunker Hill.

At the outset of the Revolutionary War, circa 1777, collective memories remained alive of the French and Indian Wars whereby, during the late 1760s, New York State, the Ohio Valley, Nova Scotia, Montreal and Quebec City had been battlefields. In both Britain and Canada, the conflict was referred to as the Seven Years' War. Britain's myopic handling of the war's aftermath bred resentments and misunderstandings that grew into rebellion. In its attempt to keep Quebec loyal, Britain instituted the Quebec Act 1774. Quebecers saw it as protecting their French/Catholic rights within a system of government they understood. American rebels considered it as among what they called "Coercive or Intolerable Acts" because it was another example of Britain denying democracy to its colonies, yet another precursor to revolution.

President John Adams explained that in order to protect their northern flank, Quebec City would need to be attacked and a liberated Quebec should be persuaded to join the revolution. In 1775 Benedict Arnold let an ill-fated expedition to seize the city, but his December 31 assault was not successful. Since they had travelled through Maine, blazing a trail through the Megantic mountains, their route later became known as the Arnold Trail (and is also part of an old Indigenous peoples' pathway to Quebec City).[1]

By the fifth generation many Heards and their descendants owned large enterprises such as salt refineries and distilleries; others were shipwrights, cordwainers, surveyors, blacksmiths and silversmiths; some were in the import/export businesses. These were the Heard descendants who elected to stay in the new United States of America. These entrepreneurial enterprises demonstrate how our ancestors were, by the fifth generation of settlement in the New World of virgin lands, already expanding in new directions.[4]

***

John Heard, grandson of Daniel (Edmund[3] Heard), always the dominant partner in the Turkey Shore Distillery business in Ipswich, became sole owner around 1769-70. The rum produced at the distillery was made from West Indies molasses, and by 1775 John began contracting vessels to sail from Ipswich with lumber and fish and return with cargoes of molasses, sugar, coffee, and other delicacies for the town. During the Revolution, he served on the "draft board" for Ipswich, conscripting men for service. On the business side, in 1776 he took to privateering, the legal warfare of private ships against "belligerents." The privateer ship's owner was allowed to keep a portion of the loot, and usually bought the crew's share before sailing to ensure payment whether or not booty was taken. John bought the shares of many Ipswich sailors who belonged to crews of ships fitted from Salem, Newburyport, and Gloucester. Between 1776 and 1781, he bought shares in at least 23 vessels, and in 1779 equipped and armed his own privateer, the brig "JOHN," with wooden guns and painted ports as well as her real armaments.

The Heard House on South Main Street in Ipswich was built in 1795 by wealthy John Heard. Before the Revolutionary War he had invested in the rum factory on Turkey Shore Road along the riverbank where they unloaded barrels of West Indies molasses. He later helped start the Ipswich Mills. His son Augustine Heard owned clipper ships and competed with those of Salem and Boston in the China trade. Augustine retired and started the Ipswich Manufacturing Company in 1828 with Joseph Farley, building a new dam and the old stone mill.

The Ipswich mansion remained in the family until 1936 when it was sold to the Ipswich Historical Society, which now uses John Heard House as its headquarters and as a federal-style living and China trade era museum.

Heard House, Ipswich, Mass. (photo by Sandra Hurd)

Aside from the mansion house on South Main Street, John Heard also invested in Ipswich real estate, including a farm at Jeffries Neck, which eventually consisted of 60 acres of upland and 40 acres of marsh. There was also an investment in the purchase of the Swasey Tavern, which was later transferred to his son Augustine in 1823 (unrecorded deed at the Ipswich Historical Society). The Turkey Shore Distillery, as it was later known, was transferred to his youngest son, George W. Heard, in 1818, ending an almost 50-year connection with that business. There were also other real estate dealings outside of Ipswich: in Boston; at Hallowell, Me.; and in the Ohio territory as an investor in the Ohio Company and Associates.[4]

One of John Heard's sons, George Washington[6] Heard, graduated from Harvard College in 1812 and received his M.D. in 1815 but never practiced medicine. He lived partly in Boston but spent most of his time in Ipswich. He was school master in Ipswich in 1824 and in 1833. He served in the Massachusetts House of Representatives from Ipswich in 1826, 1830, 1831 and 1833. He was a partner in the Ipswich Manufacturing Company with his brother Augustine and was also the first president of the Ipswich Bank, established in 1833.[4]

Augustine was employed by one of the principal merchants of Boston, part time from 1803. In 1805 he sailed to Calcutta on a merchant vessel belonging to his employer. This trip caused him to be absent from his studies at Philips Exeter Academy for two years, and it appears he did not graduate. He continued seafaring, and sailed for the first time as ship's master on the *Caravan*, entrusted with $80,000 in cargo. He became a navigator and merchant of such high degree that he soon became one of the foremost captains in the East India trade and had some of the best ships trading in the Orient. During the War of Independence his business suffered, as did all American firms doing business offshore, as the country and families were torn apart by differing beliefs and objections.[4]

Many of the Heard families served in the various military factions as Minutemen and/or officers, some on opposing sides. Augustine's half-brother Daniel (1778-1801) also worked in foreign trade with the West Indies and China.

Augustine had been able to build up a comfortable fortune through his numerous ventures, and in 1829 completed his active maritime career. In 1830, at age 45, he sailed for Canton, China, to become a partner in the famous firm Russell & Company, in which he had a three-sixteenths interest. His work was marked with success. However, experiencing health issues, he returned to America in 1834 at the end of his term. He then settled in Boston from where he continued to direct his business and investments.[4]

Augustine Heard (painting by William Morris Hunt)

The Ipswich Museum also holds a portrait of Augustine Heard (painted by William Morris Hunt), a copy of which is in the Ipswich Public Library. In 1828, with his brother, G. W. Heard, and Joseph Farley, he incorporated the Ipswich Manufacturing Company. In 1852 he became its sole owner. He founded and endowed the Ipswich Public Library, providing it with the building it is (as of 1995) still using. In 1916 the Ipswich Historical Society published a book by Thomas Franklin Waters, titled *Augustine Heard and His Friends*, which gives a detailed account of Augustine's personal and business life. An account of the business, *Augustine Heard and Company, 1858-1862*, by Stephen C. Lockwood, was published by the Harvard University Press (Cambridge, Mass., 1971).[4]

Owing to internal friction, Russell & Company was reorganized in 1840. The new firm of Augustine Heard & Company was established with Joseph Coolidge, formerly of Russell & Company, as the active partner in Canton.

The Opium War was in progress when Augustine returned to China, and during this period of hostilities his place of business was attacked by a mob which caused him serious loss, although his coolness and fearlessness enabled him to save a large share of his goods and coinage. Later he was compensated for his loss by the Chinese government. Carrying on the general merchant and commission business common to the China merchants of his day, he had the confidence and respect of the Chinese, as well as of his competitors and employees.[4]

In contrast to the sharp but unscrupulous negotiating practices of the small firms, he maintained high standards of business ethics in conjunction with the few large trading houses at Canton. With those of Samuel Russell, D. W. C. Olyphant and W. S. Wetmore, his firm was one of the four to survive the decades of competition in Canton.

In that highly individualistic period of American foreign policy, Augustine Heard & Company had an important influence in shaping the Far East policy of his U.S. Government. Augustine returned to America in 1844 and never returned to China, although he made several trips to Europe. He settled at Ipswich in the mansion of his late father, which he furnished with a large number of costly and elegant mementos of his time in the Orient. The paintings included many Chinese port scenes, clipper ships and other paintings by the noted artist George Chinnery; these paintings were purchased from the Heard Estate by the Peabody Museum in Salem, Mass., in 1931 and 1937.[4]

Meanwhile, each of Augustine's four nephews served their turn as manager of the firm in China. As long as Augustine lived, the business prospered. However, after the American Civil War, the company suffered from the same conditions that affected all American firms in the Orient.

The Ipswich Public Library itself is an ever-present reminder of the generosity of the Heard family. Augustine gave funds for the creation of a library. He selected the site, bought the land, supervised the plans, gave an endowment, and selected the first 300 books. He died in 1868, just before the library opened. *(History of Early Ipswich, A Walking Tour booklet, 2003)*

> *Author's note: Actor John Heard, whose ancestors built what is now the Ipswich Museum, starred in critically acclaimed movies and TV series, the blockbuster "Home Alone," and "Sharknado & the Sopranos," died in late July 2016. His ashes were laid to rest on August 4, 2017, at the family plot in Ipswich.*

***

Antipas[5] Bowker married Ester Rice at Worcester in 1757 and lived there for a year before moving to Northborough, Mass., for a job in lumbering. Their first son, Gideon[6], was born there in 1760. *(Florence (Bowker) McVetty, Bowker family history)*

***

Nathan[5] Heard, son of Daniel (Edmund[2] Heard) and his wife Dinah, had moved to Worcester in 1777, just after the Bowker[5] family had moved to Chesterfield, N.H. Nathan held the position of jailkeeper for the town of Worcester from 1798 to 1824. The list of prisoners which he kept from 1808 to 1824 and submitted to Thomas Walter Ward, Sherriff of Worcester County, are in the Ward Family papers, Antiquarian Society. Nathan was also appointed keeper of the house of correction for Worcester County.[4]

They were risk takers; entrepreneurs competing for the key to the richness of the natural resources of these vast lands, trading with the Old World. These were people whose forefathers had the ability to withstand the hardship of crossing the Atlantic Ocean looking for a new life and accepting all the uncertainties that might bring. What started as economics in this New World began a change to a more permanent settlement during this period.

***

It was during this time that rafting lumber from Grand Isle to Quebec City was initiated, and where Capt. Ephraim[3] Sawyer was engaged in moving lumber down to a point in the Richelieu River; the lumber shipped from there to England. In 1792 a William Farnsworth, whose family name will show up in Newport at a later time, was one of the men hired to work a rafting trip for a lumber dealer, William Moffett, taking a log raft down Lake Champlain, through the rapids of the Richelieu River to Quebec City.

Farnsworth's receipt, in his own handwriting, tells us the following:

"South Hero, Grande Island, Feabuary ye 20th 1792—Received one pound ten shillings of William Moffett towards my wages for to go to Quebeck with him. [Signed] William Farnsworth" (Vermont Historical Society)

"To Captain Ephraim[3] Sawyer—Please let the bearer Mr. William Farnsworth have six bushels of wheat. He is going aboard with me to Quebec. The wheat is for his Family in his absence. And on my return, I shall settle with you for the same. Your immediate compliance will much oblige me. [Signed] William Moffett" (Vermont Historical Society)

The descendants of both these men would become well known in both Eaton and Newport townships.[23]

Josiah[4] Sawyer, who grew up in Lancaster, was adopted by his mother's brother, Joseph Wilder of Leominster. At age 34 he commenced on his quest to "found" a town as his great-uncle had before him. After the War of Independence, he found himself as others had, trapped between two worlds ... the Crown and the self-governing Americans. He was an opportunity-seeker and saw Lower Canada as being rich in natural resources. Lower Canada and Upper Canada, still a part of Great Britain, had immense tracts of old-growth forests of eastern white pine and hardwoods, all of which were in high demand in the Old World for shipbuilding. First, the mighty trunk of a tree with a girth of at least 10 feet was needed to make the great stem and stern posts of a ship. Oak, the preferred wood for the main body of the ships, was in abundance in Upper Canada, and could be shipped down the St. Lawrence River in huge rafts to Quebec City for export to England. The ship's wall planks were made of beech wood, the masts and spurs were made of fir and spruce, the keel was elm – all woods growing in abundance in Lower Canada. Lumber from Lower Canada could be shipped from Nicolet, connecting with the great rafts already being guided down the St. Lawrence from Upper Canada. Josiah was an opportunist; in his vision, the region was essentially a gold mine.[23]

***

John[4] French, a second-generation member of the Thomas French family originally from Ipswich, had been born in Enfield in 1739 after his family had moved there. He was one of those who pioneered such a move to Lower Canada as an Associate with Josiah[4] Sawyer and was a leading light in the founding of Eaton Township with Josiah and his Associates. "His son, John[5] Sage French, was to drown tragically at Brompton Falls on the St. Francis River in 1814, exactly 100 years before my grandfather's death. John[5] Sage French's son, Horace Hall French was born in Cookshire in 1812 and married Harriet Bixby Ward in 1838 in Cookshire. I understand that they moved to the house at 315 Craig St. South in 1838, where generations of the family lived, and where my mother was born! Horace and Harriet's child, Charles Ward Bailey French was, therefore, my great-grandfather and we have come almost full circle." *(Roger K. Lancey)*

***

In 1773 Gideon[6] Bowker married Hannah Fletcher. A year later they moved to Chesterfield, N.H., where their first children were born: Solomon in 1781 and Johnathon (John) in 1783. They moved again in 1784, northwest to Guilford, Vt. Where five more children were born during the following 12 years between 1784 and 1796.

Their first-born in Guilford was a daughter, Lucy[7], born in 1786, the same year they had moved. Among the four children born in Guilford was another son, Lyman[7] James, born in 1794, 14 years after his brother Solomon and 11 years after his brother Johnathon – the two brothers who first immigrated to Newport. *(Florence (Bowker) McVetty, Bowker family history)*

The Bowker[6] family finally moved north with their family of seven children to Lunenburg, Vt., a town situated near the Connecticut River where there was ample work in the lumbering business. They raised two more children in Lunenburg, born between 1799 and 1804, for a total of nine children. Three were destined to find their way to Newport, Lower Canada, and start a new life there. The first in the family to make the move were Solomon[7] and Johnathon (John[7]), at ages 16 and 18 and eager to start an adventure in a new land. Their daughter Lucy, who had been born in 1786 in Guildford, married John[7] Lyon in Lunenburg; their two sons also found their way to Newport sometime later. Solomon and Johnathon made the trip from Lunenburg, following the Connecticut River north up through Lake Francis and the two Connecticut lakes, arriving in Newport through the Indian Stream path. They signed their application for land grants in Newport, Lower Canada, in 1799. Their signatories are evidenced in the *Newport first Records* of 1800, as acknowledged by the signed document of the Committee Regulators, Capt. Samuel[6] Heard, William Hudson and John Lebourveau.[20]

> *Author's note: I have been unable to find any record of them marrying and staying in Newport beyond these early days when they had applied for a land grant and worked to build their future in Newport. It appears that John may have left Newport, first returning to Lunenburg, Vt., sometime after 1815, but Solomon remained for some time thereafter.*

Solomon and Johnathon built a small cabin on Lot 3 of Range 6 in the central section of Newport, part of the quarter-section granted to Colonel Edmund[5] Heard.[20]

Author's note: Lyman[7] James Bowker, born in Guildford, Vt., in 1794, married Betsey Merriam and they, too, moved to Newport Township, following his two older brothers, but much later in 1834. The author does not know at the time of writing if Lyman acquired one or two of the original lots claimed by his brothers, but it would seem reasonable that Lyman would have acquired his brothers' lots if they had in fact abandoned them. There is sufficient evidence, referencing both the dates and locations of the Bowker family within the time frames, to suggest that Lyman would have surfaced with the certificates that had been issued to his brothers earlier for these lots. Also apparent is the fact that the Bowker families have occupied these exact same lots since the beginning of the settlements in Newport Township as assigned by Col. Edmund[5] and Capt. Samuel[6] Heard, who was to become Clerk of Newport Township in 1798.[20]

***

John[6] Lyon, born in 1740 in Dedham, Mass., had moved to Lunenburg, Vt., in 1799. John had served in the French and Indian Wars, his commission signed by George Washington. He and his wife had only one child, John[7], born in 1770. When John's family had moved from Dedham to Guilford, they had met the Bowker family, and their son John[7] found his love with Lucy Bowker, Gideon[6] and Hannah's daughter.[32]

John[7] Lyon married Lucy Bowker[7] in 1804. They raised two sons, Eliphalet and Orra, who were also destined to find their way to Newport. Orra would build a mill in the Island Brook region.[32]

***

As a result of the War of Independence, documents that made any reference to Great Britain were routinely destroyed. For that reason, our ancestors kept and retained, for their own personal reference, every piece of paper that related to their lives. Included in this collection of documents is the original Heard family "Coat of Arms," written documentation of the earliest Heard settlers in the New England Colonies, as well as Col. Edmund[5] Heard's venture to Newport. These events initiated an exodus of United Empire Loyalists to find a new life in a new land, and they looked north to a place they called Canady. Explorations towards British-held Lower Canada and Upper Canada began.[11]

Author's note: These documents have been kept within the family and passed from generation to generation – items which until now have been generally undisclosed.[4, 11]

These settlers would start a life from scratch in the wilderness in Canady (known as the "waste lands of Lower Canada"), as compared to what could be described as relatively civilized decades in the Colonies. They were to learn that records also would have to be kept after receiving the land grants for the loosely formed "British" government, at that time situated in Quebec City.

***

From the first Heard family settling in the New England Colonies and later in Ipswich, Mass., by the fifth generation there were approximately 58 families bearing the surname Heard. During this same period there were an additional 36 families who were direct descendants of the Heards of Ipswich through the female Heard marriages: names such as Somerby, Boardman, Leighton, Dillington, Lord, Boyton, Bragg, Stickby, Willington, Hodgkin, Gilman, Willard, Wheeler, Baker and Burnham, to name a few.

Many of these families had moved from Massachusetts towns such as Newbury, Newburyport, Gloucester, Salisbury, Worcester, Holden, and Lancaster; outward to other surrounding towns such as Wells and Portland in Maine; and west to Vermont and north to New Hampshire.

Edmund[5] Heard married Sarah Willington in June 1765, who was born in Worcester in 1743. Sarah bearing three children, Sarah, Edmund[6] and Luke[6]. Sarah died six months after giving birth to Luke, leaving Edmund with three young children, 1, 2 and 4 years old. Edmund married second Elizabeth Andrews in June of 1772, Elizabeth birthing two children, Samuel, and Hannah. Edmund and Elizabeth would raise a family of five children, three of whom would find themselves in a new land in a new country at an early age. Edmund, cordwainer of Lancaster, Mass., sold to his brother William[5], husbandman (a man who cultivates the land; a farmer) of Holden, his brother Thomas's portion of their father's estate, the late Edmund[4] Heard. In 1775, he also privately conveyed a considerable part of his property to Skeensborough on Lake Champlain in support of the British forces.

Edmund obtained a letter from General Gage at Boston, addressed to Capt. Delaplace, Commanding the British forces at Crown Point, to *"afford your petitioner aid and support on his intended rout." Unfortunately, Captain Delaplace and his troops, "were surpprized and taken prisoner by Allen Arnold and Co., all goods and effects seized at the lake and distributed among the Rebel forces."* Edmund, supplying the effort was also *"taken prisoner and carried to Crown Point where he was held prisoner until the month of October when he was sent back into the States and committed to close prison."* Because Edmund was considered a man of wealth and influence, he was released on his own cognizance, his movements and activities clearly documented for further scrutiny.[3]

Edmund[5] was later commissioned as an officer of the British, the commission as colonel *"to the first Regiment of Cavalry in the seventh Division of the Militia"* by John Hancock in 1791. The commission document is held in the Byington Collection Society for the Preservation of New England Antiquities, Boston.[3]

Edmund's brother William[5] Heard, born in Ipswich in 1755 was the fifer for Capt. Phineas Moore's company of Minute men in Col. Doolittle's regiment, before marrying his second wife, Thirza Williams, in 1797. He had six children with his first wife, Betsey Dix of Holden Mass., who died young in 1794, leaving William with six young children. His second wife, Thirza, and these children would all find themselves soon to be settling in a new land in a new country, escaping the clutches of the Patriots of the new United States of America.[4]

All of these hardy pioneers were about to embark on a new adventure for them, some for just cause, others for opportunity but all for the anticipation of settling a new land for themselves and their families. They became settlers as did their predecessors, perhaps this time on their own terms of experience.

With this background, we can better understand our forefathers, and the brave women and children who pioneered these early New England states. They appeared to value education and took great care to provide, where possible, guidance to their children towards this end. It was during this period that the Colonies of New England had seen five generations of settlers who had built their communities to a point of relative comfort. Now a few of these families were to start over again, settling in a virgin territory of harsh landscapes with virtually no amenities and total isolation. These were essentially a fifth generation starting as the first generation in a new land, as did their ancestors before them.

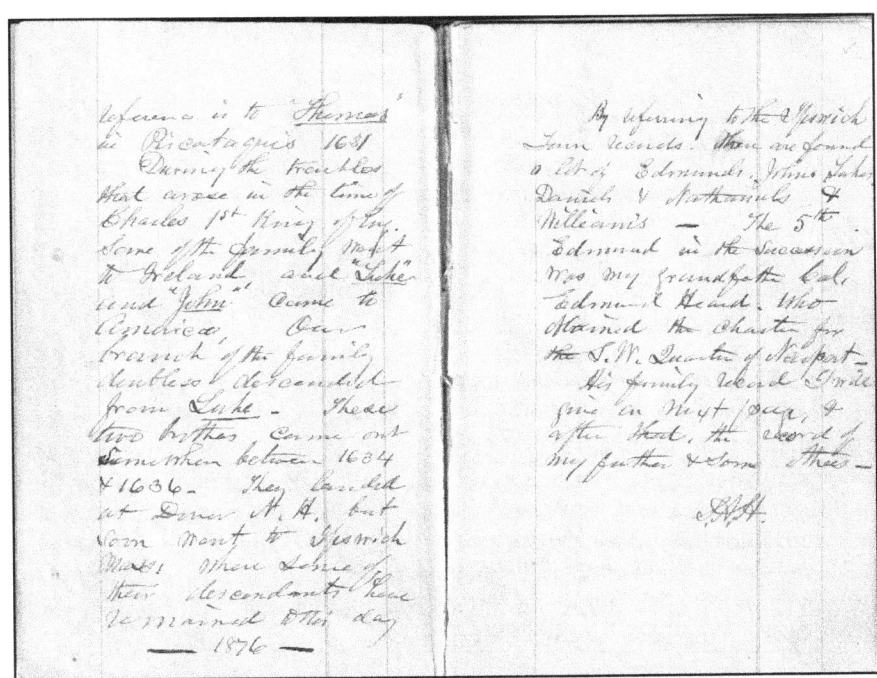

Pages 1 and 2 of the Samuel[7] A. Heard Manuscript (Heard/Hurd family collection)

These settlers did not find life overwhelming because their life was built on dreams, building a life for themselves. Under siege, their lands were taken, but they had the stamina and drive caused by past failures to start all over again. Without their perseverance, Canada would not be what it is today. It is amazing how a few pioneers like these could help shape this country. And so, a new generation of rebels and entrepreneurs was created, competing for the land's resources, while others would battle to protect them.

Author's notes:

(1) I have attempted to track the families who joined Col. Edmund[5] Heard and Capt. Josiah[4] Sawyer and connect the many branches of their ancestors on both the male and female lines. This story is also making the connections between the families of Newport from inception as they progressed through their lives.

(2) I will concentrate on the "lives lived" of those who inhabited Newport Township; however, some names will have originated from the surrounding communities of adjacent townships and so there will be a mixing of stories interchanged as people moved back and forth.

(3) A source I have drawn upon for subsequent chapters is the manuscripts of Samuel[7] A. Hurd, a direct descendant of Col. Edmund[5] Heard, who later compiled some 45 pages of family history into a booklet, the cover of which presents the official "Heard Coat of Arms." This booklet is also part of the Ancestral Heard/Hurd Collection. Samuel, born in Newport, became justice of the peace in Eaton Township for some years. Samuel communicated with Augustine Heard of Ipswich, Mass., via letters written in 1850 that are archived in the Heard Collection, Vol. AA-1, Baker Library, Harvard University. Samuel was also cited in the Biographical Review *titled* Containing Life Sketches of Leading Citizens of Essex County, Mass., [Boston, 1898] 28: 295-297.[11]

Samuel[7] A. Hurd Manuscript booklet with Heard Coat of Arms on cover

(4) Further information is provided from an inordinate supply of documents, related accountings (credit and payment), military documents and family-owned written works. Included in these are the personal diaries and letters exchanged between the families of Newport Township settlement and the New England states from which they had come.[3, 4, 31]

Our present and future is informed by the values of the past, as well as by the principles that have guided all our individual families' growth for the past 14 generations. Our ancestors wrote the blueprints by which we still live our lives, ethically and culturally.

And so, we will return to the start of our story of the early settlers who came to Newport Township. The fifth Edmund in the succession was Col. Edmund[5] Heard, who obtained the charter for the southwest quarter of Newport Township, Lower Canada. He and Capt. Josiah[4] Sawyer, whose adventure to the "waste lands of Lower Canada" would be joined by the French, Bowker, Lyon and many other families from the southern New England states as well as directly from England, Scotland, and Ireland. Still others, many originally from the same New England communities but who had initially moved to other parts of Lower Canada, would finally settle in Newport and join in its continuing development. These were our connections to the past and they would continue to make family connections in the future. They brought a culture developed from five generations of settlement in the New England Colonies that still exists today in the genes of their descendants.

***

Chapter 6   Migration from the South (1790–1815)

We will continue our journey with Colonel Edmund[5] Heard, his wife and children, and Edmund's brother William[5] Heard and his family. William had accompanied Edmund on both his third and fourth trips to Newport, Lower Canada.

Edmund[5] first moved from Ipswich, Mass., to Worcester, Mass., where he had married Sarah Willington. They had three children: Sarah (born 1766), Edmund[6] (born 1768) and Luke (born 1770). Sarah died in 1770 at age 27.[4]

Edmund married his second wife, Elizabeth Andrews, in 1772; they had two children: Samuel[6] (born 1773) and Hannah (born 1775).[4]

Because Edmund[5] had been commissioned as colonel to the 1st Regiment of Cavalry in the 7th Division of the militia, he and other commissioned officers had an income of one-half regular active pay during times of inactivity. They therefore always had income, usually 100 English pounds per year, which was considered a significant sum, especially if one could use it to build their own business. They also had the option of selling their commission to the highest bidder for a lump sum at any time. Because of this they were able to acquire goods without barter, as they were considered a good risk in their ability to pay later. Some might do this if they had become successful at farming or another vocation, or if a skirmish were pending and they did not wish to be committed to go fight again – although the latter would have been considered treasonous and was therefore unlikely.[3]

Upon receiving the promise of 1200 acres in the Township of Newport, Col. Edmund[5] Heard moved his second family– his wife Elizabeth and their two children, Samuel and Hannah – to Newport in 1793. This is commemorated by a plaque at the entrance to Maple Leaf Cemetery, in the village of Randboro, Que., near where he and Josiah[4] Sawyer slashed the first 10 acres of land on Pleasant Hill. The cemetery land was donated for the purpose intended by Edmund's brother, William[5] Heard, in 1802.[18]

From the time Col. Edmund[5] and Josiah[4] Sawyer had arrived in the spring of 1793, Edmund had taken all the necessary steps to secure his promise of the land grant. After the first year's scanty crops had been planted in the newly cleared land, they had built preliminary housing in the spring of 1793 for both their livestock and themselves. However, a more permanent residence was required for the family. The original building that they had been living in was needed to house the growing number of livestock, and their own habitation was now of utmost importance. With his family, Edmund built the first house in Newport Township in the spring of 1794. It still stands today and has been designated a "heritage home."

The cavity for the cellar was made in the centre of the spot chosen and lined with flat rock set in clay. At one end of the cellar was a stone base to support a large open chimney. This was built up a short way with stones and clay, to resist fire, then continued up through the bark roof with small sticks crossed at the corners and filled in with clay. The whole inside of the chimney was plastered with a thick coating of clay and flat stone. The largest flat stones they could find were laid around the hearth. Note the wide boards that were hand-split and the notched logs in the crossmembers.[17]

Wide floorboards in Heard heritage home, Newport (photo by Sandra Hurd)

The floors, doors and partitions were hewn planks, fastened together with wooden pins. The building was built as were the barns, using the "stick" style of building method of the day. The beams were also pegged together using round pins and corner braces. The floors were essentially hung throughout the building on these cross beams. This method of building was one of the reasons so many lost their lives in fires in these early days. If a fire erupted on the lower floor, the walls provided a direct channel to the upper floors as there was no blocking between the outside walls at each level.

Edmund and Elizabeth's house was approximately 12 feet wide by 24 feet long, with the roof pitch on the short side. The front door was positioned to the north, approximately 6 feet from the east side, allowing for a steep staircase to the loft. Since there was no "knee wall," the top floor lost about 2 feet on each side, making the "loft" about 20 feet long by 12 feet wide. The staircase from the main floor was positioned between the second and third crossbeams running east to west, essentially in the centre of the house. The last step sat on a raised platform, allowing for a turn toward the front door. Two more steps were added to the bottom of the platform.

The loft was one large room where everyone slept. The first year that included not only Edmund and Elizabeth, but also their daughter Hannah, their son Samuel and his wife Miriam, while Samuel and Miriam were building their own home on their lot on the opposite side of South River. For privacy they hung rugs or heavy tapestry they had brought with them from New England. Since there was no running water into the house, they would have collected water from a cistern, located near their first original house-barn, for the first year in their new home. An outhouse would have been strategically located near the outside kitchen for easy access both day and night.

A small window on each of the gable ends of the house provided light and air circulation; the chimney provided some heat passing through to the roof. The main floor was also just one large room with the fire hearth, eating and sitting areas.

The kitchen was located on the south side as an outside summer-style with no cellar underneath. Here is where they cooked and ate their meals in the summer, moving into the larger, heated main room in the winter. Beyond the kitchen was the outhouse.

Early houses were frequently built with one large room with a fireplace and cooking hearth on the ground level with a matching room above. As settlers were able to afford to, or if simply the time and resources allowed them to build a larger house, a matching set of rooms was added on the opposite side of the fireplace and stairway.[14] *(Brief History of Ipswich, Mass., third edition)*

Our ancestors were adept at learning whatever they needed to know to survive and to improve their lives. Hand saws were often passed lengthwise through the joints of the rough-hewn board floors when they were frozen to prevent any unevenness of the sides. When the planks thawed the natural expansion would tighten them even more. If there were any nails, iron door latches, hinges, glass, or other fixtures of this kind they would have been brought in at great expense and trouble, so many of the tools and fixtures of this time would have been fashioned by local blacksmiths or other such handymen. Many of these first houses burnt down and the settlers would carefully comb the rubble to collect any metal such as hasps, nails, hooks, and latches, as metal was not readily available and these items could all be reused.

Heard heritage home in Maple Leaf, Newport (photo by Sandra Hurd)

The original farmhouse had an outside wall just beyond the wall of the current staircase to the cellar. A matching set of two rooms was added on the south wall, which is evident today with the addition of both the kitchen and dining room along with the two upstairs rooms. At the time, it would have been one large room, both downstairs and upstairs, matching the other side. This added part of the house was built circa 1840-45 by Luke[7] Heard, Edmund[6] Heard's son and Edmund[5] Heard's grandson.

The original hearth chimney was located in the approximate centre of this south-facing outside wall. When the addition was built the "hearth fireplace" would have been replaced with a "double-topped stove," which provided heat for the house and was also the cooking stove, with a warming/baking oven on top. This stove used the same chimney as the earlier hearth fireplace, but with the addition, is now located in the middle of the house, as can be seen in the current-day photo. The early part of the house, built by Col. Edmund[5] Heard, was exactly one-half the size of the house today.

It is reasonable to assume that this addition was done circa 1840-50 by grandson Luke[7] Hurd, who took over the original homestead – the building methodology was the same style; however, the materials suggest a sawmill had been available for better flooring materials, as is evident on the addition side in the current structure.

**

The initial French family and Heard family connection:

> *Author's note: In the spring of 1796, John[4] French and his eldest sons, Luther[1] and Levi[1] of Enfield, Conn., part of the newly formed United States of America, came exploring in Eaton Township in the early spring of 1796. This was after Capt. Josiah[4] Sawyer and Col. Edmund[5] Heard had explored the townships of Newport and Eaton earlier, having applied for the land grant allocations open for settlement in the "waste lands of Lower Canada" in 1792-93. As the story unfolds, John's youngest son, John[5] Sage French, would have an unfortunate incident involving Edmund's son Samuel and John Lebourveau.[16]*

John[4], Luther[1] and Levi[1] French had first cleared a parcel of land around a region we now know as Eaton Corner and had planted some potatoes that year, perhaps the first clearing of land in Eaton. If they had attempted to settle on this first land, they would have been considered "squatters," so they returned to Enfield to make a formal application as Associates with Capt. Josiah's group. John[4], Luther, Levi and John[5] Sage and their families formally immigrated to Lower Canada in 1798, returning to Eaton Township. They made their way through their previous clearing, continuing further east to where Sawyerville is today.[16]

John[4] French, his wife Abigail Sage, and his family settled in Eaton Township in 1798 and became three of Josiah[1] Sawyer's Associates. They were granted lands in Eaton Township under the same parameters as Col. Edmund[5] Heard. John[5] Sage, now age 22, was the "Mr. French" who would be referred to by Samuel[6] Heard in his letter to his brother Edmund[6], who was still living in Holden, Vt., in 1802. Samuel[6] had wanted to send the letter via John, along with some items he had wanted to send to his brother but could not find them in the woods where he thought they might be.[10]

John[4] French and his sons, along with Josiah[4] Sawyer and his two older sons, Peter and Josiah[5], made many trips through the wilderness on foot, guided by marked trees, transporting materials to their new lands in Eaton Township. They had been raised in a lumbering industry and were practical and energetic in making their life generally successful. It was not uncommon to apply for a son or daughter to be included in these applications at this early stage as the applicants had to have at least 14-20 Associates to qualify for these grants.[23]

Many of the Frenches today occupy the same lands their forefathers carved out of the wilderness. Further in this story the author will connect Levi's son Luther[2] Sage French, who years later built a lumber business in Newport, operating as a millwright and lumber manufacturer.[10,17]

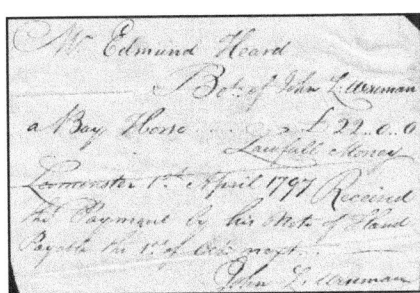

Bill of sale for Bay horse

Edmund[5] Heard had been contemplating building a mill ever since he had built his home three years prior. In April 1797 he made his first trip to Lancaster to search out mill parts that could be transported back to Newport by oxen. Unfortunately, his longtime companion and trusted horse Jess, who had served him for so many years, died during the trip. Edmund[5] bought a *"Bay"* horse in Lancaster *"for £22 (pounds)"* on his return to Newport. The original bill of sale is pictured to the left.[31]

Author's note: I found no information on the significance of a "Bay" horse.

In March 1799, Col. Edmund[5] Heard and Vermont resident Asa Waters commissioned for the formal surveying of Newport Township by a Christopher S. Bailey of Leamington, Vt. The township would have a total of 308 lots of 200 acres each in 11 ranges, for a total of 61,600 acres.[20]

The Township of Newport is credited with executing the first documented municipal business in the Eastern Townships. Early records from 1791 to 1814 were recorded by Leader Edmund[5] Heard and his Associates for a period of 23 years in a "Minute Book" of first records. These documented minutes of their meetings and voting procedures were the first in the colony demonstrating a partially elective system of government while establishing the Township of Newport. These early settlers were a law-abiding people, and as there was no law for carrying on Township business, they met together and organized under their own rules on the same lines as the law provided in the New England Colonies, more specifically under the governing laws of Massachusetts.[20]

Entered in the *Newport first Records*:

> *On the 28th day of September 1799, the Associated Applicants of the Township of Newport convened in the house of Asa Waters, where three persons were chosen to be on a Committee to inform some necessary Regulations in order to preserve the good order and understanding of the Association and the associated applicants. The regulations would outline the methods necessary for keeping and recording all matters relative to the Lands in said Township and all other matters belonging to the Association and to lay the framework before the Associated Applicants for their signature at their meeting on Thursday the third day of October next at the same location as above mentioned.* [20]

The terms of *"The Agreement of 1799"* were laid out in this document which set the stage for all further meetings to be held: *"The Regulations which your Committee think expedient and proper to adopt, as tabled in the document, under three separate articles. [Signed] Samuel Heard, William Hudson, John Lebourveau."* [20]

Signatories to the document included the following applicants:

> *Edmund Heard, Elisha Hudson, Wm. Williams, Solomon Bowker, David Ward, Wm. Heard, Wm. Hudson, John Harvey, N. Harvey, Nathanial Beaman Jr., Elijah Hudson Jr., Samuel B. Hudson, Samuel Heard, Seth Norton, David Metcalf, Joseph Kenny, Josiah Preble, Jeffrey Maynard, Timothy Holmes, Jonas Beaman, H.H. Ward, Edmund Heard Jr., Nathan Write, Wilden Wendel.* [20]

The 1801 book *Laws of the Commonwealth of Massachusetts* was brought to Newport by Col. Edmund[5] Heard. It became the guide that the settlers would use to develop their own rule of law for these early years. The organization disbanded after the driving forces, Col. Edmund[5] Heard and his son Capt. Samuel[6] Heard, died in 1814 and 1815 respectively, and the Township was to come under the newly formed governance of Lower Canada.[30]

In 1801, Samuel[6] Heard was elected "clerk" for the newly formed Township records-keeping. The first piece of business was a vote to open a road from the post of lots 7 and 8 of ranges 9 and 10 to Sawyers Mills in Eaton Township. A committee was proposed to explore the options and to post a notification requesting all freeholders and other inhabitants to a meeting at Edmund's house for debate.[20]

The municipality did not receive any government assistance for the building of roads or bridges. Local inhabitants built everything they needed without grants or modern tools, creating an impressive network of roads through the wilderness. These roads needed to be connected to roads in adjacent townships, so negotiations were required, concessions were made, and land grants were altered for accommodation. The costs of these undertakings were borne by the Associate Leader, which was essentially in payment for the additional grants given to these Leaders. This was another reason why these records of trade in labour and produce were so well tabulated.

Col. Edmund[5] made an agreement with the Associates that a three-acre parcel of land be set aside for burial purposes. This was the first reference to land set aside as "common" for the community. William[5] Heard, Edmund's[5] brother, was asked to donate three acres. An additional acre for the purpose of schooling was documented in 1804: They voted to build a schoolhouse and place it on the northeast corner of William Heard's lot, and that it would be

20 feet by 26 feet. They also voted that the terms of Edmund[5]'s donation be extended for two years longer than what was in place currently.[20]

The author's research revealed that part of a one-acre addition was to accommodate a continuing road access (now Route 210) adjacent to the proposed burial grounds, and that this wedge of land was the site of the first schoolhouse, circa 1804-06. As evidenced by the First Records of Newport, indeed a schoolhouse subscription was issued in 1804 for lumber to build it.

The promissory note pictured opposite pertains to the *acquisition of lumber – "500 12-ft. Birch planks" – for the schoolhouse from Sawyers Mills (Rufus Sawyer)*. The note identifies William Heard, Elisha Hudson and Johnathon Bowker, for a double-term note and 11 signatories for the standard-term note as per amounts subscribed. The 11 were Jonas Beaman, Samuel Phelps, Nathanial Beaman, Edmund Heard, Edmund Heard Jr., Samuel Heard, Samuel Beaman, Jonas Beaman, Samuel Hudson, William Heard, and William Hudson.[20]

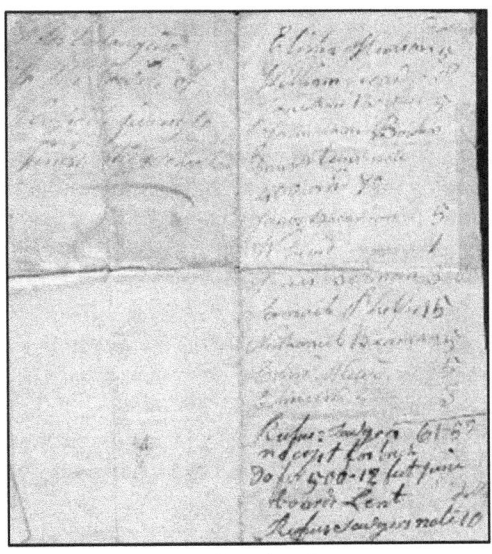

Promissory note and settler signatures pertaining to acquisition of lumber for the schoolhouse

At an 1804 meeting of the Associates, a burying ground for the Maple Leaf community was discussed and documented thus in *Newport firſt Records, 1800*:

> *Whereas great inconvenience has arisen in new towns in not reasonably providing some plot of ground to be appropriated for a burying yard & other Public uses. On this day it be agreed by and between Edmund Heard, Leader of the Township in the one part and the Associate Grantees of Newport on the other part, that a free square plot be given at the corner of Lot No 7 in the 10th range containing "Three acres" and adjoining the range line and running across the lots towards the "Mill Falls" on Lot 3, range 10, to be used & occupied by the aforesaid Grantees & others so long as they continue to improve it for the purposes as states.* [20]

At the same meeting, Article 2 documented: *"Voted to accept one acre as a present from William Heard as an addition to the above as common land."* This entry refers to acquisition for road allowance running from the north corner of Lot 8 and Lot 7, site of the current cemetery, down to Randboro to the proposed mill site[20].

Edmund[5] was still expecting his son Luke[6] to move to Newport, but Luke's wife, Polly, was ill, and he was struggling to pay off his debts. In an 1802 letter to his sister Hannah, who had returned to the New England states, married, and was then living in Lancaster, Luke[6] Heard wrote about his proposal to leave his home in Kennebec, Me. He mentioned that he knew Hannah was contemplating that she too might move her family to Canada by next winter. He suggests that if he could leave his wife Mary "Polly" with her for a bit (she was sick), it would allow him to go to Canada with their brother Edmund[6]. He could then make arrangements with Edmund and move his goods to Boston by water. He would then come up with them and bring his wife in May. He planned to make some provisions for her and their son while he tended to the Tower, and then he would come back to Lancaster and work his trade until they could all go to Canada together. [10]

> *Author's note: The Tower Luke Heard was working on was a timber-framed ship-to-shore signal tower utilized in the era before lighthouses and Morse code. It was completed in 1806.*

Meanwhile, our early ancestors harvested whatever they could. The easiest way to feed their families and survive was to hunt game. Squirrel pie was an acquired taste; bear could pass for beef; bear grease gave bread and piecrust a coveted sweet flavour. Fishing with nets, shooting deer and taking fowl while swimming were common practices.

During this era, whether they were walking in the bush, rowing a canoe or driving a wagon, the settlers carried a loaded gun. No creature that could fly, walk or swim was safe. Game and fish were plentiful and necessary for their survival. Some settlers kept meat through the summer by storing it in an icehouse, a small stone-lined timber box covered with earth and sod, filled in winter with ice from ponds and rivers. Others fashioned wooden boxes they placed in the water which ran continuously from the springs, acting as refrigeration. They would place their perishables in metal and wooden containers which they then placed into these wooden boxes to keep them cold.

To survive, the wives of the new settlers in Newport worked hard to make butter, cheese, wool, and flax, always trading a portion for such things as salt and tea. Samuel[6] Heard's wife Miriam, with her eight children, must have been under great pressure trying to run a household in essentially both a primitive and isolated environment of simple survival. They had already lost two of their children: a daughter, Hannah, at 2 months old; and a son, George at only 1 year old.

Samuel[6] and Miriam's children grew up in virtual isolation in Newport with few other children around, perhaps only meeting other children whenever a gathering of the Associates took place. Toys were often made by the children themselves: a clothespin made a small doll; a spool cut in two crossways made two spinning tops . . . with a little help from Samuel[6] and his jackknife. Empty spools from knitting looms made great wheels for a wooden cart. The children learned early on to create their own makeshift toys, paving the way for inventive minds that would serve them well in later life.

The furniture of their new house was an improvement on the house-barn they had lived in with Edmund[5] during their first year in Newport – it was movable rather than built-in because the house now had floors. They say "necessity is the mother of invention," and the settlers effected many improvements to their beds, tables, chairs and benches, as necessity had taught them to rely on their own efforts. To survive, they had to be creative and inventive. Besides their bedding and a few utensils of iron and earthenware, some small articles of furniture became useful items within the family, most of which had been kept as mementos of departed friends or relics of bygone and better days. These were generally more prized for their connection with past associations and were cherished with great care.[17]

Faced with the eternal mud from clearing the land, the men tracking in dirt every day from their work in the fields, along with the chores of the day, the women were not compelled to keep their houses spotlessly clean as they would have been used to when growing up in the New England Colonies. Their life now was entirely different. Outdoor "privies" and no running water caused their own problems, but thankfully they did not have to clean them. The outdoor privy was usually located as close to the house as possible and could be challenging during the cold winter months. The "potty" under the bed and "bedside wash basins" were the norm; of course these had to be cleaned out every day and in every season. Brooms were made from cedar boughs, favoured for the pleasant scent they gave off. The settlers used coarse, clean sand mixed with hot water to scrub the tables and floors using a homemade "mop" (made from old clothing), usually once a week.

Most of the clothing worn by the newly settled families was made in the home. The women spent many hours spinning and carding wool and weaving it into garments. They would exchange clothes with other families as their children grew out of them; typically the younger children wore hand-me-downs until the clothes were so thin they would be used as cleaning rags. Flax was grown and the linen spun from it woven and made into summer clothing or bedding.[25]

In these early days there was a feeling of mutual fellowship among the settlers. A family in difficulty or need could always expect help in times of sickness or death. "Bees" for building, harvesting and road building were common, where everyone got together to work on a project. Fires were not uncommon, most usually a barn where hay had been stored without first drying it properly. If it had not been cured properly, the hay would heat up and ignite due to spontaneous combustion, causing a firestorm of sparks and flying debris. It required a huge effort to save the animals and the house. These early settlers were resilient; within hours the entire neighbourhood would come out to help in the rebuild, bringing food and clothing, even though most had little to share.

The 1800s saw the start of industrial growth. This was the beginning of a new era when Canada was beginning to stand on its own, and stable government was being established. Canada was beginning to use its own resources to build a nation and was becoming more and more self-supportive. Great Britain was purchasing goods from its colony, not simply taking them as their own as it had previously. One of the first official documents for the Township of Newport, Edmund[6] Heard Jr. in account with Samuel Heard, was an accounting reconciliation titled and reading as follows: *"Province of Lower Canada, Newport the 13th of May 1806. This day reckoned and tabled this and all Accounts Notes and demands in full to this date. [Signed] Captain Samuel [6]Heard & Captain Edmund [6]Heard."* [31]

Sawmills needed to be established to support the newly arriving settler families; with them would come carpenters and joiners. The need for wagons brought wheelwrights and blacksmiths. Many of the settlers who came as Associates took on these tasks and became experts in their respective trades. Initially the men wore moccasins from imperfectly tanned animal hides, but in time the shoemaker made his appearance, along with the harness maker and saddle maker.

William[5] Heard was a tanner and shoemaker by trade when he arrived in Newport and became an Associate with Col. Edmund[5] Heard. He practiced his trade while settling and clearing the timber on his land grant in the settlement. Part of his income was generated by the sale of his shoes, boots, mitts, gloves and other leather products to settlers. William also made the occasional saddle and horse collars for settlers who had riding horses, including his brother, the colonel, and for those who had brought sleighs with them from the southern states.

William had built a tanning hut where he processed deer skins and bear, fox, beaver and otter pelts. The tanning process is a smelly business, so he built his tannery down on the bank of the South Branch of the Eaton River away from his homestead. The bark of the hemlock tree was referred to as "tanbark" and was the best source of the tannins used in the chemical soakings used to convert the animal hides into soft and pliable leather. William found stands of hemlock growing in abundance at the southern tip of his property adjacent to the lowland meadows and banks of the South River. Having his tanning hut near the river gave him easy access to the water and a secure and sturdy building in which to store his tools of the trade.

The skins had to be repeatedly rinsed in tubs of fresh water before they were set out to dry. The location was ideal as the smell carried on the wind downstream from his work; however, the drying racks had to be hung high after the skins were stretched to prevent wild animals from chewing the wood because of the lingering smell. The corrosive smell from the lye and bark, along with the stinking, rotting flesh, made tanning one of the least sought-after trades. However, this was his trade that he brought with him from the Colonies.

"William's fingers, roughened from the tanning and chalk he used, would run them experimentally over the hides of any excess bull calves he had slaughtered for meat. If it were of good quality, he made a sturdy saddle and if the leather stitched good, he made soles for the shoes and boots that he made." [10]

Much more valuable, however, were the deerskins William worked during the winter months into jackets, mitts and leggings for sale within the community. A tanner was a very necessary addition to any community during these times of early settlement. He also made snowshoes, stripping the bark of willow and "wiccopee" bushes and weaving these strips for the mesh, then adding leather bootstraps to secure a perfect fit for the user.

William made his own wooden wheelbarrows which he used to haul away the unwanted skin and animal parts, which he buried deep in the natural gullies in the meadows. He made a point of covering them with the plentiful river rock, which he also hauled in the wheelbarrows from the riverbanks, to prevent animals from digging them up. He even made the wooden wheels for his wheelbarrows, initially of solid wood and attached with a wooden dowel through wooden hubs. A dab of bear grease or pig fat lubricated the hub. As time went on, these were replaced with small wooden wheels made by the wheelwrights or smithies. These were rimmed with steel, making them last longer.

Since most people who engaged in trade knew each other, exchange was fostered through an extension of credit – the processes of reciprocity or familial "communalism," where each takes according to their needs and gives as they have. William might trade or establish his sale of goods as a credit for other services. An accounting for these services is evident by the IOU he issued to John Heard in 1799.[31]

There were no taxes when the settlements were first formed in Lower Canada. The British Government's mandate was to get as much of the "waste lands" (lands that they deemed of no value to the Crown for industrial purposes) of both Lower Canada and Upper Canada settled with people. These new settlers would be subject to paying taxes once settled and when their respective communities were starting to prosper.

Under the land grant policy, the "Leader" (in our case Col. Edmund[5] Heard) had to fund every aspect of land development prior to when the British American Land Corporation (BALC) would take over the territory sometime in the mid-1800s. During this time, a "clerk was established" (Samuel[6] Heard) who was responsible for keeping the records of all transactions, including using the "barter system." There were no banks where financing for a project could be acquired, or even monies available for the settlers to purchase goods outside of their own communities.

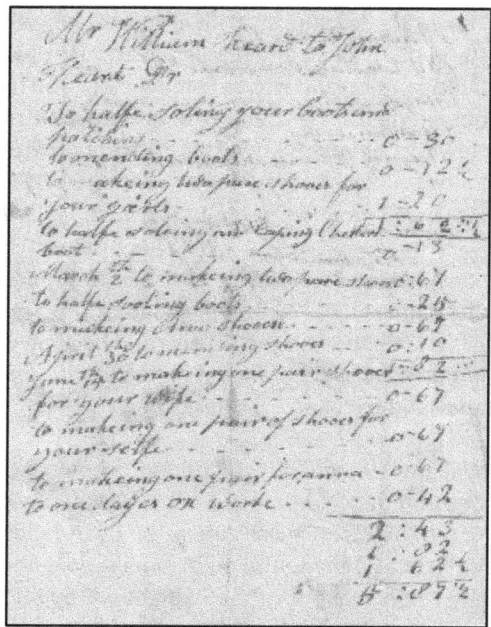

Accounting ledger to John Heard by William Heard

Bartering (Wikipedia; drawing by F. S. Church, published in *Harper's Weekly*, 1874)

The only way to account for work performed within the group was by the barter system. Bartering is an exchange of goods or services (labour) for other goods or services. A barter may be made "in kind"; an example is "labour." Subscriptions were issued as a contract with the settlers, whereby the community as a whole might benefit from a schoolhouse, meeting house, road or bridge, used by all settlers within a community. A settler could subscribe by stating a certain amount of time that he may have available to work on a community project, payable by barter of his/her time, materials or labour.

From time to time, a call for subscription would be issued for a community project. Each of the settlers would then commit to the project, usually calculated as a proportionate percentage of their own land holdings. In this way everyone was committed fairly. The barter system could then be used to pay the subscription. Those who participated could elect to pay their share in cash or in kind, with their labour or with excess produce they had grown. The produce would then be either purchased or traded in the same manner by another party.

When individuals began to specialize in specific crafts and became, for example, blacksmiths or wheelwrights, they had to depend on others for goods which perhaps they specialized in, such as farming wheat, or livestock, or hens and eggs, etc. These goods and services were first exchanged by barter, where perhaps banks were not yet established and coins were not readily available. This was an era when essentially "trade" was the marketplace.

The produce – such as wheat, for example – would be evaluated and become available to another settler at an established price. That settler may also pay for the wheat in kind with his labour on a particular project at the going market value of a set valuation per day. In another example, a settler might trade his horse team's work for a set market value and trade that credit value for wheat if he needed seed for planting.

Roads were barely more than footpaths hacked through the wilderness. They were cut through ominous forests and dismal swamps, and around or over outcroppings of rock and mountains. They were strewn with ruts and even tree stumps, and mostly impassable in rainy weather when they were transformed into a muddy morass. When a road crossed a bog, it was literally floated on a "corduroy road" of logs laid perpendicular across the road. Any wheel crossing over these were tasked to their fullest and many would break down en route.

The impressive characteristics of the landscapes experienced along their travels back and forth between Newport and New England must have inspired our ancestors. The mountains rising high beside them as they navigated along the river shorelines, opening up to long meadows stretching out before them and as suddenly converging into dense forests must have been magical. The experience must also have been quite daunting if the weather did not cooperate. In dense fog and rain the trip would have been quite different. There were a few stagecoach inns which were not necessarily strategically located, and so they might just have had to keep moving on in order to meet their timelines for the day's journey. Most often they stopped at simple log homesteads along the way where they would be welcomed to eat, rest, and feed their oxen or horses. Many of the routes they travelled, however, must have been long, arduous and lonely for our early ancestors travelling through these regions on their many trips taken for trading goods.

Sometime early in 1801, Col. Edmund[5] Heard and his associates were now in the process of assembling the metal and grinding wheel parts for the building of a "water-driven" mill in Newport. During the spring they made another trip to Lancaster, N.H., to purchase machinery for the mill. On behalf of the Associates of Newport, he purchased these parts and transported them along the Connecticut River and on up through the lakes beds of Indian Stream (later known for a short time as the Republic of Indian Stream) through the region of New Hampshire."[3]

Edmund[5] and his men used "ox carts" to transport the iron castings for the mill. These ox carts were equipped with a sturdy box strapped on a wooden crossbar, with two exceptionally large wheels, 48 to 60 inches in circumference, rotating on slightly tapered wooden spooled axles, connecting to the oxen by poles strapped to their shoulders on a wooden "yoke."

Ox cart (BAnQ)

The larger the wheels the easier the oxen could pull these heavily laden carts over rough terrain. Edmund[5] noted that *"the load was so heavy and the road was so rough, that the axel-tree of the cart gave way three times and was on the point of breaking a fourth time, when they arrived at their destination; the axel being replaced each time by the driver, who carried with him both axe and auger, from the hard timber which was so plentiful along the way."*[31]

This explains why one of the busiest and most important craftsmen in early Newport and along the travel routes leading from the New England Colonies to Lower Canada was the wheelwright, whose specialty was making and repairing wheels. At this time there was no wheelwright in Newport or the surrounding region, so settlers had to travel to Sawyerville, through East Clifton to Norton's Mills in Vermont where there was a wheelwright who could do the repairs. Because of this, Edmund[5] and his Associates purchased spare wheels to carry with them at all times, which in themselves added to the weight of the load. Because oxen pulled these carts at such a slow pace, the wood-on-wood wheel to axle worked well and did not tend to heat up due to friction when lubricated with lots of lard. When horses came on the scene, this would not be the case – horses moved much faster, and the hubs would heat up and burn out. Another decade or two would pass before workhorses became more widely used and steel axles began to be in demand.

There is mention in the first Township records (*Ancestral Heard/Hurd Collection*) of a mill located on Lot 3, on the 10th Range, which would position the mill on the South Branch of the Eaton River in Randboro. If that were the case, the first mill was a gristmill (as evidenced by visible artifacts) located immediately west of Randboro, just past the gorge and rapids on the second bend in the river. The area was then known as Grove Hill, situated where the village of Randboro is today.

In his letter of November 6, 1802, to his son Edmund[6] who was still living in Lancaster at that time, Col. Edmund[5] mentions that *"our Mills are likely to be built soon"*; *"the Mill is expected to be running by next August."* This would put the first gristmill in Newport circa 1803. Documents in the Ancestral Heard/Hurd Collection show that Col. Edmund[5] Heard made several trips to Lancaster, N.H., purchasing mill parts by way of many IOU's, between 1797 and 1801, on behalf of Newport Township; as well as an agreement for credit established with a Jonathon Newell in Lancaster in 1801.[10, 31]

In the paperwork pictured opposite, compiled by a James Carter and dated 1801, *"16½ days' work on the Mill"* was documented and *"paid in full on January 22, 1802."* [31]

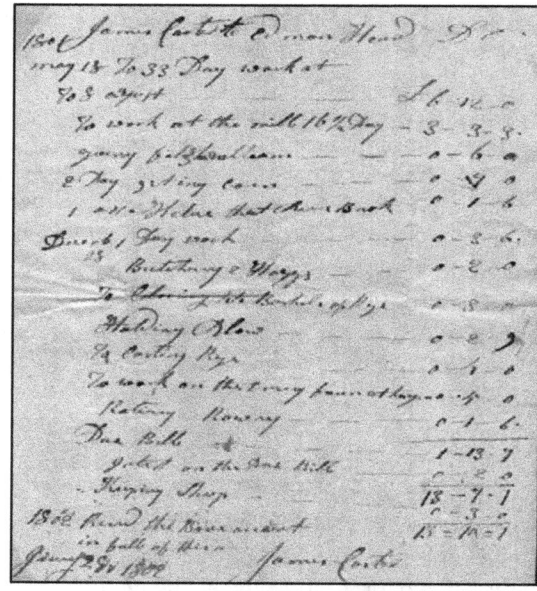

Accounting for mill labour, James Carter to Edmund Heard, 1801

***

The first Rand family and Heard family connection:

> *Author's note: Artemas Rand appeared in the original records in Newport circa 1800 but did not appear as one of the Associates of Col. Edmund[5] Heard (circa 1794-1810). Although he wasn't mentioned as an Associate, he became an integral part of their group in the development of Newport and his family became intricately associated with the Heard/Hurd families over several generations in Newport.*

Artemas[6] Rand, the son of Solomon[5] Rand and Deborah Dodge (lineage: Daniel[4], Zechariah[3], Robert[2]) was born in 1763 in Shrewsbury, Mass. Artemas[6] Rand, his wife Louisa Spring and their son, Artemas[7] Dodge, born in 1794, a young boy at the time, immigrated from Connecticut in early 1798. The family settled on Lot 3 of Range 9, above the bluffs of Grove Hill. They had two more sons born in Newport: Gardner[7] Wheeler (born 1798 and died as an infant) and Marshall[7] Spring (born 1810). *(Florence Osgood Rand,* A Genealogy of the Rand Family in the United States, *New York, 1899)*

The original Lot 3 of Range 10 was set aside as a land grant for Nathanial[1] Beaman Jr. (an Edmund[5] Heard original Associate), and a portion of the lot on the river side would have been set aside as "common" land.

Entered in the *Newport firſt Records, 1800*:

> *A vote (Article 5) was initiated to open the road from his [Beaman's] eastern line through the Public lot to the Mills. A vote (Article 6) that the road now passable southwardly from the main road leading from the Town line between Eaton and Newport past the road to "Norton's Mills" through Newport, grants on the line of division between Nathanial and Sam Beaman's on the public lot west of them commonly called the road to Edmund Heard, or "The Edmund Heard Road," shall be an open and established Town Road.* [20]

Based on these records, research indicates that Artemas[6] Rand, Nathanial Jr., and Samuel Beaman, with Col. Edmund[5] Heard and their Associates, as a group built and operated the first water-driven gristmill at the foot of Grove Hill, beginning sometime around 1803-04. The area of the actual mill had been set aside as "common river side land," meeting the prerequisite of the original land grants. All river access, including a 20-foot parcel or "leverage" on both sides, were set aside as "common" to all. The river served as a general conduit and purpose for both the lot owners and a surrounding community. The terrain between Grove Hill and Parker Hill (a name given to the region immediately south of Grove Hill) was in effect a gorge (probably made during the last Ice Age) that ran central to the existing South Branch of the Eaton River. Large banks rose on either side, creating a sort of valley where the community of Randboro would soon become a small hub of activity.

Millstone discovered on bank of South River just west of the gorge in Randboro (Eastern Townships Roots, courtesy of Danny Bousquet)

Those who lived in Newport in the 1950s would recognize this property as the land where Billy and Roberta Graham lived. The location has also been verified by Denis Palmer, who commented, "I was down at the river right there one day looking for some flat stones for the walkway at my house, and I found an old millstone there in the river."

The original Lot 3, Range 9 had been set aside for Hannah Heard, Edmund[5] Heard's daughter; however, she declined the land, married, and moved back to New England. Her brother Luke had hoped to move up to Canada with his sister in the spring; however, both of their circumstances had changed during the past year. Edmund would have been hard-pressed to ensure that this lot was occupied soon. With neither Hannah nor Luke coming to claim the lot, it could have been deemed as one of speculation and would have been declined. For this reason, Edmund would have wanted to find a suitable settler for this lot as soon as possible.

The author can find no evidence that this lot had been granted to Artemas[6] Rand; the lot located at the top of Grove Hill Road, which included part of Lot 3, Range 10 at the bottom of the hill, encompassing the river site. Artemas may have then become an addition to the Associates for the land grants of Col. Edmund[5] Heard, notwithstanding that Artemas may well have purchased this lot in kind, in trade or in cash.

Nonetheless, Artemas[6] Rand obtained 200 acres on Lot 3 of Range 9 (the southern tip of the property was where a small dam and the first gristmill was operating), and this was where he and Louisa raised their family.[47] He built his homestead at the top of Grove Hill, and his sons Artemas[7] D. and Marshall S. would see this land become developed during their lifetimes. Their homestead was the only house in the immediate area for some years, other than the Beaman family on the south side of the South River, on their Lot 3 of Range 10. The gristmill was located directly below both these properties on the common land associated with both a road and the river. Artemas[6] Rand's eldest son, Artemas[7] Dodge Rand, served in the military at the age 18-20 in the war of 1812-14 on the British side. He served in the same militia group as Capt. Samuel[6] Heard.[16, 20]

Artemas[6] died in Newport in 1837; his wife Louisa died in Newport a few years later in 1854. Both are buried in Grove Hill Cemetery.

Retrieval of a Fenian cannon at the border (Eastern Townships Roots)

It was not uncommon in this era for many children who had lost their parents to look for any kind of work simply for survival. Although many of these children would be taken in by other families, more often than not there was not even enough food to sustain their own families. Once the male children were old enough, they would be called upon to supplement their board. A call for arms would be considered the patriotic thing to do, but the driving force was that they simply needed the money. During this era there were many skirmishes along the border which caused many of these young men to serve in the protection of these lands.

One of William Heard's sons, Jerimiah, and nephew, Edward Heard, served in the Newport Militia. "It was during the many years after the war of 1812, that Irish Americans (the Fenians) raided all along the Canadian border with the intention of exploiting Canada's poor defences, instigate trouble with its southern neighbours and weaken Britain's rule. In the end, these years of Fenian raids ended up solidifying public opinion in favour of Confederation and a desire to strengthen our national defence . . . something that politicians had up to that time struggled to accomplish." *(April M. Stewart, Quebec Heritage News, QAHN)*

Meanwhile, circa 1804-05, Josiah Sawyer built the first sawmill in the village of Sawyerville on the South Branch of the Eaton River, downstream from Grove Hill. Later, Josiah built a gristmill on the southwest side of the road to Flanders.

***

The *Newport first Records, 1800* records that a meeting was convened on November 5, 1801, at Col. Edmund[5] Heard's house with a majority of the Associates of Newport present. Article 1 states: *"Voted to open a road from the corner post of lots No 7 & 8, Range 9 &10, on the south side of the Range 9 to Sawyers Mills in Eaton."* [20]

> *Author's note: This road is currently known as Route 210. I suggest the road runs from the current corner of Maple Leaf Cemetery to Randville, through the village at the bottom of Grove Hill Road and then on to Sawyerville. The junction of Grove Hill and the path leading towards Sawyers Mills in Eaton Township, then known as the Heard Road, was referred to as the Grove Hill community. A cluster of homes began at this location and become known as Randville. Sometime circa 1875-1900 the name was changed by its founder, Gardner Stillman Rand, to Randboro.*

When the first settlements were made in Newport, the roads leading to communities were merely bushed out. The next step was to open crossroads from one location to another. These original roads were maintained on a voluntary basis and had been in deplorable shape for years. Due to a lack of any real road-building equipment, and for simplicity itself, the roads generally followed the topography of the region, winding around large rock cliffs and avoiding high levels that even their oxen and horses would have trouble climbing. Sections of these roads that traversed swamps and lowland areas were constructed as "corduroy" roads: large logs were placed lengthwise across the width of the road and covered with course river gravel topped off with a sand/clay mix.

There is a respectable amount of evidence and later-dated verifications of old mill parts to suggest that there was a mill situated at the bottom of Grove Hill Road across the highway on the South Branch of the Eaton River, just past the gorge. The location of the mill was just west, past the second curve on the road to Sawyerville. This mill would also attest to the creation of a vibrant settlement in Grove Hill and the beginning of a hamlet. With a gristmill in the community, it would eliminate the need for settlers to travel the distance through East Clifton to "Norton's Mills" on the border of Vermont to have their grains ground into meal.

The 1802 document pictured, from Joshua Turner to Edmund[5] Heard, accounts for the use of his horse (Shirley) for work on the mill site.[31]

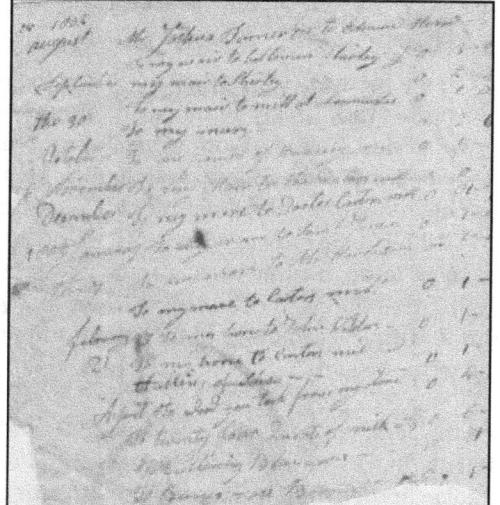

Tally of time for payment document between Edmund[5] Heard and Joshua Turner, 1802

This record would have been an accounting of work done and could represent a part of Joshua's subscription for community work on the mill. If it was not a subscription, and he was just working for Edmund on the mill, he might take payment in the form of wheat or whatever else might be on account with the "Clerk" (Samuel Heard at the time).

***

Edmund[6] was still living in Holden, Mass., when his brother Samuel[6] wrote to him to advise what they were doing to maintain the land grant agreements. They were anxious for him to decide on his move to Canada. In a letter from Samuel to Edmund, dated November 22, 1802, Samuel wrote *"you mentioned that your children had been sick with the measles and I hope they are all well by now."* Samuel also mentioned in his letter *"I had missed Capt. Sawyer when he had come by earlier in the summer. I had conversation with Hannah (his sister who was still single) and she was insistent that she would not consent to any partners in the land business and that she would not risk her* support as only 'one person' and after much debate I felt it proper that I should undertake it alone. I have burnt a portion of your cleared land and looked forward to a good crop of wheat or corn next year. Mr. [Johnathon] Bowker has offered to help me clear off the burn in the spring as everyone is busy at this time."* [10]

Postal service was yet to be developed within Lower Canada. Letters were still being carried via other settlers who may be travelling. This communication conduit to their relatives and Associates within the Eastern Townships and in the New England states was a very important part of their lives. Not only were they kept informed of each other's lives, but letters were also a way in which they might acquire goods and services.

Samuel[6] also tells us in his letter that *"they made their decision to clear a road to Three Rivers, that his (Edmund's) contribution would be $1.00 and that he should dispatch that to him as it must be paid immediately in money or wheat at $1.00 per bushel." That Elisha Hudson, William Hudson, Samuel Hudson, and William[5] Heard were to complete the work on the road, which was to be paid proportionately by the Inhabitants of Newport,"* now numbering 18.[20] New names included as Associates in the settling of Newport and who signed up as participants in the road building were *"Solomon and Johnathon Bowker, Samuel & Elisha Hudson Jr., Jeffrey Maynard, Rudolphus & John Harvey, David Metcalf, Nathanial Beaman Jr., Benj Allen and Asaph Williams."* [20]

Payment for the construction was by subscription proportionate to their land holdings, payment in kind by labour and wheat; 107 bushels of wheat and labour were collected as credit. [20]

> *Author's note: A more direct road to Three Rivers would eliminate boating down the St. Francis River, portaging around Brompton Falls, loading up again for the trip to Nicolet, and then by boat again to Three Rivers on the north shore of the St. Lawrence River. A road would also cut out the portage north from Nicolet to a point of crossing on the south shore of the St. Lawrence, directly to Three Rivers on the North Shore.*

In a meeting of September 12, 1803, *"regarding continuation of road from Mill Falls,"* the mention of Mill Falls was perhaps either a contemplation of building, or the gristmill was already in operation at the time. Edmund[5] had written in his letter of November 1802 to his son Edmund Jr., *"I expect the mill to be in operation by August of next year."* [10] Records show there was both a gristmill and a sawmill operating at this site later in Randville (Randboro) circa 1850-1869.[45]

At the same meeting, Article 4 documented: *"Voted & chose Col. William Williams to our committee to examine & mark a Road on the nearest and best ground from the Mill Falls, near William Hudson's to intersect the road from Eaton to the Town line near Col Williams's perlash."* [20]

> *Author's note: This would be a continuing road from Grove Hill (Randville) to Sawyerville and since there was no bridge at that time, I suggest they may have had a portage area on the meadow where the river was shallow on the west bank.*

From early 1801 to 1810, a provision for a burial ground and a schoolhouse for the community, including maintenance, were proposed. Meetings that had been held at peoples' homes could now be conducted at these more public places. Record keeping became a necessity at this time to ensure each of the inhabitants was credited with their contribution to the overall community. In a letter to his son Edmund[6], Edmund[5] mentions that he had put aside five bushels of wheat and promised to pay for some road building out of his harvest. Commencing October 1, 1803, a public auction was initiated to speed up the road building. A subscription for lots of five days of labour was offered, payable by bushels of wheat to the lowest bidder. Each of the landowners was listed by lot number and the number of bushels they could bid on.[10, 21]

In a letter to his son Edmund,[6] dated September 24, 1803, Edmund[5] wrote:

> *Samuel has just returned from laying out a new road to the Connecticut River and the Towns of Newport and Eaton subscribed very well. The people of Hall stream had subscribed largely in the work, which will begin the 1st of October. This work will provide a good wagon road before winter."* He also advised his son that he had *"put your name down for five bushels of wheat and you should be able to*

> *pay for the labour out of your crop; the crop being harvested already, well stacked and I estimate that you will have about 30 bushels this year. A great crop indeed . . . . Samuels's wife has a lovely daughter now and all are well. [Signed] Edmund.*[10]

In 1803 Luke[6] Heard wrote to his brother Samuel, telling him of his circumstances in his own style of spelling. It is important to note from this letter that Luke's wife, Polly, had died and he had married her housekeeper and caretaker, Hannah, and so Luke was still struggling to survive there with his children and would not be coming to Newport just yet:

> *I received a letter from you dated last September 19th and received it at Portland, the letter being directed to me at Salem but previous to the date of said letter, I was obliged to leave Sallem on account of my credottors running on me all the opportunity when I could not pay them, after being at a grate expense in sickness and brought down very low after losing my wife, sum of my credettors by the advice of my grate friend Emmonton would not give me eny time to put myself in business so as to pay them, so I thought it was my best way to leave the Town and let them take my house and contence and make the best of them thay could. I am in good business in Portland to worke for my worke at my trade and have married the woman that long ceep my house and toock care of my wife.* [10]

In 1803, Capt. Edmund[6], his pregnant wife Lucy, and their four children finally moved from Holden to Newport, where his younger brother Samuel had settled earlier with his father and Samuel's sister, Hannah. He had been appointed an Associate with Edmund[5], now able to settle on Lot 9 of Range 11 in Newport. Through his father as Leader of the Associates, he had claimed additional lots 11 and 12 of Range 7 and Lot 8 of Range 10. Edmund[6] had married Lucy Bennett at Lancaster in 1792 and they had nine children. The first four were born in Lancaster: Edmund[7] (1795), John Bennett (1797), Lucy (1799) and Luke[7] (1801).[4]

Their eldest son, Edmund[7], was only 8 years old when they moved to their new land in Newport's wilderness. Edmund[6] himself was 38. Their next five children were all born on their lot in Newport: Sarah (born 1803), Tyler Wellington (born 1806), Betsey Eaton (born 1810, died at age 18), Leander Curtis (born 1813, died at age 9 months) and Samuel[7] Andrews (born 1815).[4]

Their lots bordered the Township of Auckland and the South Branch of the Eaton River. The fertile land contained a variety of hardwood trees such as maple, beech, white birch and yellow birch, and softwoods as the land progressed to the southern part of the property down to the river. Over several years, and as the family grew in age to help out, they were able to cultivate several acres of good grasslands. They harvested excess lumber and floated the logs downriver in the spring to Sawyers' mill in Eaton Township.

The family had a good stand of maple bush, from which they harvested maple sugar each spring, boiling the sap in a huge cast iron kettle held above the fire by large poles fashioned as a tripod. They farmed a mix of cattle, sheep, some chickens, geese, and turkeys. Edmund was a hunter and an excellent shot, his accuracy formed from his training in the military. He bagged a few deer each fall, which helped to feed his growing family. This family virtually lived off the land. Lucy, an ardent gardener, planted a variety of vegetables each spring, with the girls giving a helping hand as they grew older.

Their second son, John B.[7] Heard, developed an interest and excellence in trapping. Over the years this skill came to serve him well financially. His mother, Lucy, would fashion the skins into a coat which provided excellent warmth in the cold winter months. It became a fashion itself in the years to come and an excellent trading commodity. A bearskin rug was a welcome addition to a cabin floor and the beaver trade was still flourishing during this era.

Their youngest son, Luke[7], was an ardent outdoorsman who accompanied his brother John B. on his wilderness forays in trapping but was more interested in fishing. He enjoyed nothing better than bringing home a basketful of trout for the family. These trips took them to the east on the South River into Ditton and Emberton townships.

Tyler enjoyed the farm; he chose to stay home and help with the chores and make improvements around the settlement. He was keenly interested in the raising of livestock, which served him well in his future as a farmer.

These families stood by each other as the seasons came and went. They looked forward as individual families to reaping their first harvests together. They had a frontier spirit and took pride in their accomplishments. "We are making it our land, laying a foundation for the rest of our lives."[31]

It had been 11 years since Edmund[5] had built his own first barn in 1793. Now, on June 16, 1804, Edmund[5] entered into an agreement with Elisha Hudson to cut the timber and prepare the framing to build a sufficient barn, 30 by 40 feet, to be completed on or before the twentieth day of August, on Lot 10 in the 11th Range for his son Edmund[6]. He indicated he would pay the sum of 41 "Spanish dollars," paying 20 for the timber frame and the balance of 21 on completion. A promissory note stated that upon completion, he (Edmund) would *"pay 6 dollars in money and the balance of 15 remaining in 15 bushels of good clean salable wheat."*[10]

One might wonder why and where the "Spanish dollars" were used. At the end of the Seven Years' War and the subsequent War of Independence, the new United States of America was essentially broke. The Continental Congress, the rough equivalent of the federal government in revolution-era America, lacked the power to tax. The nascent U.S. government raised cash by borrowing from other countries under all sorts of authorities. Due to the recent wars, they could not borrow from Britain or France, but could borrow from other countries, including Spain. The Spanish, rich in gold from their exploits in Peru, Chile, Mexico and California, loaned funds to the new Americans who were yet to develop their own monetary funds. These Spanish dollars were used to pay those agencies that were basically working for the government, i.e., payments to run the country along with certificates issued by the Registrar of the Treasury, Commissioners of Loans and States, Commissioners for the Adjustment of Accounts of the Quartermaster, the Commissary, Hospital, Clothing and Marine Departments, Paymaster General, and Commissioner of Army Accounts. Hence, those settlers who were in the military were paid in Spanish dollars.

In order to acquire financing, land grants that had been set aside for settlers in Ipswich, Mass., were called back by municipal governments. This was an example of the debt load incurred by these wars. *"In 1788, the majority of the commoners voted, though vigorous opposition was made by the minority, to resign all their interests in common lands, etc., to the town of Ipswich toward the payment of the heavy town debt incurred during the War of Independence, the grant estimated to be worth about £600."* (Thomas Franklin Waters, Ipswich vol. 1, Ch. 1)

***

Entered into the *Newport firſt Records* :

> *Whereas great inconvenience has arisen in new towns in not reasonably providing some plot of ground to be appropriated for a burying yard & other Public uses. On this day be it agreed by and between Edmund Heard, Leader of the Township in the one part and the Associate Grantees of Newport on the other part, that a free square plot be given at the corner of Lot No 7 in the 10th range containing "Three acres" and adjoining the range line and running across the lots towards the "Mill Falls" on Lot 3, range 10, to be used & occupied by the aforesaid Grantees & others so long as they continue to improve it for the purposes as states.* [20]

As specified in the "grant" regulations for lot allocations, existing lot owners whose lots might become severed by a road might be granted a similar piece of property, of exactly the same acreage, elsewhere as compensation. And so, a road would cut across the top portion of William Heard's property at an angle, creating a portion to the north and a wedge to the south. These two wedges, with the road running between them, would become the future gravesite and the schoolhouse properties for the community of Maple Leaf. On May 20, 1804, William Heard signed the Agreement for these purposes, given as a donation to the Community.[6]

At a meeting of Associates in 1806, it was *resolved as follows:*

> *Article 1. Voted to accept one acre as a donation from William Heard as an addition to the above as common land.*

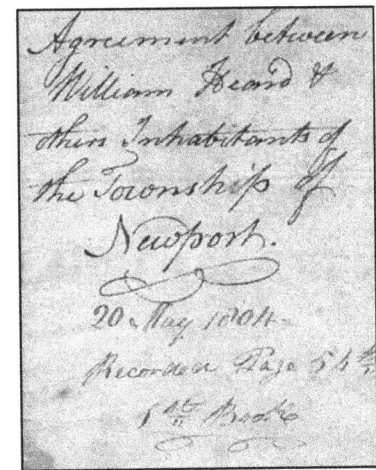

1804 agreement between William Heard and inhabitants of Newport

Article 2: Voted to build a house on the Granted part of Newport suitable for the education of youth.

Article 3: It was voted that the dimensions of said house shall be 20 by 26 feet.

Article 4: Voted that Edmund Heard be requested to lengthen the term of his donation two years longer in addition to what may be expressed therein.

Article 5: Voted to set the schoolhouse above referred to on the North Eastside corner of Mr. William Heards donation. [20]

At a meeting in 1807: *"Agreement to extend the limited provision in the agreement of 1804 referencing land set aside for burial purposes, until the first day of September 1808." "[Signed] William Heard"*

At an 1808 meeting of the Associates of Newport, as entered in the *Newport first Records*: Article 6: *"Voted that the House be built in the present season."* They voted on an *"estimate of expenses to be put forth for the next meeting and a Committee of three persons to arrange and to choose five persons to build the schoolhouse."* [20]

Author's note: A committee was voted to officiate until the next annual meeting as follows: Mr. Artemas Rand, Capt. Samuel[6] Heard and Mr. William Heard. The document was signed by 18 Associates for the Township of Newport.

At a meeting of the Associates of Newport, as entered in the *Newport first Records, 1809:* [20]

Article 4: Voted that the committee take security of the Common Ground (authorized by Col. Edmund & donated by Wm. Heard) to the resident inhabitants of South West Quarter of Newport for and on behalf of said inhabitants.

Article 5: Voted to sell to the highest bidder the improvement of three acres of the Common Ground for two years to plough, harrow & cultivate in handsome and husbandman like manner & seed the same in grass; by all in attendance, sold, the improvements to Wm Heard for eight dollars.

Article 6: Voted that the Burying Ground be leveled, ditched & fenced within one year from this time.

Article 9: Voted & chose Mr. Solomon Bowker for sexton to dig graves for the year coming.

And thus, the burial grounds for the Maple Leaf community were established in 1810.

The inhabitants also voted in favour of the requirement for all families to provide the Clerk with notification of both births and deaths in the community which simultaneously provided a venue for census taking.[31]

Notice boards were established for all to read to inform the community of meetings and any notifications.[22]

At a meeting on October 19, 1810, with Solomon Bowker as moderator, it was

resolved that a committee be formed to immediately secure such persons as may be infected with Smallpox and to make suitable arrangements to prevent the spreading and to prosecute any persons residing or coming into the or within the limits of the Township not conforming to the regulations appointed them by the committee.

Voted Article 3, that Mr. Artemas Rand, Captain Samuel Heard and Mr. William Heard be a committee responsible in prosecuting all such offenders & we will each of us pay our proportion of the expense of such Prosecution. Signed by 19 settler participants, Solomon & John Bowker, Elisha, Robert, and William Hudson, Benjamin, Israel & John Hicks, Nathanial & Jonas Beaman, Caleb Hardy, Edmund Sr, Edmund Jr, Samuel & William Heard, Ebenezer Grant, Samuel Morse, David Perkins and Artemas Rand. [20]

A notice was posted the following day, October 20, 1810.[22]

In 1798, a smallpox vaccine was developed, the first in a series of vaccines. The smallpox virus was a very real threat to these early settlers, both young and old. The vaccine, however, was not available in Newport during this era and for a long time to come. For years, since there were no public houses for people to meet, every family dwelling was open to a traveller, and a cordial welcome was extended to friends or strangers alike. If there was any indication of a sickness such as smallpox, notices would be posted in these communities to advise both traveller and homesteader to be wary of people wanting to stay over. Samuel[6] Heard, as "Clerk for Newport," recorded these events as a means to determine the affect or threat any type of communicable disease might have on the overall community.[24]

Article 10 of a further meeting, *"Voted that Messrs. Bowker(2), Samuel Heard, Hudson & Williams, be a committee to mark out and determine where a bye road will accommodate both Bowker's, Hudson and Williams to travel into the main road, near the School common land."* [20]

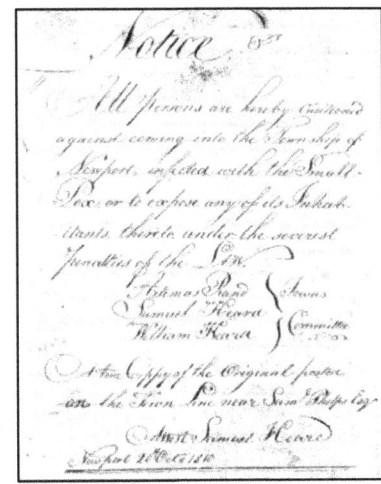

1810 notice pertaining to smallpox

This proposed "bye road" would have run through two lots no. 7 on the 9th and 8th ranges, directly north to connect to the North River Road. (The term "bye road" is determined as a road that is established solely for the purpose of connecting two main passageways to accommodate a shorter or faster route. A bye road or sideroad would not be maintained in the same manner as a main road and is usually used as a temporary solution.

There is sufficient documentation to suggest that this proposed road would connect the Bowker lands and others settling in the northcentral region of Newport so they would be more closely associated with the community developing in the Maple Leaf area. The only other route was by way of Grove Hill Road. The hill running north from Randville was only accessible by oxen and was much too steep for horses pulling loaded wagons or sleds. The road that was surveyed and ultimately built in lieu of the bye road, connected to the North River Road as we know it today. It turned off on today's Route 210 further to the southeast, (*at the location of the new schoolhouse circa 1901*), and then turned north back to the 9th Range line and on up through the 9th and then 8th ranges, through lots 10, 11, 12 and 13. Road connections in this more easterly quadrant of the lower part of Newport allowed for many more homesteading lots to be opened up that would enhance the growing community of Maple Leaf.[20]

The lack of a more direct road meant that the only other way to the northern lots was on Heard Road from Grove Hill, fording the South Branch of the Eaton River at the Newport-Eaton town line, through the town of Sawyerville, and taking a path northeasterly to these more northern lots in Newport. Hence the slashing out and use of the quasi-logging road was most likely used as a shortcut for some time.

Author's note: Evidence of an old logging road is still noticeable at Maple Leaf Cemetery. After the BALC purchased the unclaimed lands in Newport, the company assumed all road and bridge planning. The company appeared to simply follow the old logging roads, and if a road happened to ford a river that is where they built a bridge. They did not appear to lay out a planned road scenario but instead took the simplest route, so the roads followed the lay of the land. The contemplated "bye road" was never built.

Bye road proposal entered into the minute book of *Newport first Records, 1800*

***

In a letter of August 1, 1810, *"to the Senior Officers of the Militia, Captain Samuel Heard, in the Township of Newport, from The Grand Voyer of the District of Three Rivers, an order to cause to be chosen & elected between the first of September and October 15th following, five persons to serve as Overseers of the highways and bridges therein, [Signed] John Antrobus G. V."* [3]

The southwest part of the now-settled Township of Newport was divided into five districts for the purpose of road and bridge maintenance. This creation of districts was the beginning of an attempt by legislators in Three Rivers to exercise control over these early Loyalists settlements. They did not want these settlements to structure their lots in the style of the Americans, arguing that it could lead to unrest in the region, given the current climate with the new American states. The French legislators in Three Rivers were pressing the British to structure the townships in the same style as the seigneury land-lot system that had been allocated in the districts that bordered the St. Lawrence River. Their underlying intent was to discourage the Americans from perceiving that this was strictly a British settlement. Events such as this were the beginnings of subtle changes in British/French government attitudes and relations towards the existing Newport settlements and the surrounding townships. Naturally, this was disturbing for the now-established Loyalists who had just fled the United States. Meanwhile, the newly formed United States sensed that the loosely formed British/French governing bodies were still unstable and this might be the opportune time to take over these British colonies to the north.

District 1 encompassed lots 1 and 2 of ranges 6, 7, 8, 9, 10 and 11, under David Metcalf. District 2 was made up of lots 3 and 4 of ranges 6, 7, 8, 9, 10 and 11, under Samuel Hudson. District 3 took in lots 5 and 6 of ranges 6, 7, 8, 9, 10 and 11, under Samuel Morse. District 4 comprised lots 7 and 8 of ranges 6, 7, 8, 9, 10, and 11, under William Heard. District 5 was lots 9 and 10 of ranges 6, 7, 8, 9, 10, and 11, under Nathanial Beaman Jr. *"Attested by Samuel Heard, Capt. Militia, a due return made by me to the Grand Voyer, [Signed] Samuel Heard."* [3]

"Newport, April 1812, Rec'd of Edmund[6] Heard Jr. his note of hand for one dollar and ninety-two cents and William Heard for his note of hand for four dollars and seventy-one cents which I accept for his full charge of boarding Master Preble while he taught the school in Newport. [Signed] Nathanial Beaman Jr." [31]

> *Author's note: While boarding with the William Heard family, a young family of eight children from ages 1 to 14 years all living in a crowded log house, Master Preble must have thought he was in school both day and night. Thirza was pregnant with another child; three of their older daughters from his first marriage were still living there as well.*

The first meeting of the inhabitants of Newport was held in the little Maple Leaf community school on August 18, 1811. This building is one of the oldest landmarks associated with the earliest history of the community. The school was located adjacent to Maple Leaf Cemetery, on a piece of land donated by William Heard, Col. Edmund's brother – on the wedge of land on the south side of today's Route 210, on the north edge of Lot 8, just past the bend in the road and opposite the cemetery. As a one-room schoolhouse, it was built of logs and retrofitted with a chimney for heat in winter. The schoolhouse now served the community as a meeting house and venue for many other activities. This addition to the Maple Leaf community ended the practice of meetings and church services at various homes.[20]

Entered in the Minutes of October 13, 1813:

> *Article 1: [Voted] to fence the burying grounds was made at a meeting in the schoolhouse on the first of October 1813, the fence to be post & picket; the posts to be made of Cedar, Red Ash or Hemlock, six feet long and not more than five inches in diameter.*
>
> *Article 2: [Voted] that the lumber for said purpose be brought forward in the winter and paid for out of money due from Wm. Heard for rent of Common Ground and that the trust of the business be given to Lieut. Wm Hudson to say that the timber bought forward by any person he shall agree with and at such a price as he shall agree to.*
>
> *Article 2: [Voted] that M. S. Bowker repair the schoolhouse chimney and receive from E. Heard 1 dollar therefor.* [20]

In their first desperate years of homesteading, our ancestors' survival meant they needed to devote every effort to clearing and cultivating enough acreage to provide for the family. Each family needed to clear enough land to provide feed for livestock, both as grassland in summer and for the cultivation of hay, corn, and alfalfa for winter use.

***

As time progressed, tools that had been in constant use became broken and the necessity to repair them made a blacksmith perhaps the most important man in a new settlement. Many of these tools were made or repaired by Jonas Phelps, the first blacksmith in Newport.

An accounting from Jonas for one year of work, from June 1812 to June 1813, was given to Edmund[6] Heard *"for shoeing horses, sharpening a plough share, repairing horse traces several times and mending a brass skittle."* (Ancestral Heard/Hurd Collection) This shows the degree of trust that was prevalent with our first settlers, i.e., holding a bill for a year before submitting it for payment. Jonas settled at the foot of Grove Hill where he built his blacksmith shop beside his cabin. Blacksmiths were generally referred to in the local communities as "smithies" who fabricated all manner of tools and other articles, including axes, adzes, shovels, rakes, wrenches, horseshoes, knives, hammers and even nails. Jonas also made a host of other metal items relating to various equipment, such

Use of oxen drawing a buckboard wagon for transportation (BAnQ)

as the steel rims for wagon wheels and hubs, sled runners and a multitude of steel rings for yokes and chains.

A "broad axe" was used to split the logs in a fashion to make rough boards. An adze was used then to square and shape a beam. These tools were made by Jonas Phelps. The author has these original tools as part of the "Ancestral Heard/Hurd Collection."

Owning a horse was a luxury few could afford at this time in the settlement. Instead, oxen were the draft animals of choice. They were more powerful than horses; under heavy load an ox will tug and twist, using the wagon's tongue as leverage to good advantage, especially when ploughing or pulling rocks. Horses are more likely to lunge forward with all their weight on the harness collar, breaking leather straps which were hard to come by. The two-toed hooves of oxen were much better adapted to slippery conditions such as boggy ground and snow. They were less likely than horses to fatigue over long journeys or heavy workloads. Oxen were not as skittish as horses, especially when a bear or other wild animal might suddenly break out of the woods. For all these reasons oxen were the settlers' first choice in that era for the various tasks that required brute strength and endurance.

Leather harnesses were not readily available at this time, and so using horses as work animals would have been too expensive to maintain. Another advantage with oxen was the quick and easy way to harness them; a wooden hoop under the wooden yoke was slid up and attached to the shoulder yoke with wooden pegs.

Samuel Farnsworth's oxen yoke, 1799 (photo by Sandra Hurd)

Taking only a minute or so, the yoke was simple to attach to the wagon tongue. The one harness rein was attached to the "lead" ox through the nose ring attached through their nostrils. This ox yoke shown in the photograph belonged to Samuel Deacon Farnsworth and was used by him when he migrated to Eaton Township in 1799 with his wife and three sons from New Hampshire. "It was William Farnsworth, likely an ancestor of John Farnsworth, who, seven years earlier, had exchanged a promissory note with Captain Ephraim[2] Sawyer for six bushels of wheat to leave for his family while on his trip to Quebec in 1792."[23, 29]

The yoke in the photo on the previous page was donated to the Compton County Museum (now known as Eaton Corner Museum) by Samuel's great-great-great-grandson, John Arthur Farnsworth. An ox yoke was easy to make from hardwood that was in abundance, usually birch or elm. A yoke would be stronger if taken from the outside of a large branch; these old-growth trees had a much larger branch circumference than most trees today. They usually made the bow of the yoke out of ash, then steamed the wood to bend it into a bow. Green wood was preferred as it was easier to work with; once made, it was left to dry (cure) to keep it from cracking or splitting. They would typically place it in a haystack to dry more slowly over the winter.

As the land became more cultivated, farmers began replacing oxen with workhorses. However, oxen were still used for logging operations. The loggers need the oxen's strength to break sleigh roads through the woods and for hauling the huge logs out to the edge of the woods. For horses to pull sleighs loaded high with logs, the roads would have had to be frozen solid. Getting ground to freeze requires breaking the ground of insulating snow – a task that oxen excelled at. And so, in this era, the settlers were able to establish good productive farmland with oxen, using horses for lighter work if horses were even affordable to them.

Free-flowing water was sought after in these early days and considered essential for homesteading success. The reasons the houses seemed to be built in the middle of their lots were twofold; a spring located above the rise of the house would allow spring water to feed by gravity to the house. There were no handpumps at this time. Wood troughs layered over each end were used to provide water flow to the livestock and for household needs. To keep the water from freezing in winter the water had to continuously flow; the settlers used a wooden barrel, usually placed outside the barn, as a cistern for the water to flow through. In most cases they built their homes and barns near a spring-fed brook so they could simply let the cattle out of the barns in the winter to drink their fill. In summer fences would allow the animals to graze on land surrounding a brook. Meadows where the rivers flowed through were especially perfect for their cattle to graze during the summer months.

The roads or paths the settlers used went around swamps, and to some extent around major hills, and were usually the shortest route from settlement to settlement. Each settler was required to set aside a road allowance in front of their homestead as part of the agreement upon settling. These roads ended up being rather twisty as they paralleled where the settlers found water on their lands. Some settlements ended up located far off the main roads, while others may have a main path right in front of their house. In later times, when roads were established by the BALC, they simply followed the same footprint. In many cases the newer roads would have better served had they been established at the perimeter of some of these lots or directly on the range lines so the farms would not have been cut in half. This would have made for longer driveways, but at that time would have been less of an issue for future generations than crossing a highway to work the other half of their properties.

This was still an era of "gathering," hunting, fishing, and searching for foods to supplement their crops, from what the land could offer through the different seasons. Food storage was minimal; "store-bought" foods were non-existent. Metal cans were invented in 1810; however, it would be another generation before canned foods began to trickle into Newport. Barrels and wooden buckets were the only choice to carry liquids if the settlers travelled somewhere. These were hand-carved, usually during the winter months, always used and reused, and were in great demand amongst the settlers. They made cisterns of wood sealed with spruce gum to hold water; these became their refrigerators when cold spring water was allowed to run through them.

In 1810, in a note to Samuel Beaman Jr. who was going to be passing through Ascot, Edmund[6] Heard requested *"to bring back eleven or twelve yards of "tammy" or anything suitable for making a bed quilt."* This was but one example of the lack of material available to them. He also asked for *"three hundred nails if they had them and to send the bill from the Merchant in Ascot with it."* [10]

As a community, the settlers had a genuine passion for working "bees," a practice quickly adopted as a social reason to get together. Isolated for much of the year in their own homes, the women treasured any chance to be together, to quilt, sew and to card wool. They would also gather in the fall to prepare and preserve foods, such as apples that would be pared for drying. These bees could be to build a barn or house, clear land, build roads or harvest their crops. Attended by many men, women and their families, these "bees" also gave them a chance to cook large amounts of food, share recipes and exchange leftovers to take home.[35]

By 1810, new inhabitants of Newport had joined the original group: Benj Hicks, Israel Hicks, John Hicks, Caleb Hardy, Ebenezer Grant, Samuel Morse and David Perkins. Artemas[7] D. Rand was now growing to an age, along with other young men, to take their places among the new inhabitants ready to work and defend their lands.

***

Samuel[6] Heard had received a letter from his sister-in-law Hannah, dated July 31, 1808. (Hannah was Luke[6]'s second wife, as Polly had died.) Hannah had written him, advising of the passing of his brother Luke[6] in a drowning accident in Kennebec, Me. Luke[6] was planning to bring his family to Canada to settle by the next summer.[10]

> *Luke and John Larrabee had gone out fishing in an open boat, such as often used for the purpose here; before next morning, however, when a violent storm came on and caught them in open water. They were forced to ride out the storm over night and in attempting to gain access to Wells Harbour in the early morning they were caught on a sand bar, the boat filled and the boat capsized. They sought safety by swimming, but oh! my brother with the most acute pain, I tell you my husband was unable to gain the shore where liv'd his now disconsolate widow, endeared to him by her little prattling, Martha, and a babe at the breast; joined by the most tender ties of conjugal affection; judge my grief; and judge of my situation, left without a sufficiently for myself, or my little innocents, in a place where we had liv'd but a short time, without connections on my side, of whom to expect relief. I look up to the family of my husband and beg of you, not to support, but only to come down and see me without delay. Until then I trust to the mercies of Heav'n. I know the love you bore your deceased brother and the friendship you have professed for me, together with what I have already informed you will be sufficient inducement without saying more. My son Edmund sends his re aspects to you and your family, with a request you remember him to all his friends there. Hannah. Heard.*[10]

Edmund[5] was devastated by the news that his son Luke[6] had drowned at Kennebec in 1808 and would not be moving to Newport as he had longed to.

Edmund had been living alone after his second wife, Elizabeth, and their daughter Hannah (Barnard) had moved back to New England, unable to tolerate the harshness of frontier life. Edmund had been anxious to have his sons with him. He had been living alone with Samuel[6] and Miriam, his youngest son and family, and his brother William[5] and family for a few years before his eldest son Edmund[6], Lucy and family arrived. Two of his grandchildren, Samuel and Miriam's children, sadly died in infancy and were the first to be buried in the new community burial grounds.

Col. Edmund[5] Heard died in 1814, 22 years after he had first slashed a clearing on his settlement. He was the first Heard/Hurd to be buried in Maple Leaf Cemetery in Newport Township, other than his two grandchildren who had died in 1810 and 1813. He would have been even more distraught had he known he would lose yet another son (Samuel[6]) merely one year after his own death. In his 71 years he had seen his vision, investment, and hard work come to fruition on behalf of his own families. He saw them and also his "Associate" families prosper in this new land. Col. Edmund[5] died the way he lived, putting his all on the line to ensure the success of his family and his fellow Associates in settling Newport Township. These were people who put their absolute trust in him to guide them in their transitional move to an uncertain life in a new country. He was a man of action and honour, and one might suggest he made the world a better place by being in it. The cemetery, a part of the original land lots first granted to the Heard families, is a part of the first community established in Newport Township in 1801. Edmund died in a land he could call his own, surrounded by people he loved and who had worked with him to create a thriving community out of what was originally called the "waste lands of the Crown."

> *Author's note: The lettering on headstone no. 1 in row 5, lot 29, is currently unreadable and is listed in the cemetery archives as "unknown." I believe that Col. Edmund[5] Heard is buried in that location. It makes no sense that he would not be buried in this cemetery – he was the driving force to establish it so there would be a common burial place for all the new settlers in Newport. He authorized the transfer of that land parcel from his brother, William Heard, for that very purpose.*

Perhaps it was just as well that Edmund[5] did not know that his wife, Elizabeth, would sue his estate for an inordinately large sum of money, perhaps assuming that the land in Canada had similar value to that of the New England states at the time. Part of the land granted to Edmund[5] Heard was applied for under his wife's name, and the names of other Heard children and their wives, so it was not improbable that Elizabeth might want to secure her fair price for the land in question.

The plaintiff Elizabeth (Andrews) Heard filed her suit in *"Three Rivers Kings Bench the 17 of March 1820. The court having heard the parties by their council are hereby condemned to execute and deliver to the plaintiff good and sufficient titles to the lots of land mentioned in the plaintiff's declaration thereof that they do pay to the plaintiff the sum of three thousand, five hundred- and ten-pounds currency nevertheless without cost by the court."*[31]

As executor, Edmund[6] Heard Jr. was obliged to secure the monies as noted by the continuing court notifications – documents held in the Ancestral Heard/Hurd Collection. He and Edmund's heirs would have been hard pressed to honour the debt load that this might have incurred upon their families and the settlement at that time.

Sherbrooke and Lennoxville, then known as Upper Forks and Lower Forks respectively, were centres of trade for the surrounding counties where the settlers could exchange their salts, furs, and other produce in exchange for the most-needed articles. Trade was carried on at great disadvantage to the settlers in the earlier years, but after it was found that the St. Francis River could be plied with larger boats accessing through the portage to reach the markets at Three Rivers, there was a renewed incentive for trade. The first idea was taken from the Indians, who frequented those parts on their hunting and fishing expeditions, and for a time their paths and "portages" were followed by the boatmen in their birchbark and log canoes. The business had increased to such an extent that larger boats were required. An enterprising man named Elim Warner built the first large boat that descended the river. It was 60 feet long, built of pine timbers and planks, and designed to carry six tons. "The launching of this began an era in the lives of these backwoodsmen and created almost as much excitement and interest among them as the launching of a steamboat would have been circa 1899."[17]

There was only a narrow path around the falls at Brompton on the St. Francis River until Warner cut a road by which the boat could be portaged. In many places, portages were unavoidable and in others where the current was strong, slow progress was made by "doubling the rapids." This phrase, common among the boatmen, meant landing the boat halfway, leaving part of the freight on shore, making the load lighter before descending the current in the rapids. At the location where the goods were off-loaded and left on shore, oxen would pull the boat out of the water onto skids to be portaged back by oxen for the balance of the load, and the process was repeated.[17]

The earliest and most important industry for the settlers was the rafting of timber down both the North and South branches of the Eaton River which connected to the St. Francis River, onwards to the St. Lawrence River and then to Quebec City "for His Majesty's ships." The dense forests of the Eastern Townships contained huge stands of virgin pine and spruce ideal for masts and spars. Oak for shipbuilding was already being rafted down the St. Lawrence from Upper Canada to Quebec City, bound for England and European ports. It was a band of hardy men who conducted this very early lumber trade. Timber was used frequently for trade, barter or in lieu of money to pay bills for the new settlers that were homesteading in the various townships.[29]

Often a settler, in addition to his farming labour, would cut a quantity of lumber from the forest and deliver it to a dealer who was making up a larger raft. It took the hardiest of men to go into the woods in the fall and winter and cut the trees and hew the required squared timber. At this time there was a shortage of sawmills in the immediate regions of Newport, Ditton, Auckland, Eaton and Bury, so the logs had to be floated downriver. In the spring the "river men" would collect the timber onto one or more great rafts and make the trip to Quebec City where they either sold the timber directly or consigned it to dealers. These were known as the river men. People such as Ephriam[2] Sawyer manned these rafts down the Richelieu River, connecting with the St. Lawrence River and then adding to their load where the St. Francis River meets the St. Lawrence. These rafts would be connected together similar to a train, forming a series of very wide and long rafts as one. They were equipped with tents or shacks sitting on the top, along with provisions and utensils that would survive the long, dangerous, and tedious trip to Quebec City.[29]

It was well known that, on the trip down the St. Francis River to Nicolet, Brompton Falls was the most difficult place for the boatmen to maneuver. It was always necessary to "carry by" (portage) in both directions. The stories of accidents and narrow escapes were numerous with those who had to travel this route to meet the raft going on down to Three Rivers.

***

It was during one of these trips in 1815 that a sad and devastating accident took place when two lives were lost at Brompton Falls. John[6] Sage French and John[1] Lebourveau from Eaton Township and Capt. Samuel[6] Heard (son of Edmund[5]) from Newport Township were on expedition down the St. Francis. At the falls, the freight was removed and the three men remained with the boat to pass downstream. Unfortunately, the boat struck a rock and capsized; John[6] S. French sank with the boat and drowned at once. Samuel[6] was seen to strike out for the shore, and being an expert swimmer, hope was entertained by those on shore that he might make it across. However, due to tremendous turbulence, he sank out of sight and was lost. John Lebourveau, who survived, at first sprang up onto a rock to which he continued clinging as he saw his companions drowning. He could neither save them nor help himself until a rope was thrown from the riverbank, which he fastened around his waist. When plunging into the boiling current, he disappeared at first, but was finally pulled to safety onto the riverbank.[16] *(with correction, from ref. 31 documents)*

Samuel[6] Heard had been one of the most active and public-spirited men in the township. His death cast a gloom and melancholy over the people in Newport, who now realized how much they had depended on him and were concerned for the prospects of the settlement in which he had been such a ruling spirit. Among his other duties Samuel[6] had acted as "clerk" for the better part of five years. His wife Miriam was now left with a young family in this great new but inhospitable land. Their eldest son, Henry Hershel, was 16 and their youngest daughter was only 4 months old. They had already lost a daughter, Hannah, in 1810 at age 2, and a son, George Augustus, in 1813 at age 1. Miriam, 45 at the time, brought her remaining six children up as best as she knew possible, remarrying seven years later to Rev. Simeon in 1822. Her son, Henry, grew up in Newport and has been mentioned many times in various documents relating to business and public affairs. The author has no further information other than he was connected to the Congregational Church in Berlin, Mass., and died there in 1863. *(letter from Mrs. Ardel Gilbert (1956) to E. L. Hurd, quoting family Bible)*

Their second son, Samuel, took over their original homestead. He continued clearing the lands, married and raised his family there.

> *Author's note: Capt. Samuel Heard/Hurd, at age 42, Captain of the 5th Eastern Battalion of East Newport, son of Col. Edmund[5] Heard, was buried on February 17, 1816, in Eaton Cemetery in Eaton Township. The presiding minister of the Presbyterian Congregation of Eaton, Jonathan Taylor, buried Samuel in the presence of his wife Miriam, Samuel Phelps and Edmund Heard. It may seem odd that he was buried nine months after his recorded date of death; however, because he drowned, it may be reasonable to assume that his body was not retrieved or identified for some time.*

John[5] Sage French, the younger brother of Luther[1] and Levi[1], lived in Eaton Township, had married Amy Hall, and had raised three children when he drowned at Brompton at only 35 years old. Amy, along with their daughter Abigail Sage and sons Horace Hall and John[7], were left to tend to the homestead. The farm was located on the Bury road just up from the railway tracks in Cookshire. Ward Bailey, now a young man, had moved to Eaton Township from Leamington, Vt., with his parents at age 4. He married, as his second wife, the widow Amy (Hall) French, and together they brought up the three French children and raised four more of their own on part of the original farm settled by his father Orsamus and mother Margaret (Whitman) in 1797.[4, 16]

***

David Metcalf and his wife Candace (daughter of John and Mary Stratton) were first Associates and settlers with Col. Edmund[5] Heard. They had nine children, four boys and five girls, losing one son and two daughters at young ages. David Metcalf served as Township Clerk in 1813. David made the last entry in the *Firfh Records of Newport* in 1816 where he listed the death of his daughter Candace in October of that year, his last duty as Clerk of Newport Township. He had listed all his family members' births, including those of the three who had died young. The Metcalf families had settled on a farm near Grove Hill; however, due to the "short crop" of 1816, David abandoned his farm and moved back to Vermont in the spring of 1817. His son Horace later moved to Cookshire in 1852, married and taught school there. Horace later moved to Learned Plain in Newport in 1866, thus the family name Metcalf appears again later in Newport activities.[20, 16]

During this period, many second- and third-generation Heards in Lower Canada were moving to townships other than Newport. Samuel's sister Hannah married William Barnard and had moved back to the New England Colonies. Her husband, however, was engaged in a scheme for settling a new town near Three Rivers, but that plan never came to fruition. Eunice, daughter of William[5] Heard, married Isaac Burnham; both are buried at Maple Grove Cemetery in Melbourne, Que.

Nancy, daughter of William[5] and Thirza Heard, married Ezra Brainerd; they settled on a farm in Wickham, Lower Canada. Both are also buried at Maple Grove Cemetery. Another son, Jeremiah (Jerry), moved to Barnston, Lower Canada, when their two boys and a daughter were youngsters and raised his family on a farm there. One of their sons, John, took over the homestead there when he married. After William[5] died in 1829, his wife Thirza went to live with her son Jerry where she died. Thirza is buried with her husband William[5] in Maple Leaf Cemetery in Newport. Their other son, William[6] John Hurd, moved to Boston where he married and opened a successful farm hardware and equipment business, Wm. J Hurd & Sons.

Another son of William[5] and Thirza, Chester[6] Heard and his wife Hannah moved to Massawippi in Lower Canada. Chester was a Free Will Baptist. *"On his 16th birthday, he knelt by the side of a stump and began his first prayer, but 'O Lord' was all he could say; there was such a lost feeling that he turned to the Bible and erected a family alter and from then on he began religious work in town."* This was the beginning of a revival that continued for years. Tough and though young in the ministry, he sustained his position and lived to realize the fruit of his labours in the comparative restoration of the Church in Hatley, Lower Canada, to its original state. They were later buried in the cemetery there.[4]

As they did in the in the New England states, these Heard/Hurd descendants also distinguished themselves in business, commerce, the militia, and as laymen, blacksmiths, farmers, builders, scholars, medical doctors, nurses, teachers, surveyors, carpenters, wheelwrights, and educators.

> *Author's note:* Glimpses into the Past, *published circa 1950, was a compilation of articles written by local writers and submitted to the Sherbrooke Daily Record. The following is an excerpt from p. 146:*
>
> In the history of the families who came into the Townships during the early 1800s can be found some very weak spots. It would seem that there was a long space of time between their coming and the establishment of historic records. There were no registry offices, no notaries, no town clerks, and so our history of the earliest days must depend on the individual, the family Bible, the burial grounds, where perhaps rudely marked stones might share some insight into the past. Letters to and from members of a family gave much help to a historian but they could not give authentic history of general events and so years passed before what we term local history could be put together.[24]
>
> *Author's note: During early settlement years, the Newport first Records, 1800 document, referenced throughout this book, was held by the Heard/Hurd family. Its existence was not disclosed to the governing bodies and, therefore, remained generally unknown. Sufficient evidence suggests that the reason was perhaps an underlying uncertainty as to the governing bodies' stability at the time as mentioned earlier in this story. It has not been until the writing of this book that these records are now being disclosed. This 77-page document and hundreds of other documents and letters have been a guiding force in weaving these facts together. As quoted in* Glimpses into the Past, *there indeed has been a shortage of authentic material for historians to draw upon. I have identified much of this material as "hidden history" because it was indeed kept hidden. We are fortunate and thankful that the material has been kept secure and preserved for some 228 years by the Heard/Hurd families. Because of these records, we know that both Col. Edmund[5] Heard and his son Samuel[6] were key figures in the formation of a Minute book documenting the first settlements in Newport Township.*

***

Chapter 7   Invaders from the South (1815–1820)

In the early 1800s, Canada was invaded by its neighbour to the south. The loosely configured border between Canada and the newly formed United States of America was about to become a battlefield. Following its independence from Britain, the U.S. started a massive expansion outward from its 13 states. Canada was in its sights, as were the lands west of Canada. Americans made attempts to expand into Canada (the War of 1812-14) but they were repelled by combined British and local forces. Battles raged in the border regions of the Eastern Townships. Once again Loyalists on the side of Britain migrated north to fight their American neighbours, and others came seeking land in Lower Canada – both increasing the area's English-speaking population.[26]

Britain was not prepared to lose these northern colonies at any cost, so they initiated the formation of provinces: Nova Scotia was split to create New Brunswick, and the region known as Quebec was divided into Upper Canada (Ontario) and Lower Canada (Quebec). Those settlers who were long established in the now suddenly growing British Colonies, along with newcomers arriving from the British Isles, had a deep respect for British political values and an abhorrence of the ideals and aspirations upon which the American Revolution had been based. They were determined to remain separate from the United States and their determination would be tested once again during this era.[26]

Americans saw the struggle as a war of liberation; Canadians, however, believed this threat to be a war of survival. Our ancestors, concerned with a repeat of the past and worried that their homesteads and records might once again be burned, hid the Minute Book (*Newport firſt Records, 1800*) and all their formal documents and letters.

> *Author's note: Referring to the book* Loyalties in Conflict *by Professor Jack Little, a reader might have a fuller appreciation of the* Minute Book's *historical context. "For one thing, it was clearly no accident that the New England-style town meetings were not sanctioned in the Eastern Townships, and that the* Minute Book *recordings ended at the outbreak of the war."* (Jack I. Little, Professor of History, Fraser University)

In some cases, ancestral patriots of the United States now found themselves fighting American relatives and British loyalists who had fled to Lower Canada and Upper Canada. For our ancestors, it was a war amongst cousins . . . and it was horrible! Once again, the Heard/Hurd, Rand, Bowker, French, Sawyer and other Newport families were finding themselves pitted against their own families who had remained in the United States.

Families fighting on different sides are exemplified as follows:[4]

Robert and Moses Heard, both sons of cousin William[4] Heard (a descendant of Edmund[2]) served in the war of 1812 for the United States of America, and yet, Captain Edmund[6] Heard, now living in Newport, served for the Canadian side of the conflict.

Robert[6] Heard served for the United States during the War of 1812 in Capt. G. Coomb's company; Lt. Col. E. Foot's regiment, September 3-9; at Camden and Thomaston, September 20-25, 1814; and in Capt. T. Kenney's Detached Company; Lt. Col. E. Foot's regiment serving at Camden, Me. from October 1 to November 9, 1814. (Records of the Mass. Militia in the War of 1812-14; 204, 206). Robert Heard was a farmer who lived at Ash Point, Me.

James[6] Heard served briefly during the War of 1812 as a private in several Wiscasset, Me., companies of the Massachusetts Militia, including Capt. A. Potter's company and Lt. Col. E. Cutter's regiment, which saw service at Wiscasset and Boothbay, Me. It was about this time that the spelling of the family name changed from Heard to Hurd. James Hurd was listed on his death certificate as a real estate agent. He was actually a deacon in the Free Will Baptist Church.

It was also at this time that "Lt. Col. Cull recommended Captain Samuel[6] Heard of Newport Township to head a company of volunteers in 1812, thereby sidestepping Oliver Barker of Compton Township." *(Jack I. Little,* Loyalties in Conflict: A Canadian Borderland in War and Rebellion, 1812-1840*)*

Many years later, on April 29, 1871, Hannah[2] Hurd Willard Rand had applied for a pension based on her husband Artemas[7]'s service in the War of 1812. Artemas D. Rand served in the company of Capt. Samuel[6] Heard during this period. The petition was rejected in December 1872 *"for want of proof of service & presumptive abandonment of the claim."* (Military Records Service, (United States) National Archives)

Meanwhile, *"Under the call made for soldiers to defend the coast of Maine (War of 1812), five men were drafted from each company of the regiment of militia in the northern part of York County, and Capt. Ayer, the Senior Captain of the regiment, marched with them to Kittery."* [4]

Among the draftees was John Heard *(History of York County, Me., 2:353)*. His name appears as a private on the muster lists of Capt. James Ayer's Company of Massachusetts Detached Militia in the Regiment commanded by Maj. Simon Nowell, dated October 31 and November 9, 1814, Kittery Point. It showed him enlisted on September 29, 1814, for a period of three months. In a company payroll for October and November 1814, his expiration of service is shown as November 17, 1814, having commenced service on October 8, 1814, for which he received a total of $12.18 pay, including travel home. He was called "Captain" at the time of his death many years later as shown in the Morning Star, August 17, 1832. *(Military Records Service, (United States) National Archives)*

During this period the United Empire Loyalists, disenchanted with the newly created governmental system in the New England states, once again began fleeing to Canada as had their predecessors. Land grants were once more offered and began to be established in this area for settlement. Between 1810 and 1820, the urgency which dictated the departure of thousands of Loyalists from the New England Colonies resulted in a crisis when they arrived in Canada with very few possessions. Most of them had only the clothes they were wearing. The families arriving found everyone ready to share, not only their provisions but also stories of their journey north. There was hope and anticipation in the faces of all of them. They were united with husbands and fathers who were anxious to build and establish homesteads on the New Frontier. One woman, Mrs. Buck, asked "if any of the new arrivals had brought a newspaper," which when shared was the centre of interest for many hours. The region around Lennoxville, known then as Little Forks, at the junction of the Massawippi and the St. Francis rivers, was settled by many of these refugees around this time frame.[2, 29]

Cities and towns on both sides of the border were burned and civilians on each side were killed. Our ancestors were steadfast in their desire to remain loyal to their beliefs. When the war finally ended in 1817, Britain's flag was still in place and Canada remained. The war had given the Americans a national anthem and the symbol of Uncle Sam. For Canadians, it afforded them a certain pride borne of having defended their land and their ideals. It was from this point in history that a new, unifying, and unique nationalism was to take root.[26]

The Battle of Lake Champlain was fought in September 1814. The Treaty of Ghent was signed in December 1814, officially ending the war. Immigration from the United States was halted, but trade and smuggling continued with great sacrifices. A map of 1812, the Craig map (the Craig Road figured prominently during the administration of Governor Craig) shows the paths and roads that had been carved out of the wilderness by our ancestors while trying to create a trade path for their produce in exchange for goods coming into Quebec City and Three Rivers.[24]

At this time more Heards began the move to Lower Canada, joining brothers, sisters and cousins in claiming land and envisioning opportunity in a new country.[4]

An historic venture in Eastern Townships road-building was the "Craig Road," shown on the map on the following page. The first "verbal process" of a road was made by the "Grand Voyer" Mr. Whitcher, from Three Rivers. He was a man of power in the land, to a large extent his word was law. Acting as a surveyor in 1812, he laid out a portion of the Craig Road from the north line of Dudswell Twp., to Canaan, Vt., passing through Cookshire, Eaton Township, Eaton Corner, Sawyerville, Clifton and Hereford.[24]

Author's note: The reference used in the publication describing him as a "Grand Voyer" may have been chosen to reflect a certain amount of dissention with his role. The "sur" suggesting a person of grandeur and the "veyor" conveyed as "Voyer," hence the term Grand Voyer. The name "Grand Voyer" is correct as verified in a further document written by Jack I. Little, with reference to Lord Dalhousie's survey of the Eastern Townships of 1821.

Many residents of the Eastern Townships were not happy with this arrangement, as evidenced by the following excerpt: "In January 1820, for example, 45 residents of Hatley township submitted a petition complaining of the inconvenience and expense in bringing out the Grand Voyer to establish Roads and Bridges. For a public road to be opened, proprietors had to petition to have it homologated by the district Grand Voyer, an officer whose position dated to the French Regime and who was based in far-away Trois-Rivieres." *(Jack I. Little, "The Fostering Care of Government")*

According to Ivanhoë Caron (*Histoire des Cantons de l'Est*, pp. 101-102), "the 1796 law making inhabitants legally responsible for all local roads was not recognized outside the seigneurial zone and attempts to pass legislation to remove all doubts in the matter succeeded only in 1823." *(Caron, "Colonization of Canada," pp. 538, 541)*. This excerpt demonstrates the dissention of the settlers, leaders and associates who had been responsible for mapping out and building the roads in the Eastern Townships; they were clearly being usurped by the French bureaucrats based in Three Rivers during this time.

Charles Whitcher, the Grand Voyer, was over six feet tall weighed nearly 300 pounds. He travelled through the forested territory in a heavy ox cart, with only one pair of oxen, creating quite a stir amongst the sparsely settled countryside. The reason for his trip was he had gotten the idea that Eaton Township would derive more benefit from this piece of road than Lennoxville or Ascot would, so he needed a "verbal process" that Eaton Township should build one-half of the connecting bridge across the Massawippi River. The arm of the law prevailed, however, and it was settled that Eaton Township would help build the road, but not have to pay half the cost of the bridge as was first proposed. The new road was to become a huge improvement from the spotted trail, the corduroy road and bridge path that these early settlers were currently using.[24]

Author's note: Baileys Path is the road heading northeast to Megantic County to the east of Craig Road. The road to Three Rivers heading northwest is to the west of Craig Road. Craig Road continues south to Kilbourn Mills (later known as Norton Mills) at the border. A reader may note that another part of the Craig Road, heading southerly but to the east towards the Connecticut River, abruptly ends at the river. This had been the path that our ancestors most commonly used.

This was when Eaton Corner, located on the old Craig Road leading across the border, became a bustling stagecoach stop for those travelling between New England and Quebec City. From Quebec City, this road was 110 miles long, just to Newport and Eaton townships. The road continued to the border of the New England Colonies and to Kilbourne Mills, Vt. By mid-century, "the crossroads" (to Three Rivers, Sherbrooke, Quebec City and the borders of Vermont, New Hampshire and Maine) was a busy and prosperous agricultural and commercial centre. Merchants, blacksmiths, tanners, milliners, and seamstresses plied their trades, while innkeepers, doctors, teachers, and clergy were now able to serve the needs of the growing communities.[16]

1812 map of the Eastern Townships showing administrative districts and the Craig Road (sites.rootsweb.com)

***

Around the same time, however, the weather changed drastically making for extremely hard times for our ancestors looking to settle in this new land.

> *The 6th of June 1816, it snowed killing all the newly sprouted leaves and many birds. This extreme weather lasted for three to four years in succession, forcing many to leave. Many of the farms were left vacant and half of the settlers left the Country. Even the people who remained were on the point of leaving when the weather suddenly began to change in the spring of 1820, finally giving relief.[16]*

The year 1816 has since come to be known as "The Year Without a Summer." The phenomenon, experienced across the Northern Hemisphere, has been attributed to the 1815 volcanic eruption of Mount Tambora in what is now Indonesia. This explains why many of the land grants issued to the some of the original Associates were abandoned, leaving those lands open to reassignment or sale to other settlers. There were indeed speculators who had taken up some of these land grants, and the government was poised to ferret them out because these speculators had no intention of actually settling on the lands.[20]

Col. Edmund[5] Heard appeared to have had an acute understanding of this probability and had taken steps to ensure this did not happen on his part of the lands in Newport. There was also considerable uncertainty mixed with anxiety over the Canada-U.S. border conflicts in the region, with people moving in and people moving out. The author will continue the story with Edmund[7] Heard, eldest son of Capt. Edmund[6], John[7] Bennett, Luke[7], Tyler W., Samuel[7] A., and their sister Sarah, and follow them as our story unfolds.

> *Author's note: If someone moved from Newport, they will be referenced in the story if they lived in Newport as children. They will be re-introduced if they returned or are mentioned in letters.*

***

Chapter 8   Settling In (1820–1850)

Edmund[7] Heard, (the eldest son of Captain Edmund[6] Heard), born in Lancaster, Mass., had moved to Newport in 1803 when he was 8 years old. He grew up with his family in Maple Leaf and later married his first wife, Mary Willard, the eldest daughter of Longley Willard and Hannah[1] Hurd, one of the first Associates with Colonel Edmund[5] Heard. They raised three children: Mary Maria (born 1819), Lucy Minerva (born 1824) and Matilda Rosetta (born 1827). Unfortunately, Mary died in 1828 leaving Edmund[7] with their three children, aged 1-9 years old. He had a tough time looking after the needs of his young children, household chores, clearing his land, planting and harvesting crops, plus the added responsibility for certain militia duties. This was a time when the other women of the community had all been pitching in to lend a helping hand with his children, even doing laundry at times.[4]

Three years later, in 1831, Edmund[7] married his second wife, Abigail Haskell, who had been living in Lennoxville. Abigail bore two children: Edmund[8] Haskell (born 1836) and Abigail Susanna (born 1839). When they married, the family settled on Lot 9 of Range 11, one of the lots his grandfather, Col. Edmund[5] Heard, had assigned to his son Edmund[6] in 1797. The lot ran adjacent to his father and mother's farm on Range 10, and so their homesteads were located essentially side by side. The children would follow well-worn paths over to their grandparents' home, finding all kinds of exciting and interesting things to collect or capture along the way.[4]

Record-keeping of accounts amongst the settlers and other communities continued. This was vital to the success of these early settler families, as they did not have the resources readily at hand to pay for materials or products essential to survival. These records were important monetary mechanisms in keeping track of who owed whom, since much was bartered in labour and produce. These practices promoted the value of real-life experiences and common-sense qualities that are found in abundance in the areas of the New England states and Newport Township even to this day. The settlers based their knowledge on experiences of what they saw and what they felt at the time and they busied themselves doing it.[31]

An example of these records follows:[31]

In a letter to Edmund[7] dated December 1817, Charles Goodhue of Hereford was inquiring of Charles Ward whether Edmund had informed him that, while in his employ, he had delivered him 12 flats of lye in November 1810, which was never recorded on either book or note, asking him to confirm if they were ever paid for. In his reply to Mr. Goodhue in January 1818, Mr. Ward's letter tells us:

> *Edmund has been to me concerning some salts which he says he delivered me while in your employ. I have no recollection of the salts. He declares that in no way he ever received pay for them. If he never has, he states that you will find some record of them with William Heard as he sent them with him. It is possible that William got credit for them which you will be able to ascertain by looking at your Eaton Books.* [10, 31]

When Lucy (Bennett) Heard, wife of Edmund[6] Heard, died at age 71 in 1875, she left a tract of land in Lancaster, Mass. Her heirs were listed as Edmund[7] Heard, John Bennett Heard, Luke Heard, of Newport; Tyler W. Heard and Samuel A. Heard of Eaton; and Lucy (Heard) Gibson of Melbourne, Lower Canada. This was part of the land where severances had been previously sold in 1846 and late in 1853, some of which were sold to help finance the family's later endeavors in Newport Township.[4]

When the first school opened in Cookshire in Eaton Township, circa 1820, Edmund[6] and Lucy Heard's daughter Sarah, who had been born in Newport, taught school there for three years, from 1824 to 1826, before she moved with her husband Gardner Bartlett and family to Chicago in 1831. They had three children, two sons and a daughter, born in Illinois where their family members were raised and married.

John Bennett[7] Heard, the second son of Edmund[6], also emigrated from Lancaster at an early age with his parents in 1803. He married Poly Sawyer (granddaughter of Capt. Josiah[4] Sawyer). They operated the farm adjoining his father's farm (on lots 9 and 10 of Range 10), which remained in the family for four generations. They had six children: Augustus[8], Catherine Jennete, Gratia, Bartlett, Cyrus Alexander and Maria Lily. Bartlett died of cholera at age 20 after moving to Chicago to live with his aunt Sarah.[4]

Simple survival continued to be the settler's main preoccupation. The concept of mixed farming began out of necessity for these early settler families in order to provide a variety of foods for their families. Every family had to reserve a portion of their potatoes, grains and seeds for next spring's planting. Meat, grains, vegetables and fruit were carefully preserved for winter consumption. Luckily, game was in abundance and hunting skill sets became as much of a necessity as farming. Our ancestors already had a history of having to define and find solutions to the most challenging problems over decades and centuries, so this just became another normality for these settlers.[17]

The only "hay" in the country when our ancestors arrived was the wild grass that grew in the meadows on the inside of river curves and in the ubiquitous old beaver meadows. Early farmland selection was made for this very reason; they could settle close to these lowlands where the land was essentially already cleared and thus could plant immediately. In most cases, however, the better farmland was above these lowlands. If one's lot comprised both topographies, they were fortunate.

Luke[7] Heard, the third son of Edmund[6], was born in Lancaster and grew up in Newport. He had spent his first few working years working in the mill in Stanstead Township. He met and married Persis Hubbard of Stanstead. They had seven children: Sarah Ann (born 1828, died at age 3), Lucy Gibson (born 1830), Achsah Hubbard (born 1834), Samuel[7] Newell (born 1834), George Gibson[8] (born 1838), Phineas Hubbard (born 1842 and died in 1843 just over 1 year old), and Julia A. (born 1844). When he married, Luke and his family lived and farmed on the adjoining farm on the original lots 6 and 7 of Range 10 where his grandfather, Col. Edmund[5] Heard, had built his first cabin in Newport. Luke served on the first school committee for the combined townships of Newport, Eaton, Ditton, and Clifton.[4]

These early families of Heards and their Associates had, after five generations, retained the independent culture of their New England colony upbringing. They had a certain direct and open character, were self-reliant and not afraid to try new things. They were entrepreneurial in how they approached their lives, creating new things to make their work easier, and inventing better ways. They were all to have one thing in common: they strived towards educating themselves. By contrast, the culture of many of those emigrating into the Townships directly from the "Old World" had come from a background of servitude, meaning they had usually worked for someone else where the "gentry" had run everything. They had come seeking opportunity for themselves in the "New World."[31]

The settlers were adamant and dedicated to ensuring that their children were educated, so schooling was considered a mandate for all their children's futures. They recognized that their children also needed to know how things worked, how to survive. They continuously taught both their young boys and girls the practical hands-on workings of daily living required for them to be independent. They placed an importance on a more formal education, such as reading, writing and arithmetic, recognizing these would be essential to round out their basic knowledge – hence the push to get a school established with suitable educators.[13]

Nature conceded to clear-cutting because the settlers were clearing the land to enable as much cultivation as possible. It would not be uncommon to see stumps as far as one could see, especially in winter. This would remind the settlers of the massive "stumping" job awaiting them in the spring. In winter, when they could not work the land, they cut wood to sell. The smaller trees would be kept for their own use, stacked upright so they could be found in the snow and cut into firewood lengths for the following year. They also took the opportunity in winter to hunt for deer and set up traplines for snaring rabbits and other small game; these were dressed and frozen to provide a fair bounty of food during the winter months and well into spring. Beaver, muskrat, mink and fox pelts were furs in demand, providing for both clothing and trade.

In much of Newport Township, as in other regions of Lower Canada, the "rock maple" or sugar maple was found in great abundance; in some areas it was the most common tree. It is a very hardy species; the wood itself is particularly hard and is commonly known as "hard rock maple."

There are maple trees in other areas that are referred to as softwood maple. While these may still be tapped, the sap is not as sweet and the syrup produced does not have the same unique taste. In many instances these locations were chosen by those who knew the products these trees would produce, both in terms of maple syrup and prime timber. The Indigenous peoples were harvesting sap from the maple tree long before the settlers arrived, and they were responsible for teaching the settlers how to harvest this precious liquid. They called it "sweet water" and boiled it down to chewy taffy. It has been said that "a thrown hatchet lodged itself in the trunk of a maple tree and the rest is history."[17]

Edmund[7], John[7] B. and Luke[7] all had farms with large maple groves. They recognized these were trees that they would conserve for harvesting maple syrup. Not all settler lots had maple groves, and settlers from those that did not would come to help in the spring season, trading their labour for some maple product. These trees were still virgin forest and were already hundreds of years old, producing ample syrup and sugar which was an excellent food supplement. Their wives, Abigail, Polly, and Persis, looked forward to replenishing their pantries each spring as they used the maple products in their daily cooking year-round. Homemade donuts and maple syrup became staples.

In the first few years, the settlers followed the example of the Abenakis when they passed through the region on their way northwest to their summer lodgings. The men made small troughs, roughly hewn out of almost any kind of timber, to receive the sap as it oozed from a small slash in the bark. These troughs would be connected by reeds to a sack made from the stomach of a deer. The sap would drip from the tree along the reed or trough and collect in the sack. The process evolved and "later they started making small buckets from wood staves that they would simply hang under a handmade carved spout; these spouts would be driven into holes that were drilled out." They would gather the sap in small buckets and boil it in large kettles over an open fire to make syrup.[17]

There was no romance in making syrup: it required an enormous amount of labour and the smoke from the cook fires blinded one's eyes. But the sweet end product was a welcome commodity for use in making other staples. In later years, the end-of-season "sugaring-off" parties were a much-anticipated time of year for the pioneers, especially the children, who were allowed to indulge in a sweet treat. A typical sugar shack would consist of many outdoor fires with large cauldrons hanging above each fire. The walls of the shack provided shelter from the wind and offered a more controlled environment. Families and neighbours pitched in and worked together collecting the wood, branches, and logs to keep the fires going. Oxen – and after few years, horses – would pull low-slung sleds to transport the sap in barrels to the camp for boiling.

The women from the community all joined in keeping the fires hot, while cooking food to feed the hungry men. It was a time of togetherness; hard work, sweet smoke, eating, laughing, games, taste-testing, and maple sugar highs. *"Pickles were served to cleanse the pallet."*[17]

***

By 1820 the system of granting lands was now entirely through a township agent. The agent superintended the settlement of each township and was obliged to reside in or near the tract of lands that were being developed for settlement. At no preceding period did these townships show so rapid a growth as between 1820 and 1828. Nevertheless, the government disbanded this method in 1827 in favour of land companies, such as the British American Land Corporation (BALC). The company was formed to manage this process to enable the government to sell the lands directly to a purchaser. The BALC also took on the responsibility of road building and bridge planning. Later the company imposed a tax system on the inhabitants to pay for these, much to the chagrin of the settlers.[16]

Our ancestors were experiencing a time of extreme hardship in Newport, and some were now moving back to New England. Hard winters became the norm, making the seasons unfavorable for the growth of grain, vegetables and even grass. Extreme cold and frost, either late in spring or early in autumn, ruined entire crops. If that didn't do it, their crops were destroyed by wild animals. Many of our ancestors became discouraged. To make things worse at that time, food prices were very high: flour was $18 per barrel, wheat was $4 a bushel and corn proportionately high in the market.[25]

This was a time when civic duties beyond the borders of Newport were coming into play. Using typical British terminology in 1824, Edmund[7], Artemas[7] D. Rand and his brother Marshall S. Rand were summoned as "yeoman" of Newport to be grand jurors at a Court of General Quarter Session of the Peace, in the District of Three Rivers.

Author's note: Marshall was only 14 at the time, which demonstrates that "children," as we know them today, were considered "of age" much younger in these times. Perhaps this was why the census specifically categorized those aged 14-17.

The 1825 Census of Newport recorded 86 inhabitants. It is interesting to note the manner in which the age breakdown was recorded: 14 under the age of 6; 9 under the age of 14; another 11 who were 14 but under the age of 18; and so on. A listing specific to the ages of males and females was separate. The confirmation was signed by M. Nichols.[31]

***

Many of the settlers' letters indicated signs of loneliness, mostly on the part of the womenfolk, as described by those who had left to settle elsewhere. One example is Lucy (Heard) and her husband George Gibson. They had moved to a settlement in Melbourne after they married. They still longed for news from loved ones. In a letter of 1829 to her father, Edmund[6] Heard, Lucy wrote:

> *This is a dull way of communication compared with verbal intercourse, but it is better than none. I am upset that I could not come home because of my schooling and I am worried that you may think affection towards you is misguided, but this is not the case. Nothing but death will cut the tender chord that links my heart to my parents, brothers, and sisters. My brother Luke[7] (Heard) and Persis intend on going to Newport and Shipton. I often feel pained to think I did not do more to alleviate the sorrow of that dear brother while with him, although I often thought I did what I could. [Signed] Lucy* [10]

***

Around this time wooden candle moulds were introduced, replacing the time-consuming task of repetitively dipping the candles. This important innovation was not only much faster, but it also meant the manufactured candles were uniformly shaped. Some candle makers would travel from towns to settlements, taking their moulds and equipment with them, making candles on demand. Area settlers would bring their tallow to them, and candle making became an event in the form of a bee. The women delighted in getting together as a group to hear and tell stories of their children, their hopes and their dreams. Discarded moulds were reminders of the dim flame glowing in early Newport when farmsteads were widely isolated settlements and the families were struggling.[42]

Edmund[7], John[7] B. and Luke[7] Heard had immigrated from the New England states in 1803 as children with their father, Edmund[6] Heard, who was already at age 38 at the time. Due to their father's quick escape from the New England states, he had not been fully equipped with all the necessary farming implements they needed. There was no place where one might purchase these farm tools, so borrowing, exchanging or creating something new was normal for them. Farms adjacent to each other lent well to the practice of passing along equipment from farm to farm, including the labour of the sons and daughters. No money was needed to change hands; however, each family assigned one person in the group to prepare ledgers of all such transactions.

Prior to 1840 there was little money in circulation in Newport and nearly all trade was by exchange. The families would purchase the necessities on credit for three or four months, reimbursing in excess produce from their farms. Produce might consist of ashes, used in the making of potash or soap, grains for flour, seed for a next-year crop, potatoes as seed or to eat, cheese, hides for making clothing and leathers, maple sugar, or even excess livestock, hens, geese, and eggs. These items would be put against each family's credit, and any balance used to pay out their credit.[25]

Author's note: The Ancestral Heard/Hurd Collection has copious sets of these records created during those early years. Not only were implements exchanged but also labour was paid out in produce, each farmer growing or making something another may not have.[31]

After friction matches were invented in 1827 and found their way into rural homesteads, flints were slowly abandoned. It was not uncommon, even in this era, for the settlers to keep coals smothered for months on end to be revitalized to start their fires each evening. Their homes had little or no insulation and the bedrooms would be cold in the winter. Bedwarmers made sleep more bearable. The basic form of a bedwarmer remained unchanged for centuries: a lidded pan for holding coals or embers with a two-foot-long handle for safe carrying and a protruding hook for hanging it up. It resembled a large and deep copper frying pan with a lid perforated with numerous holes. The first warming pans, an innovative step forward, emerged in the 1600s. The design was simple but effective. Hot coals were placed in the pan. Closing the lid prevented the coals from escaping and reduced the available oxygen necessary for further combustion, thereby extinguishing the fire within. The air holes in the lid allowed the necessary circulation. Few would consider it an attractive or even a safe item, but on cold nights in years past people were thrilled to have one. They would slide it under the sheets to chase away the chill of the night. People in these times felt that the bed warming pan was a godsend. Almost universally, it would be hung by the fireplace from which the coals were taken.[42]

While there is no doubt the bed warmer chased away the chill, there were drawbacks. Embers or charcoal would leave the bed smelling and there was the risk of scorching the linens, certainly not an enviable place to have a fire start. Almost every home had one or more as a matter of convenience, their popularity driven by both practicality and publications such as the 1853 book *Domestic Economy*, which took pains to note the value of a good bed warmer: "A copper warming pan is indispensable to a household. Take care to have a big enough quantity of embers, above all some red cinders, when you want to heat a bed. Get it smoldering well before you use it, otherwise the fire will soon go out and the bed will not warm up. You must move the warming pan constantly to avoid scorching the sheets." Many of these early settlers would simply heat a brick or stone by the fireside, wrap it in cloth and place it in the bed. While rudimentary, the brick or stone approach was a much safer and more effective means of providing comfort while sleeping than were live embers.[42]

Some of the settlers, including Luke[7] Heard, devised a unique method to keep food and milk cold in the summer months. They made a wooden box sealed with spruce pitch; water would flow continuously through this box, from the cistern at the barn to the outside kitchen. These boxes acted as refrigerators into which they would place containers of milk, meat and cheeses to keep cold both in both summer and winter.

Author's note: I remember seeing this water box in the original Luke[7] Hurd home prior to the kitchen being refurbished in 1946.

The three women – Abigail, Persis and Catherine – must have found it difficult trying to survive with their young families in this virtual wilderness of Newport. Luke and Samuel's wives, the sisters Persis and Catherine, had grown up in Stanstead, while Abigail, Edmund's wife, had grown up in Lennoxville, both earlier-established towns. John[7] B.'s wife, Polly (Sawyer), had been raised with her grandfather Josiah[4] Sawyer and her father Peter Green Sawyer[5] in Eaton Township. Polly had a good understanding of life in an isolated community and was influential in keeping the new wives content by passing on pioneer "life lessons" on how to manage living in a wilderness. Polly took them and their children out into the meadows to show them where the natural healing herbs, such as "wiccopee bark" for laxative, grew in abundance. Many other herbs, both medicinal and edible for use in flavouring their food, were available. Wild carrots and certain mushrooms could be eaten, along with wild strawberries, raspberries and in some locations, where the lumber had been cut recently, even blueberries were abundant.

The Indians ate the root of the "jack-in-the pulpit," but to us it is known as a poisonous, but pretty, plant found in the damp woods. The Indians used blue flag for earaches, and we used sweet flag root as a kind of candy that children liked if it was boiled in maple sugar. The Indians used it in quantities to dispel fear. They also knew that pitch from the balsam fir trees would cure wounds and they were the first to brew a tea from "pipsissewa" (prince's pine), drinking it to break up gallstones. Who were the first to stuff the dried leaves of tobacco into a hole in a piece of wood, draw the smoke into his mouth and said, "Mmm, mmm that's good"? That's an easy question; we know the Indians of our country tried these things as did many of our early ancestors who might say when they were suffering greatly, "I'll try anything once," and try them they did.[24]

In the late 1820s, however, during several years of extreme winters, famine persisted throughout the region. One beef bone could be boiled repeatedly with a little bran. Our ancestors soon learned which wild roots and leaves could be eaten. Snaring rabbits and hunting deer once again became necessities to conserve their own domestic livestock for future growth. Practically every homestead had a few sheep from which the wool was used to spin into yarn to be knit into warm socks, mittens, scarves, hats and even coats, which served to keep them warm. A few of these families would slaughter an older sheep, making a mutton stew last for many weeks.[17]

These were indeed hard times. Gathering wild berries and vegetable tops to eat was a necessity. The women would gather nuts in the forest, and cowslips, nettles, pigweed and even leaves to boil. Many of our early ancestors were from the New England Colonies and had already met with these hardships. They would have had a better chance of survival than some of the newer immigrants arriving directly from the Old World that had offered a more mature civilization and cultured environment.

It was a hot summer day when two of Luke's sons, Samuel and George, decided to visit their cousins at John Bennett Heard's farm. Over the spring and early summer, they had been busy slashing a more direct trail through the woods than the road from their place to their uncle and aunt's farm. When they arrived, the boys were greeted heartily by John himself, who offered the boys to join them for supper. They waited in anticipation to see their girl cousins while Polly cooked their meal over an open fire in the outside kitchen. Polly must have wondered what the boys were doing here because *"it made no sense to Polly that these boys were interested in visiting them, so it must be one of their three girl cousins, Catherine, Gratia or Maria."* The girls were out picking berries down in the meadow and would be home soon for supper. Children in this era were not required to work as much as their predecessors and found time to do some of the things children liked to do. They did, however, emulate their parents, creating and doing projects that were in many ways beneficial to the family as a whole. Once children were in their early teens, it was not uncommon for them to go visit neighbouring farms on their own. At this age they delighted in pretending they were explorers, finding or making new trails as shortcuts to another farm in the woods, fishing and swimming in the river and climbing the cliffs of the riverbanks. Another few short years later, in their later teens, they would travel on horseback along these same trails they had cut earlier, this time more likely going to a neighbour's to help out with a farming chore.[31]

Both Luke and John found turnips to be an ideal crop for cultivation similar to the experience of the New England Colonies in earlier times. The need for turnips was very real; not only did our ancestors depend on them as an inexpensive food, but turnips and turnip tops provided rich high-quality forage for their livestock. You would have found several acres of turnips or the closely related rutabaga mixed throughout the stumps that were prevalent everywhere. Many regarded turnips as being only fit for livestock, but in reality, these nutritious roots were an important foodstuff for our early ancestors. Many a family in Newport had to subsist on a monotonous diet of turnips and potatoes through long winter months until such time as they could coax a more varied crop of vegetables from their stump-riddled fields. In most cases in these early times they needed to preserve their livestock for breeding in order to increase the numbers. To slaughter an animal would not be prudent, simply because it would diminish the family resources.

The settlers could often get two crops per season from the same field by sowing in early spring and then again in late summer, as turnips could withstand the cooler temperatures of both seasons. The harvested crop would store well in a frost-free cellar or stable. The first barn that Edmund[5] Heard built on his lots 6 and 7 of Range 9 had a hidden cellar in which the family had lived their first winter with their livestock keeping them warm. This same cellar later became the storage cellar for the turnips Luke harvested on the original Col. Edmund[5] Heard farm when he took the farm over when his grandfather died.

Many early ancestors and settlers had a razor-sharp utensil intended solely for cutting turnips.

> Author's note: I remember this very tool sitting in the shop and used it to cut turnips on this same farm where I had lived during my childhood days with my father, Edmund[10] Lionel Hurd.

The importance of turnips explains why turnip slicers were viewed as vital utensils. When vast quantities had to be cut, it was essential to have a tool that completed the job effortlessly. Some would creatively fashion hand-cranked equipment that could cut large turnips in a fraction of the time.

***

Sarah (Hurd) Bartlett (Edmund[6] and Lucy's daughter) moved to Chicago in 1831 when she married and where she raised her family. She sent a letter home to her brothers, dated December 23, 1849, writing that:

> *I am sorry that I have not answered three letters that were finally delivered to us by a young Mr. Rodgers, mainly because they have been like shifting planets. We have purchased a lot and we are now a resident of "Lynnd's Block," six doors north of Rands lift bridges on the East side of the river. We are again in the most crowded part of the city, where nothing is heard from Monday to Saturday, but the rattling of carriage wheels, the trampling of footmen on the sidewalk and the ceaseless din of business. For weeks after we arrived, I lived alone with my little family while my neighbours were dying amounting to 15-20 and some of the time between 30 and 40. My own neighbour, upon waking in the morning, having cramps at 8 AM, was dead at 4 PM. Just the next day, his brother, had diarrhea at seven in the morning, commenced cramping half an hour after, while helping himself to meat and potatoes at the breakfast table, past the reach of medicine in one hour and dead a quarter before eleven o'clock in the evening. Such is the rapidity with this dreadful sewage problem, our friends and fellow citizens are being sent to the tombs. I had it slightly myself but survived. For weeks I would look out the window and see nothing but hearses moving bodies. I am most gratified for Lucy's letter and will answer her immediately. I send my love to you and the girls, Luke and family, Edmund and family and Tyler and family. [Signed] Sarah Bartlett.* [10]

Author's note: By the sound of the letter, it seems they thought this sickness was in the air from the continuous smell of sewage.

After reading the letter from Sarah, many in Newport likely believed themselves lucky to have fresh air to breathe and pure spring water to drink. Even though times were tough, food was fresh, air was clean and their settlements as silent as the forest. People in the cities, however, were not doing so well simply because of overcrowding and inadequate sewage facilities. Cholera was the cause of thousands of deaths in the cities in this era and continued until the cause was determined to be the contaminated water they were drinking.

This is also time when many children in Newport and the surrounding townships were dying of a "lung fever." Sarah's brothers, Luke and Tyler, lost seven children between them. Maple Leaf Cemetery lists this cause of death as "consumption," a term that referred to tuberculosis or simply "TB." Vaccines did not yet exist.

Many other such health scourges plagued the communities during these times, causing great anguish for the families simply because the settlers did not know what they were or how to deal with them. Doctors were "as scarce as hen's teeth" in these early settlements, and if they had access to one, he usually lived several miles away. To get to a patient a doctor would have to travel by horseback through mud-soaked paths, hoping they were travelling in the right direction. Many a baby was born long before the doctor arrived.[32]

Because of this, many mothers of the communities had become nurses out of necessity. There was a common ailment whereby the patient would sweat and tremble, then shiver and burrow under the covers to keep warm, then vomit, throw off the covers and sweat again. Their bones ached and teeth chattered. The illness might last for weeks; yet months later the chills and fever would reoccur. They called it "the ague" and believed it arose from the soil when it was first broken or from unhealthy beaver swamps. They were not far wrong. Ague is a type of malaria caused by mosquitoes carrying the disease, and mosquitoes were indeed plentiful in these times as the men were clearing the swamps and woodlands. This was just another unpleasant reality our ancestors had to deal with. Beaver fever was also common at the time, and if not treated could prove fatal.

Some of the remedies used from the earlier days well into the mid- and late-1800s:[31]

- *Sore heads: a little creosote ointment applied to the forehead every night.*
- *Poisonous rash: Simmer Lilac flowers in cream and apply.*
- *Earache: Tobacco & roasted onion . . . drop one drop into the ear*
- *Shingles: 1 dram of sugar of lead to one pint of water, dress them with it 3 to 4 times a day and plaster with lard and keep the bowels open*

- *Piles: apply warm treacle, or a tobacco leaf steeped in water twenty-four hours or varnish which perfectly cures both the blind and bleeding piles*
- *Croup: Take the white of an egg, stir it thoroughly into a small quantity of sweetened water and give it in repeated doses until a cure is made, if one egg is not enough a second or even a third may be used.*

Author's note: "Sugar of lead" is not a typing error. It was made by boiling cherries in a lead pot. The solution absorbs lead from the pot, becoming a salt brine that would draw on a wound, like a poultice. They might also use this salt as a sweetener, albeit a deadly one. Perhaps they knew nothing about the effects of lead poisoning when they consumed it. There is a suggestion that this process was used in Roman times to sweeten wine.

Potatoes, another staple in our ancestors' diets – but scorned by the French-speaking communities in Canada who described potatoes as "food scarcely fit for pigs" – was considered an excellent vegetable for the dinner table. Every farm grew hills of the starchy tuber, and our ancestors strove to find new varieties that would mature earlier or keep longer. Abigail, Polly, Persis, and Sam's wife Catherine, as well as the other wives of the settlement, relied on potatoes in many ways: to improve the yeast starter they used to make bread; for soup, potato cakes and dumplings; for the most standard of meals, salt pork and potatoes; and even for laundry starch.

Settlers planted potatoes using a single ploughshare, drawn by an ox or horse, to first turn over the earth. This was followed by a steel-toothed cultivator and then a tiller to mound furrows into which they would hand-plant the dried "potato eyes." These tillers were just one of the tools they used, most of which they had brought with them from New England. The potatoes had been stored in sand in the dark cellars of almost every farmhouse during the winter, a proportionate amount set aside to cut in quarters for planting, their eyes already sprouting by spring.

Spring planting was labour-intensive, and so was fall harvesting. The potatoes were dug by hand, placed in huge baskets and carried from the field. The baskets were woven by the womenfolk from bullrushes gathered from the swamps in the fall. Much later, farmers in the "potato business" would progress to machinery that would both plant and harvest, using horse-drawn equipment that was much less labour-intensive than what these early settlers had to deal with.

By 1829, Irish immigrants made up one-fifth of the population in Quebec and were now settling in Newport Township. They had always planted potatoes in Ireland and considered them a treasured food source.

When Sherbrooke was but three houses where the city now stands, the settlers travelled to the nearest market at Three Rivers. At that time, travel to the market was principally over the ice. Many travelled on the frozen rivers at the tender age of 17. There were stories of narrow escapes from falling through the thin ice. They carried pearl ash and other produce of Newport in a boat down the St. Francis River to Port St. Francis, as did their forefathers, returning with necessaries for the settlers.

***

A marriage with the first French family, and second Heard/Hurd and Fraser/Frasier/Bailey family connection:[4]

Author's note: As the Eastern Townships were being settled and with more road and bridge connections being built, more people were moving between townships. Families from different areas were becoming intermixed with the older families who had been isolated for many years within their own communities. The connections between the French, Bailey, Hurd and Fraser families were proof of these extended families of the day.

Ward Bailey, born in Leamington, Vt., had moved to Eaton Township at age 4 with his father, Orsamus, and mother, Margaret (Whitman), travelling some 30 miles into the woods with no guide other than a spotted trail. Orsamus, who had been a child soldier in the American Revolutionary War, now with his wife and family, was among the group of first settler families in Eaton. They became part of Capt. Josiah[4] Sawyer's "Associates," and secured a 1200-acre grant of land, some of which later became generally known as Pine Hill Farm. Their second youngest daughter, Abigail, married James Fraser, a native of St. Giles, south of Quebec City. Abigail was an American who apparently thought the family name too "Scotchy" and made James change the spelling from Fraser to Frasier. *(Winston Fraser, Cookshire's Pine Hill Farm: The land, the people)*

Ward Bailey married Sally Rogers in 1816 but she died the following year. Ward married as his second wife the widow Amy French, the wife of John[5] Sage French. John had drowned at Brompton Falls in 1815 with Samuel[6] Heard while going to market with a boatload of produce. Amy French already had three children: a daughter, Abigail Sage, and two sons, Horace Hall and John[6] L., both of whom would become well known in Eaton Township in later years.

Ward and Amy had four more children with the surname Bailey. One of their grandchildren, William Ward Bailey, a son of Cyrus Bailey, was well educated in business and spent his life in the business of lumbering and contracting in Island Brook, Newport. William Bailey married Naomi Weston, daughter of James Weston of Newport; they raised nine children. He was a Newport councillor for eight years and acted as mayor part time. Once the children were grown up, they left Newport when William accepted a position with the Cookshire Mill Company.

Abigail Sage French, born in 1811, the daughter of John[5] Sage and Amy (Hall) French, married Tyler[7] Wellington Hurd, (the fourth son of Capt. Edmund[6]). Abigail's grandfather, John[4], his wife Abigail, along with their three sons Luther[1], Levi[1], John[6] S., and three daughters, had emigrated from Enfield, Ct., in 1798 to Cookshire, becoming settling associates with Capt. Josiah Sawyer.[4]

Tyler[7] Wellington and Abigail S. Hurd had nine children. Their first born, Sarah Malvina, was born in 1836 and married William Donald Fraser, a farmer in Eaton Township, in 1837. A son, John F., was born in 1838 and was accidently shot in 1852 at age 14 by the discharge of a gun in the hands of an Indigenous boy while hunting together on the meadow near the house. Their second son, William B., died in infancy. Their third son, Wellington F., was born in 1843. Their second daughter, Cynthia J., was born in 1845 and died at 10 years old. Their fourth son, Leander V., was born in 1848 and died at 3 years old of "lung fever." Their fifth son, Theodore Augustus, was born in 1850. Their sixth son, Charles H., was born in 1853 but died at two years old. Their seventh and last son, Frederick[8] Augustine, was born in Cookshire in 1857.[4]

> *Author's note: I have discovered through the genealogy prepared by Edward Hanson that Tyler[7] Wellington Hurd is my wife's great-great-grandfather; her great-grandfather was Frederick[8] Augustine Hurd, whose daughter married Lloyd Leslie Planche. For Sandra this is another connection to the Planche family of Cookshire.*

Even in this era, life was still fragile and the author could merely have written that only four of Tyler[7] and Abigail's nine children had survived. The impact of simple survival is clearly evident by the sad losses through accident, disease, childbirth and childhood mortality. This was also, however, the first reference to "lung fever."

The 1881 Census of Eaton, Que., listed William Frasier, Scottish, 44, born in Quebec, farmer; Sarah Frasier, English, 45, born in Quebec; Abigail Hurd, widow, English, 70, Church of England; Charles W. Taylor, Irish, 28, carpenter. (Note the name change from Fraser to Frasier.)[4]

By way of this marriage, Hiram French (a son of Levi[1]) and his cousins Horace Hall and John[6] French were now also cousins to William[7] J. Hurd of Boston and John[7] H. Hurd of Dover, N. H. – and so again, another family association with the Heards/Hurds. These two Hurd brothers were born in Newport, the sons of Jeremiah[6] (Jerry) Hurd, who was a son of William[5] and Thirza Heard of Newport. When the boys and their daughter were still young children, Jerry had moved with his family to Barnston. Years later, on one of his trips to Boston, Hiram had met and asked William[7] Hurd about the relationship/connection of the Hurds of Newport to the "Hurds of Dover."

William Hurd wrote a letter of explanation and attached the business card of *J. H. Hurd & Son*, another distant relative, who lived in Dover, N.H., a manufacturer of farm equipment with an office in Boston. In his letter, William tells us of the connections with the first Heards/Hurds who landed in Dover in 1632-63. An earlier John[1] Heard, brother of Luke[1], had been quite a prominent man in the early history of New Hampshire and was captain of Heards First, a place of safety from the incursions of the Indians, raising a family of 15 children. The history written in this letter meets with the same information as prepared by Edward Hanson in his thesis "John Heard of Ipswich, Mass."

A further note attached, written by Hiram's son *L. W. French, Insurance Agent, Eaton, PQ*, stated that Hiram was very sick at the time the letter arrived and so he had forwarded the letter, dated 1892, to Augustus[8] Hurd. This letter of inquiry suggests that even at this time in history, as members of these families grew older, there was an interest in securing information to find connections to their extended families.[16,24,31]

> *Author's note: In 1898 it was reported that "Mr. John T. Hurd of Boston, Mass., has in his possession a Bible printed in 1599. It was brought from England to Ipswich by Luke[1] Heard, the ancestor of the Ipswich Heards. John T. Heard received the Bible from his grandfather, Nathanial Heard, who received it from his father, who was a grandson of Luke."* (The Maine Historical and Genealogical Recorder, 9(1898):209) *Efforts to determine the whereabouts of this Bible have not yielded fruit.*[4]

Our ancestors suffered many hardships during this time: they lost children from diseases such as typhoid fever, diphtheria, scarlet fever, measles and general influenzas, and during childbirth both mother and child were at risk. In a letter to Sarah Hurd, her cousin Catherine, who had apparently experienced much, wrote:

> *I suggest that for the health of your brothers and sisters, that they must preserve an opposition to weakness and pain and languor in a cheerful frame of mind and spirit. They must not let come anxiety or sorrow to depress them. Gentle exercise is beneficial but hard labour must be avoided, the bowels kept free and regular. If this can be done without medicine, the better for molasses and milk is a very good drink. Spirits of any kind and of any quantity hastens and aggravates the disorder. Flannel should be worn in the winter but taken off come spring when the weather warms."* [She goes on to suggest that] *dandelions are excellent. Eat them as greens or dry them as any other herb and make a tea of them. I have found them to be more beneficial than anything else I have ever taken . . . Catherine.* [10]

***

It was not until after 1830 that settlers began to arrive in the northwestern section of Newport. The first settlers in this region (lots 1, 2, 3, 4, 5 and 6 of ranges 2 and 3) were the Learned families. Abijah Learned and his four sons Abel, James, Royal and Ebenezer had moved from New Hampshire to Lower Canada, settling around Lake Memphremagog. The youngest son, Ebenezer, is said to have been the first white child born in Columbia, N.H. He and his brothers James and Royal moved to Eaton Township in the spring of 1799. Ebenezer and James began clearing a plot of land adjacent to their brother, Royal, an "Associate" of Josiah Sawyer who had received 1200 acres of land as part of the Eaton Township land grants. Ebenezer married the widow of his brother James in October 1799, and they raised seven children. The first grain he harvested he carried on his back to Colebrook, N.H., guided only by a spotted line, to be ground into flour there. Clearly this family was not unique in living through all the hardships being suffered by other settlers during this era.[32]

In 1823 Alden[2] Learned, one of Ebenezer's seven children, became the founder of the "Learned homestead" in a small settlement in the northwestern part of Newport Township, then called Lapingham but soon changed to Learned Plain. His home, a palace in the wilderness amongst a stretch spruce and fir trees, was later given the name "Evergreen Farm."[32]

And so, the first opening in Learned Plain was made by Alden[2] Learned in 1823 and named after him. Alden spent the better part of 10 years clearing the area, living in a small log cabin on Lot 1 of Range 3 before initiating a settlement in 1833. He married Sally Mallory of Eaton Township and together they raised their family. "The first I can remember, there were about 15 acres cleared, a log house with a stone chimney, two fireplaces and an oven. The house was divided into two rooms and featured three six-paned windows. There was a 26 by 30 framed barn with stable, floor and bay, no floor in the stable. The only buildings in sight were on Lot 12, occupied by Elias Gates. At that time, my father owned a pair of steers (oxen), two cows, and three or four sheep."[16, 32] *(quote: Alden Learned)*

Alden soon decided to build a larger and better house, so with courage born of desire, he set to work. He made his own bricks and hauled lime on an ox sled in the winter from Lime Ridge, a distance of 35 miles. He built his new house with heavy cedar beams and solid brick walls, a fireplace with an oven and a brick chimney. It was a house of unusual distinction.[24]

Alden was the postmaster in Island Brook for 23 years.[24]

Author's note: A comment from a descendant whose ancestors lived nearby: "Across from the old swimming hole further up the river road was a brickworks. I remember that the Bowkers 'hayed' that field and there was a barn there." (Eric G. R. French)

Alden's brother, William[2] Learned, who was already settled in this country, married Margaret Keenan in July 1841. Once married they lived on his father Ebenezer's original Eaton homestead.[32]

Alden Learned home in Island Brook (*Island Brook: Then and Now*)

Author's note: This marriage is mentioned only because there is a fascinating story found in a newspaper clipping (dated 1894) stuck in the back "First Records of Newport 1800." While it did not occur in Newport, the story demonstrates the resolve, determination, courage, and stamina these folks displayed. It also fits in with the theme of "lives lived" in the region, and so the story must be shared.[20]

This is the story of Margaret Keenan, born in March 1821 in the town of Enniskillen, County Fermanagh, Ireland. At 13 years old she left Ireland to follow and rejoin her father, arriving in Eaton Township, Lower Canada, in July 1834. This part of her life must not become a lost history:

> Sixty years ago, amongst a group of immigrants landing at Quebec City outpost was a young 13-year-old girl. In those days this section of the country was a vast wilderness and its streams were uncharted, travelling was unnecessarily hazardous and difficult. From Quebec to Cookshire there was a road known as the "Craig Road," 110 miles in length. It passed through interminable woods, which were not altogether devoid of danger, yet this young girl traversed the whole distance on foot in three days, an apparently incredible short space of time, eventually arriving at the Eaton River. She forded the river at a point opposite George Cook's settlement (now Cookshire). From here she continued her doubtless wearisome journey until at last she arrived at her father, Mr. Keenan's home. The site, occupied today by Mr. Belanger, the identical situation of the old residence being marked at present by a solitary birch, where her father had arrived in this country three years earlier. Margaret's trek was in July, and we can well understand that walking at such a pace, in the sultry heat of a summer sun, the newly arrived stranger must have wondered a thousand times what the outcome of such a journey might be. She was in a land where everything was different from the verdant pastures of Ireland from which she had just sailed.

"Yet this journey was an eventful one, as over sixty summers had flown by when the young immigrant died to her eternal rest. Mrs. William Learned spoke her last farewell on February 28, 1894, at the age of 73, leaving behind a noble example of what it is possible for a good woman to accomplish."[20] *(clipping from unidentified newspaper)*

When Margaret died, she left behind their three sons: Alden[3], one of the best-known men of the region; Henry, who was a county warden, an Eaton councillor and the first mayor elected after the incorporation of Cookshire; and John F., a major in the 5th Dragoons, who continued living on the original homestead.[32]

***

In 1822, Ensign Edmund[7] Heard wrote a letter to the Reserve Militia of Newport to verify the men, officers, and their ages: *"Commanding you to notify and warn all those persons whose names are listed on Military Rolls, to appear at the dwelling house of Paul Phelps on Monday the tenth day of August, with firearms and accoutrements as the Law directs therein to wait further orders hereof. Fail not and make due return of this warrant with your doings here on to me or one of the Commanding Officers on or before the day of the meeting."* [3]

The Newport Militia Roll of 1824 listed 24 men. The calling for this notice indicated that conditions were ripe for another conflict. The assembly of men was to verify who might be available to muster should an event require defensive action in Newport.[3]

***

In a letter dated 1827 from Shrewsbury, Mass., Sarah (Heard) Hemmingway wrote to her uncle and aunt on her mother's behalf as her mother could no longer put pen in hand. Sarah wrote that they *"were disappointed not to have been able to see Luke[7] last winter as he went through on his way to Boston. Her brother, Robert, did see him for a moment at the Tavern as the "Stage" passed through, so no time spent with him. My mother [also a Sarah] would still very much like to visit them in Canada and it would give her so much pleasure and satisfaction to meet her only brother [Edmund[6]] once more in her life. My mother says that she would very much like to see where her father [Edmund[5]] spent his last days and where his natural kindred have been residing."* Sarah wrote that she did not think it probable that her mother would be able to undertake such a long journey, given her advanced age. *"[Signed] Sarah."* [10]

> *Author's note: The letter exemplifies the separation of families during these times and the strong longing to reunite. The roads were poor and travel difficult so the only way to reach out with news was by letter. Many of these letters were still carried by people travelling from one place to another.*

***

During the 1830s cholera epidemics were affecting both sides of the Atlantic, and Grosse-Île was established as a quarantine station to inspect all ships coming to Quebec. Due to its strength and widespread use in the settlements, common homemade lye soap made by our ancestors likely helped curb the spread of cholera.

The menfolk in this early Maple Leaf community were all good hunters; however, some made hunting and trapping a business. Although there were a few panthers, wolves were numerous and continued to cause losses in lambs, calves, turkeys, chickens and geese. However, bears continued to be the most destructive. Often large domestic animals, yearlings and sometimes colts were killed by bears in the pastures. Most of the settlers kept a few sheep – mainly kept for the wool, and when old, mutton for stew – that remained a choice target for the wolves. The government at this time offered a large bounty on bears and wolves, which helped control the number of these destructive animals.[24]

Our ancestor, John[7] Bennett Heard, trapped beaver, mink, fox and rabbits, and provided the furs to make clothing for their families. Any excess served well to sell or barter for other necessary staples. There were large tracts of land created by beaver dams in the area that provided excellent trapping. When the beavers were trapped out the lands were ideal to drain. Left vacant for three or four years, the settlers began to cultivate an extraordinarily rich soil. The new land produced well, and after the first few years of labour, grain was usually in abundance.

Bedstead frame from John Bennett and Poly Heard home (photo by John Hurd)

"Wiccopee," a member of the willow family, is found only at the edges of hardwood forests. From these bushes, John would make a small cut at the top of a branch, which allowed him to peel strands off the full length of the bush. These strands were virtually impossible to tear against the grain and thus were perfect for fashioning ropes. The end of a strand could be woven to another, allowing long lengths of extraordinarily strong rope of any size. Our ancestors used these wiccopee strands and ropes for a multitude of purposes, including handles on boxes or dresser drawers, shoelaces, and snowshoes. Another use, as shown in the photograph, was to make a mesh for their beds instead of slats. This mesh would serve to support the harvested straw they would put in flour bags to make mattresses. For more comfort, Polly also used the leaves from beech trees as a mix with the straw. The bed in the photograph on the page opposite was inherited by John Alan Hurd and was an original bed in the house of John B.[7] and Poly (Sawyer) Heard.

The sap from the wiccopee bush served as an excellent laxative. Willow trees themselves were abundant in the lowlands around the rivers and swamps; their leaves were boiled down to a strong tea for use in the treatment of extreme headaches caused by measles.

During this era of no running water in the house, most bedrooms were equipped with a basin and pitcher of water, set on a dresser known as a washstand. They might use this convenience for washing up before bed or in the morning. Most of the men wore beards but if they did shave, it was usually done at the outside kitchen basin.

Watering the animals was a chore as there was no running water in the barns either. In earlier days the settlers would have to go to a spring, where water bubbled out of the ground, or to a river to "hand-pail" their water. Even in this time they continued to fashion troughs to bring water closer to their buildings. They had wooden barrels to receive the running water and then would pail the water from these barrels. The water ran continuously through the barrels to keep it from freezing in winter. Early houses and barns were built at a lower elevation than the springs to allow gravity to feed water to the buildings.

***

Splitting shingles with a froe and hand-crafted mallet
(P. Follansbee)

When John[7] Bennett Hurd and Polly built their first house of spruce logs, they were able to use shingles for the roofing. The final touches in homebuilding were homemade shingles (a.k.a. shakes). Making these shingles required a specialized tool called the "froe" or shake axe; an L-shaped tool with a long, narrow, rectangular steel blade head set at a right angle to a short wooden handle, called a "half." Unlike an axe, the froe can be placed exactly where the user would like the split to begin. This enables the user, even one with relatively little skill or experience, to have enough precision in his work that shingles of uniform dimension could be cut. Just as important, froes are far safer to use than a splitting axe. After a bit of practice, even an unskilled individual could make a few dozen well-crafted shingles in an hour. The froe became a vital tool to help the settlers create adequate shelters for cabins and homes. The most important part of making shingles was not the labour itself but finding the right material. Shingles had to be made from blocks of straight-grained timber, and cedar was prime material. Once a straight-grained tree was located, it was cut into 24- to 36-inch lengths using a crosscut handsaw.[42]

Using a froe, a settler could make enough shakes to cover a roof in as little as a day. By now the older boys of the Heard families, Augustus, Cyrus, Edmund[8] and Luke's two sons, Samuel and George, were often pressed into service making shingles. They would make enough to trade to other settlers within the Maple Leaf community of Newport. To make a shingle, the edge of the froe blade would be hammered into the end of one of the blocks along the grain. When the blade is driven in, level with the end of the bolt, you pull or push the half, using it as a lever to multiply the force and split the wood wider. The froe is then pushed down another three to six inches. Twist the handle again and the shingle pops off. At this time, shingles began to be used to cover the sides of the homes, as board lumber was becoming available from sawmills at Kilbourne Mills, Vt., Island Brook, Newport, and Sawyers Mills in Eaton Township.

***

On his infrequent trips home to the New England Colonies, John B.[7] would try to visit as many of his aunts, uncles and cousins as he could. They were always anxious to hear news from his father, Capt. Edmund[6], and what life was like up in Lower Canada. They welcomed him into their homes and plied him with more food than he could possibly eat. Each family made sure he met the children born since his last visit, so he could take this news back home. Sugar and flour bags, common in the New England Colonies, were washed and bleached and made into pillowcases or tea cloths, trimmed with colourful embroidery. It was during this time in the New England states that the flour companies, recognizing that most women were saving the bags, decided to make them really colourful. Sure enough, the most colourful bags were the ones they bought. Competition waged between the producers as to whose bags would be most in demand. Flour? Who cares! On one of his trips, the women gave John these new bags to take home with him. These colourful bags would have caused a sensation in Newport at the time, giving a much-needed boost to the morale of the households.[10]

***

Most of the floors in the stable part of the barns, up to this era, were still hard-packed dirt with stacked flat stone walls. These stables were a dark, dingy and mouldy environment, usually with small windows situated at the top of the walls. The settlers soon began covering the stable floors with elm, an extremely hard wood which was abundant in Newport. The lumber, when fashioned in hewn planks, was the perfect wood for cattle and horse stalls. It had a hardiness and toughness that allowed for the constant movement of their domestic animals' feet without wearing out. They also began using elm to make floor-style platforms to cover the packed dirt in the cellars of their homes. Elm wood was also found to withstand the rigours of lumber sleds extremely well. It was also used extensively for "stoneboats" and floorboards for "buckboard" wagons.

***

In this era, the horse-drawn buckwagon replaced oxen (Newport Homecoming 1801-1996)

Edmund[7], John B[7], Luke[7], Samuel[7] and their sons who were now old enough to drive the horses found that indeed gravel was preferable to mud for the roads, and would draw gravel from the riverbeds. Usually after the spring freshet there would be a beach of gravel to the lee of each bend in the river which offered this great opportunity. They also found great banks of gravel further out from the riverbeds, suggesting the river flows were much larger in more ancient times. Steel-rimmed wagon wheels were now used on wagons they called "buckboards" to haul gravel. These wagons were constructed using wide hardwood elm planks, each hand-hewn using an adze, laid lengthwise across the width of the wagon; two similar boards positioned on each end and the sides. To make a load they would shovel the gravel by hand from the river side onto the bed of the wagon. The boards were not fastened down for a reason which was quite intuitive.

When they reached their destination, John and Luke would position themselves at each end of the buckboard. They would each grasp one end of the unfastened board and turn it, releasing that board of gravel. They would repeat this procedure with each board until the wagon was empty. An inherent negative to this loose board hauling was that the sand would slowly filter through the boards during travel, leaving only coarse gravel and rock for the roadbed. In most cases this type of gravel served the purpose best: the roads were just paths of mud; the course gravel would sink into the mud and ultimately make for a better roadbed. The men found that a layer of gravel was perfect when added to the corduroy sections of the roads through the swamps, creating a much-improved ride.

Many of the old roads were surfaced with gravel from the original Edmund[5] Heard farm, which by this time was the Luke[7] Heard farm. They retrieved ample gravel from a natural gravel bar in the meadow on his farm. Edmund had built a road from the gravel pit up to the farm buildings, which at that time was a relatively easy climb for the horses. It seemed that no matter how much of this stony gravel was put on the roads, the spring thaw would eventually turn the roads back into mud.

During this time and pretty much until the First World War, the wheelwright was as essential to this life as a blacksmith was to everyday living. Wagon wheels, including the steel band surrounding the wheel, needed constant repair. The wheel jack in the photograph, a hand-built tool of invention that would have been contrived differently in almost every community, was entirely created by the person on the spot. Broken spokes were so common that almost every village now had a wheelwright or at least a blacksmith who also dabbled in wheel repair. John Phelps and his group of men in Grove Hill were such tradesmen. During this era John had expanded his blacksmith business, employing several men specifically in the trade of a wheelwright, all working on both wagons and lumber sleds.

When John needed to make a wheel rim, he usually sawed it out of an oak, elm or maple plank, the pattern outlined so that the pieces would form a complete wheel when put together with pins and dowels. The half-circle pieces they used give us an indication of the immense size of the virgin trees our ancestors were still cutting during this era. He then used a spoke auger to bore the hole to fit the spoken in the rim. Then next step, called "ironing off," was fitting a metal rim over

Wheelwright removing a wheel to repair – if you don't have a wagon jack, you make one (*Handy Farm Devices*, 1910)

the wooden rim. John would measure a bar of metal for size, then heat the bar and pass it through rollers of the tire (rim) bender to obtain the desired shape. He then welded together the two loose ends. The "tire" was then heated until it was almost white hot, then dropped into position over the wooden wheel. The rim sometimes would burst into flame, but before any damage occurred, his men poured water over it and as the metal contracted, a very tight fit was ensured over the wood. The men might use three different kinds of wood, depending on the availability. In a perfect world, elm or maple would be used to make the hub or "nave," their interwoven grain making it resistant to splitting.

When available, ash was preferred for creating "felloes," sled runners that could be substituted for the wheels on a wagon for winter use. They would be fit over the same hub as the wheels and secured with the same large washer and nut. The sled runners were made in the same general way as wagon wheels, the steel being hot-fit over the wooden runners. The same concept was applied to wood-hauling lumber sleds. When placing the wheel on a wagon, the axles were lubricated with a mixture of tallow, pine tar and lard. Because horses were becoming more predominant in pulling wagons, and were much faster than oxen, wood-on-wood wheels-to-axles would burn out because of the heat, and now blacksmiths were beginning to make metal axles and hubs, which were much more durable.

Note in the photograph above that the front wheels are smaller than the rear wheels. The methodology behind this was twofold. The front wheels needed to be able to turn on its centre fulcrum and, for a tight turn, would need to pass under the box. The larger wheels in the rear allowed the wagon to run over rough terrain more smoothly and made it easier for the team of oxen or horses to pull. The larger the wheels the smoother the ride for the load and their riders. The heavier part of the load was always placed towards the rear of the wagon. The front wheels generally had 12 spokes and the rear wheels 14-16 spokes; the spokes bearing the greatest load pressures broke most often. The most common repair made by wheelwrights was spoke replacement. They used a "spokeshave" to shave the spokes to size. Every farmer would have one of these tools fashioned by hand at their own farm's blacksmith shop.

To enlarge a hole, the men reamed it with a tapered blade to ensure the hole was tapered to match the hub. Often, as when one is cutting a barrel bunghole or wheel hub hole, a reamer was needed to ensure a matching working piece. The biggest of all the reamers was the wheelwright's hub reamer, often 3 feet long and weighing as much as 25 pounds. Some of these can still be found without handles and with strange hooks. Oddly enough, experts have not decided just how these hooks were used. When the men rigged up a wagon wheel on a wheelwright's bench, they put a hooked reamer through the hub, which they weighted down with 75-lb. bags of rock.

With two men turning a very long detachable handle (which might explain the missing handles on so many of these blades), it worked nicely. With an ordinary reamer, a man exerts about half his weight downward, however, this can be better served by adding a 75-pound weight to the 25-pound weight of the tool itself. Tap auger and hub reamers were usually sharpened on the inner side of one blade. *(Courtesy of Royce Rand, Compton County Museum Society)*

***

In April 1828, Commanding Officer Lieut. Col. W. B. Telton of the 5th Battalion, Buckingham Militia, again called for an annual roll of the men of the Township of Newport in Reserve. A letter in a general order addressed to Lt. Ensign Edmund[7] Heard related: *"that the Commanding Officer had not yet received the annual Rolls of the Militia as directed by the ordinances to be returned to him by the reflective Captains of Companies, directs all Officers in Command to make their reports immediately."* [3]

The 1828 Militia Roll listed 29 married men of Newport that could be mustered for duty to the Crown. By an order of Ensign Edmund[7] Heard: *"Order number 8, all men are to appear on Newport Common Ground, for military duty on this day as the law directs, [Signed] Samuel A. Heard., County Treasurer and Justice of the Peace."* Included in these names were: *Artemas[7] and Marshall S. Rand, John B[7], Samuel A., Edmund[7], Jeremiah, Edmund[8], Wilder, Henauder, and Henry Heard/Hurd, Ancob, Charles and Ancel Annibal, Garfield Woodward, Jeffrey, Yovick and Amherst Maynard, James Patterson, Silas, John, William and Edmund Harvey, John McGuire, Francis Orofetd, Paul Perceval, Paul Phelps, Neater Williams, Rufus Sawyer, and Daniel Sunbury.* The men ranged from 12 to 52 years old. It was not uncommon during this era for a muster to occur from time to time to ensure they had men ready and willing to go to battle if called. It appeared to be important to know who was married and who was not; and of those listed, who may be of an age where other duties could be assigned to them other than at the battlefront.[3]

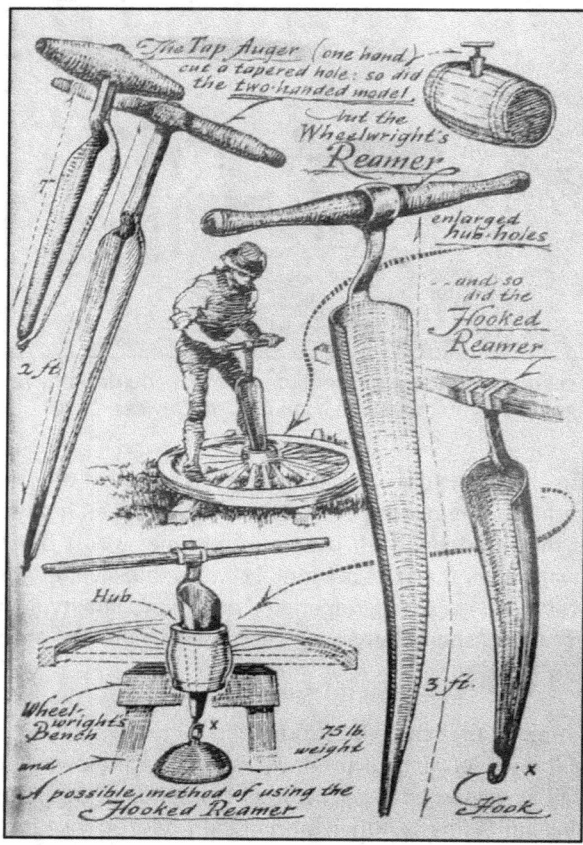

Artist's conception of typical wheelwright tools (photo by Sandra Hurd)

William[5] Heard died in 1829, leaving his wife Thirza and their youngest son, Jeremiah (age 20) and daughters Statira (17) and Lois (15) still living with her at the homestead. Her older son Wilder and Jeremiah had both been on the Newport Militia call of 1828, as noted above. William[5] Heard was the last of the three original first Heard settlers in Newport. He is buried in Maple Leaf Cemetery, headstone 5 in Row 3. He had set aside this land from his homestead as burial grounds for the community of Maple Leaf in 1804-06. Thirza and their children continued living on the original homestead until the children eventually married and moved on. Thirza sold the homestead to William G.[2] and Jennete (Planche) Heard and went to live with her son Jeremiah "Jerry" and daughter-in-law Abigail after they had moved to Barnston, Lower Canada, circa 1855.[18]

Edmund[7] was promoted from ensign to captain in 1831, the document bearing the "Great Seal of Canada" signed by Matthew Whitworth-Alymer, His Excellency Lord Aylmer, *"Knight Commander of the Most Honorable Military Order of the Bath, Captain-General and Governor in Chief in and over the Province of Lower-Canada, &c. &c. &c."* or, in today's language, the Governor-General of Canada.[24] Following this and during the 1837 Rebellion, when the French attempted to overthrow the Canadian Government and burned the Parliament Buildings in Montreal, Edmund[7] Heard was stationed at Fort Chambly, as a captain in the local militia. There was also heavy fighting in the Napierville area (just west of the Richelieu River) where homes and farm buildings were plundered and burned. The rebels were soon defeated and captured by the regular army. Many other men from the Eastern Townships region volunteered to fight for the government. Once again, this was a skirmish that called for the involvement of one or more of the Newport families.[3]

***

In 1833, the newly formed British American Land Company (BALC) soon purchased extensive land in the Eastern Townships from the Crown. The company was now establishing the available land lots that had not yet been assigned in the surveyed townships. The goal was to sell parcels of land for profit to settlers coming from the British Isles. BALC stipulations were that all "Lots" must have a "Grant Certificate" of proof, either granted or otherwise purchased; and if not, the lots were open for purchase.[16]

This was also a time when the governing bodies wished to attract more settlers to the lands. David Thompson, originally a fur trader and by then a highly accomplished surveyor, had taken on the job as surveyor in 1833 for the BALC. David arrived in the area around 1834 to explore and survey its newly acquired lands in Lower Canada, expressly in the region of the Eastern Townships. David was 64 when he came to explore the Townships and had already retired from the West where he had explored and charted nearly one-fifth of the North American continent. David had also worked from 1817 to 1829 as the principal surveyor for Britain on the International Boundary Commission.[27]

This new exploration brought David Thompson through Newport Township while surveying the Township of Ditton. On May 27, 1834, he had trusted the map he had been given to take him and his party close to the Ditton and Hampton township line. In his calculations as to where he was, however, he was surprised to find that the river they had taken landed them on the east side at an old Indigenous peoples' path. They had indeed advanced to within seven miles of Ditton's west line and about 15 miles from Capt. Edmund[7] Heard's home near the southwest corner of Newport.[27]

> *Author's note: To clarify page 62 of this reference, "Captain Edmund[7] Heard was the grandson of Col. Edmund[5] Heard, who had received the Land Grants in Newport in 1801," not the "son" as referenced.*[4]

David had received a letter dated June 2, 1834, from the office of the BALC, *advising him that his supplies had been sent to Mr. Heards.* After a month of exploration of the Company lands in Ditton and Megantic, David Thompson once again found himself close to Newport and proceeded on July 3 to retrieve his supplies, which he had been advised had been shipped and left with Edmund[7] Heard in Newport. They found the same old Indigenous path that our ancestors had taken following northwest arriving at a branch of the North River. At six o'clock in the evening they came across a clearing of farmers' land in Newport Township and heard the sound of a cow bell – the most welcome music to their ears. This was part of the original settlement of the Maple Leaf community where Col. Edmund[5], his brother William[5], Samuel[6], Edmund[6], their families and their sons John B.[7] and Edmund[7] had all settled earlier.[27]

The next day, on July 4, 1834, David and his survey party arrived early at Edmund Heard's farm, where they were put up for a few days. This farm was located at the junction, known today as Route 210 and Morrison Road, leading west to the Auckland town line. Three of his men were dispatched to meet the mail wagon that afternoon in Eaton with his documentation for the company. He asked Edmund for some men to help him get his equipment back from Ditton. Edmund advised him that the very next day he expected 30 to 40 men to be arriving to help erect a large barn and that perhaps some of them might be available.[27]

On Monday, July 7, a hot and sultry day, David Thompson with two other men and Edmund Heard as guide trudged through the wilderness to identify for David the "Post Markings" in Newport which separated the township lines of Auckland, Emberton and Ditton. They travelled "about eight miles eastward of this place, which is necessary to be known, as the point of departure to survey the Company's lands (BALC) in the west part of Emberton and the south part of Auckland." After settling with Mr. Heard, they set off in the wagon for Lennoxville, passing through Eaton and Ascot. They noted that the land in Newport has the strongest soil, a rich brown loam.[27]

***

The second immigration of the Bowker Family to Newport:[20, 32]

> *Author's note: This segment will introduce Solomon, Johnathon, Lucy, and Lyman Bowker. It will also introduce Lucy's sons, Orra and Eliphalet Lyon, who came to live in Newport at different times.*

The Bowker family of Gideon[6] and Hannah (Fletcher) Bowker had finally moved north from Guildford, Vt., with their family of seven children, to Lunenburg, Vt., in 1796, a town situated near the Connecticut River, where there was ample work in the lumbering business. They raised two more children in Lunenburg, born between 1799 and 1804, and were now a family of nine children. Three of their boys were destined to find their way to Newport to start a new life there. Solomon[7] (age 18) and Johnathon[7] "John" (age 16) were the first in the family to make the move to Lower Canada. They made the trip from Lunenburg, Vt., following the Connecticut River north through Lake Francis and the two Connecticut Lakes, arriving in Newport through the Indian Stream path. They signed their application for land grants in Newport in 1799. Their signatories are evidenced in the *Newport firſt Records, 1800*, and acknowledged by the signed document of the Committee Regulators, Capt. Samuel[6] Heard, William Hudson and John Lebourveau.[20]

A daughter, Lucy Bowker, born in 1786 in Guildford, married a John[7] Lyon in Lunenburg. They raised two sons, Orra and Eliphalet, who later also found their way to Newport. Orra would build a mill in the Island Brook region.

A younger son, Lyman[7] James Bowker, also born in Guilford, in 1794, married Betsey Merriam in 1818, in Lunenburg, Vt., where they raised five children: Louisa Adeline (born 1820), Lewis[8] Leander (born 1821), Hubbard William (born 1824), Charles Bingham (birth year unknown) and Sarah Jane (born 1834). Lyman and his family had done well in the lumber trade in Lunenburg. Perhaps they saw the opportunity that the lumbering business had to offer in this new territory in Lower Canada. The lumber from virgin timber shipped from Canada was in great demand in the rapidly growing New England states. Lyman[7] James Bowker was 40 years old and 13 years younger than his brother Johnathon when he immigrated to Newport with his wife Betsey and their family of five in 1834. They settled on the same lots his older brothers, Solomon[7] and Johnathon[7], had begun to clear earlier.

Previously entered into the *Firſh Records of Newport* in order to create a system for *"Keeping and maintaining good order & understanding of the recording of the land lots among the inhabitants of Newport, as being read by the Clerk during subsequent meetings, the inhabitants unanimously voted to accept of the said Committees' Regulations & ordered the same to be recorded."* [20]

The meeting was held, and on September 28, 1799:

> *the Associated Applicants of the Township of Newport signed an agreement containing three articles, outlining the rules pertaining to the granting of lots assigned by a committee of three, Samuel Heard, William Hudson and John Lebourveau.*
>
> *Article 2. That each associated Applicant or any other person who shall have sufficient Voucher & pitcheth or taketh up any Lot of Land in said Newport shall immediately make return of the number of the Lot which they so pitch or take up and the no. of the Range in which said lot is situated to the Clerk who shall Record the same in a book containing the Regulations of the Association & give a Certificate of the same to the person making such return upon the payment of one Shilling& three pence, Quebec currency, which shall be a sufficient pay for keeping the Records of said Association. The Certificate shall be allowed to be a sufficient security against any depredations committed by any other persons and that shall not be considered as having any pretentions to any particular Lot in said Township until a return be made to the Clerk. That the person having applied shall be allowed one month & no longer to renew their pretention to take a Certificate of said Lot and if no Certificate be granted, the Lot shall be deemed Vacant.* [20]

These regulations had been drawn up to accommodate the original Land Grant Obligations of 1799, which had now been incorporated into the new BALC regulations. These regulations were now being brought forward to identify those potentially abandoned lots, in accordance with the original grants that were assigned. Lots that had been abandoned were recorded as such, and reassigned so the BALC would now be able to sell them for profit.

> *Author's note: I cannot find evidence that Solomon and Johnathon (John) Bowker's lots were indeed the same lots that were abandoned by Peter Trueman. However, the signature of Solomon Bowker appears on the application to the above regulations, indicating that Solomon, for one, had the opportunity to claim one or more of those lots, and likely did so. There are no further records that Johnathon (John) stayed in Newport after 1816. However, Solomon appears to have remained in Newport as evidenced from later documents*

that he had signed a few years before he might have also returned to New England. There is sufficient evidence to suggest that the two brothers likely built a cabin to live in and cleared part of at least one of their lots while working on the various roads, as evidenced in several supporting records.[20]

The fact that their younger brother, Lyman[7] James Bowker, settled on two of these same lots would indicate that this would have likely been the case. Lyman would have heard about the lots from his brothers, Solomon and John, when one or the other returned to Luneburg, Vt. There is sufficient evidence to suggest that the certificates they had indicating ownership also would have been passed to Lyman, the lots claimed at the time of his family's arrival.

There had been speculation that a road would be opened up from Maple Leaf Cemetery, north to the boundary of Range 8, connecting through Range 9 to the more northern quarter lots that had been assigned to Longley Willard, Peter Trueman, Edmund[6] Heard, William Heard, William Hudson, Sam Hudson and John Squires.

The community had contemplated building a "bye road" to connect the Maple Leaf community to the growing community to its north. Oxen were able to navigate the hill on Grove Hill Road out of Randville (Grove Hill) but horses could not. A bye road direct from Maple Leaf Cemetery north to North River Road posed no problem and was easily accessible. However, when the BALC took over all road building they opted to extend the road (today's Route 210) up past the 10th range and on toward North River Road, simply because it opened up more settlement along that route.[20]

It was during this time that settlement became noticeable in the northwestern part of Newport. Until the BALC built bridges in Sawyerville and Cookshire, circa 1826, residents of those towns also had to ford the rivers. During the spring freshet, the settlers were virtually cut off from supplies they would normally have retrieved at these centres. Building these bridges would ultimately give this section of Newport direct access to Sawyerville and Cookshire, both in Eaton Township. The northern quarter of Newport, under the direction of Col. Edmund[5] Heard, was inaccessible to the southern section for some time, leaving Grove Hill Road as the only access. The inhabitants were exploring the terrain for a better route from the Maple Leaf community to the northern part of Newport. The residents of Grove Hill and the community that was beginning to flourish in Maple Leaf would continue to have to travel for some time up the Grove Hill Road during the spring months when the river was raging. Also, the hill was an ongoing problem, hence the discussion of a bye road.

A meeting of the Associates in 1807 is confirmed as evidenced below:[20]

> *At another previous meeting of the Associates on Friday, the 26th day of June, 1807 it was voted on the 1st Article, Edmund Heard Sr. act as moderator and 2nd Article, it was resolved that the whole house be a Committee to take under consideration the situation of certain Roads in the Township of Newport & point out a method of opening & making them in future. 3rd Article, voted that Messrs. John and Solomon Bowker, Sam Hudson and Wm. Williams be a Committee to mark out & determine where a Bye Road will accommodate the said Messrs. Bowker's, Hudson's, and William's to travel into the main Road near the school common.[20]*

> *The Committee reported on Article 3, on June 29th, that the Road to accommodate Messrs. Bowker, Hudson and Williams shall commence or begin at the post of lot No 7 & 8 in the 10th Range Line & continue Northward on the line of division between them so far as the Northwest corner of Mr. Sam & B. Hudson's present improvements & thence on the West side of the Ledge so called in a convenient direction to Messrs. Bowker's, agreed by unanimous vote to establish same as an open Bye Road.* [20, 31]

This documentation would lead us to conclude that both Solomon[7] and Johnathon[7] Bowker indeed had acquired those lots at the earlier date of 1799.

And so, Lyman[7] and Betsey Bowker with their family of five (three boys and two daughters, the youngest, Sarah Jane, a baby), all born in Lunenburg, Vt, arrived in Newport in 1834, settling on lots 3 and 4 of Range 7 on North River Road. These were the lots that Peter Trueman had originally been assigned in 1797, as an Associate under Col. Edmund[5] Heard. As one of the original Associates applying for land grants in Newport at that time, Peter had been assigned lots 1, 3, 4, 5, 7 and 8 of Range 7. Peter and his heirs had abandoned his application for these lots sometime between 1797 and 1799. Without a certificate they would have been deemed vacant, and so were reassigned to the younger Bowker boys.

What a scene it would have presented if we could envision the landscape as it unfolded during this family's progress up the Connecticut River that summer in 1834! As they followed the shores of the Connecticut River, emerging from the narrows at Coos Junction, they would have entered the broader expanse of water moving slowly downriver through the towering highlands of the Blue Mountains to the east. They would have passed the spectacular rugged grandeur of the Monadnock Mountains to the west where the full glory of the Beaver Brook Falls would have burst upon them near where Colebrook stands today.[44]

A view of where Col. Edmund[5] Heard first settled in Newport Township (photo by Sandra Hurd)

As they crossed into lower Canada, the view would have drawn their attention as they continued through the valley, the mountains on each side offering a breathtaking view before them. Excited but exhausted, the family would have seen many scenes that would be replaced by another of even greater beauty as they continued on through Clifton/Auckland townships. Imagine their excitement when looking over to the east at the valley towards their destination, perhaps anticipating where they would be settling in the Township of Newport. His family might have been reliving his older brothers' stories from a few years prior when they too had travelled this same path. This photo represents what one would see driving north on the Clifton-Auckland Road today. The scene in 1834 would have been virgin forests as far as the eye could see, except for a small clearing where the current highway to Maple Leaf is barely visible in the photo.[44]

Of course, alternatively, one might imagine that this trip may have been just the opposite if the weather was rainy, cold and foggy. The oxen might have been plodding through mud and the wagon wheels getting stuck in the bogs. Rain could have been pelting down and mosquitoes feasting on them while camping along the trail. They could have experienced their clothes wet with no way to dry them and perhaps food running scarce. This trip could have been an arduous, extremely slow voyage in which they really didn't or couldn't take in any scenery.

Lyman and his family began clearing their land and built their cabin in the summer of that same year. The following spring Lyman and his eldest son Lewis[8] returned to Lunenburg with his oxen to bring back some pigs, a riding horse and other livestock, including a Holstein bull to begin a herd of Holstein milking cows. That summer he used his lumbering skills and began to harvest the virgin forest that surrounded him to build suitable housing for his family and for their livestock.

They raised pigs for pork, which was usually packed in brine. Salt pork was a staple on the pioneer supper table and was as important as any other food for the family. Pork and beans and turnip soup with a piece of salt pork for flavour made the meals much more palatable. They used pork fat for greasing the axles on their oxen carts and the turnbuckles on their lumber sleds. They used tallow for candles, although pig tallow was not deemed the most desirable for candle use simply because it was smelly – but it would do in a pinch if needed.

Using three-tined pitchfork to bundle hay in a field of stumps (Newport Homecoming 1801-1996)

***

Newport Township now had five communities: Maple Leaf, Randville, New Mexico, Learned Plain and Island Brook. Maple Leaf, the centre of a farming community, now had daily mail service. Randville (previously referred to as Grove Hill) was a small village with a gristmill, a store, and a post office. In 1832 Artemas[6] Rand passed on his share in the mill to his son Artemas[7] D. Rand. That same year Nathanial[1] Beaman Jr. divested himself of his share of the mill, which Artemas[7] purchased for his son Gardner[8] "Stillman." Later in his life, Stillman Rand expanded the gristmill, circa 1860-65, to include a sawmill.

That same year one of Nathanial Beaman's sons, Jonas[2] F., also divested his family landholdings of part of Lot 10 in the 10th Range in Newport. Jonas sold 50 acres to John[7] B. and Polly (Sawyer) Heard; this was adjacent to their own Lot 9, resulting in an addition to their own homestead. The other half of this partial Lot 10 of Range 10 on the north end was owned by his sister Eliza Beaman. Jonas Beaman and family moved to Shipton Township in Lower Canada and purchased a farm there.[31]

New Mexico and Learned Plain, in the northern part of Newport, were predominantly farming communities, both edging on the Borough of Island Brook. New Mexico was centred in Newport just southeast of Island Brook and encompassed ranges 6 and 7. Learned Plain was northwest of Island Brook and encompassed ranges 2, 3, 4 and 5, located not far from the railway junction in Cookshire.

It was through Alden Learned's efforts that the roads from Cookshire to and through Learned Plain, including the road to Island Brook, were first built. On the road continuing through to Ditton Township is a small stream called Christmas Brook, so named by the road surveyors on having reached this brook on Christmas Day. The roads were really no more than logging roads when extended beyond the communities they served.[32]

It was circa 1830-34, after the schoolhouse was built in Island Brook, when roads were improved and bridges were built. This was prompted by a wave of new settlers who began to arrive in the northwestern region of Newport. The schoolhouse in Island Brook was built of logs, located near the town hall on Lot 10 of Range 6. Children attended this school and continued to attend, after it was expanded, until 1878-80. These first schools were sometimes referred to as "grammar schools" with perhaps only two classes, the teacher focusing on the basics of reading, writing and arithmetic. These early schoolhouses were small log cabins, perhaps housing only a smattering of children local to the settlement. The boys would sit on one side of an aisle and the girls on the other. The classes were sometimes divided into "A" and "B," where the two classes might be pitted against each other and questioned about what each class had been studying. This activity would enhance their grammar exercises, keeping everyone on their toes, much like a spelling bee.[24]

Many of the children would be in bare feet during the summer as shoes were scarce, especially for growing children. Both shoes and boots would always be passed down to the smaller children as the family grew. "Sometimes other children with shoes would step on the bare toes of those with none, causing much friction." The children would have to dodge cow patties on their way to school through the fields, and if the roads had gravel on them, they would walk on the grassy edge as they made their way to school.[24]

Author's note: The original schoolhouse established in the Maple Leaf community circa 1804-06 is currently located on Tannahill Road off Grove Road on the property of Michael Lister. Although some online sources indicate a schoolhouse in Island Brook was the first schoolhouse in Newport, that one was actually built later, circa 1834-35.[31]

***

The fifth son of Edmund[6] Heard was Samuel[7] Andrews Heard, born in 1815 in Newport. Samuel married Catherine Hubbard, a sister of Luke's wife Persis. (The Hubbard family were living in Stanstead, Lower Canada.) In their late teens, Sam had gone to Stanstead to further his education while Luke had worked in the mill. Sam and Cathy raised five children in Newport, three daughters and two sons: Edward Payson (born 1838), Ellen Corilla (born 1840), Lucy Jane (born 1845, died at age 26), Laura Ann (born 1848) and Samuel[8] Augustine (born 1850).[4]

Samuel[7] A. would serve as chairman of the school committee for Eaton Township. He owned a farm at Eaton Corner and became an elder in the Congregational Church at Eaton. His general merchandise store "proved a fairly successful venture" and he was instrumental in "providing a percentage of funds to support education in the Maple Leaf School." Over time, he had acquired a good property and owned much valuable real estate.[4]

It was Samuel who compiled the manuscript of family history corresponding with Augustine[7] Heard of the Ipswich branch of the family. His works were entered in the "Heard Coat of Arms" booklet containing some 45 pages. Many of his musings are now in the possession of the author. The following is an extract from that correspondence:[11]

> *I was cast upon the world without resources except what I found in my own breast and being fond of study left home where I had enjoyed little or no privileges for mental improvement & commenced study with an eye to the ministry, but my health & eyes failed me and I was forced to relinquish study. I then with my brother Luke (Luke had inherited the farm in Newport from his father Edmund[6]), bought a small farm and I continued at that three years, and my inclination leading me to some other employment I went into a store as clerk where I served 3 years for a small salary barely enough to support myself & family, since which time I have been the acting partner in a small retail business here.*[11]

Contrary to his humble musings, Samuel was successful.

A school subscription was made to support a teacher for the Maple Leaf School on December 2, 1833:

> *This may certify, To Whom It May Concern, that for the support of a school for the term of three months in this town, the ensuing winter, we the subscribers do agree to pay for the number of scholars hereinafter affixed to our names and all that we send over. Furthermore, we do agree to hire Matilda French and give her 5% per week out of the stores general profit at Eaton Corner, provided she gives satisfaction to the majority of the subscribers for the above stated term. Signed by the parents, Jeremiah E. Heard, one student, Edmund Heard, three students, Daniel Sunbury, three students, William Heard one student and Peter G. Sawyer, one student.* [31]

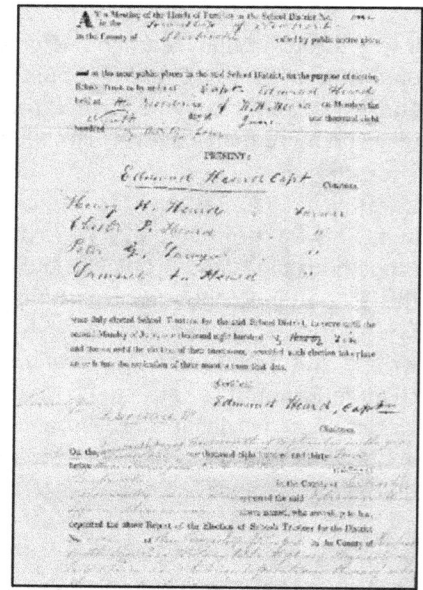

At a meeting of the Heads of Families in School District No. 1, held at the residence of Henry Hershel Heard (Samuel[6] and Miriam Heard's eldest son) on June 9, 1834, Notice was given by Capt. Edmund[6] Heard, Chairman, for the election of school trustees. They were *"Henry[7] H Heard, Farmer, Chester[7] P Heard, Farmer, Peter[6] G Sawyer, Farmer and Samuel[7] A Heard, Farmer, to serve until the second Monday of June 1836."* [31]

Maple Leaf school subscription

Parents in this era knew the importance of literacy. They took it upon themselves to teach their children that education was important and that they needed to study at home as well as at school. Earlier generations were brought up with the boys learning how to make things and the basics of hard work while the young ladies learned the basics of homemaking. In this era, however, parents encouraged both boys and girls to learn reading and writing as basic skills. The children were made to understand they had to study if they wanted to compete with other children when it was time for them to attend school. It was at this time that George Parkin, a Canadian, created the famous world map on which all the lands the British Commonwealth had control over were shown in red; some seven million square miles. As a "Mercator projection" map, northern and southern regions appeared larger than the equatorial zone, which translated into a sprawling Canada, accounting for a disproportionate but impressive expanse of red. England's Cadbury Chocolate Company sent thousands of Parkin's maps, printed with its name and logo, to schools throughout the Empire. Scholars during this era would have grown up with the notion that Canada was the largest country in North America in size.

Generations of Newport and adjacent township students were schooled in classrooms where the large map, typically on a side wall, enabled alluring geography lessons and daydream fantasies. "One can imagine that most Canadians subliminally learned that the British Empire and Cadbury were synonymous, which they effectively were, because imperial and commercial exploitation were entwined as one, the prime rationale for having colonies." *(J. Patrick Boyer, writer, journalist and P. C. Member of Parliament, 1984-1993)*

In early years the school would open in May, since the school was not heated. This changed after stoves became popular and one could be afforded its place in a schoolhouse. Once the lessons were learned and the chores done the children could play as they wished. At this time there were 13 Heard girls, and sometimes they would all be together on a Sunday afternoon or on special occasions. They would play hide-and-seek in the barns, enjoying a great pastime with so many places to hide. One might speculate that the 10 boys in the family would be involved in aggravating the girls as much as they could in these endeavours. In the winter they might play "fox and geese" or "run sheep run," or build a snow house, or hunt for hens' nests in the barn.

It was rare for the children to visit other farms other than on a Sunday, unless they were taken by buggy or sleigh. Because of this they were quite isolated, since it would be a 2-3 mile walk each way to a neighbouring farm. So, during the week they amused themselves with ingenuity and creative activities which would serve them well in later years. They had an insatiable appetite for improving whatever they faced. As a result, as they grew older, they created new ways of doing things, engaged in time-saving ways to repair and improve existing methods – practices and innovations that would improve life not only for themselves but for future generations.

Many of our female ancestors became prematurely old and care-worn during these times; and because they were isolated, they bore a certain loneliness. Some were desperately unhappy and unable to cope with separation from family and friends, afraid of the wilderness, upset with the change in their lifestyle from their well-ordered lives they may have had in the old country or in the New England Colonies. This may explain why so many of the original settlers' daughters returned to New England to marry and live there. Some of the wives left as well, but most stayed on, implying it was "God's will." Those coming from the Old World, however, viewed their new lives in Canada as opportunistic and in most cases far better than what they had in the old country.[35]

Sarah Heard, second-eldest daughter of Edmund[6], was born in Newport and had experienced the life of pioneer farming as a child and teenager. But when Sarah became of age, perhaps she too wanted out. She moved first to Knoxville, Knox County, Ill., where she married Gardner Bartlett. They became Baptist missionaries in Chicago where they raised all their children.[31]

If a homesteader's workday was long and difficult, equally was that of their wives. One of these pioneer women's never-ending chores was washing clothes – caked with dirt and sweat; smelling of body odour, farm animals, lumber and composted hay. Worse yet, these filthy shirts, pants and undergarments all had to be washed by hand in a process more laborious than we of today can even imagine. Catherine and Persis (Luke's wife), who came from Stanstead, were not used to this. They would first have to build a fire in the yard, then haul buckets of water to the house from the well, spring, or nearby stream and pour it into a kettle to be boiled over the fire. Coming from Stanstead they must surely have wondered what they had gotten themselves into by marrying these two Heard boys. They gathered the washtubs outside, placed them away from the ever-shifting smoke, and then carried the kettle to pour the water into the wash tubs. The women added one whole cake of lye soap into the wash tub. The

Washboard and tub (Andrew Hind)

women engaged their children to help, as this was treated as part of their learning experiences in these early years.[32, 42]

Before even contemplating any washing, they would have had to make the soap. They threw scraps of pork, rinds, and fat into a barrel; when enough had accumulated, Catherine and Persis would have added the lye that had been leached from hardwood ashes. They would boil the mixture in a large iron kettle hung over a fire outside, adding a bit of tree resin to improve the consistency of the soap. Hard soap is made from this soft soap by adding a few handfuls of salt to the boiling mixture. They would leave it overnight before boiling it again, adding more resin and salt until the mixture would begin to thicken. They would then pour it into moulds for cooling.[32, 42]

The women would generally separate the clothing into three piles for washing: whites, coloured and heavily soiled work breeches. They started with the undergarments and whites first in the cleanest water, rubbing each piece on a washboard, and then placing it back into the kettle to boil. The coloured group would be next, rubbing them on the washboard, wringing each piece out and then starching them. Of course, Catherine and Persis would have made their own "starch" ahead of time too, by stirring flour into cool water until smooth and then thinning the mixture down in boiling water, setting it aside to cool and then placing the liquid in pots for storage.[32, 42]

Finally, the women would wash the dirtiest work clothes in the same water and hang everything out to dry. Then they would make use of the remaining hot soapy water to scrub down floors, washstands and of course the privy seat in the "outhouse." The tubs would be turned upside-down to dry and brought back into the home. If the washing went smoothly they might have had just enough time to prepare dinner for their husbands, Samuel and Luke and the crew, coming back from their work in the woods or fields, along with the older children.[32, 42]

> *Author's note: It is no wonder that a few of the womenfolk really longed to go back to the more advanced civilization of larger towns or back to the New England states.*

These pioneer women continued to play an important role in the family beyond that of wife and mother. They were involved in all parts of the daily running of the farm; in reality, the beginning of businesses even during these times. They were midwives, medics, teachers, accountants, chicken raisers, egg collectors and fox catchers. They were also the great protectors of the children and of course they got the men to Church, arranged the marriages, sewed the bodices, knit the socks, hemmed the trousers, tended the gardens, cooked the food, nurtured and coddled their young, and of course the babies: *(pre-birth control)* there were always more babies!

The presence of the other woman, such as mother-in-law Mary, and aunts Polly and Thirza, their older daughters along with the other wives in the community, was always a huge boost to the women in these settlements. They were all locked into an exhaustive and endless cycle of annual childbirth, a number of whom would die in childbirth. Some families would have as many as 14-19 children, but with each new arrival they would be *"the joy of my heart and the delight of my eyes."*[10]

It was not uncommon for both the men and women of this era to hold many superstitions. An accidental drop of a dishcloth on the floor was a sign of company coming. To drop a utensil might mean someone was coming by hungry; a knife meant one might expect a gentleman caller, a fork meant a lady, a spoon meant a child. An itchy nose was a warning you were to kiss a fool, and a burning ear meant someone was talking about you.[33]

Samuel[7] Andrew Hurd was born in Newport Township. Owing to the newly settled condition of the country, his opportunities for early education were extremely limited. Through his own energy, determination and indomitable perseverance, he succeeded in acquiring a good English education and some knowledge of the classics. For several years as a young man he supplemented the earnings of the farm during the winter months by teaching school, an endeavour in which he was quite successful. Circa 1840 he moved to Eaton Corner and engaged in a commercial store business, in which, with one or two interruptions, he continued until the spring of 1874 when he moved to Sherbrooke. Samuel died in Sherbrooke at 62 years of age.[31]

"Of his character as a public man, it is scarcely necessary to speak. His readiness as a writer and speaker together with his sterling business qualities and his unwavering honesty gave him a leading position in political and social movements. For years he held the position of justice of the peace, was the secretary of Compton County and, until his death, was a member and secretary of the Sherbrooke Board of Examiners. He was a deacon with the Congregational Church of Eaton for more than thirty years:

> He was superintendent of the Sunday school and in everything connected with the subject of the Gospel, at home and abroad, he invariably took a leading part. Especially in connection with the support of the cause in Eaton, his services will long be remembered as having an important influence in the perpetuity of the church in Eaton Corner. He was a great lover of plainness, depreciating everything that savoured of show and affectation. Life for him was too real and earnest to be trifled with. A man of the people and yet foremost among the people, beloved by his friends and by all.[31] *(Sherbrooke Daily Record, 1877)*

***

It was during this time when jurors were beginning to be selected from the townships. The District of Saint Francis, County Sherriff sent out notifications to Newport Township for its first call for jury duties in 1834:

List of Grand Jurors for the Township of Newport for July 1834, in the District of Saint Francis for all persons qualified to serve as Grand Jurors in the Superior Courts in criminal matters and of loyal and service refuted proprietors of real property of the yearly value of twenty-five pounds currency. [Listed as] 1. Heard Edmund 2. Rand Artemas 3. Rand Marshall. [Signed] Whitcher, Sherriff, 10 July 1834."[31]

Author's note: Marshall Rand was now 24 years old, rather older than his first call when he was only 14.

List of jurors, 1834

***

A community in the north part of Newport, just south of the Newport-Bury township line, was beginning to attract settlement. It was called Knicky Knocky, though some in the community resented this appellation so they and some others referred to it as "The Hills." The Newport side of the road was generally known as the Woods Road, leading south to Island Brook. "No one is sure just how it came to be called Knicky Knocky but according to legend, it has been said that it is because you knicky up one hill and knocky down another." Around 1836, a group of settlers with the family names Dorman, Parsons, Lawrence, Reeve, Prince, Dawson and Herring arrived and settled on lots 16, 17, 18 and 19 of Range 1.[33] *(quote: Nina (Parsons) Rowell)*

When William and Elizabeth Parsons came to Canada in 1836, they brought their four grown children: sons George, James and Stephen, and daughter Caroline. Their other six children, all married, chose to remain in the old country in Motcombe, Dorset, England.[33]

Stephen (1809-1873), their ninth child, was married in 1833 to Prudence Maidmont (1817-1896). They had one child, Louisa, also born in England, who was 2 years old when they immigrated to Newport Township. Upon arriving in April, circa 1835, they immediately took up their Lot 16A of Range 1 in Knicky Knocky. The family started building their log cabin, clearing the land, and settling in to carve their living in this new land. Stephen and Prudence had six more children (two of whom died young), raising their five children, Louisa, Caroline, Ellen Jane, Thomas William, and James Alexander, on their Knicky Knocky homestead over the next 13 years. The children were assigned to watch the few livestock while they grazed because they had no time to build fences to keep the livestock safe from wolf packs that were always prevalent at the edges of the forest. They were an industrious family who cleared the land, built their barn, and sold any excess timber to make ends meet.[33]

Newport was on the verge of receiving a particularly large influx of English speakers to Quebec, notably from Ireland, Scotland, England and Wales. Many were motivated to migrate by the Irish Potato Famine in the 1840s, representing some 60 percent of the settlers that were of Irish descent.

The letters and diaries suggest mothers of the era clearly loved their children but tended to take them for granted, much as they did with childbirth. As soon as the little ones were old enough they were taught to do simple chores around the house or left to look after their younger siblings. The younger children dressed themselves, fed the chickens, and did whatever other chores they could; older sons worked with their fathers in the fields or woods, while older daughters were responsible for spinning wool, working in the gardens, and tending to the chickens, amongst other chores. Mothers taught their daughters to sew, knit, clean, and prepare and cook various foods. Mothers often doubled as teachers when there were no schools in the immediate area, or when the weather was such that the schools were shut down, often for weeks at a time.[35]

Cradle scythe (George A. Driscoll collection, BAnQ)

After many years of using a sickle to cut hay and grasses, very slow and tedious work which required always bending over, the introduction of the scythe was a welcome invention. With the scythe they could now stand up to cut hay, but the hay would just fall loosely on the ground, requiring considerable raking. Ever creative, our early settlers came up with the "cradle scythe," consisting of a scythe to which wooden sticks were attached. Usually ironwood branches with a similar curvature as the scythe, and found along the wetlands, were selected. The bark was stripped off, and the resultant cradle was bolted to the scythe. This tool allowed grasses, hay, and grains to be cut and swathed in a single operation. The swaths were then raked with a wooden-tined rake into sheaves that were bound with strips of red willow or reeds.

It was not uncommon to name a hill or a curve in a road after a settler, particularly if they lived in close proximity to the feature, or if something unusual or unfortunate had happened there. There was "Charlie Hill" where young Charlie Prince died while felling a tree; "Crooked Hill" by the Dawson's farm where the road by-passed sharply around the hill; and "Frog Pond Hill" past a particular marshy area.[33]

***

In November 1837, only three years after the "call to arms" in 1834, a rebellion started in Upper Canada and the Lieutenant Governor called upon the local militia to assist in putting down an armed confrontation. Rebels in both Upper Canada and Lower Canada were fighting for representative government. William Lyon Mackenzie was at the head of a ragtag army of rebels, challenging the British rule of law. It was not long before his offensive was coordinated with an uprising of supporters in Lower Canada, led by Louis-Joseph Papineau, who was demanding more control over the Colonial Government. This was a time when both French- and English-speaking citizens joined together to fight against an oppressive British Colonial Administration. This was the event that essentially triggered French-Canadian nationalism in Quebec, resulting in a later exodus of English-speaking Quebecers to other parts of Canada. The issues were remarkably similar to the issues of taxation imposed by the British administration in the New England Colonies, who appeared to be unyielding in their views. That event had instigated events leading to the "Boston Tea Party" rebellion in 1777 and an exodus of United Empire Loyalists to Lower Canada.[2]

Settling In

For some of these settlers, the call to arms was thrilling. Soldiering was their business; it represented the jangle of harness, the bark of orders, acknowledgement of their officer status . . . as well as regular meals and jovial male companionship. It also meant an escape, albeit temporarily, from the backwoods and suffocating poverty. While they loved their wives, the opportunity to defend the interests of the motherland was for them irresistible. Another important reason to sign up was the stipend they would receive; earning money to buy extras they otherwise could not afford was also equally irresistible. Also, in 1837, it had extra piquancy because Britain had a new Monarch, Victoria. For the first time in their lives, the rallying cry for these soldiers was "God save the Queen."[24]

This was appalling for the women; the idea of duty was swept aside by dismay at the prospect of their husbands' prolonged absence. They had infants to nurse and children to feed, and now they would be doing all the men's work in the fields: keeping fires lit, woodpiles filled, animals fed, and paths cleared in winter. Rumours reverberated through the settlement at Newport, and for many of the older women this represented a remake of the past; that armed rebels might burst out of the bush at any moment intent on rape, pillage, and murder. They were lucky because the rebellion fizzled out almost before it began, however, it was not to end in its entirety for some time.[24]

> *Author's note: The document that follows has the individual names listed, however, for the purpose of space, I have condensed the material as follows: "The Militia Roll of 1837 under Ensign [Captain] Edmund⁷ Heard for the Township of Newport."*

Ensign Edmund[7] Heard, age 32, and 26 militiamen, ranging in age from 17 to 52. Marshall Rand and Edmund Harvey were the youngest at age 17. Of the 26 militiamen, 12 were bachelors and 14 were married. These men were considered *"effective Militiamen and bearing arms"* and thereby ready for active duty. Also listed in reserve as *"Militiamen"* but considered *"non effective and incapable of marching"* were 42 men. These men ranged in age from 20 to 73, *six listed as exempts* from 60 to 100, and only one exempt by law if war broke out. Artemas[6] Rand, age 59, and William Heard, age 73, were listed in this latter category.[31]

The settlers of Newport were once again prepared to defend their lands. Having come from a recent past history of having their lands and their honour taken from them, the 27 active militiamen knew they could count on the older members of the community to provide a defence if need be. The Rebellion, however, petered out rather quickly and while our Newport defenders "mustered," they were not called upon for active duty, to the absolute relief of the womenfolk. The 1840 Act of Union united the colonies of Upper Canada and Lower Canada into the Province of Canada, comprised of Canada West and Canada East. This was to become the impetus for Confederation.[31]

During these uncertain times, the passion of our ancestral womenfolk with their marriages were undimmed, despite the hardships of the past several years and the arrival of several children. Their families, children, grandchildren and indeed their intimate communities coupled with their staunch belief in their faith, served once again to unify them. Their letters pulsate with both buoyancy and the seriousness of the times.[10]

***

Meanwhile, in 1840 Nova Scotia geologist Abraham Gesner distilled coal oil for the first time, which he named "Kerosene." With this innovation came the invention and introduction of kerosene lamps which burned brighter and cleaner than candle wax. Women in rural Newport would come to cherish this new mode of lighting, allowing them to both read and sew during the long winter evenings. Some of these settlers had brought weaving looms from the south when they settled; these had been passed on to the younger women, but these women could still only use them during daylight hours, which were already busy. If they had sufficient light, evenings could be put to good use weaving or spinning yarn after the children were bedded down.

The men generally went to bed at sundown and arose at sunrise, as the only light in the stables was the sunlight coming through the small windows. Because of the introduction of kerosene, candle-making would slowly become a chore of the past for these women and many would not regret the change. Unfortunately, Newport would not see kerosene lamps for some years; they were still not affordable to those still struggling just to survive this harsh land.

The farmers were now growing flax to produce linen which was commonly used for bedding and summer clothing before the availability of cotton. Nearly every farmer now had a small flock of sheep which provided wool for the warm clothes and winter bedding. Also, the sheep furnished the tallow for making grease for their wagons and tallow for their candles that would still be used until they could afford these "new-fangled" kerosene lanterns.

A slaughtered animal was usually shared amongst neighbours so there would be no loss from spoilage. In the winter they would store their meat in barrels to be frozen. To keep the meat from sticking together, they would lay each piece separately on shelves, let them freeze and then place the pieces into the barrels for storage. Pigs were usually slaughtered in the fall, the meat placed in a salt brine to cure and once cured, placed into pork barrels, and used as part of their food source throughout the year.

Bulls and male horses were frequently sold or traded among neighbours to change the breeding stock. The offspring were trained for pulling carts, wagons, sleds, stoneboats and other uses.[25] Heavy workhorses were also becoming popular for pulling wagons, buggies and sleighs; however, oxen still continued to be used widely for the heavy work.

Stumping was the settlers' most tedious task (BAnQ)

"Stumping" was by far our ancestors' most tedious task. Help was needed by family or neighbours to drive the oxen while a hook was anchored to one large stump root at a time. Oxen were well-suited for this type of work because of their low centre of gravity; they were strong and exerted a slow pull. The process had to be repeated several times to remove the large stumps of the old-growth forest.

All our ancestors built and used a "stoneboat" to haul stones from the newly cultivated fields and stumps to a place to be burned. They made these sleds of hardwood, usually by attaching three or four 4-inch-thick elm planks together. They would select the bottom half of large trees to include the curve into the root system, so that when hewn out these boards had a natural curvature at the one end. When attached with a cross-board it created a toboggan-like front extending 6-8 feet long. The stoneboat sat flat on the ground to facilitate rolling stones or root masses onto it. It was pulled by oxen or horses, with the driver standing on the boat. Simple in construction, the stoneboat was one of the most important tools these early settlers had to facilitate clearing their land. It was used well into the 20th century.

In all aspects of early settlement, farm children were familiar with both the animals and hard work. They learned at an early age the value of caring for animals. It was not uncommon to see children riding cows as well as horses during and after work. A mixture of both work and play for the children was now becoming an important part of the learning experience; this was somewhat different from the past generations where it was generally all work and no play.

Every settler would try to have several apple trees. Apples were an excellent source of vitamin C, and applesauce and apple pie soon became staples of the daily meals.

Between the ages of 8 and 9, all the girls in the settlement learned how to sew and do handicrafts for the home. A girl learned the simplest braiding and weaving techniques, often passed down by her grandmother who usually lived under the same roof. Knitting was a common evening activity for the women. Most girls learned to knit when quite young and were so adept when grown up that they were not dependent on any light.

The safety pin was invented in 1849; it helped hold cloth diapers in place on babies and made for many fewer accidental pin pricks. These diapers were made of old underclothing, ripped up and repurposed – perhaps their last use before burning in the fireplace.[18]

Families in these earlier days depended on the older generations for many chores, including teaching their children. It was expected that the grandparents would stay on as their children took over the farms that were being passed down from generation to generation.[35]

Late fall was a time when harvesting was complete, winter preparations had been done, and general activities began to wind down. Grandparents began to relax, talk about the weather, brag about the harvest, tell tales of their youth, and predict the future. Grandsons and granddaughters would listen intently as traditions, tales, legends, beliefs and ancestral values would be passed on while sitting on the porch or by the fireside. Later a grandchild would find him or herself saying, "My grandfather used to say . . . " sometimes embellishing an already exaggerated story.

With the influx of Irish settlers, potatoes now became an abundant crop in the township and were in surplus until two stills were set up in Eaton Township where a drink called "potato whiskey" was produced. One of these stills was near the crossroads at Sand Hill, the other a mile east of the village of Eaton. In addition to the sale of whiskey, the mash was repurposed to fatten beef cattle prior to their being driven to market in Quebec City. And so, the potato became a commodity in Newport, generating much-needed income during this era.

In July 1840, Lucy (daughter of Edmund[6]) wrote to her mother from Melbourne, Lower Canada, saying, *"my husband George [Gibson] will probably be gone most of the summer as he is driving cattle up to Quebec City to sell them for the land company. I have been successful in making butter, more than enough for my family and so I will be sending a tub with George to sell."* [10]

After several years, taverns or public houses were generally introduced into the more thickly settled localities and on the more frequently travelled routes. Initially reasonable places where travellers could stay overnight, they soon degenerated into common "grog-shops" – not the best place to stay if one wanted to sleep. It was not uncommon for travellers to feel most welcome to stay at various settlers' homes, as sharing in these times was quite the norm.

As more land was cleared, there was more pasturage and more winter forage for an ever-increasing number of livestock. As a result, butter and cheese became exportable products. Some of the farmers would gather produce and, once winter had set in, load their sleds and make the trip to a market in Montreal. Such a trip took about eight days, during which the travellers could count on settlers along the way to assist them by feeding and accommodating them and their horses. As time progressed local merchants would provide this service, hiring local teamsters to take the settlers' produce to market and bring back essential goods to sell to the settlers.[17]

***

The Loveland/Beaman family Connection: [31] *(also: Shirley Loveland and Raymond Loveland family history)*

> *Author's note: This was an era when many Newport families married those who were immigrating from other parts of the New England states and as well parts of the British Commonwealth. William[2] Loveland of Newport was to meet Nathanial Beaman's daughter, Eliza, in a most unlikely place on a trip to Quebec City.*

William[1] Loveland was a shipwright living in London, England, in the late 1700s. He worked at the London dockyards on the Thames, circa 1830, when shipwrights were in transition from building wooden sailboats to iron boats powered by steam. These ships were built to cross the Atlantic at a higher speed than their predecessors, destined for Boston and New York, and were called "boiler ships." It was also not unusual for shipyards to have "liveries" since horses had been used to move heavy timbers and now were used to move heavy pieces of metal. His son William[2], born in 1821, had a love of horses from an early age and had virtually lived with the horses in the livery while his father worked on the ships.

William[2] Loveland was already working by 1835. His father knew the captain well and arranged for him to get a job on one of these new boiler ships as a cabin boy at age 14. The ship was heading to Boston. This was an era of great opportunity in North America because of the growth of the New World. Times were tough in the Old World where many children had no choice but to work just to feed themselves. Many of these children would try getting on board as a stowaway in these ships for the chance of a new adventure. This is a snapshot into how many young children lived their lives and would seize any opportunity to leave home and begin working towards their own future.

William[2], however, did not fancy working on a ship for the rest of his life, and so on arrival in Boston, he left the ship to work in a shoe factory.

During that time William[2] boarded with a Mr. Tucker who had taken him in. It appears that Mr. Tucker was engaged in the horse-trading business within the New England states, and as William was used to handling horses, he was indeed an asset. William was fortunate that Mr. Tucker took an interest in his well-being and taught him how to read and write. It was through this association that William learned of the settlements in Lower Canada from Mr. Tucker, who saw an opportunity for trading in horses between the two countries.

William[2] Loveland arrived in Newport, circa 1840 at about 19 years old, bent on acquiring some land and perhaps starting a trade in horses with his friend Mr. Tucker. He was able to acquire a lot in the Maple Leaf region in Newport Township and soon became acquainted with the other families of the area; the Heard/Hurds, the Rands, the Planches and the McCurdys. He immediately built a log cabin and began clearing the land for what he believed would be his start of a new life, perhaps with a horse farm. For this reason, he kept in touch by mail with Mr. Tucker and some others in the Boston region. He intended to acquire a horse in the near future from his mentor, Mr. Tucker, and was waiting to hear from him as to when he might be able to start a horse-trading business with him. And so, the story has been passed down from generations that "he walked to Quebec City twice a year to get his mail."

It was not uncommon for horses to be frequently sold or traded among neighbours. By 1837, we learn of the sale of horses to the militia. These horses had to measure a certain height at the shoulder. If a horse was slightly under the required height, the owner would simply re-shoe the horse at the blacksmith by lengthening the corks on the shoes for the added height requirement. There appeared to be a good market in the United States for surplus riding horses and this could become another opportune business for the settlers in Newport.

Haying before mechanization – hay was raked by hand into bundles then lifted onto the wagons (Newport Homecoming 1801-1996)

Another story evolving from this was that "an American buyer by the name of Wakefield, who bought horses in the Townships had a devious way of getting them across the border. He would mount one horse, lead the others to a place on the boundary line unknown to the customs officials, then on to a hidden farm in the Ossipee Mountains. On one occasion, having crossed the boundary, he was warned that he was being watched by customs officials. After his lunch, he saddled up and leading the other horses returned to the boundary, trailed by the customs man who was dressed as a farmer. After reporting to the Canadian Customs of his mistake because he had miscalculated where he was, he continued into Canada, however circled and reentered the States by another trail and headed to the hideaway."[17]

William[2] Loveland first started in the business of trading in horses in 1843. The horses our early ancestors had brought with them when they settled in Newport were mostly light riding horses, used for travel back and forth between the two countries. These light horses were not often used during this later period since this kind of travel had greatly decreased. Oxen had always been the working muscle required for clearing the lands but were now being slowly replaced in Newport with heavy workhorses. Loggers were beginning to look to New England to purchase or create a trade for these horses. Conversely, lightweight driving horses were in demand in the more-settled United States, where the people were more affluent, the roads in better condition, and general travel between villages more frequent. And so, horse trading was to become a growing business for William. During this time he was living

Settling In

in Newport but had worked occasionally for Mr. Tucker in Boston to make extra money. Mr. Tucker was now looking to buy horses in Lower Canada for resale in New England, so the match was lit. Life was hard in the early settlements during this time and any way to earn a living was taken as an opportunity. William saw that opportunity and took it.

In a letter written to Edmund[7] Heard in April 1843, when he arrived in Boston with some horses, William mentioned that James[2] Beaman had sent him a letter stating that he was planning to move down and wanted him to see if he could find him a place to stay while he searched for work there. William wrote in his letter that *"times are awfully hard in Canada right now and since I have lived this long, I can't imagine times any tougher there than they have been here this past year. Normally you would hire men for 14 dollars a month for the season but now farmers are hiring men for 5 dollars a month. We have had the worst winter I have ever seen and one that has not been known for thirty years."* He mentioned in the letter that *"the trip down from Newport took me eight days"* but that Mr. Tucker was very glad to see him.[31]

It appears that this was one of William's earliest trips back to the Boston region with some horses to barter. He had brought some horses from the community of Maple Leaf to sell. He complained to Edmund Heard in his letter:

> *Because the horses were not used to walking on cobblestone, they were afraid of it. I am going to have to git the horses shod [referring to shoeing the horses] and that is going to cost. The way horses were selling down here now, the most I could git was sixty dollars. Mr. Tucker said that he had enough hay and that I could keep them in the barn if that would help. I kept them until March 21 and sold them for ninety dollars, so I felt that was a good lesson for me. I shall be back next spring if my health remains and tell James [Beaman] if he hasn't left yet, to be content where he is, as it is not much better here . . . [Signed] William Loveland.* [10, 31]

The Beaman family was one of the first families to emigrate from the New England Colonies, a member of Col. Edmund[5] Heard's Associates in the settling of Newport. Nathanial Beaman's daughter Eliza[2] decided to move to Melbourne sometime after Lucy Heard (Edmund[6] Heard's daughter) had married her husband, George Gibson, and were living in Melbourne. It was a chance for Eliza to see another part of the world, so she went to help Lucy out with her young children.[31]

Once again many of the sons and daughters of the original settlers moved to various parts of Canada, with some moving back to marry in the New England states. There was considerable communication and travel between the two countries and as the families began to branch out there were those who elected to stay in Newport. These women appeared to be a staunch group with families determined to reap the benefits of their ancestors' hard work in settling this new land north of the former New England Colonies.

For those left behind, loneliness perhaps affected the women more than anyone else, as friendships they had built were now gone. With a huge workload and travel so difficult, they knew they may never see these people again. Letters were frequent during this time but eventually they too would dissipate over time, leaving the womenfolk doing their chores with only memories of the good times. Mail was still hard to come by and when it did come, often it was brought by other hands, by people who might travel to different locales and pick up the mail for the whole community, some of which may be hand-to-hand and left at certain homes for eventual pickup.

"It was on another trip when William[2] Loveland walked to Quebec City, by way of the Craig Road, to pick up his mail, travelling through Melbourne, Que., where he happened to meet Eliza Beaman at the George and Lucy (Heard) Gibson home. Meeting her again on the way back, William was persuasive in convincing her to marry him and so he brought her back to Grove Hill, where her family had settled earlier." *(Shirley Loveland, family archives)*

In 1853 William[2] Loveland married Eliza Beaman in Grove Hill (Randboro). They settled on Eliza's part of Lot 10 of Range 10, right beside the lot where William had built his small cabin. They prospered, built their homestead, cleared the land, and had six children, four boys and two girls. They lost one daughter, Ida, and a son, Herbie, in infant deaths as well as their eldest son, William[3], when he was 6 years old. Their youngest son, Victor, died at 24 in a farm accident.

Their daughter Augusta married Henry Phelps, a descendant of John Phelps the blacksmith who had operated his business for many years in Grove Hill.

William and Eliza's remaining son, Charles[3] "Charley" Helmsey Loveland, continued to live in Newport and carried on the Loveland name. Charley was postmaster in Maple Leaf for several years. He and his wife Charlotte Goodenough, from South Ham (north of Marbleton in what was then Wolfe County) raised their six children in Newport and were well remembered by their neighbours. Their family had become a valued part of the growth in the Maple Leaf community. They were married at South Ham in 1881 by the Rev. Thomas Shaw Chapman of St. Paul's Church, Marbleton. After the children had grown up and his term of office in Maple Leaf expired, they moved to Sawyerville to retire.[24]

Charley's father William[2] was in his mid-fifties when he was raising heavy (draft) workhorses and renting out teams to the lumbering businesses. It was considered a mark of progress when one now acquired workhorses – oxen were beginning to be phased out of use on the farms and these heavy draft workhorses were preferred for the lumbering business. With roads becoming more travelled, horses were much faster than the plodding oxen, so the shift began from old to new. Augustus[8] Hurd and Marshall[8] Spring Rand were building roads together and were heavily into the lumbering business in Newport when William was renting his teams of horses in peak times. William[2] in his early 60s gave his support to the building of the Anglican Church that was built in Randboro in 1883. Their son Charles Hemsley Loveland became one of the wardens of this church in 1895.[31]

***

The Lyon/Bowker family connection:[32]

> *Author's note: Lucy Bowker was a sister of the two Bowker boys, Solomon and Johnathon, who had settled in Newport in 1799. Their younger brother Lyman had moved to settle on their land grants on the now North River Road. While Lucy never came to Newport, two of her sons would immigrate and settle on lots in the Flanders and New Mexico regions.*

John[2] Lyon was born in 1770 in Lunenburg, Vt. He married Lucy Bowker (daughter of Gideon[6] and Hannah (Fletcher) Bowker) in 1804. He had served in the French and Indian Wars, his commission signed by George Washington. John and Lucy had several children; two of their sons, Orra and Eliphalet, both experienced lumbermen, decided to explore their opportunities and headed north to the new lands being offered in Lower Canada. They travelled through the woods from New Hampshire and found themselves in the areas of New Mexico and Flanders, in Newport Township. They built a cabin on Lot 4 of Range 7. Eliphalet returned to Lunenburg. A year later he and his wife Jane came by portage, horseback, and boat across Lake Champlain to Newport with all their worldly possessions and settled on their new homestead. Orra later built a sawmill on Lyon Stream in Island Brook on the site known today as the John Westgate place.[32]

Eliphalet and Jane built their homestead across the North River on a meadow where they had to wade the river or ride horseback through it. They raised seven children including Levi and Lucy (twins), Ann Rosetta and Amanda. They raised flax to make thread and/or yarn with which Jane wove cloth. A linen tablecloth known as "Lucy's tablecloth" is still a family heirloom.[32]

In 1840, seeding tools improved and the steel-toothed dump rake was invented. Horse-drawn mowers were getting better and better, and by 1845 hay makers were now successful in compressing hay for transport. Our ancestors in Newport bought these new implements only as they could afford them, many over long periods of time. Those who could afford to purchase them would share them within their communities. However, except for the mower, these particular farm implements would not be used in Newport until a later era, simply because they were too expensive.

***

The Morrow/Cable family connection:[32]

> *Author's note: This was a time when many immigrants from Ireland were settling on lots in Argenteuil County, Lower Canada. Many were to marry in Argenteuil, some raising their families, others moving with their families perhaps looking for better opportunities, many of whom moved into Newport.*

Henry Morrow came to Canada, settling first in Argenteuil County in 1844. He married Ellen Wilson in 1844. It was not until 1871, however, that Henry and Ellen and their family of eight (seven boys and a daughter) decided to move and settle in the New Mexico region of Newport. Only the two eldest boys, William W. (born 1856) and John (born 1861), stayed in Newport. The two remained as bachelors; the other three boys and the daughter all married and moved on. John settled on the homestead in New Mexico and at 30 years old had not yet married. He had a hare lip which marred his chances in the area and so he decided to advertise for a wife. He felt he might have a better chance if he enclosed a photograph of his brother William. Elizabeth Dawson answered the ad and became John's wife, raising four children there.[32]

John's brother, William W. Morrow, married 24-year-old Hattie Jane Cable circa 1889 in Island Brook. They raised six sons: Renford (born 1895), Irwin (born 1897), Earl (born 1899), Raymond (born 1901), Kenneth (born 1903) and Justin (born 1905). Hattie had been born in Auckland Township in a log cabin, just across the South River bridge on today's Route 210, where her father and mother, Lewis and Mary Cable, had settled.

Surnames arising from marriages and new settlers in this era were Bartlett, Bowker, Cable, Dawson, Dorman, French, Gibson, Haskell, Herring, Hubbard, Lawrence, Learned, Loveland, Lyon, Morrow, Munn, Parsons, Phelps, Prince, Reeves and Willard.

There comes a time in any story relating to historical background when a reader will begin to recognize names, times and places that perhaps they had heard about or experienced in their childhood. This would be especially noticed if the reader had spent their youth in a given region, such as the Eastern Townships, throughout their younger years. Those of us who grew up in Newport or perhaps attended school in the immediate surrounding area can perhaps more readily relate to the names we will be referring to as the story unfolds in the next several chapters. These were families who had forged an inextricable connection and culture with their neighbours and the land. They then passed their experiences in life along to their children who in turn have passed them on the next generations.

> *Author's note: During this next generation, the Heard/Hurd families would become integrated with the Rand, McCurdy, Planche and Bowker families. These families became interdependent as a community, both as friends and in business, not only to survive but to thrive as well. Note the "Family Charts" at the end of this book.*

***

Chapter 9   Progress and Family Connections (1850–1875)

The developing world started to experience the advances of the Industrial Revolution during the 1850s. Steam engines, railways and the telegraph transformed travel and the production of food, textiles and weapons, giving industrial powers a decisive edge over traditional agricultural societies. In the 1850s more than 90 percent of families in North America were engaged in agriculture, logging and associated businesses operating in the more rural communities in townships such as Newport. The advent of new business entities, including electricity, created unheard of problems as well as unprecedented opportunities. Indoor plumbing became available in the 1850s for urban homes, but only new homes built after that time would likely have had this luxury, if it was even affordable in this region of Lower Canada. The indoor potty and outhouse were still alive and well in Newport; some by now had been expanded to become a "three-holer" or a "four-holer."

During the 1820s, urban areas began seeing the first wood-fired, hand-built cast iron cookstoves, however, these stoves were not in widespread use in the rural areas until well into the 1850s. Innovation began by using a simple wood block mould but the real key to this invention was the beginnings of mass production that initiated the first factory of its kind. The first full-scale manufacturing of wood stoves in Canada began in Three Rivers with the creation of multiple moulds coupled with new methods of investment. Matthew Bell was the first to offer "employment with a salary" in Lower Canada, thus the "Bell stove" was a game-changer for people living in a cold climate. This Canadian stove was the key to a level of prosperity which would include the communities that surrounded it, and Canada became at that moment in our history an industrialized nation. These stoves were available to everyone by the early 1880s and there had been an immediate rush earlier to get these more efficient modes of both heating and cooking into every household.

Heating stoves were the first to be introduced into homes, followed by cookstoves with ovens. A stovepipe would run along the ceiling in the kitchen and feed into the chimney that the heating stove had been connected to, eliminating the old hearths of the past. Since these new stovepipes also emitted heat, during the summer months a kitchen could become quite unbearable. This was especially true for anyone who cooked meals for very large families. The introduction of these new stoves also changed the style of new houses – the kitchen was now incorporated within the main house, and the former "summer" kitchens became woodsheds. The same concept became true for any adjoining (riding, buggy) horse stables that would be converted to car garages in future years.

In 1851 Singer sewing machines were patented, but it would be another generation before most of the women in Newport would have the resources to purchase one.[32]

Another important development was the invention of "safety matches" in 1855. The match head had to be struck against a corresponding material in order to light. These matches were much safer that the first matches our ancestors were using just 20 years prior. Many fires had occurred in homes simply because mice would sometimes chew on the match head which contained both ingredients required to create a spark.[32]

Sawyerville Mills dam before the floods of 1942-43 (Sawyerville 2018 calendar)

A flood of mechanically engineered equipment entering the marketplace created excitement during this period. Sawmills built to use waterpower had been started in the more rural areas, including Newport. Larger dams were now built to create more vibrant waterfalls that would drive larger water wheels to power the larger saws. Mills were now expanding with more lumber being drawn from the eastern parts of Newport and those townships bordering Newport, where the virgin timber was still standing in the outer reaches of Emberton, Ditton, Chesham and Auckland townships. Lumbering operations and mills continued to provide prosperity for our ancestors for several generations to come.[16]

It was also during this period that the Atlantic salmon spring spawn was beginning to ebb. These larger dams were not constructed with ladder steps to allow the salmon to reach the smaller tributaries to spawn. Our ancestors simply thought they were becoming fished out. To add to that theory, salmon were fished out below these falls as they collected in the turbulent eddies below the falls in huge numbers. The local settlers perhaps did not realize that these fish were trying to move upriver to spawn their next generations. They would likely have thought they had simply come across a bonanza of a fishing opportunity every few years. For them, these salmon were a uniquely different food source for their families from the usual chicken, mutton, pork or beef that they dined on for most of the year. Even these foods were available only if they had an excess of one or the other.[39]

There was also progress in farm equipment automation. Newer barns were being built with inside hay storage in the lofts above the stables. Some of the barns were built with ramps to the second floor so that horses could pull the loaded hay wagons right up to the barn floor. The men would then have to fork the hay off the wagons by hand into the lofts on each side. Large hay forks were developed in 1865 as a method to lift large amounts of hay off the wagons using a series of cables and pulleys. The fork was designed such that a man would plunge it into the load of hay, turn a handle sideways, thereby locking the fork into the hay. A carriage and track were attached to the inside of the peak of the roof, so that when the hay fork was hoisted by cable to the carriage, a mechanism triggered the carriage, allowing it to move forward down the track. A long rope attached to the fork allowed a man to trip the fork, so the hay would drop off into a loft at the end of the barn. By 1875 hay loaders were also beginning to emerge in the rural farming communities. When attached to a hay wagon, the loader picked up the hay and delivered it via a conveyor mechanism of small forks up a rack and onto the wagon. This piece of equipment became a huge time-saver in getting the hay in from the fields; however, it would not become common in Newport for some time to come. Our ancestors who were born in this era would have also experienced major changes in their lives with the introduction of steam engines, water pumps and the move from candles to kerosene lanterns and even later, for some of their grandchildren, to naphtha gas lamps.

Pasteurization of milk was developed in 1856, entering the market first in urban centres where milk was beginning to be delivered in glass bottles. People in Newport were still milking their cows by hand; the milk and cream were both consumed "whole" without any processing other than separating the milk from the cream.

***

In this century it was not uncommon for some families to have 15-20 children. The oldest girls would invariably take care of the younger children. Sadly, even in this era, many young children were still dying of diseases due to the unavailability of vaccines. Having large families was still considered part of solidifying the future for a family's survival.

This chapter begins with the children that were growing up in the previous chapter and the subsequent generations created through marriages that followed over the next several years. The associations that many of these families developed through marriages, children and grandchildren all provide an intimate snapshot into the bonds and ethics that formed who they were. A reader might reflect and remember their own lives, who they knew, how and why relationships shaped their own communities and began to shape the character of who they are today. Character, trust and attitude matter as much as skill and knowledge. As their descendants, we have been shaped by our ancestors' values which still run through many of us. This is who we are and this legacy is very much a part of us.

This is not just a story about history – it is more about the connections people have with special places and more importantly the people within those places. The purpose of this story is to bring our ancestors to life. They and their stories belong to a people who have handed down a legacy of heritage and culture from generation to generation; much like the First Nations peoples did, and that is equally as important to be told. This was a time when the many children of our ancestor families were now marrying others from within and outside the local communities. These marriages were to form connections with many of the Eastern Township families that would become familiar surnames serving in various businesses and establishments.

The author will continue with the seventh and eighth generation of Heards and others who were forging their new lives in Newport. Note that this generation is only the third/fourth generation that was born and lived in Newport. The advance of industrial progress throughout the region brought major changes in how our ancestors lived their lives during this next time frame of settlement.

***

The first Rand family and Heard/Hurd family connection: [4] *(also: Rand Family history)*

Author's note: The first Rand family that had become one of the later Associates of the Colonel Edmund[5] Heard settler group was Artemas[6] and Louisa Spring Rand. Their youngest son later married the eldest daughter of Captain Edmund[7] Heard and Mary (Willard). Mary's father, Longley Willard was one of Col. Edmund[5] Heard's first Associates who settled in Newport in 1795.[20]

Artemas[6] and Louisa had three sons: Artemas[7] Dodge Rand, born in Connecticut; Gardner Wheeler, who died young; and Marshall Spring Rand. Both Gardner and Marshall were born on the farm in Grove Hill. When Artemas[6] and Louisa built their home at the top of Grove Hill Road, circa 1799, their homestead was the only house in the immediate area, so they were alone on the top of the hill for a couple of years until another home was built by John Phelps, a blacksmith, at the bottom of the hill. Their only neighbours were the Nathanial Beaman Jr. family, who lived on the south side of South River, later known as "Parker Hill," on Lot 3 of Range 10, their lots backing onto each other at the river.

Ingenuity in building perhaps the first bridge in Newport across the South River (Eastern Townships Roots)

The small valley below both settlements would be the start of the small hamlet of Grove Hill, which then became Randville circa 1870-90, which ultimately became Randboro as we know it today. Artemas[6] had been operating the mill at the bottom of Grove Hill with Nathanial Beaman Jr. until he died in 1837. It was at this time that Nathanial divested of his share in the operation and retired. Nathanial died 11 years later, in 1848. He is buried in Maple Leaf Cemetery in Newport, headstone no. 2 in row 5.

Artemas[6] and Louisa's eldest son, Artemas[7] Dodge Rand, married Hannah[2] Hurd Willard, the younger daughter of Longley[6] Willard and his wife Hannah[1] Hurd, circa 1829. They had three sons: Gardner[8] Stillman Dodge (born 1830), Horace E. (born 1832) and William Willard Seaver (born 1836). Artemas[7] and Hannah[2] had taken over the original Longley[6] Willard homestead on lots 3 and 4 of Range 8. They acquired this farm after Longley died and Hannah's brother William married and moved to Barnston, leaving the farm to Hannah. They raised their family here, developing the 400-acre farm until Artemas[7] died in 1878 at age 84.

Author's note: Longley's eldest daughter, Mary[2] Willard, had married Edmund[7] Heard earlier in 1818, raising their family on the original lots granted to his grandfather, Col. Edmund[5] Heard in Maple Leaf. This was to be the same farm that would be taken over by their son, Edmund[8] Haskell Hurd.

After her husband Artemas[6] died in 1837, Louisa Rand continued living on the original farm property at the top of Grove Hill, on Lot 3 of Range 9, with her son Marshall S.[8] Marshall married a couple of years later, and so Louisa lived alone for a few years in the original home until she passed on.

Mary Maria Hurd, the eldest daughter of Edmund[7] Heard, married Marshall Spring Rand (Artemas[6] and Louisa's third son) in Newport in 1839. Mary Maria bore 10 children, including two daughters and a son who died at a young age. The other seven grew up and became an integral part of Newport Township's development. They were: Lucy Eleanor (1841-1874), Hannah Elvira (1848-1922), Newell Clement (1850-1922), Austin Spring (1852-1895), Willard Stedman (1854-1915), Frederick George (1858-1875) and Gardner ("Gardy") Wheeler (born 1866). The family settled on a property originally granted to Capt. Edmund[6] Heard, which had been part of the original land lots arranged by Col. Edmund[5] Heard.

Capt. Edmund[7] Heard (1795-1852) died at 57 years old. He had previously bequeathed these particular land lots that he had inherited from his father (Edmund[6]) to his daughter Mary Maria and Marshall Spring Rand when they married, circa 1839. These lots were located just off today's Route 210, and on the road to Auckland/Chartierville. Travelling on this road towards the Auckland Bridge, Lot 12 is on the right and Lot 13 on the left or east side of the road. They cleared the land on the south part of lots 12 and 13, bordering on Route 210; the homestead was built on the west side of Route 210. These references to Route 210 are how we know those roads today.

> *Author's note: A map of Newport at the front of the book indicates the surveyed lot numbers in relation to the ranges of Newport. With this reference, a reader may have a better understanding as to the location where their ancestors had settled and later farmed. These original lots were surveyed in 200-acre parcels, north to south. However, as time passed from generation to generation, many of these lots were severed into smaller parcels of land.*[28]

Marshall[8] and Maria went to work, first building their homestead while clearing their lot for two years before their first daughter, Lucy Eleanor was born in 1841. After they lost their second and third daughters, Minerva in 1845 and Luvia in 1850, they raised seven children in Newport, but lost another boy in 1863. During these early years on the homestead they cleared enough land to cultivate and produce ample food for their growing family as well as fodder for their livestock. Marshall became a farmer, a lumberman and a road builder. As time progressed, he began to work with his neighbour Augustus[8] Hurd, the eldest son of John B.[7] and Polly (Sawyer) Heard, in clearing, lumbering and opening up new roads in both Newport and Ditton townships.

John Phelps resided in Grove Hill where he had built a significant blacksmith shop at the side of his house. The tools used in the neighbouring settlements were all made locally by John who had established himself as the resident blacksmith throughout his earlier years. John was approaching 55 years old when he found his business was booming because of the lumber business. John expanded his blacksmith facilities and was now forming sled, whiffletree and harness metals for horse-drawn equipment. He employed several younger men from the area, making axes, saws, horseshoes, peaveys, "cant dogs," sled runners and chains as well as many other metal parts. As his business flourished, he sold his goods to a demanding market.

Around this time, Marshall Rand recognized an opportunity to make extra money by constructing the wooden part of the sled runners. He began looking for curved tree root knurls which were perfect for making one-piece sled runners for timber sleds. John Phelps and his men would cut and form the steel, applying them hot onto the wooden runners, cooling them quickly to form a tight fit. These steel runners were then bolted in place for longevity. Wooden sled runners soon became a big business for the farmers who were clearing the forests of these large hardwood trees. They would always be keeping an eye open for root knurls or curved branches and Marshall would buy them on-site, digging out the roots and rough-cutting them into proper lengths. He would then work the wood in his shop into sled or sleigh runners and harness "hames" (for the horse collars). When finished, he sent then off to "John the Smithy" to add the steel part.

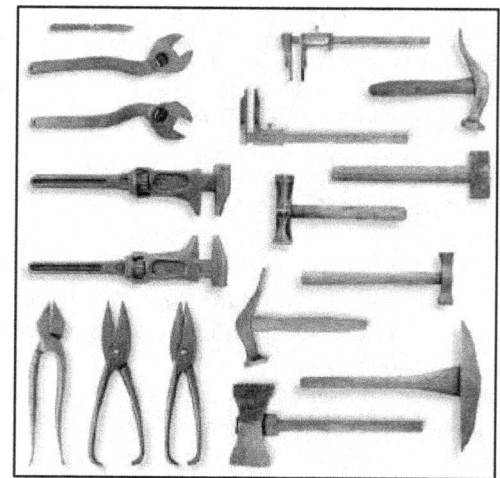

Typical tools of the day (antiques.ca)

Because steel was still hard to come by, any equipment containing steel that had broken down, such as whiffletrees, spokeshaves, pullies, and axle turnbuckles, would have the wood burned out and be repurposed. Many other farmers would also make wooden parts and send them to John to reconfigure any excess metal into new tools. Steel was a precious commodity, so all the metal, including nails, latches, hinges, wheel hubs, clevises and tools, were always retrieved from the ashes of any buildings that burned down.

As the communities in and around Newport began to grow, lumbering became a major business opportunity for the region. To just survive, the families sold any excess produce to other businesses, such as the lumber camps; any extra fodder became food for the horses in the lumbering operations, including meat and vegetables that they would sell to the working lumberjacks.

Lumberjacks first harvested the virgin hardwoods. However, from the mid- to late-1800s there was a graduation to softwoods which grew adjacent to the hardwood forests. A proliferation of logging trails throughout Newport leading to adjacent townships enabled year-round felling of remote spruce, hemlock, cedar, and some pine. Later, the winter logging trails merged with common roads in order to get the timber to specific markets. This activity would soon become a road issue with the farmers in these regions.

Lumberjack standing on a pile of virgin timber logs, heading for the mills
(Ken Burns documentary "The National Parks: America's Best Idea")

Hardwoods such as maple, elm and white birch were still in demand as charcoal for iron manufacturing and again for export to New England. Note the immense size of the virgin timber loaded on these railcars circa 1850-75. It was at this time that the settlers began to use the sawdust from the sawmills to insulate the outside stone foundations of their buildings in the fall in preparation for winter. This was a time when the mills were glad to get rid of the sawdust at their mill sites, as it was a fire hazard. The settlers also used sawdust to preserve ice in the summer months.

These immense trees were felled using only an axe and a large two-man crosscut saw. The saw had two upright handles on each end where a man positioned on each side would alternately pull/push the saw through the base of a tree. The woodsmen would first notch the tree in such a way as to direct its fall so it would not fall onto another tree or otherwise get hung up. These trees, as large as they were, required a similar but smaller saw to cut the notch. Then, using the axe they would chip out the notch. Once the tree had fallen, the branches would be cut with similar but shorter saws. They used a "bucksaw" to cut the smaller branches at the top and saved this wood to cure for their own use as firewood to heat their homes.

Many of these hardy men were professional lumberjacks, others were farmers from the local community. Many died or were severely injured from accidents in these trades. It was not uncommon for a wife and family to suffer from the losses and injuries of their menfolk. There were no handouts and no government assistance but there were compassionate communities of people who would always band together to help out. Regardless of these tragedies, the settlers managed to keep up their courage and continued to flourish by moving forward with their lives.

Men who worked in the logging business might work on a farm during the spring, summer and fall. Some were hired with their horses as a package. If their mares were in foal, it was not uncommon for both the mare and the logger to be housed by the settlers during the summer months. Many of these loggers would work for the farmers off-season in exchange for room and board. If a mare had a colt, a farmer would often house the young horse for the following winter as well, as explained in the letter on the following page. They would skid the huge logs out of the forests with a team of horses to a cleared area. The logs were then rolled and placed in piles for other men and their teams to load onto sleds, their job to take these large loads to the trains for shipment. They might also ask the settler family to house a colt or younger horse for the winter, creating a bartering tool to pay for its keep in exchange for labour the following spring.

On September 13, 1858, Edmund[7] Heard received a letter from the *"Indian Village"* in the St. Francis region, and was asked:

> *As I am again on the eve of leaving for the woods, I will not be able to go after my Mare and Colt before fall, but in the meantime if you can find a buyer you may sell the mare for $80. And the colt you may judge of the value according to its appearance of course and try to sell for cash but if a good man's note was offered at 3 months you may take it. Please let me know how much your amount will be for the keeping of the mare till fall as I might not be here. Mr. Gill will send a man and pay you at the same time. [Signed] John Watso.* [10]

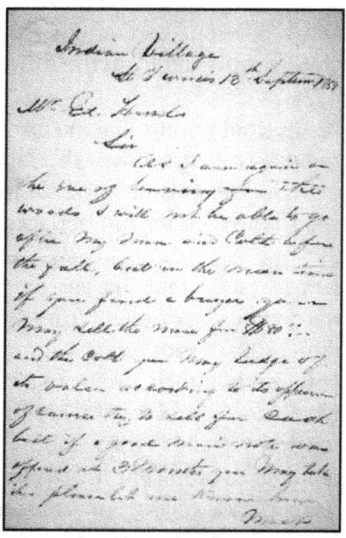
Letter from John Watso to Edmund[7] Heard

Horse-drawn timber loads had to be manageable on uneven and winding winter roads leading to the mills. They were hauled to Sawyer's lumber mill in Eaton Township, to French's and Lyon's mills in Island Brook and as far as the Cookshire Mill in Eaton Township. To groom these winter logging trails, snow was sometimes converted to ice by water sprayed by horse-drawn water tank sleighs. This process made for excellent lumber trails; however, it created a need for special horseshoes, providing another booming business for the smithies.

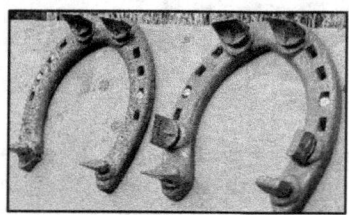
Horseshoes with ice picks (Eaton Corner Museum; photo by Sandra Hurd)

Because of new lumbering operations opening, horseshoes were now common. They were required to provide grip for the horses now hauling on harder surfaced roads, and an absolute necessity on winter snow-packed roads, particularly on ice. On the right is the shoe that would be placed on a horse's left hind foot, the inner picks being dull while the outer picks are sharp. This was intentional to prevent the horses from inadvertently cutting their own feet.

The smaller shoe on the left would be placed on the left front hoof and that horse would be placed on the right of a team of two. Steel-wheeled wagons, used in summer and fall, became the norm in this era along with steel pulleys, chains, winches, and steel wrenches for equipment. *(Royce Rand, Eaton Corner Museum)*

Newport Township was beginning to expand as roads opened in the northern part of the township. This was evidenced by the sale of a property by Jacob M. Annable to the Corporation of School Commissioners of Newport in 1857 for the sum of five pounds. Even in this time frame, the elders of Newport were anticipating a school might be needed in this area. The land was located just above the Grove Hill Road, bearing northeast at the junction of the road to Flanders and to North River Road. This property acquisition was anticipated to accommodate future settlement in this region of the township. *"Distinguishable as being all that part of lot number one in the eighth Range, bounded as follows: Commencing ten rods North of said Eighth Range line thence running North along the road seven rods with a depth of two rods. Signed in the presence of Joshua Nourse & Augustus[8] Hurd."* The Grove Hill School, however, was not established until circa 1870.[31]

***

Samuel Heard, born in 1805, the second son of Samuel[6] and Miriam, had taken over the homestead on Parker Hill, Lot 7 of Range 11, after Miriam remarried and left Newport. His father had drowned at Brompton Falls in 1815 when he was only 10 years old, but Miriam had brought up the family of five, with the help of her eldest son, Henry H., who was 15 at the time. Henry Herschel Heard later moved to Berlin, Mass., as a Baptist minister and married there. Samuel's younger brother, Alexander, born in 1808, died at 21 years old in a farm accident. Samuel stayed on at the homestead, farming and in the winter working in the lumber camps in Ditton and Emberton, until he met and married Sophronia (surname unknown), who was also born in Newport. They had one son and five daughters: Samuel A. (born 1831), Sarepta (born 1830), Annet (born 1831), Elbs (born 1835), Elvira (born 1839) and Ann Maria (born 1845). All were born and raised on this original homestead overlooking his cousin's farms across the South River valley to the north.[4]

Author's note: Henry Alger, the son of Asa and Abigail (Sawyer) Alger of Eaton, married Sarepta as his second wife, creating another Heard connection with the Sawyer family. Abigail Sawyer (1795-1885) was the third daughter of Capt. Josiah[4] and Susanna, the founders of Sawyerville. Samuel's third daughter, Elvira, became a teacher in Eaton Township.[4]

It was at this time when our ancestors and other settlers in Newport were beginning to complain that the lumber companies were cutting "cadge roads" to their camps, sometimes even across a farm to get there. The two groups were co-dependent, so the situation was complicated. Farmers provided food for shanty gangs and hay for their horses and oxen which provided winter employment and cash for the farmers. Despite these differences it became clear that the logging industry had become an integral part of the overall success of these communities.

By 1865, the British American Land Company (BALC) was now fully in charge of building roads for the settlers. The loggers, however, were destroying the roads before the roads had a chance to settle into a compact state in springtime. It took at least 100 heavy loads of provisions to supply a single logging gang, causing the roads to be ploughed into deep ruts and mud holes by the lumbermen's heavy loads, evident during the winter thaws. This issue was further impacted if the loggers were to go through a farmer's field during spring thaw, causing much grief and downright antagonism on the part of a farmer. The roads of this era were still basically hard packed mud with some gravel in certain areas.

Road graders for the common roads started to be used to provide a smoother road surface. These horse-drawn graders were supplied by the BALC. Farmers could now work these graders, sharing the duty from farm to farm, making extra income payable from the BALC who in turn billed the logging businesses. By adding gravel to the roads, coupled with this grading process, the graders were instrumental in keeping the farmers happy for the time being. The graders used in this era were constructed of heavy logs cut square, each about eight feet long and fastened together with chains; the chains fed through augured holes equally on both sides of each timber. The timbers were positioned so that they were perpendicular to the road. There could be as many as 8-10 logs hauled behind a team of horses. They would increase the weight by adding flat rocks on top which made the square edges of the logs dig down into the roadbed enough to create a flattened surface. Several passes and decreasing the rock load allowed for an even and smooth roadbed. These roads, however, lacked ditches and when heavy rains occurred, the roads would pool with water, the horses sometimes wading knee deep to get through.

Typical mud roads of the day; note the absence of ditches (Shutterstock)

The streets in the villages were also a mixture of mud and horse dung; great when well-packed and dry. However, when it rained heavily, and during the frost release in the spring, these streets and roads essentially became quagmires of stinking horse dung mixed with mud, rutted and certainly impossible for travel by foot. The towns constructed raised wooden sidewalks made of sawn elm so the ladies could step out of the buggies directly onto a relatively mud-free walk and by lifting their skirts slightly, and they would lessen the necessity of continually washing the hems. These raised wooden sidewalks allowed the farmers and shoppers to park their buggies and wagons alongside and tie up the horses to a hitching pole.

***

The first Bowker family and Heard family marriage connection: [4] *(also: Florence (Bowker) McVetty, Bowker family histories)*

> *Author's note: Names that would become associated with the Bowker families of Newport through generations of marriages were/are Ferguson, Hodge, Heard, Farnsworth, Draper, Gilman, Gill, Boynton, Buck, Aldous, McVetty, Lowry, Drouin, McBurney, Daly and Parrington.*

Lucy[8] Minerva Heard (second daughter of Edmund[7] Heard) married Lewis[8] Leander Bowker in 1845. Lewis was born in 1821 and had emigrated with his parents from Lunenburg, Vt. He was the son of Lyman[7] J. and Betsey (Merriam) Bowker. Lewis and Lucy began clearing their land and raising their family on a second Bowker lot on the North River adjacent to his father's farm. This Lot 4 was one of the original lots applied for and registered by his great-uncles, Solomon[7] and Johnathon[7] Bowker, in 1799. Here they raised their four children: Edmund[9] Heard (1849-1929), Lyman[9] James (1853-1924), Herbert Rice (1857-1950), and Luvia Amanda (1855-1944). All three boys left Newport when they married, two to the U.S., but Herbert, who had moved to Eaton Township when he first married, later returned to Newport to take over his father's farming operation. Lewis and Lucy raised their family on this lot following in his father's footsteps with the dairy farm and was now cutting both pulpwood and hardwood lumber from the land.[4]

Lewis and his father Lyman were now sharing the use of horse-powered machinery to cut hay, which allowed them to harvest 7-10 times more than they could by hand. By growing more feed, they were able to increase their herd of dairy cattle, which provided them with more income. Lyman had built up a good herd of Holstein milking cows, some of which Lewis had acquired before he was married, giving them a good start to their own farming operation.

The steel-toothed riding dump rake and the hay tedder were both introduced in the early 1860s. These two new farm implements became "must-haves" which further increased haying efficiencies.[31]

The beginning of mechanization in farming, combining machinery with live horsepower (Heard/Hurd family collection)

Lumber continued to be in demand in the growing New England states. From those proceeds both families were able to buy some of the newest farming equipment that was becoming available. Over time and as the children were growing, Lewis and Lucy grew their herd of Holsteins and became significant milk producers, each year clearing more of their farm for both pasture and cultivation.

***

The grindstone wheel was introduced and came into fashion during this era. It became another must-have implement for every farmer and logger to quickly sharpen their axes, ploughshares and cutting blades of the new mowing machines. No longer did they require the blacksmith to sharpen their tools as they had before. One would find the grinder, an abrasive stone wheel which was turned by hand in a trough of water, ready for use in almost all farms in Newport. Some of these wheels, which started off with circumferences of perhaps 16 to 20 inches were still used as they wore down to little more than four or five inches. They would be repurposed in smaller troughs for sharpening men's razors and kitchen knives. Sharpening became another chore for the young teenagers, both boys and girls, to help in the running of the farms and logging operations.

Grindstone wheel (Pinterest)

***

The first Planche family and Heard/Hurd family marriage connection: [4] *(also: Planche family history)*

Author's note: The Planche family, generally known as the "Planches of Cookshire," immigrated from England to Leeds in Megantic County. Their children married into the Heard/Hurds of Newport, their children in turn connecting with many of the families of both Eaton and Newport.

John Paul[1] Planche (1788-1889) was born in England and married Elizabeth Aden when he was 23. They had one son, William[2] ("Willy") George (1811-1888), born in England. Elizabeth unfortunately died giving birth, leaving John Paul to bring up their infant son. Willy was 11 years old when John Paul married his second wife, Charlotte Gooding (1798-1876) in London, England in 1822. They had three children in England: Charles (1823-1847), Eliza Ann (1825-1893), and John[2] Paul Jr. (1829-1893). The family immigrated circa 1830 to Leeds, Megantic County in Lower Canada. In Leeds they had four more children: Edward (1831-1907), Charlotte (born 1834), Emily (born 1838), and Frederick (**born** 1842). John Paul[1] Planche became a government teacher at public schools in Leeds, a position he held until he retired.

John Paul[1] (known as "JP") Planche, with his wife Charlotte, his first son William[2] (Willy) and their family of four boys and three daughters) had travelled many times on the Bailey Path from Leeds to Newport and Eaton townships between 1833 and 1860. During these travels they met the Heard/Hurd families in the southwestern part of Newport in the small farming community of Maple Leaf. His children were of the age where they were looking to settle in this new region of opportunity bordering Newport and Eaton townships. After their children married and moved to Newport and Eaton townships, JP and Charlotte continued to live in Leeds. They travelled back and forth on this road many times to see their children, until they themselves moved to Cookshire sometime after 1860-62 when JP retired at 74 years of age. He died in Cookshire in 1889 at 101 years old.

JP and Charlotte came at a time when the Eastern Townships were experiencing extremely cold winters and would have found living conditions a challenge. Charles Planche, the second son, was the first Planche to marry a Heard. Charles married Matilda Rosetta Heard (Edmund[7] Heard and Mary Willard's third daughter) in 1844 and settled on Lot no. 12 of Range 10, one of the original lots assigned to Capt. Samuel[6] Heard. They built their first home there. Conditions began to improve during the following years; the lands were cleared, lumber was in abundance to sell and crops beginning to flourish.

Charles and Matilda Planche had a daughter, Mary Elizabeth, who was only one year old when her father Charles died in 1847 at age 24. Matilda continued to live at their homestead with Mary for four years, until she remarried. She married William Stevenson in 1851, and moved to William's family homestead in Learned Plain, Newport, where he had been living with his parents. Matilda and William had four children: three daughters and a son. Their son, Herman Alton, born in 1867, later became a farmer and held the offices of school commissioner, a prominent officer of the I.O.F., and organizer for the Patrons of Industry.[4]

Matilda's daughter Mary married Elijah Leggett in 1870 and moved to live with him and his parents on their farm in Auckland Township. Elijah's parents, Robert and Mary (Folsom), lived on Lot 10 of Range 11, across from the Rand farm on the Newport side of the South River, on the other side of the covered bridge.[4]

Author's note: As an example of land values during this time of settling Newport, it was noted that the original sale of the 200-acre farm to Robert Leggett had sold for 14 shillings and seven pence, the sale officiated by Samuel[7] A. Heard, Secretary Treasurer of the Corporation of Compton County at the time.[31]

The next occupied farm up the road from Auckland, on the Newport side of the river, was the home of Marshall[8] and Mary Maria (Heard) Rand. The two families could visit but had to ford the river while the water was low in the summer and fall months. Lewis Cable and his family also lived just across the river, as did as her sister Suzanna, who had married Lewis's son Charlie. These families were becoming a community in themselves as their children grew up together. The mothers would get together with the children often during the long winter months, passing the time remaking clothes for the coming year while the children played together.

Author's note: Interestingly, four of the Planche children married into the Heard/Hurd family . . . so not only did they live at nearby farms, but they were to have continuing close family ties. Two Hurd sisters and a brother married two of the Planche brothers and a sister; another Heard/Hurd cousin married the eldest Planche boy.[4]

JP and Charlotte Planche's eldest son, William[2] (Willy) George Planche, was 32 when he married his young bride of 17, Catherine Jennete ("Janet") Heard (daughter of John B[7] Heard) in 1842. They resided in Newport as farmers, on Lot 8 on the 10th Range. This farm was the original settlement and homestead of the William[5] and Thirza (Williams) Heard family. They raised seven children on this homestead: three sons and four daughters.[4]

During the summer and fall, Janet took the children out with her to the woods to hunt for certain herbs that she would dry and use for medicinal purposes. They often found little mounds of beech nuts which had been gathered by squirrels and picked them up for drying later. These trips were an exciting time for the children: running through the woods, exploring a brook or moss patch, watching for rabbits and birds, and of course the occasional snake. Janet was a young mother and so brought her children up almost as her friends, taking them everywhere she went. From an early age, Janet taught them all to swim; every summer they spent time swimming in the river. The old tanning hut that William had used for many years was still there by the river and had been converted to a change hut.

Janet made fresh bread early Sunday morning to take with them to the river where they had lunch on a table and bench that William had made some years before to work his leathers. The children would explore under the rocks for salamanders and perhaps a bug they had not seen before. If they saw berries, they would stop and pick them, hoping to pick enough for everyone for supper. Sometimes they saw a bear and would steer clear of them especially in the spring when they may have had cubs. This was the beginning of a time when children were treated more like children rather than extra farm hands, which allowed them to foster both imagination and ingenuity in learning life's lessons.

William (Willy) G. Planche operated the first post office in Maple Leaf during their early married years. Later they resettled in Eaton Township at Currier Hill before moving to Massachusetts for a time. They returned to Newport again after their children had grown and married. William[2] was a councillor in Newport as well for several years. He died in 1888 in Newport at age 77, one year before his father died in Cookshire, Eaton Township. Jennete (Janet) died 10 years later in Bridgewater, Mass., in 1899, at the home of her daughter Lucy.[4]

Surnames originating from the marriage of William[2] Planche and Catherine Jennete were Planche, Williams, Jordon, Lothrop, Copeland, Seale, Waterhouse, Stone and Hurd.

***

The Rand/Cable/Planche/Leggett/Heard/Hurd family connections:[4]

Author's note: These five families – Rand, Planche, Hurd, Cable and Leggett – were to bond with a close relationship in their own community at the junction of South River/Auckland and Newport as well as within that of the Maple Leaf community just down the road towards Randboro. Clusters of farms closely associated became mini communities. Matilda "Tilly" (Hurd) Planche and Mary Maria (Heard/Hurd) Rand were sisters. Jenette "Janet" Heard was a cousin of the two sisters and Eliza was the sister of the three Planche boys. (Note the Heard/Hurd name change.)[4]

Abigail Susanna Hurd, the fourth daughter of Edmund[7], married Charles ("Charlie") Cable. They raised two daughters: Flora, who married Abraham Lafleur, and Emma, who married John Arnott. They lived on a lot just off today's Route 210, across the South River in Auckland, next to the Leggetts. Surnames originating from Abigail's marriage were Arnott, Cable and Lafleur.[4]

Circa 1850 the BALC built a wooden covered bridge over the South Branch of the Eaton River which now connected the two townships of Newport and Eaton. This bridge allowed the closely knit families to visit more freely. Marshall,

Mary and family, who lived on the Newport side of the bridge, could now walk over to visit with Mary's niece, Mary Elizabeth and husband Elijah Leggett, her sister Susanna and Charlie Cable and their families as well – at any time.[31]

On the left side of the bridge was the site of the log home built by Charles[2] and his father Lewis[1] Cable. Charlie married Abigail Susanna Hurd, the fourth daughter of Edmund[7]. They had one daughter, Flora, who married Abram Lafleur. Both families continued to live in Auckland Township just south of the Newport line, across the road from the Leggett farm. Hattie Cable, a daughter of Lewis[1] Cable, married William Morrow in 1870; they raised their six sons in Island Brook.[4]

Covered bridge crossing the South River at the junction of today's Route 210 and the road towards Auckland Township, circa 1955 (The covered part of the bridge burned down in 2001.) (photo by author)

Surnames originating from the marriages of these women were Cable, Lafleur, and Morrow.

Author's note: Flora and Abram Lafleur had a son, Charles[3] (Charlie) Lafleur. Charlie married Grace Graham of Parker Hill; they lived in the hamlet of Randboro beside the original home of Charlie and Lottie McCallum, who had traded their home for a farm owned by John Jones on Parker Hill.

Ships knees used in the McDermott covered bridge (photo by Sandra Hurd)

Circa 1875 to 1880, most bridges in the area were renovated; after extensive repairs to their wooden infrastructure, they were covered with walls and a roof, ostensibly to protect the base and foundations from the elements. The construction of these covered bridges further added to the general economy of the Township providing the lumber and more expressly, "ships knees." These unique knee-shaped braces provided the strength to withstand the heavy snow loads in winter, and also provided a more solid framework necessary to withstand the continual vibration from the many horses and sleds passing through the bridge every day.

The origin of the term "ships knees" stems from their use in shipbuilding and were exported from both Upper Canada and Lower Canada. They were essentially the roots or large branch curvatures that provided a sturdy one-piece brace, using the same concept that Marshall Rand was providing for lumber sleds. The brace could be angled on the back side to match a ships curvature, providing tremendous strength for the hulls. As this style of the shipbuilding started to wane by this era, a new use for ships knees began to emerge in covered bridge building. Many of the lumbermen in Island Brook and surrounding townships were now collecting and making ships knees as an additional business and shipping them out with other lumber for export south to the U.S. market. In the reconstruction of the old bridges all over the New England states, covered bridges using ships knees were now becoming big business.

In 1855, the first principles of law in Newport came into force. On July 23, 1855, the following residents became councillors: Alden Learned, Charles[7] Sawyer, Samuel[7] A. Hurd, William[2] G. Planche, Gilbert T. Williams, Charles B. Hawley and William Stevenson Jr.[32]

It was also during this era that a "bridge tax" was initiated by the townships in order to pay for both their construction and ongoing maintenance. A receipt of payment by Augustus[8] Hurd was *"[dated] November 21st, 1855, [signed] C. H. Harvey, Sec-Treasurer, Newport."*[31]

Augustus[8] Hurd (eldest son of John B.[7] and Polly Sawyer) married Eliza Ann Planche (eldest daughter of Willy and Charles Planche) in 1847. They had six children, two sons and four daughters: John Bennett[9], Augustus[9] Frederick, Ella Jane, Edith A., Ellen, and Eliza Mary.[4]

Surnames originating from the marriage of Augustus[8] and Eliza's daughters were Jones, Lindsay, Beecher and Nourse.

Augustus[8] and Eliza Hurd's eldest daughter, Ella Jane, married Lorin Jones. They resided in Sawyerville and had no children.

Eliza Ann (Planche) and Augustus[8] Hurd

Their second daughter, Edith A., received her diploma at the age of 18, *"to teach elementary schools in the district of St. Francis and Bedford,* passing all the requirements of *"Reading, Geography, Sacred history, History, Canada, Arithmetic, Dictation and Grammar,"* from the Board of Examiners, *"this second day of May in the year 1876, [signed] N.R. Doan, President, S.A. Heard, Secretary."* Edith A. married Charles Lindsay and they moved to the U.S., where they raised two children.[4]

The third daughter, Ellen, taught school for a few years before meeting and marrying Hazen A. Beecher at Richmond. They moved to Augusta, Me., and had no children.[4]

Their fourth daughter, Eliza Mary, married Henry J. Nourse. They moved to Coaticook and also had no children. Unfortunately, Henry died in middle age of his injuries after a ram butted him into a fence.

> *Author's note: Augustus[8] and Eliza Ann's children are my great-uncles and great-aunts. Their youngest son, Augustus[9] Frederick, was my grandfather. This was a connection that I have to the Planche family. The other is through my wife, Sandra. Kate Marie Hurd, daughter of Frederick Augustine[8], son of Tyler[7] Hurd, married Lloyd Leslie Planche in a later generation. Kate Marie and Lloyd Leslie Planche were Sandra's grandparents. Kate Marie Hurd was a direct-line descendant of Capt. Edmund[6] Heard.*

Augustus[8] and Eliza lived on the original farm of Edmund[6] and John[7] B. Heard/Hurd. A bill of release, dated 1856, from Polly Sawyer (Hurd) to her son, *"Augustus[8] in the sum of two hundred and twenty-five dollars was made on the 29 July 1856, witnessed by James Beaman & William Loveland."* Augustus[8] was a farmer, lumberman and businessman in Newport Township. During their lifetime, Augustus[8] and Eliza accumulated several hundred acres of land in Newport, Auckland, Eaton and Ditton townships.[31]

On February 2, 1857, Augustus purchased a one-half acre Lot 13, on the 11th Range, beginning on the northeast corner in Auckland. This lot fronted on the South River just across the bridge from Newport to Auckland from today's Route 210. In February 1858 he bought another 50 acres of Lot 11 in the 10th Range of Newport. That same year, Augustus purchased the standard 200-acre Lot 13, on the 11th Range in Auckland. He acquired several additional lots in Newport, and in 1861 purchased another 200-acre lot in Ditton Township. His purchases were from both the BALC and the *Municipality of the County of Compton*. Augustus served on the Newport Municipal Council and opened up many new settlements by building connecting roads.[31]

On July 26, 1859, John Paul[1] Planche Sr. wrote a letter to his son-in-law, Augustus Hurd (who was married to JP's eldest daughter, Eliza A. Planche) immediately after he had returned home to Leeds from his trip to Newport. He described his trip and confirmed he wished to buy the land Augustus had offered to sell him. He bought the land in Auckland, where his son, John Paul[2] Planche Jr. set up his first sawmill, circa 1860-65. The land was located on the South Branch of the Eaton River near the existing bridge on today's Route 210, which took them into Newport Township where the Hurd family lived. This was the lumber mill that would be sold to Lester Wooten, who by the early 1900s employed 40-60 men in his operation.[31]

Author's note: The structure of the letter itself is interesting (referenced above, shown below). It is written on a sheet of lined paper which was normal even at this time. When folded, the letter become the envelope. What is interesting is that as late as 1859 people were still writing the letter so that it could be folded to become the envelope. This was the practice in the early 1700s because paper was scarce, and the practice clearly continued until 1859 and later.[10] The letter is reproduced here:

Leeds, July 26th, 1859

My dear children,

We arrived here at home about 8 o'clock much fatigued on Monday end. We had hail, thunder and heavy rain and we were nearly wetted to the skin. I rejoice to say all here are well by God's mercy, the crops of wheat and barley on the way are good. Potatoes middling, buckwheat miserable the same of the hay on our farm. The wheat splendid, the potatoes cover the ground. Buckwheat hardly worth cutting, good barley about average, rather short, some very fair the greater part hay. An average crop of turnips, carrots, cabbage, and onions look well. If no accident takes place with the wheat, we shall have enough for bread on the whole. I may say it is wonderful after what I have seen and I feel that I am most unworthy of what am I, that the Lord should grant me so many helpings. The love of my children whilst with them caused my heart to sing with joy, may God help you help them. Surely the Lord has been about my paths on Monday. I would have written but the Post had left before I arrived at home Tuesday. I scrawled a few lines to Fred and began this letter but could not finish it. I only feel that I have recovered from my journey this day Thursday. Your mother has stood the journey better than I have and now my dear Augustus I have spoken to the boys about the 200 acres of land in Auckland that you offered to sell to me for ten pounds. I will take it at that price and pay you five pounds this fall and five pounds next year and you will please do me the favour to write and let me know if the payments will suit you. It may be a means of our ultimately being near you. It rained all day yesterday and today we have not cut any hay and shall not till the weather is more settled. I pray you help the dear children. I hope Johnny and Ella will sometimes think of us and try and love us.

Your mother and each one here desire to give their most sincere love and now dear Augustus and Eliza believe me, your affectionate parents.

J. P. & Charlotte Planche

The letter was received by the main post office in Eaton Township, located in Eaton Corner. The letter would have then been sent to the post office in Randboro, operated by Samuel[7] Newell Hurd, to be picked up by John Paul's son, Willie Planche, who was the postmaster in Maple Leaf at the time. At this point, the addressee paid for the mailing as no stamps were used.[10]

Date-stamped folded letter without envelope, as had been done years earlier (Hurd family collection)

Author's notes: *July 26: Letter authored by John Paul Planche, Sr.*
July 29: Stamped at "Leeds Township" in Megantic County
July 30: Stamped "LC" (i.e., Lower Canada)
Aug 2: Stamped Randboro P.O.

John Bennet and Polly (Sawyer)'s second daughter, Gratia Hurd, married Edward Planche, the fourth son of John P.[1] and Charlotte. They moved to Cookshire, along with his third brother, John Paul[2] Jr. and his wife Jane McIntyre. This part of the family was to thrive in self-made businesses in Eaton Township, and became known as the "Cookshire Planches."[4]

It was during this era, after canned goods had been available for some time, that the can opener and Mason jar were invented. These two products became the mainstay of any household in Newport, with canning and preserves being "put up" each fall. Many of the women in the Maple Leaf community, Eliza (Beaman) Loveland, Matilda (Heard) Planche, Eliza (Planche) Hurd, Mary Maria (Hurd) Rand, Jennette (Heard) Planche, and Eliza (McCurdy) Hurd, the Leggetts and the Cable families would all get together on a farm and hold a preserving and canning day. This was another way for the women to have the opportunity to share in the news of the neighbourhood children, their husbands, and their own troubles. This was also the "era" where some stores were beginning to sell canned products, so tin cans were the first metal garbage of the day, beginning the "tin can era." Since there was no organized garbage disposal at the time, farmers tended to bury them in land depressions, usually found in meadows. Rusty cans in abundance can still be found in these depressions today; some collectors still pick through the piles and resell the cans at far higher prices than they were ever sold for filled with product during these times.

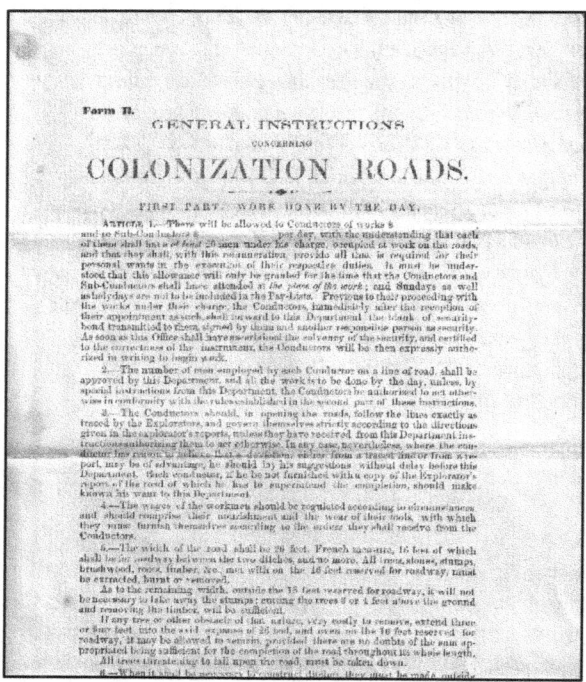

General instructions notice for contractors pertaining to colonization roads

Augustus[8] Hurd was operating multiple businesses at this time. He was farming with his family, raising cattle, sheep and the usual chickens. He also grew and sold hops each year to a market in Montreal. He was heavily into the road building business, building "colonization" roads – the connecting roads within and to adjacent townships. He was also in the lumbering business, or "logging" as it was referred to. In the process of building new roads and opening up new lots for new settlers, trees need to be felled so there were logs to sell. Augustus found himself on both sides of the fence: operating a farm and empathizing with the farmers on poor road conditions, but at the same time operating a lucrative lumbering business, hauling the heavy loads which rutted the roads he was in charge of building for the township – a lucrative business indeed.[31]

This was also when Augustus Hurd and Marshall Rand began working together building roads for the BALC in Newport.

On September 2, 1862, the Office of the Municipal Council for the Municipality of Newport wrote: [31]

> *Messrs. Marshall Rand and Augustus Hurd.*
>
> *You having been appointed as a committee to let the building of a portion of the highway on the fifth and sixth range line of Newport—I therefore have the honor to submit for your guidance the following detailed statement of the available means at your disposal for the contrition of the said road.*
>
> *The detailed statement indicated that the road assessments were as follows:*
>
> *Township of Newport $452.02, Township of Ditton $129.36, Township of Clinton $719,73.*
>
> *The amount payable on the first of November next $260.40 The balance of $459.33 will be mostly collected so that it can be paid on the first of December next, and that there will perhaps be $75.00 that it will not do to promise before the first of February 1865.*
>
> *[Signed] Charles H. Harvey, Sec. levy Treasurer. Municipality of Newport.*

Augustus[8] Hurd and Marshall[8] Rand worked together on two fronts, building these colonization and connecting roads as well as the lumbering operations resulting from clearing the lands for the road building. Their wives and older children were pretty much running the farms during this time.

Building these colonization roads was not without certain specifications. Each township mayor, under the presidency of Warden Lewis McIver, was sent the notice:

> *It was ordained and resolved by Law of the Council circa 1883, to regulate the width of winter roads in Compton County. Width of single and double sleds be not less than forty inches from outside to outside of runners and that the width of sleighs, single or double be not less than thirty-six inches from outside to outside of the runners. That all sleds used by one animal be in a manner that the left runner follows in the track of the animal. By order of Lewis McIver and Sec Treas. Cyrus A. Bailey.*[24]

A detailed guide for the building of these roads was provided to each township. It included several pages of rules and regulations and 32 articles of general instruction. The document was produced by the Department of Agriculture and Public Works, signed by *E. Moreau Inspector of Colonization* in 1871.[31]

Lumbermen and typical virgin forest logging sled using both horses and oxen (Andrew Hind)

Augustus and Marshall built a logging road through to Ditton Township following the Newport-Auckland border line to the South Branch of the Ditton River. Each spring they floated logs downriver on the South Branch of the Eaton River to either the mill at the junction of today's Route 210 and Auckland Road (operated by his wife Eliza's brother, John Paul[2] Planche), or to Stillman Rand's mill in Randville.

Augustus had been advised on August 14, 1866, by the Secretary General of Newport, Ditton, Chesham, Clinton and Auckland, Charles Harvey, that *"His Excellency the Governor General wishes to inform you, that you are appointed a valuator for the Municipalities of Newport, Ditton, Chesham, Clinton and Auckland effective the 8th instant, September 1866."* The document was certified on August 22, 1866, *"that he would faithfully perform the duties of Valuator agreeing to the foregoing named appointment. [Signed] S. A. Hurd, J. P."* [31]

Now that BALC was providing roads throughout Newport, Augustus was challenging the location of a "highway" that was proposed to follow the travelled "path" road running right through his property. When these original roads were initiated, in his grandfather's time, these roads were built by the settlers as part of the prerequisite of the "land grants" of the time. *"Each settler had to set aside a "common" road allowance running in front of their homestead which could be connected by adjacent settlers."* [31]

Most often these roads were built around swamps, large hills, or other obstacles and so they essentially followed the lay of the land. Another factor was that homesteads were built on elevated areas where possible, but lower than the springs that were to ultimately provide a downhill supply of water. The roads leading to the homes also may run right through a property. Since these first roads were simple with no ditches, farmers could drive across them at any point with their wagons, buggies, and sleds anywhere on the property, almost like an extension to the fields.[20, 31]

Given this, it would be a reasonable argument that Augustus would prefer that the proposed "highway" be surveyed closer to the edge of his lot line. He would prefer that the proposed road would not cut through a part of his farm, which in this case would cut a corner of 50 acres off the top end of his lot, accessible only by crossing a ditch. There were no culverts to cross over these ditches. He didn't care that it might mean a longer driveway from his house and barns to the main road.

An excerpt from the Council meeting of October 7, 1867:

> *Survey made in June last, of a highway from what is known as "Beaman's Turn" on the line between lots number 9 on the 10th Range of Newport from there recording the survey to the Town line of Newport and Auckland. After discussion, it was proposed and agreed to by the parties interested and also by this Council to leave the matter to Arbitration. Moved by Councilor Wm. Stevenson and seconded by Councilor McGee and resolved that James Munn and William Sawyer of Eaton Township hereby be appointed as arbitrators in said matter and report back to this Council next session.*
>
> *[Signed] Charles H. Harvey Sec. Treas.* [31]

An excerpt from the Council meeting of November 4, 1867:

> *Municipalities of Newport, Ditton, Chesham, Clinton, and Auckland.*
>
> *The matter of establishing the highway, as surveyed by C.E. Towle, June last for discussion.*
>
> *The establishment of said survey was opposed by Augustus Hurd and after deliberation upon the matter, it was moved by Councilor Samuel Hurd and seconded by Councilor Paquette (Auckland), that it be resolved that Alden Learned is hereby appointed as special Superintendent with a view to establishing a road according to the survey as stated first in June of last.*
>
> *That is to say to commence at the Northwest corner post of Lot No. 8, of Range 10 of Newport, thence according to said survey to the place of Russel Sunbury, thence commencing at the Beaman turn on the side line between lots No. 9 and 10 until it strikes the line dividing the N. and S.1/2 lots of 9 and 10, thence to return into the now travelled road at a distance of 8 rods South of said, thence on the now travelled road until it reaches a distance of eight miles North from the N.E. corner of the South 50 acres of Lot No. 9 in the 10th Range and to return to the said survey of the said corners from thence to follow the said survey to the Town line of Newport and Auckland Township.*
>
> *[Signed] Charles H. Harvey Sec. Levi Tres. M.C. of Newport.*[31]

And so, the road as we still know it today was established in 1867, running from the corner (Maple Leaf school of circa 1901), northeast up to Cora Austin's farm, and from that same corner south past the Morrison farm to the Auckland Township Line, right through the middle of Lot 9 in both ranges 10 and 11. The road continued from the junction point of Morrison Road, across lots 10, 11 and 12 in a southeasterly direction to the Newport-Auckland town line, where a bridge was to be built to cross the South Branch of the Eaton River into Auckland Township.

It was at this time that the Hon. John Henry Pope was asking Augustus if they could have a daily post at the Rand farm location so he could pick up his daily tabs from his mining operations. The proposal was that if Marshall Rand could pick up the daily tallies and mail deliveries from the mine, Pope could then pick them up from Rand's. Augustus and Marshall were in fact cutting through that region building logging roads and so were already there. Marshall was to bring the mining tabs back from the mine and use his place as a temporary post office for mail pick-up. Augustus[8] Hurd was having a direct dialogue with the Hon. J. H. Pope in establishing and providing a sort of special delivery service from the Ditton Gold Mine.

An excerpt from the letter written to Augustus:

> *. . . that the trail can be made wide and that you will provide service for $25 dollars per annum. That if you want it all the way up to your place then we can do that for the same price. But if you want the service carried from Sawyerville to Rands, you must write to me and you must name your Postmaster and your Post Office. [Signed] J.H. Pope, House of Assembly.*[10, 31]

***

Lumber mills had now become the economic driver, operating in Island Brook, Randville, Sawyerville, Cookshire and East Angus, and offered a ready market for the settlers' surplus lumber. Softwood, commonly known as "pulpwood," was now in demand for the paper mills in East Angus and elsewhere. Augustus and his men were to capitalize on this continuing opportunity.

***

It was during this era that property insurance became available. Up to this point when buildings were lost to fire or storms, the loss to a family was one of complete destitution. The communities then, of course, would gather together and help rebuild a house or barn, however the materials would have to be paid for by the homeowners and so the loss to a family was severe.

If livestock were lost then it might take years for a farmer to acquire sufficient replacements to allow themselves to prosper once again. Policies issued by companies such as the *Stanstead & Sherbrooke Mutual Fire Insurance Company*, established in 1835, available for businesses, were now becoming affordable to the farming communities.[31]

A policy no 11845, for Augustus Hurd, dated December 17, 1860, with Stanstead & Sherbrooke Mutual lists insurance coverage for the term of five years (1860 to 1865) on his property; listed as two barns, hay & grain therein, for the commitment sum of 400.00 dollars, 20 dollars and 60 cents, payable in installments at 3% interest.[31]

***

This was a time when very few farmers had a clock. In the winter, the school children waited until they saw smoke from the chimney of the schoolhouse before starting their trek to school. Augustus and Eliza bought perhaps one of the first clocks in the community, a novel wooden geared unit. This helped the children get to school on time when the warmer weather began in the springtime and there was no smoke for them to see.

The school was just up the road from Augustus and Eliza's home, however, many other children in the community had a long walk to get there and would not necessarily see the smoke in the morning on a cloudy day. Having a clock in the house, showing the correct time, was also helpful on cold winter days. It allowed Eliza time to hitch up the horse and sleigh to pick up some of the other children who lived further along the road.

Pratt & Frost clock in Ancestral Heard/ Hurd Collection

Two clockmakers named Daniel Pratt and Jonathan Frost formed a partnership in 1832 and operated their businesses in Reading Square, Mass. An unusual feature of the clocks was they often had the date of manufacture printed on a label pasted to the inside of the cabinet. Often old labels continued to be used for the next year or so, with the original date on the label crossed out and the new year inscribed. Pratt & Frost dissolved in 1835, each partner going his own way. Frost continued making clocks until about 1850 and Pratt until 1858.

All wooden clock mechanism

At that time these clocks sold for $7. Pratt provided many families with reliable clocks at modest prices for that time, relieving settling families from dependence on the sun or the smoke from a chimney as a gauge of time.

You may note that the working mechanism was made of wooden gears which was significant to make them more affordable. *"After the clocks were next wound,"* (meaning that they had to be wound every day) was just another in the daily chores before starting the day. Augustus[8] and Eliza were given one of these as a gift in 1847 when they married and set up house in the old John Bennett[7] home.

***

Much to the annoyance of the families in Newport, the school administration was guided under Eaton Township jurisdiction as part of Sherbrooke County. They felt they deserved their own methods of running the school that had been initiated and built to serve their community by the original settlers and had been operating satisfactorily since its beginning in 1804. Hezekiah Austin, who was a councillor in Newport and held the office of school commissioner for Newport during this time, joined forces with Augustus to challenge this jurisdiction. In 1867, they received the following letter[31] from the Commissioner of Schools for the region, winning their battle for independence:

> *Augustus Hurd Esq., Newport 1867.*
>
> *I have the honor to inform you that his excellency the Governor General was pleased on the 16th instant in a virtue of the 1st Clause of the Act 12 U & 50.*
>
> *To separate the Township of Newport, County of Sherbrooke, from the scholastic Municipals' of Eaton and to create it into a separate scholastic municipality with the name and limits it has as Township aforesaid and to let subside the said Municipality of Eaton with its former limits that had been distracted as aforesaid, the said erection to have effect on the first day of July instant.*
>
> *The landowners in said Township will then be authorized by law to make an election of School Commissioners in virtue of the 5th & 6th Clauses of the Act 12 U & 27."*
>
> *Your obedient servant, [Signed] S. W. Williams*
> *County of Sherbrooke* [31]

***

Home of Augustus and Eliza (Planche) Hurd (Hurd family collection)

Augustus[8] and Eliza had a large chicken coop on the farm and the girls would delight in getting up early to collect the eggs which supplied the farm. Any overage would, of course, be for sale. Sometimes split wood was used in summer to create a temporary corral for their chickens to run outside. These wooden fences sometimes protected the chickens from foxes which were a real threat.

Occasionally the children would find a "stolen nest," i.e., a cache of eggs, as hens will try laying eggs outside of the fenced area. This of course became an exciting event. Foxes are always on the alert for both a stray bird and/or a cache of eggs. This would surely be a reason for the foxes to be ever close to the chicken house, and so the girls were always on the lookout for these nests and for foxes. There was a recipe for catching foxes handed down from their great-grandmother Lucy Bennett Heard: *"Mix oile of amber and oile of spike beeswax, goos oile and bevers casters, all simored together in the goos oile and then oint the trap with the same and put a little in the bead but not on the gate."* [10]

Even during these times when parents were strict, children willingly tested their limits. Augustus received a letter from the schoolteacher dated November 28, 1861, regarding the conduct in class of his son John B[9]:

> *I take the liberty to send you a note, to inform you of the conduct of your son. He has already taken the liberty to tell me he will do as he likes, in spite of all I can do. Now I wish very much to maintain order in school, and in order to do so, such things must be attended to immediately. I therefore inform you of it and wish you would reprimand him as I think you could have more influence over him than I could. I don't wish to have trouble but must insist on obedience. [Signed] A. H. Harvey* [10]

***

Edith A. Hurd, the second daughter of Augustus and Eliza, married Charles Lindsey in 1852. Charles was born in Eaton Township, the son of Robert and Emily (Alden) Lindsay of Eaton. They had two daughters, both born in Eaton. They all moved to Hallowell, Me.

***

By this time, in the third generation of Newport residents, candle-making became much easier. Kerosene lamps were available but were expensive and were not yet in widespread use in Newport. Tin moulds had now become available for sale and quickly became popular, becoming another item sought after by the communities. A cotton wick was stretched through the mould, tied in a knot at the pointed end and attached to the base plate at the large end. The mould was filled with melted tallow and set to cool. When hardened, the candles were drawn out and put away in a candle box. Eliza and her daughters Ella, Jane, Ellen, and Eliza Mary could now make several hundred candles in a few days – enough to last all year. The disappointing part of this new, efficient process was it eliminated the necessity for the womenfolk to gather for their annual candle-making bee.[42]

***

John Paul[2] Planche Jr. married Jane McIntyre; they moved to Cookshire circa 1850 where they raised three sons: Henry A., James and Lloyd Leslie. They opened a general store under the name of *J. P. Planche & Son* that, over time, became a very prosperous venture. JP had also established a flour mill which was sold later to the Standish family.[16]

Edward Planche, (JP's younger brother) married Gratia Hurd in 1855 and they had two children, Ada and John Harold. By 1860 the family had also moved from Newport to Cookshire. Edward was a staunch Methodist and was serving on the church board in March 1860 when they were considering building a church in Cookshire.

Surnames originating from the marriage of Edward and Gratia Planche were Gates, Goodenough, Planche, Ross and Studd.

***

The Hurd, McCurdy (Makurerdy) and Rand family connections: [4] *(also: C. Rand family history)*

> *Author's note*: The name *Makurerdy* dates back to 1400 in Ahoghil, Ireland, with a name change to McCurdy circa the 1600s. Petheric McCurdy married Margaret Stewart, a direct descendant of the Stewarts who go back to Sir John Stewart, born in 1360, a descendant of King Robert of Scotland. Their son, David McCurdy, married a Margaret Laughlin in Ireland from a refugee Scottish family. At a couple of points in the genealogy, the Irish men married Scottish women. John McCurdy (1774-1858) married Sarah Howard, whose mother's maiden name was "Knox," a direct descendant of John Knox, the Scottish reformer.
>
> *Thus the McCurdy family was a combination of Irish and Scottish descent. A grandson of this family, George, married Laura Haskell, daughter of John and Lucy (Hutson) Haskell. They were from the same family as Mark Haskell (1658-1691) who had immigrated earlier to the New England Colonies. Mark's granddaughter, Pricilla Haskell, born in 1718 at Gloucester, Mass., married Edmund[4] Heard in 1742 at Ipswich, Mass. They were the parents of our Col. Edmund[5] Heard of Newport. And so, the connections amongst these families went back a long time.*[4] (Rand family history)

The first generation of McCurdys to come to Canada came directly from Ireland. George and his wife, Laura Haskell McCurdy, and their children Eliza, William and Laura, settled in Ascot, Lower Canada, circa the early 1800s. The George McCurdy family was the beginning of yet another family that immigrated from Ireland but that already had a connection to the Heard family and were now to make connections with both the Heard and Rand families.

By the latter part of the 1870s most families were now branching out to other communities and, while roads were still rough, these families travelled between the communities of Maple Leaf, Island Brook, Sawyerville, Bury, Eaton Corner, Birchton, Bulwer and Ascot/Lennoxville. The region surrounding the Maple Leaf community indeed was growing as one large family of relatives and now beginning to mesh into these other communities.

Author's note: When one family's siblings marry multiple siblings of another family, tracing the lineages can get very confusing. However, new blood lines were essential for an ever-increasing group of relatives living in rather tight communities. I will try to unravel this new assortment of people and hopefully make it understandable. Capt. Edmund[7] Heard and his wife Mary (Willard) Heard had a son, Edmund[8] H. Heard, and four daughters. Their eldest daughter, Mary Maria[8] had married Marshall S. Rand; and one of their daughters Hannah Elvira and a son Willard S. married into the McCurdy family. Edmund[8] Haskell Heard also married into the McCurdy family. The community generally referred to Edmund[8] by his second name, Haskell, mostly to keep the names they were referring to straight, with so many Edmunds circulating.

Edmund[8] Haskell Heard married Eliza McCurdy in 1863. They had four daughters: Laura Abigail (born 1865), Mary Maria (born 1870), Sarah Eliza (born 1875) and Jessie Minerva (born 1878). Unfortunately, Eliza died young at age 46 in 1888 from tuberculosis, only 10 years after Jessie was born.[4]

Edmund[8] Haskell and Eliza (McCurdy) Hurd

Surnames originating from the marriage of the daughters of the Edmund Haskell Heard line were Hurd, Lawson, Riddell and Swail. In 1871, William H. McCurdy married Hannah E. Rand, a daughter of Mary M. (Hurd) Rand; and William's sister, Sarah McCurdy, married Willard S. Rand (Hannah's brother).

The 1871 census of Newport shows that a Roland Larrabee, aged 14, born in the U.S., was living with Edmund and Eliza and their family at that time. It was not unusual during this time that many children who were left homeless, their parents having died young of disease or accidents, would be taken in by other families who may have befriended their parents or may have worked with their parents at some juncture.

In a letter to Edmund[8] a friend visiting from the U.S., Thomas Colby wrote: *"I forgot to leave that thimble for you but will send it next writing and let me know how you make it catching foxes. I have not tried to catch any yet on account of being here in Hereford. I have cut my foot awfully bad so I have not been able to do anything for a week and do not know when I can. I have not got back to Free America yet and don't know when I shall."* [10]

***

During the 1850s, a torrent of books poured forth into Canada, detailing everything that should be done in the house and how to do it. Household skills that a previous generation had taken for granted were now carefully defined in astonishing detail. Books detailed how and when to receive guests in "the parlour," how to cook every piece of an animal's carcass, and how to bind a wound. These were all tasks our ancestors most assuredly would have been able to do to survive, without even needing to pause as to the why or how. Imagine how the settlers must have felt to read it all from a book that any one of our ancestors could have easily written. Nevertheless, to see this written out may have provided a certain degree of substantiation. Urban homemakers at this time were looking for more modern ways of doing things and these books exposed them to any number of ideas they could pass on to their daughters simply because it was in print. And so, with books becoming more readily accessible, many of the recipes our ancestors just knew would no longer have to be passed on verbally, as they were able to forward them to various publishers for printing.[35]

***

Gathering hay was another chore for Edmund and his family when weather dictated the timing that would ensure a successful harvest. Earlier, the settlers simply used a scythe to cut the hay but now they were using crude mowers drawn by horses. The whole family would follow behind with handmade wooden-toothed rakes, essentially raking a whole field into bundles. Using three-tined pitchforks, they would load a wagon, placing bundles on each of the four corners, then filling in the centre so the hay would tie into itself and stay on the wagon. They would then head for the barn. Gathering and storing hay was a very strenuous and laborious operation.

Loading hay the traditional way so it wouldn't fall off the wagon was an art in itself (BAnQ)

In haying season, timing was of the essence, and it was critical to have good quality hay. Haskell, Eliza and his oldest daughters would strive to get the hay cut, dried and raked ready for storing before any rain. The girls were just children at this point, so the parents would call on neighborhood boys to help them during this critical time. Haskell was not yet able to afford the new hayloader that had recently been invented, which would have greatly improved the speed of loading the wagons. Some of the hay may have been put directly into the barns, though most was piled high just outside, since these original barns were built with little space over the stables.

Edmund and Eliza had built a "root cellar" on their farm similar to those in the New England Colonies. Root cellars were often built to preserve the family's fruit and vegetables from winter frost. The cellar was positioned as a dug-out cavity into the side of a slope not far from the house. The front was built of stones layered like a foundation and accessed by a heavy hand-built wooden door, the roof covered with earth and sod. Their home was still an original log home which sat on a stone base with no cellar. This was a deciding factor as to why many of the first homesteaders had built the root cellars. The original homesteader's main preoccupation was to get a roof over their heads and build suitable housing for their livestock before winter set in. They had no time to devote to digging a cellar first. Over time, these old log homes were replaced by newer sawn-lumber homes with stone cellars.[42]

Keeping the fires burning was another challenge for the women. This task was made dramatically easier by the invention of the safety match in 1855. Another first in this era, baking powder, available from mid-century, put an end to the heavy, flat cakes that had been the norm. The girls delighted in the chore of making bread for the family as they got to sample the first out of the oven. New three-tier stoves that also heated the houses were being installed in the homes, replacing the hearth fireplaces of the past. A baking oven was incorporated in the middle section for the very purpose of baking bread, pies, etc. A small bit of bread dough was saved from one baking to the next and served as a yeast culture. Later in the day the bread dough would be set in the warming section to rise. Sometimes the "hasty pudding" would be placed there to keep warm. Hasty pudding was made of yellow cornmeal, simmered in an iron pot on the front section of the stove for the day, ready for a snack before bed. These new stoves were unique in that they had a top "warming shelf" that could be used to keep warm the food that had been cooked earlier on the stovetop. This was especially helpful when cooking for large families.[18, 31]

***

Edmund H. and Eliza did a brisk business selling both hardwood and softwood lumber as they cleared more land to cultivate. They also raised hops for extra money and had a herd of sheep and Ayrshire cattle. The Ayrshire breed is believed to have originated in Ayrshire in southwest Scotland. In the early years they were known as Cunningham's then Dunlop's. With so many people immigrating from Scotland and Ireland at this time, the Ayrshire breed was a natural to be imported into the region. They were known for the ability to convert grass into milk efficiently and had a hardiness about them. The breed's strong points were the desired traits of easy calving and longevity. Ayrshire cows were good milkers; the bulls and steers were suitable as oxen; and the young steers were a good source of beef for the table. Ayrshire milk was considered the ideal drinking milk.

Haskell Hurd was a farmer but his love was woodworking, and he was good at it. He built a large workshop where he built himself a large wagon and lumber sled that he put to immediate use both summer and winter, hauling produce, hay and logs. He made tools and fashioned equipment. Many in the community came to him to help them fix an article or make something new. When his youngest daughter, Jessie, was born in 1878, he made her a little rocking chair of yellow birch he had cut from the woods. He also was a staunch Methodist, and he and the family did not miss the services held at this time in the Maple Leaf schoolhouse on Sundays. With busy daylight hours and poor light after sundown, most Bible reading was done on Sundays. In his letters he often wrote of travel to secure funding for the church and missionaries, as well as having church meetings at the schoolhouse.

Haskell and his family had many visitors from around the township, and they did like a good party. Many of their visitors would come to visit and have a cup of tea and biscuits, or simply to have something made or fixed. They mostly included his immediate neighbours, Marshall and Mary (Hurd) Rand and William[1] and Eliza (Beaman) Loveland and families. The Planche family farm was also nearby, along with that of his cousin Augustus[8] and wife Eliza Planche and their children. His sister, Abigail, and her husband Charlie Cable lived just beyond the fork of today's Route 210 on the way to North River. Charlie and Abigail would later move to a farm in Randville (Randboro), just up Parker Hill from the South River on the left-hand side of the bridge. One of his cousins, George Hurd, and George's wife Amelia, were living on his father Luke's farm just down the road towards Randville. They were a closely-knit community of family ties as well as friends who could call upon each other or share in times of need.

Children's rocker, crafted by Haskell Hurd in 1882 from yellow birch from his farm for his 4-year-old daughter Jessie

Lewis[8] and his wife Lucy Minerva (Hurd) Bowker and their children often paid a visit even though it was a long trip for them from North River Road. They had three lively boys – Edmund[9], Lyman and Herbert – and a daughter, Luvia, who loved to visit with Haskell and Eliza's daughters, enjoying hide-and-seek in the barns and around the yard, and lots of homemade bread and sweets to end the day.

Another cousin, Samuel[8] Newell Heard, (a son of Luke[7]), married Persis D. Williams. Persis was the daughter of Gilbert P. Williams of Newport. Samuel and Persis operated a small farm in Randville while also owning a general store there and serving as postmaster for 23 years. They had one son, Phineas, born in 1862, who unfortunately died at age 21. Samuel held the office of Mayor of Newport for 12 years, was school commissioner for several terms, and was also the justice of the peace. Samuel and Persis were also staunch Methodists.[4, 16]

***

It was during this time that vendors loaded with all kinds of household commodities began to flood to the rural communities. They were in the business of selling anything that made them money. Carter's Little Liver Pills were said to cure sick headaches, dyspepsia, indigestion, dizziness, nausea, drowsiness, bad taste in the mouth, coated tongue, pain in the side and a turbid liver. There were tonics, blood purifiers, and many other cures with various ointments and, of course, sweet candies that were so different from what was perhaps made at home. They carried whatever was new for a rural market, which was not necessarily new in urban settings. In these settlements travel was for necessity, never merely for pleasure. Many of these wares were new to the area and required a certain scrutiny. Our ancestors were an honest and God-fearing group and so trusted others to be the same; however, once tricked the community would not be tricked twice so it was "vendor beware." Besides, the rural families worked on their land continuously and had no time to travel much beyond Newport to purchase anything. These vendors would arrive at the store front with the local children all vying for a spot to see what Samuel and Persis Heard might be stocking their store with, in the hopes that candy might be available for sampling.

Stores were not self-serve in these days. Behind the counter were shelves right up to the ceiling, packed with a wide range of canned food and Mason jars of pickles, beets, carrots and more. When you came in to shop at their general store in Randville you sat down on a chair and called out your grocery needs while Sam or Persis or a helper would fill your order. Bread, usually baked on site, was placed on side tables along with a variety of baked goods that may have been purchased from other farmers' wives from around the community. Newspapers and magazines were available, along with candies in huge Mason jars placed in full view of a child's discerning eye. String hung down within easy reach from rolls of twine held in wire hoops near the ceiling. Sam or one of his helpers would wrap the purchases in brown paper and tie up the parcels with twine. The brown paper was hung under the counter in huge rolls with a cutter that simply laid across the roll. They would pull on the paper and rip off what was required to wrap the bottles so they wouldn't break on the way home.

Now that they were cultivating more land, many of the farmers were now expanding to acquire more livestock including horses, cattle, pigs, sheep, and fowl. Butter and eggs drew a weekly source of income after the needs of the household were met; any surplus would be taken to surrounding stores and sold or traded for other goods. In the fall, pigs were slaughtered, the meat salted and packed in pork barrels which were now standard in every household. Any excess of produce from the Maple Leaf community was taken to the store in Randville and offered to the town of Sawyerville for sale in the general stores there. The farmers in the Island Brook region generally took their produce to Cookshire, much of which was loaded on trains for an ever-expanding urban trade.

With some canned foods and many dried foods now becoming available, Samuel and Persis provided a robust service of groceries, a variety of dry goods, cleaning supplies, nails, bolts and some clothing. Rubber boots and a variety of leather boots and some shoes were also part of the array of goods available. Because the store also operated a post office, the store became a meeting place where one could read or buy newspapers and magazines and get caught up on all the news and gossip of the area. At the rear of the store Samuel had a shop where he sold harnesses and farming and logging tools. He also operated a harness and leather repair shop there as part of his business.

***

For Eliza and her daughters, tending to the bedroom had changed from the earlier days of settlement when they used corn husks to bulk up their mattresses. Geese had become another popular farm commodity, grown for eggs and meat. The feathers were used in their own households for pillows and mattresses; any excess feathers were sold. These mattresses had to be aired frequently and fluffed up, hung in the shade, and taken in before nightfall – yet another task for the household.

Because running water was gradually being introduced inside the older homes, the use of chamber pots was being discontinued – along with the constant smell of urine. Older houses were being retrofitted with steel pipes connected inside the building's outer walls and along the ceilings. With this piping innovation, inside bathrooms began to replace the outdoor privy. New houses were plumbed with lead-soldered steel piping at the time of construction.

Introduction of the laundry roller
(Andrew Hind)

Laundry was made somewhat easier with the introduction of the "laundry roller," which eliminated the need to wring out the laundry by hand as Polly, Mary, Sarah, Persis, Abigail and all the women before them had done. Unless homes were retrofitted with the new piped water systems, the water still had to be brought from a large outside water tub, poured into a large, galvanized tub, heated on the stove, and finally carried to the shed or wherever the laundry was to be washed. To wring the excess water from the clothes, Eliza or one of the girls had to feed the wet laundry through the roller by cranking the handle, a very tedious job requiring a strong arm. Once the water was squeezed out, they hung the clothes on laundry lines stretching from a pole or tree to a corner of the shed.[32, 42]

Just up the road from Haskell and Eliza's homestead, Newell and Laura (McCurdy) Rand, now married, had taken up residence on Lot 12 of Range 11. They had cleared the land and had built both their house and barns. Their excess timber was either sledded to the South Branch of the Eaton River and sold to John Paul[2] Planche to be rough-sawn in his mill or floated downriver to his cousin Stillman Rand's mill in Randville.

By this time, Marshall S. Rand and Mary Maria (Hurd) Rand's children, Newell Clement Rand, and his wife Laura (McCurdy), their daughter Hannah and son-in-law William McCurdy, and even young Austin were coming to visit and help out with some of the extra chores. Austin was keenly interested in woodworking and began spending time with Haskell learning building skill sets which were to become more than a hobby for him in his future years. Laura's young sister, Sarah McCurdy, appeared to be smitten by Austin's younger brother, Willard S., and was becoming a constant visitor at Laura's or alternatively at Eliza's house if she thought Willard might be there. Sarah married Willard Rand in 1878 when she was 24 years old.

In early spring and late fall, our Newport community farmers were faced with long days working outdoors while the children were making long treks to school and spending their days studying. They'd be sure to wear bonnets or a knit hat, mittens and a shawl or scarf before setting out in the cold for the day. Edmund, Augustus, Marshall, his son Newell and William McCurdy all raised a few sheep to provide the wool for these essentials. Sheep were easy to care for as they needed little pasture to graze on and a trained dog for some protection from predators. Our ancestors coveted their dogs, trained for this very purpose of protecting not only the sheep, but the domestic fowl and even the young calves. These family dogs became their constant companions. When the children were returning home from school at the end of the day, it was not uncommon, when the dogs would hear the children let out of school, that all the dogs in the community raced to the school to accompany them home. It was a joyous time indeed for both the children and the dogs.

The process of creating wool usually commenced on a sunny and warm spring day, simply because the smell of damp sheep's wool covered with mud and dung was not particularily inviting. When the men selected a sheep from the flock for shearing they had to work quickly. The trick of the job was to turn the sheep over on its back while grabbing all four feet and holding them high with their left hand, while using the right hand to clip off the winter coat of fleece with large hand shears. Once all the sheep were clipped – if you think that was hard – the real work would now begin.

The wool had to be sorted and bits of sticks, burrs and matted wool pulled or cut out. Keep in mind that the wool would contain feces as well, so it was not nice and white; in fact, it was downright dirty. Usually the men and young boys would help to carry the water and build the fires. Some families in this community, like Edmund who had daughters, also needed the young men to help them with their seasonal chores, especially with early spring planting and fall harvesting. And so, out came the women, both Eliza Hurds, Eliza Loveland, Mary Maria Rand, Hannah McCurdy, Jennette Planche and all neighbouring daughters, organized themselves much like a "bee" from the neighbouring farms. Once the water was heated in large cast iron or tin buckets on the outside fire, the wool was first rough-washed. It was then washed in another bucket in hot soapy water to remove the wool's natural oils. Yet another large wash bucket was used to thoroughly rinse out the soap from the heavy mounds of wool. Some of the wool might then be separated into water-filled iron tubs to be dyed. Indigo was used for dying it blue, sumac blossoms for brown, onion skins or goldenrod for yellow, and so on.

Whether the wool had been dyed or merely washed, once dried yet another chore remained. They had to work lard or oil thoroughly into it with their hands. Throughout this process the wool was fluffed up; this helped mix it evenly, facilitating the next step, carding the wool.

Carding is the process of brushing the wool to clean it and straighten its fibres. To accomplish this task the women used a "carding" tool, typically a square or rectangular paddle, perhaps 4 x 4 inches or 4 x 8 inches, with small bent wires or nails (fashioned like a brush). A small amount of wool fibers would catch on the nails on one brush; the carder they would remove the fibres with the other brush. In our day one would hardly imagine that this process was considered a *"calming, pleasant task,"* that was often done by the mothers and their older daughters in the evening while rocking by the fire. Once the fibres were separated, the process was repeated again and again until the mounds of wool were processed and the straightened wool fibres ready for spinning into wool yarn.[42]

***

Sometime during the late 1860s, photography became available, usually in studios. With the advent of the camera, hand-painted family portraits were abandoned. Photographers soon found a lucrative business in bringing photography to the farm and began to ply the farmlands and villages by horse and wagon or buggy, taking both individual and family portraits. The photographer would have to wait until the farm chores were done and the farmer, his wife and their children washed and dressed in their best "Sunday going-out clothes." They would all stand, children in front, and have to remain perfectly still for 10 seconds or more . . . and they often looked rather grim in the photos. The idea of a picture taken of them was completely foreign and caused a certain amount of anxiety. This was serious business, and in their view the parents needed to look like they were in charge and the children were to look straight ahead with no fooling around. A second shot would cost more money and that was just not about to happen. They might not see the photo until several weeks later when the photographer would return with the photos framed, ready to be placed in proud display over the mantel in the guest or parlour rooms of every house. This was the first time people were able to make connections with others of their families simply because they could now see familial resemblances.

A photograph was much more powerful than a painting because it captured the moment both politically and geographically. These photos documented what people looked like for later generations but, for them, photos were a reflection of themselves. Up to this point our ancestors' only vision of themselves was by viewing themselves in a "looking glass," a term in this era for "mirror." The photograph gave them the sense or impression that when they entered the room they were breathing the same air as the person in the picture. Many would have private conversations with a loved one who had perhaps passed on. The photograph gave our ancestors a sense of comfort in many ways.

These photographs also gave them a sense of who they were, not a perception of a painter's view. For a time some of the photos were painted over in colour to look like paintings. Overpainting was done only by those who could afford it, as many thought they were enhancing these lifelike photos. Regardless of whether in black and white or painted over, everyone was totally enamored by the realism. It was the first time they thought realism was even possible.

Canada's history from 1867 on has been documented by photography. This photographic heritage gives us an astonishing history of what people saw as they lived through a decade. Photography also provided a reflection of who we think we are, and as photography started taking on the scenes of everyday living, one was given a sense of what one did as well.

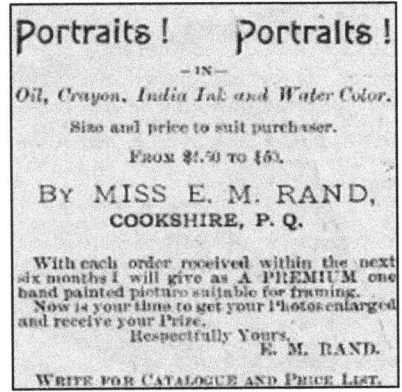

Elvira Rand newspaper ad, *Cookshire Chronicle*, 1898 (Hurd family collection)

Artemas[7] D. and Hannah[2] Hurd (Willard) Rand had three sons. Their third son, Willard. S. Rand, moved to Cookshire where he married Dorothy M. Hall, becoming a "dealer in firearms and ammunition."[16] Their daughter Elvira became an accomplished artist and the owner of the Cookshire Portrait and Art Studio. Elvira did fancy painting of all kinds, making a specialty of enlarging portraits. Family paintings were the norm for centuries; however, when actual portraits or photographs became more common, many people still wanted colour so there was a certain demand from wealthy people to have their photos painted. This is exactly what Elvira did – then, of course, people wanted the portraits framed, which became an additional business.[31]

Elvira's brother, John, did an extensive business picture framing, including huge gold-leaf mirrors, which were in vogue during this era. Many of the richer homes had 10-foot ceilings and these mirrors and paintings adorned most of the more affluent homes of the day. He was also a general agent for his sister's art studio. He also provided frames for all types of studio photographs taken by Wilkinson Bros. Studios, also located in Cookshire. John and Millicent Wilkinson were the author's maternal great-grandparents. John Wilkinson and his brother Alfred had bought the studio from H. H. Weedon in 1892.

***

By the mid-1800s, 40 percent of the population of Quebec City and most of the Montreal and Eastern Townships population were English-speaking. After 1850-60, the influx of English-speakers to Quebec steadily declined.[45]

Much of the wild land in various parts of the Eastern Townships still belonged to the BALC. Roads had been opened to Ditton on the east and to Auckland on the south. For the year 1866, $451.27 was levied for schools and for that same year, the government grant was $45.56 along with some other assistance from the "supplement fund" in aid of poorer municipalities. There were five district schools in Newport and its population was now 403.[17]

The communities of Maple Leaf included a one-room schoolhouse and a cemetery. The area southeast on today's Route 210 to Auckland had a sawmill on the left-hand side of the South River. A bit further down the road, southwest on today's Route 210, was the small hamlet of Randville, with a general store and a Baptist Church. A gristmill had been built there at the foot of Grove Hill. Amongst these three communities had resided all the original first settlers of Newport, with many of their ancestors still living on the same properties. The community at this time included Parker Hill Road, which ran south to the Auckland border.

***

Newport was principally settled in the northwest and southwestern parts, though a few families had settled near the Bury line in the mid-northern of Newport, forming a community referred to as "Knicky Knocky." The lower part of the road leading from Bury (Bury Township) was known as the Woods Road or sometimes referred to as the "back road" to Knicky Knocky.[33] *(Nina (Parsons) Rowell)*

William[1] and Elizabeth Parsons came from England to Lower Canada in 1836 with their adult sons George, James, and Stephen; their daughter Caroline; and Stephen's wife and daughter. Their second-oldest son, James Alexander Parsons (1850-1927), married Mattie Bailey who died young. James's second wife was Hattie Wilson; they settled in Bury Township. William and Elizabeth's six other children, all married at the time, had chosen to remain at their homes in Motcombe, Dorset, England.[33]

Stephen Parsons (1809-1873), William and Elizabeth's ninth child, married Prudence Maidmont (1817-1896) in 1833; they had one child, Louisa, born in England. Louisa was 2 years old when they immigrated to Newport Township. Upon arriving in April, they immediately took up their lot in Knicky Knocky, Lot 16A of Range 1, and started building their log cabin. Stephen's father, mother, two brothers and sister settled on the Victoria Road near Bown in Bury Township. The women and children stayed in Sherbrooke until July of that year until suitable dwellings for both families had been constructed.[33]

Stephen and Prudence had seven more children, two of whom died young. Louisa (1835-1910) married John Fisher. Caroline (1837-1914) married Thomas Dorman. Thomas William[2] (1840-1840) died in infancy. Ellen Jane (1842-1923) married George Bennett. Thomas William[3] (1845-1887) married Jane Ellis and they also made their home in Knicky Knocky, on Lot 15B of Range 1. Charlotte Elizabeth (1848-1853) died of typhoid at the age of 5 years. James Alexander (1850-1927) married Mattie Bailey then Hattie Wilson.[33]

Even in this era, young children were dying of diseases we take for granted as no longer a threat because of the continuing development of vaccines. Those who advocate the discontinuation of vaccines need only read stories of past lives to surely realize the importance of how lives are saved, especially for young children.

Thomas William[3] Parsons (1845-1887) met Jane Ellis, a daughter of Luke Ellis who lived on the Victoria Road; they eloped and were married in 1866 in the Free Will Baptist Church in Hatley. They made their home in Knicky Knocky and lived on an adjoining farm next to his parents. Thomas had previously served in the Fenian Raids. He was well known as a great hunter. As the story is told "he hunted and caught the bear after it had bit Alex Lennox's hand off and he disposed of it."[33]

Stephen Parsons (Thomas's father) died in March of 1873 at the age of 64, crushed by a falling tree while working in the woods. His wife Prudence continued to live at the old homestead, milking cows and doing all the other farm chores. She helped as midwife for the birth of many of her grandchildren. Prudence was a woman of high moral standards, a regular church attendant and a meticulous housekeeper. Prudence died on the homestead in 1896.[33]

***

Until 1859 there were only two small banking agencies in the Eastern Townships, both branches of the City Bank of Montreal. These were located in Sherbrooke and Stanstead to serve the business and commercial interests of Montreal rather than the financial needs of the Townships. Credit was withheld by the City Bank of Montreal because of a lack of appreciation for the possibilities that the District of Compton County could offer. Businessmen in the Eastern Townships believed that if the scattered capital could be combined into a local banking institution it could be deployed to foster local manufacturing and other industries.[16, 34]

The Hon. John Henry Pope of Cookshire was instrumental and successful in obtaining a charter for a proposed bank. In 1859, under the chairmanship of John Henry Pope, the first statement of the bank showed that 6,816 shares of

Eastern Townships Bank dollar bill (Hurd family collection)

the 8,000 permitted by Charter had been subscribed. Ninety-three percent of the capital had been raised in the Eastern Townships, and of that, 47 percent had been raised in Compton County. And so, the first bank of the Eastern Townships was born, allowing citizens of Newport Township and adjacent townships to access full banking services and to acquire credit as well.[34] The photograph is a copy of a "one dollar note" issued by the Eastern Townships Bank. As a result of this initiative, investment was now being pursued more vigorously in the Townships for both land development and business entities.[34]

***

A "Public Notice" issued on June 22, 1863, by the Department of Crown Lands, stated that *"Referenced claims to any of the lands to which claims shall not have been substantiated, or if substantiated and the required installment or arrears have not been paid previous to noon of the 15th of October 1863, will afterwards be offered for sale at Auction."* [31]

At this time, there were several unclaimed and/or partial lots in Newport and many in other townships that appeared to be in arrears for payment of their land and thus might come up for auction. These were once again hard times, and the residents of Newport were struggling to make ends meet. Since this was a pre-Confederation period, this sudden activity may have been in preparation of solidifying land ownership to conform to pending new governance policies for the townships.

***

Other than the records of the southwestern region of Newport, i.e., the *"Newport first Records, 1800,"* there appeared to be no official municipal records for Newport until 1855, when the first principle of law came into force and the government began to establish municipal councils. This was when the Municipality of Newport began to keep

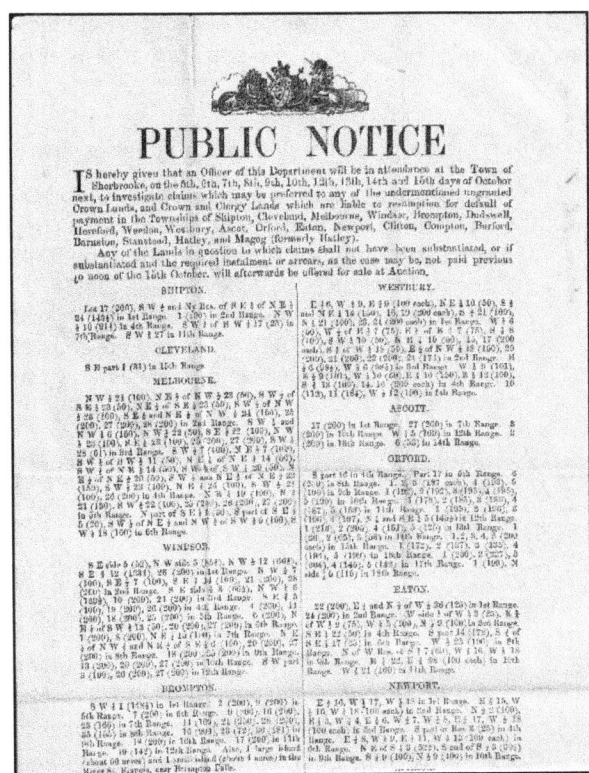

Department of Crown Lands public notice of default, June 22, 1863

their own records in Island Brook and record the names of the mayor and councillors. Council chosen for 1855 was comprised of Alden Learned, Charles Sawyer, Samuel N. Heard, William Planche, Gilbert Williams, Charles Hawley, and William Stevenson Jr. Mayors recorded after 1855 were Alden Learned, Samuel[7] Heard, William Planche, Joshua Nourse, C. D. Chaddock, W. W. Bailey, George[8] G. Hurd, Samuel[8] A. Hurd, and E. Learned.[16, 32]

The first mayor of Newport was perhaps Charles D. Chaddock in 1866. Following his tenure, the records show William[2] G. Planche was mayor in 1868, followed by William Bailey in 1873.

Lucy Gibson[8] Hurd, born in 1830 and the second daughter of Luke[7], married Charles D. Chaddock in 1850, settling and farming on Lot 6 of Range 9, another of the original lots of Col. Edmund[5] Heard. They had seven children: a son and daughter who died as infants; a daughter, Celia, who died at 11 years old in 1862; a daughter, Laura, who died at 16 in 1873; another daughter, Ellen, who died at 19 in 1880; and another daughter, Alma, who died at age 33 in 1887. Alma was still single and lived with her parents on the farm. They were another of the families who lost many of their children to various illnesses that perhaps could have been prevented by vaccines had they been available.[4]

C. D. Chaddock

Of Charles and Lucy's seven children, only one son, George C., survived and married. He and his wife, Ida Blodgette, raised two daughters, Miriam and Pearl. Pearl grew up on the farm with her grandparents and married Clement Flaws. Then, to add to Charles's grief, his wife Lucy died at 45 years old in 1875. Charles later married his second wife, Malinda (Eastman) Cairns. Surnames from the marriage of Lucy and Charles Chaddock were Chaddock, Flaws and McGargle.[4]

Charles H. Harvey held the position of secretary treasurer from when the government established these new municipal records in 1855 until the appointment of R. H. Wilford, who served in the position until he died in 1897.[32]

R. H. Wilford was born in Cookshire in 1829 and married Eliza Dexter in 1862. With the opening of Island Brook circa the 1840s, and the rush of settlers to the northwestern segment of Newport, he moved there and opened a general store. For several years he held the position of postmaster and secretary treasurer of the municipal council and school commissions.[32]

***

Two excerpts from *History of Compton County* by L. S. Channell:

> At the time of the organization of the British American Land Company (BALC) in 1833, no settlement in the County had been made east of Eaton. There was no bridge across the Eaton River giving access to the eastern part of the County until the BALC built one in Cookshire in 1836. The first settlement in Learned Plain was by Alden Learned in 1823 and named after him. Not until 1830 did other settlers begin to arrive. Shortly thereafter, the first school was started. It was thought that no Municipal records were known until 1841, when the government established Municipal Councils. It was not until 1855, when the first principals of law came into force that Newport recorded its first official Municipal Records.
>
> The first inhabitants located in the southwest corner around Randboro.[32]

Author's notes: There is no date included in the second excerpt, and neither quote matches the documented records in the Ancestral Heard/Hurd Collection.[31]

I have referred many times to a "hidden history." Had I decided against writing this book, the records held by the Heard /Hurd families of 1792-1814 may well have been lost and we would not have known any of the rich history of our extended ancestry in Newport. It appears that these municipal records (Newport first Records, 1799), which appear to have been considered nonexistent according to the excerpts above, will be an important addition to reference material for historical researchers. To learn that indeed there was a settlement in the eastern part of Compton County (Eaton and Newport townships) prior to 1836, and indeed prior to the settlement in Learned Plain in 1823, is critical to understanding the local history. To find an irresistible trove of information has been like the discovery of a dusty old box in the attic of a dilapidated old house packed with heirlooms. The disclosure of these records is as important for our descendants as it might be for a reader unfamiliar with the region; simply because it is a missing chapter in life that is now being revealed.

***

By 1866, the economy of Newport Township was growing, driven by the four mills in operation: a shingle mill, with a lathe and a mill to plane lumber; a gristmill for grinding provender (grist) for animals; a lumber mill, milling rough-cut studding and beams; and a sawmill.

The lumbering business in Newport was continuing to flourish. The logging trails were heavily travelled during the winter months, providing the mills in the surrounding area with lumber to saw. Many men were now away from home and living in logging camps. Supplying and cooking for these camps became another whole industry, the men judging the camps they would work in by the food they served.

Author's note: The first gristmill had been built in Grove Hill (Randville/Randboro) circa 1810, organized by Col. Edmund[5] Heard, and built by Artemas[6] Rand, Nathanial Beaman Jr., and others of the Maple Leaf group of Associates. The original mill was built and owned by the Associates as a community. It was purchased in equal shares by Artemas[5]Rand and Nathanial Beaman Jr., who operated the mill for several years before Nathanial retired and divested his half of the share in the Mill to Artemas[7] Dodge Rand. The mill essentially was operated from circa 1804-06 to the late 1890s by members of the Rand family.

Gardner (Stillman) Dodge[8] Rand, the eldest son of Artemas[7] Dodge and Hannah[2] (Hurd) Willard, was born in 1830. Stillman married Celestia Annette Williams and they resided in Randville. In the intervening years, while the mill business was steadily forging ahead, Stillman had built a fine new house in Randville where he brought his new bride to live. He was the first to build a kitchen inside the house. He also built a small room adjoining the kitchen, commonly known in the New England states as a "keeping room." In Newport it was referred as a "borning room" and was essentially a maternity ward. Because it was close to the kitchen and the stove, the warmth transferred to this room, making it a convenient and ideal birthing room. Stillman's mother Hannah[2] lived with her son and family until she passed on.[4, 18]

Stillman Dodge[8] Rand held the offices of councillor and school commissioner for several years. When Stillman (he was always referred to by his middle name) took over the gristmill in Grove Hill (Randville) from his father Artemas[7] at 35 years old, he expanded the operation to include a sawmill, all run by waterpower, circa 1865.[16]

Stillman and Celestia raised seven children: Flora Arrabella (born 1855), married her cousin Austin Rand; Corilla Frances (born 1857), married Archie G. Jones; Hollis Gardner (born 1858), moved to the U.S.; Alice Adella (born 1861), married Moses H. Cairns; Luna Myrtilla (born 1865), married Benjamin Seale; Lucial "Lucy" Adelia (born 1867), married Moses H. Cairns; and Myrtle Maria (born 1875), married Alfred W. Swail. The daughters married people whose names were already familiar in the communities of Newport. Surnames through these marriages were Rand, Jones, Cairns and Seale.

Gardner Stillman Dodge and Celestia Rand (courtesy of Carol Rand)

Author's note: Moses H. Cairns waited a year after the unfortunate death of his first wife, Alice A. Rand, at age 30 years, to then marry her younger sister, Lucial A. Rand.

Stillman was the founder of the first borough in Newport (known as Grove Hill community, first named Randville and then Randboro).

Stillman was an exceptional man, full of ideas and energy to execute them. He was a skillful farmer and workman in many trades. He had always dreamed of building a village or even a small town. The lower segment of the farm, Lot 3 of Range 9, previously owned by Stillman's grandparents, Artemas[6] and Louisa, bordered on Randville below the escarpment we know as Grove Hill. Stillman began subdividing this part of the farm on this lower level of land. The larger part of this lot was the 50 acres where Louisa Rand had been living and was part of the escarpment at the top of Grove Hill Road. The mills were on a part of the common land assigned in 1799, bordering the South River at the ends of both Nathanial Beaman's lot to the south and Artemas[6] Rand's lot to the north.

William Graham was born in 1866 in Falstone, Northumberland, England, and immigrated to Newport with his wife Hannah (Reed) Graham circa 1890. He purchased this small subdivided 50-acre parcel from Stillman Rand. Stillman sold the top or north end of the farm to George Coates and family circa 1900. *(Graham family history)*

Stillman divided the rest of the property below the escarpment into 1-, 2- and 3-acre lots through which the Edmund Heard Road, now Route 210, passed. Stillman was selling lots to newcomers arriving from England, Ireland and Scotland. In total he sold 12 town lots. The buyers contracted to have their homes built on these lots, adding outbuildings, small barns, henhouses and even a pigpen, all very necessary at that time. Stillman planted a white pine on each corner of his lots, some of which still stand today.

Randville was expanding with a store, harness shop, post office, schoolhouse, church and blacksmith shop along with several new houses. Stillman's cousin Austin S. Rand was the contractor for building these houses prior to his untimely death at age 43 in 1895. It was the addition of these new homes that would make the village large enough to be designated a "borough." Sometime between 1875 and 1895, during Stillman's continued expansion of the town, its name was changed to Randboro.[47]

In 1866 the population of Newport, Lower Canada, was 403 persons, an increase from 86 in 1825.[31, 45]

Surrounded by acres of unbroken forest in Newport, the settlers were still clearing the lands. Wood was a plentiful commodity, and the mills filled an urgent need in the community. Roads were still virtual mud paths so hauling logs over long distances was not an easy task. The closer the mills, the easier it was to get the timber in and out of the community.

Stillman Rand's mill operated as an up and down "rip" sawmill, designed to rough-cut lumber into planks. Before the mills were powered by water, four men taking shifts were positioned on two floors to work the gigantic rip saw. The two men on the top floor positioned over the log and two men on the bottom floor under the log carrier, each taking turns pushing and pulling the saw as the log was slowly cranked forward on the carriage. The two men on the bottom floor had the hardest and perhaps the dirtiest work in the mill: when pulling down on the saw, the sawdust would cascade down on their heads. These men wore large, brimmed straw hats so the sawdust would fall past their shoulders. And so, it was a great step forward when waterpower was added to the mill and this process was converted to a mechanical system of up and down sawing, powered by the waterwheel. Sawmills at this early stage were operated using these ripsaws, which were essentially the same style as the crosscut saws used to cut the trees in the forests. This was the type of saw used before the circular saw was invented and came into general use.

The new mill was powered by the same wooden water wheel that had powered the gristmill operation, but with the addition of another sluiceway and a larger water wheel. The operational aspect was set up so the wheels could be engaged in alternative cycles. The saw blade was robust and narrow, positioned in a frame which moved up and down by means of a crankshaft below the floor. The logs were held in place by an "iron dog" driven into the end of the log, the log being pulled along on a carriage. The carriage had to be stopped about two inches from the end to prevent the saw cutting into the "dogleg." These two inches on every board were split and were known as the "stub short" or "stub shot." With this new automation, 1000 feet of lumber could be cut by one man in a 12-hour day. This mill operated at peak during the early spring runoff and ran 24 hours a day from early March to mid-summer. In the fall, only the gristmill part of the operation was open for business due to the reduced flow of water.[43]

***

Just prior to Canada's Confederation in 1867, the United States was engaged in its second Civil War (1861-65). Many of our ancestors in the New England states were caught up in perhaps the most devasting war of all, pitting Americans against Americans. While the author's intention is not to write about the wars themselves, it is important to mention that indeed some of our ancestors of several eras had been and were engaged in these efforts. The libraries are full of history books relating to all wars and I wanted to write only about the subsequent effects on our many families' lives that permeated from these engagements. Many of our ancestors who had left the New England Colonies earlier had raised their children in Newport and surrounding townships. Some of these children, or their children, had returned to the new United States and now became embroiled in this war. Not unlike previous generations, they found themselves pitted against their own cousins, some of whom had moved to the southern states, or as far west as Wisconsin, or as far south as Texas. These same ancestors were also still in communication with their cousins in Canada and so there was much anguish shared on both sides of the border.[4]

***

Manlius Holbrook was born in Leamington, Vt. in 1844. He was Sergeant Major of the 2nd Regiment, United States Sharpshooters and served four years in the Civil War (1861-65). He was wounded at Antictam and later seriously wounded at Gettysburg. Manlius married Persis A. Wheeler in 1868; in 1871 they chose to homestead in the Island Brook region of Newport, leaving conflict behind. They raised six children. Two boys were born in Leamington before they moved: Horace H. (born 1869) and Mark M. (born 1870). Three daughters and another son were born and raised in Newport: Florence M. (born 1879), Olive L. (born 1882), Ernest W. (born 1888) and A. Pearl (born 1889).[32]

Manlius and Persis were a couple with religious principles and daily devotions. They were active in the Methodist Church in Island Brook and were talented musicians. Florence and Pearl were both music teachers and along with Olive served as church organists. Olive and Pearl accompanied old-time fiddlers at any social gatherings while Horace and Mark sang in the church choir. Horace married Ida Kerr, Mark married Lavina Buchanan, Florence married H. J. Wells, Olive married Charles Alden and Pearl married Charles's brother, Fred. They all remained in Island Brook. Manlius was talented at writing poetry and wrote a clever poem about the people in Island Brook.[32]

Author's note: There are two poems included at the end of Chapter 17 that capture the thoughts of our ancestors in both the communities of Island Brook and Maple Leaf. One was written by Manlius and the other in a similar style by Ray "Sliver" Griffin. The Methodist Church in Island Brook was built circa 1869 and changed to a United congregation in later years. The Island Brook cemetery was established at the same time and was located right behind the church on a separate part of the property.

While researching the Manlius poem, the author discovered another poem offering a glimpse of "lives lived" during these troubled times surrounding the Civil War. It is a handwritten poem in the Heard/Hurd files that speaks of the times. It was written in pencil on blue paper found amongst the Heard/Hurd ancestral letters. The fact that it was in these files indicates there was continuing communications between our ancestors of both countries. In order to identify the writer of this poem, the author examined the files in the Heard/Hurd genealogy including those who were living in Newport; none were ordered to go back to the States. Some Heards/Hurds living in the New England states, however, did die in battle defending their positions during this era. The poem was written on the battlefield by Corporal George Hurd, a direct descendant of Edmund[2] Heard. Following is a short biography of George:

George Hurd, clerk in a hardware store in 1858, enlisted in the Union Army on May 7, 1861, as a private for three years. On June 20, 1861, he was mustered as of "Williams Light Guard," Company D, 5th Regiment, Excelsior Brigade, 7th New York Infantry. This regiment was formed in Massachusetts, but when their quota was filled, the Company was sent to New York. On May 5, 1862, George was wounded at the Battle of Williamsburg. He was promoted to corporal on March 1, 1864, and on May 6, 1864, was wounded again at the Battle of the Wilderness. Corporal Hurd, the company poet, was mustered out on June 19, 1864. The 1870 Cambridge City Directory listed him as a soap-maker of the firm Cooper & Hurd. An obituary in a Cambridge newspaper noted that "he had considerable literary ability but was unfortunately brought out in such a modest way that few besides his relatives and most intimate friends were favored with his works."[4]

When one reads his poem "The Soldier Boy" (reproduced on the following page) it is plausible that his injured comrade was telling George Hurd his story, believing he was dying, and George simply formed the story into a poem, uncertain as to his comrade's fate.[31]

The Soldier Boy

The sun was sinking in the west, and fell with lingering rays
Beneath the branches of a forest, where a wounded soldier lay
Beneath the shade of a palmetto, beneath the southern sultry sky
Far away from his New England home, they laid him down to die
A group had gathered near him, a comrade in the fight
A tear coursed down each manly cheek, as bid his friends good night.
A friend and dear companion, was kneeling by his side
Trying to stop the life blood flow, but alas in vain he cried
His heart was filled with anguish when he found it was too late
Appear that dear companion, the tears fell down like rain
Oh, Harry spoke the soldier, Harry, do not weep for me
I am crossing the dark river, where all beyond is free

Stand up comrades listen, to the words I have to say
It's a story I will tell you, ere me would pass away
Far away from her New England home, underneath the pine tree state
There is one for any coming, with saddened heart will wait
A fair young girl my sister, my darling and my pride
I loved her from my boyhood, I've no girl besides
I've no mother, she is sleeping beneath the church yard sod
It has been many a year, since her sprit went to God
I've no father, he is sleeping beneath the cold blue sea
I've no brothers, we've no sister, there was only Nell and me.
When our Country was in danger and she called for volunteers
She threw her arms around my neck and bursted into tears.

Saying go my dearest brother, drive the traitor from the shore.
My heart it needs your presence, but your Country needs you more.
Although my heart seems breaking, I will not bid you stay
Upon this dear old home porch, I'll await thee day by day.
Now my comrade, I am dying, and I never shall see you more
She will vainly avail my coming, at the little cottage drive.
I have loved my Country dearly; I have given to thee cry all
If but for darling sister, I would be content to fall.
A smile radiant with its brightness, a hail across his head
One quick convulsive shiver, and the soldier boy was dead.
Down beside the Potomac, where they laid him down to rest
With his pinafore pillow, and his musket on his breast.

End

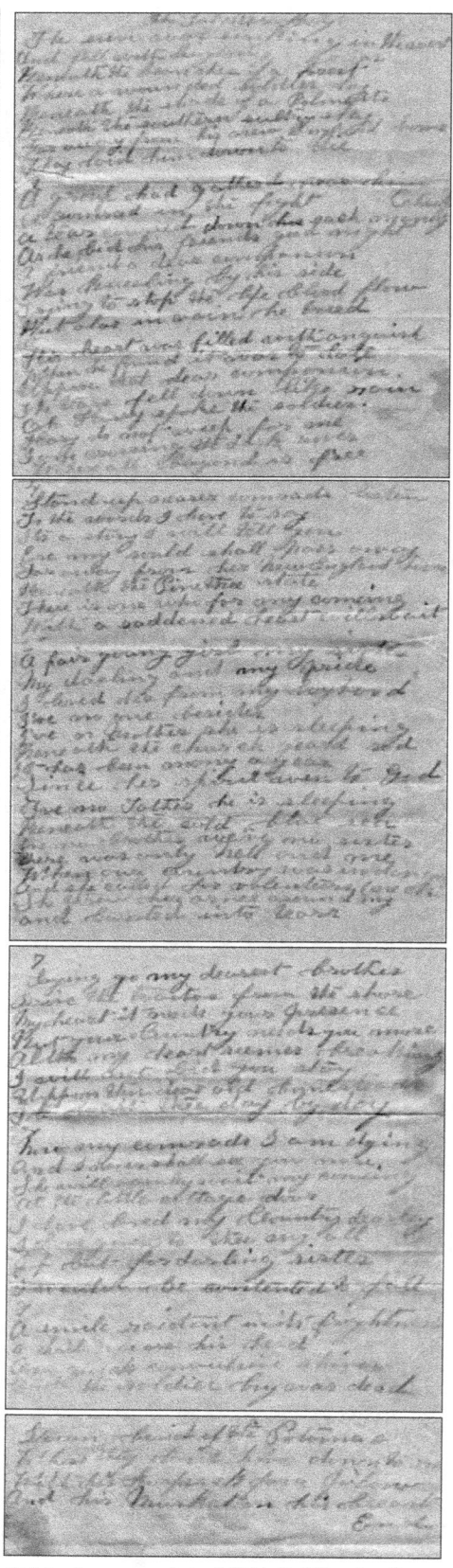

Original manuscript of "The Soldier Boy"

***

Confederation in 1867 saw Canada become a country, and the country kept building on this through to the end of the 19th century. On July 1, 1867, Canada comprised the provinces of Ontario, Quebec, New Brunswick and Nova Scotia. From 1861 to 1867, the population in this region grew from 3,090,561 to over 4,000,000. "Specifically, in Lower Canada the population had grown from 9,000 in 1676, to 1,111,566 inhabitants in 1867."[31] *(The Globe newspaper, 1867)*

"With the first dawn of this gladsome midsummer morn, we hail the birthday of a new nationality. A united British America, with its four million people, takes its place this day among the nations of the world. Stamped with a familiar name, which in the past has borne a record sufficiently honourable to entitle it to be perpetuated with a more comprehensive import, the DOMINION OF CANADA, this First day of July, in the year of our grace, eighteen hundred and sixty-seven, enters a new career of national existence. Old things have passed away. The history of old Canada, with its contracted bounds, and limited divisions of Upper and Lower, East and West, has been completed and this day a new volume is opened. New Brunswick and Nova Scotia united with Ontario and Quebec to make the history of a greater Canada, already extending from the ocean to the headwaters of the Great Lakes and destined ere long to embrace the larger half of this North American continent from the Atlantic to the Pacific."[31] *(The Globe)*

> *Author's note: An original Globe newspaper, the edition of Monday, July 1, 1867: Vol. XXIV, No. 156, referenced above, had been saved as part of the Ancestral Heard/Hurd Collection. The years 2020 and 2021, for example, will be history a century from now . . . Save a newspaper!*

"There is much to be said for the value of old newspapers in which writers tell of the past and prophesy as to the future. A newspaper of over 150 years ago, reflected the opinions of the day . . . and they were writing history. We are doing the same today; a century from now, readers might be interested in what we are doing today."[24.]

Where did the name "Canada" originate? The answer may be as quoted from the Globe issue celebrating Confederation. "The discovery of Canada is generally attributed to Jacques Cartier of St. Malo, France. There is a sort of legendary story, however, which makes the Spaniards prior discoverers, and derives from them the name of our new Dominion. It is said that the Spaniards were the first Europeans who visited this country, but that finding no gold in it – not having penetrated as far as Madoc – they speedily retracted their steps. When the French came afterwards, the first nation Iroquois so frequently repeated the words – *Aca Nada . . . Here is nothing* – which they had heard uttered by the Spaniards, that Cartier fancied it was the name of the country and hence the origin of the appellation 'Canada.' A somewhat more probable derivation of the word is from the Iroquois language, in which 'Canada' signifies a village or collection of houses. Cartier, it is believed, hearing the Iroquois apply this name to the village of Strathcona on the site now occupied by Quebec (City), extended the designation to the country."[31] *(The Globe)*

The process of becoming a fully independent nation was much more evolutionary in Canada than in the United States. While Canada was established as a country in 1867, the transference of governance from Britain to a fully independent Canada evolved over the period from 1867 to 1982. And so, Canada gained its independence from Britain relatively peacefully through an evolutionary process spread over a long time span. There was no war of independence against Britain, relatively little blood spilled and very little violent demand for personal liberties; independence was gained in an orderly and measured way. As a result, Canadian society today is more dedicated to "peace, order, and good government."

A form of self-government in the U.S. was put in place as early as 1840. The United States, or "America," occupying the most bountiful part of North America with the most benign climate, grew and prospered, becoming the economic and cultural centre of the modern world. It was a place with ample opportunity for an individual to carve out their own destiny. Canada, on the other hand, with its much smaller population spread out over a massive land mass and having a much more hostile climate, was less amenable to success as individuals. Canadians had to work together and to depend on each other to succeed. In Canada, individual liberties had to mesh with communal needs. Our ancestors found that the border between the New England states and the New Canada might divide us physically, but not in spirit. We are a similar people who likewise share cultures, challenges, and goals in a climatic way. It is a relationship rooted in trade, and most importantly in family tradition.

Our pioneer ancestors, however, had been living uneasily in an unsettling period following the break from English rule while living amongst the Patriots of the new United States. Col. Edmund[5] Heard had been uneasy because of his political views and alleged insubordination. He had always been a strong supporter of responsible government and so he, and many of our other ancestors and others who had chosen to move to the "waste lands of Lower Canada," would have been pleased to learn that Canada had indeed ultimately become a country.

With that change, provincial governments begin to take over responsibility for roads; our municipal governments began to govern our communities at large. Canada's population grew by almost 50 per cent between 1871 and 1891. In 1871, just one Canadian in five lived in a town or city, but by 1900, it was close to two in five.[35] "The population of Lower Canada by this time was now 1,111,566."[31] *(The Globe)*

***

Earlier in this era, a Baptist church had been built in 1866 in Grove Hill; Rev. A Gillis was pastor.

Newport's population was about 1,700 by 1881; a huge increase from the 403 in 1866.[45]

Because Cookshire had grown more quickly than Sawyerville, it had become the commercial hub. Island Brook was a direct link to La Patrie, in Ditton Township, and the Maine border. Logs were moving from east to west through Cookshire, from Ditton Township and beyond. Chartierville, also in Ditton Township, was still a rough logging road and Randboro had no land on which to expand as it was in a valley surrounded by an escarpment. Sawyerville was not expanding in the same way as Cookshire. When the railway lines came into Cookshire, it became the new crossroads, linking commerce to the west, south and east. Island Brook was able to expand as the land on both sides of today's Route 210 was relatively flat.

> *Author's note: La Patrie is a French word used for fatherland. The ideas of La Patrie (the fatherland) and le citoyen (the citizen) emphasized the notion of a united community enjoying equal rights under a constitution. It was initiated by French revolutionaries to create a collective sense of belonging among the countrymen.*

***

Chapter 10   Expansion and New Connections (1850–1875)

After Colonel Edmund[5] Heard and Associates settled the southwestern quadrant of Newport circa 1793-1814, the next settlements were towards the northwestern section, near the Bury and Eaton line. While sparse settlements had started earlier in this sector, such as Learned Plain and Knicky Knocky in 1828, settlement was slow after most of the wild land had been secured by the BALC. It was not until around 1869, when a more permanent settlement commenced around the Island Brook region, that the pace of progress increased significantly. During the years 1869 to 1881, Island Brook gained a town hall, Good Templars Hall, two sawmills, a gristmill, an Episcopal church, a Methodist church, a hotel and a school. School was held for four-month terms with scholar fees at 40 cents a month and a half a cord of wood per student, which had to be delivered to the school and piled by the door before the first of February.

There was an early Irish Catholic community that settled on Ditton Road. These were the families of Flanagan, Corrigan, O'Farrell, Donahue, McCarty, Gaughan, McGrath, McKenny, Thompson, Green, Dougherty and Hebert. Some of these folks moved away, others lie in Thompson Cemetery on Mexico Road, most of their land reverted back to forest. Also, some of the first settlers in Island Brook who had immigrated from Ireland were Protestant. These settlers had first settled in Morin Flats (known today as Morin-Heights), Argenteuil County, northwest of Montreal, so they all knew each other from that settlement. Many of their sons and daughters had married prior to moving to the Island Brook region of Newport, circa the 1850s. Their surnames – Seale, Byrnes/Burns, Westgate, Painter, Kerr and Millar – all became well-known in Newport communities.

Seale, Byrnes/Burns, and Westgate/Painter family Connections:[32] *(also: Ilah (Westgate) Batley family history)*

The Seale family was one of the original families in the Island Brook area. They were descendants of one of two brothers who came from County Down, near Belfast, Ireland. Joseph[1] Seale, his wife and family of 11 children – six girls and five boys — settled in Morin Flats. One of their boys, Joseph[2] (1845-1921), moved to Island Brook with his first wife Mary Westgate (1848-1884), where they raised a daughter, Matilda, and two sons, James and Joseph[3]. The two boys moved west when they grew up; Matilda married James Christie; they settled on New Mexico Road. Joseph[2] married his second wife, Kate Hammond (1853-1930), and they raised four children: twin daughters Eva and Mary and sons Wilbert and Howard. Wilbert enlisted in World War I and was killed at the Battle of Vimy Ridge in 1916. Eva married William Henry Hammond of Island Brook where they settled. Mary and Howard never married and continued to live in the Island Brook region. They were very active in the Methodist Church and prominent in all community affairs.

Another family, William[1] Johnston and his wife Margaret Byrnes, immigrated to Lower Canada from Ireland and also settled in Argenteuil County with their two sons, William[2] and Henry, who kept the Byrnes last name. They had two more sons born in Argenteuil, John and Thomas, and as with others within the same family spelled their family name as Burns. William[2] Byrnes (1852-1917) married Peggy Jekyll (who also immigrated from Ireland) in Morin Flats. They had one son, William[3] (1852-1914), who was born and raised there. After the death of his wife Peggy, William[2] married Isabella Grant (1834-1910) from Montebello and later moved to Island Brook to live with his son William[3] and daughter-in-law Catherine.

William[3] Byrnes married Catherine (Kate) Seale (one of the daughters of Joseph[1]) in Morin Flats in 1872. They had nine children. Five boys were born in Morin Flats: Joseph (1872-1960), William Alexander (1874-1943), Isaac (1876-1879), Richard H. (1879-1973), and Isaac V. (1882-1969). The younger two boys, Charles H. (1887-1964) and Thomas (1892-1973) and two daughters, Maggie (1884-1972) and Florence J. (1890-1990) were born in Newport.

William[3] Byrnes also changed his name to Burns before the family moved and settled in Island Brook in 1885. Their first years in Island Brook were busy ones as they cut trees, cleared the land and laid the foundation of their farm. Their second-oldest son, Richard, married Ethelyn Millar. He knew the history of the Seale family as well as his own family and was proud of the fact he knew the names of his 64 first cousins on the Seale side of his family. Their first daughter, Maggie Burns, who was born and raised in Newport, married George Seale.

Folks in the neighbourhoods remember William[2] Byrnes (Burns) as a genial old man who was fond of spirits from time to time. Since William[3] and his wife Kate disapproved of it, he used to get his grandson Richard (Dick) Burns to buy a bottle of gin for him occasionally. He confided to Dick, "I don't drink it, I just wet my finger on the cork and lick my finger." However, as Dick said, "He must have had a good many licks, because the bottle didn't last very long." *(Ileana Lowry Burns, 1993)*

The family of James Westgate (1818-1897) was born in County Mayo, Ireland. James immigrated to Lower Canada in 1835 at age 17 and settled with other Westgate families in Morin Flats, Argenteuil County. He married Letitia Stapleton (1819-1889) and they moved sometime after 1865 with their family of eight (six boys and two girls) to Island Brook. Three of the boys married and moved away from Newport; two of the boys remained single; and the youngest boy, Isaac, later married and stayed in Newport.

James and Letitia Westgate's eldest daughter, Mary (1834-1884), married Joseph[2] Seale. They raised three children, James[2], Joseph[3] and Matilda, on their farm on the New Mexico Road in Newport; however, both sons moved west after they grew up. Matilda, the second daughter, married Charles Rydeberg and had two sons, Harold and Howard. Matilda later married Donald McPhee and they lived in Montreal. Both Matilda and Donald are buried in Island Brook Cemetery.

Westgate family portrait, shot at Isaac and Ellen's farm, New Mexico Road (visible in background)

L-R, rear: Lulu, Isaac, Bertha, Ellen; front: family dog, Issac "Roy," Milton, Byron "Maple"

The photograph is on a postcard addressed to Lulu from her brother-in-law Earl Young and sister Bertha, postmarked 1912.

(courtesy of Ilah (Westgate) Batley)

James and Letitia's youngest son, Isaac, married Mary Mooney who died in 1888 two days after the birth of their first child, Bertha. Isaac married, as his second wife, Mary's sister Ellen (1865-1930). They reared eight children: Bertha (1888), Mary (1891), Howard (1892), Lulu (1895), twins Beatrice and Gladys (1896), Isaac Roy (1898), Agnes (1900), Byron Maple (1906) and Milton (1908), all born in Morin Flats but raised in the Island Brook region. This family moved to Newport with many other Westgate and Parker families.

Isaac trained and worked as a police officer in Montreal for a period before moving back to Island Brook with his family. His defensive training proved useful as many local disagreements were settled by having a boxing match. John Patton and Isaac were often in disagreement and would set a time to meet at Wilford's General Store, where a ring was set up for these occasions, "so the story is told."[32]

It was not uncommon in these large families that the children would leave home to find work or marry at a noticeably young age. Byron, known by his middle name Maple, weighed only three pounds when he was born. He was looked after by his older siblings, who dressed him in dolls' clothes, put him in a shoe box, and placed it on the open oven door to keep him warm. The girls certainly learned how to care for children in their adolescent years and were thus well prepared for the time when they would be raising their own families.

Thomas Painter was born in Bristol, England in 1839, a brick layer by trade. He married Elizabeth Jane Grey in 1867. They came to Lower Canada in 1870, enduring a six-week voyage, encountering much sickness, and losing a baby on the way. They first settled in Ditton Township. Thomas found a job hewing timbers in Bulwer, and on Saturdays he would walk home, crossing Newport Township, carrying provisions for his family. He travelled on "spotted" trails through the woods as there were no roads most of the way. He moved to the North Road near Island Brook in 1883.

His six children – Agnes, Arthur, Alice, Oscar, Ernest and William – all attended the little red schoolhouse in Island Brook across from their home.

Alice married Richard Kerr; Oscar married Gertrude Laberee; and they continued living on the original homestead. William Painter married Florence Patton and together they had two daughters, Verna and Shirley. These three families all remained and cleared their lands in Island Brook.

Ada Hume and Myrtle Learned were two teachers of this era that William Painter, one of their students, knew well, perhaps too well, as they had to keep tabs on his boisterous and disruptive activities during school hours.

William and Ernest Painter often spoke of their father's donkey that he used for work on the farm. This donkey became part of their everyday life. It was a sad time when this faithful servant died, and so the family gave it a proper funeral. His parting words were, "Here lies an ass that carried the stones, Sophia cried, and Old Man Painter buried the bones."

Thomas Painter loved to read and recite; his solace was his Bible and his clay pipe was his enjoyment. He requested that his tombstone be inscribed as follows: "Here lies the remains of Old T.P., who never more will bother thee, where he has gone, and how he fares, nobody knows, and nobody cares."

Horses were important during this era in Newport, both for farm work and transportation. They were always well cared for and always a source of great pride. For Isaac Westgate, his desire was to have a fast-driving horse. Neighbours in the community were always comparing their horses. Referring to a return trip from Cookshire (in Eaton Township) to Island Brook, the story is told: "On one of these occasions, Isaac Westgate left Cookshire ahead of William (Willie) and Florence (Florrie) Painter with their baby, Verna. Isaac loitered until Willie caught up to him and then let his horse take the lead. The race was "on" as Willie did not have any slough of a horse, caught up to him and then kept his horse's head over Isaac's sleigh seat all the way to Island Brook. When the Painter's turned into their drive, they discovered Verna's head was bare as she had lost her hat sometime during the excitement of the race and no one noticed."[32]

Later, Isaac Westgate decided it was time to hitch his two-year-old colt for a drive. Isaac was amazed at how well the colt accepted being driven and bragged at the store about his smart colt. Everyone laughed and told him that his son Maple had had that colt to the village many times visiting Verna Painter. Verna was born in the village of Island Brook in 1908 and was the daughter of William Painter and Florence Patton. *(Ilah (Westgate) Batley)*

***

The Millar family moved to Island Brook in 1868. James Millar was a veteran of the Fenian Raids, belonging to the No. 5 Company of the Argenteuil Rangers, for which services he received a Fenian Raid medal. The Ontario Government had offered a free land grant to all Fenian Raid veterans. James Millar was one of those who did not accept the offer as he believed that what they offered was very poor land. Later it became the site of the fabulously rich gold fields in the Kirkland Lake region. During his younger years, James and his brothers had travelled with the farmers taking their produce to Port Royal (Montreal), as security guards against Indigenous warrior attacks.[32]

James Millar and his Irish wife Mary (née Henderson) moved from Argenteuil County to Island Brook in 1868, accompanied by their son Alexander, who was 3 years old. The trip was made by oxen, a distance of approximately 200 miles. Even at this later date, it was evident that oxen were still being used extensively by some communities. At that time there were no settlements east of the stream known as Island Brook.

James and Mary raised three daughters in Island Brook: Naomi Jane (1868), Charlotte (1874), and Ethelyn (1881). Naomi married John Burns in 1887; Ethelyn married Richard Burns in 1912; their eldest son, Alexander, who was raised in Newport, married Elizabeth McVetty in 1887. Alexander and Elizabeth later moved to Alberta.

In the early years Mary worked with her husband James clearing the land on Lot 8 of Range 5, taking the children along with her. They burned the trees they cut down and often baked potatoes in the hot ashes from the fires; that would be their main meal. James worked on trails through the woods to La Patrie in Newport or to Cookshire in

Eaton Township (each about 12 miles in different directions from Island Brook) to get groceries which he carried on his back. James later worked on the railway lines and also worked on designing houses and barns by making scale models for construction. He was a rural mail driver for 34 years; his route covered 22 miles from Island Brook to Learned Plain to Cookshire. On occasion, when the roads were blocked by snowstorms, he carried the mail on his back. There were no statutory holidays in these times, the mail went through every day of the week except Sundays.

Mary Millar was the local midwife in the early days of settlement in this part of Newport. She brought over a hundred babies into the world without losing a single mother or baby. One time, a member of the Irish settlement on the road to Ditton Township to the east, came for her on a "stoneboat" (a flat platform made of heavy planks used for hauling away large stones when clearing a field). We can only imagine how rough a ride that would have been! "There would have been nothing to hold on to and the worried father-to-be kept whipping the horses to make them go faster, putting Mary in danger of falling off without the driver even noticing; but hang on she did, although badly shaken up." Mary acted as a nurse when there was sickness and laid out the deceased after a death. She seldom received any pay for her services, although people often gave her a pretty dish from their cupboard or a chicken or some meat. This is just how things were done during these times. *(Ileana Burns)*

Surviving the winter, even in the mid-1800s, defined our ancestors perhaps more than the other three seasons. Up to around 1870, houses were heated and food cooked in open fireplaces. Most houses had a summer kitchen built at the back of the house where foods would be prepared and cooked during the three seasons. In winter, this separate unheated area away from the house would be the winter larder for frozen foods and the preparation point for any game needing immediate carving. Many of these buildings burned down in the early years because these open fireplaces operated non-stop to heat the house and cook food.

An example of the first homes built using sawn lumber instead of logs (unknown Internet source)

Houses that had been built of logs and the newer ones that replaced them, now built of sawn timber, board-and-batten style, were not painted. When newly built they looked great, but as with all untreated wood, after a few years the sides would become weather-beaten and turned black. So, there was not much colour surrounding the farm buildings other than the trees and bushes – a dreary time indeed. Creosote, a smelly chemical solution, was sometimes used to help prevent the wood used in the stables from rotting. A "whitewash" solution of lye and water was used to brighten the dim stable areas and at the same time cover some of the manure splash prevalent everywhere in these low roofed animal sanctuaries called barns. Most of the chores, i.e., feeding, watering and bedding down the livestock, had to be done at the end of a day's work with little or no light, so whitewashing the ceiling, walls and livestock pens really did brighten up the work area.

This was the era when visionaries were preparing to establish industries in Canada, and Canadians began to flourish. Manufacturing of paint, stoves, lead water piping, farming machinery and many other manual labour-reducing opportunities would lead the economy and change the landscape forever.

This was also an era when women were becoming eager to work and do things for themselves and not be so dependent on the necessity of having a husband they may not necessarily be in love with. Unfortunately, there was little work to be had outside of the family home, and even at this time women still found themselves having to settle for the notion of finding a suitable partner and husband who would support them in a manner that they had set their dreams to.[35]

***

Author's note: Austin, Sunbury, Hurd, Willard, French and Planche connections: The communities of Maple Leaf, Randboro, New Mexico and Island Brook were expanding their reach and these families were all becoming interconnected in both working relationships and in marriage. I was unable to find any references to a brother George Austin, born in 1859, the second-born in the Austin family.[4]

Hezekiah L. Austin (1820-1892), a farmer, was born in Maine. He followed the sea for a living from the age of 19 until he was 30, when he returned home, and remained there until 1863. He had married Sarah Harlow in 1851 in Dixville, Me., and they had five children. Three were born in Maine: Emma in 1853, Flora A. in 1856 (she drowned at a young age) and George in 1859. The family moved to Newport in 1863 where Byron was born that year. Their youngest daughter, Florence, was born in 1869 on the farm they cleared in the New Mexico region. Hezekiah served in the offices of councillor and school commissioner and was a road inspector.[16]

Emma J. (Austin) and John Bennett[9] Hurd and daughter Flora (Hurd family collection)

Hezekiah and Sarah Austin's eldest daughter, Emma J. (1853-1939), married John Bennett[9] Hurd (1850-1907) in 1870, the first son of Augustus[8] and Eliza Hurd. They cleared and lived on the farm on Lot 9 of Range 10, in Maple Leaf. They had a daughter, Flora N., born in 1872. Flora married Clark S. Willard and they raised their five children on the farm there. This farm became generally known as the Willard farm with the two generations farming the land for over 60 years.[4]

Apple cider was as synonymous with rural life of yesterday as barn dances and wholesome food. It was a common refreshing drink when John would take a break from haying or ploughing, wipe his forehead with a handkerchief, and have a swig of cider. While Emma and John built up a herd of Yorkshire pigs, their main source of income from the farm was apples. Over several years they created a sizable orchard behind their house. The reason had been simple: apple trees provided a host of valuable food sources. The first apple to grow large enough to cook in late summer made what was called "green apple pie." This distinguished the pie from one made from dried apples. They dried the apples as a winter food store or made applesauce or apple butter. Often in the fall when the apples were harvested the women in the neighbourhood would have an apple-paring bee. They sliced the apples and strung them on stout linen thread, after which they were taken back to the other homes where they were hung in festoons from the beams above the fireplace where the fruit soon dried out and could be stored for pie-making in spring and summer. Any apples that were rejected for these purposes provided an additional food source for their horses and their ever-expanding pig farm. Once the best of the crop was harvested, they made cider.[18]

Since only inedible crab apples are native to North America, the New England colonists brought apple seeds with them from England. Our ancestors in turn brought apple seeds from the New England Colonies when they migrated to Newport. These were hardy varieties, producing apples well-suited to cold climates and winter storage in cellars. They were ideal for apple cider sauce since appearance did not matter. Cider was popular because of its full flavour and nutrients and was easily stored for months on end. Cider sauce was made by long, slow cooking the apples with plenty of cider added, resulting in a thick, rich syrup sauce. It was stored in an earthenware crock and kept in the cellar where it was well preserved all winter. A variation was "shoe peg" applesauce, with blackberries added.[18]

As their orchard grew, Emma saw an opportunity to sell cider. It was not long until John and Emma had purchased a cider apple press and were in the business of supplying the communities in the area with cider. The work was not easy; apples had to be gathered, washed, cut into quarters and the seeds removed to use for later planting. The apples were put into the hopper and ground into pulp. Cheesecloth was placed at the bottom of the press, acting as a filter. Several layers of apples and cheesecloth were placed, until the press was full. A handle was turned to "rack down" the cider press onto the apples, extracting the juice which filled the vats. The drink, known a "soft cider," could be enjoyed immediately but the bulk was stored in wooden casks and allowed to ferment for several months, providing a more vibrant drink. Some was made into cider vinegar for cooking. This was another example of how our ancestors became entrepreneurial in their day, seizing any opportunity to enhance their livelihood.[42]

Hezekiah and Sarah Austin's youngest daughter, Florence M., married Edward Dawson, and they resided as a family in the New Mexico region of Newport. (New Mexico was an area surrounding the road running through the community of farms of Ranges 6 and 7, lots 12, 13, 14, and 15.)[32]

Hezekiah and Sarah's third son, Byron, who was born in 1863, married Cora I. Sunbury (1865-1966) of Maple Leaf in 1883. They lived on the farm on Lot 11 of Range 9 in Maple Leaf that Cora's father Russell had cleared and built on in early 1856. The house Russell had built was larger than most in the region with 14 rooms, some of which housed the hired hands. He had built up a large sheep farm and needed considerable help running the farm. By 1890 they had together amassed a large sheep herd. The excess wool the farm supplied allowed Russell to purchase a large sewing machine from John McNichol's store in Sherbrooke. Cora and her sister Kate had both learned to use the sewing machine when they were young girls and made clothes they sold to the surrounding communities.[31]

Russell Planche and pets (Hurd family collection)

Cora's sister Kate Sunbury married Henry W. Planche, a son of William and Jennete (née Heard) and they moved to New York, raising their daughter Tracy O. and son Russell W. there. They were Cora's only niece and nephew. Cora was an icon in Maple Leaf, living to 101 years old, never having gone to hospital until her last week of life. "I have lived high and dry and have had plenty of fresh air," she said as she celebrated her 100th birthday on November 5, 1965. "She lived her entire life on the same farm and slept in the same bed where she was born in 1865." *(Stevenson,* Sherbrooke Record*)*

Byron and Cora continued to raise and operate the sheep farm for many years, hiring help when needed in shearing season, selling both the wool and excess mutton and lamb for butchering. Cora had a large spinning wheel and loom in her house on which she spun the wool after carding it all by hand. She then used the wool to make blankets, window coverings and other woven materials. She still had her father's large sewing machine which she continued to use to make clothing. She sold many of her works in Newport as well as Auckland, Eaton, and Bury townships. Over the years, many of her knit wool articles of clothing found themselves in almost every part of the township. Byron cut wood for their own use as well as to sell. As Cora often would often say, "A farmer always has wood to cut, gardens to harvest and something to sell, so we never worried about starving."

Cora kept alive the homey virtues she practiced all her life. She was a simple country woman with a limited education who was always there for anyone in need. She knew the histories of every pioneer from the very beginnings of settlement in Newport. She was always a friend to the children of any families in need in the "Lawrence Colony" settlement beyond her farm. During the First World War, she knit socks to send overseas to the troops, all double-stitched wool with 12-inch legs to keep the men warm in the trenches. "You have not got a trunk big enough to hold all I have knit." *(Cora Austin)*

Cora loved the young folk in her community, and those who moved away over the many years always remembered her so well for her kindness. When any came back to visit, she was delighted to see them. After Byron passed on, Cora boarded a few men who were working the Lawrence Colony and Ditton Township lumbering operations. Arthur Lowry and Frank King stayed on after the winters' lumbering and worked for Cora as farm hands for a few years. Frank drove Cora anywhere she wanted to go in her old car, keeping the car washed and polished. Over time he became her constant companion. Eventually Frank King became a part of her life, continuing to help Cora well into her nineties until he too passed on, and Cora was alone in her home for many more years.

Cora was acutely aware of how many children suffered from poverty in the colony. How many of us remember being coerced by Cora into buying the wild berries that the children had picked so they could earn a little money? She insisted everyone, even children, call her by her first name. How many remember she always had a meal for anyone who knocked on her door? Her gifts were many for they were given with a loving heart. "She was proud to say she lived alone in the 14-room farmhouse, looking after the house and heating it with her woodstove." Cora neglected to say that she really lived in the kitchen, her single cot located in the little room off the kitchen, known as the "borning room," which she referred to as her parlour.

Author's note: I remember that in her later years, the mailman of the time, Jimmy McVetty, would tell me he would bring Cora a "mickey of brandy" from time to time. Cora always said she needed it to cook with. Later Wells Bishop told me he was also bringing her a "mickey of brandy" from time to time as she needed it to give her heart a jolt once in a while. One has to wonder if or how many others were doing the same.

The author with Cora Austin, 1964 (photo by Sandra Hurd)

Cora related many stories of when they cleared their farm of stumps with teams of oxen.

She told the story of an Indian man from the Indian village in the St. Francis region of the Megantic Mountains, arriving at their door one cold winter night travelling on snowshoes. He asked for permission to stay in the barn overnight in exchange for doing whatever chores they might give him to do. The next morning, he was gone, and the chores were all done. A few days later he came back, his knapsack loaded with supplies and a large bag of meal. He was so loaded down that Cora could not believe he was walking this long distance on his way to back to Megantic. Again, he stayed overnight in the barn, doing the chores as requested and, in the morning, he was gone. *(Robert Burns)*

The original barn built by Cora Austin's father, Russell Sunbury, circa 1845-46 (photo by Sandra Hurd)

***

During this same period, Charlie Headley Loveland (1854-1952) met and married Charlotte Goodenough (1860-1947) of Island Brook and took over the farm adjacent to Charlie's parents, the William[2] and Eliza (Beaman) Loveland homestead. The farm, located next to Byron and Cora Austin, had belonged to Charles and Matilda "Tilly" (Heard) Planche. Charles had died at 24 years old and the farm was sold. It had not yet been cleared of virgin forest, and what was cleared –about 25 acres – had not been worked, so now needed to be brushed and cultivated. Clearing the land must have been a daunting task for even the most stout-hearted, strong-backed, and enthusiastic of men.

Charlie and Charlotte raised their family of six children, four boys and two girls: Roy (born 1885), George (born 1886), Mildred (born 1889), Charlie Victor (born 1891), Ruth (born 1893) and Arthur (born 1895). The family continued to clear the farm for cultivation and to build a "mixed farm" of Shorthorn cattle, sheep and a few pigs. The family's focus was the breeding and raising of both (heavy) workhorses and some riding horses. Riding horses were becoming popular now in the Townships as the towns were growing, the roads had been improved, and many farmers could now afford buggies and sleighs. The churches were full on Sundays and many people were using these light riding horses for extended travel.[31] (*Loveland family history*)

Since Charlie's father, William, was heavily engaged in the business of horses, now buying and raising his own horses to sell, Charlie was housing and feeding several horses on his land as well as his own team of Belgian workhorses.

Marshall Newell W. Rand and Shetland pony (Hurd family collection)

Oxen had been mostly phased out during this era, and Charlie's Belgium heavy workhorses were used to clear the stumps in a different way than when oxen were used. The trees were massive and seemingly endless, and the chore made more miserable by the clouds of mosquitoes that hung over the landscape like dark rainclouds. They usually "brushed" during the winter months when the farming workload was considerably reduced and the bugs were gone. The large trees were felled, branches cut up and piled high, and the logs sledded to the roadside for sale. When spring arrived, the branch pile was set afire. The sale of potash had pretty much dried up during this time and the farmers realized that the ash was much better to remain in the soil than sold as had been the custom of their forefathers. The addition of ash would make the soil nutrient-rich for a few years, resulting in exceptional harvests.

The hardest part of clearing the land was yet to come: removing the stumps. Small stumps could be dug out with a pickaxe. The stumps of evergreens, which have lateral roots, could be pulled out fairly easily with one horse. Others would have been so large and heavily rooted that Charlie would have simply ploughed around them for several years. Eventually they had to go, and these large stumps needed to be forcibly pulled. Horses were ill-suited for this task because – unlike oxen – they tended to jerk-pull; the handler would attempt to calm them so they would not break a rope or hurt themselves. And so, Charlie made the horses' job easier by using a stump-puller mechanism: a tall, tripod-shaped device that pulled the stump straight upwards from the ground.

Pulling a stump was not a one-man job so Charlie's father William and other neighbourhood men (four to six men) would come over to help on these "stumping bees." Byron Austin, Newell Rand and his father Marshall "Spring" Rand, Willy Planche, the Hurds – i.e., Augustus, George, John B. and Edmund H. – all neighbours in the community of Maple Leaf, were often part of the stumping bees, giving a helping hand. First, "grub axes" were used to dig around the stumps and cut off smaller roots. A "pickaxe" was used to hack through larger roots. A cable was attached to the stump, run up to the peak of the tripod, which pulled around a roller winch, then stretched out to the teams of horses. The horses walked around the tripod in a circle, pulling the cable tight, with the winch lifting the stump free from the ground. Because the process was all about leverage, there was very little strain put on the horse, so they could repeat the process all day long. This was very different from the days of oxen when stumps were pulled horizontally out of the ground. The stump remover was efficient and inexpensive and used throughout this era when horses became the norm. Most of the boys in Newport learned horsemanship in handling these heavy workhorses during their teenage years, both for this process and for hauling timber. Marshall Spring and Augustus were in the lumbering business during this era and so the logs were hauled to mills by their teams of lumbermen. Roy and Victor were also becoming older and were there to help in guiding the many teams of horses.

Charlie and Charlotte Loveland's children all grew up knowing how to handle horses and prided themselves with their ability to train young colts. The light horses were trained for riding as well as for pulling light loads such as buggies and sleighs. The draft horses were trained for logging in the woods, both hauling large loads and also "snapping." When they needed to pull single logs from where they fell, they would use one or two horses to pull them one at a time out of a tight area like a swamp or heavy bush and brush. This process was referred to as "snapping out" a log. A large steel clevis with sharp ends was clamped to a log, connected to a long set of rope or chains, using long reins to keep away from the end of a log being pulled. They would literally have to dance, running along as the horses pulled these logs out to where they could be handled.

Charlie and Charlotte's children all attended the little schoolhouse in Maple Leaf just down the road from their farm. Their schoolmates and friends in the community were Marshall Rand Jr., Rufus Riddell, Raymond Wood, Frank Morrison and Louis Boisvert. For Mildred and Ruth, their friends were the Charest sisters (Marie and Clara), Rosalie

Boisvert, Louise and Annie King, Edith Morrison and Gertrude Riddell. Jessie Hurd (daughter of Haskell Hurd) was their schoolteacher during this time.

Charlie's father William had imported small Shetland ponies as more of a hobby horse to teach the young children how to ride at an early age. The Shetland pony was a breed of horse popular as a child's pet and mount. Originating in the Shetland Islands archipelago in the far north of Scotland, the breed was adapted to the islands' harsh climate and scant food supply. Charlie sold one of these small horses to Clement and Laura (McCurdy) Rand for their son, Marshall N. W. Rand. From that sale a small trade in these horses developed in the surrounding townships. The children in this era had to walk to school and both Marshall Rand and Rufus Riddell rode their Shetland horses everywhere, including to school circa 1901. Mary Maria (Hurd) Rand was a daughter of Edmund[7] and his wife Mary (Willard) Hurd, whom William Loveland had worked with in his first horse trade business in 1843.

***

The Lyon family and Bowker family connection: *(Florence (Bowker) McVetty; Bowker family history)*

> *Author's note: Solomon and Johnathon (John) Bowker, the two oldest sons of Gideon[6] and Hannah (Fletcher) Bowker, had grown up with their parents and siblings, a family of nine children, first in Guilford, Vt., and later in Lunenburg, Vt. Their younger sister was Lucy. Both Solomon and Johnathon had applied for land grants and had already settled in the southwestern part of Newport in 1799.[20]*

John Lyon married Lucy Bowker, who was 18 years old in 1804. By this time John's family had moved to New London, N.H., while the Bowker family had stayed in Lunenburg, Vt. John and Lucy raised their two sons, Orra and Eliphalet, in New Hampshire. When they became of working ages, Orra and Eliphalet decided to explore opportunities for land grants in this new land of Lower Canada. They travelled through unknown territory along the Indian paths through the woods from New Hampshire and found themselves around the New Mexico and Flanders region of Newport.[32] Orra and Eliphalet Lyon built a cabin on the North River just south of the New Mexico settlement. Eliphalet returned to New Hampshire to retrieve his wife Jane and family. Orra built a sawmill circa 1864 on Lot 17 of Range 8, on what was then called Lyon Stream, a branch of the North River. The site was on what we might know today as the John Westgate farm.

The following year, Eliphalet returned with Jane and built their cabin across the North River in Flanders, on a meadow where the French farm (as we might know it today) is located. They had to either wade the river or ride on horseback to get to the road. They had seven children, including Levi Lyon and his twin sisters, Ann Rosetta and Amanda.

Eliphalet and Jane's son Levi Lyon (1842-1923) married Lucy S. Wheeler (1841-1932) in 1864. Levi built a log cabin in which they began their life together in the wilderness with only one small dwelling between their home and Ditton Township. Here Levi and Lucy had three daughters: Laura (born 1865), Jane (born 1867) and Mary Amanda (born 1871). "Their daughter Laura was the first child born in the Island Brook region in 1865."[32] In early 1878 Levi and Lucy moved to his brother's farm in Flanders to care for Eliphalet and Jane, who had an extended illness. Lucy was pregnant at the time with another daughter, Mabel Lucy, who was born in 1878 at the farm in Flanders. They later returned to the Island Brook farm where a son, Edward Nelson, was born in 1881 and another daughter, Myrtle, was born in 1882. In this location, they cleared the land and started a farm, later known as the Todd farm. The family raised flax to make thread and yarn with which Lucy wove cloth. A linen tablecloth, known as "Lucy's tablecloth" is still a family heirloom.[32]

Ralph Todd, born in 1830, married Ann Rosetta Lyon (one of Eliphalet and Jane's twin daughters) in 1855, raising 10 children on the farm which they took over from Levi and Lucy as they grew older.

"The horses had worked so hard that when flour was needed, Levi would let the horses rest while he carried the grain on his shoulders through the woods to Lake's gristmill on the Eaton River where he had it ground; and carried the flour back home. Levi was hard worker, a farmer, carpenter, and most of all a great gardener, always trying one more item each year. Lucy was a homemaker, mother, nurse, seamstress and tailor for both men's and women's clothing. Their most important interests were their family and their church, donating materials and labour to both." *(Aileen (Todd Rowe) Morrow, granddaughter of Levi Lyon, 1993)*

An 1884 cookbook, owned by Lucy, contained recipes for dye formulas. The ladies spun their own yarn and wove their own blankets. They raised sheep, grew flax and made their own linen and thread. They would knit long stockings for the girls, socks for the menfolk and mittens for all the family. Ruth (Burns) Morrow knew of a lady who knit underwear for her husband: "By the way, he had only one such suit."[32]

> *Author's note: If one were able to look into the "shed chamber" attached to one side of many of the old houses, they might discover there was often a large, unfurnished room above the woodshed. It became temporary quarters for the "hired man" and also where unused articles were stored, which became "attic fashion." In exploring these unexpected treasure troves, one might come across a pair of wooden skates hanging from a rafter, a candle mould, numerous calendars, an old tin ladle or lantern, or a flax spinning wheel, all items evoking memories.*

By the 1870s the convenience offered by the cast iron cookstove triumphed over affection for the hearth, and now most families' meals were cooked on top of the stove or in the oven. Many of these stoves were placed right into the original hearths, the pipe simply placed inside the original chimney flue, but most found their place in a hallway between the kitchen and living room. This provided a more even heat distribution throughout the house.

Flatiron, Eaton Corner Museum (photo by Sandra Hurd)

By the late 1870s, water jackets as part of the wood cookstove were invented and hot water could now be piped to a tank. This was much easier than heating the water on the stovetop or over a fire. Flatirons could now be heated on the stovetop, always ready for use if the stove was hot, which was most of the day. From breakfast to dinner to supper, these stoves operated, even in summer. As mentioned earlier, this was an era of indoor plumbing when steel piping was installed in existing homes. Rather than running between the walls, the pipes ran along the wall and ceiling. At this same time, piping now led through a water jacket in the stove to a hot water tank and on into an indoor bathroom. Homes that were being built in this era would have these pipes installed inside or between the walls as we do today. In existing homes, they built a subfloor on which both the bathtub and the toilet were placed so that the piping could be installed in the cavity underneath them.

***

Island Brook was the first officially recognized "town" in Newport. It was established circa 1872 on the original Lot 12, straddling ranges 5 and 6. At this time there were four communities in Newport Township: Maple Leaf, Grove Hill (renamed Randville), New Mexico and Island Brook. As each farmer was responsible for maintaining their portion of the roads running in front of their farms, an inspection took place during each of the seasonal changeovers:

> *At the General Session of the Municipality of Newport held on the 3rd of November 1879, it was moved by Councilor Todd and seconded by Councilor Learned have; Resolved that a pair of horses shall receive the same price per day for Road work as a pair of Oxen or a horse and cart and that the Secretary Treasurer do provide each Road Inspector with a copy of this Resolution. [Signed] R. N. Wilford, Secretary Treasurer. To: Edmund H Hurd Esq., Inspector Road Division No 13 Newport.* [31]

Island Brook was named by the first settlers because there was an island right in the middle of Island Brook stream, which at that time (the early 1800s) was a river large enough that the settlers were able to float sawlogs down to the North River. By the late 1800s to early 1900s it had become smaller, but still had sufficient flow to float pulpwood downstream. By the late 1900s the "river" was a stream, and at the time of writing it is now not much more than a pathetic brook. *(Robert Burns)*

***

Hannah Elvira Rand (1848-1922) married William Howard McCurdy in 1871; they had a son, Marshall McCurdy. They lived on Lot 9 of Range 11, their homestead at the top-east corner of the lot, beside the Edmund[8] Haskell Hurd homestead, where they were engaged in the business of sheep farming. They had a ready market in the wool trade, and with the coming of trains they could now send their wool to Cookshire to be carded. The finished product

Hannah Elvira Rand (Hurd family collection)

was then shipped out by train to an ever-increasing market. Hannah would now be relieved of hand carding the wool that she, along with her neighbours Cora and her sister Kate (Sunbury) and Eliza (Beaman) Loveland had done for so many hours in the past.[4, 31]

Their sheep business grew, mostly for the wool that now found markets abroad. They had a steady supply of lamb and mutton meats, which they used in stews and supplied to other local entities, providing another income stream. Most farms now had flocks of sheep, usually shorn in the spring. Their wool, dirty from the winter months of being cooped up in indoor pens, had to be thoroughly washed. This was a big job usually handled by all members of the family. The wool pelts were then sent to the mill at "Slab City" in Eaton Township where it was carded into rolls, quality identification tags attached, then stacked for shipment.

***

Newell Rand family, L-R: Edna S., Laura A., Marshall N. (seated in front), Alonzo A., Newell C., Mary M. (photo courtesy of Carol Rand)

Newell Clement Rand (1850-1922) married Laura Adeline McCurdy (1843-1913) in 1873. Laura was a sister of Edmund[8] Haskell Hurd's wife, Eliza. They had four children: two sons, Alonzo Alton (1883-1932) and Marshall[2] Newell Wesley (1888-1939) and two daughters, Mary Maria (1879-1928) and Edna Sarah Eliza (1885-1944). The family always lived in Newport on the severed part of the original "Rand Homestead" that his father Marshall and Mary Maria (Hurd) Rand had cleared, i.e., lots 12 and 13 of Range 11.[4]

Surnames originating from the marriage of the Rand daughters were Riddell and Williams.

Newell and Laura Rand cleared the land and built their home on Lot 12, on the south side of today's Route 212, on the road to Auckland, just west of where his parents had settled on Lot 13 of Range 11. Their house was one of the first in this area to have an indoor washroom. This was the era of transformation from the "outhouse" to indoor plumbing facilities with the availability of lead piping. During this same period many of the attached "summer kitchens" were being converted to become a normal part of the house and became part of any new house plan when building.

The first duty of this era was still the continuance of clearing the lands, building new dwellings, and expanding shelters for their livestock. With sawmills in the area, the settlers now had sawn wood available and could build wood-framed houses instead of log homes. It was also a mark of progress to move from using oxen to working with a heavy workhorse. Through specialty breeding, horses that replaced oxen became known as "draft" horses. Stumps were now being hauled into big piles with enormous piles of brush and burned at night, leaving broad fields of level ground that was more-easily worked by equipment, which was also starting to find its way into Newport.

Newell and his family expanded the farm into a mixed livestock farm of cattle, sheep and some pigs. Cattle provided milk and cream, and one was slaughtered each year for their own consumption. The sheep gave them wool and again the opportunity for the odd lamb stew. The pigs ate the household food waste and provided income from time to time, as well as bacon, hams, pork roasts and suet for making head cheese. They had a chicken coop that Laura was very partial to. She harvested the eggs and sold the surplus eggs to her neighbours. She would hitch up the horse to the buggy and deliver the eggs once a week, as far away as Randville. She always had orders to fill for Samuel and Persis Heard's little store in town. She would pick up other groceries, some in trade. She would also spend some time visiting Newell's brother Austin and his wife Flora, his cousin Gardner and Celestia Rand, and his father Artemas[7] and Hannah, along with friends in town. Randville was becoming a busy hamlet with new people from the region moving in and new houses being built.

As did many of the farmers in the area, Newell Rand spent a good part of the winters lumbering with his father Marshall, hauling logs to the riverbank for the spring river run. Laura and the children would do the chores, feeding and watering the livestock. In the winter, with Newell away, Laura would hitch up her horse to the "pung" sleigh and take the children to the Maple Leaf schoolhouse, sometimes picking up some of her neighbours' children along the way. Many of the women took turns taking the children to school in the winter months.

Newell was a councillor for Newport Township and secretary of the "Patrons of Industry." The "Granger Movement" was begun in the late 1860s by farmers who called for government regulation of railways and other industries whose prices and practices, they claimed, were monopolistic and unfair. They were referred to as "Patrons of Industry."[24]

When Laura (McCurdy) Rand died at 66, Newell married a cousin, Randboro native Flora Arrabella Rand (1855-1935). Flora was the daughter of Newell's first cousin, G. Stillman D. Rand, and had been Newell's sister-in-law. Edith Morrison referred to her Aunt Flora as "three times a Rand; born a Rand . . . married a Rand . . . and married another Rand." *(Edith (Morrison) Rand diaries)*

>*Author's note: Newell was 74-75 years old when he married his cousin Flora circa 1914-15. They continued to live on the original Lot 12 of Range 11. Flora's parents, Stillman and Celestia Rand, took over her home in Randboro that Austin had built and that some years later was purchased by Charlie and Lottie McCallum.*

In a "debt transfer" dated March 24, 1879, a debt of $300 owed by Matthew Boyd to Stillman Rand *(Cert # 4594)* was transferred to Austin Rand, named in the document as a "Carpenter." Was Stillman Rand in need of money (not likely) or was he aging and deciding to begin transfer of his estate prior to his death? It was not uncommon then for debt to be transferred if the debtor was reliable – it was as good as money in the bank. It was also not uncommon for successful people to lend money rather than for those borrowing trying to secure temporary loans from a bank. However, Austin died before Stillman Rand did, so the note would have passed to his wife Flora.[31]

"I knew the Stillman family well when I was young, as fine upstanding and aging citizens. They were all married, had children, and farmed in the neighbourhood except for one son who had moved to Boston to become a railway engineer.[47] Whenever he came home to visit, we as children looked at him as today's children might look at an astronaut. Stillman was fond of children and one of his favourite joys was to make a batch of fine hard candy and toss large flakes of it to school children on their way home from school." (Ernest "Ernie" McCallum)

Original home built by Austin Spring and Flora Rand in Randboro, later the home of Gardner Stillman and Celeste Rand (courtesy of Carol Rand)

Newell's younger brother, Austin Spring Rand, had married his first cousin Flora Arrabella Rand but died early at the age of 43 and they had no children. Austin, with the help of his brother Newell, built their home in Randboro beside the Baptist (later Methodist then United) Church. Austin was a builder and carpenter, building most of the homes in the region for his cousin Stillman and as well doing the finishing work, making doors, cupboards, tables and chairs. The partial Lot 3 of Range 9 was considered "common ground" under the initial "Grant Rules of 1810" and set aside for the very purpose of starting a town. His cousin, Gardner Stillman Rand, had inherited Lot 3 of Range 9 from his father and had begun the development of the town. After Austin died and Flora married Austin's brother Newell, Stillman and his wife Celestia moved into their home in Randboro. Readers might remember this house as Charlie McCallum's. Later, Charlie's son Ernie McCallum and his family moved back from Ottawa and bought the house, taking care of his parents in their old age.

Austin Rand (1852-1895), a carpenter in his earlier days, made horse "hames" when he began his trade. He saw an opportunity to make these hames for the loggers in the area who needed these as replacements due to the extreme pulling force on the hames when using single horses to pull logs out from these dense forests. When his father Marshall S. found curved branches of maple hardwood, he saved them for Austin. Marshall in his younger days had furnished many curved hardwood pieces for sled runners for lumbering. Austin was taking over part of that business, making horse hames which had a small curvature at both the top and bottom ends. Two of these hames were attached to the horse collars with adjustable leather straps, one at the top and the one at the bottom, which cinched the hames in place on the horse collar.

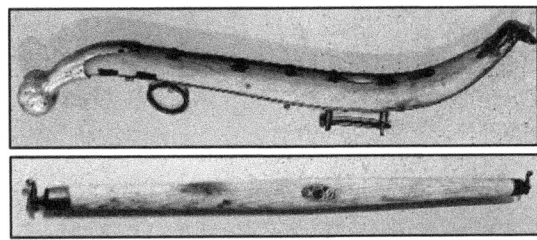

Horse harness hames and whiffletree (Hurd family collection; photo by Sandra Hurd)

Today, one might recognize them for the brass knobs placed on top of the hames that would be later put on for show. The hames were the part of the harness that carried the full pulling power of the horse. The softer collar was set in place directly on a horse's neck and cinched tight enough so that the combination collar and hames would take the full weight of pulling a load. The wooden hames were encircled with metal that was screwed on for strength. A clevis and pin would be positioned on each side where the "traces" are attached. These two traces, one each side of the horse, are a wide heavy leather harness strap directly connected at the rear to a "whiffletree." If a pair of horses were hooked up to a sled or wagon, the whiffletrees (one for each horse) were connected to a longer hardwood whiffletree, attached to the sled pole with a single bolt, providing a seesaw movement. This method of attachment allowed the horses movement flexibility. Since each horse required two hames, this provided an excellent source of income for both the woodworker and the smithy who had to form the metal surrounds. It was lucrative because hundreds of horses were required to support the lumber industry in addition to the farmers' own use.

Willard Stedman Rand (1854-1915), the third son, married another sister, Sarah McCurdy (1854-1941) in 1878. They always lived in Newport, and cleared more land for cultivation on Lot 11 of Range 11, on both sides of today's Route 210. He built his home on the north side of the road on a knoll, and his barn on the same side but just below the knoll. Willard and Sarah also ran a farm of mixed livestock, having a good team of workhorses, a herd of Ayrshire cattle and some pigs. The original Rand farms were located just up the road on lots 12 and 13 of Range 11, the original lots formerly owned by Edmund[6] Heard Jr. Willard was a school commissioner and later a valuator at Newport. They had one son, Scott Rand, who first moved to the Maritimes, and later he and his wife moved out west. In a later era, Clinton Rand (a son of Marshall[2] Newell W. Rand) purchased this farm from Renford Morrow just after World War II.

***

The Hon. John Henry Pope's interest had been aroused during the summer of 1862 when it was reported that an Abenacki Indian had found gold in the Township of Ditton to the east of Newport. Pope, accompanied by William Bailey and two other friends, set out by horse team to reach the Salmon River.[16]

"Mr. Bailey fished and Mr. Pope and the other two explored. Eventually John returned with a comical smile on his face remarking; 'Look here Bailey, you are having all the fun; I guess I'll fish too.' At dusk however, Luther Weston returned exclaiming, 'By George, I have found it,' displaying a small piece of gold. They camped overnight and the next day they all went exploring with the excitement of gold on their minds, not fishing." After more gold was washed from the stream, the following day the men returned to Cookshire and filed their claims and so the Ditton Gold Mining operation was born. It was during this time when Cyrus Hurd (Augustus's brother) operated the Ditton Gold Mine for the Hon. John Henry Pope near the village of La Patrie in Ditton Township, circa 1862.[34]

***

Cyrus Alexander and Mary E. (Langdon) Hurd (Hurd family collection)

Cyrus Alexander Hurd, grandson of Edmund[7], son of John Bennett[9], was born in 1842 in Newport, and married Mary E. Langdon in 1865. They had one daughter, Nellie, who died at 14 years old.[4]

By the latter 1800s, gold prospectors were already active on the Ditton River adjacent to Newport Township, referred to as the "El Dorado" of the Eastern Townships. The area is as fascinating for its history and landscapes as for its natural riches.[16]

Augustus[8] Hurd Sr., being quite entrepreneurial, reasoned that if there was gold in the Ditton River near La Patrie then perhaps there might be gold downstream, and so he investigated to see if he could acquire the riverbed rights. Not to let this opportunity pass, Augustus was trying to stake a claim in a part of the south end of the Ditton River, but John Henry Pope maintained he had claimed it all.[31]

In a letter dated June 8, 1876, from Samuel A. Hurd, Compton County Treasurer and Justice of the Peace, to Augustus Hurd, *"I send herewith thirty-two dollars and twenty-five cents ($32.25) proceeds of gold you left me which the bank declined to take and I sent it away to be cashed. This is a little better than you may be offered here. I hope it may prove satisfactory. [Signed] S. A. Hurd."*[10]

In his letter dated June 11, 1876, Augustus Hurd requested two licenses *"to dig for gold in the bed of the little Ditton River, downstream from the LaPatrie operation."* The request was rejected in a reply dated July 27, 1876, from *"Gold Mining Inspector"* S. S. Rinard: *". . . the laws through which that river flows, in the 9th range of Ditton Township, were Patented to Mr. Horace Sawyer in 1866. . . I have declined your proposal unless I receive further information on the subject."*[10]

Augustus replied on July 31, 1876, that he did not want the land; he simply wanted the license to mine the bed of that part of the Ditton River. He went on to say that:

> *The Hon. Pope has been mining for the last 10 to 12 years, employing from 6 to 15 men, thanks to me. I surmise that nobody knows how many thousands he takes out yearly. That Sir Pope refuses to let anyone dig in the bed of the river, claiming all the bed of the river himself with one or two friends. If you will grant me license to work in the stream, I am ready to pay for license and royalties if I am successful in finding gold.*[10]

Author's note: Both several small gold nuggets and the original medicine bottle that stored the nuggets originating from this mine are in the Ancestral Heard/Hurd Collection, indicating that Augustus must have had some success.

The author has no information as to whether Augustus succeeded in getting a license; however, in a letter to Augustus in March of 1879, J. H. Pope wrote:

> *I do not object to your prospecting or working anywhere above little sluice falls on Little Ditton [River], which I suppose must be the place you refer to. I hope to be home before you would want to go on and I can notify or see your brother Cyrus about it. We are trying to redeem our pledges and I think most of our friends think we have done so hope it will improve after a little. Remember to Mrs. Hurd and family. [Signed] J. H. Pope.*[10]

Author's note: The letter is written on official "Agriculture Canada, Ottawa" stationery.[31]

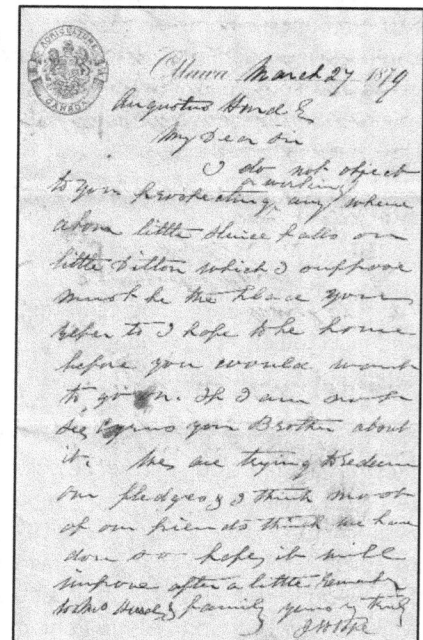

Letter to Augustus Hurd from Hon. John Henry Pope (Ancestral Heard/Hurd Collection)

***

A local blacksmith made a tool called the "broad axe," which was still being used in forming beams. It had a relatively short handle attached to a wide (14-inch) blade angled slightly, allowing the user to split a log lengthwise, creating a long slab of hewn wood. Hewing a log was hard work, but Cyrus Hurd was good at it. The log was first laid on the ground and with a regular axe, cuts were made into it about 2 feet apart, all at equal depths. Then the broad axe was used to square the log. The previous cuts facilitated this task, as chunks between the cuts would easily fly off under skilled blows until the log was squared and ready to use for construction. The outside slab that had the bark intact would be nailed to the side of a building much like siding today. The inside boards, usually elm, would be hewn with the broad axe, creating heavy but wide planks. They were rough but excellent for wood floors.[31]

Broad axe (top) and adze, both stamped C. A. Hurd (photos by Sandra Hurd)

Of course, there was always a story to tell about the skills of these hardy men and their beloved tools as sort of a rite to passage: Following a few libations at the local watering hole, near the gold mine, some of the workers would start boasting and squabbling about their expertise in the use of the broad axe. Loose tongues would encourage betting abouts one's accuracy and expertise with this axe. The challenge was to place a wooden match on the floor, then from shoulder height, swing the axe downward with full force to split it lengthwise. Cyrus collected on many more occasions than he had to pay . . . so the story goes.

Cyrus built his barn in Newport using both the broad axe and an adze, another tool used to square timber logs for cabins, houses and barns. After using the broad axe to make a first pass on the log, the builder would essentially square the logs by chipping with the adze while standing on two other logs, swinging it between their legs, a most dangerous task that required much skill. Prior to mill saws, the adze and the broad axe were used together to form supportive beams. Both required a great deal of skill to use, and more than a few men struck themselves on the foot or leg, causing much irreparable damage. These tools were made by Richard Parker, who was both a farmer and blacksmith and lived just down from the Haskell Hurd Homestead on Morrison Road. These tools would have been loaned out and therefore the name, C. A. Hurd stamped on the base as identification, would increase the likelihood that he would get them back in due course.[31]

In September 1871, Augustus[8] Hurd was contracted to build the colonization road for the second and third ranges of the Township of Emberton. The contract, *"number 4807, reference number 13438"* was issued by the *"Department of Agriculture and Public Works, [signed by] E. Lebourveau, Inspector of Colonization."* The letter requested that Augustus *"send an accounting every eight days, the document to include the pay lists of the work performed."* The Colonization Road instructions contained 32 specifications, by which the contractor of operations was to abide.[31]

An addendum noted as follows: *"To avoid heavy postal charges, the pay lists accounts, statements of disbursements, receipts and other vouchers of expenditures, shall be drawn up in duplicate and with other voluminous documents, except letters, must be forwarded wrapped in a slip or band of paper open at each end and not in an envelope or under cover of a letter."*[31]

Markets for wheat, lumber and potash continued to grow until the 1860s, with preferential tariffs in Great Britain still favouring Canadian imports. However, when England revoked the tariffs, Canadian exporters looked increasingly to the United States to sell their goods. A new dynamic primarily for English-speaking business

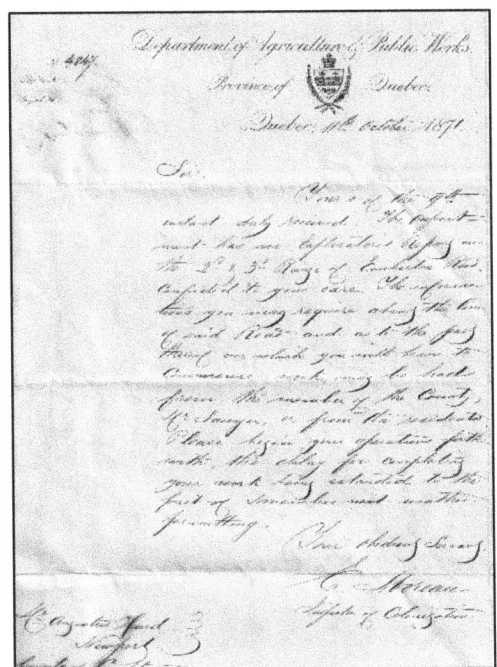

Road contract no. 4867 to Augustus Hurd, signed by E. Moreau, Inspector of Colonization, 1871

elites began to develop a more diversified economy based on importing, exporting, manufacturing, and retailing. That diversification also included enterprising French-speaking Canadians who were building high-tech shipyards and dry docks in Montreal.

It was through this era that Augustus[8] Hurd, dealing with the new Eastern Townships Bank, received a postcard in 1882, noting his interest had been deposited in his account for a note he held. There are two interesting factors that stand out with this notification: the size of the postcard, only 4 in. by 2.5 in., and the fact that there was clearly no privacy then, as everyone who handled the mail would know he was receiving interest on a note he held in the bank. It was a very trusting time indeed.[31]

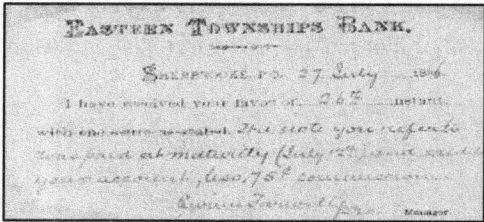

Postcard of notification from the bank, the info available for all to see – a trusting era

***

The town of Island Brook, located 12 miles east of Cookshire, closest to the railway station, had daily mail, with annual postal revenue of $187.50. It had a town hall and an office for the secretary treasurer for Newport Township. A natural attraction, one-half mile downstream from the bridge crossing the stream known as Island Brook, is the Island Brook Falls, with a chute of about 100 feet from top to bottom. The stream descends in a quick chute of 60-70 feet from the head to the bottom, before it joins the North River.[32] North River and South River merge downstream to form the Eaton River.

A particularly happy time for the children in the summer months as soon as the work was done was to head to these rivers to find the best swimming holes. Some of the fondest memories were these times spent at the river, basking in the sun, learning to swim, or simply trying to catch a fish underwater. There was always a slope from the shoreline that ever so slowly descended into the depth where a speckled trout or rainbow trout lurked.

Newport had four sawmills in operation by 1866: one made shingles, another was a lathe and planing mill, a third ground provender for animals, and the fourth was a lumber mill. By this era, mill owners were able to ship their finished product by rail to outside markets beyond Newport and adjacent townships. The Industrial Revolution of the 1850s and '60s was a period of rapid growth, and the Eastern Townships, including Newport, enjoyed their share of that growth. Eaton Township was also flourishing and the saw and gristmills of William Sawyer, the grandson of

William Sawyer's gristmill and original sawmill on the right, Sawyerville (Eastern Townships Roots)

Island Brook Falls (Conception Graphique, Rene Roy, 1995)

Capt. Josiah Sawyer, had taken over the operation of the Sawyerville mills from his father John circa 1869-1889. Much of the lumber from Newport was also sledded to his mill. William Sawyer and his wife Julia lived in Newport. William was the MLA for Compton County from 1871 to 1886.

***

The late 1800s was also a period of evolution in the art of candle-making, which had changed little in the previous hundred years. Around 1850, paraffin made from coal tar was discovered and starting to become commercially viable for making high-quality candles that burned bright, clean and without odour. In the decades that followed, new machines that could make more than 1000 candles per hour were introduced to the marketplace. As a result, manufactured candles became another item to be sought after and purchased by those who could afford them. The braided wick was also invented in the late 1800s. Wicks before this time were made simply of twisted strands of cotton, which burned poorly and required maintenance in the form of a snuffer to cut off the charred part to make the candle burn better. The braided wick, however, was tightly plaited and a portion of the wick curled over, enabling it to be completely burned, eliminating the need for the snuffer process.[42]

Kerosene lamps had now become the norm in urban centres, burning much cleaner and safer than candles. They were brighter, almost odour-free, and easier to use in lanterns that would light up every room like never before. With enough light, our ancestors would be able to sew, crochet and knit in the evenings. Patchwork quilts and fancy embroidered handkerchiefs were now available for sale in the more urban centres. Many of these were being made in the rural areas and sold for additional income to the larger populated towns and cities. This new way of lighting, however, would take several more years before finding permanent use in Newport simply because of the added expense. Only those who were in businesses would be able to afford the new lanterns that would eventually come to light up the many rural farms of Newport in the coming years.

***

Gardner Wheeler Rand (born 1866), the youngest son of Marshall S. and Mary Maria (Hurd), married Lily Parker in 1890. Lily was the twin sister of Lottie McCallum and sister-in-law of Charlie McCallum. They operated a farm with her son Roy from her previous marriage to John Cable. Unfortunately, Roy died in 1912 at age 15. The farm was in Auckland Township just off Morrison Road in Newport at the 11th Range border of Auckland and Newport townships.[4]

> *Author's note: I remember the farm as the Morrow/Stickles farm below the Morrison farm on the 11th Range Road when I was going to school. Rodney Hillman remembers his grandfather, John Jones, taking him there and to Frank and Mabel Morrison's farm up the road. Rodney believes that this farm was owned by his grandfather John Jones before "Gardy" and Lily owned it. (Rodney Hillman)*

Gardy and Lily (Parker) Rand holding baby Barry Berwick, son of Hilda (Rand) Berwick; the boy at the far right is Rodney Hillman (courtesy of Carol Rand)

***

The word "housewife" appears to have come into common use in the 1880s, referred to in a multitude of books as the "frugal housewife," the "careful housewife," the "patient housewife," and the "faithful housewife."[35] Most young women in the region were brought up in the strict moral atmosphere of their respective religious faiths, the young bride was imbued with high standards of conduct, kind, amiable and industrious, readily assuming her rightful place in the households of the local communities. Books became more readily available now that postal services became available in the more rural areas such as Newport. Books were gathered and traded around the communities with great anticipation. This was an era when women themselves were reading about other women and the perception of how they were being viewed by the writers of the time.[35]

***

The French (surname) families of Newport connections: [25, 16, 32] *(also: French family history)*

> *Author's note: There were two French families that settled in Newport. I have referred to the first French family as the family from whom Edmund[3] Heard had purchased a lot from John[1] French in Ipswich, Mass. I have researched this family as connected to John[5] Sage French, who drowned with Captain Samuel[6] Heard at Brompton Falls. The second French family immigrated from Cornwall, England, first to Boston and then circa 1857 to Newport. and are included later in the chapter. The two families became known and referred to as the "English Frenches of Newport."* [24]

John[4] and his two older sons, Luther[1] and Levi[1] French of Enfield, Conn., part of the newly formed United States of America, came exploring in Eaton Township in early spring of 1796. This was after Captain Josiah[4] Sawyer and Colonel Edmund[5] Heard had explored the townships of Newport and Eaton a few years earlier, having applied for the land grant allocations open for settlement in the "waste lands of Lower Canada" in 1792-93.[16]

John[4], Luther and Levi had first cleared a parcel of land in 1796 around a region we now know as Eaton Corner and had planted some potatoes that year. They returned to Enfield that fall.[16]

John[4] French (1739-1822), his wife Abigail Sage and his family, Luther[1] (born 1775), Levi[1] (1777-1858), John[5] Sage (1780-1815) and three daughters, officially immigrated two years later, in 1798, from Enfield. They returned to Eaton Township, made their way through to their previous clearing, then travelled further north to where Cookshire is today. They became part of the group of Associates under Capt. Josiah[4] Sawyer. During their two years back in Enfield they had applied for the land grants as Associates with Josiah, receiving a total of 2,400 acres. John[5] Sr. was granted 1,200 acres, Levi 1000 acres, and Luther 200 acres in Eaton Township.[25] If they had moved back to their original parcel of land they had previously cleared, and unless they had applied as part of an Associate group, they would have been considered "squatters." The family settled on the east side of the Eaton River and built a log cabin near the foot of the hill on the Bury Road, as we know it today.[16]

> *Author's note: John[4] French's third son, John[5] Sage French Jr., was the person Samuel Heard[6] was to meet in the woods in 1802, to give him a letter from Col. Edmund[5] Heard addressed to Josiah Sawyer, as he was travelling back to Lancaster, Mass. This was the same John[5] S. French who later drowned with Samuel Heard at Brompton Falls in 1815. Interestingly, Mary[3] Ellen Lebourveau, a granddaughter, would marry a third-generation French, but of the second family of Frenches who settled later in Newport.* [31]

Levi[1] and Martha (Osgood) French had eight children; however only two sons, Hiriam, born in 1808, and Luther[2] Sage, born on their homestead in Cookshire 1828, survived. Hiram French (Levi[1]'s son), married Sarah Williams of Newport. The family moved from Eaton Township to Newport where they raised their 10 children. Hiram was a farmer and Insurance agent in Newport Township.[16]

When Luther[2] Sage French married Margaret Stevenson, the daughter of William Stevenson, in 1876 they too moved from Eaton Township to Island Brook where they raised their seven children. Luther[2] Sage was a millwright and lumber manufacturer. He built two sawmills in Newport, which became the Mills of Luther French and Sons, an important business in Island Brook. In 1876 he dammed the stream on the north side of the bridge in town where he built and operated a lumber mill (on Lot 1 of Range 6). His house was situated close to the mill just opposite the Island Brook Post Office. A surveyor from Three Rivers, named Whitcher (the "Grand Voyer") had laid out a road from the town of Island Brook, where Luther operated one mill, to his second mill, located just above the juncture of the North River and Eaton River.[32]

Luther and Margaret's seven children were George William (born 1852), Horace (born 1854), Alice (born 1856), Levi[2] (born 1858), Clyde W. (born 1861), Elon (born 1863), Thomas[4] F. (born 1866) and Anna (born 1869). Two of Luther[2]'s sons also had an interest in the mills and worked with him in their expansion of the business. George W. and Thomas[4] French continued to operate the sawmill, and the shingle mill located about a quarter of a mile downriver from the sawmill, from 1883.[16]

Luther's son, Lieutenant George Washington L. French, born in Cookshire in 1852, moved to Newport in 1878 to operate the mills with his brother Thomas[4] F. They employed 15 men. At this time the lumbering part of the operations were taken back by their father, Luther, as this was his preference and area of expertise.[32]

George W. French married Ida Jane Willard at Grove Hill in 1879. She died during childbirth the following year, in 1880. Their daughter, named Ida Jane as well, died young at age 12. George married his second wife, Mary Louisa Lothrop, in 1887. Their daughter, Alice Maud, was born in 1888. George held the offices of both councillor and school commissioner for Newport for several years and served as justice of the peace for the District of St. Francis.[31]

> *Author's note: A reader might notice that many of the female surnames originated from many of the other Newport settlers. Ida Jane Willard was a great-granddaughter of Longley[6] and Hannah[1] (Hurd), one of the first Associates with Col. Edmund[5] Heard. One of Longley's eldest daughters, Mary, married Ensign (Capt.) Edmund[7] Heard, and Artemas[7] D. Rand married her sister Hannah[2] Hurd Willard.[4]*

Thomas[4] F. French, the other son of Luther and Margaret, married Emma Learned. They and their family built a shingle mill in 1883, about a quarter-mile downstream from the first sawmill operated by his brother.[32]

In the spring when the water was high there were river drives. Pulpwood (small second-growth spruce trees cut into 4-foot lengths) was floated downstream from where it was cut to as far as the pulp and paper mill in East Angus. The men who worked for the French mills on these river drives boarded at various homes along the river.

One of Luther French & Sons sawmills, Island Brook (Newport Homecoming 1801-1996)

The Luther[2] French & Sons mills were an important factor in the business of Island Brook. When the spring runoff began, so did the "drive" as scores of lumberjacks accompanied the churning mass of timber down the swollen rivers.[32] "When I was a young girl, I watched the pulpwood and logs tumble over the falls. Sometimes the schoolteacher would take the pupils to watch this sight." *(Ruth (Burns) Morrow)*

The lumbering business continued to flourish in Newport. There was a blacksmith shop right across from French's Mill, where horses were fitted and shoed in order to work in the surrounding woods and on the farms. The story was told that "Alex Buchanan came to Island Brook when he was 12 years old and he remembered how he had tried to fish in the mill pond without anyone seeing him, but he could never do it without Mr. French seeing him and letting out a big yell." In later years Alex became part of the Lumber Board Sawers and Millwright group working for Luther, who continued to yell at him from time to time.[32]

Levi Lyon bought the mills from the Frenches around 1901, adding a clapboard mill in 1903, which were later sold to Brompton Pulp & Paper Co. This mill burned down around 1915-16. Around 1908, Levi and Lucy Lyon built the square house next to the Anglican Church in Island Brook and lived there until 1918. Levi died in 1923; Lucy lived with their daughter, Myrtle, until she died in 1932.

Across the road from the sawmill in Island Brook was a cheese factory. Area farmers did all their milking by hand and took their milk to the cheese factory where it was made into cheese. Each farmer who brought milk to the factory took his turn taking a load of cheese, packed in veneer boxes, to the train station in Cookshire.[32]

Most farmers had pigs at that time, so every time they took a load of milk to the factory, they brought back "whey" (the skim off the top of the processing vats) for the pigs. The kids accompanying their fathers on these trips would love to stand around eating curds. Flies were, of course thick and always present around the whey vats.[32]

***

Author's note. The second French family that settled in Newport were two brothers circa 1848. They purchased lots 2 and 3 of Range 6, and in later years Lot 1 just off Flanders Road. These three lots were original lots taken up by Caleb Sturdivant and granted under Col. Edmund[5] Heard and Associates. Caleb Sturdivant abandoned his claim circa 1801-14 and the lots were reopened to new subscribers when Newport became a Township after 1801. After the BALC purchased the unsubscribed lots circa 1834, these lots became available for sale.[20, 32]

William[1] Victor French (born 1826) and his brother John[1] William French (born 1824) emigrated from Cornwall, England, to Lower Canada in 1848. They both came to Newport that year and purchased their lots on Range 6 in the Island Brook region. John stayed on one of the lots, cleared the land, and built a homestead. Meanwhile, William moved to Boston in 1849 where he worked for about for 12 years as a cabinet maker. William met and married Margery McGee in Boston in 1850; unfortunately, Margery died. They had no children. William married her sister, Elizabeth McGee, in 1857 and four years later they returned to Lower Canada where they settled on the lot beside his brother John. The two families worked together to clear and farm their individual lots on Range 6 in the mid-southwestern part of Newport where the North River and Statton Brook ran through their farms. Their descendants have lived on these farms since these early settlement days.[32]

William French family gathering at the wedding of William and his third wife, Eliza Seymour Damon (courtesy of French family archives)

The William[1] V. French Family:[32]

William[1] Victor French married Elizabeth McGee in 1857 in Boston where they had two children, Margery (1857-1954) and Mary (1860-1933). They named their first daughter after Elizabeth's sister. The family moved to Island Brook in 1861 where they extended their family on the new homestead: James W. (1862-1947), William[2] (1864-1939), Robert[1] Foster (1866-1961), Margaret "Maggie" L. (1870-1950), Henry (1873-1947), and Elizabeth "Lizzie" W. (1875-1965). William served as valuator, councillor, and road inspector in Newport for nine years after he arrived in 1861. William married his third wife, Eliza Seymour Damon (pictured), in 1907 after moving in retirement to Dixville, Que. The photograph taken at their home in Dixville where they married.

Only two sons remained in Newport after their siblings married: William[2] married Ester Burns of Newport, and Robert[1] Foster married Mary Ellen Lebourveau of Eaton Township.

The John[1] William French family:[32]

John[1] William French married Emma J. Parsons, daughter of George Parsons of the Knicky Knocky community near Bury, in 1858. They raised nine children on their homestead on Range 6: Frederick W. (born 1859), John[2] W. (born 1866), Charles D. (born 1870), Abel E. (born 1876), Ella (born 1861), Alice (born 1862), Annie E. (born 1864), Emma C. (born 1873) and Ascha.

Author's note: Research indicates that Ascha(h) may have been adopted by John and Emma. She was known as Aschah Sunbury and she married Levi D. Chamberlain. (ref.: Linda (French) Oliveras)

With John[1] and his brother William[1] and their families living in homesteads that were side by side, it allowed them to bring up their children together. The families were able to help each other with the continual clearing and lumbering of the land, the farming chores; the children playing together almost as brothers and sisters. Coming from Cornwall, they had a strong tradition of cattle breeding, and so both brothers began their stock of Shorthorn beef cattle. In the late 1800s, they transitioned to the Friesian and Ayrshire breeds. These breeds were becoming more attractive than the once-dominant Shorthorn which were predominately a beef-only breed. The Ayrshire breed yielded a higher milk and cream advantage and therefore was a good choice for early settlers.

There is an immense rock in one of their fields, a "glacial erratic" relic of the Ice Age, the only known specimen of its kind in that area. It is estimated to weigh 100 tons. A story has been passed down through the century that a particular spot near the bridge where a popular swimming hole has attracted many over the years was in fact an Indian encampment; also, an Indian graveyard as they were then called.

Glacial erratic on Aubrey and Blanche French family farm field (courtesy of Mildred Waldron, from *In Poetry*, circa 2002)

One could see several sunken spots on the brow of the hill even today. Rob French recalled "having seen several bones protruding from the ground as he pointed out a worn footpath from the brow of the hill to the spring and the river's edge." A short distance from the bridge (always called the French bridge) is a large meadow, tree bordered, still referred to as the "tan yard meadow," a place used by the Indians to tan their skins. "Several poles were still standing when we visited the place."[24]

"The swimming hole was up the River Road beside the meadow farm fields at a point where there was once a bridge over to what had been a brick works, down the hill from Austin Bowker's on the North River (the "Wells Bishop road"). The other popular swimming hole was at the bridge at bottom of the hill (down from Grant/Harris Nugent's place). The water was deeper there . . . and it was fun to dive off the bridge. The field on the other side of the bridge was called the tan-yard. I also found it interesting that halfway up the hill to Harris Nugent's, there were the remains of Abenaki houses, which Grandpa said were the Maynards and the Rainys. The last of that group were the Sharbees. I remember "Long Tom Sharbee" and seeing their cabin on the Bowker road back in the late 1940s /early 1950s – another whole side of "pre-history" perhaps never explored." *(Eric R. French, great-great-grandson of William V. French)*

Author's note: The "brick works" referred to by Eric French was most likely the area just off the banks of the North River on the clay flats, where Alden Learned had his ovens for curing and assembling the bricks he was making when he built his home referenced in Chapter 8. His children carried on this trade, building chimneys and other brick and mortar projects in the surrounding communities of both Newport and Eaton townships.

The swimming hole by this bridge was populated on hot summer days by as many as 75 or more enjoying one of Canada's popular sports. People visiting from as far as Portland, Boston, New York and many other places would gather here; fathers bringing their sons and daughters to a place where yesterday and today were bound by friendly ties. Grandpas, grandmas, grandsons and granddaughters came to visit the scenes of yesteryears and revel in the friendliness on all sides, making it easy to understand why people would on a Sunday after church head towards the "old swimming 'ole" on the "English Frenches'" farm.[24]

***

In 1865, the Island Brook Methodist Church was being constructed, and by 1870, it was completed; Island Brook now had its own parsonage and resident minister. The church was 46 feet long, with 9 x 9-inch framing, the beams all hewn by hand. The belfry materials were cut by circular saw, indicating that part of the church was perhaps added later. The Rev. E. Sweet, presided in Island Brook, the church acting as a mission by itself. The cemetery, located at the back of the church, served the Protestant communities in this region and was developed during the same period.[32]

***

Methodist Church in Island Brook
(Newport Homecoming 1802-1992)

When Tyler[7] Wellington Hurd (the fourth son of Edmund[6] Heard) married Abigail Sage French (John[5] Sage and Amy (Hall) French's daughter), they moved to Eaton Township onto part of the original homestead lot of Abigail's grandfather John[4] French. Both Abigail's brothers, Horace Hall and John[6] French, continued to live for some years with Tyler and Abigail while they were young, on a now-divided part of the farm. Their family enjoyed a one-storey framed home just outside of Cookshire, and operated a 300-acre farm, 150 acres of which was under cultivation –half with crops and half used as pasture – and 150 acres forested woodland. Their farm was located near the bridge in Cookshire on the Bury road. This demonstrates the progress and hard work that these early settlers and the two generations behind them had made by 1851. Tyler served on Eaton Township's first municipal council in 1855 and as chairman of the school committee.[4]

When Ward Bailey married the widow Amy (Hall) French, they took over a divided part of the original John[4] French homestead (1200 acres) on the Bury Road from Cookshire, raising four more children with the surnames Bailey. The families of French/Frasier/Fraser and Hurd were to be connected and were a closely knit group of families throughout the following era.[16]

The 1881 and 1891 censuses of Eaton showed that the widow Abigail S. Hurd (1836-1898) was living with her daughter Sarah Minerva and son-in-law, William Donald Frasier (Fraser).[4]

> *Author's note. The first Hurd/Fraser/Frasier connection: The surnames Fraser and Frasier are one and the same. Apparently when James Fraser married Abigail Bailey, an American, she thought the name Fraser was too "Scotchy" and wished to Americanize it, so she had the parson insert an "i" in Fraser when they were married. (Winston C. Fraser,* Cookshire's Pine Hill Farm: The land, the people*)*

Augustine Samuel[8] Heard, Samuel[7] A. and Catherine's youngest son, born in 1850, became a partner with J. A. Camirand and H. A. Fraser circa 1880 in the company Camirand, Hurd & Fraser Advocates. Circa 1895 he partnered singly with Harry Fraser in the company Hurd & Fraser Advocates, Barristers Inc., located in Sherbrooke, Sherbrooke County, Que.[4]

***

Lucy (Bennett) Heard, wife of Edmund[6] Heard, died at 71 in 1875, leaving a tract of land in Lancaster, Mass. Her heirs were listed as Edmund[7] Heard, John Bennett[7] Heard, Luke[7] Heard of Newport, Tyler[7] W. Heard, Samuel[8] A. Heard of Eaton, and Lucy[7] Gibson (Heard) of Melbourne, Que. This was part of the land where severances had been previously sold in 1846 and later in 1853 which probably helped finance the later endeavors of the Heard families in Newport Township.[4]

***

The promise to build a railway in 1871 connecting British Colombia would finish the task of uniting Canada coast to coast. After many feeble attempts and the election of Sir John A. Macdonald as Prime Minister, William Cornelius Van Horne, an American, was hired by the CPR board to get the job done. In 1885, the last spike was driven on time by Donald A. Smith, and Canada became a nation.[45]

In 1871 Canada there was almost as many Irish as there were French people.[45] *(The Canadian Atlas, 1888)*

***

The years following the completion of the transcontinental railway connection across the West was a time when there were long and severe labour shortages on the Canadian prairies, and these became extreme during the weeks of the fall harvest when millions of acres of crops needed to be brought in during a very short period of time from September to October. In 1890 "harvest excursions" were organized by the Canadian Pacific Railway in which special trains would transport workers from eastern Canada to various "Prairie Centres." There they would be hired by agents and travel to farms across the prairies. The labourers were given low fares by the CPR as the railway knew it would later earn a great deal of money from transporting the harvest. The CPR was also the largest landowner in the West, and it hoped that some of the excursioners would decide to settle in the West and buy some railway land. The bulk of the labourers came from Ontario, Quebec and the Maritimes. Wages were high – certainly the highest a labourer could earn in Canada. A season's work could pull in up to $300 and as room and board were normally provided, the only expense was the $30-40 for the train trip west. There were many farmers, both men and women from Newport and surrounding townships, who went west on these excursions from time to time, up to and until just after the First World War. Some folks, such as George Loveland, stayed and bought land there, returning years later to retire back home. Once harvesting combines began to replace binders and threshing machines, this practice began to wane, simply because much less manpower was required to harvest the grain. *(ref.: Robert Irwin, "Harvest Excursions" in The Oxford Companion to Canadian History, 2004)*

Harvesters in Western Canada (Glenn Wright, *Legion* magazine, 2001)

Author's note: This has been an amazing record of large families that, from humble beginnings and with no educational advantages, made good use of their limited resources. They progressed from one generation to another with members of their families ultimately achieving distinction in creating new businesses, working in the lumbering, agricultural, industrial, educational, and various professional fields. These same people offered their time serving the municipality in which they "lived their lives." The inspiration in writing this book on their lives comes from the ancestors because in writing their stories, it felt as though I was living with them in their times, like finding an old friend you hadn't seen since childhood.

***

PART TWO
The Diaries and the Letters

Maple Leaf Cemetery (photo courtesy of John Hurd and Elizabeth (Hurd) Richardson)

Maple Leaf Cemetery is located on today's Route 210, about one mile east of Randboro in the Municipality of Newport, Que. It is a quaint, triangular-shaped rural cemetery. Almost all stones are legible. The cemetery dates from about 1804-08 and it is still in operation today.

> *Author's note: I believe there is sufficient evidence to suggest that Col. Edmund[5] Heard (1743-1814) is buried on Lot 29, Row 5, headstone no. 1. This particular headstone is unreadable and archived in the cemetery records as "unknown." Col. Edmund's wife, Elizabeth (née Andrews), is buried in Deerfield, Mass. It is highly likely that his burial would have been the first in the cemetery, given the date, and so, the mystery is . . . where exactly is he buried? As the records show, he was the driving force to establish a cemetery in Maple Leaf.*

MAPLE LEAF CEMETERY

The community-minded culture is evident today, just as it was in so many years past. Following is the list of current members of the Maple Leaf Cemetery Board of Directors, courtesy of Linda (Graham) Fisk:

- Barry Loveland, director for 25 years, 24 as president
- Gladys (Graham) Fisk, director for 22 years, 19 as vice-president
- Linda (Graham) Fisk, director for 21 years, 19 as secretary/treasurer
- Sidney Morrison, director for 40 years
- John Hurd, director for 22 years
- Shirley Morrison (recently deceased), was director for 20 years
- Cheryl (Nugent) Graham, director for 19 years
- Trudy (Rand) Doherty, director for 19 years
- Jamie Berwick-Rand, director for 11 years

Bernie Taylor has been the diligent caretaker for 17 years.

Author's note: It is striking that the surnames of all the directors listed above are descendants of those whose surnames were a part of the original settling families in Newport. Bernie's ancestors had settled in Eaton Township. Those who have served in the past, as well as this current Board have dedicated themselves and taken pride in the preservation and integrity of Maple Leaf Cemetery.

Chapter 11   Growth in Newport (1875–1900)

Railways were to shape the economy and electricity began to influence politics.[16]

During the industrialization period, railway-building became a predominant project. By 1876, railways began to crisscross the provinces. Lumbering had progressed from fording logs downriver to the lumber mills to hauling them to the mills in horse-drawn sleds, greatly increasing efficiencies. These tandem horse-drawn lumber sleds were great for local winter transport; however, now the excess of milled lumber needed new ways to get to market. With the ever-growing demand for building products, a quicker and all-seasonal transport method became the priority of the day. Shipping by train guaranteed a more direct pickup and delivery into the marketplace to the south. By 1885, the transcontinental railway had been completed through the Rocky Mountains to the West Coast, allowing lumber to be shipped to the Prairies and creating even more demand for Eastern goods. Lumbering was now a major economic driver and railways provided the conduit to a burgeoning marketplace.

In the newly formed Eaton Township, men were working quietly but impatiently towards a short railway that would connect vital points, one of them being through Cookshire to link up with the New England states. William[6] Sawyer, ex-MLA (and grandson of Captain Josiah[4] Sawyer, the founder of Sawyerville) and his confreres spent considerable time and money in this effort, which was kept quiet for as long as possible. William, who married Julia Smith in 1839, owned both the Cookshire and Sawyerville sawmill operations.

The railway project was kept quiet because there was much resistance to this progress, specifically from those who were prospering from horse-driven long-haul logging operations – the railways would cut into their businesses. The lumbering industry, however, was rallying for railways to get their pulp, timber and lumber to markets more quickly and more economically. Railways also threatened the peripheral and supportive businesses of the small towns along these long-haul routes. The teamsters, who hauled the timber using double-tandem sleds many miles utilizing various men along the way, would be in jeopardy. These teams of horses and their men needed to be fed and housed at way stations, usually in the form of taverns. Harnesses and sleds needed to be purchased or repaired, other goods bought and sold. The people who relied on these peripheral businesses felt threatened; felt they stood to lose if railways were built.

Many farmers also opposed railways at that time. They would lose land to expropriation; perhaps their farms would be cut in two. They would have to cross railway tracks to pasture livestock or tend to their fields on the other side. Trains would spook their livestock and horses would bolt; animal deaths were inevitable. Furthermore, their land was likely to drop in value if severed by a railway.

The consortiums developing these plans required surveys and financing. The railway required a square timber for ties, which necessitated cutting more lumber. Bridges and stations had to be built, resulting in economic activity that would boost the economy. Nevertheless, the planners met with huge protests, some of which were violent, which hindered and delayed progress. For this reason the proponents kept their project quiet for as long as possible. The Granger Movement was begun in the late 1860s by farmers who called for government regulation of railways and other industries whose prices and practices, they claimed, were monopolistic and unfair. The farmers and others who owned businesses connected with the current methods of lumber transport were often referred to as "Patrons of Industry."[16]

> *Author's note: The map of Compton County (on the following page), from H. H. Miles in his book* Canada East at the International Exhibition, 1862, *is reproduced by L. S. Channell in his book* History of Compton County. *It shows the progress of the railways built during this era. Note the junctions in both Cookshire and Sherbrooke and the lines towards Canaan, Vt., and Lake Megantic. During the 1800s people had begun to migrate to Canaan, as it was strategically located on the border between Canada and New Hampshire. With the initiation of railway transportation, the regions surrounding the railways were beginning to expand.*[16]

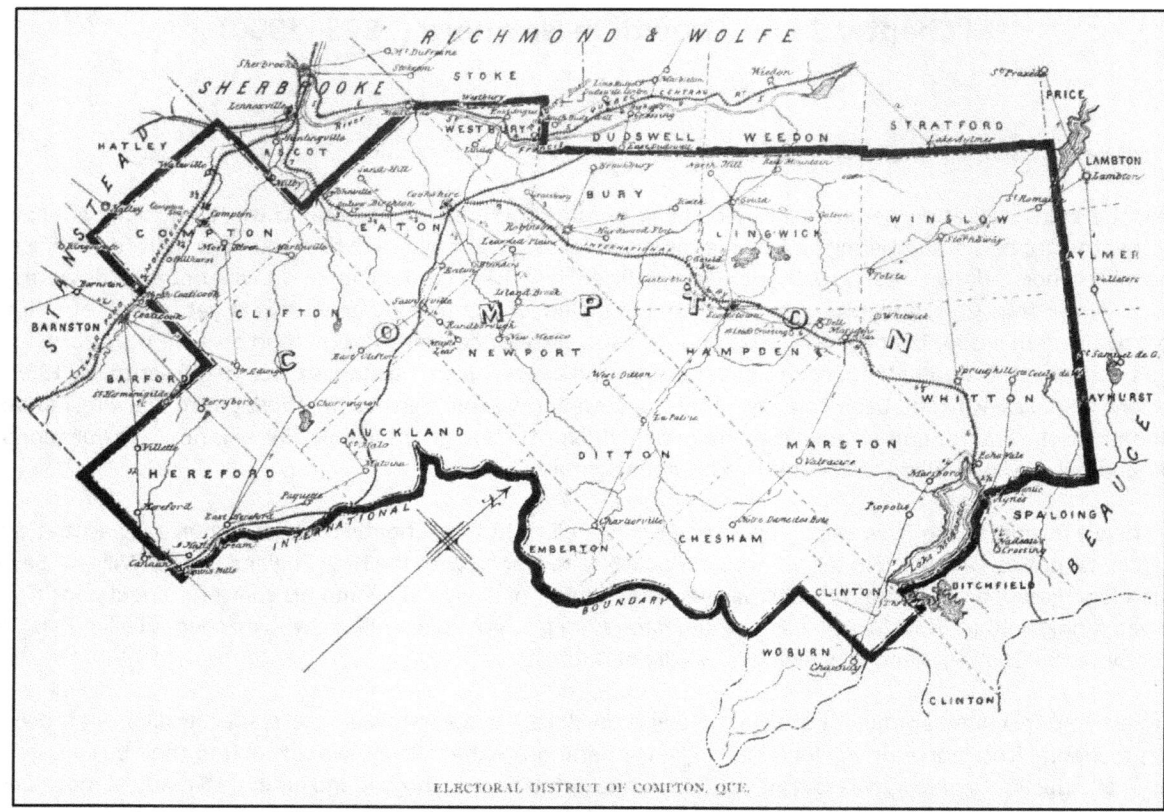

Map of "Electoral District of Compton" (L. S. Channell, *History of Compton County*, 1896)

During the late 1800s, work was in progress on a railway from the New England states, crossing the border at Canaan, Vt., along Hall Stream in East Hereford and north through Auckland/Clifton townships. It would pass the edge of Newport Township and on into Sawyerville, arriving at a connecting point in Cookshire. This would allow trains to connect from Montreal through a large station junction in Sherbrooke, passing east through Ascot, crossing Eaton Township with stations at Birchton and Bulwer, and continuing east to the Cookshire Station Junction. From Cookshire running directly east, tracks were soon to be laid, running through the townships of Bury, Ludwick, Hampton, Marsden, and Whitten, crossing the Eastern Townships' eastern border at Beauce County and Megantic and on into Maine.[16]

These early entrepreneurs' vison was to create a major hub in Cookshire with connections south to Vermont, east to Maine, and west to Montreal. They envisioned that timber harvested in Maine and all the townships in between could be shipped for processing from all the local lumber mills along the way. The many end products could then be shipped west to the growing Montreal market and south to Vermont and the huge U.S. market would provide a huge economic draw.

Author's note. The boundary line between Vermont and New Hampshire was not finally established until 1934; the border between Vermont and Canada not until

Coal-fired steam train engine plowing spur track, late 1880s (Roger Cook and Karl Zimmermann, *Magnetic North*)

1925. Until the lines were firmly drawn, there were several border skirmishes. (Canaan, Vt., municipal website)

Many of our early settlers, even in the late 1880s, were living difficult lives as food not obtained from the wilderness soil, forests or waters had to be transported from seaports great distances away. The railways would prove to be an efficient and effective conduit for a wide range of products (other than lumber) from both the Port of Montreal and the border junction in Maine.

John Sawyer, a son of Capt. Josiah, had taken over both the sawmill and gristmill operations in Sawyerville from 1869, after his father died, to 1889, after which John's son, William, took over.

The original Cookshire sawmill had been built by Henry Dawson in 1881; however, he unfortunately went bankrupt.[24] The mill was reorganized in 1882 by subscriptions that were taken up by W. B. Ives, R. H. Pope, A. W. Pope and H. B. Brown. All through these stirring years, the prominent men in the Eastern Townships had their hands full of business projects and proved themselves men of distinction and determination. In 1889 the Cookshire Mill Company consortium bought the Sawyerville sawmill from William Sawyer, a grandson of Josiah. William kept the gristmill, located on the southwest side of the bridge.

Sawyerville postcard showing the lake created by the dam, circa 1890 (Hurd family collection)

When the demand for lumber exceeded supply, the Cookshire Mill Company erected a larger and more modern sawmill in Sawyerville in 1889, with a capacity for sawing 100,000 board feet every 12 hours. The expansion included machinery to produce clapboards, laths and barrel staves. The first shipment of finished product by rail was made in January 1889 by the Cookshire Mill Company. Much of the lumber sledded or river-rafted during the spring runoff to the Cookshire or Sawyerville sawmills came from Newport and other surrounding townships.

The Sawyerville sawmill burned down six years later, in 1895, causing the Cookshire Mill Company to again expand its operations in Cookshire. The Sawyerville mill property was then purchased by George and Mary ("Mamie") Matthew of Sawyerville. George rebuilt and expanded the mill for milling lumber. He also operated a sash and door factory on the west side of Flanders Road. The milled lumber was taken up the street to the railyard at the Sawyerville train station where it was stacked for shipment. When George Mathew died suddenly of pneumonia after his second trip to the Yukon to claim a gold deposit, the mill was managed by his wife Mamie and operated by George's brothers, Tom and Rob Matthew, for many years. The mills were purchased circa 1919 by Alonzo Hurd of Newport. Alonzo expanded the operation under the umbrella of the Sawyerville Manufacturing Company.

Stagecoach travel in the mid-1800s (Eastern Townships Roots)

With trains came a more efficient mail service. Gone were the old stagecoaches delivering mud-soaked bags placed on the rear platform of these stagecoaches and delivered to the local post offices in rural communities. Mail would be placed in special mail bags from a central mail-sorting depot in Montreal and each bag would be tagged to be dropped at a certain station stop. From there, the mail would be picked up and delivered to a general store where it would be sorted and placed in mail slots. There was no mail delivery to homes at this time, so recipients would travel to town to pick up their mail. These train stations became mail and passenger drop-offs (junctions) where business opportunities developed. People who disembarked the train may have needed a place to stay or perhaps had to be driven somewhere; this created a need for accommodation and/or a ride to their end destination. Mail dropped off at a train stop needed to be picked up, so perhaps a local store might be built which would include a mail facility. The general store was the place to shop for groceries and hardware, buy harnesses for the horses, pick up the mail, buy the newspaper and catch up on the local news. The general store became the new community meeting place.

***

At this same time, women who essentially ran the households were becoming economic drivers as never before. They were reading the newspapers, taking note of the advertising and buying these advertised products as general stores in their communities began to expand and carry them in inventory. Kit Coleman was the first woman correspondent in Canada to create a "women's section." Women wanted a voice in society, sent in their letters to advocate their position in the society of the day, and were reading letters they had sent in the newspaper.[31] *(Sherbrooke Daily Record, 1889)*

The Ladies' Guild, an affiliate of the Anglican Church, was organized in Newport well before the 1890s, the first women's church organization in the new settlement of Island Brook. Some of the first members were Mrs. S. Wood, Mrs. William Dawson, Mrs. R. H. Wilford, Mrs. J. Weston, Mrs. Tom Painter and Mrs. John Patton. As the community grew, ladies from outlying areas joined the guild. They raised money to help maintain the church, as other communities did, by holding church suppers and selling handmade items such as knitted socks, mittens, needlework and quilts.[32]

These ladies were renowned as excellent cooks and freely donated their time to prepare food for various fundraising dinners. People came from miles around to attend these bountiful meals held in the local church basements and halls in the various communities. Christmas was especially festive with platters of dried fruit, pies, butter tarts, shortbread cookies and maple sugar cake that resembled fruitcake. They always had a Christmas tree for the children. They made green and red cheesecloth candy bags and filled them with a variety of candy and nuts, always ensuring that each child received one.[32]

The early days of December were spent by the young mothers and daughters happily addressing Christmas cards, putting those received as decoration on the fir tree that had been brought in by the man of the house. There were no lights then, although some brave souls apparently put candles on the trees, or so it has been said! The young ladies would write notes of interest to their sisters and brothers who had married, moved away and were raising their own families, anxious to receive a letter in return. And then there was Valentine's Day, Mother's Day, Father's Day, birthdays, anniversaries and milestone events that would prompt someone to write. To receive something in the mail brought great delight for the whole family. The children crowded around to hear the news that would always be enclosed in the cards. This was also the telegram and postcard era where memories were documented by a traveller and, of course, the receipt of one of these brought genuine excitement for all the family.

In this era, each community supported a Ladies' Guild and as each generation passed on, the Guild would be revitalized by the next generations of women – in the 1920s by women such as Verna Westgate, Freda MacLeod, Hazel Ewing, Jessie Hume, Jessie Spaulding, Edna, Margaret and Evelyn Lister and Althea Statton.[32]

***

The Lister family roots are in Lachute, Que. William Lister came to Newport in 1890 to join his brother James who had bought a farm in the Island Brook region on Lister Road. He bought 50 acres behind the Spaulding farm which would become known as the Lister place. After a few years working on his land and for other farmers in the region, William built a house on the property.

William returned to Lachute where he married Martha Silverson in 1896; they took up residence on the small farm in Island Brook. Martha bore four children: Allen (born 1897), Garnet (born 1898), Clarence (born 1902) and Gladys (born 1904). In 1905 they moved to Montreal, where William worked for three years for his cousin in his wood yard, splitting and delivering wood by horse and wagon. Wood was sold by the bag in Montreal at this time and delivered from house to house. Their son Walter was born in Montreal but died at age 18 months. William was unhappy with city life; he returned to Island Brook to check on his house and informed his neighbour, Mr. Cassidy, that he would be moving back.[33]

The William Lister family threshing with true horsepower (courtesy of Lister family)

And so the story has been told that William and his family took the night train, arriving at the Cookshire train station in the middle of the night. He walked all the way to Island Brook, arriving at his neighbour Mr. Cassidy's home at 4 a.m. Mr. Cassidy immediately harnessed the horses and went to pick up Martha and the children who had been waiting with their baggage at the train station. They stayed at the Cassidys' home until their furniture and other belongings arrived by train several days later. The next morning William went to Bury to purchase windows and doors for the old house which had been broken into while vacant and boarded up. Later he got a job at the lumber mill in Island Brook, owned at this time by Levi Lyon.[33]

To help the family out, 12-year-old Allen and 11-year-old Garnet took a job, using a horse and sled to haul slabs from the mill, bringing some home for firewood from time to time. A few years later William and Martha bought 15 acres across the road for pasture for a horse and cow. Another son, Gordon, was born in 1908 at their home, now called "the Lister Place." They sold it in 1910 to his brother Jim and moved to Bury where they bought a house where another son, Arthur, was born in 1911. Four of their children remained in Newport where they raised their children.

Allen went to England in 1918 and enlisted in World War I. After the war he married Ada Brown; they raised four children there. Garnet married Evelyn Spaulding (1902-1993); they took up residence in the village of Island Brook where a son was born in 1935. Garnet worked for various farmers and in lumbering.

Clarence married Edna Young (born 1925); they bought the Simpson farm on the road from Island Brook to Bury in 1926 and built a barn – which still stands today – from lumber cut from his father's farm on the Lister Place. Clarence and Edna had one daughter. In their later years, they cared for his parents, William and Martha, with help from other family members. William died early in 1956 and Martha died later the same year. The farm was sold to William's brother James. Clarence died in 1990.

Gladys married Foster Laberee; they raised three children. Gordon married Marguerite Largy (1920-1988); they raised three children in the village of Island Brook. Gordon ran a milk truck operation and they both worked at the post office for many years. Arthur married Vera Mosher (1922-1983); they raised 10 children on a farm in Lawrence Colony.[33] *(submitted by Edna (Young) Lister, 1994)*

***

And then there was "old-time courting" which was sparked at the annual "corn husking bee." Most of the corn was a golden yellow, so when an ear of red corn suddenly appeared, often in the hands of the prettiest girl in the party, by custom there was a mad scramble among the otherwise-bashful young men to kiss the holder of the red ear. This was not always an accident; the genial oldster hosting the neighbours who were helping husk his crop of corn had been known to "plant" a few red ears where some young lady would be sure to find it. The red ears were originally a variation that occasionally appeared in an otherwise yellow crop, but it was well known that some farmers would grow a few stalks of red corn for the very purpose of livening up their annual corn-husking party. When the corn was all husked the party trouped into the house for cider and donuts. Typically, Charlie Alden and his wife Olive, or Fred and his wife Pearl, accompanied each other, the men playing fiddles and ladies playing pianos; providing the music for a few dances for all to enjoy.[18]

For the next 25 years, Newport and the surrounding townships would prosper with many mills operating. Clapboards and machined lumber were produced in great quantities, and much of it was shipped by trains to larger markets. This was a boom time in Newport, when new houses were being built to replace many of the old log homes, churches were being built, and schoolhouses were being expanded or rebuilt to support the many new arrivals into the township – people seeking work or perhaps a new life in a different part of the Eastern Townships.

Sadly, this was also an era of great pain and suffering with a new disease referred to simply as "lung disorder," as they did not know what it was. Little cabins started dotting the landscape where people who were sick were isolated, their meals brought to them until they either died or recovered; it was a time of anxiety for every family as well. We know many people died during this period, and the affliction was typhoid fever or tuberculosis, the latter typically referred to as TB.

> *Author's note: William Sawyer wrote a note to Abigail S. Hurd, daughter of John[5] Sage and Amy French and wife of Tyler Hurd, originally of Newport. (See letter below.) Tyler and Abigail were living in Eaton Township at the time of this letter. William Sawyer was MLA for Compton County for several years; he and his wife Julia (Smith) lived in Newport on Grove Hill Road at the junction of the North River Road. William and Julia were staunch Methodists.[23]*

Religion played an important role in the lives of each of the families during this era as well, regardless of the particular faith. Everyone was there to help people through hard times, and men and women played a role in finding ways in which to help those in need. In a letter dated June 1858, William Sawyer wrote:

> *Dear Sister [Abigail] Hurd*
>
> *The sisters of our Society are making an effort to aid the Planches by way of a Tea Meeting. They feel confident of your sympathy and would be very glad of your cooperation so far as you are willing to give it. We know you feel an interest in these matters and many of the sisters look to you as one of the eldest and leading members for an example and have no doubt you will give them our worthy of invitation. If you can please send us a note of what you will do so that we may know what is required of others in order to have the preparation complete. There is a Class Meeting at Mr. Chaddock's next Tuesday evening, we shall be glad to meet you there. We trust you are advancing in Holiness.*
>
> *Yours Truly,*
> *[Signed] Wm Sawyer*[21]

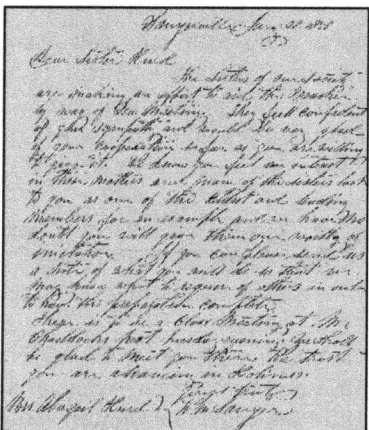

Letter from William Sawyer to Abigail Hurd

> *Author's note. You may notice reference to the women in this society as "sisters." In a later letter written by Haskell Hurd, his reference to "sisters" was not referring to "relatives" of a specific family as one might assume. One may also note that many gravestones during this period are marked "died of Consumption" simply because at first it was known simply as a lung disorder, until they learned of its medical name as TB.*

Many times, when the menfolk were sick, the entire family had to rally around to do the chores, because no matter what happened, the livestock had to be fed, watered and cleaned. Often the women had to take charge of everything around the farm – cooking, laundry, haying and all other manner of daily life activities – while looking after the children when they too were sick. In many cases the women died from overwork and as well from these illnesses, in which case the men would remarry if only to keep the family together.

***

George Gibson[8] Hurd, son of Luke[7] and grandson of Edmund[6] Heard, was born in Newport in 1839. He married his first wife, Mary Lorinda Sawyer, in 1861. Mary was the daughter of Josiah[5] and Susan Sawyer and was 25 years old

when she married George. They settled on his father Luke's farm on lots 6 and 7 of Range 10, Newport, the original farmland granted to Colonel Edmund[5] Heard. Mary took great pride in their herd of Angus cattle, a breed originating in Scotland. She was unable to have children and they were married for only 12 years before she succumbed to TB and died at age 37.[31]

Author's note: The marriage of George and Mary was a second marriage of a Heard/Hurd to a descendant of Capt. Josiah[4] Sawyer. The first was John Bennent[7] Heard, who married Polly Sawyer, the daughter of Peter Green Sawyer, Capt. Josiah's son.[4]

Mary Lorinda Sawyer and George Gibson[8] Hurd

George Hurd, a stockbreeder and farmer, took great pride in his herd of purebred Angus cattle, particularly his Angus bulls, which he showed at the annual Cookshire Fair. The first recorded importation of this breed from Scotland was in 1859 by Sir George Simpson, Governor of the Hudson Bay Company. Angus cattle began arriving in Montreal by 1860 to feed an ever-increasing demand for sturdy beef animals. Breeders in Eastern Canada were expanding their purebred herds and exporting Angus cattle to Western Canada.

George looked to harvesting wood as another source of revenue. Wood was a staple in a farmer's life; selling the logs provided income and the large branches provided much-needed wood for heating. George built a woodshed attached to the house for easy winter access. He cut hardwood during winter months, as the logs could be pulled out of dense forests, pulled through wetlands, and rolled onto the logging sleds much easier when the land was frozen. Logging sleds would be pulled by a team of horses and transported to the roadside or directly to the mill for sale. Usually a year's supply of burnable wood for household use would be transported to a spot behind the house. Since they had to split the wood by hand with splitting axes, they would split it when frozen as the wood generally split easier. Once cut up and then split, the wood was piled to "cure" or dry until the following winter.

Clipping from the Canadian Atlas of 1881

> **TOWNSHIP OF NEWPORT.**
> Annable, L. H., M.D., physician and surgeon. Commenced practice here in 1878. Graduated in Vermont, 1865. Was born in Compton Co., 1837. Residence and P.O. address, Sawyerville.
> Hurd, G. G., farmer and stockbreeder, residing on Lots 6 and 7, Con. 10, and owning 260 acres. Has been Mayor of the Municipality, and is now a Councillor. Has lived in the township since 1839. P.O. address, Sawyerville.

George used his horse team on a treadmill which connected to a large circular saw that had now become available at this time. George would hire a live-in helper along with a couple of other men and together they would prepare the logs for cutting. They used a "cant dog" to roll the logs onto a long wooden tray, attached to a base. A cant dog was a tool with a long wooden handle equipped with a metal bracket that had a small steel grip on the front end of the bracket to bite into a log. This tool allowed a man to turn and roll large logs with relative ease to position them for sawing. Sawing logs was another of the farm tasks that needed to be done.

Two horsepower engine (Hurd family collection)

The word "horsepower" originated from the use of horses before engines were born. The treadmill, patented circa 1886, used horses walking on these treadmills to provide power for sawing wood, threshing grains, turning poles for making cedar water conduits and many other jobs that required rotational motion. The treadmill shown would be classed as a "two horse-powered" machine, simply because there are two horses on the treadmill.[31]

Before the days of steel pipes, augured logs were used to deliver water. A system for auguring pipes, once set up, worked the same way as a lathe, except on a larger scale. A treadmill powered the "pump log auger," which was a long boring bit. The log was placed on a sliding platform running the length of the log. A worker would use the cant dog to continuously push the log into the rotating auger. Once the pole was fully augured, he would attach a "pump log reamer," a tool with cutting edges to enlarge the hole. About 40 logs at a time would be bored. Next, the ends of the logs were shaped with a reamer at one end and a "bummer" at the other end (like a giant pencil sharpener). The logs were then ready to be laid in the ground below the frost level, the tapered end of one log driven into the blunt end of the next log to create a tight fit. These wooden pipes provided a continuous conduit for water from a spring to both the barn and the house.

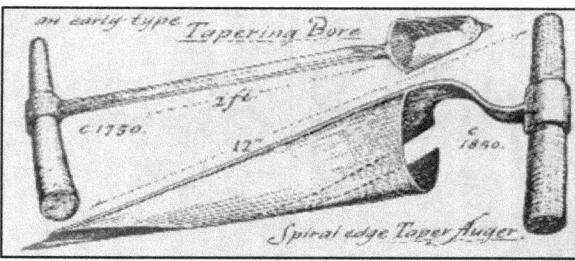

Illustration of wheel hub reaming tools, Eaton Corner Museum (photo by Sandra Hurd)

This was also a time when various styles of water pumps were entering the marketplace. It was not uncommon now to see a handpump attached to a kitchen sink; this allowed water to be pumped from a cistern of continuously flowing water. Since not all the farmers in the community could afford a "treadmill," George would farm the unit out to his neighbours for various jobs where it made the job faster and easier to manage.

> *Author's note: It was on George Hurd's farm as a young boy in the summer of 1946 that I became aware of the wooden piping. Entering the original Edmund[5] Heard house, there was a large wooden box carrying the water directly through the kitchen, in and out again; the water never stopped running naturally, summer or winter and therefore never froze. One of the pump logs in the Eaton Corner Museum's collection, dating to the 1920s, was made by Horace Cable, who lived on a farm between Sawyerville and Randboro. Dug up in 1997 and donated to the Museum, it was a part of a waterline approximately 250 feet long, from a spring to the house and barn.[31] (also: Royce Rand, Eaton Corner Museum)*

George Hurd married his second wife, Achsah "Amelia" Hodge, born in Eaton Township in 1855, the daughter of Samuel B. and Lois Katherine (Hall) Hodge. Amelia was 21 and George was 37 when they married in 1876. They raised two children: a son, Alonzo George (born 1882) and a daughter, Julia Lois (born 1893).

George and Amelia grew hops. He built a large combination hop house and meat dry-aging room just to the right of the original house. On one side of the building he dried his hops; on the other side he built in a wooden winch to pull up a carcass to hang to dry-age before carving it into the various cuts of meat in preparation for freezing for the winter. Animals were typically slaughtered in the late fall when nights were getting cold before winter set in. Once carved, the meat was positioned on shelves to freeze, then stored in wooden barrels. If they had ice, they might have packed the meat in layers. If the cuts had not been individually frozen prior to packing they would have stuck together, making it impossible to select a particular cut to cook.

Amelia Hodge (courtesy of Gillian (Hurd) Anderson, great-granddaughter)

George and Amelia's hop house and meat dry-aging facility (photo by author)

This was the fifth building positioned in front of the house. The four barns were positioned in a square so that the barnyard was basically fenced in on all four sides by the barns. The cattle, pigs, sheep and horses could be let out in this barnyard for watering from a large wooden trough. The chickens, geese and turkeys could also be let out to feed and water. Colonists built their homes facing their barns for the simple reason that they would be able to keep an eye out for any mishap that might befall their livestock. In this case, if one were to turn the house 180 degrees, the view all the way down the valley towards Randboro would have been stunning. Clearly, having a good view had not been considered when his great-great-great-grandfather, Col. Edmund[5] Heard and his family had first built the house in 1793-94.

In the autumn after the harvest was brought in, George ploughed his fields to prepare the land for next spring's seeding. In this era, farming implements were drawn with one or two horses. George had a one-furrow plough, so it took him a long time to completely turn over the earth in a field of any size. Since George did not favour manure piles around the barns, during winter he would clean out the gutters every day and would spread the manure by hand from a horse-drawn sled onto the ploughed fields as fertilizer for the following spring's crops.

Spring would call for "harrowing" the ploughed fields, followed by the seeding process. Harrowing was another tedious but necessary process to break down the ploughed soil and manure and even-out the furrows.

The harrow of this era had circular disks arranged in a row on each side of the horse-drawn pole. These disks were running at an angle to the pole (like a snowplow but at an opposite angle on each side) so that, when pulled, the disks turning at this angle caused a circular ploughing effect, breaking down the furrows. After this process, George would hitch up to another style harrow that was simply a series of spikes welded on bars that would further break down the furrows but were used more for leveling the field for seeding. George, and later his son Alonzo, would weigh down these cultivators by adding rocks on top, not unlike what they did in the past with the road graders. Harrowing was but one of the tasks that had to be done before seeds could be planted and expected to grow.

***

Author's note: Since the Township of Newport was growing rapidly, the requirement for a municipal town hall became essential to serve the communities with both municipal offices and public meeting facilities.

R.W. Heneker, the BALA Commissioner sold land to the Municipal Corporation of the Township of Newport for a Town House for the sum of $25.00 on January of 1871. The I.O.F. [Independent Order of Foresters] Hall Court No. 605, was instituted in 1890 by John W. Stocks, H.S. The first Officers were: A. F. Bowen; H. N. Henderson; G. W. French; M. W. Bowen; H. A. Stevenson; Wm. Morrow, Treasurer; F. Burns, Chaplain; T. F. French; R. Lavallier; J. W. Kerr; W. J. Kerr; E. Phelps; E. E. Bowen; and A. E. Orr, M.D. Physician.[16, 32]

In the years 1855 to 1891, many settlers who had served their communities as councillors were appointed to serve for intervals as mayor of Newport Township. Starting in 1855, the appointees were Alden Learned, Charles Sawyer, Samuel N. Hurd, William G. Planche, Gilbert T. Williams, Charles B. Hawley, William Stevenson Jr., Joshua Nourse, Charles D. Chaddock, William W. Bailey, George G. Hurd and Ebenezer Learned. From 1891 onward the mayor was voted (rather than selected) into the role, beginning with Artemas S. Farnsworth, followed by councillors George W. French, John Kidd, H. B. Learned, Newell C. Rand, Edward Dawson and Robert Halliday. George Hurd also served in the office of Compton County warden, councillor and school commissioner.[16]

George G. Hurd
(Newport Homecoming
1801-1996)

At a council session held on Monday, September 9, 1889, Mayor George G. Hurd and councillors Ebenezer Learned, Russell Sunbury, Hezekiah Austin and Robert French, and Secretary Treasurer Charles H. Harvey were ordered to *"notify the Cookshire Mill Company to repair by the 20th instant all damage done to the riverbanks caused by their logs last spring failing which Levi Lyon, now owner of the French's mills, may be appointed to proceed to do the said repair."*[32]

Maple Leaf was the centre of the farming community and now received daily mail from Sawyerville. New Mexico, also a farming community only four miles from Island Brook, received mail three times a week and had an annual postal revenue of $14. Randboro was becoming a progressive town with a gristmill, a sawmill, a general store, and a post office with postal revenue from daily mail at $17 dollars for the year.[31]

The *Illustrated Atlas of the Dominion of Canada,* published in 1881, showed the land purchases and recorded Newport's population to be 1,700 with land valuations of $185,000, a significant increase from the previous census.[45]

A Roman Catholic Church was built in the 1870s and served the Irish Catholic community of the Island Brook region. This church was located across the road from the newly built town hall. Covered sheds built beside each church were used to hitch the horses during the services. A Catholic cemetery was located on the New Mexico Road to serve the Catholic community.

The Anglican Church in Island Brook was built in 1875 entirely of wood at a cost of upwards of $1000 and was considered a pretty and thoroughly churchly structure. The principal people involved in its building were Messrs. S. Wood, William Dawson, R. H. Wilford and James Weston. William. L. French and R. H. Wilford were the wardens; the Rev. E. C. Parkin was missionary of the district; and the Rev. A. H. Moore was the incumbent pastor.[16]

***

Author's note: Henry Morrow and his wife, Ellen (Wilson) Morrow, had immigrated from County Derry, Ireland, in 1844. They settled first in Argenteuil then moved to the northcentral part of Newport, near Island Brook, where they raised their eight children. Their eldest son, William W., was born in 1856 and was the first of their children to be married in their new homeland. The Morrow families would join the families of McVetty, Bowker, Farnsworth, French, Burns, Nugent and Westgate in the continuing economic growth in the regions of Learned Plain (Flanders), Island Brook, North River and New Mexico. Education was becoming more widespread amongst this generation of farmers; their children able to attend facilities beyond the borders of Newport Township.

In 1894 William Morrow married Hattie Cable in Island Brook. They raised six sons: Renford, Irvin, Earl, Raymond, Kenneth and Justin. Unfortunately, Hattie died young at age 40 and William was left with a family of boys ranging in age from 4½ to 15 years old. William instilled the boys with good moral values. His son Kenneth often recalled that once when he was visiting an aunt he had taken a minor item. When his father saw the item and inquired where he had gotten it, he drove him back the same day, six miles by horse and buggy, to return it. Kenneth was about 7 years old at the time. William was a disciplinarian and sometimes harsh. He was often heard saying, "If I get a hold of you, I will tan your butt, Ken." Another time, Ken had taken some apples from a neighbour's orchard, and William took him to Nahum Todd, the neighbour, to confess what he had done. William and the boys attended the Methodist Church in Island Brook where he taught Sunday school.[32]

William hosted church (community) picnics for many years; these took place at his maple sugar bush as he was one of the best sugar makers in the region. William was also an exceedingly kind person; when one of the neighbour's daughters was sick and could not attend, William put himself out to bring her some ice cream – a favour children do not forget. Hattie's sisters, Hannah and Alice, were especially kind to Kenneth, Justin and the other four boys, sometimes spending their holidays with them. Kenneth and Irwin completed their elementary schooling with their cousins at the Island Brook Elementary School, while Justin boarded with his Aunt Hannah and attended the Sawyerville High School. Earl had left home at an early age and went to work in Western Canada. Kenneth was needed on the farm, so he stayed to begin a farming career, going on harvest excursions in Western Canada with his brother Earl for a few years to make some money. Kenneth was only 14 when he went on his first trip out west to work. Renford and Irvin both completed their education at Stanstead College.[32]

James McVetty, another farmer living on Learned Plain Road, was born in Megantic County and arrived in Newport with his second wife, Elizabeth (Colvin), circa 1884. They raised their three children – James A., Elizabeth and Emily – on their homestead on lots 1 and 2 of Range 2. Elizabeth married Alexander Miller; they raised three children and continued to live in Newport. James[2] also married and continued living on the farm, raising his children there.

Author's note: The Bowker/Heard family connection by marriage: The Bowker family homestead was first settled by Solomon and Johnathon Bowker, who had immigrated from Luneburg, Vt., circa 1799 and were part of Col. Edmund[5] Heard's settling group of Associates. They had acquired two original lots (lots 3 and 4 of Range 7) that had been previously abandoned by Peter Trueman. One of these lots was then cleared and developed by their younger brother, Lyman[7] Bowker and wife Betsey. These two lots are located on the North River Road about three miles from Sawyerville.[4]

Lucy Minerva[8] Heard, (the second daughter of Edmund[7] Heard) married Lewis[8] Leander Bowker in 1845. Lewis was the son of Lyman[7] J. and Betsey (Merriam) Bowker; he was born in 1821 and had emigrated from Lunenburg, Vt., with his parents. Lucy and Lewis had four children: Edmund Heard (1849-1929); Lyman[8] James (1853-1924); Herbert Rice (1857-1950); and Luvia Amanda (1855-1944).[4] *(also: Florence (Bowker) McVetty family history)*

Edmund Heard Bowker married Lucy Minerva Ferguson and they moved out of Newport.

In 1879, Lyman[8] James Bowker married Clarinda Lenora Harvey (1853-1919). They had two children: a daughter, Lucy Minerva (1880-1951), who married Walter W. Sherman; and a son, Elwin Lewis (1884-1959), who married Minnie Smith in 1915. They lived in Eaton Township. Lucy and Lewis continued farming on the original Bowker homestead and expanded their herd of Holstein milking cattle. They often went to visit their uncle Edmund[8] Haskell Hurd in the Maple Leaf region, the families always looking out for each other in times of hardship and sickness. In a 1919 letter from Edmund[8] Haskell Hurd to his daughter, Mary, in the U.S., he mentions that *"Lyman has been hit with a bad bout of pneumonia."* If a cold or flu migrated into pneumonia it was considered a severe sickness and without antibiotics available, it caused many deaths in the communities.[31]

Art Farnsworth

Luvia Armanda Bowker married Artemas ("Art") Farnsworth in 1884 at the Bowker home on North River Road. They raised six children, three boys and three daughters: Lewis Bowker, Charles Albert, Agnes Stevens, Henry Alton, Luvia Minerva and Dorothy Maria. Art established the Farnsworth farm about two miles beyond the Bowker homestead. Apparently the Bowker family was not too happy about Art taking Luvia to "the stumps," as they called his farm because he had cleared his farm from virgin forest.

Their daughters, Agnus and Dorothy, were both diabetics which caused their early deaths. Art had heard that there was a new miracle drug called insulin being introduced on an experimental basis in Edmonton, Alta. He was en route to Edmonton with Agnes in the hope of procuring medical help for her but, unfortunately, she became extremely ill and had to be taken off the train in Winnipeg where she died.

Art was a faithful and reliable agent for the BALC (British American Land Company), a position which made his family worry for it was his job to expel "squatters" from Company land. These squatters were sometimes very abusive and threatening to any authority that might remove them from what they now considered their land, having lived on it for some time. As well as farming near Flanders, Artemas Farnsworth was Mayor of Newport for three years and a councillor for eight years. Art was appointed secretary treasurer for Newport Township circa 1888, a position which he filled until his death in 1934. His son Lewis took over the position until around 1976, so father and son served in the position for about 88 years.[32]

Herbert Rice, the third son of Lewis[8] and Lucy (Hurd) Bowker, was born in the house which still stands today and is currently owned by his great-grandson Jeffrey Bowker. Herbert married Ormasinda "Sinda" Cornelia Farnsworth (1861-1897) of Eaton Township in 1888. They had two sons: Edmund Heard (1891-1973), who in 1917 married Naomi Maybell Gillman (born 1897); and Austin Stevens (1896-1990), who in 1922 married Ruth Ethel Gilman (born 1899). *(Florence (Bowker) McVetty family history)*

Herbert and Sinda carried on in the dairy business that both his grandfather and father had developed through the years, building up their herd of Holsteins to one of the largest milking operations in Newport. They continued clearing the land and were now cutting pulpwood as second-growth timber, shipping it down the North River then the Eaton River to the pulp and paper mills of East Angus.

> *Author's note: Those who were in the pulpwood business as their sole livelihood knew it as a darned tough life. Many men had lost their fingers from frostbite or chainsaw/axe cuts or broken their legs trying to free logjams in the rivers or when chains broke on their sleds and the pulpwood cascaded onto them. It was considered if a man and his chainsaw were able to cut 9-10 cords a day, only then was he worthwhile hiring.*

Sinda died five months after the birth of their second son, Austin. She died of pneumonia after "taking a chill" at the funeral of Mrs. William French (née Ester Burns) in Island Brook on January 10, 1897.

It was not uncommon when sickness struck a family, that a team of horses would suddenly arrive carrying men and women who would bring everything needed to perhaps cut a woodpile or to prepare food for the kitchen. They would go into the house and help with mending, sewing, and knitting; anything to help a stricken family in their time of grief and need. These people were neighbours, the kindest and truest friends anyone could wish for. Many tears would be shed during these times of sickness, and with no doctors or hospitals anywhere close, people had to depend on each other's knowledge and assistance to survive.

Herbert R. Bowker married his second wife, Jennie Gertrude Draper, in 1897. Their daughter, Edna Mary (1899-1993), married Ernest Middlemiss in 1920. Ernie and Edna Middlemiss operated a farm just off Grove Hill Road in Randboro during the early 1950s. Their only child was stillborn in 1924. Many years later in 1949, Gordon "Gordy" Hodge remembers when his brother Kenneth, who was working for Ernie at the time, convinced Ernie to hire Gordy to work for a couple of days with the threshing crew. Gordy was 9 years old and Ernie paid him $1.00 a day which included food and board. Edna was thrilled to have Gordy there as they had no children and so that was a special time for both Edna and Gordy.

***

Although the Herringville and Knicky Knocky communities north of Island Brook were separated by only a short piece of woods, they had distinct social lives. This was true of all such early communities, where isolation led the residents of each community to form their own social circles. Knicky Knocky was unique in that it straddled two townships and was isolated from other more mature communities through a lack of roads at the time. The first generations kept to themselves, creating a bond that held a tightly formed group of people, all entirely dependent on each other . . . not unlike the earliest settlers in Maple Leaf. This settlement was distinct in its social life only because it was a much later settlement, and yet the community was living in a more backward time . . . simply because of its isolation from the larger, more progressive and now established communities. (Another example of these social differences was the later establishment of Lawrence Colony.) Some of the first settlers who arrived around 1836 were named Dorman, Parsons, Lawrence, Reeve, Prince and Herring. The Herrings settling in Herringville, just north of the Newport Township border with Bury; the Dormans settled in the upper part of Knicky Knocky; the Parsons, Reeves and Princes settled further down the road in Newport.[33]

Hop farming was once an important Eastern Townships industry and for an area of Knicky Knocky in Newport, hops were indeed a lucrative sideline to the regular farming business. Around the timeline of the 1880s and the 1890s, one of these hop raising enterprises was established by Thomas Dorman on his farm, situated on the town line road between the townships of Bury and Newport.[33, 43]

In this venture, Tom Dorman was assisted by his two younger sons, Walter and young Tommie, and an adopted boy, Alfred Coates. The hop seeds were planted in rows and cultivated much the same as any root crop and being perennial, once planted they multiplied year after year. Since the plant is a twining, climbing vine, slender poles were inserted beside each plant and by the time the vines had attained full growth, it gave the yard the appearance of a young forest. The leaves were a dark green and quite rough.

Hop harvesting. Prudence Maidmont and her daughter Jane Ellis Parsons, ancestors of the Lyle Rand and Fay Parsons family, are both somewhere in this photo (*Island Brook: Then and Now* booklet by Ruth Burns)

The flowers were of a greenish colour and conical in form. Both were used in the production of beer, ale and porter as well as having medicinal value.[33]

As might be expected, crops such as hops added a great deal of extra work to the farmers' already heavy workload. The plus was that the hops were harvested in late August, after haying but before grain harvesting. Many extra helpers were called in from the surrounding farms to pick the hops before they were nipped by frost. This offered an opportunity for the women and girls to earn a little money to keep for themselves.[33]

The farm became a veritable beehive of activity. Mrs. Dorman catered to the workers' appetites with an abundance of the best food ever; known as an excellent cook, she took great pride in setting a lavish table of food. One of the highlights of the day always occurred at four in the afternoon when a lunch was sent to the fields: not an ordinary snack; indeed, a sumptuous repast.[33]

The harvest began by taking down the poles and clipping the vines near the ground. They would then be placed in deep large wooden boxes, 8 ft. x 3 ft., which were positioned near the pickers, the boxes being moved along the rows. Once full they were transported to the hop house, a wooden building with an upstairs floor of narrow boards set edgewise about an inch or so apart. These were covered with cheesecloth to prevent the hops from falling through. The hops were spread out in a shallow, even layer and turned from time to time for drying. On the floor below a fire was kept burning day and night in a big box stove positioned to direct the heat up through the floor. As each day's picking was dry, the hops would be packed in bales by a hand press, and the floor would be ready for the next pickings.[33]

With the influx of young people, there was a dance every night at one or another of the homes around, so the hop picking season was hailed with great delight by both young and old, while the work was enlivened with social chat and friendly gossip. Since the aroma of hops would permeate the air, the boys felt that the girl's clothes should too. Apparently one of the best-remembered features was the fun the boys had in ducking the girls into the hop boxes, or so it is told. It was not long before many farmers in Newport grew hops behind their houses to make their own special brew.[33]

***

Thomas[1] William[2] Parsons (1845-1887) was one of the children of Stephen and Prudence Maidmont Parsons, who had settled in Knicky Knocky. He met Jane Ellis, a daughter of Luke Ellis who lived on the Victoria Road. They eloped and were married in 1866 in the Free Will Baptist Church in Hatley. They made their home in Knicky Knocky on the farm beside his parents. They raised nine children, two of whom would make their home in the Knicky Knocky community: Sarah Jane (1869-1949) married (James) William Dawson (1865-1949), and George Thomas[2] (1885-1964) married Nellie Annabella Lefebvre (1885-1975).

Thomas had previously served in the Fenian Raids. He was known as a great hunter. As the story is told, "He hunted and caught the bear after it had bit Alex Lennox's hand off and he disposed of it."

Thomas Parsons
(courtesy of Carol Rand)

A keen believer in education, Thomas William[2] Parsons donated, around the year 1878, a small piece of land from the corner of his farm on Lot 14 of Range 1 in Knicky Knocky for a school. Records show that Thomas was paid $10 for a box stove and pipes, and $1.25 to set them up. The following year, James Price was hired to build a fence around the school, and Thomas was paid $4 to build a privy.[33]

Other wood was purchased for 75 cents and $1 per cord delivered. Neighbours were paid $1.50 for building the fires during these four-month terms in the winter. "Other expenses were a cup and pail at 30 cents, a broom at 25 cents, and nine lights with glass went for 45 cents."[33] The lights used in the school were kerosene lamps having a wick and a tubular glass chimney, the light emanating from the wick.

Unfortunately for his family and the community, Thomas died at the age of 42 from blood poisoning caused by a carbuncle, leaving a young family, the youngest son only two years old. Jane remained on the farm, managing with the help of her growing children and by boarding the schoolteacher. Jane also built the fires and cleaned the nearby schoolhouse on the corner of the farm. After her youngest son, George, was married, she made her home with them for a few years, frequently visiting at the homes of her other children and helping out wherever possible. Jane died at her daughter Sarah's home at the age of 76. Although she never had the privilege of attending school, her knowledge acquired through experience was a great asset to her and her family. She had learned by doing things herself. In her later days, she went out and cut down the apple tree, simply because it obstructed her view.

Knicky Knocky school, 1894. Back row, L to R: George Parsons, John Parsons, Walter Dorman, Scott Parsons, Annie Hamilton, Mary Boyes, Janet Boyes, Jessie Bennett, Ivy Parsons, Maggie Bedard (teacher). Front row, L to R: unidentified boy, George Dunsmore, unidentified boy, Will Boyes, Douglas Dunsmore, Wilfred Lizotte, Maggie Boyes, Annie Allison, Viola Allison, Emma Lizotte. *(Verification: Carol Rand)*

In 1888, Inspector William Burns visited the Knicky Knocky school to check on how many students were attending. He reported there were 15 children who could attend school now in the summer, all living in Newport. He noted that a Mr. Dorman, who was living in Bury Township, does have 100 acres in Newport, and that he is claiming the right and privilege of being able to send his two children to school there. He also noted that there was a Scotsman, whose name he did not know, who had three children fit to attend school.[33]

***

The first schoolhouse in Island Brook was a log building, built circa 1834-35 and attended by children until around 1878-80. Then a one-room elementary school was built and those students wishing to further their education attended Cookshire Academy in Eaton Township. One of these young ladies, Mabel Lyon, (a daughter of Levi Lyon), received her teachers permit in 1896. She taught her first three years in Island Brook. There were periods of time when classes were held, i.e., between the snowmelt and planting, then again between planting and haying and yet again from harvesting to snow-fly. The children were needed to help on the farms in the spring, mid-summer and fall. The inspector always visited during the fall sessions. The photograph on the following page shows students attending Cookshire Academy circa 1891-92, some of whom were from Island Brook and Learned Plain regions.[31]

As with all the women of Newport, they were a skillful, thrifty, and hardworking lot, often helping their husbands in the fields and in the bush. They were excellent seamstresses. They made clothes for themselves, their husbands and all their family members. Some created their own dye formulas for the colours. An 1884 cookbook formerly owned by Lucy Lyon had recipes for these dyes. They spun their own yarn and wove their own blankets. They raised their own sheep, grew flax and made their own linen and thread. They knit long stockings for the girls and socks for the menfolk.[32]

Nothing was wasted. Scraps of material were used to make quilts. The womenfolk would get together in "quilting bees" when the best quilters would be invited to quilt. Materials not suited for quilts were used to hook or braid rugs. "My mother often dyed discarded materials for her hooked rugs." *(Ruth (Burns) Morrow)*

In this era families still made their own laundry soap. They made their own bread with hops. When young people tasted beer for the first time, they noted the flavour was similar to the bread they had been eating all along.

***

Author's note: In 1876, Alexander Graham Bell invented the telephone, and in 1879 he invented the light bulb. These two inventions began to make

Cookshire Academy students, circa 1891-92 (Hurd family collection)

their way into Newport and surrounding townships by the late 1890s. "Opportunity is missed by most people because it is dressed in overalls and looks like work." (Thomas Edison)

John[1] W. French was one of two brothers who had emigrated from Cornwall, England, to Newport in 1848. He married Emma Parsons in 1858. They had nine children, four sons and five daughters: Fred, John[2] W., Charles D., Abel "Abe," Ella, Alice, Annie, Emma and Aschah.

Fred French married Elizabeth "Jenny" Bridgette; they lived in Sawyerville, Eaton Township, where Fred operated the gristmill for William Sawyer at the time. They had a son, Reginald "Reggie," and a daughter, Dorothy. It was said that Fred was a bit of a prankster and kept a BB gun (which shoots small lead balls like bird shot) behind the door.

When a horse was tied to the hitching post at the mill, he would give the horse a "peck" or two with his BB gun. The frightened horse would break loose and run up the street, leaving its owner bewildered. In the photograph note the covered bridge on the right; this crossed over the South Branch of the Eaton River in Sawyerville. This was the road leading to the northwestern part of Newport Township from Eaton Township, and was the route to Flanders, the North River Road and Island Brook.[31, 32]

Author's note: Both the sawmill and gristmill in the photo were owned at this time by John Sawyer and his son William (MLA for Compton County), Capt. Josiah Sawyer's grandson.

Sawyerville sawmill and gristmill (Eastern Townships Roots)

Two of John and Emma French's sons, John[2] W. and Charles D., had a deep interest in telephone lines and electric lighting. It was John[2] and his brother Charles who introduced electricity to the region. In 1891, these two brothers started a telephone line connecting Scotstown to Bury, Cookshire, and Lennoxville. Later the line was extended to serve Sawyerville, Island Brook, Bishop's Crossing and Marbleton. The switchboard was on the dining-room wall at John's farmhouse and their sister Emma operated it.

John[2] W. and Charles D.'s youngest brother, Abel, wanted to help them, so he developed a unique way of marking the distance between the poles by taking a horse and buggy with a rag tied to a spoke of the wheel; when the rag went around 14 times, he would put a mark for his brothers to put in another pole.[32]

In 1895, they contracted to build a line from Sawyerville through East Clifton to Beecher Falls, to the border at Vermont for the C.D.D. Telephone Company. In 1899, John and Charles built a dynamo and installed the first "electric light" plant in Sawyerville, later selling that plant to W. A. Worby of Sawyerville.[32]

After they sold their telephone operation to the Bell Telephone Company, John moved to East Angus and became the electrical engineer where he worked to change the Brompton Pulp and Paper Company mill in East Angus from waterpower to electricity. He continued as the substation operator for many years. He then became an employee of the Southern Canada Power Company. Charles moved to Colebrook, N.H., and built a telephone line connecting Colebrook with Canaan, Vt.[16, 24, 32]

As mentioned above, John[1] W. and Emma French had five daughters. Ella graduated as a nurse and married Ben Farnsworth. Alice worked in California for a few years, then returned home and married Eugene Baldwin, who had the largest Jersey herd and cattle farm in Canada at the time. (Jersey cattle were first introduced to Canada in 1868 in Quebec. The American Jersey Cattle Club provided registry services to Jersey owners and breeders in Canada until the Canadian Jersey Association (established in 1901) began its own herd book in 1905. Jersey cattle produced milk with a high cream content and were chosen by the creameries starting up in Newport and surrounding townships to produce cream, butter and cheese. Emma was talented in music and remained single; Annie married Alonzo Hodge; Aschah married Levi Chamberlain.

Abel "Abe" French, the youngest son, married Alma Patton from Island Brook, taking over the farm of William and Emma on Lot 2 of Range 6. They raised their five children in Newport: Elgin, Colin, Gordon, Emmerson "Aubrey" and Rita.

Known to be adept at woodworking, Abe French could make 53 rock maple axe handles in one day. When he retired from farming, he kept busy building boats and making bowls and plates. He and his wife Alma, along with his brothers John, Fred, and Charlie, contributed their talents to the Island Brook United Church Choir and were also members of the Sawyerville-Cookshire Concert Band. Frederick Augustine Hurd was leader of the band for many years and a member of it for some 60 years. In 1926 Frederick was presented with a silver cup by the members of the band for his many years of faithful service. So once again the French and Heard/Hurd families were interconnected.[32] *(quote: Aubrey French, grandson of John W. French)*

Abe and Alma French and family (courtesy of French family)

The William[1] V. French family:[32]

The second French brother, William[1] V. and his wife Elizabeth McGee would see only two of their eight children stay in Newport. They were William[2], who married Ester Burns of Island Brook, and Robert F., who married Mary Ellen Lebourveau. Mary was a granddaughter of John and Sally Lebourveau. Mary's grandfather was also with John[5] Sage French (of the first French family in Newport) and Capt. Samuel[6] Heard at Brompton Falls when both John French and Samuel Heard drowned in 1815. Their son, Henry, married Emma Chaddock. I have no information on their other son, James. Two of William and Elizabeth's daughters, Margery and Elizabeth, married two Farnsworth brothers: Margery married William; Elizabeth "Lizzie" married Thomas. Their daughters Mary and Margaret "Maggie" married into the Chamberlain and Fuge families respectively; all moved to adjacent townships. After Elizabeth passed away, William married his third wife, Eliza Seymour Damon, and they lived out their retirement years in Dixville, Que.

William[1] and Elizabeth McGee's son, Robert[2] "Rob" Foster French married Mary[3] Ellen Lebourveau. They raised four children on the Flanders Road, Lot 1 of Range 6: James[3] H. (born 1894), Archibald[3] W. (born 1897), Elena[3] (born 1902) and Lloyd Robert[3] (born 1910).

Harvesting wood continued to be one of the most important jobs to ensure there would be enough stove wood to heat their homes through the winter months, as evidenced in the circa 1900 photo opposite at the farm of John and Emma French.

"In our time in the 1950s while going to Sawyerville High, the Frenches' farms were variously located at the Wilfred Grapes place, Frode Nielsen's, down the hill into the valley (the place I remember as the family farm) i.e., the Meadow and up the hill on the other side of the valley, i.e., towards the Latimer place." *(Eric G. R. French)*

Woodpile at John William and Emma (Parsons) French home (courtesy of French family)

The French families all enjoyed fishing, especially at the mill site and bridges which crossed over the three waterways. During this era, there were abundant rainbow trout in both the South and North branches of the Eaton River and speckled brook trout remained prevalent in the streams upriver.

> Our earlier ancestors had relied heavily on an abundant supply of fresh salmon plying these rivers and they may have simply not noticed this as a diminishing source over time. Fish were abundant in all the rivers leading into the St. Lawrence, especially salmon. Small dams built or relied on by our pioneering ancestors resulted in the loss of half of all Atlantic Salmon habitat by 1850. This was not only because dams prevented fish from reaching their breeding grounds, but because salmon trapped below these dams were easily speared or netted in large quantities during these early days. The early mill sites encouraged overfishing as well; the thought at the time perhaps was not one of conservation. However, there were movements during this time in favour of laws to be passed that sought to forbid the dumping of waste logs into rivers and lakes, although no sanctions against the spewing of sawdust and bark were imposed. *(paraphrased from an article by Dwayne Wilkin in the magazine QAHN)*

***

Robert Buchanan was born in Ireland in 1828. He came to Canada and settled in the New Mexico region of Newport in 1871. His previous occupation was a shipbuilding carpenter. He and his wife had five children, however, only four survived. Their daughter Annie married Willard Parker (of the Parker family of Parker Hill) who was residing in Sawyerville, while the others in the family had moved out of the region.

Patrick "Pat" Redman owned and operated a general store in Island Brook, facing the North Road across from the Tom French house. (Thomas[4], Luther's son, was a descendant from the first French family in Newport, John[4] French). Pat was a big man and when he went into town for supplies for his store, he carried heavy articles such as barrels of flour, up steep hills just to make the load lighter for his horses. The building owned and occupied by Pat Redman was destroyed by fire on February 16, 1912.[17.]

When R. H. Wilford died in 1897, the post office was moved to Mark Holbrook's home. At the turn of the century, Sam Miller and his wife, Maggie Dawson, bought the Luther French property and operated the post office and small store during that era.

Learned Plain, 4½ miles east of Cookshire, was now the centre of a good farming community, having daily mail with an annual postal revenue of $41.

The New Mexico region of Newport, just southeast of Island Brook, began to open up by the late 1880s and became a busy agricultural settlement comprised of mostly Catholics, both francophone and anglophone, including recent immigrants from Ireland. The community's first settlers were from Mexico, Me., a farming town at the confluence of the Androscoggin and Swift rivers at the western end of the state. They came to Newport to take advantage of cheap land and abundant forests, and it seems they brought the name of their community with them, naming it "New Mexico."[39]

It is always interesting to know the origins of place names. Most of these towns and villages were named after places the settlers formerly lived. Newport was likely chosen from the early Heard settler group who came from the New England Colonies. Towns named Newport existed in Maine, Rhode Island, New York, New Hampshire and Vermont, as well as Newport Center in Vermont.

Reports of ghosts were common around New Mexico in the 1800s. Farmers living in the vicinity of New Mexico Road, just a couple of miles east of Island Brook on ranges 6 and 7, were dismayed to discover that their cows were no longer giving milk. Suspecting that someone or something was stealing the milk, a few of the farmers set a trap and, during the night caught a large white hare suckling on their cows. Apparently suspecting that supernatural forces were at play, the farmers released the animal, but not before notching its ears. A short time later, an old woman named Peggy Green died and it was obvious at her funeral that her ears were notched in the same way as the captured hare. These events confirmed suspicions that all was not as it seemed. Following the death and burial of the old woman, the farmers expected that their cows would start producing milk again. Only after they returned to the cemetery and walled in Peggy Green's grave did things return to normal and the cows again begin to yield milk.[32, 39]

The elements of the Peggy Green legend are well rooted in the folkloric traditions of the British Isles. Identified by folklorists as the "witch as hare" motif, the tale conforms to a constant formula with only minor variations.

***

In the latter part of the 1800s, people living close to or in urban centres typically went to a studio, such as in Montreal or even as far as Boston, for a professional portrait. In rural areas, photographers would instead travel throughout the rural communities to take a family portrait, then return to their local studios to process the film. The arrival of the photographer was considered a major event. Everyone would dress in their best clothes for a photograph, simply because no one had a picture of themselves. If they could even afford a picture, then this was a great opportunity for the whole family to be included in the portrait for the same price. These rural families were extremely busy farming so typically the photographer would arrive on a Sunday because they were more likely to convince a family, surrounded by their peers, to agree to a photo. Another major reason was that they would already be dressed in their "Sunday best." When they did go from farm to farm, it was not uncommon for a photographer to have to wait for the farmers to finish their chores before agreeing to sit for picture-taking, and for some with a great deal of prodding from their wives. The photographer would usually stay for supper, the evening spent in telling stories of his travels from town to town, children sitting in rapture listening and absorbing every moment.

Photography was now being used for special events such as marriages. Portraits of individuals and family groups became a source of comfort; a reminder of people they missed who had passed away. Some folks even talked to these portraits. They reminisced with these coveted photographs of their parents, their own families, and celebrations. Photos gave them visual recordings of their families to treasure. As their descendants, through this photography we have a better visual understanding of what their lives were about.

Family portrait (E.T. Resource Centre, Herbert Derick Collection)

***

The southwestern part of Newport:

Sunday was considered a day of rest and a day to dress up for the trek to the closest church. Families were remarkably closely knit within the community with a strong belief in the Sabbath as a Holy Day. Within these communities were sensible people who worked hard, went to church, paid their bills, and remained suspicious of bombast, public displays of emotion or foolishness of any sort. To play cards or anything frivolous on a Sunday was considered sacrilegious at best, so Sunday was a day when all families banded together for morning church services.

The Free Will Baptist Church had originally been organized in 1822 with a membership of 22 from both Newport and Eaton townships. Congregants included Samuel[7] and Sophronia "Sally" Heard, William and Joanna Alger, Gordon Percival, Edmund and Hulda Alger, Rodolphus Harvey, Simeon and Mary Alden, Nathanial and Martha Currier, and Mallory and Betsey Morse.[16]

By 1890, there were 108 Baptist residents in the two townships. One of the original churches was in upper Newport in the Maple Leaf community beside the school. After a few years, the Free Will Baptists became weak and were not able to keep up regular preaching. Sometime in 1891-92 the then-members of the Free Will Baptist Church decided to fall into line with the regular Baptists. By 1895, the combined sects felt it more advisable to have the churches in a more central location, so a new church was built in Randboro.[16]

Randboro, located on the north end of the original Lot 4 of Range 10, was the second town established in Newport. As the area of Grove Hill began to flourish with business and settlers, Grove Hill became known as the hamlet of Randville. Later, the name changed to Randboro. It was nestled between two large riverbanks on the South River, referred to the north as Grove Hill and to the south as Parker Hill. The terrain to the east slowly rose towards Maple Leaf Cemetery, and westward levelled out towards the town of Sawyerville in Eaton Township, where the same old Ice Age riverbanks were in place, but much further apart.

There were two churches in Randboro: an Anglican and another which would transition from a Baptist to a Methodist and then finally to a United Church. The Baptist Church was located at the intersection of Heard Road and the road to Parker Hill. It served the early community of Grove Hill. Austin S. Rand, son of Marshall S. and Mary Maria (Hurd), was the contractor for the building of this church, circa 1895.[31]

> *Author's note: The Baptist church in Randboro took over the congregation that were attending the original Baptist Church in Maple Leaf. This church is evident in the background of a schoolhouse photograph circa 1901. The church in Maple Leaf then became the first Methodist church in Newport soon after this changeover. This church was closed in 1922, as noted in Edith Rand's diary.*

Methodism, already established in Eaton Township largely due to efforts of William Sawyer and Albert Farnsworth, was to enter Newport by 1896.[16]

> *Author's note: The book* History of Compton County, *by L. S. Channell, first published in 1896, indicates that the Baptist Church in Randboro had already changed denomination by that time, becoming Methodist. The book suggests that this church also had a Roman Catholic chapel within the same building.*

The construction lumber for both churches would have been sawn in the Randboro mill, the logs hauled from within the community. The churches of the time were often used as community meeting houses and celebration facilities. Church volunteers contributed lumber, timber, and boards. They formed bees to work in groups; carpenters to construct the basic building, artisans to craft pews and others to landscape the land; the labour in most cases was voluntary as it was merely considered a part of the community effort.

The first Presbyterian Church was erected in Sawyerville, circa 1889, contracted and erected by Austin Spring Rand of Randboro.[16]

St. Matthews's Anglican Church in Randboro, a pretty "Gothic" church, was built entirely of wood in 1883. This church owes its existence to the missionary ardour of Rev. A. H. Moore and to the support given to his efforts by

Asher B. Jones Sr., William Loveland, Augustus[8] Hurd, Richard Dawson and Asher B. Jones Jr. In 1893 the interior ceiling was finished in tongue-and-groove hardwood and the church was now considered to be exceedingly pretty. In 1896 the church wardens were Messrs. Herbert H. Hunt and Charlie H. Loveland. The Rev. A. H. Moore resided in Randboro and served both the Island Brook and Randboro churches under his charge. The church was located at the top of the first hill, on the left-hand side, leaving Randboro on today's Route 210.[31]

St. Matthew's Church, Randboro (Hurd family collection)

The Baptist Church was a larger building than the Anglican, with a basement hall. A platform served as a combination choir and altar platform as well as a small stage on the main floor. Music drills, small plays, songs and recitals were performed by all the children in the area on special occasions such as the Harvest Home Supper and Christmas celebrations. "Whenever a student minister preached a sermon on the ten wise and the ten foolish virgins, he was really preaching to the converted." *(Ernest "Ernie" McCallum)*

The churches were busy places on Sundays, on choir practice nights, and of great interest when weddings or funerals took place. Activity prevailed everywhere, school children (called scholars in those days) going to and from school; a few from the village but mostly from surrounding farms.[47]

Sundays were generally a time for extended families to connect. After the church service they would plan visits in town. While church dinners were being prepared in the basement by the womenfolk, with lots of laughter and gossip ensuing, the men were supposed to be looking after the children playing in the barns. In reality they holed up in the stables, traded stories about their week's work, and shared locations of great hunting and fishing holes.[47]

Box socials were immensely popular to raise small sums of money for one good cause or another. Single women and girls would fill a nicely decorated box with good things to eat, like a piece of mince pie which was much favoured, and place their name inside. At these social events, always held in someone's home, these boxes would be brought in secretly and placed in the pantry. After a period of singing, playing games or dancing had ended, the boxes would be auctioned to the single men and boys. The buyer would find the lady whose name was inside the box and the two of them would find as private a corner as possible and eat supper together. "Sounds interesting, simple, and innocent? Do not think for a moment that conniving and skullduggery did not exist as men and boys tried to learn whose lunch was up for auction. Many a fate was sealed over a box social supper for as the good Lord knew, and it seemed so did the ladies, the way to a man's heart may in fact be through his stomach." *(Ernie McCallum)*

***

It was during this era that the BALC built a new wider wooden bridge in Randville (Randboro) across the South River. From the bridge a road led south to the Township of Clifton and on through Hereford towards Norton Mills in Vermont. It became known as the Parker Hill road, connecting with the Auckland Township line road, running south and then west to the village of Clifton. This bridge eliminated the need for residents of Randboro or Maple Leaf to travel to Sawyerville and up the Clifton Road to get to Clifton. The road also connected with the Auckland Township line road, running east to the Morrison Road, providing another road connection to the Maple Leaf community.

The construction of this bridge connecting to Randboro at the foot of the Parker Hill Road allowed for excellent bobsledding during the winter months. This had been impossible before simply because a sledder would slide right into the river. Now with the bridge in place they were able to slide down the hill, across the bridge and up a small slope right into Randboro, ending at the front doors of the Baptist Church. "The hills that sloped down towards the village from the north and south were filled with children, and even some adults on winter afternoons, after school let out, each with his or her bobsled or a many-passenger double bobsled. High speeds and sometimes risky coasting made the blood run faster." *(Ernie McCallum)*

***

Haskell and Eliza Hurd's home, built in 1875 (Hurd family collection)

In the summer of 1875, Edmund[8] Haskell Hurd and his wife Eliza built a new house. Edmund had fabricated all the doors and windows, inserted the glass, and made the sashes to hold them. During this era, houses were now constructed with rough-cut 2 x 4 or 2 x 6 studding between large 8 x 8 square-sawn spruce timber. The second floor was now positioned to sit on the framework for the first floor as we build them today. Clapboards were now available from Stillman Rand's mill in Randville or Lyon's mill in Island Brook. The clapboards were nailed horizontally much the same as we do today. Free sawdust obtained from the huge piles surrounding the local sawmills was now being used as insulation. Since a vapour barrier was non-existent, the walls were "lathed" then plastered, providing a much warmer house inside that those homesteads built only a decade earlier. Laths were long thin boards cut about 2 inches wide and nailed horizontally across the stud walls approximately 1 to 1½ inches apart. They were produced at the Sawyerville Mill in the sash and door factory, which was a separate part of the mill operation. Lath and plaster construction allowed the plaster to sink into the slots and thereby stick to a wall while the plaster dried. Another final coat of plaster was applied for a perfectly smooth surface. These new-style homes were much safer that the "stick-style" homes that had previously replaced the log homes of earlier settler families. A fire in the lower level could not travel up through the walls as easily as in the previous houses because of the upper floor barrier.

The general frames of barns were still being built with 8 x 8-inch or 10 x 10-inch spruce, however they were now being mill-sawn. These beams were mortised at the connecting points. Each beam and supportive cross beam were hand-drilled with large augers. Spruce pins 2-3 inches in diameter and 10-12 inches long were hand-fashioned with a two-handled spokeshave-style razor. These wooden pegs were shaved generally round, held secure for this process on a specially made bench. The pegs would then be driven into each of the holes, securing the two mortised beams together. Now that the farmers could buy or trade for mill-sawn board lumber, the boards were nailed vertically on the outside walls of these beams similar to the board-and-batten style we are familiar with today.[31]

Haskell Hurd's 1875 diary (courtesy of Mary Hurd Lawson, Haskell's great-granddaughter)

Author's note: We are fortunate to have the one-year diary that Edmund[8] Haskell Hurd wrote in 1875. This diary provides a snapshot of "lives lived" in a section of Newport in the late 1800s. Edmund was always referred to as Haskell, perhaps because there were so many Edmunds in the family, a situation that resulted in confusion for everyone around them. His wife's name, Eliza, also created confusion in that there were also many with that name. Haskell also named his third daughter Eliza.

The following information is excerpted from Haskell's 1875 diary which reflects "a year in the life" of a Newport resident.[41] Haskell appeared to have a hired hand named Leon, who surname remains unknown.

Early in 1875 Haskell had been building his own wagon. He had the steel part of the wheels made by the blacksmith Richard Parker, who lived just down the road towards the Auckland Township border. Haskell even made his own wagon gear, having the steel part made and then fitting the axle in place. *"I bought some used steel from George Hurd, and paid Gardner D. Rand $1.06 for a bar of iron, which I will have Richard Parker fashion into a workable piece of the wagon."* He listed in his diary that the total paid for the steel parts used to build his wagon was $52.33.[41]

He also built his own logging sleds and used them during the winter months for hauling timber for sale to the mills in Randboro or Sawyerville. During this summer of 1875 he was building their new house and traded some of the logs for cut lumber.[41]

Haskell was appointed for several terms as road inspector for the township. He also was engaged in "breaking the roads" in the winter, which at this time was simply driving his team of horses through the drifts to make a hard sled track as a base. If he was not hauling logs, he was splitting wood or in the summer hauling hay, buckwheat, oats, peas and hops. He spoke of "travelling to Randville often, stopping by George Hurd's for a visit or to help him with something." He also mentions that he and Eliza went to Samuel (Hurd's) in Randville often where Sam had a harness shop at the back of his general store. Haskell could pick up what he needed and Eliza could shop in the store for her needs. Austin Rand, who was 23 years old at this time, came to Haskell's shop often and they would make tools together. Newell would even come to mend his sleigh at his shop. This was a time of companionship in Newport and Haskell would always take time to go to "see a sick horse at Newell's or a sick cow at Willy's."[41]

"Preachers Pearson and Gillies appeared to command a fair crowd and were well liked in the community." Haskell canvassed for monies to support the various ministers from Newport and Auckland townships. He also was a supporter of the school, *"canvassing for support for the teachers who were teaching in Island Brook, Maple Leaf, Randville and also Auckland Township."* [41]

"Paid $0.40 for one year of service to Willy [William Planche]." . . . *"Willy paid me $3.25 today on behalf of Mary Ann McCurdy."* Willy Planche ran the Maple Leaf postal service. He was the eldest of the Planche boys and had married Jennette Heard. They lived in Newport when they were first married before moving to the U.S. After their children were grown up they returned in their later years to live in Maple Leaf where Willy died in 1888 at age 74.

"Gussie [Augustus[8] Hurd] sold his oxen for $150 for beef today and Robert Leggett sold his oxen to Gussie for $125, quite a switch. I'm so glad that Eliza [Planche] and Gussie are doing so well."

"Newell Rand had a surprise party [in March of 1875] and so George & Jennie McCurdy stayed with us that night and William Stevenson came with his mother. Lewis [Bowker] and Lucy Minerva, Sam [Hurd] and Persis, George [McCurdy] & Aunt Persis also visited today and we all went to the party."

In his diary, Haskell tells us that *"Spring is the time cows and heifers are calving and the scattering of buckets for the start of sugar season is upon us. Later, Gussie had a sugaring off and all the families were there."* The sugaring-off was followed by one at Newell's' and then at Willy's and finally at his own farm. He noted that after he had gathered the buckets, *"we had made seven hundred lbs. of sugar this year."*

Lucy Chaddock, Lucy Gibson Hurd, Luke[7]s daughter, died in the spring of 1875 and coming back from the funeral, Edmund broke a wagon wheel on his new wagon; *"the roads were so bad. I had to go to Richard [Parker]'s shop to buy two new ones which I paid $5.00 for. Gussie bought a mare from W. Wilford for $141."*

The farmers were busy in the spring, ploughing out the hops and cultivating the fields. They used poorer weather to build or repair their "slash fences," fences built of cedar rails in a zigzag fashion. *"I bought four bushels of grain and four bushels of potatoes from George Hurd. I planted potatoes and finished sowing oats today. Leon is drawing manure for the hops and preparing the garden. I went to Auckland today to raise money for a minister."*

"The spring [of May 1875] was very cold & unpleasant. There was nothing sown as the ground was too wet and it was too cold for the cattle outdoors, grass had hardly commenced to grow." If the weather was bad, people from the surrounding region would visit each other. *"William & Hannah [McCurdy] visited with us many times in May."*

By June, Haskell mentions *"we were planting beans, tying the Hops, and sowing buckwheat. Lewis [Cable] came to shear the sheep."*

"I gave a note to Austin [Rand] for $100 payable in 6 months to help build our new house" . . . [In June 1875] *"I commenced digging the cellar for the new house. I cleared the dirt with the oxen. Worked most of the month digging the cellar. Needed a stone boat to haul the stones away, so went over to get some planks from John [B.[8] Hurd, Willard farm] to build it with. Roland [Larrabee] helped with laying rock for the cellar wall. Hired George [Hurd] paying him fifty dollars for three months to help in the general construction of the house and laying a foundation to include a root shed."* . . . [By July they

were] *"cutting frame timber and hewing with Charlie [Cable]'s new saw. We finished the cellar but it is not yet lined with stone."*

In July, *we were framing the house,"* [and by this time Haskell] *"was hauling timber to the mill and returning with cut boards to keep up. William McCurdy and Haskell's hired hand, Leon were busy laying stone on the inside of the cellar. Austin [Rand] came to start on the house today. Bought barrel of flour $6.00 so Eliza [Haskell's wife] could make some bread this week."*

"Lucy Ann Planche [Lothrop] had come up from Massachusetts to visit her cousin Mary Elizabeth [Planche] Leggett on their farm in Auckland, and as they passed by the Rand farm, they connected with Marshall Rand and William [McCurdy] who wanted to see how the house was coming along. They were disappointed however, because they missed Eliza as she was at a quilting bee making quilts for winter."[41]

In August they were still haying, while Haskell was working on the house. On rainy days he was making window and door mouldings in his shop. It was indeed a busy time, *"working on the house in the morning, haying in the afternoon. Newel, Marshall [Rand], and Charlie [Cable] came to lend a hand with the haying today."* Having finished haying, he was *"now drawing and hauling sand for the stonework."* They were now starting to "put the clapboard siding up." *"I travelled to Sawyerville to get a load of clapboards from the Mill there."* Haskell was using rough-cut 2 x 4 lumber for the walls, and Leon was filling in with sawdust and nailing laths on the inside to hold the plaster, *"the plaster oozing through the slats [laths] on the inside and forming a bond working well."* Austin Rand was nailing the clapboards on the outside. Haskell was hauling the sawdust from Stillman's mill in Randboro – at this point the mills were pleased to get rid of the sawdust.

"A couple of hop buyers came by offering only 15 cents a pound for our hops" and now Haskell had to think about how he was going to start picking and harvesting his hops. Before he could start, *"I went to Lennoxville to buy some hop sacks, paying $4.25 for them. I was hauling oats and peas off the fields today. I needed some money so I sold a heifer to George W. French for $21.00."*

"Finished harvesting just before an early snow in September. Hauling granite stone for the fireplace and chimney... "Willy [Planche] and Leon brought us a load of lime from Lennoxville and Charlie came to work in setting the stone. The roads were terrible and the wagons and horses strained to get through the mud. Austin [Rand] still finishing the inside of the house. Charlie [Chaddock] came from Island Brook today and commenced splitting the granite and placing it in position."

October *"had a rainy start but the stonework got done. Austin was pretty much finishing up the plastering. I bought 736 feet of floorboards from the Mill at twelve dollars per thousand ft. While I was there, I had my buckwheat ground. Lucy [(Hurd) Bowker] and Lewis [Bowker] came to visit us today and to see how the house was progressing."*

In November *"I went to the Maple Leaf Post office to collect $38.65 from Willy. He paid me $38.65 in State's money being the amount owing me by G Abbot.* From those funds, *"I paid Robert [Leggett] $18.18 for the repairs he had done on my barn."* Some of the farmers at this time had small threshing ("thrashing") machines they could move around without much difficulty. *"Newell [Rand] was thrashing peas for me, it was slow going, however it did the job."* He mentions that *"Eliza is sick."*

> *Author's note: Interestingly, in the diary Edmund[8] Haskell Hurd referred to his wife, Eliza, as being sick in November and then confined to bed. This made me wonder the nature of her illness. After checking the dates, I discovered it was clear she was pregnant and due at any time. Edmund and Eliza's third daughter, Sarah Eliza, was born on November 20, 1875, in the old house.*

By this time, Haskell had finished the clapboards and painting the outside of the house, and *"just in time before a big snowstorm today, Nov 11th. Continuing to work on the inside of the house putting in the doors and the sashes which I am making in the shop. Eliza [Planche (Hurd)] paid us a visit to see how Eliza [Haskell's wife] is doing today. She is confined now being so sick and not yet ready to move into the new house. I butchered a hog today, dressing the meat and placing it* *the ice box for winter use." "I paid Newel $30.00 for his work thrashing the oats and peas and to Charlotte Loveland, $4.75 for weaving today."*

Haskell notes that in early December, *"the roads are blocked. I spent a lot of time today with the horses breaking roads."* On off-days he was making window sashes in his shop. *"I bought a box of glass-setting mixing mortar and pointing grout, am painting inside of house, working hard every day to finish."* On December 7 he wrote *"Fredy Rand took sick,"* and on December 17 *"Fredy died today."*

Haskell's last entry for the year was on December 30, 1875: *"Sold two tubs of butter to Harvey and Annabell, sold some flocking to William Sawyer, sold some pork to Richard Dawson for $1.00."* [41]

***

In February 1880 Haskell subscribed to *The Illustrated Household Magazine* for one year and three months for $1.25. The subscription receipt was signed by George Stinson.[31]

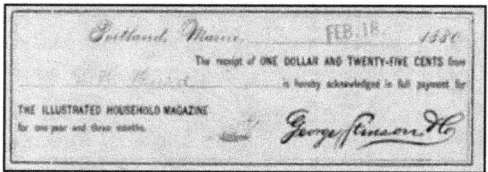

Receipt for Haskell's magazine subscription

At the time of Eliza's death in 1888, their youngest daughter, Jessie, was 10 years old, so now Haskell was raising three daughters, ages 18, 13 and 10, alone on the farm. His eldest daughter, Laura Abigail, 24 at the time, had married Valentine Swail two years earlier. Val and Laura operated a farm in Newport on lots 11 and 12 on the 9th Range.

Edmund[8]Haskell Hurd married his second wife, Adeline Stevenson, in 1892. They had no children and continued to operate the farm on lots 9 and 10 on the 11th Range (one of the original granted lots from his grandfather, Capt. Edmund[6] Heard). By 1899 his second daughter, Mary Maria, had moved to Boston to train as a nurse; she later furthered her studies at the Sloane Maternity Hospital in New York City.[31]

***

In 1884, the first T. Eaton & Co. mail-order catalogue was published and the first agitator washing machines were developed. The catalogues were not delivered to the homes at this time, but rather to the local post office and local stores. While our ancestors in Newport flocked to the stores in Randboro or in Island Brook to get a peek at the Eaton's catalogue, electric washing machines would still be a distant dream for most of the womenfolk in Newport. Battery-operated radios could be ordered from the catalogue and would soon become a must-have in every household. This mail-order business would soon thrive, as women had a chance to order clothes that would be different. Women in the countryside were still wearing home-knit wool stockings and hand-knit woollen petticoats with homespun skirts. These were a necessity for warmth, which outweighed any pride about their bulky appearance. When young folks tried to do with more streamlined attire, their elders would say, "Pride won't keep you warm." Men's clothing included stout homespun wool pants, which they were happy to have; no inclination to change. Wearing these "catalogue dresses" for the women, however, would become a status symbol as there were many who could only dream of wearing those clothes.

The next year, in 1885, the transcontinental railway was completed to the West Coast, carrying with it a burgeoning mail-order business to every rural community from coast to coast.[16, 35]

It was also at this time that Gratia (Hurd) (1829-1874) and Edward Planche (1831-1907), their daughter Ada, born in 1857, and son John Harold, born in 1865, moved from Newport to Cookshire. Ada married Alexander Ross, born in 1850, becoming his second wife. Ada and Alexander became an influential couple in the affairs of Eaton Township and Compton County, as her parents, Gratia and Edward, had distinguished themselves in the politics of Eaton.[4]

Author's note: Responsibility started young for our ancestors during these early days.

Alexander Ross was only 16 years old when he was appointed secretary treasurer of the school commissioners, a position he held until he was 21. He was then elected a member of the board, holding that office for 12 years. For 17 years he was a member of the council of Lingwick, 15 years as mayor. In 1887 he was warden of Compton County.

He was in trade in Gould and Scotstown, first with his father and later with his brother until 1889, when they went out of business.[4]

Alexander held the appointment of mail clerk for five years and accompanied the very first mail car on the new International Railway. In September 1890 he received the appointment of secretary treasurer for Compton County when the family moved to Cookshire. On January 1, 1891, he was appointed collector of customs for the Port of Cookshire when it first opened. He was an officer in the 58th Compton Battalion of Infantry for about 28 years. He was appointed ensign of No. 2 Company when it was organized in 1866 and was later promoted to 1st lieutenant then captain. He received the brevet rank of major in 1884 and was promoted to senior major of the battalion in 1890. He retired in 1894, retaining his rank.[16]

**

Frank Leslie Morrison (1894-1970) and his sister Edith Mary Morrison (1889-1968) were born in Lachute, Que. Their parents were Henry Morrison, born in Lachute, and Margaret Young, born in St. Louis de Gonzague on the south shore of the St. Lawrence River near Valleyfield and Beauharnois. Henry died when Frank was a baby and Edith was just 6 years old. Richard[1] Parker, who owned the farm on Morrison Road and had come from the same area in Argenteuil County as the Morrison family, became their stepfather. He died in 1902. *(Rand family history, Carol Rand)*

Richard[1] Parker was also born near Lachute, in Lakefield, Que. He married his first wife, Sarah Peppin Jones, a daughter of Asher Jones. By way of this marriage, Richard became a part of the Gilbert Jones families of Parker Hill. The Joseph, Allen, James and Bill Parker families all lived on Parker Hill, hence the name of this community of farmers just south of the village of Randboro. Richard was not living on Parker Hill, but further east on what became known as Morrison Road. He married Margaret Young as his second wife. Richard was not only a farmer, but also a blacksmith whose work included metal forming for sleds and general farm equipment repairs around the community.

In a letter to his daughter Mary Hurd on August 9, 1902, Haskell Hurd's diary made mention that *"Richard [Parker] was taken to a hospital in Montreal last Monday and had an operation on Tuesday, the first report was that it was a very critical operation but successful and he was doing well. Yesterday they telegraphed to Margaret to come at once, that he was very bad and so we are all very anxious to hear again what his condition is."* Richard died in 1902 when Edith was about 13 and Frank was 8 years old. Margaret, their mother, was a widow again. She raised her children on the farm on Morrison Road, named after her first husband, Henry. Frank inherited the farm when he was older.

Margaret (Young) Morrison and children Edith and Frank (courtesy of Carol Rand)

Author's note. I will periodically highlight certain facts that may be interesting to the reader who is familiar with the region, or connections that will lead to families identified later in the story. Many "stories" abound within regions and certainly Newport Township was not exempt from these enticing collaborations.

It was normal for teenagers to date in this era, but instead of cars they would hitch up a driving horse and buggy to pick up a young girl and take her to a local church play. The buggies were equipped with bells to alert anyone else on the road, but the driver mostly relied on the horse to navigate the roads without lights. There were two spots for lanterns on either side of the front dash panel; however, they were not there to illuminate the road as much as to provide a light for others on the road to see. Once arriving at the church, these lanterns provided the illumination from the hitching posts to the church doors and were then used indoors as well. The boys had to be careful not to become too detracted with their date for the evening, ensuring the horse reins were securely fastened. Sometimes the horses would become bored waiting, and if the hitch were not secure or became loose, the horse would find itself free and decide to head home. Once out of sight, and with no one yelling "Whoa!" the horse would head home at a full trot. Sometimes other boys might even unhitch a horse as a prank, so he might then offer himself and buggy to accompany the young girl home. This might afford him the opportunity to try to woo her with some engaging and lively conversation on the trip home. This ploy might work, especially if the boyfriend was in anyway shy, which was often the case on first dates. This situation would be very embarrassing for the boyfriend, feeling already at a most distinct disadvantage in his relationship with his girlfriend.

Of course, it was not unusual for horses to know the way home; and once home the horse would stand at the barn door and wait for its owner to unhitch him. Sometimes late at night a young boy's family might see the horse and buggy out by the barn and wonder where he might be or if something had happened to him. To meet your parents while returning along the road with the buggy you had begged to use would not have played out well. Farmers tended to go to bed early and get up at daylight, simply because they were tired after a hard day's work, and with no lights, why stay up? A tired and rather grumpy father disrupted from his sleep, who really did not want to be there, would not be an ideal encounter for a young boy trying to impress.

Author's note: While this was the horse-and-buggy era, life in these farming communities was not that different from when I was growing up in the 1950s, except we were now driving cars.

***

Mary Jane Hamilton grew up in a log cabin located a bit north towards Grove Hill (Randville) on Lot 4 of Range 10. When she married Harold[1] Leggett they stayed on in the cabin, raising their two children, Luvia and Harold.[2] Harold, however, died young so Mary was left to bring up the two children alone for a period of time. Mary Jane then married Joseph[1] Parker (a brother of Richard) and they moved further south, settling on Lot 4 of Range 11. They were the first settlers in this region of Newport that became later known as Parker Hill. *The lot had been first cleared by Mary Jane's uncle, John Hamilton, but never settled on. It was on this homestead that Joe and Mary began to farm, raising their 10 children. Two of those children were twin sisters, Lottie and Lila. Lottie married Charles A. McCallum and Lila married Gardner "Gardie" W. Rand, the youngest son of Newell C. Rand.[47]

*Author's note: *This was the lot that a subsequent neighbour, Gilbert and Hannah Jones's son John would buy years later in 1909, and trade for a house that would belong to her future son-in-law Charlie McCallum in Randboro. And so, the land would come full circle, becoming once again in an associated family.*

***

Demmon Munn, a farmer's son, was born in Hereford in 1835 and had moved to Eaton at 20 years old. In 1862 the family purchased a farm in Newport, about 1½ miles from Sawyerville on lots 1 and 2 of Range 9, with a sizable meadow on which excellent meadow grasses grew. Demmon married Abigail Phelps, a daughter of Paul Phelps who was living in Grove Hill in 1861. Paul Phelps was the son of John Phelps, the first blacksmith in Newport. They had three children: a son and two daughters that both died in their early 20s. Abigail died at 42 years old. Demmon married his second wife, Elizabeth, a daughter of Bill Cairns of Clifton, and they raised two more children: a son, Fred, and a daughter, Mary Ella. Demmon held several public offices both in Newport and Eaton townships.[16]

There was an area in the meadow of Demmon's farm where the South River branch of the Eaton River was fairly shallow. Horses at the time still had difficulty at the best of times pulling any kind of load up the Grove Hill Road, so this tract had been used as a crossing for many years by the settlers in both Maple Leaf and Randboro to get to Sawyerville and north to the northwestern part of Newport.

An old logging road ran on the line between Eaton and Newport townships from the junction of Grove Hill Road and the road (later known as Grapes Road) to the northeastern part of Newport from Sawyerville and the Grove Hill Cemetery, down past the Munn farm, connecting to today's Route 210 at the river. This path was never developed as an official road; however, it may have been used during the winter months as a shorter connection to the northcentral part of Newport before the bridge was built. The outline of this old logging road is still visible today.[31]

It was a great moment for the inhabitants of Randboro and Maple Leaf when the BALC constructed a wooden bridge over the South Branch of the Eaton River circa the mid-1840s. The bridge was located on the south end of Demmon Munn's farm, at the border of Newport and Eaton townships, on the meadow where settlers had been fording the river for some years to get to Sawyerville. The bridge was not covered; many of these early bridges soon needed major repairs because the wood soon began to rot, rendering it unsafe. For this reason, covered bridges later became

Munns Bridge over the South River (Eastern Townships Roots)

the norm. The bridge became known as Munns Bridge, not because he built it, but because it was located on a corner of his farm.[31]

Grove Hill Cemetery is located on the south side of Grove Hill Road, near the intersection of Grove Hill and Flanders roads. It is in Newport Township, on the border of Lot 1 of Range 9 of Newport and Eaton. It was established sometime before Artemas[7] D. Rand and Hannah[2] (Hurd) Rand's deaths. It was not uncommon for people to be buried on their own farm properties in earlier times, as evidenced by the burials of Artemas[6] Dodge and his wife Louisa earlier. In this case the cemetery grew as a community burial ground. Artemas[7] Rand married Hannah[2] Hurd Willard and they took over the farm. This farm would be known in later times as the Smith farm.

Author's note: The original cemetery is located on Lot 2 of Range 9, originally owned by Longley[6] Willard and his wife Hannah[1] (Hurd). When Longley Willard died, he left the farm to his son and two daughters, Mary and Hannah[2] Hurd. Their son William[7] had moved to Marbleton and was raising his family there. One of their sons, Lockhart[8], was to have a son, Clark S.[9] Willard, who married Flora Hurd of Newport, the family coming full circle two generations forward. The Lot 1 beside their farm, and the land adjacent in Eaton Township, was originally owned by William Sawyer, a grandson of Capt. Josiah Sawyer who had acquired all the lots west of Newport, which included his mill site.

Grove Hill Cemetery (photo by Carol Rand)

***

Author's note: A Hurd/Frasier/Fraser connection: Tyler W. Hurd (son of Edmund[6] Heard) married Abigail[2] Sage French (daughter of John[5] S. French) and moved from Newport Township to a farm in Eaton Township. Their only surviving daughter, Sarah Malvina Hurd, married into the Frasier/Fraser family of Cookshire. Many of the Hurd ancestors who were born in Newport, both male and female, moved to other townships as opportunities manifested themselves with improved local roads and businesses.

Tyler and Abigail[2] Hurd's three surviving sons, Wellington[8] F., Theodore Augustus[8] and Frederick Augustine[8], as well as his only surviving daughter, Sarah[8] Malvina (1836-1898), were all born in Cookshire, Eaton Township. The 1861 census listed his family thus: Tyler (55), farmer; wife Abigail (50); daughter Sarah (25); son Wellington (18); son Theodore (11); and son Frederick (4). Sarah married William Donald Frasier/Fraser (1837-1897) and they took over the original (John[4] and Abigail[1] French) farm on a separated parcel of the original homestead lot that had belonged to them on the Bury Road. Sarah's widowed grandmother, Abigail[1] French, continued living with them on the farm. The Eaton Township censuses for both 1881 and 1891 show the widow Abigail Hurd living with her daughter and son-in-law Sarah and William Frasier. These three boys and daughter were direct descendants of Col. Edmund[5] Heard who founded the first settlements in Newport, Lower Canada, in 1793.[4]

Tyler and Abigail Hurd's eldest son, Wellington F. (1843-1870) married Ester M. Cook (1848-1869) in Cookshire. They had a son and daughter who both died in infancy. Ester died while giving birth to her daughter, Amy, who also died a year later in 1870. Wellington also died that same year at age 27. Tyler and Abigail had lost five of their children at young ages and now they lost two grandchildren, a daughter-in-law and another son.

Theodore "Theo" A. Hurd married Ellen Anerbella Alden and farmed on the original Tyler Hurd farm. They had two sons, Montie, who moved to the U.S., and Rufus, who died at age 12. Theo served on the municipal council for Cookshire. When Theo took over the farm Tyler was in the dairy business. Theo and his family expanded and operated a huge Holstein dairy farm. Holstein cattle originated in Holland and were introduced in Canada in 1881. Today they comprise over 85 percent of Canadian dairy cattle. The breed is characterized by its colour (shiny black and white), large size and exceptional milk production. During this era, milking the cows was a huge chore, whether one was in the "milk and cream business" or simply providing for their own consumption. Milking cows by hand may take upwards of an hour, depending on the size of the herd. If they were in the business of selling cream, some of the milk would go through a process of separation to extract the cream. The cow was one of the most prized possessions for the homesteader. In the earliest days of Newport settlement, the settlers would have painstakingly herded one or more cows of various strains north with them when taking their grants of land. Once settled they would expend a great deal of energy to protect them from predators, keep them well fed and expand their herd every year with new calves.

Tyler and Abigail[2] Hurd's third son, Frederick Augustine[8] (1857-1950), was born in Cookshire and married Hattie[1] Eva (Davis), who was born in North Stratford in 1858. They had three children: Harry (born 1880), Kate Marie (born 1883) and Hattie[2] Eva (born 1892). Hattie died young in 1892 in childbirth. This image opposite is the only known photograph of her.[31]

Hattie (Davis) Hurd and daughter Kate Marie (courtesy of Sandra Hurd)

Frederick A. Hurd was leader of the Cookshire Concert Band for many years and a member of it for over 60 years. In 1926 he was presented with a silver cup by the members of the band in recognition of his faithful service.[32]

> *Author's note: Frederick and Hattie[1] Hurd's daughter, Kate Marie, married one of Henry Planche's sons, Lloyd Leslie, of the Newport and Eaton Planche family. Lloyd would have been a great-great-grandson of J. P.[1] Planche who had moved from Leeds, Megantic County, to Eaton Township circa 1860, and so yet another later connection to the original Planche family of Newport.[4]*

Frederick Augustine Hurd married his second wife, Agnes Amanda Baker; they had a daughter, Florence Agnes.

The ladies were skillful, thrifty, and hardworking people who helped their husbands in the fields and in the bush lots. They made clothes for themselves, their husbands and all their family.

As soon as school was out, one of the children's jobs was to weed the garden or dig dandelions greens, pick strawberries, or pick potato bugs off the potato plants. They put the potato bugs into cans filled with kerosene, which was an effective way to kill them.

Frederick Augustine Hurd and Agnes Baker (courtesy of Sandra Hurd)

The women, of course, would always be with the children during these work periods, telling them stories of the past or sharing jokes that were passed along from generation to generation. Children of this era were considered part of the workforce, expected to help in the everyday chores, whether it was doing laundry, preparing food or working in the fields or barns. They would take on whatever chore had been assigned them with an attitude that whatever the chore was, it was an opportunity to learn. As they became older, it was a chance to feel grown up.

Sick or not, idle times were spent whittling maple sap spouts, whistles and many other small items that would help in their daily activities. Children continued from an early age to work diligently alongside parents and others in a closely knit community. The girls made candles and soap, fetched eggs, milked cows, cooked food, washed and ironed clothing. Young boys ploughed the fields, weeded gardens, split firewood, carried water, learned to hunt, and kept an alert eye for livestock predators, all just a part of growing up in rural Newport and Eaton.

***

Author's note: The children of JP Planche, his first wife, Elizabeth, and his second wife, Charlotte (Gooding) Planche from Leeds Township, who had married into the Hurd/Heard families earlier, would find their children and their grandchildren continuing to have family ties in both Newport and Eaton townships.[31]

The Hurd /Planche/Frasier family connection: John William[2] "Willy" George Planche (eldest son of and Elizabeth Planche) married Catherine Jennete "Janet" Heard and they raised seven children in Newport and Eaton. Their son John William[3] took over the post office job from his father after his parents left for Bridgewater, Mass., for several years. They later returned to live at Currier Hill in Eaton Township. A grandchild would later connect with another Frasier in Cookshire.[31]

John William[3] Planche, eldest son of "Willy" and "Janet" (Heard) Planche, married Lenora Williams. One of their daughters, Eva (Planche) married Robert Seale; they continued farming on the Seale homestead in Newport. A son, Frederick Arthur (1871-1939), married Ellen A. ("Nellie") Frasier of Cookshire in 1926. Another daughter, Florence, married Ernie Taylor of Newport.[4]

Willy and Janet Planche's second son, Charles Edward, married Kate Sunbury, sister of Cora (Austin) and daughter of Russell[1] Sunbury of Maple Leaf. Charles and Kate adopted a son, naming him Russell after Cora and Kate's father. Russell[2] was born in Newport and moved with his parents and sister to New York.[4]

Willy and Janet's youngest son, Henry (1853-1929), married first Jennie Grant, then Matilda "Tilly" Smiley of Lennoxville. They operated a small farm first in Maple Leaf then later in Randboro, where they raised their four children: Roy, Leon, Ada, and Fred.[4] Willy and Janet's other children all left the region and settled in other parts of the Eastern Townships.[4]

Planche sawmill on South River in Auckland Township bordering Newport (Eastern Townships Roots)

Sometime after 1860, Willy's father, JP Planche, retired from his teaching post in Leeds, Megantic County. He moved to Cookshire with his second wife, Charlotte, and his son John Paul[2]. Father and son started a sawmill on the Auckland Township side of the South River, just past the covered bridge, on a 200-acre parcel of land JP had purchased earlier from Augustus Hurd. John Paul[2] (1829-1893) married Jane McIntyre; they raised seven children: Henry A., Harriet, James, Charlotte, Evangeline, Bertram A. and Edward J.[4]

John Paul[2] and the Planche families operated the mill for

several years before selling it to Lester Wooten circa 1930. The mill later became known generally in the area as (Lester) Wooten's mill; early in 1931 the mill was up and running again, employing 50-70 men. *(Edith (Morrison) Rand diary)*

The Planche family owned several businesses, amongst them a general store and a flour mill in Cookshire. In later years they sold both. John Paul[2] left other businesses and another store to his son Henry A. (1853-1896). Henry married Harriet Theodotia Taylor and they had five children: Lloyd Leslie, Clifford, Howard, Norman and Evangeline. They established the prosperous firm H. A. Planche & Co., a general store in which he was a senior partner. Through his able management, the business grew from that of a small village store until it deservedly gained the reputation as the largest commercial establishment of its kind in the Eastern Townships.[31]

Sketch of Henry Planche (*Compton County Chronicle*, Dec. 1893)

Henry was elected a councillor for Cookshire in 1892. Unfortunately, he died at age 43, only three years after the image opposite was published in the 1893 Christmas Supplement of the Compton County Chronicle. His brother James and James's wife, Edith Pratt, owned a bakery in Cookshire until 1895, before they moved to East Angus where they formed a partnership with James Wilson and his uncle, Edward J. and Gratia (Hurd) Planche, under the name of Planche, Wilson & Co.[16]

***

Edward Payson Hurd, a son of Samuel[7] A. and Catherine Heard, was born in Newport in 1838 and married Sarah E. P. Campbell of Newburyport, Mass., in 1865. They had five children; three daughters and two sons, but by 1869 had moved to Newburyport. Edward Payson Hurd "was educated in the common schools at Eaton Corner, Canada, and at the Academy, then under W. W. Bishop Niles of Concord. He studied the classics from 1852 to 1855 and then entered St. Francis College, Richmond, and later in 1861, McGill Medical School at Montreal."[4]

In his book *Reminiscences of Student Life and Practice*, local doctor E. D. Worthington writes:

> I think I had the honour of performing the first capital operation made in Canada under the influence of sulphuric ether, and subsequently chloroform. On March 14, 1847, I amputated below the knee, in the case of a man named Stone, at Eaton Corner, in the presence of Dr. Rodgers of Eaton, Dr. Andrews of Cookshire, Rev. Sherrill and Mr. Samuel Hurd, father of Dr. Edmund Payson Hurd, now of Newburyport, Mass. The effects of the anesthetic were the most successful and remarkable character. Stone during the whole time of the operation retained his consciousness, talked rationally. At one time he had a 'presentiment of pain,' for he gave a word to 'pass the bottle' which he cherished as a bosom friend. *(Sherbrooke Daily Record, March 20, 1847)*

Edward Payson Hurd remained at McGill for four years, graduating in 1865. He began practice in Danville, Que., but moved to Newburyport, Mass., in 1870. From 1871 to 1881, Dr. Payson Hurd was one of the city physicians appointed by Mayor Hale and served as city physician until 1885. In 1893, upon the death of Dr. Snow, Medical Examiner for the Third Essex District, Dr. Hurd was appointed to that position for seven years by Governor Russell. The same year he became "pension examining surgeon" for Newburyport and surrounding towns. He wrote many articles for medical journals and translated several texts from French and German. (A list of these texts appears in *Biographical Review: Containing Life Sketches of American Medical Biographies*, published in 1920, on page 396.)[4]

Dr. Payson Hurd died of pneumonia, an illness he developed after being trapped on a train that was stalled near Newburyport during a huge snowstorm that virtually closed down the eastern seaboard in 1899. He was 61 years old. The spring floods from this heavy snow melt affected all the eastern seaboard; Newburyport was no exception. The following spring remained cold, and the summer was cold at the turn of the century in 1900, with much water remaining in the lands.[4] *(Newburyport newspaper, 1899)*

Train buried in snow for several days (wbur.org)

***

Author's note: Following is a segment that played out in the northcentral part of Newport, narrated by the late Ruth (Burns) Morrow of Island Brook, author of the booklet Island Brook: Then and Now.[32]

Mr. and Mrs. Morgan lived in the house just west of John Burns Jr. in Island Brook. They had only one child, a daughter Etta, born in 1867, whom they spoiled so badly that she did not learn how to do any of the basic chores in dealing with the necessities of life. When Etta grew into womanhood, she advertised for a man in the newspaper. A man answered her ad, but he obviously did not enjoy life with Etta, unfortunately committing suicide by hanging himself. Etta advertised again and soon got another response. After a short time, this man simply disappeared and was never heard of again. She advertised a third time and this man, Joe Clark, stayed with her, dying a natural death. There were different opinions as to why Joe stayed, he had been a navigator on a ship, seeing much of the world; saying little about any family except a brother who visited him only once.

When her mother, Mrs. Morgan (Julie), became ill and bedridden, Mr. Morgan was the one who had cared for her. Their neighbours helped as much as they could by washing her hair, changing the bed sheets, and bringing them food occasionally. Mr. Morgan would often come across the field asking for food in the early morning. The neighbours would feed him and send food back to Julie.

After the parents passed on, Joe and Etta were left alone to run the farm. Joe really worked hard to make it work, trying to teach Etta how cook and help out on the farm and he even tried to teach her how to milk the cows, but the milk just would not come out. The young neighbourhood girls, Ruth Burns being one of them, were always welcome in their home. Joe had many interesting stories to tell about his travels. He was a good singer and one of the girl's favourites was "The Cat Came Back." Etta would sometimes sing "Skitter Seeds of Kindness."

Joe, having been a navigator, knew rope tricks, how to tie rope knots and how to splice ropes. In this era, farmers used large hay forks, called "horse forks," to carry sections of the hay load to the hay mow. Large ropes were used for this purpose, sometimes breaking, and needing repair. Joe could splice the rope so well that no one could tell where it had torn apart.

One-time Joe had a toothache, so taking a pair of pliers he went to a neighbour's barn where a young man was working and asked him to pull his tooth. The neighbour said "No, I'm not going to pull your tooth," but Joe insisted and the tooth was pulled. Joe left the barn bleeding but singing a happy tune.

Etta was unique – one of a kind. She was always popping in on her neighbours. She was not harmful; however, she could be a nuisance and so she was seldom a welcome person in any home. Etta often carried a few eggs to the store in her bosom, where Joe would not see them, to exchange for a bite to eat. If some of the local boys thought she had eggs, invariably one of them would try to hug her to break the eggs. "My parents didn't approve of anyone harming Etta and so we were always kind to her."

Their buggy wagon had a convertible top to shade Etta from the sun and weather. When she went to the Fair, or any other outdoor activity, she carried a fancy parasol for shade. She loved to dress up and wear fancy hats and rouge. She made her own rouge using crepe paper.

One of the neighbours was having a church supper, which women often had in their homes in this era to raise money for the Church. Etta always attended such events. On one particularly stormy winter's night, the hostess asked her son to take Etta home. He hitched up his horse to the sleigh and took her home, leading not driving the horse for a distance of about a mile and getting lost in a snowstorm, but the horses seemed to instinctively know the way. Ruth Burns had remembered "a stormy winter's night when her dad thought it was his duty to see that Etta got home safely, and he was nearly hit by the snowplow."

When Joe and Etta became senior citizens, and were not able to care for themselves, Mr. and Mrs. Fred Gagne took over the farm in 1931 and cared for them. Joe predicted he would die, and his death occurred exactly at the time as he had said it would. Joe was 72. The Gagne's took care of Etta as long as was possible until they had her admitted to the Wales Home in Richmond. She fell down the stairs in 1947, dying from the accident. She was 80 years old. *(Ruth (Burns) Morrow; unpublished booklet)*

***

In June 1893, Archdall (Archie) Buttemer and his wife, Florence Richardson, set out for Canada from England. They landed in Quebec City 10 days later then proceeded to Bury where they stayed at Murray's Hotel while making arrangements to purchase a farm, which they did, in Knicky Knocky. Archie was a well-educated man and kept a daily diary. They raised seven children; unfortunately, May, who had been born in England, and her brother Frank both died of scarlet fever only a day apart in the last two days in December 1900. Their surviving children were Beatrice, Bernard, Ethel, Reginald "Reggie" and Ronald, all of whom moved to Eaton Township in 1902.

Author's note: Ethel and Reggie married Ord family siblings: Ethel married Arthur Ord and Reggie married Pansy Ord. Arthur and Pansy's siblings were Mamie (Ord) Matthew of Sawyerville, Lena (Ord) McCarthy of Sawyerville, and Harry Ord of Clifton. [33]

***

Author's note: The Graham/Jones family connection and a Hurd family connection in the southwestern part of Newport. The information provided with input from Rodney Hillman, a descendant of both the Jones and Graham families, and information from the Graham family history, courtesy of Carolyn (Graham) Grapes.

William[1] Graham was born in 1866 in Falstone, Northumberland, England, where he married Hannah Reed. Hannah was born in 1864 in Bradley Farm, Corbridge-On-Tyne, also in Northumberland. William and Hannah immigrated from England, leaving their eldest daughter, Catherine Anne, in England to live with her grandparents. The family purchased a small, subdivided farm from Stillman Rand late in 1890. The farm was situated at the top of Grove Hill Road in Randboro. Here they raised their five daughters – Mary Eleanor (Nellie), Hannah Louise, Elsie Anne, Diana Grace, Ruth Lillian – and a son, Robert Reed.

Author's note: Artemas[6] and Louisa Rand had raised their two boys on this farm, Artemas[7] D. and Marshall S., who was 16 years younger than Artemas. Marshall married Mary Maria Hurd in 1839, a daughter of Edmund[7] and Mary (Willard) Heard, taking over an original Hurd property in Maple Leaf. Note the name change in this generation from Heard to Hurd.

Gilbert Jones married Hannah Cable; they raised three children, twins John Asher and Corilla (born 1888), and Archie (1891-1959) on an original settlers' farm on the south corner of Parker Hill and Statton roads. When Gilbert and Hannah retired, circa 1910, their daughter, Corrilla, moved with them to their home in Randboro. Their farm was later purchased by James Parker and his family.

William and Hannah Graham's second daughter Mary Eleanor "Nellie" Graham was born in 1890 in England and had immigrated with her parents to live in Newport. Nellie met John Jones and his family many times in Randboro when John's family came down from their farm in Parker Hill to get their mail and shop at the Randboro store. Nellie married John Asher Jones in 1910; they lived on his parents' original homestead on their farm until they were able to settle on their new farm. Directly across the road was the original settlers' farm of Joseph and Mary Jane Parker, on the north side corner of Parker Hill and Statton Road. The Joseph Parker farm had been sold to John Jones in 1909, however the old house needed major repairs, so they continued living on his parent's farm on Parker Hill where two of their three children were born: Vera Vivian (Jones) Lowell (born 1910) and Rita Elsie (Jones) Hillman (born 1913). Their only son, Milton Asher, was born several years later in 1925 on a different farm.

***

It was in this era that the BALC, still managing lands to the east in Newport and Ditton, began contracting out the lands for clearing in these regions. These were lands that were generally uninhabited. The company would generate income from the lumber and once cleared, sell the land back to the government for resale. The company hired the local farmers who had good horse teams to augment the lumbering crews in hauling the lumber out to the roadsides or directly to the various mills. William Graham, a skilled horseman with his team of Belgian workhorses, spent many winters hauling out timber for the BALC.

In an effort to not damage the main roads and reduce hauling distances, Joseph Riddell, along with other logging contractors in Newport, were beginning to build logging roads along the backs of many lot lines. This worked well in the winter months. They brought these roads out to or close to the main roads to form shipping junctions. From here they sledded the logs in tandem loads to the nearest railway, where the logs were stockpiled for shipment. This arrangement provided valued additional income for the farmers' lands through which these logging roads passed.

One of these shipping junctions was at the back end of Lot 8 on Range 9 (on a property later purchased by John and Nellie Jones) where a logging mill/plant was built close to today's Route 210 at the halfway point of the lot. This particular mill was created to cut logs into specific lengths, squared on two sides, for use as railway ties. These were referred to as "square logs." Some of these logs were "imperfect" for the railway beds, so were purchased outright by some framers in the area for use to shore up building foundations on their farms.

Typical long-haul tandem sled log train, drawn by double- and triple-horse teams (Newport Homecoming 1801-1996)

This operation employed many men and teams of horses. Farmers such as William Loveland, William Graham, and others in the area hired themselves out to these lumber contractors with several teams of horses as "sledders" just for this purpose. This generated extra income during the winter months. Logs were loaded on the sleds at random by the sledders, wherever they might be located and sledded to a railway site for shipping. Usually a man would be employed to mark and tag the logs before they were moved from the cutting sites so the logs could be identified later. These marks were then recorded, verified, scaled, and classified by the employees of the BALC just before the logs were loaded onto the trains. The lumbermen would be usually paid at the end of a season.

On spur lines, cheaper wood like pine and cedar was used, while hardwoods such as elm were used on curves and switches – these woods all available in abundance throughout Newport Township. A creosote application process was added at this mill; once cured the ties were shipped to Sawyerville for transport on the railways.

This arrangement would carry through the 1920s and 1930s when the BALC traded the cleared lands back to the Crown. The Crown then offered lots out for farming during the Depression years. A settlement that had been cleared was to become known as the Lawrence Colony and would be another new community in Newport.

***

For as long as farmers have been raising livestock, making hay has been one of agriculture's basic chores. Haying was a laborious and exhausting process. John Jones used a horse-drawn sickle mower which helped increase the amount of hay and grain he could now harvest, but he was still pitching hay up onto a wagon as they had done before.

As new mechanized implements came onto the market, farmers in Newport began using machines to harvest grains. Initially the harvester would only cut and leave the grain in swaths but, after 1875, the binder came on the scene, cutting and binding in sheaves. Initially, one of these machines would be purchased by one farmer and then hired out to surrounding farmers to help pay for it. It was not long before most farmers would own one as it greatly improved the efficiencies of production and allowed for harvesting larger fields. These sheaves would be "stooked" in bunches to dry before the next process of shaking the seeds out. The resulting straw would serve as winter bedding for livestock.

The hand-held scythe that our ancestors had used to harvest hay for many centuries was now obsolete, although still used around the buildings. With these new-style mowers and binders, the process of haying and harvesting grains was greatly speeded up, however, much hard work remained. These newer farm implements such as seeders, mowers, tedders, rakes and binders were all self-powered by the movement of the wheels they rode on, as the

Sheaths of grain stacked in stooks to dry (BAnQ)

horses pulled the equipment. Usually one of the wheels was designed with a connecting gear which meshed with the mechanism that operated the mechanics of the unit itself. These steel wheels usually had an added tread welded on, designed to grip with the ground much like a tire tread in today's world. If the machine had acquired too much of a load, then the wheels may simply slide along with nothing working. If this occurred, it was usually in a muddy area where the wheels might lose their grip. With the introduction of these more modern farm implements, fields and crops were expanded, however the workload increased, simply because it increased another job that had not yet become mechanically invented. You've never experienced discomfort and fatigue until you've spent a hot August day pitching hay onto a wagon with a fork, or spent a day pitching hay in the hay-mow of a barn under the heat of a tin roof, covered head to toe in dirt and hay, your nose clogged and your mouth dry as chalk. After several days of this exhausting work, shoulders would ache and hands were blistered from wielding the hay fork.[42]

William and Hannah Graham's fourth daughter, Diana Grace Graham, was born in 1897 married Charles "Charlie" Lafleur in 1916.

Author's note: Charles was born in 1892, the son of Abraham "Abram" and Flora (Cable) Lafleur. Flora (Cable) Lafleur was the daughter of Charlie and Abigail Suzanna (Hurd) Cable. Abigail Suzanna Hurd was the daughter of Edmund[7] Hurd, and hence the tie to the Hurd family of original settlers in Newport. Abigail died in their old homestead in Auckland Township in 1910.[4]

In 1920 William and Hannah Graham's fifth daughter, Ruth "Lillian" Graham, born in 1899, married John "Irvin" Graham, born in 1900. John's parents were Robert John and Jessie (Cable) Graham from a different branch of Grahams and not related. John, who had a good team of horses, followed his father-in-law, William, in augmenting his farm income by hauling logs and when needed to work on various farms during peak times both in winter and summer. He also hired himself and his team out for work with the BALC. New roads were being built across the township, and John was hired for road repair and road building, including the old logging road to Ditton Township. These jobs were beginning to become full-time employment for many in the township who were able to handle good horse teams.

Author's note: Louisa Rand continued living on the Rand farm property, Lot 3 of Range 9, after Artemas[6] died in 1837. Their share of the gristmill and lumber mill operations in Randboro had been passed on to her eldest son, Artemas[7] D. and Hannah[2] Hurd (Willard) before Louisa died. Their son Gardner[8] Stillman bought out the half-share ownership of the mills from Nathanial Beaman Jr. when he retired and continued to operate the mills for many years. Stillman divided the same lot on the east side of Grove Hill into town lots below the ravine in Randboro. The northeastern part of the lot was then divided into two farms: the farm just above Randboro was owned by Ernie and Edna (Bowker) Middlemiss in the early 1920s; the one further north belonged to Edward "Eddie" and Ester (Speck) Tannahill at that time.

Stillman Rand had taken over the mill operation circa 1850-55, and later expanded it to include a sawmill in the early 1860s. After Artemas[7] D. died in 1877 at the age of 83, Stillman subdivided the original family farm – the farm at the top of Grove Hill, where his grandparents Artemas[6] and Louisa had lived all their married life – into lots. A portion of that farm was purchased by George Coates and his family circa 1900.

Irvin and Lillian Graham were living on the 50-acre lot on the south portion of this original lot which crossed the road (today's Route 210), below the ravine to the edge of the South River. This area below the escarpment was the original location of the first gristmill in Newport.

Author's note: Irvin and Lillian Graham's son, Billy and his wife Roberta and their family operated a small campground for many years on the small meadow on the side of the river, providing a fun place for many visitors to the region. (Carolyn (Graham) Grapes family history)

Stillman Dodge and Celestia Annett (Williams) Rand raised six daughters and a son in the town of Randboro that he had founded. Flora Arrabella Rand (1855-1935) married her cousin, Austin S. Rand in 1876. Austin died at age 42, and Flora married Austin's brother Newell C. Rand, after Newell's wife Laura (McCurdy) had died at age 61. (Flora had no children of her own). Corilla Frances (1857-1885) married Archie G. Jones in 1881. Their son, Hollis Gardner Rand, born in 1858, married Florence Helen Milldram in 1887 and they moved to South Braintree, Mass. Alice Adella Rand (1861-1891) married Moses H. Cairns in 1880. Luna Myrtilla Rand (1865-1952) married Benjamin Seale in 1885. Lucia Adelia Rand (1869-1935) married Moses H. Cairns in 1892. Myrtle Maria Rand (1875-1928) married Alfred William Swail in 1896. Surnames generated from the daughter's marriages and their children were Jones, Cairns, Seale and Swail.

Author's note: The Rand daughters married men that had all been born in Newport and their surnames would continue to be well known in the region for many years, their own children becoming a significant part of the families of Newport. You may note that Alice Adelia had died young at 30 years old and Moses Cairns married her younger sister, Lucia, a year later.

Ephriam and Hamilton Cable had purchased a severed 100-acre farm some years later (part of Lot 2 of Range 10) sandwiched between Nathanial Beaman's lots 1 and 3. This lot had been left vacant, deemed as "common" from the original lots granted to Col. Edmund[5] Heard and his Associates in 1799. The lot was adjacent to John "Irvin" and Lillian Graham, the buildings situated below the ridge on the north side of South River, beside today's Route 210.

***

The last half of the 19th century began a major shift in how our ancestors lived their lives in Newport. This was an era of introduction to baking powder and gelatin, cast iron wood-burning cookstoves, hand-cranked washing machines, running water and the medical discovery of bacteria and germs.[35]

Rolling the road in the winter with four teams of horses, as was done in tandem sled log hauling (Eastern Townships Roots)

There were no idle hands during these early years in the communities of Learned Plain, Knicky Knocky, Island Brook, New Mexico, Maple Leaf and Randboro. The large families of young men did not have to go far to find work as several sawmills, clapboard mills, along with the gristmill, each employed 15-20 men. Lumbering operations were expanding in both hardwood and pulpwood, and now the excess and liability of sawdust in massive piles emanating from the mills was itself finding a market – it was being collected and shipped to the train station depots where it was loaded into railcars headed for the urban centres to be used in icebox fridges. The winter roads in Newport were still being kept open by rolling, using the teams of horses provided by different farmers along the way. Lumbering roads were also rolled because it made it easier for horse teams to pull the heavily loaded logging sleds to the various depots and the mills.[31,32,33,43]

***

The cheese factories, one in Island Brook and one in Randboro, employed a few people and the blacksmith shops that were now thriving each employed 2-3 men. Many other related jobs were "farmed out" to service these businesses and more, adding to those jobs in the lumbering, building, and servicing of the road and bridges, harness shops and leather works. Down the road past the fork from Island Brook on the road to Sawyerville, a glove factory was located not far from the corner. Add to this a growing farming industry and the demand for beef, sheep, pigs, fowl and eggs, along with crops such as hops, buckwheat, potatoes, corn, wheat and barley, and collectively it meant that almost everyone in Newport had work.[32]

People in this era were in a sense still pioneers; they were not subjected to the hardships of the first settlers, but were still pioneers in the way they lived in the rural areas. There was no electricity and wood stoves heated the water in pots placed on the top of the stove. They were now using kerosene lanterns in their homes and in the barns. Horses were their mainstay for working the lands and travelling the roads. They were, however, now able to draw upon the experiences and resources of nearby communities that were all now expanding out from the earlier pioneer stage.

Typical wall-mount kerosene lantern; note the protective shield attached to the back (Hurd family collection)

***

Author's note: As with any community there are always characters that appear to live on the edge and provide much gossip and perhaps a certain degree of entertainment that may be enhanced as time moves on. The Fallon family of Maple Leaf would carry on that tradition. My father remembered his neighbours well and often spoke of their shenanigans with great laughter. "Bill and Fred Fallon were the youngest of the family and the most irresponsible characters, who were well known for entertaining and practicing in the use of alcoholic beverages. Their abode lacked any kind of cleanliness or sanitation. The drink finally caught up with them and they were to die in their eighties on the farm." [31] *(quote: E. L. Hurd)*

The older generation of Fallons had come to Newport from Ireland in 1820 and raised a large family. When Edward died he left his sons John, Bill and Fred a well-equipped farm on Lot 8 in the 9th Range. Edward Fallon had earlier sold a parcel of his land (the east half of the south half side of Lot 8) to George Pitcher in 1872. He had also sold the southwest quarter of Lot 10 on the 6th Range; however, 50 acres remained.[31]

Edward had bought 50 acres, a severed portion of the north part of Lot 9 in the 9th Range, from the BALC in 1864 for $150. A letter from the BALC in 1887 called for payment in arrears. Times were tough for the Fallons. By 1870, in order to survive, John Fallon leased the farm to Louis Sevigne for a term of two years, furnishing three cows, a yoke of oxen and a horse in foal. John, generally known in the community to be "tighter than bark to a tree," paid only half the price for the service of a stallion. All animals, including any newborn animals, equipment and materials, were to be left intact on the farm during the two-year lease. After Edward died, John decided to leave. He moved to Alton, N.H., his last will dated there in 1888 in which he appointed George Pitcher to dispose of all his assets.[31]

Dorwin Pennoyer of Colebrook, N.H., assigned Bill Fallon a one-half interest in a new and improved fire and waterproof paint and on January 25, 1870, consummated the deal for the sum of $4,000. The assignment listed the states in which the letters patent would apply for territorial rights.[31]

Author's note: The bill of sale for parts of their land and the patent assignment referred to above are part of the many documents referencing the Fallons in the Ancestral Heard/Hurd Collection. I could find no evidence as to whether Bill Fallon ever actually paid or received any revenue from this endeavor; however, the two brothers remained on a reduced acreage of the old farm for the rest of their lives.

The Fallons' next-door neighbours, in earlier times before they moved to Randboro, were Henry W. and Matilda "Tilly" (Smiley) Planche. Their home was not much better than the Fallons' in cleanliness; however, Tilly – who was considered "not the sharpest tack in the box" – would kindly prepare food for the crews while they worked the two farms. In those days, the grains were threshed from farm to farm by crews comprised of the local neighbours. "When it came time for the crew to work at the Planches or the Fallons, I remember as a boy the crew coming half-starved to my mother's as they could not stomach Tilly's fare."[31] *(quote: E. L. Hurd)*

***

William and Hannah McCurdy sold a portion their 100-acre farm to Haskell Hurd for $125 on December 14, 1883, keeping 25 acres at the northeast side of the original Lot 9 of Range 10. When Haskell Hurd had built his new house across the road earlier, he had planned to build a new barn if he could acquire this lot. Hannah had been ill with TB and was recuperating in Bradford, Penn., at the time of the sale. Her father Marshall S. Rand had acted as her agent for the sale. The document was signed by M. S. Rand and witnessed by Willard S. Rand. Hannah and William rented the severed homestead during the time she was ill in the U.S.[31]

> *Author's note: An example of monetary values in the early 1900s: Haskell Hurd sold seven head of cattle for $195, six two-year-old cattle for $25 each, the old grey mare for $45, and an additional 13 cattle and a young colt "horse" for a grand total of $390.*[4, 41]

Eliza (McCurdy) Hurd died in 1888 of tuberculosis (TB). Her husband, Edmund[8] Haskell Hurd, married Adeline Stevenson three years later in 1892. They were still farming on the original farm where he and Eliza had raised their four daughters. Two of his daughters were married; his second daughter, Mary Maria, was training as a nurse in Boston, and Jessie was teaching in the Maple Leaf schoolhouse up the road and still living on the farm.[4]

Adeline (Stevenson) Hurd, circa 1895 (Hurd family collection)

During this era, TB had taken its toll in Maple Leaf with the deaths of George Hurd's wife Lorinda (Sawyer), Tyler and Abigail Hurd's three children, six of Charles and Lucy (Hurd) Chaddock's children, Willard Rand, and many more in the surrounding communities. In the early days of this sickness, it was referred to as a "lung disease" and the cause of death was labelled "consumption." At the height of the TB epidemic, small cabins began to appear all over the Townships to house the sick away from other members of the family.

Haskell Hurd wrote continuously to his daughter Mary when she was studying in Boston. One letter describes how far-reaching TB was in the region. He wrote to tell her that *"your Aunt Margaret had died and your Aunt Eliza [Planche] had gone to take care of her at the house and was taken sick soon after and also died."* He went on to say that *"Your Aunt Laura [McCurdy] went and took care of Eliza during her sickness, a very singular thing to do, and she died too. All three sisters have died in the same house. Your aunt Hannah [(Rand) McCurdy] has gone to Boston to a sanatorium last Friday as she is not well."* By the tone of his letter, Haskell was very distraught, as one could imagine, as it was happening all over the world.[21]

> *Author's note: Haskell referred to the ladies as "sisters" in his letter when in fact they were part of a group of both men and women "brothers and sisters of a society" who met to enhance their religious beliefs and lend helping hands to people who were sick or in need of food in the various communities. These societies were quite prevalent in this era, usually connected with churches, and in this case the Methodists. The "Educational Society," also orchestrated by the Methodist Church, was comprised of men and its members referred to as "brothers."*

***

By the 1880s, Eastern Township farmers formed the largest occupational group of English speakers in Quebec. At the same time, the Eastern Townships Colonization Society was established to recruit British immigrants. As more and more English-speaking settlers were immigrating directly from the "old country," this was a game-changer in the overall development of an English-speaking group of townships.[16]

The Newport Council in 1895 was formed as follows: A. S. Farnsworth, Mayor; councillors George G. Hurd, William L. French, John Kidd, H. B. Learned, Newell C. Rand, Edward Dawson, and Robert Halliday.[16]

The 1891 Census of Newport Township showed a population of 1,121.[16]

***

The Court Island Brook Independent Order of Foresters ("I.O.F.") was instituted by John W. Stocks in 1890. Meetings were held regularly and with good attendance from the surrounding communities. Many of its members are referenced in this story of lives lived and include: Herman and Charles Stevenson; George W. and Thomas French; William Morrow; Arthur Dawson; Alvin Lebourveau; Henry, William, and John Nourse; Mark Holbrook; Richard and Joseph Seale; Arthur Alden; and Isaac Westgate. These were just some of the officers and members during this era.[16]

Island Brook I.O.F. members (L. S. Channell, *History of Compton County*, 1896)

Chapter 12   Families We Knew (1875–1900)

The settlements in Newport during this era were principally in the mid-west and southwestern parts of the township, with a few families in the north, near the Bury line. In the northeastern quarter there is a section of swampy land, but most of the other parts were suitable for cultivation. Roads had been opened through to Ditton Township on the east and to Auckland on the south. Much of the wild land in the eastern section was still the property of the BALC and continued to be open for settlement. The existing settlements were now becoming well established and the small communities that had been seemingly stretched out and isolated were now coming together as one. With the introduction of automobiles, Newport Township began to connect socially with the other townships that surrounded it.

Laura Abilgail (Hurd) Swail and Valentine Swail

Laura Abigail, the first daughter of Edmund[8] Haskell Hurd, married Valentine Swail of Randboro in 1886. Both were born in Newport. They had three children – two sons and a daughter – and lived on lots 12 and 13 of Range 8. Their first son, Lawrence, became a doctor; he married Mildred McFee and they moved to Edmonton to set up his practice. Laura and Valentine's second son, Emerson Henry, died of pneumonia at age 16. Their daughter, Evelyn, became a schoolteacher in Parker Hill and soon after married Rufus Riddell. Surnames originating from Laura's marriage were Swail and Riddell.[4]

Up to a week before his death, Emerson had been in his usual health and attending school in Sawyerville. On Wednesday he returned from school feeling unwell, an acute form of pneumonia rapidly developed. In spite of all the medical skill and devoted nursing one could have done, he never rallied but passed away early on the morning of March 28, 1914. Despite the weather and nearly impassable roads, the community gathered to grieve in the Methodist Church in Randboro, the service rendered by Rev. G. H. Forde.[31]

Spring in Newport was a time of certain exhilaration as the snow started to melt and rays of sunshine and warmth shone through the forest. This was a time when Valentine and Laura Swail made preparations for the maple sugar season. Trails needed to be broken through the maple bush to begin tapping the trees. The earlier days of lumbering had not affected the maple bush lots, as they were carefully managed and kept intact with great pride on almost every farm. They were considered a necessity for the production of maple syrup, maple butter and sugar. By the late 1800s and early 1900s, harvesting these products provided a welcome income boost for the farmers. Our early ancestors soon began to refine the sugaring process of previous generations. Most households kept a tub or more of soft maple butter and sugar for baking, along with several gallons of maple syrup for the table.

Collecting sap (courtesy of Carol Rand)

Each spring Valentine would hire a couple of young lads to help tap the maples. Each tree had to be drilled by hand and handmade wooden spigots hammered into the holes to collect the precious sap. A specially designed low horse-drawn "sap sled," carrying homemade wooden buckets, would follow. Valentine would drop the buckets at each tree for the boys to hang on these spigots to collect the sap. Later, a large tub would be positioned on the sap sled, filled from the smaller sap buckets collected from each tree, and taken to the sugar shack for boiling down.

Author's note: The photo opposite depicts the sap sled and collecting barrel; however, the sap buckets and carrying pail are of a later era.

Earlier sap buckets were made locally by hand by a cooper, a man who made washtubs and barrels. (The cooper's name was usually stamped on the bottom of the bucket.) Later in time, the sap buckets were made of wooden staves as "stave mills" began to appear in the Townships. The closest stave mill was soon to be established in Sawyerville, where they could produce barrels, wash tubs and buckets, all made by huge stave-making machines.

The men made a shoulder "yoke" which allowed a person to carry two sap buckets at a time from the trees to pour into the barrel on the sap sled. The yoke hung on the shoulders across the back of the neck, continuing out on each side from where a bucket would hang. The men would move around a tree on snowshoes, reach out to a tree bucket, pour the sap into their shoulder buckets, one side then the other, keeping the buckets balanced. This was innovation at its best. It still took time for a person to get the hang of this process, and much sap was lost in the learning. Once the skill was mastered, a person could become very adept at collecting sap.

Most of the time the "crew" had a packed lunch prepared by "Mother," and when the sap began to run "Father" pretty much stayed at the camp to oversee the boiling of the sap.[31]

Everyone worked all day collecting sap and delivering it to the sugar camp, where it was emptied into a large storage container. This storage container was usually located at a higher elevation than the camp, so the sap could be gravity-fed. The sugar camp was usually located near or in the sugar bush. It housed the equipment to boil the sap, along with the firewood needed to keep the fires burning.

To make good syrup a sugar maker had to ensure the fire was burning exactly right to keep a constant boil. Valentine, Laura and the boys usually strived to acquire "slab wood," a residue from the sawing process not unlike the sawdust, which was piled near the mills. Slabs were the sides of the logs left over after the boards were cut. Slab wood, often with the bark still on, generated the hottest fires and was considered the best for this purpose. Every log that was sawn produced four slabs the full length of the log, so slabs were plentiful. There was an area in Eaton Township known as "Slab City" where slabs were piled sky-high. Most of the mills where softwood (spruce) was sawn had piles of these slabs available for burning.

In the peak of the season, Val might stay and boil all night, and supper was brought to him by one of the boys. Laura would not only feed everyone, but she and the boys took care of the barn chores: the cattle, pigs, chickens, and horses still had to be fed, watered, and cleaned for the night. Sometimes Lawrence and Emerson would sit up all night boiling syrup for their father, which they considered a real treat. They sometimes would bring eggs to the camp and boil them in the sap and see how many they could eat. The eggs would absorb the sweet flavour from the sap, enhancing the taste considerably. One might wonder if the boys kept their bedroom window open to vent the air after eating so many eggs.

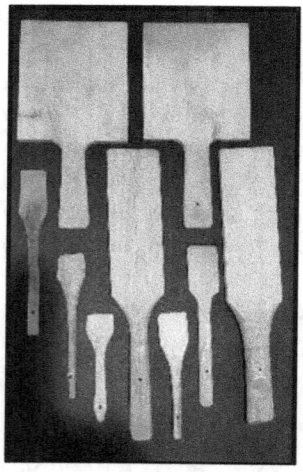

Maple syrup paddles, part of AHH collection (photo by Sandra Hurd)

In mid-April, the sugar season would draw to an end when the weather became too warm, the sap slowed and the rains came. This was the time when the farmers would invite all the neighbours to a "sugaring-off" party. Children would never miss this event as they crowded into the sugar camp looking for the syrup paddles; every sugar camp kept a supply of paddles on hand as part of their supplies. Boiling the syrup to the proper consistency for eating on paddles or on snow was an art. Val used a large dipper to ladle the foaming contents back and forth in the pan to keep the syrup from boiling over, but always at a foaming boil. Once the syrup became of a consistency where it would sit and gel on snow, a large bucket of clean firmly packed snow was brought in, and the syrup was ladled onto the snow in long strips. The sugar syrup would immediately congeal into a taffy-like material for all to enjoy.

Often at these events the farmer would have prepared a table of packed snow to pour the syrup on. Everyone would dive in and roll the toffee-caramel-like syrup with forks and eat it that way. Sometimes one of these forkfuls would be offered to the farm dogs, which they accepted with enthusiasm. Giving a dog a ball of soft maple toffee, however, caused the dogs to run around frantically trying to unstick their teeth with their paws. The children always reacted to this effort with squeals of laughter and delight, as the dogs would run their noses into the snow, trying to get their mouths working again. Once successful they would come back for more.

If the snow was sparse or dirty, folks might use the wooden paddles to dip directly into the boiling syrup instead of using the snow. These paddles were always handmade; everyone in the surrounding community made them and would bring their own paddles. Once the syrup was boiled down into a thicker consistency, they would take a turn dipping their paddle into the syrup. The children would have a smaller spoon-size paddle to scrape the thick syrup off the larger paddles. Children, of course, would get the taffy-like syrup all over their clothes, but everyone would have a great time. When the pan was empty, everyone who still wanted more would scrape the sides of the pan with their paddles until all was gone.[31]

Most of the farmer-producers were very generous, and often had sugaring-off parties at the end of the season. Ruth (Burns) Morrow mentioned: "I remember as a schoolgirl when the teachers and schoolchildren would be invited to one of these parties. We loved the treat and the half-day school holiday. There would be ham and sour pickles with the noonday meal and we would go to another camp in the afternoon to another party."[31]

With their appetites for sweetness sated, the boys (always the boys) would seek further entertainment: rubbing their fingers on the soot-ridden pan bottom then trying to blacken the girls' faces with it. This was the climax of the sugaring-off party. And then there was "wiccopee" for those who knew of its medicinal properties, i.e., that of being a laxative. This knowledge had been handed down from the First Nations to our earliest ancestors. The older boys seemed to have retained this knowledge and would strip the bark off a branch and quietly swish it into the pan. The greedy ones, again mostly the boys, would eat their fill, and would soon be looking for a private place in the bush to contend with diarrhea from the wiccopee.[43]

This was also the time to clean the equipment and wash the buckets. Everyone who attended the sugaring-off party would pitch in to help. The buckets were washed on site and carefully stored in the camp, ready for the next year's run. The syrup toffee was delicious, and it was a great chance for everyone, young and old alike, to get together and celebrate the end of a great season.

Sometimes these celebrations instigated a party which might take place in the barn over the stables. The haymows were mostly empty at this time in the spring; the barn floor that separated them was swept clean of chaff and the floor was perfect for a big barn dance and potluck supper. Out would come the fiddles, mouth organs, guitars and banjos, with drums made of various tin buckets. Dancing would start with both the young and older folks participating, and many times the children fell asleep in the hay while the party continued. "Pure living, good earthy clean fun, fresh, rosy cheeks left everyone tired but happy to be alive."[32] *(quote: Ruth (Morrow) Burns)*

The first maple sap evaporator was patented in 1858. Since that time there have been many tweaks and improvements to the syrup-making process, but it remains largely unchanged. Maple syrup quickly became another profitable industry for the farmers. It is one of only a few agricultural products in the northeast part of North America that is not a European colonial import, therefore emblematic of Canada.

Later in this era, with these new evaporators, maple sugar-making became a business with significant revenue for farmers in Newport. In earlier years, when sugar sold for about three cents a pound, most of the sap was boiled down into sugar. Perhaps a few gallons of maple syrup or maple butter would be saved, mostly for home use. Because it was inexpensive, there was little demand for it. Sugaring-off parties were an enjoyable social event, but white sugar was becoming more readily available in stores, so maple syrup started to become more of a novelty. This started a slow increase in demand for the product in urban centres that increased rapidly as shipments by rail made maple syrup more readily available to a much wider market, especially in the cities. Over time syrup-making became a significant money-making proposition and syrup was viewed now as more of a luxury product than it had been in the past. This precipitated the demise of sugaring-off parties as social events, as producers no longer felt inclined to invite the general public to take their fill free of charge.

Author's note: Sugar camp visits later became a tourist attraction where farmers were able to charge admission to individuals or groups for social events and to sell their products directly. For those familiar with the syrup industry, the various hardwood rock maple species each produces their own specific flavour, not unlike grapes, wines, and vineyards. The maple tree varieties and the soil variations create different tastes that can vary from neighbour to neighbour.

***

By 1900, the population in Canada was 60 percent rural, comprised mainly of woodworkers, loggers, carpenters, blacksmiths and farmers. This generation of our ancestors lived a hard but simple life, while a new wave of immigration from the British Commonwealth began. These new settlers were an order-loving and efficient class of people who were mostly people of religious principals and good morals. They worked hard and overcame many obstacles while raising large families, becoming prosperous in their new homeland in Newport Township. As these new settlers immigrated, they bought their property through associates and commissioners of the BALC. The original 200-acre lots were now being subdivided into 100-acre lots selling for $500 and 50-acre parcels for $250.[32]

This era was also the age of factories, with thousands of people working nine-hour shifts. There was no such thing as a weekend; people worked non-stop, seven days a week, and shift work was becoming common in urban communities. Newport Township was not immune; many of our ancestors moved out of the rural communities to urban areas to find work during this era. Electricity was a key factor in the growth of factories. Known as the "Gilded Age of Opportunity," it was a period of hope when younger people began moving to where the work was with expansion going on in almost every industry – railways, lumber and steel industries, to name but a few.

Immigrants were seeking jobs in the metal trades and in the ever-expanding shops of the Grand Trunk Railway and other companies such as the Angus Shops of the CPR, Canadian Steel Foundries and Canadian Vickers Shipyards. The demand was high for boilermakers, machinists and blacksmiths. Some companies began bringing most of their staff over from Britain. It was also a fractious time if workers could not feed their families; a sense of desperation separating poverty and wealth in the more urban areas, creating stark new divides between the "haves" and the "have-nots."

This was also a time when the number of people who depended on a paycheck exploded, working 12-hour days, six days a week in these smaller businesses, including stores. Unfortunately, tuberculosis (TB) was still raging throughout the countryside, causing much loss of life and creating anxiety when anyone new arrived in a community. Just the fear of the unknown caused people to be acutely aware of any worsening sickness related to their lungs.

Charles Albert, the second son of Art Farnsworth, contracted typhoid fever soon after starting his fourth-year science studies at McGill University in the fall of 1909. A vaccine for typhoid had been developed in 1909 but may not have been readily available. After recuperating, he went to work in the office of Dominion Bridge Co. in Lachine, Que., intending to resume his studies in September 1910. He was, however, stricken with pleurisy and pneumonia due to a weakened immune system resulting from TB, and passed away after only six days, his life cut short by this disease.[31]

***

Having moved from relative civilization in the New England states, education continued to be a high priority, important not only for the male lineage but also for the females. Throughout the earliest years and despite the minimalist existence in these new settlements, the emphasis on education did not wane. If the training they sought was not readily available locally, folks would not hesitate to look south to New England and be away for periods of time to further their education.

The Maple Leaf schoolhouse had served the community from the early 1800s. Part of it was the first cabin built by Colonel Edmund[5] Heard on Pleasant Hill, where he had lived while he explored the Township of Newport lands. It started out as a simple log cabin, which in 1805 was moved from Lot 6 to Lot 8 and placed adjacent to Maple Leaf Cemetery. A new larger log building was erected in 1807-08, and the smaller cabin then served as the entry foyer to this new school. By 1810-11, community meetings were being held in the schoolhouse. Several schoolteachers taught in the school from this period on through several eras, including Augustus[8] and Eliza Hurd's daughter Edith, who had graduated on May 2, 1876, as an elementary school teacher at 19 years of age. Edith received her diploma from the Board of Examiners of St. Francis, signed by N. R. Doar, President, and S. A. Hurd, Secretary.

Sometime in 1870, the Maple Leaf schoolhouse that had been located adjacent to Maple Leaf Cemetery on the original William[5] Heard property was moved. The Maple Leaf community was ever-expanding, and the school needed to be as centralized as possible to accommodate this shifting and increasing population. The larger school allowed for a continuation of its uses as both school and meeting house. The building was now approximately 24 feet by 34 feet, with a front-door entry room. There were hooks for the children to hang their coats on, a shelf over the hooks for lunch pails, and a place for boots.

The circa 1901 photograph opposite shows people that both the author and some readers would remember from Newport in the early 1950s.[16, 31, 41]

Author's note: The Charest children are related to the former premier of Quebec, the Hon. Jean Charest.

Thirty teams of oxen were required to relocate the schoolhouse to the corner of today's Route 210 and the road to North River on Lot 11 of Range 10. The building was expanded again; the original log construction was replaced with a post-and-beam construction using rough-sawn 2 x 4 lumber, complete with clapboards and real glass windows. The lumber was milled at Stillman's mill in Randville; the clapboards were from Lyon's mill in Island Brook.[31, 40]

Maple Leaf schoolhouse, circa 1901 (Hurd family collection)

L-R, back row: Marshall Newell Rand, Rufus Riddell (both on Shetland ponies they used to get to school), Raymond Wood, Mildred Loveland, Jessie Hurd (teacher), William Howard McCurdy, Sarah Hurd, Hannah Elvira (Rand) McCurdy

Middle row: Marie Charest, Clara Charest, Evelyn Boisvert, Gertrude Riddell, Louise King, Annie King, Edith Morrison, Rosalie Boisvert, Arthur Loveland

Front row: Louis Boisvert, Frank Morrison, Charlie Loveland, Roy Loveland

> *Author's note: A church is barely visible in the background of the photo above. From letters written as late as 1875, the people in Maple Leaf were still using the schoolhouse for church services, which would suggest that the church beside the school was built sometime after 1875. The church was first built as a Free Will Baptist Church, but due to lack of support, the diocese became weakened, circa 1890-92, and the congregation changed to regular Baptist. When a Baptist Church was built in Randboro in 1866, some of the congregation in Maple Leaf changed entirely to Methodist. After that, in 1883, the Anglican Church was erected in Randboro and many of the residents of Maple Leaf were attending that church, so congregations were spread out rather thinly. Eventually the Baptist Church in Randboro changed to Methodist, and then later to United.*

The desks were long, narrow tables with benches for seats. The benches had been constructed from hand-hewn pine or spruce planks, and could be as wide as 24 inches simply due the enormity of the virgin timber in the earlier days when our ancestors first settled in Newport. They made the planks for the tables, benches and flooring by first starting a split on the round top surface of the log along its entire length. They then carefully used wooden wedges along the split, adding a wedge on each of the ends. Once the split started, they pounded down on the wedges along the top and added more wedges on the ends, producing a perfectly thin 2- to 3-inch plank the full length of the log. When the schoolhouse was moved, the section of original floor was still distinguishable from the sawn lumber floor used in the expansion. It was not uncommon in this era to see a single-board door on these older buildings, measuring 32-34 inches wide. The crosspieces on the door kept the door from warping over time and still included the hinges which had been made of wood knurls. This is where many of the older folks of this era had gone to school as well as the three generations before them. These ancestors' genes are part of our DNA today.[24]

Charlie and Charlotte Loveland's children all attended the little schoolhouse in Maple Leaf, just down the road from their farm. Four of them are pictured in the photo on the previous page; the other children are their schoolmates and friends in the community who also attended this school. Many of their own children attended the school up to the early 1930s. Jessie Hurd, daughter of Haskell Hurd, was their schoolteacher during this particular time frame; her tenure continued until she was married in 1902.[31]

***

This was an era that was a game changer in the way people lived their lives. Railways progressed and allowed product to be sold in ever-expanding markets. Lumber was necessary and in heavy demand during this era, and farmers' children could now move anywhere. Innovation abounded, and those who had been raised on the farmlands knew how to work and were creative, simply because they always had to make do with what they had. They knew how to create tools and fix equipment and were very innovative in creating simple ways to do things. In 1904, tea bags were invented. The first canned pork and beans, peanut butter in jars, and Canada Dry Ginger Ale were available and on sale in stores everywhere. In 1905, the first gasoline tractor was introduced, and the electric toaster was invented in Canada. In 1907, the first Hoover vacuum cleaner was introduced, and cars were becoming more common. Men in the factories, many of them farm boys, were making these products. Farmhands were in demand as never before.[35]

People were on the move to find better jobs and better living conditions. Transportation by train allowed for easier movement between the cities and rural areas and offered an expanding market for goods in every direction. Men from the farmlands had always worked on trust and honour with their neighbours, but the ability to handle money was becoming a new challenge simply because they were not used to it. Many new families that found themselves in Newport and surrounding townships worked at the mills or were building new roads, bridges and railways. With these changes came new opportunities, for example in cheese-making, as farms were expanded and production increased to meet the growing demands of rapidly expanding urban markets.

New equipment was becoming available for farmers. The knotter was invented around 1866, which allowed hay to be bound automatically, but it was not until around 1900 when Cyrus McCormick incorporated the system on his binder machine that the novel idea took off. From that point on, hay binders began to find their way into Newport. At first the bales of hay were simply dropped into the fields to be loaded by hand onto a wagon. Then a conveyor attached to the unit allowed the hay bales to ride up and drop off directly onto the wagon. A man would then lift them up and pack them as far as they could reach. A similar conveyor at the barn would transport the bales up to the haymow where a person would distribute them into breathable piles.

About this same time, a new system of cutting and binding oats and barley had entered the market, allowing farmers to hook their horses up to a machine that would harvest these crops automatically, tying the grain stalks into small sheaves. Farm hands would then "stook" several sheaves into a group to dry. Both men and women were now able to follow alongside a wagon, pick up several stooks at a time with a three-pronged fork, and toss them onto a wagon. The sheaves of grain would be arranged on the wagons with sheaf tops placed towards the centre of the wagon. Once the wagon was unloaded, the "chaff" was swept off the wagon before the next load. The chaff, a combination of grain and straw bits, was collected to be ground up as cattle feed. The sheaves were taken to the barn to be threshed, usually on "threshing day," a day set aside when the thresher crew was assembled to do the final harvesting process of separating the grains from the straw. The grain shaken out by the thresher was bagged in burlap bags to be sold or emptied into a storage unit, usually a cedar-lined room free of mice and rats, to "winter" as seed for the coming year.

***

Meanwhile, Mary Maria Hurd, the second daughter of Haskell and Eliza Hurd, had graduated from the Massachusetts General Hospital Training School for Nurses in Boston in 1901 and had received further training at the Sloane Maternity Hospital in New York City. Her father, Edmund[8] Haskell Hurd, wrote to her faithfully every few weeks all through her studies, after she married, and until his death in 1923. After Haskell died, his daughters, Laura Abigail (Hurd) Swail, Sarah Eliza (Hurd) Hurd and Jessie Minerva (Hurd) Riddell all continued to write letters to Mary.[21]

Mary Maria Hurd, circa 1901 (Hurd family collection)

Author's note: This letter exchange provides a snapshot into the lives of these family members and the lives of others who lived in Newport over a period of many decades, much of which frames the content of this part of the book. These letters reflect "lives lived" – during the early 1900s from Haskell's letters, then the 1920s, '30s, and into the war years of the early '40s from Mary's sisters' letters. It is through these letters, much like a diary, that mention the names of Newport neighbours and community events, that give a reader a significant glimpse into their lives and how those lives were changing.

This was also an era where many could travel by train and see places the previous generation could only dream about. In a letter to his daughter Mary in 1905, Haskell Hurd mentions *"there was an excursion to Ottawa on the 20th, and so, Newell and Marshie Rand, Charlie Cable, George Hurd and myself, took the train and took it all in, getting back on Friday. The tickets for the round trip, was only $3.40 from Cookshire. We had a very nice time."* [21]

With the railways came prosperity. However, as time progressed, pricing for goods became highly competitive. The railway consortiums extracted higher profits for goods moved, squeezing the factories, mills and warehouses, who in turn squeezed the sources and producers. The rapid expansion during this time was mainly due to the extensive railway network being developed; however, this rapid development ultimately negatively impacted the next generation. Competitive market forces would be keen, as produce was bought and sold in an ever-expanding market.[16]

***

Grove Hill School was originally built on land that had been set aside as "common" as per the land grants issued circa 1801, (Lot 1 of Range 8) on the crossroad that ran from Grove Hill Road to Flanders Road. Today one might recognize the intersection of Grapes and Boutin roads as the general region in which the school was located. In the photograph, note that the road – even at that time – was still rough and narrow with some gravel surface.[31]

***

Southwestern Newport:

Mail was now being carried by railway to and from the larger

Grove Hill School, circa 1900. Standing, L-R: Ethel Harvey, Alma Boyd, Frances Harvey (teacher), Annie Buck, Leo Desrocher. Sitting, L-R: Edmund[9] Bowker, Russell Planche, Donald French, Mary Waldron, Grace Buck.[40]

urban centres and boroughs that had railway stations. The mail was then picked up from these train stations and delivered to the smaller communities. John William Planche, a son of Catherine Jennete "Janet" (Hurd) Planche, was postmaster in Maple Leaf and was also a Newport councillor, a position he held for several years. The postmaster's position was recognized as a prestigious public role; the postmaster was considered "well-informed," likely because they always had the opportunity to read the newspaper first. John's marriage to Leonora Williams produced three children, one son and two daughters, their marriages originating the surnames Seale and Taylor.[16]

In the foreground of the photograph on the following page is the very latest gas pump of this era, in front of the Randboro store. A vigorous back and forth motion on the lever at the side pumped the gas up to fill a calibrated glass cylinder (the glass protected by a wire mesh). The operator would fill to what the customer indicated: "I'll only need a gallon today, Sam." The gas would then be drained into the vehicle's gas tank by gravity. The charge would be kept on the store's books until the crops were sold or the milk products delivered and paid for.[31]

The Methodist (United) Church is visible in the background on the left. Samuel[8] Heard and his wife Persis were devout Methodists. Persis's brother and his wife, Hiram and Ella Williams, both ardent Baptists, had immigrated from England and were living with Samuel and Persis to help run the store during their later years. Hiram and Ella later purchased a farm up the road on today's Route 210 just left after "Williams Hill." The Williams family would have attended the Baptist Church in Maple Leaf, which was still operating at this time.

Car-truck at gas pump at Randboro store, circa 1918 (Eastern Townships Roots)

Author's note: Williams Hill was the first location of Col. Edmund[5] Heard's cabin where he and Captain Josiah[4] Sawyer had cleared the first 10 acres in that first summer of 1793. They referred to the hill as Pleasant Hill at the time. My father, Lionel, had always known this hill as Williams Hill, whereas when I was growing up, I knew it as Laroche's Hill, simply because Claude Laroche and his wife Marion and their children Verlie, Lynford and Judy lived at the top of the hill. Clearly, the resident's name had a major influence on identifying specific locations.

The photograph of the gas pump above also demonstrates the beginning of transporting milk from the farms to the cheese factories or creameries. Note the load of milk cans in the back of the car behind the driver, the car being used as a truck.

It was around this time that Charles A. "Charlie" and Gertrude "Gerty" (Hatcher) Montgomery sold their farm on Parker Hill, bought the Randboro store from Samuel and Persis Heard, and settled in town. They had been living on Charlie's parents' farm, on the west side of Parker Hill Road at the junction of Statton Road. They operated the small store and become huge supporters of Newport and Randboro for the next 35 years. Charlie and Gerty built a hall across the street that became well known as "Montgomery Hall," providing a general community meeting place as well a venue for parties, weddings, and dances.[31]

By 1910-15, rural mail service was shifting from the many small regional post offices to home delivery. Contracts to deliver the mail were coveted by local farmers, who applied for and qualified for the job to bring in extra income for the family. The applicants had to be acquainted with the territory and the residents on the various routes and have an attentive memory. These mailmen never failed to have a collection of local stories to tell, and they became the most interesting person to visit with. A good mailman always took the time to enjoy a chat along his route, and so usually there was one member of the family waiting at the laneway to receive the mail, but more importantly an opportunity to hear the news or stories of the day.[43]

Author's note: A series of articles written by the late Nellie Parsons (Mrs. George Parsons) that were published over many years by the Sherbrooke Record *was compiled in the booklet* Treasuries of Historical Articles *by her daughter Nina (Parsons) Rowell. One of these stories, recounted below, gives readers a glimpse of how "lives lived" were unique during this era.*

And so, "the story is told" that "a certain mailman's horse was so accustomed to stopping for these visits that if the horse saw someone working nearby, it would just stop and start grazing on the grass on the roadside, giving the driver a chance to visit. This particular driver over time was getting on in age and his memory was failing. On one occasion, he stopped at a box, removed his mittens, and took out the outgoing mail. He checked the postage and placed it in the receptacle he carried, put his mittens in the box and drove on. He had not gone far when he began searching for his mittens; finally realizing what had happened, returned to the box, retrieved his mittens, and deposited the mail instead. This incident did not escape the eyes of the lady he had been talking to and much to her amusement she waited for him to return with her mail."[43]

***

Augustus[9] "Gussie" Frederick Hurd (lineage: Augustus[8], John B.[7], Edmund[6]) married his second cousin, Sarah "Sadie" Eliza (Hurd), the third daughter of Edmund[8] Haskell Hurd, (lineage: Edmund[7], Edmund[6]) in 1892. Gussie was the youngest of six children and son of Augustus and Eliza (Planche). His eldest brother, John B.[9], had married Emma Austin; they were farming next door, so there were several Hurd families farming in the Maple Leaf community.

Both Augustus and Eliza were born in Newport, less than a mile apart. They had three children: Edmund[10] Lionel, Frederick[10] Karl and Arthur Haskell[10], all born on the original John Bennett[7] Hurd farm in Newport, lots 9 and 10 of Range 10. Augustus (everyone knew him as "Gussie") served on the school board and was warden of St. Matthew's Church in Randboro.

Sadie and Gussie Hurd, 1892 (Hurd family collection)

Author's note: Gussie's parents, Augustus[8] and Eliza (Planche), had purchased considerable acreage throughout Newport, in addition to properties in Auckland and Ditton townships and a home in Cookshire, Eaton Township. After retiring from their farm in Maple Leaf, they lived in their home in Cookshire. Eliza died in 1893 and Augustus died in 1905. Among the many family artifacts and heirlooms left to Gussie and Sarah were the First Records of Newport (1800), the Samuel A. Heard Manuscripts, as well as all documents dated from 1792, including his own working years. These included his own and other family letters dating up to his death in 1905. The original gun and sword that Col. Edmund[5] Heard had brought with him in 1793 were also included and are all in the current possession of the Hurd family.[31]

Interestingly, Augustus[8] Hurd left a revolver, a five-shot 0.32 rimfire; the engraved barrel reads "Remington & Sons 1873." I do not know why he owned this pistol. Perhaps it was because Augustus[8] was perceived as very wealthy. He was engaged in road building, lumbering, farming and indirectly in politics, so perhaps he needed to ensure his own protection, or perhaps he acquired it simply because he could afford it. Ammunition for this gun has not been manufactured since 1920. (Courtesy of Malcolm Haskell Hurd)

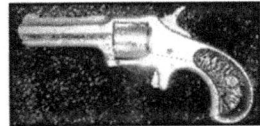
Augustus's revolver

Sarah "Sadie" had a gramophone, a "Marconi Victor" she placed in her sewing room so she could do her work listening to her opera and piano records, perhaps the only type of music recorded at that time. Sarah also had a spinning wheel which she used to spin wool for many hours until she had enough to create something. She would then take the wool up the road to Cora Austin's to be woven on her loom.

Newport residents could now buy sugar and flour in cotton bags, as it had been available for years in the New England Colonies. Women saved these bags like their ancestors did; washing then bleaching them to make into pillowcase or teacloths, trimmed with colourful embroidery and crocheted or tatted edges. In the evenings they would sit on the old rocker chair using these new kerosene lamps for light, crocheting doilies, centrepieces, edgings, and tablecloths, using fine crochet cotton that could be store bought.

When Sadie and Gussie were first married, the chore of clothes washing was still done on a scrub board, but now Sadie could wring out the laundry by passing the clothes through a "wringer" attached to the washing tub. The ironing was done with a flatiron, heated on the wood stove. There would be two or three flatirons sitting on the stovetop, ready to be used at any time. As there were no thermostats then, the fire in the wood stove had to be regulated just right for the oven to bake. Water was heated and kept on the stovetop in an oblong copper pot for use as required, i.e., for washing dishes or clothes. The hot water had to be ladled into pails which were then poured into the wash buckets – just another chore women needed to prepare before any clothing was placed into the wash. A fresh supply of water had to be "pailed" back into the copper pot to make sure there would be plenty of hot water for dishwashing later in the day. Perhaps a bath might be necessary before retiring for the night, so this copper tub pretty much stayed on the stovetop, almost as a permanent fixture.

With three boys in the family, Sadie did not have much help around the house, unless she asked for it – and you can be assured she did. The boys were expected to do their part, and Sadie provided them with a long list of chores to be completed before and after school each day. Spring housecleaning was a busy time, as everything had to be cleaned thoroughly, including the straw and feather ticks in the bedrooms, which were emptied and refilled with fresh clean straw. Her son, Fred, was good at bringing clean straw from the barn, delighted with a first sleep on freshly cleaned goose down-packed pillows and a soft mattress of new straw. Lionel, the eldest son, had to clean up the woodshed and get rid of the wood chips that had collected during the winter and mow the lawn in the summer.

Author's note: Despite all the work there was always time for frequent visits with neighbours, or to help each other in times of need. In this circa 1895 photograph, William McCurdy, who was dating Jessie Hurd, is sitting in the buggy, and Augustus "Gussie" and Sarah "Sadie" Hurd are sitting on the chairs. They are in front of the original home of Gussie's father and mother, Augustus[8] and Eliza (Planche), at the original location of the log home built by his grandparents John B.[7] and Polly (Sawyer), circa 1820.[31]

William McCurdy and Jessie Hurd visiting Gussie and Sadie Hurd (Hurd family collection)

The haying process began in spring with seeding the hay fields. In early Newport, this was done by hand, but as horse-drawn seeders found their way into the community this process was speeded up. As it was in earlier times, the equipment would usually have been purchased by one farmer in the community and then hired out to the neighbours. After ploughing in the fall, the farmers would harrow the field in the spring; a first crop such as red clover would be seeded, harvested usually in two cuttings in the summer and stored as sileage. The following year the field would generally be harrowed only and reseeded with "timothy," which when fully grown would be called "hay." Once seeded with timothy, the field would produce for several years before the process would be repeated. Usually by mid-July the hay was ready for harvesting. After the mower cut it, horse-drawn rakes gathered the hay into "windrows" where the moving air could dry it. Our earlier settlers used forks to pile up the hay into haystacks or "crofts," sometimes as high as 30 feet, beside the barns. The hay on top would shed rain and snow and protect the hay in the middle from rot, yielding dry, light green hay.

Life on the farm was not easy for Gussie and Sadie, due to its location three miles from Randboro and six miles from Sawyerville. If you did not have something you needed to finish a job, you either had to make it or wait until you could get to town. There would be no electricity for many years, and the nearest telephone was a half-mile away, at the Rand farm. The telephone was a party line, so you may have to "wait your turn," which was mighty aggravating if you were in a hurry to contact someone for something you needed. Even if you got a line, you were often faced with static and buzzing, so it was hard to hear or be heard at the other end.

Gussie owned a pung sleigh which was part of standard equipment on the farm and as essential as was the buckboard wagon. It was similar to the buckboard with a front seat which could hold three people and storage space in the back. It was built up on high runners lined with steel rather than low like a usual sleigh to avoid plowing in heavy snow. It was lightweight and a horse could move quickly while pulling it. Horses loved to get out of the barns, especially in winter, perhaps having stood idle for several days. So, getting out even in the coldest days and being allowed to run with a sleigh was a treat for them; horses being really no different than dogs in this regard. On a crisp winter's evening, it was not uncommon to hear the jingle of sleigh bells throughout the countryside as families would be out visiting neighbours or bundling up in buffalo robes just to go for a ride. The horses were equipped with these sleigh bells, (usually a cluster of four to six brass bells), which was essential to alert others on the road, particularly on a cloudy evening. Bells were deemed mandatory by law. Horses always knew where they were; however, a horse was not particular about where they might take a sleigh if they met up with another horse on the road, so a driver needed to be aware of other horses on the road. Not unlike today's world, there was always somebody who thought perhaps the sleigh ahead of them was "slower than molasses going uphill" and would be wanting to pass; the sleigh bells "humming" behind them would let a driver know to pull over.[31]

Augustus and Eliza Hurd visiting neighbours on a Sunday afternoon on a Pung sleigh (Hurd family collection)

From time-to-time Gussie and Sarah and the boys would travel to Randboro to the general store to pick up staples, the mail, the newspaper and other general necessities; it was an exciting time for the boys to get out and meet other people and peer at all the goodies that abounded in the store. The roads were still poor, and especially so during spring melt, so sometimes travel was slow and tedious but, regardless of the road conditions, they would always make it to the Anglican Church in Randboro on Sundays.

Occasionally Gussie would have to go to Sawyerville to get materials, and so "the story is told": Apparently Gussie kept a sort of diary. Sarah found it one day and was surprised to read that on one of his trips to town he had noted that he had stopped at the hotel in Sawyerville and paid 25 cents for a bottle of whiskey. Certainly, in a previously staunch Methodist and even now an Anglican household, this was very unacceptable behavior. After this revelation, Sarah would likely have been intense in her vigilance as to his whereabouts after coming back from town. A remark by Gussie was remembered well by his son, Lionel: "Doesn't that beat all hell." *(E. L. Hurd)*

***

Two old neighbours Lionel Hurd connected with in his youth were the brothers Bill and Fred Fallon, bachelors who lived on a farm next to the Hurds. Lionel recalls that when he was as a child, "Bill would come over wearing gum rubber boots with no socks, barely navigating over the rocks and fences. Only with luck, he would be carrying wheat flour for Sarah, which was considered the best for making pancakes. These were times when they had run out of suitable drink, and perhaps thought food might be more satisfying. Bill, of course, would eat as many pancakes as he could and only sometimes, he might take some cooked pancakes back to his brother Fred." *(E. L. Hurd)*

It has been told that, "In the winter of 1918, someone missed seeing old Bill Fallon for a couple of days and so Gussie thought someone should go to see if he was alright. Taking his son Lionel with him, who was 11 at the time, they paid a visit to his farm. They found him dead, sitting in his rocker by the stove where the fire had gone out. He was fully dressed in his clothes, his boots still on and his pipe still in his mouth, his body totally frozen. They figured he was probably drunk and just did not keep the fire going."[31]

A similar event happened a few years later to his brother, Fred, when in February 1934, he too was found dead. Cora Austin phoned to tell Jessie (Hurd) Riddell that "Frank King, Gussie, and Frederick were breaking (rolling) out the road passing by Fallon's and seeing no smoke from the chimney, they checked in his house where they found Fred lying on the bed fully dressed." It was not long for the story to be told that when they tried to lift old Fred from the bed his body was frozen "tighter than a bull's ass in fly season" to the blanket and so they just rolled him up, blankets and all, and took him to the undertaker.[31]

***

Author's note: Ever wonder why barns are so large? Blame hay. A cow can eat 30 pounds of hay per day, so it could take two to three tons of hay per cow to get through an average winter. Most farms in this era would have perhaps 15-20 cows, plus the one- and two-year-olds they kept until maturity. Storing that much hay required a large barn. A farm with even a modest dairy or beef herd usually had enough hay to provide for the farm's needs with some left over to sell.

During this era, farmers were beginning to have the resources to build bigger barns, quickly abandoning the old outside haystacks, instead moving hay indoors for overwinter storage.

While this process helped the farmer immensely during the winter months, by feeding the cattle inside, it made for an even more exhausting haying process in the summer. First, farmers would fork the gathered hay onto wagons to be transported to the barn. There were now two ways in which the hay was taken off the wagons. A new barn might be constructed to unload outside the end of a barn, using a specially designed "hayfork," running along a track which was positioned along the roof ridge, protruding out the end of the barn. From the wagon below, the hay fork would be lowered from the roof beam track, using a series of rope cables. A man would push the fork into the hay, turning a lever which activated a hook on each side of the fork. Horses hitched up to a rope outside the barn floor and with a series of pullies, the hook and the hay were lifted to the track, connected to a trolly, which carried the hay bundle to a haymow or hayloft. A trip rope would release the hooks on the fork and the hay would drop into the mow exactly where the operator wanted it to fall. Then, farm hands inside would distribute the mound of hay around the loft with pitchforks. When the hay was needed in winter, a farmer would go up into the mow and pitch the hay into a chute where it dropped down to the livestock below.

Barn-raising Gussie and Sarah's new barn, circa 1900 (Hurd family collection)

Gussie and Sadie built a new barn to accommodate an increasing herd of Shorthorn cattle, and of course their two workhorses and carriage pony. Barn raising was still a community affair and involved the neighbourhood men, women and children; all as part of the workforce. As many as 80 men would gather for the barn raising, the women providing their unsung support and preparing food for all. For the children, this was a time of great delight, getting together and making new acquaintances with younger children or new families that had moved into the community.[31]

Men would pass the hewn beams up to the men standing on the upper layers. Using large hardwood mallets, they would pound the round wooden pegs into place, locking the beams together. The general construction was still the same as earlier days, with each beam notched, drilled and fitted into the upright beams. These beams were then supported by 45-degree cross supports, all pegged into place, throughout the barn structure. Sawn rafters were then placed and secured to the beam construction. The sides were covered in a batten style with sawn board lumber.

Gussie decided to construct his new barn to accommodate a wharf-style slope that would allow a path for the horses to pull the load of hay up to the second floor where men would fork the hay off the wagon down into the mows on each side of the barn floor. They built the last few feet of the wharf supported by large beams and topped with 4-6-inch-thick elm boards.

Without horseshoes, the horses would not have been able to climb up this wharf and into the barn floor on the second level when pulling a load of hay. It did not take long for the horses to anticipate that they needed to pick up speed at the bottom of the ramp, using the heavy load as a sort of ballast, and had to strain hard near the top to get the load up the steep incline. Their horseshoes were their saving grace. Imagine, if you can, that they had to back up the horses with the empty wagon behind them, back down that wharf.

A load of hay, with its driver, could tip over if the horses could not quite make it to the top – the load and horses alike would slowly slide backwards; it was not a situation anyone wanted to be in. Horsemanship skills were key to this task working well, and it was a continuing challenge even for the best team and driver.[31]

***

For several years, the Methodist Church in Maple Leaf was without a settled pastor after it was abandoned by the Baptist clergy in favour of the church in Randboro. The pulpit occasionally was filled by neighbouring Congregational ministers. In 1894 Rev. Richard Hay was installed as Pastor. The Sabbath school had been reorganized, and an active "Christian Endeavour Society" had been formed along with a ladies group called "The Helping Hand Society," all part of the Methodist movement in Eaton and Newport townships of this era.[16]

Edmund[8] Haskell Hurd sent out invitations to the marriage of Jessie, his youngest daughter, to Joseph Riddell in the Methodist Church in Maple Leaf in June 1902. The community, both young and old, attended the wedding ceremonies as Jessie had been a teacher in the community for five years and many of the children she had taught were now married themselves. After the reception at the home of her sister Sadie and Gussie, they drove away in a new buggy built by her father Haskell over a long period of time in his own shop at his farm.

Gussie and Sadie Hurd's youngest son, Arthur, circa 1925-26, pulling the buggy full of straw in front of the "wharf." Note the steep incline to the barn floor the horses had to climb.

Author's note: The date of this invitation is evidence that this church existed in 1901 as a Methodist congregation and that it was indeed built and located near the Maple Leaf schoolhouse circa 1901.

Jessie Minerva Hurd (born 1878, the fourth daughter of Edmund[8] Haskell Hurd) and Joseph Riddell (born 1873, the eldest son of James and Jane (Docherty) Riddell) settled on a farm on lots 8 and 9 in the 9th Range, Maple Leaf, on the old Fred and Bill Fallon farm. Joseph's parents had taken over the foreclosure of the property earlier and raised eight children on this farm. Joseph was both a farmer and lumberman, operating in the townships of Newport, Auckland, Emberton Woods and Eaton. They built up a herd of purebred Hereford beef cattle and showed their prize Herefords at the Cookshire Fair each fall.

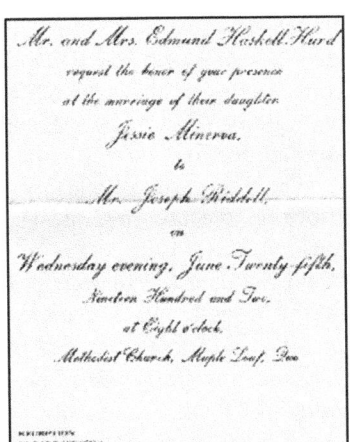

Invitation to Jessie Hurd's marriage to Joseph Riddell

Jessie Minerva Hurd and Joseph Riddell

Jessie and Joseph had no children. He took a great interest in civic duties, serving as his term as president of the Compton County Co-Operative Fair Association in Cookshire. He was also a contract builder, and later in 1933, a partner in the sawmill and the sash and door company in Sawyerville.

As a contractor, Joseph built the consolidated school in Sawyerville circa 1932. *The tender of Joseph Riddell for $18,978.00 was accepted and Alex Matthew was appointed building Inspector.*[40]

Jessie was a schoolteacher and had taught for five years in the Maple Leaf School from 1898 to 1902. Working with limited equipment, a teacher's life was active but tiring. At the end of a school day, Jessie would have had to sweep the floor and clean the classroom, bring in a supply of wood from the adjoining shed, prepare kindling for the morning fire, and empty the water pail so it would not freeze overnight.

In the morning upon arriving at the school, she would light the fire in the big box stove which sat in the middle of the one big room. The children watched for the chimney smoke, their signal that it was time to go to school. Most homes in this era did not have a clock and depended on a sun dial – which was fine if the sun was shining. Farmers generally woke at the first sign of daylight and went to bed when daylight ended, and that was their timetable, i.e., their clock. School generally started at nine in the morning and finished at four in the afternoon. Students' desks were wooden and joined by an iron frame which included the seat, bolted together in clusters of four to six desks in a row. Each desk had a small hole for an ink bottle to sit in. There were special drawing books; the paper was not pure white but more of a tan colour. Students were provided with scribblers and lined exercise books, supplies dependent on the tax levy collected for the year. The children took turns gathering water from a spring across the road, which they shared at lunch. Most children brought their own packed lunch rather than walk back home since the children pretty much walked quite a distance to school during this period. Jessie was strict; if any student misbehaved in class or at lunch break, they would have to go stand in a corner with their face to the wall or "get the strap." That was just the way it was.[40]

***

Author's note: When Gardner Stillman Rand took over the gristmill operation in Randville (Randboro) from his father, circa 1855-60, he had made a small dam in the river just southwest of the gorge. He expanded the business to make a combination sawmill and gristmill in the same location as the first gristmill which was built by his father Artemas[6], Nathanial Beaman Jr., Col. Edmund[5] Hurd, and their Associates.

Over the years Stillman had established a flourishing business, both in grinding grains for both human and livestock consumption in the gristmill operation and in producing boards, beams, clapboards and shingles in the sawmill operations. Circa 1890 Stillman sold the mills to Charles "Charlie" Stone, who was new to the area. Charlie had studied engineering and was contemplating a move somewhere to start a business. He became engaged in the lumber mill business and over time had accumulated sufficient monies to relocate and purchase a mill himself, choosing to establish himself in Randboro, circa 1890.[31] Charlie operated the mills for several years.

In a letter dated 1874, Harriet Whitcomb of Huntington, Que., wrote to Eliza (Planche) Hurd requesting information on the Stone family. Harriet mentioned that *"my cousin Leonard's second son, Charles had just graduated from College in June, and while there, had traced his ancestry, finding a record of the first "Stone family" who had immigrated from England some forty years ago."* Harriet was expressing her sorrow of knowing so little about her ancestry and wondered if Eliza *"could shed some light on the Stone family history from Charlie."*[21]

Author's note: Even in this era, people who had lost touch with family members were indeed anxious to reconnect with their ancestry. Many of the letters in the Heard/Hurd ancestry files have questions as to where (certain) people went, where are they now, did they have children, and can you give me an address?

Stillman had a vision for a town. Through his years of operating the mills in Randville he had hired many local men, some of whom settled with their families in Randville. Stillman subdivided several lots so they could live there; this was instrumental in Randville qualifying as a borough and becoming officially known as Randboro circa 1880-85. These were our ancestors; they saw what was needed and put in the effort to make it happen.

***

Author's note: Charlie and Lottie McCallum raised four sons and a daughter on Parker Hill. The eldest son, Ernest "Ernie," moved to Ottawa where he married. Some years later he returned to Newport to care for his parents. He wrote his memoirs in a small booklet titled Autobiographical Recollections: Study the past to plan the future. *Some material from that booklet is included throughout this section, as part of the story of Parker Hill and Randboro circa the early 1900s. The booklet was graciously provided by Diana (McCallum) Langworth, a daughter of Ernie's brother Leslie McCallum.*

Charles "Charlie" A. McCallum, born in 1877 on Île Brion, Magdalen Islands, Que., at age 17 already a boatman, fisherman and seal hunter, decided to leave the island. His mother had died when he was a small boy, then his father died when he was 14, leaving him and his brother by themselves. "His upbringing on that desolate island was of the wildest and woolliest sort, and completely devoid of schooling or churchgoing, but he could dance and sing old shanty, sea and war songs with the best of them."[47] *(quote: Ernest (Ernie) McCallum)*

Charlie worked for a few years as a seaman aboard coastal colliers. He had begun hauling coal out of North Sydney on Cape Breton Island, N.S., when he decided to make another change, moving to Scotstown, Que. He became a very capable lumberjack, log driver and sawmill hand, all rugged trades which suited his rugged nature. He saw a new opportunity in Randboro and came to work in Charlie Stone's new sawmill in 1906. There in 1907 he married Lottie Parker, a widow with two older children. Lottie was one of the twin daughters of Joseph and Mary Jane Parker of Parker Hill. Lottie's children from her first marriage were Harold Robert and Luvia Mildred Leggett. Luvia had already married a cousin of Charlie's, George McCallum, who had introduced his mother-in-law to Charlie. George McCallum had arrived in Newport earlier than his cousin; however, he died young, leaving Luvia a widow who never remarried. Charlie's brother Bill would follow in his footsteps 14 years later and bring with him an incredibly special talent.[47]

After Charlie McCallum married, he and Lottie (Parker) bought an uncompleted house in Randboro. "The union of Charlie and Lottie occurred less than nine months before Ernest arrived in 1908 and so it seems things change but they remain the same over the years. I remember Uncle Ernie saying at the 50th anniversary for Charlie and Lottie, that he was already almost 50 and jokingly wondered how that could be." *(Diana (McCallum) Langworth)*

Their first son, Ernest "Ernie," remembers his brother's birth. He had found some tread tacks and was busily nailing the tacks into the unfinished stairs when his father took him in hand and brought him upstairs to see his new brother Leslie. And so, Leslie was born in that house in 1910. Randboro was a busy place; with the sawmill in full operation, with teamsters coming and going, "the horse-drawn rigs of customers tied at the hitching rail at the small general store, the blacksmith shop down the road with Charlie Greenwood (Boisvert) pounding the horseshoes on his anvil, beating out rhythmic ringing sounds that were heard everywhere."[41] *(quote: Ernie McCallum)*

> *Author's note: Charlie Greenwood was generally known by two names: Charlie Greenwood and Charlie Boisvert. Perhaps he had a shady past and his answer might have depended on "Who's asking?" However, the real answer probably lies in the translation as Greenwood translated into French is Boisvert.*

Spring in 1901 was exceptionally warm, and after another winter of heavy snow, the resultant very high stream flows threatened area mills. June 27 was a bright and sunny day and exceptionally hot. Wild strawberries were at their best, and women and children took every advantage of the opportunity to "lay in a store" (i.e., secure a supply) for the winter despite the excessive heat. When the last pail was filled it was a relief to get to the comparative coolness of the house. Around six o'clock in the evening, thunderclouds were gathering in the west and rumblings of thunder were heard gaining in intensity, until they became a continuous reverberating crash. Each time the storm returned with increased vigor, the lightening which accompanied it in one continual flash was accompanied by torrents of rain without abatement until around four in the morning. Little rivulets that normally meandered through the valleys became raging torrents, sweeping everything away before them.[43]

The river flows had already been high from spring runoff before this massive thunderstorm. The cascading rivers caused huge damage to the riverbanks and flooded the meadows of surrounding farming communities all along their courses. The water cascading down the South River blew out both the dam and the mills. Everything was swept away, leaving huge boulders in the riverbed.[31]

> *Author's note: A similar spring flood destroyed the first French mills in Island Brook in 1834. The water cascading down the Eaton River also took out both the Cookshire bridge and mills. The best waterpower in Eaton Township had been ruined. The water had washed away a new mill that had been built only a year earlier and made a cut about 50 feet deep and over 200 feet wide. The abutments of the old bridge can be still seen today, high and dry. These spring floods were not unusual, so on several occasions there was a lack of sawmills to process logs until they were rebuilt.[16, 31]*

In a letter to his daughter Mary Hurd in North Middleboro, Mass., in 1906, Haskell Hurd mentioned that *"Charlie Stone built a new Steam Sawmill in Randboro last fall, some 40 teams of horses have been hauling logs and pulpwood down to his mill and some on to Sawyerville all winter. Jo [Riddell] has over twelve thousand cords of wood to float in the river run this spring, just waiting for the water to rise."* [41]

Charlie built the new dam upriver on the east side of the Parker Hill bridge. The water had flooded a considerable amount of land extending upriver as far east as the meadows of the George Gibson Hurd farm. He recognized that the new settlers and farmers would continue to require lumber for building homes, barns and new businesses. Being a progressive thinker, he built his new operations, both a gristmill and sawmill, powered by steam – the first "steam engine" mills in Newport.[31] Note the location of "Stone's sawmill" in Ernie McCallum's 1970-75 drawing of Randboro as he remembered the village from his childhood.

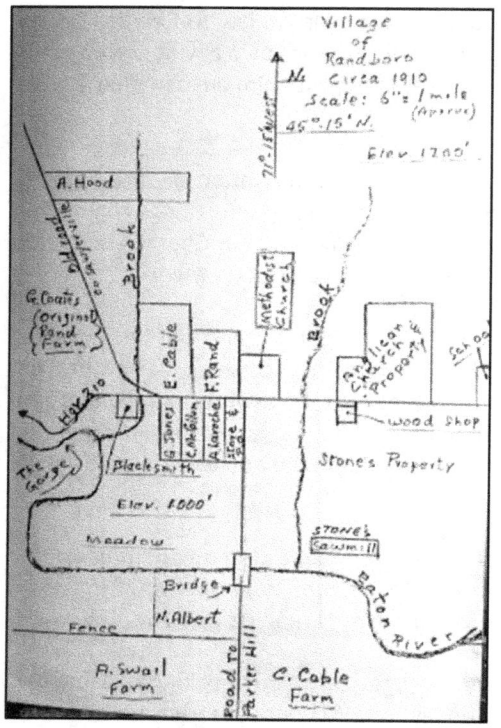

"Village of Randboro circa 1910" sketch
(courtesy of McCallum family)

By installing steam power, Charlie was able to augment the lack of waterpower when the water ran with less vigor during the summer. He installed two large iron water wheels: a larger one for sawing logs and a smaller one for shingles and thinner boards. The wooden water wheels that had been used for the previous 40 years sadly disappeared in the flood. He decided to build the new mills on his land on the east side of the Parker Hill bridge, but on the north side of the river. This mill site was essentially right in the centre of Randboro.[31]

A man of ambition, Charlie threw himself into the role of lumberman with an unbridled enthusiasm despite having no previous experience in the business. The sawmill he constructed was unique in that it incorporated some of the existing conventions of traditional water-powered mills and others of the more modern steam-driven style. The mill was freed from the constraints of requiring a heavy stream of water flow. It continued to employ a dozen or so men on a full-time basis. Charlie's reliance on farmers as "mill hands" meant the mill's operations were dictated to a large degree by crop seasons. This was a perfect match for extra work because when the water flow was at its lowest, the spring crops would be in the ground and the summer haying completed. They could work again after the fall harvesting was completed.

The mills generated ample work during the winter months. Because a lake had formed behind the dam, when frozen it was an excellent source of fun for both young and old for skating parties. Sundays in Randboro became a hub of activity after church services for outdoor winter activities; the Parker Hill road provided bobsledding while others were skating on the pond.[47]

The odour of a sawmill was distinctive, but for the residents in Randboro "the scent was pungent, heady, clearing the nostrils, even clearing your thinking," the smell becoming so normal that no one noticed. Freshly piled cut lumber emits a similar odour, an outdoor fragrance, a scent of sacrifice of trees giving themselves to make lumber for buildings as does the earthy scent when ploughing fields for grain and gardens.[43]

With each sawmill came exceptionally large sawdust piles, usually adjacent to the mills. Children used to love to climb these piles and slide down. It was as much fun as tobogganing in the winter. These huge piles of sawdust proved to be a major liability as many mills burned down from fires emanating from overheated sawdust piles. Initially the sawdust was given away, just to clear the areas around the mills. Later, it began to be used to keep ice in icehouses and as insulation between the walls of the newer houses.

Getting rid of the piles of sawdust was great for the mills, but it too became a huge business in itself over time. With the advance of rail service in these communities, the sawdust began to be hauled to train stations and shipped to the cities and out west for insulation and was also in great demand for ice storage in the cities.

In a letter Haskell[8] Hurd wrote to his daughter, Mary, now living in Boston, he relates as follows: *"In the spring of 1909, Joseph [Riddell] had 5000 cords of wood cut and nearly half hauled to the South river side, ready for the spring river run down to the mill at Randboro. There is a great business being done in square hardwood timber this winter. The timber has to be 20 feet long and not less than one foot in diameter at the small end. Gussie [Augustus[9] Hurd] is getting a number of pieces. The lumber business pays well; two men can make ten dollars a day now."* This was the start of the railway tie business which would expand in Newport and surrounding townships for many years to come. These ties, referred to as square-cut timber, were laid down on a prepared railbed for the steel rails to be spiked onto, and would serve Newport well in increasing the demand for lumber in the years to come.[21]

***

It was during this time when kerosene lamps were beginning to replace candles in Newport. The old galvanized tin candle moulds found their way to attics to become heirlooms of the future. All night-time work and social affairs took place under kerosene lamp light. Trimming wicks, polishing lamp chimneys and filling the lamps with kerosene were now daily chores.[47]

Florence Holbrook (a daughter of Manlius and Persis, who had homesteaded in Island Brook) "stood before the altar as a bride on September 21st, passed to her reward under the saddest circumstances on November 9th, 1904. An accident with a coal-oil [kerosene] lamp resulted in saturating her clothes with oil and igniting them, at the same time causing severe burns from which she succumbed after two days of extreme suffering. Florence was a bright, talented young lady of the noblest Christian character." *(the late Mabel (Alden) Mackay, granddaughter of Manlius)*

***

The William[1] Victor French families of Newport:

Robert[1] Foster and his wife Mary Ellen (Lebourveau) French raised their four children on their farm on Lot 3, adjacent to the farm of William[2] and Ester (Burns). Rob and Mary had four children: James Henry (born 1894), Archibald "Archie" W. (born 1897), Elena (born 1902) and Lloyd Robert[3] (born 1910). After he returned home from World War I James married Hannah Harvey and they purchased a farm in Island Brook. Archie married Alice Newby; they purchased a farm on Flanders Road at the junction of today's Route 212. Later in life they moved to a farm in the Island Brook area. Lloyd Robert moved to Sawyerville to begin a career in the lumbering business. All three French families farmed on lots 1, 2 and 3 of Range 6, near Island Brook; one farm bordered on the corners of the Flanders and French roads.[25, 32]

> *Author's note: Lloyd Robert French met Bertha Evelyn Hurd, a daughter of Alonzo Hurd of Newport, who owned the Sawyerville Mill in Eaton Township. This was a third Hurd/French family connection. Eric George Robert French (son of Lloyd Robert and Evelyn (Hurd) French) is a direct descendant of both William[1] Victor French and Col. Edmund[5] Heard on his mother's side.*

***

By 1905, cheese factories had started up in many small towns. Both Randboro and Island Brook had small cheese factories that provided a market for the farmers to sell excess milk in the summer. Valmore Drolet and his wife were the first cheese makers in Island Brook; they built their factory east of and close to the stream called Island Brook, facing Ditton on the La Patrie Road. Victor Burns was one of the last Island Brook cheesemakers. The cheese was later made in the building behind where Robert Burns lived in later years.[32]

Conveying milk to the cheese factory and returning with whey to feed the pigs was always a chore that delighted the children, as they could ride in the wagons and get a chance to be in town. The store was the draw for their curious minds. Whey is the liquid that remains after milk has been curdled and strained in the cheese-making process. Pigs were well-fed in the surrounding farms with this residue from the factories and, when slaughtered in the fall, provided excellent pork roasts for the table.[43]

There was a time when milk was put into pans to cool. The cream was skimmed off and used to make butter for table use and provide cream for coffee, whipped cream, cakes and biscuits. The cream was churned into butter and the skim milk fed to the calves and pigs. Later "creameries" were established, and farmers bought separators to extract the cream from the milk, the cream sent twice-weekly to the creamery, the butter being exchanged in trade. As businesses were established, the women no longer had the task of making butter at home.[43]

***

Author's note: In the northcentral part of Newport's Knicky Knocky community, Thomas[1] and Jane (Ellis) Parsons (the fourth generation) had nine children, two of whom would marry and raise their children in Newport, the daughters generating the surnames Dawson and Weir.

Thomas and Jane Parsons' son, George Thomas[3] Parsons (1885-1964) married Nellie Annabella Lefebvre in 1906. Nellie was the local teacher at the time and had been born at Hardwood Flat. They took over the old farm from his father Thomas[1]. They had nine children, all born at the old homestead: George Lynn (1907-1997) married Gladys Cook; Thomas William[3] (1909-1989) married Doris Mayhew; Una Alice (1910-2004) married Wesley Leavitt; Ruby Bernice (1912-2011) married Percy McKelvey; Myra Sybil (1914-2007) married Willard Mayhew; Norma "Lillian" (1918-2013) married Earl Thompson; Fay Muriel (1920-2018) married Lyle Ashley Rand; Audrey Frances (1922-2017) married Stuart Thomas A. Dougherty; and Nina Ivy (1926-2009) married Herbert Leslie Rowell.

Nellie Lefebvre and George Parsons (courtesy of Carol Rand)

George and Nellie farmed the old 50-acre homestead with the addition in 1908 of a sugar camp and more farmland almost a mile away, reached by a laneway that divided Russell Dougherty's farm. George spent the winters working in the woods, cutting and hauling logs from various woodlots. At one time he hauled to Ed Lyon's mill, near the railway behind Keith Smith's farm. "Mr. Lyon was a truly kind man and a special friend of all the family."[33] *(quote: Nina (Parsons) Rowell)*

Nellie, as did her grandmother Jane before her, boarded the local teacher. Gifted in sewing, needlework, rugmaking and many other handicrafts, she was able to clothe her family, usually remaking something from an unused garment.

George rebuilt the barn in 1912. In 1920 he dug a well and installed a windmill; they were finally able to have running water in both the house and barn. This was a luxury for the family after the many years of "pailing" water for every domestic chore, as well for drinking and watering the livestock. Of course, if there was no wind or the well dried up in times of drought, they had no water, so they stored rainwater in a large drum.[33]

During the years they were raising their family, their house was overcrowded but they were not able to afford to fix it differently. Now they began to fulfill one of their dreams. George, good at carpentry, remodelled the old farmhouse. The roof was lifted, allowing for two more bedrooms and a bathroom over a large kitchen, using the best of lumber for the hardwood floors, both upstairs and down, new hardwood stairs and kitchen cabinets. By this time, their family was practically all grown up and so they only spent about 10 years in this luxury.[32]

"Each spring while they lived on the farm, George made a fine quality of maple products, selling what he had left after putting aside what he felt was needed for the house, usually 50 gallons of syrup and 20 large tubs of soft sugar. The table at home was never completely set if the maple syrup was not on it. Something we never seemed to tire of was sugar rolls."[33] *(Nina (Parsons) Rowell)*

Fay was the seventh child in a family of nine children. In the summer, she and her younger sister, Audrey, had the chore of bringing in the cows from the pasture to be milked. Fay and her sisters would pick wild strawberries, raspberries, blueberries and currants for her mother Nellie to make into jam. The berries grew in abundance and the strawberries seemed to be bigger than the wild ones they picked near the railway track in Sawyerville. In the spring, during sugaring season, Fay often had the job of taking supper to her brother Tom. He would be boiling sap in the sugar camp long into the evening or night.

"A time of fun for Fay as a child was dressing in costume to be in the July 1st parade in Bury or Scotstown. At Christmas my grandfather, Thomas William Parsons, would buy a small pail of peanut butter that would be a treat for the children and a pail for himself. There would be an orange and a small gift in the Christmas stockings! My mother's older sister, Ruby, was already teaching school and she gave lovely gifts to her younger sisters." *(Carol Rand)*

The Parsons family left the old homestead in 1947 and moved to the town of Bury in the Township of Bury.

***

James William "Willy" Dawson (1865-1949), born in Lancashire, England, acquired his education in carpentry there. He came to Newport with his parents and two sisters. They decided on Knicky Knocky for their homesite and built a one-room cabin high on a hill with a small brook running below, a view of the mountains to the west, surrounded by heavy woodlands on the other three sides. Willy lived there until he built a beautiful big house where he brought his bride, Sarah Jane Parsons (1869-1949), in 1892. Sarah was a daughter of Thomas and Jane (Ellis) Parsons.

James and Sarah were destined to spend the rest of their lives in Knicky Knocky. They set their sights on making this land a family homestead, clearing the land and planting wheat, barley and corn. They farmed with a team of horses and raised a mix of cattle, pigs and sheep, along with some hens and geese. Surnames resulting from the marriage of their daughters were McLeod and Olson.

"Sarah and Willie were industrious people. Sarah prided herself on the whitest wash and putting it on the line the earliest, getting the beds made, daily dusting done, floors swept and scrubbed, all done besides her cooking, knitting, and mending. She was a faithful Church Guild and Women's Institute member. Willie helped rebuild the St. Paul's Anglican Church, was a staunch Liberal, a member of the Oddfellows and took a keen interest in politics, sitting as Mayor of Bury for 10 years. His word was his bond, no finer tribute can be paid to any man." Sarah and Willie both died in 1949.[33] *(quote: Nina (Parsons) Rowell)*

Willy and Sarah Dawson family. L-R, back: Guy Herbert, father Willy, Thomas George, mother Sarah Jane (Parsons), Clarence Walter; front: Blanche, Elizabeth Jane, baby James (courtesy of Carol Rand)

***

The farm across the road from the Dawson homestead was purchased by Alex Dougherty, born in Inverness, Que., in 1865. He moved first to Island Brook in 1877 and then to a heavily wooded tract of land, north of Island Brook and midway to the community of Knicky Knocky, their nearest settlement. At that time there was only a blazed trail from either community. Alex married Jessie Dunsmore in 1886; they lived on the Steven Parsons farm where their first two children were born. They moved to California for a time where two more children were born. The family returned and resettled on the same farm. They built a large addition to the house and new barns, making the "Dougherty place" one of the most attractive farms in the region. They continued to live there with their youngest son, Gordon, and his wife, "Lena" Parsons (daughter of John and Mary (Lizotte) Parsons), until 1947 when they moved to a house in the village of Bury.[33]

Gordon and Lena took over 300-acre farm and raised three daughters. After selling off most of the lots and finally the farm and buildings, they retired in the fall of 1977.[33]

Author's note: The following excerpt from the booklet Knicky Knocky, *complied by Nina Rowell, gives a reader an idea of the cost of building materials and labour in the early 1900s.*

In 1903, the schoolhouse in Knicky Knocky needed extensive repairs before the start of the school year and so a petition was put forth by the ratepayers to the School Commissioners to take proper steps to have the repairs done at once. Chairman George W. French was appointed to initiate this request. Extensive repairs were made to the school by William Dunsmore at a cost of $223.00 with William Dorman superintending the building repairs. The bill brought in was 26 lbs. of nails @ 78 cents, 50 ft. of lumber @ $3.75, 28 ft. of 8x8 @ $1.12, 1½ thousand shingles @ $3.75, teamwork @ $1.00 and a carpenter for two-and-one-half days @ $3.75. This school continued to serve the community until it was closed in 1924 and the children sent to Bury. They would have to provide their own transport, a horse and buggy in the summer and a sleigh in the winter, until around 1930 when school vans were brought into play. This was a special arrangement made by the Department of Education in Quebec City to allow the children of this part of Newport to join with Bury for school purposes only and their attendance would be free of any payment of school fees. Apparently, Alex Dougherty, a School Commissioner at the time was instrumental in getting this started as his grandson, Stuart was about to start school. "Alex didn't want 'the poor wee lad' to have to walk or get to school on his own."[32, 33]

***

A small woodworking and cabinetmaking shop was established in Randboro where all the work was done by hand – "no power tools here." One of the items produced was hand-made mouldings for house trim – a welcome cosmetic addition to a new home. "The man doing this work probably never thought of himself as an artisan or maybe even as an artist." For those who could afford it, adding mouldings along the edges of the ceiling and around doors and windows enhanced the interior look of a home. Embossed tin ceiling tiles were becoming popular in many kitchens; the edges were fitted with mouldings. In some cases, these ceilings were later painted, giving a look of real craftmanship if one thought it the work of a great plaster job – it was. Many homes had large mirrors with frames plastered in beautiful designs and then painted with a gold leaf flake, giving an illusion of possible wealth.[47] *(quote: Ernie McCallum)*

Ernie McCallum tells us, "When I was young, land was still being cleared on the farms about the village and the burning of brush fires went on during the spring and late fall seasons. Everyone seemed to be at work, always, and very happily so."

This was an era when people came together with a sense of strong leadership, many of whom were prominent leaders in their communities because they were infused with a strong social conscience.

Author's note: Early automobiles were known to their detractors as devil's carts, stink wagons and juggernauts of the roads. The earliest license plates were leather tags, prior to metal plates appearing in 1925. This photo is of Jessie and Joe Riddell driving their new car, a Model T Ford, circa 1926.[31]

Most of the roads were not built for motor traffic, so when cars started to appear in the early 1900s, the roads had to be reworked. The early roads were essentially carved out from the forests and were basically mud. Even the roads through the small villages were mud; add a significant amount of horse manure droppings and you had a relatively well-packed road. However, when it rained the road became a stinking quagmire of deep ruts and a challenge to drive through. Add to that the spring frost heaves, and the roads became almost impassable even for horses – motor vehicles might as well stay home.

Joseph "Joe" and Jessie Riddell out for a Sunday drive (Hurd family collection)

In winter, the roads were rolled with big horse-drawn rollers which allowed horses to travel with sleighs on a hard-packed base after each snowstorm. These rollers were made of hardwood consisting of two massive rollers hooked to a single axle, separated by a space in the middle to connect the draw pole. This pole was connected through to cross members attached to each of the outer sides of the rollers. A team of horses was connected to the draw pole. The rollers were filled with coarse sand to make them heavy and allow for a packing effect. The team would pull the rollers over the snow, packing it down and making the roads flat and smooth for sledding.

Typical road snow roller, circa late 1800s, drawn by a double team of horses (Pinterest)

Marshall Newell Rand was one of the "road rollers" in the Maple Leaf region, taking over this task from his father, Newell C., and Haskell Hurd. Marshall would roll the road beyond Gussie's farm on today's Route 210 to the Auckland bridge, up past his grandfather's farm on the road to Chartierville. In the spring, however, when the snow began to melt, these roads became an oasis of large potholes, later becoming quagmires of mud, so everyone tried to get as many supplies as possible before the roads would become basically impassible for a time. Because the roads were hard packed, the snow did not melt as quickly as in the fields, so during the late spring residents who had to travel would sometimes travel on sleighs through the drifts of snow that had collected in the fields beside these roads.

The farmers along the roads had constructed lean-to sheds at certain intervals where the rollers would be stored. Another farmer would pick up the rollers from there, carrying on rolling their part of the road. Augustus[9] "Gussie" Hurd, Marshall Rand, Valentine Swail, Wallace Boyd, Charlie McCallum and John Graham spent many hours with their teams of horses rolling the roads through Maple Leaf, Parker Hill, Grove Hill and west to Sawyerville to accommodate the school sleds and any other sleigh travel between the communities.

Horses were everywhere in Newport during this era. Men and their horses had a great affinity for each other, and with very few exceptions, horses were well-treated. There were drive sheds on the church grounds to house the horses while the attendees were inside at services, weddings and socials. Heavy workhorses were an absolute necessity for the farmers, loggers and haulers, and driver horses to draw the buggies and sleighs were the mode of transportation for the womenfolk and their children, just as cars are today. Most homes had additions equipped with horse stalls and small hay lofts overhead, just to house the driving horses. These additions would be treated like our garages in today's world. Through the seasonal farm work, both draft and light horses were used for ploughing, harrowing, seeding, cultivating, harvesting, and threshing, each succeeded the other in orderly fashion during most of this era.[47]

With freeze-up and snow, logs were hauled to farmyards and to village dooryards to be cut up for firewood, ready for the arrival of young Alonzo Hurd with his father George's horse-powered treadmill and drag-saw machine. Earlier in the fall, Alonzo Hurd would have gone from farm to farm with his treadmill, and Gussie, Lionel and John B. Hurd with their thresher machine. These two events became social affairs; each farm or home required seven or eight men to handle the job. Neighbours exchanged work from farm to farm as the rig moved along.

Without question, a hearty meal beyond imagination was "set out" by the host farm's womenfolk, where many views were often debated at these meals. Any philosophers and debaters of renown would find themselves lost should they ever take on a table surrounded by farm folk "discussing any subject under the sun."[47]

***

H.R. Cairns
1917, 1921

Horace Cairns

During this period, Newport continued to be represented by pillars within the community, each serving various terms as mayor or councillor. G. C. Chaddock held the post of mayor in 1906, followed by H. A. Stevenson from 1907 to 1916. Horace Cairns served a one-year term, succeeded by Fred W. Sunbury in 1918. Cairns returned as mayor in 1919 and served until 1922.[32]

Artemas Farnsworth was appointed secretary treasurer, assisted by his son Lewis in 1912. Mark Holbrook served as justice of the peace for many years. In 1910 John Burns Jr. was appointed justice of the peace and held this office until his death in 1945. John Burns was the last justice of the peace in Newport.[32]

Patrick Redman's store and home in Island Brook was destroyed by fire in February 1912. Augustus "Gus" Alden opened a general store across the road from the Methodist Church, managing the store for a few years as his health allowed, assisted by his son Charlie. The store was operated later by Charlie and Thomas Burns. This store also unfortunately burned in the early 1920s. Sadly, building fires were commonplace due to the buildings' wood construction and also due to burning wood for heating and cooking.[32]

Randboro was becoming progressive, with an Anglican church, a Methodist church, a general store, a schoolhouse, a post office in the small country store, a cheese creamery, a blacksmith shop, a cabinetmaking shop, a sawmill and a gristmill. The 1901 census of Newport showed 1,092 residents: 231 Catholics and 861 non-Catholics. The census was recorded and broken down exactly as it shown here.

***

Unidentified violin player – a possible Hurd or Riddell relative – wearing a suit typical of the day (Jessie (Hurd) Riddell album; Hurd family collection)

Ernie McCallum tells us that during this period, "Parties took place in many homes at which people seemed to have great pleasure. Reed organs were in some homes and here and there someone had a piano. A violin always turned up and what else but some dancing. It always surprised me to see how nimble and graceful these sturdy muscular men became when the music started and the square dancing began, the women and girls whom one naturally expected to be nimble and graceful, always proved to be all and more than expected. It was not all square dances; however, incredibly old and pretty dances are done with grace and skill, waltzes, gavottes, gallops and schottisches are names I remember."[47]

Many households in the village had a milking cow, chickens, a pig or two, a fattening young beef animal and a horse. In addition, each had a potato patch and a large vegetable garden. All these required attention and work. No wonder everyone was busy. The word unemployment had not yet been considered in this time; there was no such thing. If someone needed something everyone else got busy to make it, grow it, build it, or help someone who could.[47]

In Randboro, the favoured activities were provided by the river: swimming holes were numerous and well used in the summer; after winter freeze-up, stretches of straight, smooth ice from the bridge upstream for 200 yards or more would be kept clear of snow and used for skating. On a fine winter's night, a fire would be built on the ice and many adults as well as children would be out skating.[47]

In late spring, log drives took place on the river. Both hardwood and softwood logs were driven to mills or to be loaded on trains in Sawyerville. Logs were also driven on the North River, six miles downstream to Cookshire to the mill or to trains. Some of the pulpwood log drives continued on to East Angus on the Eaton River. "We could always look to a log jam right before our eyes in Randboro where the river curved sharply through the rocky narrow gorge. We would line up along the roadway above the gorge and watch the log drivers working in the cold, rushing water to find the key log or logs that held the jam. They would cut or blast the obstruction out of the way and guide the loosened logs on their journey downstream. A dangerous job indeed."[47]

The Standard Chemical Co. of Toronto Ltd.'s subsidiary operation in Cookshire signed a contract in the spring of 1908 with William Cromwell and Joseph Riddell to drive and load all their pulpwood held on the South River "Pond." The contract stipulated they were to share the expense equally to repair the first dam if it was breached in this operation; their fee was to be 90 cents per cord. Further, the contract stated that if it was impossible to obtain railcars, they were to pile the wood in the railyard. The extra fee for this work was to be rated at 10 cents per cord. The company would pay 40 cents per cord when the wood was driven, the balance of 50 cents per cord when the wood was loaded, the pond cleared, and the scale received. The contract stipulated the "Pejepscot scale" be used.

Protocols were put in place to standardize the grading and measurement of lumber. The Pejepscot scale, commonly known as the "northeastern scale," was one such standard used in the region. Log scaling estimates how much lumber can be sawn from the log, and is performed primarily to determine the value of individual logs. Scaling is also used to maintain accountability for paying loggers and landowners, to evaluate the financial performance of a sawmill, and to ensure the quality of logs entering the mill yard. This method of measurement and stamping assists in inventory management and quality control, and allows the tracking of logs from the cutting process to a mill site. Examples of scaling practices include measuring the weight of pulpwood to estimate the volume and measuring the dimensions of hardwood sawlogs, along with applying a log rule to determine how much lumber can be sawn from the log. Scaling estimates the log volume on a board foot, cubic foot, linear foot or cord basis. In scaling logs, the volume of available material is usually estimated from the weight of the product, where moisture content, species and other factors are considered. For logs that are to be processed into lumber, log rules are usually applied to estimate the total volume (expressed in board feet) of lumber that can be sawn. *A.F.P.A. 00. The "P" was the grading agency, the 00 space designated the mill. The letters S.P.F. indicated the species when circled: spruce, pine and fir; followed by 1, which was the assigned grade of lumber.*

> *Author's note: The Pond mentioned earlier was the reservoir created by the Sawyerville dam; it extended all the way up to the Newport line. Pulpwood cut in Newport was driven down the South River and held there with connective booms of logs chained end-to-end, circling a particular group of logs. Getting these logs over the dam without damaging them was a tricky business.*

***

When Charlie Greenwood/Boisvert died in 1912, Charlie McCallum bought the old blacksmith shop at the foot of Grove Hill that John Phelps had established and operated for many years. Charlie Greenwood/Boisvert had bought the shop from John circa 1865. And so, Charlie McCallum learned another new trade and became a "farrier." Horseshoeing was a large part of blacksmithing operations in this era, and an art in itself. Not only must the farrier shape the shoe and hoof correctly and nail the shoe in place, but also contend with cranky or younger, frightened horses that had never been "shoed" before. A farrier had to be talented at handling horses.[47]

Charlie's eldest son, Ernie, reminisced; "I remember being called to the shop by Dad, before I was 5 years old, to hold a 'twister' on a nervous horse's lower lip." A twister was a loop of hemp rope, spliced through a hole across the end of a wooden handle. The loop was slipped around the horse's lower lip and the handle twisted just enough to divert the animal's attention from its foot to its lip. "So, I would stand at the horse's head and hold the handle, twisting lightly. As the fitting and nailing of the shoe to the hoof began, and if the horse started to kick or fight, I would twist the handle a bit and that was all there was to it. I have known some lips since that time that would have benefitted from a touch of the twister."[47] *(quote: Ernie McCallum)*

Randboro, circa 1900. The photo was taken from the top of Grove Hill Road, looking down to the left as one would drive into town. The store is visible in the foreground at the far left. The blacksmith shop is indented between the two houses at the right. A woodpile is showing along the driveway towards the blacksmith shop (set back from the road). The left-hand side of the road, today's Route 210, shows towards Maple Leaf; the right-hand side is towards Sawyerville.

Chapter 13   Uncertain Times (1900–1925)

Mary Maria Hurd and Gifford Lawson Sr.

Mary Maria, the second daughter of Edmund[8] Haskell Hurd, was 37 when she met and married Gifford Lawson Sr. in New York City in 1907. After her marriage, the family moved to Middleboro, Mass., and she continued nursing at the Massachusetts General Hospital. Gifford, who had emigrated from England to the U.S., became a public utilities accountant and was sent to several subsidiaries of an electric utility company based in New York City. Gifford became a U.S. citizen on October 14, 1921, while working in Rutland, Vt. He was budget comptroller for the electric utility company in Chicago, Ill., from 1929-1933. Gifford was unemployed for a time during the Great Depression, joining the Tennessee Valley Authority in 1936 as the company was being formed to produce and sell electricity in the U.S. market.[4, 31]

***

To increase its presence on a national scale, in March 1912 the Eastern Townships Bank (est. 1859) merged with the Canadian Bank of Commerce but most of its branches remained open in the townships.[34] In 1961, the Canadian Bank of Commerce merged with the Imperial Bank to become the Canadian Imperial Bank of Commerce.[48]

***

On January 8, 1912, the farmers in Newport experienced a significant blizzard, the strength of a hurricane, that *"blew through the night."* Haskell Hurd wrote to his daughter, Mary Lawson:

> *The winds took the roof off one side of Gussie [Hurd]'s barn and carried it over to the horse barn, striking the ridge of the house and taking about five feet in depth and one half of its length in rafters including the chimney and the debris landed in the fir tree behind the house. We were all in bed but soon up and out to see what happened. Another part of the roof had struck the woodshed doing considerable damage to that building as well. Gussie, Sadie and the children had to vacate the building and go down to Stewart [Willard]'s to stay for a few days. I stayed in the house for the rest of the night and got my tools together from Gussie's shop. We had to repair the chimney and roof on the house, the weather holding around 40 below zero, but the days were bright, and we got it done.*[21]

In mid-July, Mary (Hurd) Lawson spent a day visiting Val and her sister Laura Swail, and Gardie and Lily Rand. She mentions in her letter home, dated July 14, 1914, that *"Gardie is much better than I expected after his operation."* Gardie had had an operation for cancer in Montreal a few weeks earlier and was convalescing. Mary mentions that *"Uncle Charlie [Cable] has visited tonight, and Sadie seems to be alright with her new little baby [Arthur]. He weighed 7½ pounds, not large but plump, and is so cute."*[21]

***

Newell Clement and Laura (McCurdy) Rand raised their four children – two boys, Alonzo Alton and Marshall Newell, and two girls, Mary Maria and Edna Sarah Eliza – on the original Lot 12 of Range 11 that had been granted to Captain Edmund[7] Heard. Alonzo (1883-1932) first married Catherine Jane Riddle, then later married Gladys Irene Colby. Mary Maria married Albert Riddell; they had no children. Edna, born in 1885, married Alan Williams; they resided in Bulwer, Eaton Township. Newell's wife Laura (McCurdy) died in 1913 of TB.[31]

Newell Rand as an older man (Hurd family collection)

Newell Rand's brother Willard Stedman and his wife Sarah (McCurdy) Rand, a younger sister of Laura's, lived on the next farm, just west on today's Route 210, so the two sisters, Laura and Sarah, had raised their families in close proximity to each other. In 1916 when Mary (Hurd) Lawson was visiting at Willard's farm, in a letter home she made reference to Sarah (McCurdy) Rand: *"Poor Sarah grieves so much for Willard [who had died at age 61 in October 1915] and she has aged so much since last year. Her son Scott and Beatrice and young Perry are on their way to West Summerland, B.C. Sarah has not decided just where she will live as she is so worried about Infantile Paralysis now.* "[21, 31]

Alonzo Rand's wife, Catherine, had just come from visiting the house in Brooklyn, New York, where her brother's baby just died from that disease. Sadie (Sarah) Hurd tells us in her letter to her sister Mary, *"I have not been taking the children out anywhere. Not until that awful disease is under control. They do not seem to be able to control the epidemic in New York. Lionel, Frederick, and Gifford are playing together so well."* Gifford Lawson was the only son of Gifford and Mary (Hurd) Lawson who were living in the U.S. at the time.[21]

> *Author's note: Both TB and infantile paralysis (polio) were prevalent at this time. Many of the older people were dying of the lung disease, and now this new threat to their children caused much anguish and anxiety amongst parents. This was a time of extreme anxiety and misgivings for families.*

Mary's husband, Gifford Sr., wrote to Mary in July telling her about 70 cases of infantile paralysis in Chicago. Paranoia existed in this era, not unlike today with COVID-19. He wrote: *"It is reported that three Germans were distributing 'snuff' outside the Windsor machine company, Vt., and someone got suspicious and had the stuff examined and it was found to contain some deadly germs, however it seems improbable to me. [Signed] Gifford Lawson."* [21]

***

> *Author's note: The "Great War" of 1914-18 saw many of Eastern Townships men and women volunteer their services. Newport Township played its role in the war effort, and while I will not go into detail about the war itself, I feel it important to recognize those who lived in Newport and served and whose families were an integral part of the growth of Newport Township.*

United Empire Loyalists who had immigrated to Lower Canada from the U.S. during the American War of Independence (1775-1783) and their descendants had continued with the ways in which the British military conducted its business at that time. The Canadian military of this era followed suit. When the call went out to the settlements for a body of forces, it was incumbent upon anyone capable of enlisting to do so, to have a share in the honour of serving their country. Military service was considered by many men as a rite of passage, a chance to prove themselves, to be a part of something bigger than they felt they might be individually. It also appeared to be an opportunity to see the world. Testosterone levels were perhaps another a large factor.

Young recruits from Newport were not immune to the fact that farming was a tough business; they were accustomed to hard work. Why not get paid for doing what farmers normally did, shooting rifles (in the infantry), riding horses (in the cavalry), felling trees (in forestry units) or digging ground (as sappers or trenchers)? Enlistment was their honourable ticket out. They envisioned, in the war's opening days, going straight to France or Belgium to fight and defeat the Germans; a quick trip over and back before Christmas. They had all heard knowledgeable people smugly assert, "the fighting will all be over by Christmas."[3]

When the war started in August 1914, young men of all backgrounds rushed forward, feeling the widespread exhilaration, fearing they might miss the war's adventure and encouraged by neighbours and friends to join. England was well on its way toward a commercial and manufacturing economy which would have a direct impact on its warmaking ability. This ideology was widespread; the opinion at the time reflected an unchallenged belief in the vast superiority of all things British.

The war immediately accelerated mass production and employed many more workers, including women, in the workforce. This event marked the beginning of the end of that quiet, idyllic life in Newport. Many young men, not long in Canada from the British Isles, volunteered for armed services, and in a very few weeks a huge void existed in Newport and surrounding townships. Nearly every able-bodied young man in the villages and countryside was soon in the service and had been shipped overseas, many never to return. The effect on the economy was drastic.

People with very little money set aside for their future needs hoarded it in fear of what may come. Trade dropped off and people were not buying anything but food. Some of the older men and single women went to Sherbrooke to work in munitions plants.

For those living on the home front, jobs were still in abundance, however, as the war dragged on, "most were silent, not wanting to speak of the war. Words were inadequate for their emotions. This war was about the incredible haunting madness that melted all humanity and dissolved the old-world order, one soul at a time. The British Empire exploited its colonies for Imperial purposes and the clergy exhorted local men to enlist and fight the devil as a holy war. Weaving the whole from its particulars also celebrates the capacity of ordinary people, under extreme conditions and duress to accomplish extraordinary things." *(Patrick Boyer, MPP and columnist,* Gravenhurst Banner, *Nov. 2020)*

In a 1915 letter to her cousin back home in New England, a visitor to Newport wrote, *"In the French settlements, many young Frenchmen are hiding in the woods to escape the draft, one was shot by an officer a few days ago, running for the woods. The officials are having lots of trouble with the French Canadians right now."*[21]

Thirty-eight men from Newport served in the First World War. Five were killed in action, three were wounded and many of the others returned home in shock; it took them many years to adjust to the normality of home life and none ever felt the same again. Some of the family names you will recognize from this book: Dawson, French, Harvey, Morrow, Statton, Seale, Loveland and Lister, to name a few.

Private Charles Victor Loveland, second son of William and Eliza (Beaman), was born in 1891. He had moved from Newport to Medicine Hat, Alta., where he enlisted with the 175th Infantry Battalion D Company. He was transferred to the 31st Battalion B Company in 1917 and was wounded on August 2 while retrieving the wounded at the Battle of Hill 60 in Belgium. He died there on August 6, 1917.[32]

Archie Renford Morrow, born in 1895, was the son of William and Hattie (Cable) Morrow. He enlisted with the Cookshire/Sherbrooke Hussars in May 1916 and was sent overseas with the 117th (Eastern Townships) Battalion. His battalion fought in the battles of Vimy Ridge, Lens (Hill 70) and the Loos. When this mission was complete, they were sent to Passchendale. He was wounded by enemy machine gun fire to his right knee, leg, and shoulder during the battle at Passchendaele in 1917. He had lain 36 hours in "no man's land" before being rescued by his battalion. He was flown to Epsom, England, where he underwent several operations followed by a nine-month recovery in the hospital. When he was well enough he was sent to Ste. Anne's Hospital in Ste. Anne de Bellevue, Que., to complete his recovery. Renford came home after the war, and in 1922 married Elizabeth McCormick (1897-1981) in Bury. They farmed the homestead with his parents and brother Kenneth in Island Brook. In 1927 Renford and Elizabeth bought a farm for themselves in the Maple Leaf region of Newport where they raised their family.

Archie Renford Morrow (Eastern Townships Roots)

Ernest W. Holbrook, born in 1888, was the son of Manlius Holbrook. He enlisted with the 102nd North British Columbia Infantry and served overseas. He was recommended for the Victoria Cross for single-handedly capturing a German machine gun and its crew on the Somme River in France in 1917. Ernest survived to return home to his farm in Island Brook.[32]

Private Wilbert T. Seale, the son of Joseph Seale, enlisted in 1916 with the 117th (Eastern Townships) Battalion. He was killed at Vimy Ridge in 1917 at the age of 26.[32]

Private James Henry French, born in 1894, the son of Robert Foster and Ellen (Lebourveau) French, also enlisted with the 117th Battalion but was transferred to the 5th Battalion, Canadian Mounted Rifles. He survived the Battle of Vimy Ridge despite being shelled with mustard gas.[32]

Sergeant-Major A. B. McKeage, born in 1890, the son of David McKeage, enlisted with the Grenadier Guards in 1915. He was seriously wounded in the head in 1918.[32]

> *Author's note: History books tell us much about the war years on the front; however, not so much as to how lives on the home front were impacted. The following accounts of the years to 1918 were typical of "lives lived" while the war was raging in Europe.*

Charlie McCallum had taken a job at a munitions factory in Sherbrooke, but he was an outdoors man so when offered a job with a building contractor, he accepted. Unfortunately, he fell off a ladder, hitting the ground with quite a force. "He was terribly injured and was in hospital for a long time. Imagine the situation that existed: none of the social benefits or insurance plans, so taken for granted today, were even in existence or even thought of. You were on your own, sink or swim. To add to the misery, the hospital, the doctors, even the ambulance man all sued for payment, monies he did not have."[47] *(quote: Ernie McCallum)*

Charlie was laid up for two years with his injuries, unable to work in his blacksmith shop because his right hand and arm were too severely damaged and not strong enough for him to hold anything. The family traded their home and blacksmith shop in Randboro to John Jones for his farm in Parker Hill. This farm was the original farm of Joseph and Mary Jane Parker, his wife Lottie's parents. "The farm, as our parents obtained it, was badly run-down; there was no livestock, no implements, just land and buildings. It was the best they could afford."[47] *(quote: Ernie McCallum)*

John and Nellie Jones and family moved several times, but always resided close to the communities of Randboro, Parker Hill and Maple Leaf. After trading the farm in Parker Hill for Charlie McCallum's house in Randboro, they lived in Randboro for only a short time before they bought a farm in Auckland Township, at the foot of Morrison Road and the Newport/Auckland township line. They moved from there to a farm owned by William and Hannah (Rand) McCurdy on the corner of today's Route 210 and Morrison Road, and from there to the old Randboro schoolhouse on Route 210 just east of Randboro. They settled more permanently on a farm on Route 210, about a mile east of Randboro in Maple Leaf. This farm, on Lot 8 of Range 9 just west of the cemetery, was where they continued to raise their family. They farmed pigs and a mixed herd of Shorthorn cattle, selling milk and cream. *(Rodney Hillman)*

John and Nellie Jones always lent a helping hand throughout the Maple Leaf neighbourhood. John had a reputation as a shrewd trader; everything was for sale at any time but more likely for trade. If he put a piece of equipment out on his lawn, a buyer might want to check out whether it worked before making a trade. John would sell anything, but his big thing was selling his houses. "I remember my grandmother saying that every time she would get her house decorated, he would sell it. He was into selling cows and horses and it got so no one would trust him because he would sell the animals as being young or middle-aged at most, when in fact they were ready for the boneyard. Someone checked out a horse he had for sale and found it had no teeth. He sold a stove once but took out the grates before it was picked up. When the buyer came back for the grates, John wanted extra money for them, saying they were not included. Because of this he made many enemies; however, he was still always well-liked within the community simply because most people were aware of his shenanigans." *(Rodney Hillman)* It has been said that John would skin a fart if he thought there was a penny in it.

***

As with many other farmers in Newport during this time, it was the courage, determination and resilience displayed by these men, women and children that propelled them to pitch in and work hard to attain their livelihood, always expecting better days ahead, and they did just that. This enthusiasm and positive attitude to get things done appeared to be in the genes they inherited from their ancestors – and survive they did.

The women who were running the farms while their menfolk were overseas were still suffering from tragedies with the onset of new diseases they knew nothing about; some had already lost their husbands in the war while other women would be dealing with shell-shocked and wounded husbands returning from overseas. When the war was over, they would be jubilant and looked forward to stability in their lives. They

"Welcome Home to the Soldiers of Sawyerville" (Eastern Townships Roots)

were not yet to know that another round of disease was about to hit them in the form of a pandemic, and that their men returning from overseas likely brought it with them.

***

By 1917, Joseph and Jessie (Hurd) Riddell had a couple of farms and a herd of 85 head of fine Ayrshire and Hereford cattle. Meanwhile, Laura (Hurd) and her husband, Gifford Lawson Sr., had not been doing so well in the United States as Gifford found himself unemployed and office jobs had already begun to wane.

Ayrshire cattle and one Hereford on right on Joseph Riddlell farm (Hurd Family collection)

Rural farming areas were indeed a better place to live during tight times as there always seemed to be demand for a product our ancestors could produce that allowed them to live reasonably well. Food was always available on the farm, which was not the case in the large cities to the south.

***

In preceding generations most farms in Newport grew hops, which became the subject of a rather curious tale. "Mother often told us that, when she was a young girl in the 1880s, many people, including her parents had a hop yard." The growing vines were trained around and tied to eight-foot-tall poles with wool yarn. Hop picking time came in early fall and even small children were given their work to do. Each day's picking of hop cones was spread out on the upper floor of the hop house, with a fire burning below, to cure. This provided a great place for socializing. Roasting and eating corn-on-the-cob was a happy way to round out an evening as the hops dried. It has been said that many an amorous entanglement was suspected in the far-reaching, dark corners of the hop house. Most of the people of the era past were deeply religious and, to boot, either devout Baptists or Methodists. Mary Jane, née Hamilton Parker, had two sisters and three brothers living nearby and they were all good-living, devout people. Mary mentioned that "to make the cheese more binding in the family, one of her brothers was a Methodist minister and a doctor of divinity at that."[47] *(quote: Ernie McCallum)*

Enter three hellfire-and-brimstone-preaching Methodist Evangelists. They told the hop growers they were siding with the devil by growing hops because hops were used in making beer and ale. This kept up until people became thoroughly frightened and gave up growing hops, converting their hop houses to other uses. In depriving themselves of this cash crop, their incomes were seriously affected. Many of the younger folks from established families once again moved away, mainly to the Boston area, and the Irish and English who had comprised the bulk of the early settlers also started to slowly disappear.[47]

"In my mind, these Evangelists were not well informed because hops are used in brewing simply to add flavour to the libation. The real evil in the brew is the alcohol which comes from the malted barley, but at no time did the fervent Evangelists ever suggest that these farmers stop growing barley. "Were they not straining at the gnat while swallowing the camel?" "When we were growing up, we would pick the burrs and stuff them into our pillows and mother would put a few hops into the yeast when making bread which gave it an interesting flavour. The first time I tried beer, it was nothing new or novel as it tasted just like Mother's bread." [47] *(quote: Ernie McCallum)*

***

The farms in Newport were expanding, with most farmers becoming more independent due to new equipment being available and changing their workload. These new machines replaced hired hands for both harvesting and lumbering; however, farms still needed help because many of the men had gone to war. Younger boys were quitting school because their parents needed them on the farm; they were replacing the hired help. They knew, as many of the older men had known, how to handle horses by pulling on the reins to calm the horses down that were not used to the noise made by mowers, rakes and tedders dragging along behind them. (Horses were now being spooked by a different source of noise on the roads they were so accustomed to trotting on in complete silence.) These young men learned how to repair the new equipment and took great pride in being considered an integral part of the farm, the man of the house and a sense of feeling grown up.

Mary (Hurd) Lawson wrote to her husband Gifford:

> *Here it is August and we are not seeing anything in our Canadian newspapers about the Infantile Paralysis epidemic that is infecting sections of the United States but we do not want to travel through these infected areas (Vermont is especially bad) with young Gifford. Trains are unsafe now with this disease. The phones here are not reliable as we hear buzzing from other lines and can hardly hear the voices. There are no cases here yet. Our people are suggesting that I leave Gifford here to go to school as soon as Evelyn [Swail]'s school opens at the end of the month. Sadie is improving now after her fall, taking a few steps with a crutch. Gussie has a car and so they drive now.*[21]

In a letter to his daughter Mary, in 1918, Haskell Hurd mentioned that his daughter *"Sadie is not well, has had inflammation in the veins of her left leg called 'Phlebitis' and she is on crutches."*[41]

> *Author's note: Apparently Sadie's pregnancy with her youngest son, Arthur, in 1914 had caused some concerns with her health. These cleared up sometime in 1918; however, she continued to suffer if standing for long periods of time. Working in the kitchen and in her henhouse, on her feet for many hours, caused periodic flare-ups for many years. Sarah took a fall sometime during the Second World War years and broke her hip, so her crutches served her well for many years. Haskell made her a special set of crutches equipped with a metal spike, which moved down from the foot by simply turning the handles.*

Gussie and Sarah ("Sadie") bought their first car in 1917, a model T Ford, one of Henry Ford's first cars built on an assembly line in a factory in Detroit. These cars were significantly more affordable than earlier motor vehicles, and the farmers and families in Newport would strive to be able to buy their first engine-driven mode of transportation. These first automobiles were considered "non-essential" and so were a form of pride and prestige for the families that were able to afford one.

The model T car had a hot-shot battery under the back seat, but you had to turn the crank at the front of the car to start the engine. Once it fired up, the engine ran on magneto. Magneto is a small dynamo with permanent magnets for generating electric current. If the car were moving slowly the lights would be dim but would become brighter as one speeded up, and the driver would have to continually adjust a lever on the steering wheel to increase the spark to the firing cylinders. Another lever on the steering wheel column was the gas control, as there was no gas pedal, which meant one would set the speed with this lever. There were three pedals on the floor of the Model T: one on the right for the brake; a reverse pedal in the middle to allow the car to go backwards; and a pedal on the left to shift gears from low to second and then high speed. A lever on the floor worked the brakes as well as the clutch. Driving a car was rather complicated for those who were used to driving horses and had no mechanical operational experience at this time in their lives.

If the car had a top, the side curtains slid on a wire from back to front, attached to the car roof with fasteners. The windshield came in two parts, split in the middle, easily opened and closed if you wanted more air flow through the passenger seats. If the car needed to be pulled out of a quagmire, or towed, which was often, the driver could use this feature to feed the reins through the windshield so one could hold the reins for the horse as he was being towed.

The rubber tires had an inner tube. If a driver had a flat tire, he would have to take the tire off the rim, patch the tube, put it back in the tire and fit the tire over the rim. He would then pump up the tire and reinstall the wheel on the car. This was done on-site; no roadside assistance in those days. The car came equipped with tire patches, glue, and a tire pump which implied that the tires often went flat. The size of the tire was 30 inches by 3½ inches – a large circumference but narrow wheel and tire. Because of this, these cars rutted the roads considerably; however, the narrowness and height also meant these cars could navigate deep trenches in the roads in these early times.

> *Author's note: The tires on these cars were not long-lasting, and it was a relatively short period of time before the countryside started to become the dumping ground for used tires. The war, however, dictated a need for rubber and there were many "rubber drives" initiated through the schools to collect these tires, the children exercising great delight in seeking out caches of old tires in farmers' pastures and dumps.*

These cars were bouncy (no shock absorbers at this time), so passengers had to hang on to their seats and for sure their hats. These cars were also slow in braking, so a driver needed to anticipate well in advance when to prepare to stop. The engines, however, were quite reliable, and as time went on our ingenious Newport ancestors repurposed these engines to run all kinds of farming equipment, from saws to pumps, replacing the old horse-driven treadmills.

Gussie and Sarah Hurd always referred to their car as their "open air" car. The author must assume that the canvas side curtains had not been included with this car. Gussie was a terrible driver and as his sons Lionel and Fred became older, they tried to teach their father to signal when he intended to make a turn. The conversation went like this: "When you want to turn, just put your arm out the window . . . straight out for a turn left and if turning the other way, then bend your elbow up to signal you are turning right." Gussie was adamant and determined in his reply: "If they can't see my car, how in hell are they ever going to see my arm?" *(E. L. Hurd)*

After Gussie and Sarah bought their first car, one of Gussie's first trips was to pick up his sister-in-law, Mary (Hurd) Lawson at the train station. Gussie mentioned to Sarah that he figured *"from the farm to Lennoxville will be a 40-minute trip via car to pick up Mary, so we have lots of time to get there."* Mary was to arrive from Vermont on the train and Gussie and Sarah did arrive on time. Gussie had put Mary's steamer trunk on the back seat with Sarah, for her to hang on to, so that Mary could sit up front in the new car and enjoy the scenery. The trip back was to be different however, as a heavy storm was brewing. Apparently, the Ascot swamp was the problem, not Gussie's driving. Trying to get out of a rut while meeting a team of horses, the car skidded and went into the ditch and the engine stalled. As

Gussie and Sarah in their 1917 Ford Model T, waiting for Mary at the train station (Hurd family collection)

Mary tells the story, "We all got out of the car in the pouring rain, Gussie cranked the engine, got it started and I pushed on the back of the car and by the third push, the car went back on the road and away we went, wet and our clothes all muddy but okay." Gussie was heard to say that "the car is okay in good weather, come hell or high water when it's raining, not so good."[21]

"It would have helped if he'd had some driving lessons before he took to the road. Gussie was great with horses and he had become used to the way the horses would automatically anticipate where to go and when to stop. Because Gussie always referred to his driving as he was 'going to beat the band' one might assume he meant he drove fast with it. His car apparently terrorized other horses on the road, sometimes his car careened up on to sidewalks and people's lawns, so they say!" *(Eric G. R. French)*

These cars typically motored along at about 15 miles per hour and so how fast was that! The miracle was that Gussie made it into town and around Newport Township without any serious mishaps for many years until he got used to driving. When his sister-in-law Mary was visiting one summer, she mentioned in a letter that her sister, *"Jessie has given me a nice auto cap and veil, very nice, and with straps so I do not have to hang on to my hat for dear life while motoring."*[21]

***

Sarah (Sadie) Hurd had a large chicken coop, where her pullets were housed, and a henhouse for her laying hens. She prided herself in running the whole operation from collecting the eggs to providing freshly plucked chickens for dinner. At one point she was literally running a chicken farm consisting of 200-300 Leghorn chickens. Leghorns are generally white in colour; a large breed and perfect for roasting. She let them run free-range all over the yard, resulting in an abundance of chicken poop on the lawns.

Author's note: Sadie's sons, Lionel and Fred, had the job of keeping the lawns mowed. Lionel for one was so fed-up sliding on chicken poop when he had to mow, "he vowed he would never have chickens on his farm . . . ever!" This was a promise to himself that he kept when he had his own farm years later.

In 1918, Mary Lawson (Hurd) and young Gifford[2] were back in Newport and stayed for the summer with Sarah, her sister, Sarah, and Gussie. She mentions in her letters later that summer that *"we have had some dandy rides in Gussie's car and we visited Cousin Cyrus Hurd's."* Mary states in her letter that *"wartime regulations are not allowing men to cross the line now, so even though we are only 23 miles from here to the border in Vermont, Gussie is not allowed over."*[21]

They were going to visit with her father, Edmund[8] Heard at Gussie and Sarah's farm and Mary mentioned that *"he has had some kind of accident to do with his eye which may have to be removed. He was fortunate not to have lost his life in this accident."* A few days later, in a letter written on August 21, Mary advised her husband Gifford[1]:

> *Papa has had a bad accident. He was working with Uncle Val' [Swail]'s helping hand, advising him about sinking and blasting rocks on a field of land, which Val wanted to plow. He set the fuse alight and waited and it did not explode so he thought it was not burning and was leaning over the fuse to relight it, when the powder exploded right into his face and the blast threw him back about 15 feet with rocks the size of a half bushel, down to splinters all around him. One eye looks to be destroyed, the other the Doctor hopes to be able to save. His face is badly bruised, but poor dear Papa, he is so patient. It was a miracle he was not killed. The Doctor thinks he may have to go to Montreal to have one eye removed if he cannot keep the inflammation down. I am washing out his eyes with a solution of boracic acid every hour to keep down the inflammation. Lionel and Gifford Jr. are at Jessies [Riddell] having a good time right now.*[21]

On August 24 Mary advised Gifford that *"Papa, is able to sit up. In a darkened room, his eyes are so weak and he is nearly blind in the one eye, hoping the other one will heal okay."* Their son Gifford Jr. was 8 years old on this day.

***

By 1918, under the War Measures Act, the manufacture and sale of intoxicating beverages were prohibited in Canada. By the 1920s era, Quebec had no temperance laws and those in the New England states seeking "relief" made the Eastern Townships their destination, resulting in unprecedented growth and prosperity. Liquor now selling in bottles was booming, along with their associated distilleries and filling plants.[48]

In 1918 new laws set by the government introduced rationing as a way of sharing food fairly. Sugar, meat, flour, butter and milk were all rationed so that everyone received what they needed. Each person had special ration cards which they had to present to a store when shopping for groceries. Once again farmers were better positioned than urban folk in that they had all the eggs, milk and butter they needed, so their rations cards pertained to mostly store-bought goods. Farm produce such as vegetables might be bartered for other goods, such as maple sugar, not available on certain farms.

Gifford Jr., Arthur H. and Fred K. Hurd (Hurd family collection)

During the summer of 1919, Mary and young Gifford, who was 9 years old, were again staying with Gussie and Sadie in Maple Leaf. By August 1919, Gifford Sr. left for Canada to be with his wife and son for a short vacation. He had been working for the Colonial Power and Light Company in Chicago, however, he appeared to be arranging for a new position. They had sold their house and were waiting to find out where they would be living.

In the immediate years after the First World War, as the men returned home from the front, women were sent home from the factories and businesses. Many women who had successfully worked in several occupations, doing jobs that had earlier been considered only appropriate for men, felt they had just lost their independence. Only single women were allowed to continue working, but once married they were to be considered housewives. Many still did work locally at various jobs but mostly in domestic roles and/or as caregivers.

***

By this time in 1919, the Spanish flu (also known as the 1918 flu pandemic) had become a worldwide epidemic. It was one of the deadliest influenzas in human history, estimated to have killed between 17 and 50 million people, possibly as high as 100 million people world-wide. At that time, communication to rural areas was by paper or teletype/telegraph (which was then mailed) and so our ancestors in Newport were hit hard mostly because many would not even know it was coming.

1918 Spanish flu pandemic, showing patients beds set up in an arena (Shutterstock)

The story of John and Jessie (Harrison) McCloud, who had bought the old James Prince farm in the Knicky Knocky region in 1905, was especially sad but so representative of the times everywhere. They were proud to own a double lot, feeling good about getting ahead in their lives but now their family was about to be hit hard by the pandemic. John was an excellent carpenter and had rebuilt the old house where he and Jessie were raising their seven children when the pandemic first hit in 1918. Dora, who was 11, and Bernice, who was 7, became sick for only about two days and died within five minutes of one another. Some uncles lived in the barn, doing the chores and bringing the available necessities to the house.[33]

Neighbours were not allowed near the family to help comfort them in their sorrow or in any other way. Later that winter the family, in their weakened condition, contracted whooping cough and then chickenpox. The family became so discouraged they sold the farm and moved to the "Lower Village" where John began working in Stokes' sash and door shop. This was a typical scene that reverberated all over the country during this time, when families were quarantined from each other as well as from their communities at large, and many were to find themselves like John and Jessie who had to start all over again.[33]

At the start of the pandemic people would not have known to keep a distance; in these closely knit communities helping take care of one another was the normal thing to do. This would have been yet another hurdle in the lives of our ancestors – i.e., to find a way to make things work in the face of adversity, including dealing with diphtheria, smallpox, measles and now this flu for which there was no cure or vaccine available at the time. These communities had always been used to working together as a whole, in a disciplined fashion to defeat whatever came their way, so in these times farming and local business would have carried on as usual despite the risks of becoming ill.

***

The Parker Hill schoolhouse was located on one corner of Charlie McCallum's farm, the original farm of Joseph and Mary Jane Parker a quarter-mile from the McCallum homestead. This farm was where their five children were raised: Ernie, Leslie, Stanley, Wilma and Colin. There were 21 "scholars" in September of 1919 and the teacher was Miss Evelyn Swail, the daughter of Valentine (Val) and Laura A. (Hurd) Swail. "An interesting fact prevailed as four of these scholars were our first cousins while nine others were our third cousins."[4,47] *(quote: Ernie McCallum)*

Author's note: The William Montgomery farm was located on the west side of Parker Hill Road. They raised two sons, Auvern "Vernie" and Charlie; both attended the Parker Hill school. Charlie married Gertrude "Gerty" Hatcher; they moved to the borough of Randboro and bought the small general store there. Most of the children living on Parker Hill – the McCallums, Montgomerys, Joneses, Specks, Desruisseaux and Parkers – would have started school in their earlier grades at the Parker Hill school.

Parker Hill community, circa 1910 (courtesy of McCallum family)

Auvern "Vernie" and Gladys Montgomery raised their four children – Graydon, Dalton, June and Paul – on the original homestead. George and Elva Speck's nine children – Lloyd, Carl, Pauline, Alma, Gerald, Everett, Ina, Rowena and Lois – were also raised on Parker Hill. Other children who attended the Parker Hill school in their early school years included Bill and Ilah Parker's children, Allen Parker's son Clayton, and Albert Desruisseaux's son Léon and daughters Lillian and Irene. The younger children were bused and finished their school years in the new consolidated school in Sawyerville.

Evelyn Swail, first teacher in Parker Hill school (Hurd family collection)

Some of these children walked two miles from home to school and were only 6 years old. When these half-frozen children reached school, they crowded around the pot-bellied stove to thaw out. On terribly windy and cold days, Miss Evelyn Swail would arrange the whole lot of them around the stove, with the littlest ones nearest the stove. She would teach the lessons as best she could. These schoolhouses were not insulated in any way and so the heat from the stove dissipated quite rapidly the further one was sitting away from it. Often the older children, who sat the furthest away from the stove, might begin to get chilled, their feet and hands cold from the drafty floor.[47]

It was a rugged life in this era but the children knew of no other and if anyone complained they would have constant reminders from their mothers, brothers and cousins that in *their* days there had been 45 scholars and one teacher; no desks, only benches; no paper and no pencils. "They only had slates and slate chalk with the slate held in one's lap and even more work to do once back at home as the land was being cleared and they all lived in log cabins."[47]

***

Marshall Newell W. Rand (1888-1939), son of Newell Clement Rand and Laura McCurdy, married Edith Mary Morrison (1889-1968), the older sister of Frank Morrison. They had four children in Newport: Lyle Ashley (born 1914), Clinton (born 1920), Hilda (born 1925) and Laura Edna, who died at birth.

Marshall and Edith lived with Marshall's parents for a time when they first married. Lyle was born on his grandfather Newell's homestead. Lyle was 4 years old when Marshall and Edith bought their own farm in 1919, just down the road at the corner of today's Route 210 and Morrison Road. When Newell's wife Laura died in 1913, John and Nellie Jones moved in with Newell for a time to help out before Newell married his cousin Flora Rand as his second wife.

Marshall Rand and Edith Morrison wedding portrait (courtesy of Carol Rand)

Author's note: Captain Edmund[6] and his family had first cleared this land; later his son, Capt. Edmund[7] and their family took over the farm and continued clearing the land, raising their families on the original homestead. "This is the clearing that the surveyor, David Thompson, had found in 1834, when he was trying to locate his supplies from the BALC and had them shipped to the Heard's place."[27] When Haskell Hurd built the new house in 1875, Austin Rand, Marshall's uncle, had helped with the building and had done most of the finishing work.

Edmund[8] Haskell Hurd was raised on this farm with his siblings, and he too had continued raising his family on the homestead. Haskell was 75 when he sold the farm in 1911 to Robert and Eva (Planche) Seale, who stayed only a short few years before they sold it to Marshall and Edith Rand circa 1919.

Friends, neighbours and family did not need an invitation to stop for tea at Marshall ("Marshie") and Edith's home, and overnight guests were just as welcome. "Charlie the Peddler" practiced his trade throughout Newport and Eaton townships and was a regular visitor at the home, always trying to find a way to stay overnight. He often would try to arrive there at mealtime, so Edith had to find ways to outmaneuver him. They often had a hired man who would also stay depending on how long he was needed, so Edith could often tell Charlie the house was full.[32]

The story is told that "At one time a hired man named Sam Laberee came to stay, and he always accompanied the family to church for Sunday Service. Sam was a bit of a rebel but also had some mental issues and so many in the community tried to help him along. And so, the story has been told that Sam would call out 'Praise the Lord' if he were moved by the minister's comments or prayers. Marshall felt it was inappropriate so he told Sam he would buy him new boots if he would stop calling out like that. Sam readily agreed, however, on one subsequent Sunday, Sam was so inspired he just could not resist. He called out 'boots or no boots, praise the Lord!'" *(Carol Rand)*

"[Sam's] maternal grandmother, Margaret Morrison Parker, was a large part of his life as a child, teenager and as a young man. She lived close by on the farm with her son Frank and his wife Mabel. She was often at Dad's home to give help with the household chores or whatever was needed." *(Carol Rand)*

Marshie and Edith had one of the few telephones in Maple Leaf. "Folks unfamiliar with the neighbourhood were often directed to the house by the side of the road if they needed to make a phone call." The telephone at that time housed the connective mechanism inside a two-foot wooden box. The box was usually placed on a wall, somewhere central in the house. The phone was positioned so that one would stand up to speak into a projected mouthpiece. Most people built a stool so that they could sit and talk. The box had two bells on the top face of the box, with a receiver on the side. When a call came in, the two bells would ring, perhaps a long and two short rings. Each home was assigned a different ring, so if that was your ring, you picked up the receiver and placed it to on your ear. Over time as more phones were installed the rings became the signal for everyone to stop what they were doing to see if the rings were for them. Of course, it was not uncommon for "snoopers" to carefully pick up the receiver and listen in, keeping their breathing to a minimum. It was also not uncommon for the people speaking to recognize different background noise and simply say, "Oh, Maud! Get off the phone!"

Lyle, Clinton, and Hilda Rand attended Maple Leaf School, along with Howard and Herbert Loveland, Arthur Hurd, and many other familiar names within the community of Maple Leaf. Often during the winter Lyle, the eldest, would ride to school on the snow roller driven by Frank Morrison. "In later years, after the little school had been sold in 1932 and Dad (Lyle) was a teenager, he drove a horse-drawn van carrying the 'scholars' to school in Sawyerville. Upon arrival and departure at the school, he fed, watered and cared for the horses and, unfortunately, missed first and last class each day." *(Carol Rand)*

Marshie and Edith worked the farm for many years as the children were growing up, lumbering in the winter months as with most of the farmers in the community. The Depression was having an adverse effect on all the farmers during the period leading up to Marshall's death, and while they ate well, there was no money available for purchasing other than what was entirely necessary.

Because of their frugal backgrounds, farmers knew how to survive on truly very little, and their children and families were brought up carrying this same trait. As it was in the past, family and community were everything and people banded together to lend a helping hand.

Lyle, Clinton and Hilda Rand harvesting potatoes (courtesy of Carol Rand)

Planting potatoes was a family affair. Lyle began by marking the rows, while Clinton spread fertilizer from a pail. A few days earlier, Edith would have retrieved some 200 potatoes from the cellar and cut them so each had at least two "eyes." The eyes were the protruding sprouts that that would become the tops, which when mature would blossom, producing caches of potatoes in the root system. Lyle would follow the rows, dropping a "seed piece" every 12-14 inches. Marshall would hitch up a horse and cultivator and cover them up. Each seed piece planted would produce about a dozen potatoes. At this time, Hilda would have most likely been playing with another friend, but as she got older she too would have been assigned one of the jobs.

As with all children, time is marked and measured in different ways, changing the landscape of their lives. Just as this family would come to bear the unbearable and respond to the challenges before them, some things would alter their lives forever. They took solace from the community they and their forefathers had forged before them, in a land often harsh and unforgiving. They too would find ways to adapt.

***

Gussie Hurd had a huge woodworking shop along with blacksmith facilities where he made iron and wood farm and lumbering tools. This building was between the house and the chicken coop. When he was working in his shop, he was continuously harassed by Sarah's chickens trying to get into his shop and so he too had a dim view of poultry in general. Their youngest son, Arthur, was several years younger than his two older brothers, Lionel and Fred, and so was somewhat like an only child when growing up.

Arthur was a great delight for his mother Sarah (Sadie) while he was growing up as she could now spend more time enjoying doing things that she could not have done with her two older boys. When Arthur was young, he took great delight in playing with various pieces of farm equipment.[31]

Arthur Hurd, 1919 (Hurd Family collection)

Many children who are alone because of age differences or are an only child learn to pretend and visualize, making their own fun. Arthur was no different. It was not uncommon for Arthur to use any idle farm equipment as part of a prop. He perhaps might have imagined himself as he is in the photograph opposite, as a gunner in World War I.

***

Author's note: Another family connecting the Parker/Morrison/Rand and Swail families of Newport: Mabel Seale was the daughter of Alfred and Luna Myrtilla (Rand) Seal. Luna was a daughter of Stillman and Celeste Rand of Randboro.

Mabel (Seale) and Frank Morrison (courtesy of Carol Rand)

Frank Morrison married Mabel Seale and had two children, Phyllis and Malcolm. In a letter written by Laura (Hurd) Swail on July 30, 1933, she mentions *"they had a little son, only three weeks old, a beautiful baby."*[21]

Surnames resulting from this marriage are Morrison, Dempsey and Lister.

Frank and Mabel Morrison lived on Morrison Road, halfway between the Auckland Town Line and today's Route 210, on the farm Frank had inherited from his mother, Margaret (Young Morrison) Parker. They raised a mixed herd of Shorthorn cattle and some sheep and pigs. The Shorthorn breed was a first choice during this period: they were very hardy, they produced milk and cream, and were good beef animals. Mabel raised turkeys, chickens and geese for both meat and eggs.

By 1920 many of the neighbourhood farmers were selling cream. It was picked up each morning by the cream truck and taken to the creamery in Sawyerville, which replaced the cheese/creamery in Randboro. By two o'clock in the afternoon a box car, loaded with cans of cream, all packed in ice, would be picked up by a freight train and delivered to its destination in Boston, 250 miles away, before the next morning. The price for cream in 1920 averaged 38 cents per pound, calculated in butter fat. Railways were now weaving themselves throughout the country, providing new markets both in selling and purchasing opportunities for the inhabitants of Newport and surrounding townships.

Most farmers raised turkeys, chickens and geese, and the chore of feeding and taking care of them would often become the responsibility of the children. Young fowl took a lot of care until they were able to fend for themselves, but once grown they would forage for themselves during the day, usually returning to the "chicken house" in the evening to roost. As it is with most livestock, food was the most likely persuasive factor; the fowl enticed by the outlay of corn provided by Mabel or the children. Geese also provided a source of down which they would use for pillows and quilts. Frank and Mabel could always sell dressed turkeys and geese, bringing in either income or trade for other goods.

Frank Morrison augmented his income by working with other farmers for the BALC on the local roads. The BALC was the entity that extracted both bridge and road taxes directly during this time. Frank become the first curator of the Compton County Historical Museum at Eaton Corner, where many loaned and donated artifacts from the immediate area would be placed on display.

Author's note: Phyllis Morrison married Gordon Dempsey; they lived in Sawyerville next to the United Church manse. They had one child, Donna Dempsey, who married Elton Lister. They moved back to Newport Township where they raised their children at the corner of Grove Hill Road and the road to North River. The farm became generally known as the Dempsey place. This farm on Lot 1 of Range 9, was originally the farm of William Sawyer (MLA for Compton County), the grandson of Capt. Josiah[4] Sawyer, founder of Sawyers Mills (Sawyerville). Their son Michael Lister is the current owner of the original Tannahill farm, which became the Bailey farm in the later 1950s, on Tannahill Road in Newport. This is where the original Maple Leaf schoolhouse is currently located.

Phyllis and Hilda (Rand) Berwick were of similar age and were best friends from childhood until Phyllis died suddenly quite a few years before Hilda's death. Hilda grew up on the farm at the corner of today's Route 210 and Morrison Road. Hilda was the daughter of Frank's sister Edith (Morrison) who had married Marshall Rand. *(Carol Rand)*

***

Alonzo and Eva (Robinson) Hurd (courtesy of granddaughter Gillian (Hurd) Anderson)

Alonzo George[9] Hurd, son of George[8] Gibson Hurd, (lineage: Luke[7], Edmund[6] Heard/Hurd) was born in Newport in 1882. He married Evelyn "Eva" Frances Robinson, who was born in Eaton Township, the daughter of James and Selina Robinson. Alonzo and Eva farmed for several years on the farm where he had grown up –the original Col. Edmund[5] and Luke[7] Heard farm on lots 6 and 7 on the 10th Range in Newport. They lived for a few years on the farm where he had grown up, however Alonzo's heart was in the business world.

Alonzo was educated at Maple Leaf School and Sawyerville Model School, then later attended Belleville Business College. He sold the farm to Fred French, circa 1917, as he had become heavily involved in other business activities and the family moved to Sawyerville in Eaton Township. The property went up for sale again in April 1932 and was purchased by Joseph and Jessie (Hurd) Riddell – and so the original Col. Edmund[5] and Luke[2] Heard/Hurd land remained in the Hurd family for a few more years.[4, 31]

Alonzo and Frances "Eva" had three children: George Robinson (born 1913), (Bertha) Evelyn (born 1916) and Eric James, born in Sawyerville in 1920. On hot summer days and especially on Sunday afternoons, Alonzo and Eva would take toddlers George and Evelyn, along with others from the Maple Leaf settlement, to enjoy a picnic and the swimming hole on the South Branch of the Eaton River along the meadows of this farm. Many from the Maple Leaf community went swimming in the summer in various spots on the river.

Eva learned to sew at an early age, which proved of great benefit economically and for a certain amount of pleasure. She made almost all their own clothes, not just dresses and coats but also hats. She and their daughter Evelyn would not feel fully dressed without a hat as was the custom. She made clothes for George, Evelyn and Eric and was proud to say they were often made of used materials. She would cut the clothes down or turn the material over, using clothes George had grown out of for Eric's use. She prided herself in her ability to remake lovely dresses for Evelyn from store-bought clothes. When making something over, she always took it apart and carefully washed and pressed each piece. Leftover scraps of material were made into quilts.

Alonzo Hurd was active in local business and municipal affairs and had bought the local electric plant in Sawyerville in April 1910. He later sold the plant to Southern Canada Power Company (later acquired by Hydro Quebec).

1937 hearse owned by Henry Phelps (courtesy of Melody (Knapp) Campagna)

Eric French, Alonzo and Eva's grandson, recalls: "Eaton Electric was located further down the river, below Bill Faulkner's place. When I was a child, I remember that there was a barn-like, weather-beaten house inhabited by the Royers. At the river, there were the concrete and iron remains of a shaft and the water wheel/generator. Uncle George Hurd (Alonzo's eldest son) operated the mortuary out of the white 'Hurd' house for a time. I also remember the 'Black Mariah' funeral car in the shed housing at the back of the building. There were all sorts of discarded Eaton Electric invoices in the dilapidated storage boxes." (Eric G. R. French)

Alonzo was also secretary-treasurer and one of the principal shareholders of Dudswell Electric Company, which was sold to Shawinigan Water and Power Company (also later acquired by Hydro Quebec); he was secretary-treasurer of the Village of Sawyerville; mayor of the Village of Sawyerville; and founder of the Sawyerville Manufacturing Company Ltd. circa 1920.[4] He died in 1941 at age 59.

> I remember Grandpa (Rob) French telling me (with tears in his eyes) about an incident between him and Grandpa Alonzo. The two were discussing the refusal of the Baptist Church congregation to sell the parcel of land behind the Baptist parsonage to the Compton County Protestant School Board so that they could build a new school. At the time Grandpa French was the mayor of Newport and Grandpa Hurd may have been on the Sawyerville town council and/or school board. Grandpa Hurd was upset at what appeared to be a lack of civic-mindedness on the part of the Baptists (Grandpa French being a Baptist). Alonzo got off a cheap chippy shot at him in a fit of temper, 'That's those Christians for you.' I think Grandpa French was also upset at the Baptist intransigence – hence his emotion. (Eric. R. French, grandson)

***

Shortly after the 1895 Sawyerville mill fire, George Matthew had bought the property from the Cookshire Mill Company and built a new mill in Sawyerville which operated for many more years as a lumber mill, along with the sash and door factory and the gristmill on either side of Flanders Road. The dam had created a large lake which ran upriver as far as Munn's farm at the border of Eaton and Newport townships.

Brothers George, Robert (Rob) and Tom Matthew are pictured in the sash and door factory photo opposite. George had gone to the Klondike earlier, as had many others, seeking the opportunity to mine gold. The venture had been quite successful for George and his group. Unfortunately, when George returned to his claim a year later, in 1920, he succumbed to pneumonia.

Three Matthew brothers at the Sawyerville sash and door factory: Tom on the left, at the shuttle; Rob and George on the left and right respectively of the sawdust collector (courtesy of George and Mamie Matthew family)

Everyone knew his wife "Mamie" (Ord) Matthew, who continued to manage the mill for several years. In her later years, those who grew up in the 1950s would remember Mamie managing the J. A. Lowry Store for Jim Lowry in Sawyerville.

Bert Trombley, who was farming in Newport at the time and was also an avid lumberman and contractor, purchased the mills from Mamie Matthew. Bert operated the mills for several years and had further branched out as a contractor building houses; however, he lost the mills through bankruptcy. Alonzo Hurd seized the opportunity and became the new owner of the mills circa the mid-1920s as the Spanish Flu epidemic had begun to subside. His operations consisted of two businesses: a sawmill, on the right of Flanders Road, and a sash and door operation, which became the Sawyerville Manufacturing Company, on the left.

The original gristmill operation of Capt. Josiah[4] Sawyer was also still running during this period and still owned by his grandson William[6] Sawyer. William served as MLA for Compton County from 1871 to 1886.

> *Author's note: William was in his early 80s in 1896 and I have been unable to find any documentation as to who took over the gristmill into the 1900s. I suspect his wife may have continued the business for a time; however, as they had no children, the operation may have passed on to others of the Sawyer family or sold outright. In a letter dated 1933 from Sarah Hurd, she mentions that "Deacon Sawyer used to run the mill and Allen Worby had run the shop on the opposite side of the river for a time."*

Alonzo Hurd's sister, Julia Lois Hurd, daughter of George[8] Gibson Hurd, (lineage: Luke[7], Edmund[6] Heard/Hurd), was born in Randboro in 1893. In 1918 she married Lloyd Herbert Hunt. Lloyd was born in Sawyerville in 1891, the son of Herbert Henry Hunt and Henrietta Goodenough of Cookshire. Julia was a graduate of Macdonald College and became a schoolteacher. She was an ardent pianist and volunteered for many years as church organist. Lloyd was a merchant who owned and operated Hunt's Store and served as mayor of Sawyerville for several terms. They had two sons: Bruce H., who married Charlotte M. Whitcomb; and Gordon George, who married Jean A. Robinson, daughter of Alfred Herbert and Helen Robinson. Alfred Robinson was the postmaster in Sawyerville for many years.

Surnames originating from the marriage of Julia and Lloyd are Hunt and Prah.

***

The culture in the 1920s in urban communities allowed for single women to work; however, once married they were expected to bring up their children and essentially had to leave the workplace and become wholly dependent on their husbands' endeavors, whatever they might be. The most significant departure from this culture was in the farming communities. Women, single or married, were included as an integral part of the workplace whether in the house, the barn or the fields. They were considered equally important and valued as any other part of the family. The children were an extension of that culture, all working together for the advancement and enjoyment of the family as a whole. The cultural differences between urban and rural had an enormous and positive impact on the work habits of rural children of this generation.[31]

During these years (circa the 1920s) in the Maple Leaf community, not unlike in previous times, neighbours would help each other out in the fields and barns with seasonal activities like haying and harvesting. The younger children were brought together to play at each other's homes while essential work was done. Sometimes older children looked after the younger ones, which allowed both parents to work the farm chores. Marshie (Rand) would bring his "hay tedder" to work the hay at Gussie's, as he did for Arthur Loveland, the Willards and many of the other farmers when needed.

A hay tedder fluffed the hay, allowing it to dry much faster than if it was left in swathes. And so, Lionel, Frederick and Arthur Hurd were an extension to all the other families of Maple Leaf as were the other families to them. They grew up together, played and worked together, and each family looked after each other's children whenever the need was there. This community spirit had not changed since their ancestors settled there in 1793 and was the glue that kept these families together through their losses and their disappointments, but equally importantly the community shared their good times too.

Fred on his bike, Lionel with his horse Barnie, and Arthur Hurd on his wagon (Hurd family collection)

With the introduction of horse-drawn rakes and hay loaders, the haying process became less labour-intensive and allowed the farmer better efficiencies. The manpower required for hay gathering was greatly reduced. This added mechanism meant that farmers, including Gussie, could cultivate more fields and harvest and store more hay for winter. He began clearing the lot and selling the lumber across the road from the house down to his sugar bush on today's Route 210. Farms would once again be cleared of lumber to provide more land for cultivation as farms began to grow larger with additional livestock. These newly cleared lands would initially become pastures, allowing for more grazing areas during the spring, summer and fall for cattle, horses and sheep. After a few years, once the stumps and rocks were removed, these newly cleared pasture lands became new cultivatable fields, producing hay. The farmers of this era initiated a crop rotation system whereby the fields and pastures were changed over every three or four years. The pastures may be fertilized and planted with oats or barley for the first year, followed by corn a second year, followed by red clover for silage, and finally timothy for hay for a couple of years before rotating back to pasture lands. This promoted better crops as each field was rotated in a timely fashion. Farms were starting to become more sophisticated; it was the beginning of the family farm being operated more like a business.

Gussie and Lionel Hurd would often bring in 10 loads of hay in a day, while the younger children might play together at another farm. It was during these early days that Fred and Arthur would spend time with Edith (Morrison) Rand, who might be spending part of her day picking berries or some other necessary outdoor task. Fred would watch over the younger children as Arthur, Lyle and Clinton played together, which allowed Edith time alone to do her chores. Likewise, the Rand children would often go to Gussie's and play with Arthur on these many occasions, while Sarah took care of the children so that Lionel and Fred could help with the haying. It was during these times when families all over Newport bonded together doing the same activities and became lifelong friends.

Loading hay with a hay loader, an important step towards mechanization of haying (P. Charpentier, BAnQ)

Gussie and Sarah's eldest son, Lionel, now a young teenager, often went to his Uncle Joe and Jessie Riddell's farm to help with their haying. Unlike Gussie's barn, Joe's was equipped with the new "hayfork" system, that operated on a track and allowed them to unload in quick fashion; each hayfork bundle could now be deposited towards the far end of a haymow. The pulleys themselves were all made of hardwood (handmade locally on a lathe) and attached to metal housings made by the local "smithy."

Lionel would hook the horses to a large hemp rope that led to a pully system allowing the horses to pull this large forkful of hay from the wagon up to the track. When it connected to the wheeled track mechanism, the load would careen down the track with the load to the mows at the end of the barn. Once there, an operator would trip the fork mechanism with a long rope, and the hay mound would drop into the haymow.

The process was not easy as the driver of the horses had to anticipate the moment when the load reached the track – the horses would be pulling hard when all of a sudden there would be no tension; the driver had to be ready to immediately haul back on the reins to stop the horses. The process, however, was far easier on both man and horses than hauling a wagon full of hay up a ramp to the second-level barn floor like on his father's farm. This is perhaps where the expression "Hold your horses!" comes from, although this expression was used widely in many other circumstances of general conversation.

Typical hayfork hay lift, utilizing rope and pulleys, powered by horses (Newport Homecoming 1801-1996)

Edmund[10] Lionel Hurd on his horse Barnie (Hurd family collection)

Gussie and the boys prided themselves on their ability with horses; horsemanship was a very important skill for the men of this era. It was essential to know how to maneuver the horses – whether around stumps when logging, or when pulling a load of logs across a river, or when haying or harvesting. When collecting stooks of grain, the horses had to stop and start between the stooks to allow the men on each side of a wagon time to pitch up a forkful. Over time, the horses began to figure it out on their own, which proved that good horsemanship meant that man and his horse acted as one. Most farmers thought of their horses as friends and talked to them continuously when harnessing them up. Not all men or women were good with horses: some had a knack, while for others just putting on the harness could be a chore that one might never forget. Lionel was one who had that knack and his handling of horses served him well for many years.[31]

***

The following excerpt is derived from a call to service dated March 19, 1771:

> *It is recommended as a Christian Duty incumbent on every Planter that remains at Home, to take care of, and assist to the utmost of his Abilities the Families of those Men who go on this Service, that neither their families nor plantations may suffer while they are employed on a Service where the Interest of the whole is concerned.*[3]

This call to service goes back as far as the earliest days of the United Empire Loyalists and continued as an integral part of military conscription. Some, unable to serve due to handicaps by previous service or age, either too young or old, were required to serve in different ways.

During the First World War (1914-18), the author's father, Edmund[10] Lionel Hurd (1907-2001), listed in the census as farmer, was too young to enlist, yet he was expected to follow the "call to service" as stated above. The farmers who went to war often left children, spouses or handicapped family members with the difficult task of carrying on during their absence. The "Soldiers of the Soil" were these younger boys who extended the care of their own farms to many neighbouring farms, far exceeding the normal expectation of maintaining their own domestic crops. They were expected to plant a crop to support the war effort, delivering that crop to the nearest railway station. In recognition of this service, at the end of the war Edmund[10] Lionel Hurd received a "Soldier of the Soil" badge, no. NL211-15, issued by the Canada Food Board.

Author's note: My understanding is that this badge is exceedingly rare. Issuing these badges would have been considered the natural thing to do in recognition of those who stayed at home yet conscientiously and energetically supported the war effort. This badge represents his service on the home front during the First World War. When the Second World War began, these same younger men became of age to enlist in this war as did my father. These badges were probably not keepsakes, but my father kept his. It is now part of the military artifacts in the Hurd Military Collection and has been placed alongside his Second World War medals of Honour for service in the Pacific War.

Lionel Hurd's Soldier of the Soil badge

***

Many an evening was spent studying the stars and the moon while stories were told. Children listened to these stories with great rapture and would remember them to retell when they themselves had children; there was none better than the real-life story of Bill McCallum of Randboro.[36]

Some of our settlers of Scottish and Irish descent brought with them a distinct culture and folklore. Legends and tales from "the old sod" were quite literally uprooted and replanted in a new land. While the setting was different, the characters and main elements were the same. Irish immigration to Lower Canada peaked during the Potato Famine of 1845 to 1852. Some had arrived earlier as part of the British plan to resettle the Irish "have-nots or poor," as they had been referenced at the time, in the North American colonies. Some were also seeking refuge in a new land as had our forefathers in the early 1700s. Canada experienced the arrival of many Irish and Scottish families from that era, who had settled in other parts of Lower Canada and had become established. Now many of their children were seeking new opportunities elsewhere and Newport was not immune to a new influx of Irish and Scottish settlers from these earlier settlements as well as directly from "across the pond."

Was he a miracle worker, a mystic, or a totally unique performer? Was he a charlatan, a purveyor of black magic, a super magician, or a slight-of-hand artist, or all these things? He was just a humble, self-educated, ordinary man, living a mundane life in the quite hamlet of Randboro. He was obviously an entirely unique individual, unpretentious and self-effacing, who, when he found he possessed strange powers, modestly used them to impress but most of all to fascinate. The man was William "Bill" McCallum, a town character in Randboro and surrounding communities who provided everyone with a wealth of conversational topics. His singular exploits became legend.[36]

Bill McCallum; note the bottle nailed to the tree (Eastern Townships Roots)

Bill McCallum was of Scottish ancestry, born in 1875 on Île Brion in the Magdalen Islands just off Prince Edward Island and Nova Scotia's Cape Breton. Bill had a bad fall as a child causing serious injury to his right leg. Infection had set in and he was treated by a horse doctor lured to their isolated home. The boy was strapped to the kitchen table while the well-meaning practitioner, with no anesthetic, scraped the bone, resulting in inhibited bone growth. Bill's right leg remained seven inches shorter that his left. Eventually Bill was able to fashion a seven-inch sole to his right shoe and was able to maneuver quite well with the aid of a crutch or cane.[36]

Author's note: The building in the background of the photograph opposite is the store Samuel[7] Heard operated for over 23 years. It was later owned by Charlie and Gerty Montgomery who ran it for many years, well into the 1950s, followed by the Mackay family.

It appears it was while working at a fish cannery doing repair work that Bill first learned of his unusual ability. While working on some windows, he noticed that the nails he used to fix the wooden frames would sometimes penetrate the glass. And so, Bill simply nailed the glass to the frames and discarded the putty normally used to hold the glass in place. From then on, Bill just knew he was "different" from most.

Bill came to Newport in 1921. His brother Charlie and Charlie's wife Lottie (Parker) were concerned about Bill's handicap, and had made a special visit to his birthplace inviting Bill to share their home, a farm on Parker Hill near Randboro. This was welcome news to the younger McCallums, for they knew of their Uncle Bill's talent with the violin; now they would have their own fiddler for Saturday night dances. Soon after his arrival they were to witness something far more outstanding than they could have ever imagined.[47]

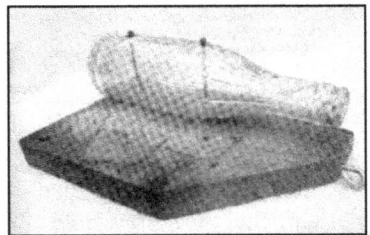

A Coke bottle nailed by Bill McCallum

Down by the sugar bush, the McCallums had a dump, a repository for the household trash. They soon noted it was being decorated by empty pickle bottles and patent medicine bottles, mysteriously nailed to the surrounding trees. They were also noticing pieces of glass nailed to the veranda posts, door frames and almost everywhere. One day, when the large kitchen mirror was broken, they were surprised to find that it was soon back in place, like a jig saw puzzle, each piece nailed in its proper place to form the complete mirror.[36]

Bill was, however, reluctant to perform "on demand" but would be quite disturbed if a viewer judged his actions with glass as a trick or sleight of hand. To dissuade an observer who suspected trickery, Bill would use any type of glass, whether a beer bottle, plate glass, light bulb, or a thin wine glass; he would pick up a rock or hammer and simply drive a nail through it, pinning the glass piece to another piece of wood. Over time he found that he could easily push a railway spike through both sides of a bottle or drive a glass wedge through other pieces of glass with his hands.[36]

A regular bottle with nails Bill McCallum simply pushed through with his hands, circa late 1930s

Townspeople walking to church on a quiet Sunday morning, on one occasion, soon realized that Bill must have been peeved at something the night before. They noticed that every telephone pole on the street had a beer bottle nailed to it at eye level. This was just one of Bill's way of showing displeasure. Soon there were bottles nailed everywhere and people started taking them down to collect them. Just as quickly as they were removed, new ones would replace them.

His unusual ability with glass was soon so commonplace that it began to fail to even arouse curiosity from the local communities. Bill would always say "the imps made me do it," and so when Bill and the "imps" were in sync, glass seemed to lose its fragile character and any outside observers were left mystified. Many stories abound about Bill "The Glass Man."

Author's note: Samples of his works had been analyzed by technical laboratory experts in the field of glass making at Domglas Ltd. of Montreal with no concrete conclusion. It was confirmed that this was the first and only time that such a phenomenon had ever come to their attention and "we still do not know how it was done." Bill McCallum has been written up in the Guinness Book of Records. Many have tried to figure out how he did it; no one has succeeded.[36]

And so, the story has been told by Lyle Rand who worked for Hurd's Meat Market for many years, that when they needed a new smokehouse for curing meats to be built, they gave the job to Bill. Bill did the job with his usual dexterity, but there was one added extra not called for in the plans. They were somehow not surprised to find a beer bottle neatly nailed to an interior wall, just Bill's trademark to say; "I was here." *(Carol Rand)*

When a local garageman, Emard Hurley, needed a hole to be made in glass, he would take the object to a shop in Sherbrooke where this was accomplished using a diamond-tipped drill. When it was learned that Bill could perform the same thing with a nail and hammer, Emard no longer needed to make the costly trip to Sherbrooke. When the former supplier questioned the reason for his loss of business, and a sample was presented, their retort was that such a hole could only be made with a diamond drill. Highly miffed and to settle the matter, Bill drove a square rod through a piece of glass, had it sent to the doubting former supplier, along with a simple request, "Ask him to drill a square hole."[36]

It was not long before their Uncle Bill became known in the small community as the "Glass Man." "A few days after Christmas 1946, Bill told his brother, Charlie, that he would die in two days . . . and he did, bringing to an end a colourful episode in the regions of Randboro and Sawyerville, writing a *"finis"* to the sometimes-bizarre activities of a most unusual character."[36]

As important to our heritage were the many "stories" that were told over and over again to whomever became a new audience. Both young and old delighted to sit around the kitchen with its wood stove and listen with rapture as these stories became legends. If one saw a twinkle in the eyes, you would know a story would soon be told, and for anyone listening, they would have to decide for themselves if the story were true or not. Regardless of the authenticity, the story would undoubtedly be retold and perhaps embellished to add zest to the scene.

***

The children of Charles and Charlotte Loveland had long grown up and moved out of Newport, married, and started their own families. Their son Roy (1885-1963) married Eleanor Lobdell and left Newport. Their son Charles Victor (1891-1917) participated in the "harvest excursion" for a couple of years, taking the CPR train to Medicine Hat, Alta. He decided to live in Alberta where he joined the militia, was sent overseas, and died during the war in 1917. Mildred (1889-1994) married Herman Lowry; they took over the original homestead of William[2] Loveland and Eliza (Beaman), later retiring and moving to Sawyerville.

> *Author's note: William[2] Loveland and Eliza (Beaman) had three children who died as infants. Their eldest son, J. Victor[1], died at 23 years old in 1891 in a farm accident. William[3] took over the farm, however, he died at 32 years old in 1902. Eliza stayed on and her granddaughter Mildred, and Herman Lowry took over the farm.*

Charlie and Charlotte Loveland's son George (1886-1983) also joined one of the annual CPR harvest excursions, travelling to Alberta to a ranch where he met and married Mary Millar. Mary had been born and raised in Island Brook; she was a daughter of Alexander Millar and granddaughter of James and Mary Millar. Her family had moved to Alberta in 1911-12. Mary was working on a nearby ranch with the many other women who participated in this part of the annual harvest excursion. Their job was to prepare meals with the ranchers' wives – cooking breakfast, dinner and supper for the many crews working the fields. George and Mary purchased a ranch near her parents and farmed there for several years before moving back east to Sawyerville to retire with their daughter Shirley.

Charles and Charlotte Loveland's daughter, Ruth (1893-1992), married Arthur Ward and moved to Eaton Township.

Their youngest son, Arthur (1895-1987), married Nora Parsons who was living in the village of Bury. Nora was the daughter of Herbert William Parsons and his wife Bertha (Mayhew). After they married, Arthur and Nora continued to farm on the original homestead of his parents, taking care of Charlie and Charlotte after they retired. *(ref.: Nina (Parsons) Rowell)*

***

John "Irvin" and Ruth Lillian Graham, the fifth daughter of William and Hannah Graham, raised one son in Newport. They lost two other sons, Aubrey and Donald, in infancy. William[2] "Billy" John Graham was born in 1921 in Randboro. The Graham family lived on the subdivided original farm of Artemas[6] and Louisa S. Rand, who had worked with the original Heard and Associates in the land development of Newport in 1796-1814. The Graham families farmed and raised three generations of families on this farm. John and Ruth are buried in Maple Leaf Cemetery in Newport Township. John's parents are also both buried in Maple Leaf Cemetery: William died at age 51 in 1927; Hannah died at age 100 in 1964. *(Carolyn (Graham) Grapes family history)*

***

Albert Riddell was the youngest son of James and Jane (Docherty) Riddell. Albert (1876-1934) and Mary (Rand) Riddell (1879-1928) first settled in the New Mexico settlement in Newport Township, circa 1920, clearing more of the land, started mixed farming with Shorthorn cattle, some pigs, and a few sheep. There was an abundance of wild berries on these farms after the first round of clearing that had taken place in earlier times. Albert and Mary had no children of their own, but they loved children and often invited the neighbouring children to accompany them picking berries on the flats where the land had been recently cleared. They grew turnips, potatoes, oats, barley and buckwheat, while the rest of the cleared land was in hay. In late fall they always spread the manure that was in a pile near the barn from the past winter over their gardens and fields as fertilizer.

Albert and Mary fashioned a sled with low sides that they would hand-fill with a "manure fork," a five-pronged wider-style fork with a short handle. Once filled, the horses would pull the sled to the fields where they hand-pitched the manure on each side of the sled, spreading it lightly over a large area. They made a pattern of this, going back and forth until either the manure was finished or the field was complete. Farmers in the region might spread as many as 30 loads in a week-long spreading session. This was the method of fertilization on all the farms in the past and continuing throughout this era. No chemical fertilizers were purchased.

Albert Riddell and Mary Rand wedding portrait (courtesy of Carol Rand)

Wild Canadian plums sometimes grew on these farms, perhaps along a stone wall. They were called "pound sweets." As part of an outing on a Sunday, Albert, Mary and their neighbours and the children from the area would spend the afternoon picking plums. The plums were cooked and mixed with maple syrup and made into preserves for use as a sauce in the winter. Another common local fruit was chokecherries, which grew wild usually along brooks or wetlands. Most were red, however on some farms they were plum-coloured, and these were considered the sweetest. Chokecherries were made into chokecherry jelly. Children were led to believe that if they ate chokecherries and then drank milk, they could choke. The author believed this to be a tale initiated so that we children wouldn't eat everything we picked. However, curiosity prevailed; one day he was brave enough to test out the theory and found it to be false.

Albert and Mary Riddell sold their farm in New Mexico and purchased the William and Eliza (Beaman) Loveland homestead on the 9th Range from Herman and Mildred Loveland where they lived until they retired to Sawyerville.

***

Author's note: An earlier branch of the Planche family children had moved from Leeds Township. Three Planche brothers had married three Hurd sisters and a Hurd son had married a Planche daughter. Further generations would be reconnected, becoming the fifth Hurd and Planche family connection. Since the family moved out of Newport, my intention in expanding the ancestral lines is to simply identify the connections so a reader may see where the sixth and final connection reverted back to the Hurd families of Newport.

Kate Marie Hurd (1883-1950) was born in Cookshire, Eaton Township, the first daughter of Frederick[8] Augustine Hurd (lineage: Tyler[7], Edmund[6]) and his first wife, Hattie Eva Davis (1858-1892). In 1905, Kate Marie married Lloyd Leslie Planche (1884-1939), Henry[1] A. Planche's son who had also been born in Cookshire.

Lloyd Leslie and Kate Marie (Hurd) Planche (courtesy of Sandra Hurd)

Lloyd Planche's father, Henry, had owned the general store (later sold to Mr. Casavant) and the flour mill (later sold to Mr. Standish) in Cookshire. When the general store went bankrupt during the Depression, Lloyd first worked for Harry Moe in the garage at Main and Craig streets. In later years, Lloyd Leslie and his family operated the garage on the corner of Main and Craig Street South for many years. The three houses across the park on Main Street belonged to members of the Planche family. Edward built the house at the top of the hill; a cousin John, a harness maker, had a harness shop downstairs in the next house; and Edward's daughter Ada lived in the third house. Arthur Planche owned the former Charlie Fraser house on Craig Street South.

During the 1930s, George Gill, who married Leslie and Kate's daughter Phyllis, owned a garage located next to a building owned by Standish on Craig Street North.

There were many Planche families, all descendants of the JP Planche family of Leeds and Newport but living in Cookshire during this era. They were generally known as the "Planches of Cookshire."

Lloyd Leslie and Kate Marie Planche had seven children, two boys and five girls: Desmond Lloyd, Harriet Aline, Phyllis Edith, Lois Elsie, Norma Evangeline, Laura Alice and Frederick Henry[2] "Harry." Their firstborn son, Desmond, born in 1906, died in infancy. The other children were all raised in Cookshire. Their eldest daughter, Harriet (1909-1946), married William (Bill) W. Parker; they had one son, Peter Lloyd.

George Gill's Model A Ford converted into a snowmobile in front of his garage, circa 1930

Phyllis (1911-1984) married George Westley Gill and raised five children, all born in Cookshire: Laura Mary, Edith Jenniss, John Westley, Georgina Ann and Robert George.

Lois (1913-1999) married John Mitchell; they had two daughters: Ola May, born in Cookshire, and Pamela Ann, born in Sherbrooke. Lois married, as her second husband, Harold Clout; they had a daughter, Linda Kathryn, born in Espanola, Ont., and a son, Harry Donald, born in Marathon, Ont.

Norma (1916-1974) moved to and worked in Drummondville, Que. She remained unmarried. Sometime after her father Lloyd Leslie's death in 1939, her mother, Kate Marie, came to live with her, where she died in 1950.

Laura (1918-1989) married Charles Leidy[1] Blair. Their family of three were born and raised in Drummondville: daughter Sandra Kathryn (born 1943), son Michael Andrew (born 1945) and son Charles Leidy[2] (1953-2017).

Harry (1924-1996) married Edmee M. A. Tessier. They had five children: John Paul[3], born in 1952 in Montreal; Sharon Marie, born in 1953 in Red Deer, Alta.; Peter Michael (1955-2017) and John Robert (1957-2008), both born in St. Jean, Que.; and Valerie Anne, born in 1961 in Middleton, N.S.

Lloyd and Kate (Hurd) Planche family. Standing: L-R: Aline, Phyllis, Norma. Seated: L-R: Laura, Lloyd Leslie, Harry (standing between his parents), Kate Marie, and Lois. (courtesy of Sandra (Blair) Hurd)

Author's note: Laura and Leidy Blair's daughter, Sandra Kathryn (Blair), married Frederick Edmund[11] Hurd (the author). Ironically, both are direct descendants of Col. Edmund[5] Heard. Fred is also a descendant of Capt. Josiah[4] Sawyer. This marriage would be the sixth connection of Heard/Hurd/Planche families now in the 11th generation.[4]

A regular visitor to the Planche's home was "Charlie the Peddler" who usually planned to stay overnight. Charlie loved children and always made it his business to try to stay overnight in many of the homes, probably because he knew what the children would enjoy. He packed his suitcase appropriately with wares before each house visit; he already knew from his last visit that there would be something the children wanted. The children could hardly wait for morning to come when

Charlie would unpack his huge suitcase with everything from underwear, socks, shirts, sweets and perhaps the occasional toy. His motto was "You name it, I have it" and if he did not have it, you could be sure he would have it on his next trip. Lloyd always bought something for every member of the family.[31]

***

The northwestern and central section of Newport:

Levi Lyon was a hard worker; a farmer, millwright, carpenter, and most of all an ardent gardener, always trying one new item each year. His wife Lucy was a homemaker, mother, nurse, seamstress and tailor of both men's and women's clothing. Lucy bought wool from her neighbours who raised sheep, carded the wool, spun the yarn, and knit wool socks, caps, leggings and even homespun skirts. Lucy even made men's wool pants by weaving the various materials on her loom, sketching out a pattern and sewing the legs together. The pants, tucked into high boots with a couple pairs of socks, made for a warm outfit. Levi and Lucy had two children: Edward "Ed" Nelson, born in 1881; and Myrtle Elvira, born in 1882. Levi Lyon bought the Luther[2] French & Sons mills around 1903; his son Ed added a clapboard mill in 1904. Levi and Ed continued to operate the mills until selling them to the Brompton Pulp and Paper Co.[32]

Levi Lyon mill crew circa 1916. L-R, back row: G. Taylor, William Shaw, unknown, Garner Lister, Fred Seale, Emerson Buchanan, Johnny Rutherford, Alex Buchanan, Charlie Burns. Front row: an unknown boy, Arnold Buchanan, Charlie Head, Jim Lister, Mr. Bailey, Richard Burns, Jim Darker. Not shown but at the side was Isaac Westgate with his team of horses. (Newport Homecoming 1801-1996)

***

Author's note: William[1] and Elizabeth (McGee) French would see their grandchildren still living on the original homestead they had settled on in 1861. The original farmhouse would now be home to their many descendants in the years that followed. The Depression, however, was especially hard on the French families of Newport.

William and Elizabeth's eldest son, James Henry French, married Hannah Mary Harvey who had immigrated from Liverpool, England, in 1909. They lived on the family farm their entire married life. They had five children, four boys and a girl: Lawrence Alfred Robert[4] (born 1920), James[4] Harvey (born 1922), Clinton Desmond (born 1925), William[4] Victor (born 1928) and Elizabeth Mary[2] (born 1931).

James and Hannah had a tough time making ends meet during the Depression on the farm. It had already been lumbered and other than the livestock they raised, there was not a lot of income generated that was not going straight back into running the farm. They raised a small herd of Shorthorn cattle which slowly grew over many years, allowing some excess beef to be sold during the time when their children were into their teen years. Hannah looked after a large garden which helped feed the family over the years. She always had chickens and turkeys producing eggs and was able to raise enough extra fowl to sell outside of the family needs.

The original William and Elizabeth French homestead; the house built by William when he first arrived in Newport (courtesy of Linda (French) Oliveras)

"The cultivatable soil on the land was run-down. I remember my father saying that in 1920 or '21, he harvested only 14 tons of hay, a dry year I think; market steers were only worth $18 apiece, but hay costs were $35 per ton the following winter. These were poor years and life was tough once again in Newport, but we were able to survive the '20s and the Great Depression of the '30s."[35] *(quote: Eric G. R. French, grandson of Robert F. French, great-grandson of William[3] V. French)*

Author's note: Robert and Ellen (Lebourveau) French raised four children on their farm, one of whom was James Henry, who married Hannah M. Harvey. Their children had now grown up, were marrying, and choosing their own lives. One of their children married into the Hurd family – yet another connection to the Heard/Hurd families of Newport.

Robert and Ellen French's eldest son, James Henry, had fought in several major battles in World War I and was gassed during the battle of Vimy Ridge. He survived to return home and purchased the lots 8A and 8C of Range 5 in Newport from William McLaughlin, then known as the (John and Mary) Millar farm. William McLaughlin negotiated the sale of the farm to James in 1919 through a loan from the Soldier Settlement Board.[32]

Archie W. French, the second son of Robert and Ellen, and his wife Alice Newby owned the farm on the west side of Flanders Road, now known as French Road, just before the junction of Island Brook Road. "They later moved to the farm next to my grandfather James H. French, down the hill on the same side of the road, across from the Fred Burns place. They raised a son and a daughter, Dorothy. Their son Kenneth married Joyce Ross and had one son, Sydney. None of their descendants remain in Newport." *(Linda (French) Oliveras)*

Lloyd Robert[3] French married Bertha Evelyn[5] Hurd (Alonzo George Hurd's daughter) in 1939. They lived in Sawyerville where they raised their three children: Eric George Robert[4], Barbara Ann and Susan J.

The John William and Emma (Parsons) French families of Newport:

Abel "Abe" French married Alma Patton and took over William and Emma French's farm on Lot 2 of Range 6, where they raised Holstein cattle and in later years became part of Quebec's milk quota system. They raised four boys and one girl: Elgin R., Colin W., Gordon A. E., Emmerson "Aubrey" and Rita C.

Abe and Alma lived on the ground floor of the family home; their son Aubrey and his wife Blanche (Dempsey) lived on the second floor. When Abe and Alma died, they moved downstairs. Their daughter, Brenda, married Ross Thomas; they operate one of the original farms on Lot 3 of Range 6 in Newport – still farming on their ancestor John William French's original farm.

Gordon French married Lavina Waldron; they lived for a short time in the second-floor suite at the William French homestead, above Aubrey and Blanche, before moving to a farm in Clifton Township.

***

Author's note: The Alden family was another family that was well recognized in the northwestern farming community of Newport for many years. Their ancestors migrated to many other parts of the Eastern Townships and served in prominent positions in municipal affairs.

Fred Oliver Alden (1882-1964) married Pearl Holbrook (1889-1965); they raised six children on a farm on North Island Brook Road about two miles from Island Brook. One of their sons, Arthur (born 1911) married Alice Brown in November 1941, just weeks before he was shipped off to the Pacific Rim with the Royal Rifles of Canada. Jessie Alden (born 1913) married Lloyd Hume; Mabel (born 1919) married Doug Mackay in 1939; Delbert (born 1921) married Alberta Warburton; Arnold (born 1923) married Patricia Swift in 1927; and Howard, the youngest (born 1929) married Mary Tiner.

Arial view of the Aubrey and Blanche French farm (courtesy of Linda (French) Oliveras)

The Alden family worked extremely hard and always had a hired hand. Pearl was terribly upset with Fred one Christmas. She gave him a pair of kid-leather gloves and he gave them to Jim Lassenba, who was working for them. Jim very proudly wore the new gloves to church, but "when he knelt down, the two holes in the seat of his pants didn't compliment the gloves at all" and so Pearl was "fit to be tied" with Fred, as the expression goes.[32]

Pearl Alden was an accomplished, talented pianist. She gave lessons in her home and had an ear for music. She could listen to a new tune on the radio, then go to the piano and play it. She played the organ in church, had a lovely alto voice, and sang many duets with Jean Dawson. She also played for dances, which meant that Garnet Lister, who played the violin, came at least once a week to practice with them. She took the children along to the dances and when they got tired and fell asleep, they were tucked under the piano or on chairs together on a bed of coats. This is how life was in the country during this era; the children grew up to love music and they all knew how to dance. "One night her daughter Mabel woke up screaming because she could not find her mother. Pearl had had her hair cut that day and Mabel being sleepy just didn't recognize her."[32]

Fred always called the square dances; the "Grand March and Circle" was always the first dance of the evening. He would dance a jig at some time during the evening, accompanied by his brother Charlie. There was always a house full of people with plenty of food shared and music making at the Alden home.

On a Sunday it was not uncommon to have 16 or more for dinner. Fred would say "There's someone coming" and Pearl would dash for the pantry, take a cup of sugar, break a couple of eggs into a cup, fill it to overflowing with cream and whatever else it took to turn out a lovely sponge cake. When lunch time came the cake was topped with home-made real whipping cream, and if it was strawberry or raspberry season, then there would be a generous topping of berries as well. [32]

Pantries had replaced outdoor kitchens of the past decade; this was where the food was stored on shelves or in cupboards. All the food preparations were done in the pantry on a large "harvest" table before being taken out to the kitchen to cook on the stove. The kitchen in this era was typically a large room with a stove and a large table where everyone ate breakfast, dinner and supper. It was used mostly for family visiting and anyone from another farm who might stop by for a quick visit and a bite to eat. The "parlour" and "dining room" were usually saved for company, meaning visitors or family who lived elsewhere and came to visit from time to time. Most of the time the furniture in this room was covered in sheets to keep the dust off – sheets quickly removed if someone considered "company" arrived. The dining room was used by the family usually only on Sundays when everyone would be "dressed up" in their "Sunday best," having just returned from church. Dinner was always served shortly after the noon hour in the farming communities. Supper was the evening meal, usually leftovers from the main noon meal.

Cellars during this era were usually dank and musty smelling, as the floors were dirt and the walls were simply flat stones layered in clay, which was the building's foundation. There was usually a cupboard, constructed of elm boards laid loosely on the dirt floor, where they stored their chokecherry, raspberry, strawberry and gooseberry jams. The cupboard also likely held a plentiful amount of maple syrup, maple butter and apple cider sauce as well. The children did not appear to mind volunteering to go down to get a fresh supply for breakfast. These cellars were also ideal for storing produce, including potatoes, carrots and other root vegetables during the winter months. Vegetables were usually placed in sand that was poured into handmade woven baskets. The baskets were usually made from dried bullrushes, the stalks of which were plentiful in marshes and roadsides. The other half of the cellar might hold large amounts of dry stove wood for both cooking and heating stoves on the main floor of the house.

***

Author's note: The Bowker children were direct descendants of Col. Edmund Heard from the marriage of Lucy Minerva Hurd and Lewis L. Bowker and so they had named their first-born son Edmund as was the custom. A reader may wonder why so many children carried the same names from generation to generation. A possible reason may have been with so many children's deaths, they felt there was a need to make sure one of a particular family would carry the name forward. The next family in the story are the grandchildren of Lewis and Lucy from the marriage of Herbert Rice Bowker and Ormasinda "Sinda" C. Farnsworth. They also carried this tradition forward with Edmund[2] Bowker.

Edmund[2] Heard Bowker (1891-1973) and Naomi Maybelle Gilman were married by the Rev. G. H. Forde on a sunny day at the Gilman home in Sawyerville, Eaton Township. They lived on Flanders Road on the farm originally owned by Henry French, situated between the Flaws and Nugent farms. They raised two children: a daughter, Evelyn Orma, who married Gordon Arthur Boynton; and a son, Wesley Herbert Gilman, who married Hope Lillian Gill, an RN. After they retired Wesley and Hope renovated and lived in the old farmhouse.

Austin Stevens Bowker married Ruth Ethel Gilman and they raised six children, two boys and four girls: Agnes became a nurse and married Theodore (Ted) Buck; Gordon married Audrey Mabel Aldrous, who was also a nurse; Hazel married Eugene Fernand Drouin; Florence married James (Jimmy) McVetty; Elsie married Lynford Clayton Lowry; and Norman married first Kathleen Monahan and second Betty Lou Schrane Biggs.

The two brothers, Austin and Edmund, had married two sisters, Ruth and Naomi, daughters of Lewis and Mary Ann (Campbell) Gilman. Austin and Ruth farmed for a short time with his brother Edmund, then moved to the Munn farm at Munns Bridge bordering on the Newport/Eaton town line (later owned by George and Eva and their son Alvin Nugent). They relocated again to the Lindsay farm (later owned by Frode Neilson) on the North River Road, adjacent to the original Bowker homestead. When Austin's stepmother died in 1929, they took over the home farm. His father Herbert lived with them until his death in 1950.

***

When Mary Burns, a talented teacher, musician, and community worker in Island Brook died at the age of 29 years in 1920, the community mourned her loss. Her mother Marinda (wife of Fred Burns) organized the "Mary Burns Mission Circle" in her memory. The girls gathered at her home once a month for a devotional period and games. To raise funds there would be an ice cream social where much of the ice cream was homemade. "It was quite often during the summer months my mother would make a large hand-operated ice cream freezer full of home-made ice cream, usually vanilla flavoured and sometimes bananas were mashed up and added to it. We all had a hand in making it, from the cooking of the custard, the crushing of the ice, turning the crank, to licking the dish when it was all finished. It was a rare occasion to have any left over, but if there was it was repacked with fresh ice and made a welcome dessert on Sundays." *(Nina (Parsons) Rowell)*

The Mission Circle would celebrate different events such as St. Valentines' Day, July 1st and Christmas.[33] One evening the girls were rehearsing in the town hall for an event they were holding. I recall that they were playing musical games like "Old John Brown" and "musical chairs." A lady living close to the hall telephoned some parents and "told them that the girls were dancing, which she thought was disgraceful."[32] *(quote: Ruth Burns)*

***

Flora N. Hurd (1872-1943), the only daughter of John B.[9] and Emma (Austin), married Clark Stewart Willard in 1893. Clark (1859-1915) was born in Marbleton, Que. They continued living with her parents on the farm next to her cousin, Gussie, the farm where her grandparents Augustus and Eliza (Planche) had lived their lives. They raised five children, three boys and two girls, on the farm that became generally known as the "Willard farm." Their children were Burton Stewart (born 1894), Keith Lockhart (born 1903), Merle Emma (born 1905), Ivy Hurd (born 1908) and Clark. Their children all moved away, Burton as far away as Albuquerque, N.M., the other five to various places in the New England states where they married. Surnames resulting from the marriages of the daughters were Bennett and Draper. Ivy married an educator and aeronautical engineer and served as a Red Cross nurse in World War II.

Author's note: The Willard Heard/Hurd/ Rand connections went back three generations. Clark Willard was the son of Lockhart[8] Hall, whose father was William[7]. His grandfather Longley[6] Willard was an Associate of Col. Edmund[5] Heard. Longley married Hannah[1] Hurd and they had a son, William, as well as two daughters. Their eldest daughter, Mary, married Capt. Edmund[7] Heard. Their youngest daughter, Hannah[2] Hurd, married Artemas[7] Dodge Rand. Edmund and Mary's eldest daughter, Mary Maria, married Artemas[7] D.'s cousin, Marshall Spring Rand. My father, Lionel, grew up with these cousins and always enjoyed any visits they made.

Merle Willard, Lionel Hurd, Ivy Willard, Keith Lockhart[3] Willard, Fred Hurd, and Arthur Hurd (in front), circa 1924

This was an era of spirituality in which card-playing, dancing and most assuredly alcohol or hard drink were considered unworthy for the proper upbringing of children by some of the more ardent and staunch church supporters of the day. Sundays were absolutely a day of rest; a day for Bible reading, attending church, and getting together for afternoon visits while the children were involved in all kinds of children's activities – everyone dressed in suits or their "Sunday best" clothes.

Author's note: Clark Willard's sister, Ida Jane, married George W. French of Island Brook at the church in Randboro – another example of how these families were interconnected in so many ways.

Randboro, circa 1890–1900. Randboro store is the third building on the left; the Baptist/Methodist/United Church is first building on the right; McCallum's home is third building on the right. (Courtesy of Audrey (McCallum) Murray and Diana (McCallum) Langworth)

Chapter 14   A Changing World (1900–1925)

This era, from 1900 to 1925, saw the widespread rollout of vaccines for tuberculosis (TB), diphtheria, whooping cough, and tetanus. In 1925, telephones came onto the market, and switchboards to operate these new devices provided work for women. The first commercial passenger flights were beginning and with them, airports were being built. The communities of Learned Plain, Island Brook, Knicky Knocky, New Mexico, Maple Leaf and Randboro were thriving; however, the situation was about to change and it would test the mettle of the Newport inhabitants.[48]

***

The southwestern section of Newport:

Arthur[3] and Nora (Parsons) Loveland were now farming on his parents' (Charlie and Charlotte's) original Loveland homestead in the Maple Leaf community with their family of two boys and a daughter: Howard (born 1921), Herbert (born 1926) and Dorothy (born 1931). The farm was located next to his sister Mildred and husband Herman Lowry's farm (the original William[2] and Eliza Beeman farm) and Bryon and Cora Austin's farm, both on Range 9.

Arthur and Nora (Parsons) Loveland

Arthur and Nora continued operating the family farm and contributing to the Maple Leaf community. They raised Shorthorn cattle, pigs, horses and chickens. Arthur bought a used Ford Model A taxi in the spring of 1930 that had 11,000 miles on the odometer. Many of the farmers had been buying automobiles during the late 1920s, which allowed them to travel further around the Townships to buy food and clothing. Farmers were always attracted to auctions to bid on used equipment and now they were able to travel into different regions beyond their reach with horses. With cars came travel; the children were exposed to new villages and people and experienced a whole new world further out in the countryside.

***

Wallace and Elizabeth "Lizzy" Boyd

Wallace and Elizabeth ("Lizzie") Boyd lived on Lot 7 of Range 9, immediately north of the Luke Hurd farm, circa the 1920-1950s. The property was originally owned by Edmund Harvey, one of the first settler Associates. Luke Heard sold a parcel of his land (50 acres) to Edmund Harvey in 1876. Edmund passed the property down to his heir, Porter Harvey, who sold the farm to Matthew Boyd. When Matthew died, the estate was left to Wallace and Lizzie Boyd. The document was officiated by Samuel A. Heard, County Clerk of Compton County. Wallace and Lizzie had no children to work their 250-acre farm, so they hired many of the younger lads from around the community to help them with harvesting. They raised beef cattle on the farm along with the usual array of barnyard fowl. They retired in the late 1950s and lived their final days in the original home they had lived in all their married lives. Wallace was an ardent hunter and bagged a deer most years, providing them with a good supply of venison through the winter months. He was also a fisherman; every spring he was out in the early morning catching his limit of speckled and rainbow trout. They both worked hard in generating a first-rate garden and Lizzie spent hours canning the vegetables as well as putting up preserves in abundance each year.

Author's note: An example of one of the small TB cabins mentioned earlier was situated on today's Route 210, just west of Maple Leaf Cemetery between the Boyd and Jones farms. The building was still there as late as the early 1940s. In 1947-48, my brother, Jim Hurd, remembers seeing someone sitting on the small porch. Circa the 1950s the building was moved closer to the house to become a small garage for Wallace and Lizzie Boyd's "Prefect" car, a small car imported from Great Britain. The left and right turn signals on this car flipped out on a lighted lever between the front and rear doors.

***

When Newell Clement Rand died in 1922 the original Rand homestead was purchased first by a Mr. and Mrs. Hollis Evans and family. Later Bert Trombley bought this farm. Bert was a farmer and lumberman and at one time owned the Sawyerville mill. He was also a contractor who built many homes throughout the area. He and his family lived for many years on this farm on today's Route 210, and later sold the farm to Emile Rouleau and his family who owned it during the latter part of the 1950s.

> *Author's note: It greatly enhanced this book to have diaries written by our ancestors and kept by succeeding families that give us a definitive idea of how people lived and interacted in these earlier days. Edith (Morrison) Rand kept daily journals from 1922 to 1968 in which she not only recorded day-to-day life in Maple Leaf but also referred to people and events in the surrounding communities – a perfect source for understanding "lives lived" in Newport during these eras. The contents of the diaries are entered in this book either directly or transcribed as part of bringing the narratives forward in this format.*

Edith's husband was Marshall[2] Newell W. Rand, known by everyone as "Marshie." Edith's recordings of daily life represent a typical year in how the families lived in Newport; people helping each other.

Edith (Morrison) Rand diary excerpts from 1922, a year in the life of a Newport resident: the entries were selected for their content as the author chose to group interesting entries to give a snapshot of the times within each month.

> January: *Cold and lots of snow, dressed chickens' and put some out to freeze. Went to Sawyerville with single team to take down 25 lbs. of butter, got 37 cents per lb. Mr. Harry Stewart was shot while hunting out on the range. The ambulance was called to move Mr. Stewart to Sherbrooke hospital where he passed away. 16 below zero at Willis Leggetts.*
>
> February: *Clinton broke his thumb in the ringer* (the clothes washer rollers used to wring out the water).
>
> March: *Uncle Charlie [Cable]'s birthday today, March 8, he is 83 years old. Marshie attended Council and I washed. Marshie gathered sap all day and made sugar [syrup] all night. Clinton had the croup. Ten little pigs born today. Marshie now has the croup. Uncle Edmund [Haskell Hurd] came and spent the day and John [Jones] came and did the chores for us.*
>
> April: *Took Lyle to school in the sleigh and I did the chores tonight. Two little lambs were born. Marshie went out to the other farm and took Clinton with him. I made twelve and one-half pounds of Butter. Marshie churned. Did two weeks ironing. Marshie split wood. John and Nellie Jones came up and Frank Morrison bought 167 pounds of pork at 0.15 for $25.05. Made 18 pounds of Butter and took out the double windows. Flora LaFleur came to visit for the day.*
>
> May: *The cream truck came for the first time this spring to collect and Marshie went out to roll the land. We planted the potatoes. Aunt Hannah [Rand] McCurdy died May 20. Marshie worked digging ditch and got the water started. He worked on the road all day. Marshie dreadfully sick with headache. Uncle Ed, [Edmund H. Hurd] Gifford and Mary [Hurd] Lawson and Sarah Hurd called here. Marshie butchered two pigs, weighing 200 pounds. Nellie [Jones] came up and we stretched her curtains. The town of Bulwer gave a play and we went. Mr. and Mrs. Hollis Evans were here to look at the farm. Charlie LaFleur came and worked all day, made the garden and picked stone. Marshie and Mr. [Demmond] Munn [who was 87] went as far as Emberton [Woods Township] to look over the road, took Lyle and Clinton with them and to New Mexico. I took wool to Sawyerville.*
>
> June: *We cultivated the potatoes today. Went to church with John and Nellie and family and had tea here in the afternoon. The men worked on the road. We moved most of our furniture to other farm, Marshie cleaned the car engine and I picked a few berries and bought more from Nellie. We left our old home for good and moved to the other farm. Mr. and Mrs. Evans took possession of their new home. Marshie, Lyle, and I went to Bury and bought 15 hens.*

Author's note: The "other farm" Edith refers was the Newell Clement homestead on today's Route 210, Lot 12. It was sold in 1922, the year Newell died. This was the year when Marshall and Edith, who had bought the Edmund[8] Haskell Hurd homestead from Robert and Eva (Planche) Seale in 1919, moved their final possessions from the old homestead to their new farm.

July: *Alonzo [Rand, Marshie's brother], Albert and Mary [Riddle; Mary was a sister] and I went to Coaticook. We cut the grain and I made brown bread.*

August: *Finished reaping today at Frank [Morrison]'s; made ginger snaps, and picked cranberries which I put up.*

September: *We all went to the Cookshire fair. An airplane made the flight from Colebrook, [New Hampshire] to the Fair. Lyle started school at Maple Leaf this year.*

October: *Marshie spreading manure. I made donuts. Thrashers are here to do our farm, we [Marshie and his brother Alonzo], helped Gussie [Augustus and Sarah Hurd], Albert and Mary [Riddell] with the thrashing. Made mustard pickles to put up. Bought oats and straw (40 cents). Fred French buried today. Marshie ploughing the fields now. Ada Planche's birthday and we are invited to a party at Planche's tonight. We did not go.*

Author's note: Fred French had bought the old Luke Heard farm which was then resold to the Chute family. The Chutes farmed there until 1932. Ada was Edward and Gratia (Hurd) Planche's daughter; she would have been 65. Her husband was Alexander Ross, so the party would have been at her brother John Harold and his wife Charlotte's home in Cookshire.

November: *Snowing now, so we are banking the house. Grandpa [James Parker]'s funeral, Ernest Parker, Clarence Cable, Archie Jones were bearers. Hymns "Asley in Jesus, Peace perfect Peace, and There is no night in heaven." The service was held in the Baptist Church in Randboro. I churned fifteen pounds of butter. Went to Sawyerville for Quarterly Board meeting. They closed the Church today. John Nellie and their son Milton [Jones] came for dinner. We went to the Randboro church and had tea at Aunt Flora [Rand]'s. A man got lost in the woods. Heavy snow. We got in seventeen head of cattle and Joe Riddell came and got his cattle. Mr. Hazelton has not been found. Marshie went to Parker hill to help dehorn some cattle. I made Pumpkin and Cranberry pies, cake, and donuts. We sold two pigs for $16.00.*

Author's note: The diary written by Edith (Morrison) Rand in 1922 clearly states "the Church was closed today." Edith is referring to the Methodist Church in Maple Leaf. The very next Sunday they attended the Baptist Church in Randboro. The Baptist Church in Randboro changed to the Methodist denomination sometime between 1922 and 1924. Documents such as this are not only revealing but also provide clarity and confirm when events in history occurred. For any author attempting to write about any history, having access to diaries such as this, coupled with other supportive material that has been preserved through time, is extremely beneficial.

December: *Alonzo [Rand] had a hard night, Neuralgia. Very cold and stormy. Marshie yarded logs all day. I dressed chicken. Our chimney burned out in the evening. Frank [Morrison] broke out the roads today for the first time this year. We are having lots of snow.*

Christmas Day: *Good sleighing. Gardie and Lilly [Rand], Albert and Mary [Riddell], Frank and Mabel [Morrison], Mother [Margaret Morrison Parker] and Rufus [Riddell] were here for dinner. The hens laid five eggs today.*

New Year's Day: *Stormy and rough. Marshie cut wood brought home one load of wood. The hens laid 6 eggs today. Frank rolled the roads. Gussie [Augustus Hurd] and Frederick [his son] came down to visit and spent the evening. I made buns. (Edith (Morrison) Rand diaries, courtesy of Carol Rand)*

***

On Sundays, the families would gather to go to church and give each other a lift, some in their cars, others in their buggies in the summer or sleighs in the winter. Church was a social event and loved by all, especially the children as they could meet their extended family as one. Another social event was going to the store to get the mail. Everyone looked forward to this as an opportunity to read the headlines in the newspaper and get caught up with the local news.

Weddings were an important social event that always took place on a Saturday and were followed by a dance. These dance parties spread to become part of any and all major celebrations and were held at the Orange Hall, Oddfellows Hall, Knicky Knocky old schoolhouse, Island Brook Hall, Randboro Montgomery Hall, and church halls wherever a band could be set up. Music was a big draw for local talent.

Charlie and Olive Alden were musicians from the Island Brook region and gave freely of their talent. He played the fife, mouth organ, Jew's harp and was an old-time fiddler. She accompanied him on the piano, and they provided entertainment for special occasions like St. Patrick's Day as well. In later years, Charlie and Gerald would play for the Calf Club dances in Island Brook, and even in later years, Wayne and Vivian Alden and Chilston Lowry would entertain.[32]

> *Author's note: A Jew's harp is a small lyre instrument that when held between the teeth gives tones from a metal or bamboo tongue struck by the finger.*

***

A typical year in the life of Edith (Morrison) Rand, illuminated by excerpts from her 1923 diary:

- *We went picking wild berries with the kids this spring. I am churning butter every second day now. The boys helped thinning turnips all day. We are having strawberries for every meal. The boys and me are hoeing potatoes and corn rows. Marshall is sharpening the scythes, getting ready for cutting. Marshie bought a force pump for the kitchen.*

- *We all went to the strawberry social at the Baptist Church in Randboro. There was an Orangemen's picnic and a big dance in the Hall in Sawyerville and we all went and had a great time.*

- *Mowed hay all day and Marshie mowed the roadside at the same time. Got in four loads then the next day six loads, which we put in the back of the barn.*

- *Peddler Charlie was here, we did not invite him to stay the night, as he usually tries for. Lyle and Clinton went to Gussies for tea in aft. Young Arthur [Hurd] was here for dinner, playing with Clinton. We went to Johns [John and Nellie Jones's] for a party in the evening had a great time,*

- *The telephone man came and put in a phone and connected the line with Frank [Morrison]'s [July 20, 1923].*

- *Went to Randboro to Church today. Marshie got Mr. Grahams horses to work today.* (John and Ruth Graham lived in Randboro on Grove Hill Road.) *It was Rita Jones's birthday today [July 24]. She is 10 years old, and she had a party and Lyle was invited.*

- *I led the horse on the hay fork today. Arthur and Lionel [Hurd] were here today, Arthur playing with Clinton, Lionel helping Marshie with the haying. We got our cream cheque today totaling 53.70. Marshie tedded the hay over at Gussies [Augustus and Sarah Hurd's] and they got 10 loads, while Frederick and Arthur [Hurd] came and spent the day, playing with the boys.*

- *Rufus Dawson motored from Barrie, Vt., got here in the evening, and started back home at 1.30 o'clock the next day.*

- *Marshie mowed hay today but broke the pitman rod and had to go town to have it repaired. Marshie and Lyle drove 10 head to Charlie [Chute's] and we got $700. Lyle walked all the way to Sawyerville,* *and so, Flora went to get him with her horses. Clinton played at Gussies with Arthur, all day and I walked to Franks [Morrison].*

- *I sent to Eaton's for a "Voile dress" Black trimmed with Henna with white spots. Peddler Charlie was here, and I bought "Gingham" for a dress. We had new potatoes for dinner for the first time this year and I made green apple pies today, along with doughnuts and cakes.*

- *Mildred Swail and Errol French were married today [August 29, 1923] at the Randboro Church . . . Rita and Milton [children of John and Nellie Jones] were here for a visit.*

- *Got in seven loads of green oats today. I picked cranberries and put them up (meaning cooking and storing in Mason jars). We mowed buckwheat all day today, starting the harvest season now. Put out manure and spread today, taking out 30 loads today.*

- *Uncle Ed [Edmund[8] Haskell Hurd] died today, March 14, at quarter to one o'clock, Marshie went up to Gussies to see them. Frank King and Cora Austin, Gardie and Lily, Eddie, and me, all went up and cleaned up the Church and made a new platform. It was a large funeral and everybody was there, the Hymns were, "Abide with me" Peace perfect Peace."* [The church had been closed; however, it was fitting to have Haskell's funeral in the old church that he had supported for so many years.]

- *We dug potatoes all day. Marshie was reaping the farms today. We cleaned buckwheat all day got eight bushels. Cleaned kitchen pipes for winter. (excerpts from Edith (Morrison) Rand diaries)*

The term "reaping" in the entry immediately above was used to describe harvesting grain with a new machine, called a binder, that cuts the stalks of grain and ties them in clumps or sheaves with binder twine, then drops the sheaves on the ground. Not unlike earlier days, the farmers in this era were there to help each other during planting and harvesting times.

***

Evelyn Sarah Eliza Swail, daughter of Val and Laura (Hurd) Swail, graduated from Maple Leaf School and was a schoolteacher in the Parker Hill region of Newport where she met and married Rufus Riddell in 1924. They lived on the farm off Parker Hill Road on the corner of Auckland and Newport townships, an area known as East Clifton. They lived there many years before moving to Vulcan, Alta., to be with their children who had moved there when they married.[31]

Evelyn Swail and Rufus Riddell

The invitation to Rufus and Evelyn's wedding in September 1924 invites guests to the Methodist Church of Randboro at "High Noon" – evidence that by then the church in Randboro had changed from Baptist to Methodist.[31]

Author's note: The church in Randboro had been a Baptist denomination as was confirmed in Edith's diary of 1922. Here in 1924 it is a Methodist church, and the congregation was yet to make another change in the future, to United.

***

The northcentral section of Newport:

William Morrow's first wife, Hattie (Cable), had died at 40 years old and now their children were starting families of their own. In 1921 William married Mary Isabelle Armstrong (1879-1929). William was town treasurer and one of the founding members of the Court of Island Brook of the IOF (Independent Order of Foresters), established in 1890. He also served the Township of Newport as fire adjuster for many years. William was a superb cook, serving meals in the lumber camps, also for many years. He had built a home for his mother, Ellen, between his house and the barn while the six boys were growing up. Ellen had always delighted in hosting tea parties for her grandchildren and inviting some of the neighbourhood girls to join them, and of course the boys. Everyone got to eat cookies and cake.[32]

In 1922 several students were ready to start high school and parents were anxious to have the higher grades taught closer to home, so an intermediate school was established in Island Brook. The first teachers in the new school were Miss Glenna B. Watson, teacher and principal at $90 a month, and Miss Edwyna Beaton, at $60 a month. This meant a consolidation of schools from several districts. Two gentlemen who devoted many hours to the benefit of their school and community during this era were Thomas Burns and Archie French. Thomas served for 24 years as school commissioner and chairman of the local school board.[32]

Students were now being picked up in the outlying regions and brought to the new consolidated school. By 1931, when the newly built Island Brook Intermediate School was ready for enrollment, Kenneth Morrow used his team of horses and van to convey students from District no. 2 to the new school. In the winter, the wheels were removed and replaced with sled runners. He also had a small wood-burning stove installed at the rear of the van enclosure to use during cold days. Archie French was instrumental in keeping the school open for the last number of years before it closed for good.[32]

***

"By 1926 when Fay Parsons began school, the Knicky Knocky schoolhouse that her grandfather had built was no longer in use, so she attended the new school in Bury with her sisters. Bury was five miles away. Sometimes they were driven in a horse-drawn van but when the roads were too muddy, they walked both ways. Other times her older sisters drove their horse-drawn sleigh to the Bury school. My maternal grandmother (Nellie Parsons) was a teacher before her marriage, and as such, according to my mother, she required her own children to achieve high grades in school, which they did! Even in her later years, Nellie Parsons would still hitch the horse to the buggy and drive herself to the Women's Institute meetings. There was no way she'd miss them." *(Carol Rand)*

In 1927 Kenneth Morrow bought the old William and Hattie Morrow homestead in Island Brook from his brother Renford and Elizabeth (McCormick). Kenneth (1903-1991) married Ruth Burns (1910-1996) in 1930 in Island Brook, where they continued to farm and lived all their lives. Kenneth served as an adjuster for the Mutual Fire Insurance Company and served as property evaluator for many years for the Township of Newport. Ruth was a schoolteacher for five years in Lawrence Colony and 24 years in Island Brook and was considered by her many students through the years as the best teacher they had had. Ruth authored the history journal *Island Brook: Then and Now*, from which much of the history of Island Brook has been drawn and referenced for this book. They raised two daughters, Geraldine and Edwina.[32, 16]

In 1928, just a year before the Great Depression that was to bring untold hardship to Newport, Renford and Elizabeth Morrow (McCormack), with their son Donald (1924-1980), bought the Willard Stedman and Sarah (McCurdy) Rand farm on today's Route 210, Lot 11 of Range 11 in Maple Leaf. They also purchased a partial section of the Haskell[8] and Eliza (McCurdy) Hurd farm, Lot 10 of Range 11, in 1941. Two other children had been born to them in Island Brook: a son Donald and a daughter Lillian, both of whom died in infancy. They raised another two sons and two daughters on their new farm in Maple Leaf: Jean (1928-2009), Myrlin (1933-1966), Waymond (1936-) and Donna (1945-). They operated a mixed farm of Shorthorn cattle, horses, some sheep and pigs, along with the usual domestic fowl.[32] *(Morrow Family history)*

***

In the 1920s some farmers began painting their barns with linseed oil to help seal the wood and keep it from rotting. Rust was mixed with the oil to keep fungi and moss from growing on the wood. This turned the oil red and so the treated barns of this era all had a light reddish tone to them. Barns are still painted red to commemorate that tradition.

Horse-drawn automated equipment such as mowers, rakes and binders were now becoming a necessity for all farmers – part of the normal farm equipment. Fall threshing ("thrashing") season was a remarkably busy time for the farmers. The horse-drawn binder cut the stalks of grain and formed them into bundles called "sheaves," tied them with binder twine, and dropped them on the ground as the cutter moved along. Men, women and the older children would be out in the fields stacking several of these sheaves (with the grain side up) into stooks to dry. The "threshing machine" was a large piece of equipment that processed the sheaves of grain through a separation process, whereby the straw would be blown into the loft in the barn for use as livestock bedding during the winter. The grains would be bagged into jute or hemp bags, or sometimes the thresher would blow the grain directly into grain bins. Because these machines were exceptionally large and expensive, a farmer might purchase one and then go from farm to farm in the fall and hire out themselves and their thresher. In this way they provided a service to the community of farmers while also recouping some of the cost of this expensive equipment. Communities in Newport, such as Island Brook, Learned Plain, Knicky Knocky, New Mexico, Maple Leaf, and Randboro/Grove Hill/Parker Hill, might each have one farmer who would buy either a binder or threshing machine and go from farm to farm.

On the day that the thresher was to arrive at any farm, the men from the community would come with their horses and wagons to pick up the stooks from the fields. Others would place the stooks onto the thresher conveyor, or bag and store the grain, or spread the straw in the loft. The thrasher was powered by horses walking on a treadmill. Meanwhile, the women and daughters were preparing enough food for the noontime dinner and suppertime meals for the crew. It was a time when the whole community got together almost as a party; men, women and their children were all participants in these events.

Elizabeth Morrow and her family were feeding at least 8-10 men with the very freshest home-cooked meat and vegetables along with pies for everyone; a feast indeed! Every woman wanted the community to know that her food was indeed the best. The men and boys were not about to let this opportunity go unnoticed, and in recognition would give their compliments to each and everyone. The boys were smart enough to seize the moment to make sure the daughters were also held in great favour, and those who were even smarter let them know it. These work bees became social community events that everyone looked forward to.

Author's note: In 1947, soon after the Second World War, Renford and Elizabeth sold the original Willard Stedman Rand farm, severing this part of their property and selling it to Clinton and Doreen (McCormack) Rand – re-establishing the Rand family name in Maple Leaf.

***

The Westgate family of Newport:

Author's note: William and Florence Painter had two daughters, Verna and Shirley, both raised on their farm in Island Brook. The following excerpts on the Westgate family have been obtained mainly from the booklet Island Brook Then and Now, *prepared by and including quotes from Ilah (Westgate) Batley and their family history.*

Maple Westgate married Verna Painter in 1928. As many others did at the time, they looked for work elsewhere. They found their future in Detroit, where Maple worked for the Ford Motor Company. Their first boy, Mailin, was born there in 1929. As happened for so many at the time, the Great Depression caused them to move back home to Island Brook. Maple took a job driving a transport truck for Lynn Transport Co. for a short period of time until he saw an opportunity for land settlement in a new area of Newport.

Newport Colony had been opened up for settlement by the British American Land Corporation (BALC) in 1931; Maple and Verna settled on a lot that same year and farmed there until 1946. They milked a herd of purebred Holsteins and raised five children: son Mailin and daughters, Patricia, Norma, Ilah and Linda. In 1947 they purchased a farm in the Island Brook region on today's Route 212 where they continued farming and increased their herd of milking cows. It was during this later period that Maple began to drive the school bus for the Eastern Townships School Board, which he did for 35 years. *(Ilah (Westgate) Batley)*

Maple Westgate and Verna Painter wedding portrait, 1928 (courtesy of Ilah (Westgate) Batley)

This region of Newport was known as "patented lands" under the control of the BALC. Once the lumber was taken off, the BALC traded the land back to the Crown. The Crown then gave out those lands during the Depression as lands for settlement.[31]

"As a result of the economic hardship of The Great Depression, there was a back-to-the-land movement in Canada that advocated for the settlement of impoverished people onto tracts of land with the view that they would be able to become self-sufficient, much like the settlers of the 18th century. Within this context the Eastern Townships Protestant Colonization Association was established in 1935 in conjunction with the government and the Anglican Church. The Association's primary area of operation was to place needy families on previously unsettled lots in Newport Township. Initially referred to as Newport Colony, it became known as Lawrence Colony in 1937. By 1940, 45 families had been settled in the Colony, but after a 'honeymoon' period of sorts, the administration of support efforts, land titles and taxes were fraught with confusion, inefficiencies and disappointments and so many of these settlers were to leave over time." *(Jody Robinson, Eastern Townships Resource Centre)*

> *Author's note: The big difference here was that the land had already been stripped of its virgin timbers, so these settlers did not have the opportunity to earn extra cash by selling lumber. They had to survive solely on their farming skills, growing sufficient crops to have surplus to sell after their own needs were met. Hence, they struggled to make ends meet, during both the Great Depression of the 1930s and the subsequent war years. Second-growth was mainly spruce and other softwoods which they harvested for pulpwood.*

Verna always grew a large garden that supplied many vegetables and fruit for Maple and her five children. She pickled and canned every fall while Maple always kept a pig to slaughter for ham, bacon and pork roasts. Her daughter Ilah remembers "going into the pantry to find a pig's head in a brine being prepared to make 'head cheese' which my father loved, especially spread on bread or toast."[32] *(Ilah (Westgate) Batley)*

Maple built a "smokehouse" where he utilized a small smoke fire method to cure the hams and bacon. Ilah recalls, "The smokehouse caught fire one day, which wasn't particularly good for the ham!" *(Ilah (Westgate) Batley)*

Homesteading was much the same as in earlier years, but occurred here in Lawrence Colony as late as the 1930s (Newport Homecoming 1802-1996)

As with all the farmers of Newport, they tried to become as self-sufficient as they could. They cut their own firewood for their stoves; they became their own blacksmith. Maple would take a piece of iron, heat it on red-hot coals and then form/hammer the hot, softened metal into a shape he might need to repair or replace on a sled or piece of equipment to keep it going.

Maple also cut pulpwood as many of the farmers did then to augment his income. He was working with Jack Laird one day, hauling the wood out with their team of horses and noted that there were a lot of bear signs where they were cutting. The horses could smell the bear scent and became uneasy. Jack appeared to be even more uneasy than the horses as he had already had some bad experience with bears. They continued to work until dark and began to haul out the lumber with Maple and his team in the lead. He pulled his horses to a stop and yelled back to Jack that the horses would not go forward. Jack yelled that maybe they could smell the bears and that Maple should put the reins to the horses. Maple would let the horses go a few steps and then pull them to a stop, hollering back to Jack that they would not go. Jack yelled 'Give 'em hell, Maple, just put the reins to them!' Finally, Maple did just that and let the horses run until they were out of the woods. *(Ilah (Westgate) Batley)*

Maple's passion was spending a day fishing on the Island Brook rivulet. The Westgate's old dog got excited as soon as Maple's fishing pole appeared, but he was not a welcome companion because he would seek out and lie down in the best fishing hole.

Deer hunting was another exciting time of the year in Newport, and Maple knew every tree, rock and river-bank scar* in the woods, always planning well in advance for the hunt each year.

> *Author's note: *A riverbank scar is formed by the spring river runoff, which carves out a space in the banks of earth, usually at a bend in the river. This leaves an overhang of grasses and hay easily reached by deer standing under the riverbank's overhang. In the fall, with the river being low, deer would lie down and rest under these food canopies.*

Many evenings were spent in the kitchen with Alton Ewing and others telling stories of the big ones that got away. It was generally known that Alton couldn't hit the broadside of a barn even if his life depended on it, so if Alton was telling the story it was generally believed to be exaggerated. In years past if the daytime hunt was unsuccessful many would continue with nighttime hunting. In later years, with new hunting laws, the local game warden, Arthur McCloud, took a dim view of the practice, making everyone quite nervous about participating in the nighttime sport. "It has been said that Arthur would fine his own grandmother!" It was also told that "It wasn't surprising that the Westgates were wild kids as they had all been raised on venison."

Verna was a talented seamstress and made all her children's clothing on her portable Singer sewing machine. Everyone wanted a Singer-brand sewing machine, perhaps because it was the only well-advertised brand. Verna enjoyed exhibiting her handiwork at the Cookshire Fall Fair along with the many other women of the community. It has been said that she would "dig up half of the garden to find matching-sized carrots to compete at the Fair."

The Irish seem to have been a superstitious lot, or perhaps they just enjoyed teasing. Playing tricks and telling ghost stories were part of their culture. And so, the story is told that when the Westgates lived at their North River farm, they had to walk by the Thompson Cemetery to get to the village. This cemetery served the Catholic families of the Island Brook region of Newport. The children had been told that Aunt Annie's ghost came out at dark and had been seen dancing on the gravestones. When young Maple Westgate got to the cemetery, he would take off running until he was a safe distance. Apparently, he sat down on a log to rest and when he looked beside him there was Aunt Annie's ghost. She said to him, "We had quite a run didn't we, young fellow?" Maple, his hair standing on the nape of his neck, was said to have replied, "Yes, and we're going to have another as soon as I catch my breath!"

***

In 1927, pasteurized milk and Kool-Aid appeared in urban centres. Milk on the farms in the rural areas such as Newport remained "raw," meaning no commercial pasteurization. Kool-Aid, however, was being introduced in the local stores, much to the delight of the children – and so began the "sugar" age. Up to this era locally produced maple sugar was widely used in Newport kitchens for donuts, preserves, cakes and pies. But now granulated white sugar was available in local stores and used freely in just about anything that needed sweetening.[35]

***

The second French family of Newport:

Rob French

> *Author's note: William[1] Victor French and his wife Elizabeth McGee raised eight children; however, only two stayed in Newport: William[2], who married Ester Burns, and Robert[2] (Rob) Foster, who married Mary Ellen Lebourveau.*

Robert (Rob) Foster French became mayor in 1923 and served until 1927.

"There were three things that stand out in my memory about my dad [Lloyd Robert[3] French]'s early experiences in Flanders on the meadow: my grandfather [Mayor Rob French]'s and grandmother's hospitality and employment opportunities to newly immigrated Canadians such as Wesley Ford and Pete Jespersen; my grandparents' aid of food, work and accommodation to depression refugees passing through; the value of things such as oranges and nuts in Christmas stockings in the '20s and '30s (simple things – not so long forgotten)." *(Eric G. R. French)*

"Wesley Ford remained a family friend for life. I remember when we were small children Wesley would often come out to the farm from his home in Montreal. On one occasion he brought a swing set with a slide for us kids and spent the day assembling it for us. That swing set lasted for many years; and my own children enjoyed it in the late '70s and '80s." *(Linda (French) Oliveras)*

Rob and his wife Mary Ellen owned a farm in the Flanders region. They had four children: James Henry (born 1894), Archibald William (born 1897), Elena (born 1902) and Lloyd Robert[3] (born 1910).[25, 32]

James Henry and his wife Hannah "Mary" Harvey had five children: Lawrence Alfred Robert (born 1920), James Harvey (born 1922), Clinton "Desmond" (born 1925), William Victor (born 1928) and Elizabeth Mary (born 1931). In 1928 Mary fell ill, and their son Desmond was taken to their grandfather (Robert[2] and Mary Ellen) French's farm when he was 2½ years old. Clinton remained there, growing up like he was their own son. Following the hurricane of 1938, Lawrence broke his leg in the sugar bush and later moved to Hamilton, Ont. During World War II Harvey served in the Royal Canadian Army Service Corps and Medical Corps. He was discharged in 1946, contracted tuberculosis, and died in 1948. Lawrence's daughter Karen now owns the James H. French homestead.

William[2] V. French earned his diploma from Macdonald College and became a teacher. He taught for several years while assisting on the farm, of which he became sole owner in 1966. He married Ruth Eleanor Corrigan in 1977; they were still living in the original Millar home on the property on Range 5 circa 1995.

Elizabeth trained as a nurse in the Sherbrooke Hospital, graduating in 1951. She married Adrian Davies in 1952; they moved to Ontario that same year then later to California.

The French bothers grading the road (Newport Homecoming 1802-1996)

It was during this era that the Township of Newport purchased horse-drawn road graders. Not unlike the wooden winter rollers, they parked the grader at different farms to be picked up by the next farmer to do their share. They would hitch up two teams of horses in tandem; each of the horse teams needed a driver who walked beside each team guiding the horses both in speed and turnarounds.

The grader itself required two men on board to rotate the blade and two men at the back to raise or lower the blade as required while the grader was moving. Two more men walked at the rear to pick up any large stones, discarding them out of the way along the roadsides. Shown in the picture are William French by the white horse and Charlie Nourse behind him. Seated on the grader are Reggie and Abe French with Rob French walking at the rear.

Up to this time most farmers had been grading the roads with the original wooden square beam system and cutting the vegetation along the edges of the roads with their horse-drawn mowers. They had always been careful where the rocks were placed. "When the Township took over road maintenance the workers just threw the rocks onto the roadside. The farmers were annoyed at the road graders for throwing the rocks on to the roadsides as it caused huge damage to their mowers, so they simply just stopped the practice of mowing the roadsides." *(E. Lionel Hurd)*

***

Gussie Hurd bought his second and last car in 1928. It was a Model A Ford which he drove until they sold the farm in the early 1950s. Gussie (Augustus) was an excellent horseman and always prided himself on his ability with horses. He drove his car like he would drive his horses, steering the car like one might pull on the reins of horses. Compared to his previous Model T, this car had brakes that worked well; Ford had installed a red triangle on the rear fender to alert other drivers that this car stops quickly . . . so one needed to be prepared. Apparently the car stopped so quickly that even horses drawing wagons behind the car could not stop in time. But Gussie somehow expected the car to behave like horses and stop if it encountered another car or a team of horses. He never put his foot on the brake pedal unless absolutely necessary.

Many of his neighbours came to know that if Gussie was on the road they had better stay alert. And so, the story goes that Gussie stormed into town with his new car, driving it the same way as he steered his horses, except that the car did not react well to his jerking the steering wheel. "Yelling 'Whoa!' didn't cause it to stop well either, until he 'got the hang of' the brake pedal." *(Eric G. R. French)*

Gussie's Model A Ford (photo by author)

Gussie and Sadie were driving down to Randboro when one of the back wheels came off on Williams Hill, rolling past the car and on down the hill. Gussie is said to have remarked to Sarah, "Well, doesn't that beat hell . . . I'll bet you a dollar to donuts that's our wheel!" They caught up with the wheel at the bottom of the hill and Gussie tossed it into the back seat and carried on to Randboro, the car slumped a bit low in back. These cars were constructed on a single frame, similar to a buckboard wagon, so would have remained steady even with a wheel missing in the rear. Gussie would have gotten some temporary wheel nuts from the store in Randboro and gone on to the garage in Sawyerville to get the proper nuts.

***

W. E. Goodenough was elected Mayor of Newport in 1928 and held the position for eight years through the Great Depression until Hollis Burns became mayor in 1937. John Burns Sr. had held the office of justice of the peace for Newport from 1910 until his death in 1945. He was the last justice of the peace in Island Brook.

The Wall Street stock market crash in 1929 triggered the Great Depression, bringing economic hard times to many Canadians; Newport was far from exempt. Many of the farmers in Newport and surrounding townships, who had recently purchased or expanded their farms or purchased new equipment and livestock, were shocked by the sudden downturn of the marketplace. Young people were hit especially hard because they were just beginning to shape their lives for the future. Many wouldn't get married because they could barely support themselves, never mind a wife and family. Those who had just started their families had to find new ways to survive.

W. E. Goodenough

While the farmers were not able to sell their produce for much money, they were always able to eat and once again the community survived on each other's generosity. Their gardens flourished with an abundance of strawberries, rhubarb, potatoes and vegetables; their poultry houses were full of new chicken and geese hatchlings and eggs; the fields were abundant with hay, corn and barley. They had ample wheat, barley, oats and buckwheat for making bread and pancakes, along with dandelions and cherries for making wine. Since they couldn't sell their livestock, they had lamb, beef and pork to eat. These communities of farmers would contribute to church suppers, which became fundraisers, helping people less fortunate and attracting families from urban centres where the men had lost their jobs.

***

Author's note: Robert Nugent (1846-1904) and Alice (Gill) Nugent (1857-1944) had immigrated and settled in the Maple Grove area (near Thetford Mines, Que.) at the start of the Great Depression. They raised two sons, Grant and George, on their farm in Maple Grove. The two brothers married two sisters, Hattie and Eva Williamson, and were trying to make a living with their families on poor farmland. Like many whose world began to collapse, they sought a better life and found excellent farmland in Newport.

Grant John and Harriet "Hattie" Edith (Williamson) Nugent migrated from Maple Grove with their four children: Hubert, Muriel, Harris and Doris Eva, who was 11 or 12 at the time. They purchased a farm in the northwestern Flanders region of Newport (near Island Book) from the BALC circa 1928-29. They loaded all their belongings onto their double wagon, making several trips on the long journey to their new farm. On the final trip with the livestock, Muriel, Harris and Doris helped guide the cattle that were singularly tied to each other behind the wagon. Hattie had loaded their chickens in pens on the wagon along with enough feed to sustain the flock for at least a month. "My Uncle Hubert drove the team of horses up from Maple Grove near Thetford Mines for the big move." *(Terry Winslow, grandson)*

Grant and Hattie's fifth child, Robert ("Bobby"), was born on their new farm in Flanders. "The story was that they moved because the land in the Maple Grove, Thetford region, was too stony to be farmed properly and they had a large family to support." Unfortunately, Hattie died of a brain tumour when Doris was around 17 years old, and so Grant was alone with his older children to bring up Bobby. The Depression years would continue to be tough years; however, the family was able to thrive on their new farm. *(Allan Hurd, grandson)*

George Robert (1888-1971) and "Eva" Beatrice (Williamson) (1892-1981) Nugent emigrated from Maple Grove to Manchester, N.H., where they raised their only son, Alvin George (1914-2000). Times were tough in the 1930s, and after Alvin graduated from high school in 1932, his first job was wheelbarrowing cement to build a mill in Groveton, N.H. The family moved to Newport in 1934 and purchased the farm known as "Munn's farm" from Austin and Ruth Bowker. It is located in the southwestern sector of Newport, on the border with Eaton Township, and is divided by the Randboro-Sawyerville road, today's Route 210. *(Bill Nugent)*

> *Author's note: Todays Route 210 from Sawyerville to the original Maple Leaf community ran through Munns farm and was originally referred to as the Heard road. Munns farm was an original lot owned by Nathanial Beaman, an Associate of Col. Edmund[5] Heard.*

"Grant used to tell his grandson Allan Hurd only half-jokingly that when it came to wives, George got the better deal." *(Allan Hurd, grandson)*

Alvin Nugent married Ruth Elizabeth (1919-1998) Matthew, youngest daughter of George (1869-1920) and Mary "Mamie" Annie Matthew (1891-1971). Alvin and Ruth raised three sons on the farm: Donald "Donny," William "Billy," and Thomas "Tommy." Alvin's parents continued living on the farm for several years after Alvin and Ruth married, so they had the opportunity to be close to their grandsons during their retirement years. Alvin built a new barn in the mid-1950s to house their ever-increasing herd of cattle. They had herds of both beef and dairy cattle along with the usual flock of chickens, operating a mixed farm that produced beef, milk, chickens and eggs.

***

Charlie Wood, a logging contractor in the region, was a forward-thinker so when tractors became available by 1927, he purchased a Linn tractor; a powerful machine with two six-foot-long caterpillar tracks powered by a six-cylinder gas engine. This meant seven sleighs of logs could be pulled from the bush at once, not just the one or two that a double team of horses could manage. By the early 1930s larger mills were in operation and lumbering sounds still emanated through the woods during the winter months. "You think troopers can swear? You ought to hear the sawmillers." Yelling is another thing that sawmillers do." Considering the decibel level of several three-foot saws and with the carriage moving the logs; it is not surprising they had to raise their voices to be heard. "Sawmillers" carried that tone into their daily life habits because they probably became deaf. Arthur Lowry, who was boarding at Cora Austin's, was a prime example of one who had worked many years in this industry and appeared to be deafer than a doornail.[43]

Charlie Woods' logging tractor, one of the first machines used in mechanical logging in the area (Newport Homecoming 1802-1996)

Lester Wooten had bought and began operating the old Planche mill at the junction of today's Route 210 and the townships of Auckland and Newport in April 1931, employing some 40-50 men in the lumbering operations. Charlie Wood, his men and other loggers were now engaged in hauling long sleighs of logs to the mills with these tractors. This new mode of "workhorse" was beginning to replace the former methods. The lumbering industry was modernizing and this triggered the beginning of the demise of many teams of horses that had been used primarily to draw lumber sleds. Many of these teamsters were operated by the local farmers for extra income during the winter month. With the introduction of tractors and even trucks beginning to show up in the summer months, farmers began to be squeezed out of a significant part of their income.[46]

***

Arthur, Eric and Evelyn Hurd and Maple Leaf Methodist Church. Maple Leaf school was just up the road from the church. (Hurd family collection)

The old Methodist Church, located beside the schoolhouse in Maple Leaf on today's Route 210, was purchased by Marshall Rand and moved to the old Haskell Hurd farm sometime between 1930 and 1932. This circa-1927 photograph shows the church. Note that the roads were now somewhat wider and able to accommodate vehicles passing in either direction. While buggies and cars intermingled on these roads, some horses still tended to be afraid of cars, especially if one passed them from behind. A team of runaway horses was not uncommon during this transitional period, the horses usually heading "hell-bent" for home. Arthur Hurd is pictured here with his cousins Eric and Evelyn Hurd, children of Alonzo and Evelyn "Eva" (Robinson) Hurd, walking back to Sarah and Gussie's home after walking to a school event. The Maple Leaf School was just up the road from the church.[31]

By 1926 Edmund[10] Lionel Hurd, the eldest son of Augustus[9] ("Gussie") and Sarah ("Sadie") Hurd, had graduated from Maple Leaf School. He was 19 and ready for a career, as were many others in Newport. He dreamed of a career in business, following Alonzo Hurd's footsteps. He attended Belleville Business College and graduated in 1929, but there were no jobs available in the business world. He returned to work on the farm and worked at odd jobs around the community.

Jobs were scarce even in Newport, so Lionel took on many temporary jobs. He worked for his uncle Joe Riddell in various lumber camps in the townships of Ditton and Emberton, sometimes deep in woodlots encompassing thousands of acres. These were difficult and lonely experiences away from family.

Lionel joined the local militia, the Sherbrooke-based 7th Hussars, a horse cavalry at that time. He continued for some time as a reservist. In 1929 he was commissioned as an officer with the 7th Hussars after training at St. Jean, Que. With the introduction of machine guns in warfare, the horse cavalry role was essentially modernized in all countries in the western world and became armoured tank units. In April 1936, the 7th Hussars amalgamated with the 11th Hussars to become the 7th/11th Hussars and were re-designated an Armoured Division. These new divisions were intended to "brush with the enemy" in reconnaissance roles.[3, 31]

Lionel Hurd, commissioned as an officer in 1929

Lionel also helped build the new Sawyerville High School in 1931, with his uncle Joseph Riddle who tendered the construction for $18,978. Later he took a more permanent job as a surveyor for the mines in Rouyn-Noranda, Que. Isolated living in lumber camps and hard physical work appeared to be his lifestyle prior to the war, which may also have helped him with survival skills during the war.[4, 40]

***

The Great Depression was the start of a long road of simple survival for most. While much of the world was without work, and their families starving, Japan invaded Manchuria. Japan was employing and training their men in the military so they in turn could feed their own families, while Germany was employing their men in building up their military.

The countries of the "Free World" were employing their men by building new infrastructure. Trade wars between Japan and Germany were further crippling many of the Free World's markets, causing a world-wide economic slowdown which began to affect Newport residents.

Opening the new consolidated school in Sawyerville in 1932 changed the landscape in Newport and ushered in a new era of transporting children to school. Prior to consolidation in 1931, parents were responsible for getting their children to school; this was why schools had been placed within each community and many students had to walk two or three miles. Now, tenders were let to transport children to town. The conveyances were horse-drawn wagons – now sporting hard rubber-tired wheels – in spring and fall, and sleds in winter. These new "school buses," drawn by a team of horses, did so on some rough roads and needed an enclosed upper body to protect the children from adverse weather conditions.

A blizzard with high winds and 2-3 inches of snow occurred during the last week of April 1931, which required the farmers to get their cattle back into the barns. Weather was as unpredictable then as it is now, and during that year the school bus drivers had already changed from sleds to wagons, causing some very treacherous driving as a result.

The spring melting of these hard-packed snow roads was a particularly difficult time for travelling. It necessitated the use of large open farm wagons which had a larger and more stable base. Frequently the driver would have to resort to travelling in the open fields alongside the roads, as the fields lost their snow much faster than the hard-packed roads.[40]

School van (Sawyerville High School Reunion 1994)

The reins that the drivers used to control the horses ran through little holes at the front of the wagon's upper box. In cold weather these "school vans" or in winter "school sleds" could be shut up tight to retain some heat provided by a small wood stove at the back. Note in the photograph, the driver sat on the right looking out a small window that could be covered with a rolled-up tarp when not in use. To keep the fire going, the driver would select one of the children to tend to the fire. This was considered an opportunity and a privilege so each year the children would vie for the job.

"A resident in the community remembers one occasion when something startled the horses so that they shied, and the van tipped over on its side. The lid came off the stove, coals spilled out and an unfortunate girl sitting near the stove ended up with burns to her bloomers."[40]

Tenders to drive these school vans and sleds were issued. The Maple Leaf route was tendered to Fred Hurd at $2.65 per day; Bert Cook had the Parker Hill route for $1.60 per day, and Austin Bowker took the route up towards Flanders and Island Brook for $1.80 per day.[40]

To assist the grades 10 and 11 pupils to deal with the heavy demands of these grades more effectively in the consolidated school, a notification was posted that school hours had been extended to four o'clock in the afternoon. An exception was made for three students who were to travel in the vans at 3 o'clock.

Entries from the 1932 diary of Edith (Morrison) Rand:

Wed. Jan. 6: *It rained hard, took all the snow away. We churned 7 lb. butter and I baked today. There was an auction sale of the Maple Leaf, Randboro, and Parker Hill schoolhouses. The Maple Leaf school sold to Ernie Tannahill for $16, the Randboro school sold to Charles Montgomery and the Parker Hill school went to William Parker.*

Sat. Jan. 16: *Colder, the ground is frozen and quite cold today. Lyle and Clinton went to Randboro to see the schoolhouse moved to Charlie Montgomery's.*

Fri. Feb. 26: *A fine warm day today. The Maple Leaf school house was moved today down to Alfred Swail's with Charlie Wood's tractor.*

Tue. Mar. 1: *It snowed last night, a wintry today. Mrs. Mary Leggett's 86th birthday. Col. Lindburgh's baby was kidnapped tonight.* [big news in the USA]

School sled, driven by Fred Hurd Sr. (Sawyerville High School Reunion 1994)

Fri. Mar. 11: *Marshie rolled the roads today. The sawers* [referring to men who sawed the logs, cut them into 12-14-inch blocks, then hauled them out during the winter for the later splitting of firewood] *finished this afternoon. Been at it since Monday. The sawers moved to Frank's [Morrison]. Sawyerville Catholic School burned to the ground this morning. Damaged Albert Riddle's house a lot.*

Author's note: Albert Riddle was married to Marshall's older sister Mary. Albert and Mary had been farming in the region of New Mexico, then later on the William[2] and Eliza (Beaman) Loveland farm, and had now retired. The house she is referring to is the home we knew as belonging to Volney Hurley in Sawyerville on the Clifton Road.

Thu. May 12: *Beautiful and warm. Col. Lindbergh's baby was found at 3:30, murdered.*

Tue. May 17: *Beautiful day today. Terrible fire in the woods up on Bert Tremblys. Marshie fought fire till nearly midnight. Also, Lyle. *Charlie and Grace were here in the evening. Also, Sarah Hurd came over."* [*Charlie Lafleur had married Diana Grace Graham.]

Wed. May 18: *Beautiful day again. A big crowd from Sawyerville and Marshie fought fire most of the day.*

Thu. May 19: *Lovely day. I washed five wool blankets. Marshie seeded for himself. Men from village watched fire all day. Also *Sam [Laberee, a hired hand]. They finally got it under control.* [*Sam had always been a bit challenged and in his old age was committed to Ste. Anne's Hospital in Ste. Anne de Bellevue, Que.]

Sat. May 28: *Marshie, Lyle [their son] and Sam worked on the road all day. I went to Mr. John Riddle's funeral with Lionel and Gussie [Hurd].*

***

This was a time when trains were becoming a main source for both passenger and commercial travel. Salespeople were dispatched by the distributors of goods to the smaller rural towns to show their huge suitcase packed with wares to the local shopkeepers. They would disembark from the train and hire a local teamster with a covered wagon or sled used then as a local taxi. Later, as cars became the norm, these salesmen would travel in "coupe" cars, commonly known as "salesmen's cars," simply because they had no backseats but a very large trunk. The store in

Randboro previously owned by Samuel and Persis Hurd had been purchased by Charlie and Gertie Montgomery and these salesmen would descend upon them showing samples of product that they could order. For the first time people of the community could buy a wide assortment of goods and, especially for the women, fashionable clothing could be purchased at a local store.

Typical store-bought clothes of the era (photo by Sandra Hurd)

***

Fred Hurd (Gussie and Sadie's second son), the entrepreneur and sportsman of the family, was 22 when he decided to farm foxes. His cousin, Evelyn (Swail) Riddell, the schoolteacher on Parker Hill, seemed to think there was money to be made in farming foxes. She was raising nine silver foxes at the time, and this idea gave Fred the inspiration to do the same. He built three large wire pens at least 12 by 12 feet each. The pens were perched as high as 10 feet off the ground so that their pee and poop fell through the wire floor. This was smart thinking on his part because he never had to clean them out.

Oddly, he built these pens just behind Sadie's chicken house, perhaps to allow the foxes to keep track of their game (Sarah's free-roaming chickens below the pens) keeping the foxes healthy in anticipation. One might wonder if the odd chicken got thrown in for the foxes. If so, the author might suspect the chicken dumper may have been his father, Lionel, when he would have come home to visit, as he so hated those chickens. Perhaps even Arthur may have had a hand because the chicken poop was all over the yard and he had now inherited the job from his older brother, Lionel, to mow the lawns. Fred was raising both red and silver foxes, housing them in the different pens. The author has no information as to why his uncle Fred was raising the foxes, unless he was selling their skins and tails to the furrier market. The depression did not seem to quell the sale of fur coats and foxtails, which became a brisk business in the cities for the affluent women who were wearing them even during this era.

***

On July 17, 1932 Jessie (Hurd) Riddell wrote to her sister Mary. Her letter tells us:

> *Sometime the first part of June, Dr. Beaton was coming home from a call out Randboro way and when he got along to the Pejepscot Lumber yard, at Alonzo Hurd's mill, he saw a fire in the lumber, so he got help at once and they put the fire out with pails of water (didn't take out hose). The fire had started in a pile of chair stock and they found a bath towel soaked with gasoline or kerosene and fine lumber (chair stock) crisscrossed over it. That was what was burning and another 10 minutes and they couldn't have put it out. Whoever did that will probably have another try at it. The lumber was so close to many houses that they would have been burned down as well.*

Not even a week later, a major fire destroyed the Sawyerville mills and Alonzo Hurd was devastated as he lost not only the mills but piles of lumber paid for and ready for final milling. Insurance covered only part of the family's losses. The mills were rebuilt and would continue operations until the floods of 1941, '42 and '43. "While Grandpa Alonzo was alive the plants down at the river underwent at least one fire and one flood. It was rumoured that these disasters killed him as he died of a heart attack in his late fifties."[31] *(quote: Eric G. R. French)*

***

Mary Hurd's husband, Gifford (Lawson) Sr., had now lost his job in the U.S. due to the Depression and they were suffering terribly. Mary's sister, Sadie, wrote in July 1932:

> *Those who came from the U.S. here, say we are not going through anything like what the people there are. We try to save in every way possible. I feel every time we go out in the car that we should not be using the gas. We are all so grieved over Alonzo Hurds loss. Last Saturday night all his mill burned, the Sash and Door factory and Dry Kiln and from 30,000 to 50,000 feet of lumber burned as well. he estimates his loss at $15,000 and had only $6,000 insurance for coverage. There are lots of mysterious fires these times, especially much opposition to contend with and danger of any small businesses being crushed by the larger ones. Alonzo is feeling pretty blue right now. We hope that the loss of income will*

not mean for George (Hurd) to have to give up going to University. He has had one year and passed fine and he is a very clever fellow." I think Alonzo intends to rebuild his mill if he can.[21]

By 1932 the Great Depression was affecting almost everyone in Newport, causing much general hardship. Thankfully, food was not as much an issue here as it was in the more urban and city centres. The army offered some refuge by at least creating jobs, so if one wanted to join, there were two weeks of military training each year. Both Lionel and Frederick Hurd applied for and went to the 10-day Military Training Camp in Valcartier for a couple of years. *"The boys had a wonderful time at the camp this year,"* Sadie wrote to her sister Mary in 1932 *"Frederick was disappointed not to have received the tender to drive the school bus for next year as he was underbid."* [21]

***

Marconi radios were available in Canada circa the late 1890s. Despite that, when the radio was first introduced in the early 1920s, many predicted it would kill the phonograph industry. Radio was a free medium for the public to hear music instead of having to buy records. It would be another decade before radio transmissions reached the rural areas such as Newport. Radios were not readily available in Newport until catalogues started to flourish in the latter 1920s.

By the 1930s, battery-operated crystal radios became popular in all rural areas when radio stations increased their wattage output, and by 1934 some 60 percent of Canadian households had a radio. It was an inexpensive way to keep up with news events of the Great Depression and as well plenty of farming news. It provided a ready means for escape from the economic hard times through sports broadcasts and entertainment programs. Many would listen to the hockey and baseball games and especially the baseball broadcast from Chicago on Sunday afternoons. Hearing the cheering and roaring applause of the crowds provided a feeling of actually being at the ballpark or hockey arena. Everyone in the family crowded into the kitchen or parlour to listen to these broadcasts that became part of their entertainment.[48]

In the U.S., Bonnie and Clyde and Dillinger were on the loose, robbing banks. The "Dirty Thirties" was a time of devastating drought and severe dust storms throughout much of the midwestern and southwestern United States and the Canadian Prairies. Newport residents relied on their radios for their news, as it was often more up-to-date than their newspapers. Even though our ancestors were going through very difficult times during this era, they would listen to the news on the radio of people starving and standing in food lines and feel blessed that they could feel safe in Canada and able to feed their families by growing their own food on their farms.

And so, during the Great Depression era of the 1930s, vacuum tube radios had become a part of everyday household listening for both news and entertainment. These battery-operated radios were now available by mail order, and those who could afford a "Philco" brand radio bought one.

There were radio stations as far as the Texas-Mexico border who had built "border blasters" with available wattage of up to 500,000 watts and these stations were heard all the way to Canada. "The signal was so overpowering you could hear the music on the barbed wire fences, the farmers would say." *(Ken Burns, "Country Music" documentary)*

From the drudgery of the day, being able to listen to the radio in the evening was an escape for the whole family; listening to country music was a favourite in almost every farmhouse. The music spoke of the times and was the same music they danced to on Saturday night. It was not long before another radio station, W.S.M, opened in Nashville, broadcasting the Grand Ol' Opry, hosted by Roy Acuff, every Saturday evening. Local talent learned to play these songs just by listening to them on the radio over time and replayed them to everyone's delight at the local dances in Newport halls and surrounding townships on Saturday evenings.

Of course, with radios came advertising, selling everything from insurance policies to baby chicks. In the 1930s frozen foods began to appear on shelves and most urban homes had water heaters. In 1934, cream of mushroom soup was available in cans starting the "canned goods" revolution in commercial foods. Home canning of produce grown on the local farms had been a major step forward for our more recent ancestors, allowing them to store more of their own home-grown vegetables for winter consumption. Now they could add store-bought canned produce they would not have canned on their own. It was a real advantage during the lean years ahead in urban centres but only if affordable.

In a letter to her sister, Mary (Hurd) Lawson in July of 1932, Sadie (Sarah) writes *"Lionel is hoping something will turn up to give him an opening but things are certainly discouraging, however we have our health, home and plenty to eat and that is what millions today have not. The hunting season has opened and Wallace [Boyd], Frederick and Arthur have both been up to the little camp on Lyon Stream and stayed all night but did not bring home any game."* [21]

Our ancestors in Newport did not say much about the depression except that having grown up on a farm, they felt that they fared better than city folks. Having land to grow their own vegetables was an advantage and there was usually an animal to slaughter. Hens produced eggs and later could be "dressed" and roasted for a meal. Milk was "separated" for the cream which was used to make butter. Anything extra could be sold or traded. Wild berries grew nearby in fields, pastures and roadsides. Most farmers had several varieties of apple trees.

As was the case for many others in Newport, both the Rand and Hurd families had hardwood maple bushes and produced their own maple syrup and sugar for cooking and table use. "My mom said that some neighbours could afford white, granulated sugar and it was special when they would want to trade a cup of it for maple sugar!" *(Carol Rand)*

Music and dances were a big part of country life during the depression. They were a diversion, an opportunity for people to get together, to socialize, to forget the hard times and have fun at minimal expense. The music was local and exceptionally talented, and all the communities by now had a hall. Charlie Montgomery, who owned the little store in Randboro, had built a large hall for just this very purpose; a place for the Farm Forum meetings, political meetings and any other type events that would bring people from the countryside to Randboro. One might suspect that "Montgomery's Hall" was paid for simply from the added income generated from goods purchased by folks coming in early on a Saturday night from the countryside for an evening of fun.

The Junior Guild held a party and dance there on November 3, 1932. Sadie and her son Fred went that evening and had a great time. Sadie wrote:

> *The Junior Guild has one of these dance parties every month except during Lent and July and August when it is too hot. . . . The Guild met yesterday at Mrs. Bill Parkers home. Frederick took Nora Loveland, Lizzie Boyd, and myself in the old open-air Model T Ford car. It was very cold riding but we were all bundled up so we were not cold. Later Fred took the car and went hunting with Wallace Boyd and when Arthur got home from school, he saw them at Wallace's with a two-year-old buck on the running board of the car, so we will have lots of meat this week.* [21]

***

As had always been the custom, and especially now, everything was used, reused, and repurposed on the farm. This included clothing. Worn wool sweaters, coats and other items were cut into strips to make hooked rugs. The base of the rug was a washed feed bag stretched over a handmade wooden frame. This generation was ingenious in how they made do with what they had. They made their own jacks out of wood by fashioning a simple circular fulcrum, with a lever, allowing one to push down on the lever which would raise a two-part block. *(Royce Rand, Eaton Corner Museum)*

Rug hooks were fashioned from a nail, which was filed to make a hook. The handle was often that of an old kitchen strainer or a piece of cutlery. Many of the women hooked rugs, made of old materials from clothes, bedding and other cloth materials that would normally be discarded in today's world. These rugs, some fashioned in round, others in oblong shapes, would be placed throughout a house, especially beside beds where it was a comfort for their feet in an early morning rather than a cold floor. Many of these rugs were sold for much-needed money in the urban markets. During these tight times, sugar bags and flour bags were pieced together and made into sheets and other bedding. "To save their shoes, the children in my mom's family often went barefoot in the summer." *(Rand family history)*

One of the activities that all young boys and girls favoured was picking wild strawberries, raspberries and blueberries, as well as high-bush cranberries. Arthur and Sarah (Sadie) Hurd would walk to their back 200 acres to pick berries, as they grew in profusion on newly cleared lands. The brush left over from lumbering and clearing the land was collected into huge piles then burned. Once the piles were burned down the land underwent a controlled burn. Once the land was burned, raspberries, strawberries and blueberries were the first to grow, the berries so plentiful the pickers would have their baskets overflowing in a less time than it took to get there. Apart from all the shortcakes and pies eaten in season, great amounts of these native berries and also apples were preserved for use in the winter. Home canning fruits and vegetables such as tomatoes, corn, peas and beans became an important household activity, both in the spring and in the fall. "The knowledge that white sugar is not good for you had not yet been discovered and so our ancestors suffered no harm at all. Most farmers though, were using natural maple sugar. Oranges were unheard of but for the one we got in our stockings for Christmas."[47] *(Ernie McCallum)*

Sadie Hurd appeared to be keenly interested in both the political and business aspirations in the region. Many of her letters speak to how the government is not working for the people and/or should be working, and how their decisions reflect on the prosperity of the local constituents. She was interested in any projects that might bring a new opportunity to Newport as reflected in another letter referencing a new "invention" she had heard about in the States that would make sawdust into briquets. Sawdust from the mills was in abundance, and with many mills that had burned down, the sawdust piles were a huge liability. Many of these piles of sawdust heated up and simply caught fire by spontaneous combustion, not unlike hay if it is put away too green (not "cured" as in fireplace wood).[21]

Sadie wrote to her sister Mary in the U.S.:

> *I hope they will be able to get the project financed and that a real start has being made. Can you find out if in using sawdust must it necessarily be fresh made sawdust or can they use it from piles that have laid for a few years. Is the machinery heavy for manufacturing, what I mean is this —could it be transported from one mill to another, using the sawdust on the spot or would the sawdust have to be transported to a central plant? If a success can be made of making briquettes from that sort of waste, surely the Province of Quebec offers an ideal place for starting such a business.*[21]

In a letter to Mary in October 1932, Sadie wrote:

> *An American firm is about to start a factory for making barrel staves in Sawyerville. It is expected that they will employ fifty to sixty men year-round. This mill will mean a local market for lumber which we all have ample to sell. Gussie intends to see the man who is head of this business as soon as possible to see if he can coordinate the lumbermen for supply.*[21]

Communities such as those in Newport were really no different than other rural areas, demonstrating a communal spirit where everyone brought their different skill sets to bear for the benefit of others. The key element that held these communities together was survival – not much different than those before them. During this era where more formal education began to flourish, there was more of a mesh of entrepreneurial, social and a hands-on common sense that was shared amongst all within each individual community. It was the sharing of these skill sets that provided a sense of well-being during these tough times in Newport.

In a letter written by Sarah Hurd in 1932, where she mentions that Milton was very ill and she looked after him one night before he died, she mentions to her sister Mary that *"Milton was Arthur's schoolmate and when he acted as a pallbearer it was the hardest thing he has ever had to do."*

Author's note: Milton Jones, the only son of John and Nellie Jones, died young at age 17 in 1932.

***

Sadie wrote to her sister Mary (Hurd) Lawson:

> *It was on this night in October of 1932, that Alonzo Rand died. It seems that he had worked all day but had not felt well and went home and right to bed. He was alone and some people that were also living in the house heard him moaning and called the doctor who came and gave him four hypo's, stayed*

with him for a couple of hours and them left him alone. Apparently, the pain he had been having was from stones in his bladder, however, he was found dead the next morning. The doctor called it heart failure; however, I don't see how they got away with it without an inquest. [21]

Author's note: Alonzo Rand, eldest son of Newell Clement and Laura (McCurdy) Rand, was born in 1883 and died at age 49.

The sale of the Maple Leaf, Randboro, and Parker Hill schoolhouses in 1932 not only meant "the end to the little red schoolhouse" in this section of Newport Township so far as Protestant education was concerned, but also made way for the new order of things. Many of the older residents of the community viewed the passing of these old schools with great sorrow as they recalled bygone days and bygone times. The old schoolhouses were now to pass into private ownership by auction. The Maple Leaf school was purchased by Eddy Tannahill and moved to his farm on Grove Hill Road. The Parker Hill schoolhouse was purchased by William Parker and the shed by Albert Laroche. The Randboro schoolhouse and shed were now the property of Charlie Montgomery.[40] On Saturday, January 9, 1932, a crowd gathered at the Knicky Knocky Parsons Schoolhouse near Bury for the auction of that building, although the sale was then postponed to a later date. These auctions marked a major change for all the communities of Newport as well as other townships in the surrounding regions.[46]

Gone were the days when the teacher went to the schoolhouse, built the fire, and when the children saw smoke, they went to school. These schools had been built through an untiring interest in education and with modest means by citizens who knew the value and the need for education of their children. There was a blackboard, a tin dipper, and a corner where outer garments could be hung and, in the winter, rubbers stored. In summer most of the children still went barefoot.

There were no more teachers boarding at homes in the community, and staying with families for days or weeks, according to the number of children in the family. The new Consolidated Schools were operating at full capacity and students enjoyed larger and separate classrooms, basement play areas and large backyard grounds for teeters, bars, and a sports field. Recesses offered the opportunity for interaction with students from all parts of different local communities providing a much broader community learning awareness.

The schoolhouse at Knicky Knocky was sold by public auction later in the spring of 1932. The old building that had served the community so well was refurbished with a beautiful hardwood floor and became Knicky Knocky Hall. Dances were held every Saturday night beginning with the Easter Dance and during the summer and fall months. Admission was 25 cents for the men, the ladies were allowed in free. Some brought lunches. Local talent provided the music and later bands such as Les Beaulieu's Orchestra were hired. Good lighting was provided by gas lamps and lanterns also hung from the ceiling. "As I remember about halfway through the dance, a light would start to dim; my father would get up on a ladder and take it down and with a special pump, give it more air and soon it would be as bright as ever." *(Nina (Parsons) Rowell)*

And so, the schoolhouse on the property where Fay Parsons had grown up now became a dance hall. "My mom remembers going to dances there. Lyle Rand finished school in the new "consolidated school" in Sawyerville in 1933. Fay Parsons finished school in the village of Bury before the end of the 1937 school year due to a serious illness." *(Carol Rand)*

***

Sadie Hurd held a great interest in world affairs and was quite vocal in her assessments during these tough times. She wrote to her sister Mary in 1933:

I have confidence that Canada will see a come-back before the U.S.A. We are more underdeveloped, and I think trade within the Empire is going to work out to our good. We would see much benefit now were it not for the exchange rates, however no doubt in time this condition will adjust itself. In the meantime, it holds our prices down and keeps them up in Britain. We are wondering what this financial crisis in the U.S.A will have on your prospects? Things are certainly moving rapidly here as our banks are refusing to accept American cheques, currency, or money orders. The Post Office is refusing to send money orders across the border. We heard today [March 23] that the Canadian dollar is worth $1.20 while the American has dropped to .80 cents. [21]

Staggs Stave Mill opened in 1933 and created many jobs for local younger men in the adjacent townships. Sarah wrote that *"Mr. Stagg the Mill Manager, says it is our Canadian Protective tariff which brought them here and that many industrials are moving to Canada on that account."* Many of the logs cut and sledded to this new mill in Sawyerville were coming from Newport. Logs had to be marked, almost as a branding, to identify ownership. Such terms such as "scorers," "scalers" and "markers" were all individual jobs carried out throughout the lumber industry and were considered key positions, held by skilled lumbermen. Some logs were marked for regular lumber, and some went for making barrel staves. Codes used in the marking process identified the source of the lumber so that the farmers, cutters, sledders and river runners would all get paid appropriately, based on the lumber markings, much like the branding of cattle in the West.[21, 31]

Alonzo Hurd rebuilt the Sawyerville mills in 1933 after the fire, partnering with Lloyd Hunt and Joe Riddell. When Alonzo broke his leg in April 1933, both Lloyd and Joe had to abandon their own work to help him run the mills.

Jessie (Hurd) Riddle wrote to her sister Mary:

> *Alonzo is getting along real well now, his leg in a cast but he moves around on crutches. He has been coming downstairs now, but it was three weeks since it was really fixed right as there was one piece of bone broken clear off and they have had quite a job to keep that in place. Alonzo thinks it is beginning to heal now.*[21, 31]

In the spring of 1933, Sadie's letter tells us:

> *Fred Fallon is getting weak now and his beard has grown to about six inches, I wish you could see him. It is Fred [Hurd]'s job to "shear" him each spring and this spring his hair is already down to his shoulders. Fred came over last Sunday and Fred clipped him. You would never know him for the same man when Fred got through. Gave him a shampoo and he has a new pair of trousers and looked the cleanest we had seen him for a long time.* [21, 31] [Fred Fallon died in early February 1934.]

At the same time, Fred Hurd bought his own horse team and hauled logs down the river road; his brother Arthur joined him many times after school when Fred passed by on his way to the mill.

> *Gussie, Norman [Betts] and Fred, hauled two loads each day and landed the logs at the Newell Rand place and when the river is up by Spring, they will river run them down to the Sawyerville Mill. They are paying $3.00 a thousand feet and so they will run the loads on Saturdays as well. Fred is driving the school van again and he gets $2.25 a day, so that is a comfort. Fred gets up at 4:30, taking care of both teams and he will go with Norman while Arthur will drive the School van out to the river road, pick up Fred so he can pick up the school pupils and take them to school. Wages are low but there is work to be had by nearly everyone who wants to work.* [21]

In May of 1933, Fred bought Arthur Loveland's car for $150. It was a 1928 Model A Ford sedan that previously had a taxi license so he would be able to use it instead of the horse-drawn school van when the roads were passable. Fred hoped he could also use it to take some fares to earn extra money.[31]

In a letter to her sister Mary Lawson in late 1933, Sadie wrote:

> *I must tell you what Frederick is doing. Two years ago, he bought some calves. He paid $12.00 each for them and after two years, he was offered $15.00 each for them by the butcher here at Sawyerville. Fred told him he would never take that for them, that he would rather butcher them himself and sell the meat. He has been doing this for a month now and has sold all the meat and three head of Gussies cattle as well. He is going to buy three or four cattle from Gussie and keep on selling. He is undercutting the Sawyerville butcher [Martin] and intends to keep on going until the weather gets too cold." We are getting a lot more than we would ever get selling them in the market. It is awful the price the farmers are having to take for everything we have to sell, and the consumer is not getting the benefit of it.*[21]

Sadie wrote in the early spring of 1934: *"We have had a long cold winter and heavy snow this year and roads are impassable this March. Arthur and I walked up to Renford Morrow's [Willard Rand's old homestead] to see their new baby boy [Myrlin]. He has the croup and we are worried for him."* [21]

Unfortunately, Lila (Parker) Rand, the wife of Gardner Wheeler Rand, *"fell down her cellar stairs in late 1934, breaking her leg."* Lila was in her 70s at the time, still storing vegetables and preserves in roughly built cupboards in the cellar. As a rule, these old staircases were steep and poorly lit, the cellar always dark. She survived but was lame for the rest of her life. These cellars were havens for spiders and other crawly creatures and were considered by the children as not a place to be: "I do not want to go down there!" or "I am not ever going down there!"[21, 32]

***

The different commnunity halls strived to provide entertainment that would bring some fun during these trying times. One notable event, which gives a flavour of the times, was held in late December 1934. The young men and boys of Sawyerville and surrounding regions put on a special entertainnment in the IOOF Hall called "Pleasures of 1934." It was a variety show and they planned all the program and carried it out themselves: music, singing, dancing and short skits. Only one girl took part in a skit, a step dance. Eight teenage boys, dressed to look like girls with coloured caps, bodices and shorts (very short), performed drills and danced.[21]

The hall was packed. In the crowd was Herbert Bowker. As he passed down the hall on his way out, Minnie Williams asked him how he enjoyed the show. "Well," he said "I don't think much of it. When girls will get up before a crowd and perform almost naked, I think something should be done about it." Minnie replied, "Do you mean to tell me that you, a man who has had two wives, don't know a girl's legs when you see them, from a boy's?" Poor old Herbert, I expect blushes every time he sees his own legs . . . perhaps he never saw his wives' legs. He certainly made a lot of fun for others through his prudishness."[31]

***

In mid-1934, Sadie Hurd suggested that her sister Mary, husband Gifford Lawson, and their son Gifford Jr. should come to live in Canada. Gifford had had difficulty landing any kind of job in Chicago for the past four years. Also, Mary seemed to be ill often, which ws a major concern for Sadie. The Great Depression was hitting hard in the U.S. and Jessie (Hurd) Riddell, her sister, wrote:

> *A cup of coffee and a donut is only enough to keep the breath of life in one, and I know you well enough to know you are not faring any better. When you need help, Maime [Mary], you know we will gladly send you assistance, as you must never get into this same fix again where you are hungry. Joe is enclosing an order for three hundred dollars on a Bank of Montreal in Chicago for Gifford.* [21, 31]

Sadie wrote that *"Fred is thinking of opening up a butcher shop this spring based on his experience last fall in selling meats,"* further suggesting that *"the family move up, even to help Fred with his new venture."* [21]

Sadie wrote in March 1934:

> *I walked over on the snow crust to Renford Morrow's place to see their new baby. He is eight months and the poor little fellow has Bronchial Pneumonia, but they got an experienced nurse in today. Renford is Hattie Cable's son* (the son of William and Hattie Jane (Cable) Morrow) *and a returned soldier. They have three children now, and this is such a beautiful baby. He weighs twenty pounds now and he seems so forward for his age.* [21]

***

Even during the Great Depression life seemed to be looking up for the Augustus Hurd family. Sadie had bought two incubators for hatching eggs, planning to increase her flock of chickens and egg production. She planned to have 100 pullets to sell by summer. Her son Frederick was in the first stages of planning to open up a butcher business in the spring of 1934. He priced out all the equipment he would need including an electric refrigerator, along with a shop to work from, located in East Angus, in Westbury Township. Customers who had supported him in the past year were asking for more deliveries and so in preparation, he cut down the back of his Model A Ford car to convert it into a truck for delivering and selling meat on the road. Sarah was ecstatic about this venture, suggesting that they would be selling much of their farm produce to Fred's store, which would include chickens, eggs, pork, lamb and beef for him to market in his business, both sharing in the profits. They anticipated he could sell for less and still make more than the current market was offering the farmers. If this venture grew, they and many other farmers in Newport were committed and ready to sell their produce to Fred as well, so supply would not be an issue.

Fred, always an avid hunter and fisherman, had learned how to butcher deer and moose at a young age. He had always participated in the butchering of any animal on the farm when they needed meat for their winter family consumption. After completing high school, and by 1934, Fred had established himself as a butcher when he opened a small shop in the town of East Angus. He was buying livestock and now delivering meats directly to the farming communities in his converted car/truck.

***

The winter of 1934 brought heavy snow. In March as the snow melted even the horses were getting stuck, limiting travel. As the story is told,

> Mrs. Lowry, a woman as large or larger than Alice (Cable) Bailey, was in the woods with her husband riding on the big lumber sleds. With the snow so deep, the going was "slower than molasses going uphill" and the sleds kept sinking to her side so much they thought the sleds would tip over. Mrs. Lowry decided she should jump off and did so. She sank deep in the snow and became stuck. Because there was no way her husband could move her, he tied a rope around her shoulders, hooked her up to the sleds and pulled her out just like a toboggan.[31]

By the summer of 1934, Sarah, being the businesswoman that she was, had already inventoried what she planned to have ready for sale by the fall, including 150 chickens, 40 of them Barred Rocks ready to market now. She was wanting to keep mostly Leghorns as East Angus was a good market for them. Sadie's letter informs us she is becoming optimistic now that the Depression is perhaps coming to an end stating, *"the men in the Mills are getting a 10% raise in their salaries right away and in Sherbrooke all industries are now running full time."* [21]

In a May 13 letter to her sister Mary, Sarah mentioned that *"Fred's store has opened in East Angus and he is selling beef, pork, ham and bacon, frankfurters and cottage roll, chickens and eggs. He expects to have fish for Friday and later veal as well. The big pulp and paper mills are running again full time, and everyone has work, which means of course pay cheques, so we hope it will be a good opening for him."* [21]

Mary Maria Hurd had her life cut short by having contracted rheumatic fever as a girl on the farm. "It resulted in lifelong heart disease (angina) and thyroid disease (a goiter that was operated on in the Mayo Clinic in 1930) before she and daddy, Gifford (Lawson) Jr., retreated to Canada for the early years of the Great Depression while grandfather searched for new employment." *(Mary Hurd Lawson, granddaughter of Mary Maria)*

Sarah's sister Mary had taken her up on her invitation to come to the farm and stay for the summer that year. "Mary stayed with her sister Sadie [Sarah] and Gussie while Daddy worked with Uncle Fred who was establishing his butcher business. When grandfather [Gifford Sr.] finally found an accounting job with TVA [Rural Electrification] in northern Alabama, he sent for Daddy to drive grandmother to their new home. After they crossed the Canadian border, grandmother had a stroke and Daddy had to drive her back to Sadie's to recuperate. Dad [Gifford Edmund Jr.] was not allowed by authorities to remain with her and so he had to drive into New Hampshire where he managed to find a job with room and board on a farm for several months. Unfortunately, after relocating to Alabama, Grandma had a massive stroke that killed her in 1938." *(Mary Hurd Lawson)*

***

Many of the women in the communities of Maple Leaf and Island Brook were organized to assist families, both locally and abroad, that were struggling to make ends meet – in organizations such as Women's Aid (WA) and Women's Missionary Society (WMS). These organizations were connected to the various churches; the meetings always started with a prayer. Two early presidents of the WA were Mary Sunbury and Martha Burns, who would hold tea each month in members' homes. Ladies active in the WMS in Island Brook included Naomi Burns (wife of John) and Glenna Burns (wife of Thomas); the latter was president for many years. Two ladies who served in office for a number of years were Miss Mary Seale and Mrs. Mary Todd. Mary was also president for many years; she was remembered as a fabulous cook and noted for the high quality of her work for church functions. Another devoted worker was Hazel Burns, who acted as sectary treasurer for many years until the end of the project.[32]

Hazel Kerr (wife of Franklin) drove her horse two miles to the meetings, never missing a meeting summer or winter. She acted as president for many years and with the help of Ilena Burns and Ruby Banks had been instrumental in keeping the church open for the occasional service.

Music always lifted the sprits of any community and there were many talented musicians, both vocal and instrumental, who organized younger generations for a choir and for displaying their own talents at various functions. Rev. Vibert's wife raised enough money with the participation of the choir to buy an organ for the Island Brook School. Old-time fiddlers David Ewing, Charlie and Gerald Alden and Garnet Lister were always available for any type of gathering or party that was organized. These functions were very much a part of their lives, giving back to their communities who needed both spiritual support and physical activities through the depression years.

Group photo of some Island Brook residents

L-R, back row: John Burns, Mrs. Jim May, Mrs. John Burns, Miss Lilla Kerr, Mrs. Horace Holbrook, Mrs. Franklin Kerr.

Middle row: Mrs. Jim Dougherty, Mrs. Hollis Burns, Mrs. Lovell Spaulding, Mrs. Thomas Burns, Mrs. N. Todd.

Kneeling: Mrs. A Burns, Elaine Kerr, Rowena Gagne, Mrs. Fred Gagne, Mrs. W. Hammond, Mrs. Jack Dawson, Mrs. R. Carr, Miss Mary Seale.

(reproduced from *Island Brook: Then and Now* [32])

This was also the time when William Shaw travelled the countryside with his horse-drawn wagon or sleigh, showing silent movies at the community halls. He told the stories of the movies and sang songs to entertain the audience. Sometimes he brought a "Marconi" phonograph record player which provided music for the movies. A sign on the back of his vehicle read "Professor Shaw." Professor of what, no one seemed to know![32]

***

By now, Lionel Hurd was mostly working for his uncle Joseph "Joe" Riddell on Joe's new farm in Eaton Township in the summers, and in logging camps during the winter. Joe and Jessie operated a huge logging enterprise that took a lot of their time in paperwork and management, so having Lionel to run the farm was a great help for them.

Arthur Hurd was growing up and at 18, he took a girl out for the first time to a dance at Charlie Montgomery Hall in Randboro in the spring of 1935. Gifford Lawson Sr. was still unemployed in the U.S. and Sarah's sister Mary was still unwell and had been sick most of the previous two years. Sarah continued to suggest in her letters that they should move back to Canada as she was optimistic that Canada would pull out of the depression before the U.S.[21]

***

By 1934 labour unions were coming into play in urban factory centres – victories for workers after much violence during the previous several years, and for owners the necessity to create safer, cleaner workplaces, albeit at additional costs to their bottom lines. By 1935, bottled liquor became a booming market thus more workers were hired during the period from 1936 to 1940, getting workers out of the food lines and back to work again. Bulldozers were beginning to replace horses in logging operations. Hand pumps were changing to mechanical water pumps drawing from a well or spring, and steel water pipes were installed in most homes.[48]

The bread winners (mostly men) were again moving to urban centres to find work. Unfortunately for many farmers like Val and Laura Swail, who were now in their seventies, and others of this generation in Newport, they could not find a buyer for their farm. Retirement for them was just not going to happen and so they carried on, keeping a few hens, a couple of horses and some cattle – just enough they could care for.

Hollis Cairns served as Mayor of Newport in 1937 and continued for the next six years into the World War II era, when in 1943 Austin Bowker was voted mayor and served until 1950. Hollis and his family lived just outside of Randboro on an original Lot 6 of Range 9, operating a large dairy farm on their 200-acre farm. The John Williams farm was located to the west on an original Lot 5, adjacent to the Cairn's farm, the hill known then as "Williams Hill."

> *Author's note: The road leading to the Cairns farm is now identified as "Chemin Lapointe," the area once referred to as "Pleasant Hill" where Col. Edmund[5] Heard and Capt. Josiah Sawyer slashed the first acre of land to build a cabin in 1793. The author remembers this hill as "Claude's Hill" simply because Claude Laroche and his family – Verlie, Lynford and Judy – grew up and lived in the original Williams family home. Matthew and Lizzie Boyd's farm was located to the east adjacent to the Cairns farm on an original lot first owned by the Harvey family, an original Lot 7 of Range 9.*

***

By 1937, the Great Depression intensified and rolled in like a thick fog. The tough times of earlier years returned with a vengeance. Gas was expensive and, in most cases, hard to get. Foods outside the normal growing cycle were becoming too expensive for most. By 1937 Japan had invaded mainland China and commanded the sea lanes between Hong Kong and Singapore.[3]

Fay Parsons was extremely sick with rheumatic fever for a year or more in 1937, followed by a neurological disorder called St. Vitus' dance. When she was well Fay worked for her brother-in-law, Earl Thompson, who had a small restaurant in Sawyerville. She also helped local families with cooking and household chores in town and in High Forest. *(Carol Rand)*

Rev. Arthur Vibert (*Cookshire Chronicle*, March 24, 1937; Hurd family collection)

Sarah Hurd writes that "*Gussie, Frederick and I went to Jessies for dinner Sunday. The Reverend Vibert was sick so we had no service and so we could go visiting with a clear conscience.*" Church in this era was vitally important in the communities and many people were referred to as "staunch" Baptists, Methodists, Anglicans or Roman Catholics. Each family had their own method of a practicing religion and so for some, even visiting without first attending church might be quite unforgiving.[31]

On Tuesday morning, March 9, 1937, the villages in the region were shocked and saddened by the news of the sudden death at his home of Rev. Arthur John Vibert. "Although in poor health for some months, Rev. Vibert had carried on his work as usual until a month ago when he gave over the Sunday services to students supplied by his beloved alma mater Bishops University. He was a friend to everyone, his good nature and even temperament being the subject of admiration and favorable comment. Over the many years he had taken a keen interest in the children and the welfare of the communities he served as well as those of his own church. John was born in 1878 in Jersey, the Channel Islands. With the Rt. Rev. Philip Carrington, Lord Bishop of Quebec officiating, the funeral was attended by almost the entire populations of Sawyerville, Randboro, Maple Leaf, Island Brook from the surrounding countryside. He was loved by everyone."[31]

***

Hauling a load of hay with repurposed car as truck on George Parsons farm (Newport Homecoming 1801-1996)

This photograph, taken at the George Parsons farm in Knicky Knocky, shows children playing on a car repurposed as a truck hauling a trailer load of hay. Old cars were never sold, they were repurposed and if they rusted out then the engines were used for anything else that required power to operate a piece of equipment!

Lyle Rand, the eldest son of Marshall and Edith (Morrison) Rand from Maple Leaf, and Fay Parsons, daughter of George and Nellie from Knicky Knocky, met at a masquerade dance in Sawyerville in February 1938. From that time and for their entire lives they dressed up for Halloween dances. "My mother always made the costumes. My dad was a wonderful dancer as were his siblings. Lyle, Clinton, and Hilda often went to dances together in the Newport locals, e.g., Island Brook and at Charlie Montgomery's Hall in Randboro. Dances were held sometimes on Fridays as well as Saturdays. Les Beaulieu's orchestra played at dances in Sawyerville. Movies were sometimes shown in Randboro by 'Prof.' Shaw." *(Carol Rand)*

***

It was during this period that Fred Hurd enjoyed fishing and hunting whenever the seasons opened. When hunting season opened in the fall of 1938, Frederick, his brother Arthur, and three friends – Wallace Boyd, Bob Graham and Jack Hillman – would go up to the Lyon Stream region or the Emberton Camps for deer hunting. *"They baged three nice bucks and so we will all enjoy venison this winter."* [21]

Jobs were scarce so Lyle Rand began working in the neighbourhood and as well as in East Clifton, helping with just about everything, including helping his father and neighbours dig graves at Maple Leaf Cemetery if help was needed there. As a young man, Lyle started work as a butcher for his cousin Fred Hurd at his meat market in East Angus. Having grown up on a farm, he and his brother, Clinton, were well trained in the slaughter and butchering of cattle, pigs, and sheep.

***

During this era, the roads in Newport were maintained by the Township and the municipalites, hiring local men in each jurisdiction to do the work. Many of these men were local farmers who looked forward to having the extra income during those tight times. The maintenance of the roads in both winter and summer were done in off-peak times from a farmers normal workload and so this arrangement worked well for all parties.

William Painter and George Malloy bought the former Levi Lyon property west of the Anglican Church in Island Brook. George built a blacksmith shop and operated his business there for many years. George was always ready to repair or produce any metal items the farmers needed, or to fix broken-down road maintenance equipment. His would be the last blacksmith shop serving the community,

In late summer 1930, Gleason Painter, with his earnings from working with the summer road crew, bought a used 1918 Model T Ford for $50. He was 18 years old at the time. Gleason would work all winter on that car, getting it ready so he could invite his girlfriend for a ride in it the next summer, and you can bet he had that car out in early spring as soon as the roads were clear.

Kenneth Morrow's horse, May, was pulling the car to John Burn's barn for winter storage. Gleason mentioned, "You didn't have to tell May what to do, she knew what she was supposed to do, she just headed for the barn." Mature horses seemed to have a sixth sense in knowing just where they had to go and how gentle or how hard they needed to pull on a load – truly a remarkable combination of both horsemanship and treatment of animals. They became a part of the family just as pets are today.[32] *(quote: the late Gleason Painter)*

William Painter was caretaker of road work circa 1939 and part of his job was to hire and arrange the work crews for the overall road maintenance in the Island Brook region. His work included keeping a ledger on the work done and by whom; the wagons and teams and the wages the men earned. Gravel was still being shovelled by hand into narrow buckboard wagons and then hauled from Gordons Kerr's gravel pit in the centre of the village of Island Brook. Gordon Kerr was paid 10 cents per load of gravel taken from his pit.[32] *(also: Ilah (Westgate) Batley)*

Positioned as the floor of these buckboard wagons were 8-10-inch boards, placed side by side forming the floor. The buckboard would have side and end boards approximately 12 to 14 inches high, forming a box. The front and end boards would be held in a slot so they could be removed. Ideally these boards were usually sawn from elm trees, which were still in abundance in Newport during this era. Elm was a preferred wood for this purpose because of its strength and endurance.

Buckboard wagon, turning the boards to release the rocks (BAnQ)

The men had an ingenious method of unloading the gravel without having to shovel it again; a technique that had been handed down from previous generations. When the gravel was loaded and hauled to the part of the road needing repair, the men would simply remove the front and back ends of the box ends and with a man on each end of the board, they would simply turn each of the boards over. Every second board was longer on one end allowing a person to grip the board to turn it over. The gravel would fall out in the exact spot they wanted. They would repeat this process with each board, sometimes moving the horses ahead to another spot until the wagon was empty. The use of this method over many years resulted in a later modification: the boards were sawn lengthwise with a tapered edge rather than a square edge; this allowed them to be flipped over much more easily than before.

This road work was usually initiated in October when the haying and harvesting was over and more men were free to work on the roads. Road repair was a community affair because it was in everyone's interest to keep the roads driveable, and it was anticipated the work provided some much-needed immediate cash for these many farmers. The ledger William kept showed wages in this era at 40 cents an hour for both the man and his team of horses, an eight-hour day paying around $3.20. This was big money even then, when the average pay for a man's work would have been less than a dollar a day if there was work at all. *(Ilah (Westgate) Batley)*

Many men in the surrounding community took their turns providing the labour force, paid at that time by the municipal government. They would generally work on the more immediate roads surrounding the town such as the Learned Plain Road, crossing the 14th Range; North Road, which leads to the Knicky Knocky community and the Bury Township line; and New Mexico Road, leading to North River on the south side of town. Fred Alden, Herb Statton, Franklin Kerr, Henry Shaw and Clarence Lister all lived on the North Road. The other men lived above or below the village of Island Brook along today's Route 212. A typical four-day work schedule as documented in William Painter's ledger included William Painter and a helper. Fred Alden would work with two men along with Herbert Statton and a helper and his team of horses on any particular day. Franklin Kerr would also work with two of his men and his team along with William Hammond, also having a man and his team of horses working on the New Mexico Road.[32]

Hollis Burns worked his team with two men along with Henry Shaw and a helper on the road to Learned Plain, while Ivan Kerr and his helper and team of horses worked alongside Gordon Kerr, his helper and team on the north roads of Island Brook and east to Lawrence Colony. Usually there were four or five men working on the same days, some staying in the gravel pit to load as a team would return for more gravel. They would back their wagons up as close as possible to the bank of gravel so the men loading would use less "elbow grease" – taking advantage of the gravel sliding down the bank as they hand-shovelled it into the wagons. With six teams of horses there would always be two loading up while four were on the road.

Other days there might be four or five men working on the same days, like Ansell Burns, Garnet Lister, Clarence Lister, Joe Kerr, Ivan Kerr, and Kenneth Morrow, who would all band together taking a portion of the roads in their immediate locale, while Ted Darker, Gleason Painter, Nakum Todd, Dick Burns and George Rutherford might work their specific areas on alternating days. *(work ledgers: Ilah (Westgate) Batley)*

It was as important in this era as in the past for these farmers to have a reliable team of heavy workhorses which would have been well cared for. Horses were still an absolute necessity as they were constantly used in farm operations as well for travel purposes. They were still considered the tractors and trucks of the day, an important part of the workforce in hauling wood, pulling logging sleds and hay wagons and perhaps loaded with goods to sell in the local markets. With the introduction of mechanical conveyances, horses would soon be relegated to living out their lives in retirement on the farms. Their horses were considered part of the family, much like their dogs, both still contributing a service to daily farming chores. They would never be sold simply because a farmer felt the need for them to retire in their old age as they themselves would want to, living in a familiar place and being with the people they had worked with and lived their lives with.

Most of the farms of the day also had one or more driving horses. When the roads were impassable for cars, these lighter and faster horses were hitched up to buggies in the summer or sleighs in the winter to travel to the larger towns, such as Cookshire or Sawyerville, to buy supplies and groceries. These horses could usually be ridden bareback (most farmers could not afford saddles) and were often used in the spring to check the fences before letting the cattle out to pasture for the summer, a job the older children looked forward to each spring with great excitement.[32]

In the summer these lightweight horses were used to pull lightweight haying equipment such as hay tedders and hay rakes. Once the timothy and clover were mature enough for harvesting as hay, workhorses were employed to pull the heavy mowing machines which left the hay in swaths and left to dry in the sun. Hay tedders were a unique invention that farmers used to lift and fluff the hay the day after it was cut, allowing it to dry better in the sun. This machine was powered by the wheels (just like the mowers) it ran on, geared to a series of offset forks; when moving forward, the forks that were just level with the ground would kick the hay up from the swath into the air. Verna Westgate was driving her horse on the tedder one day and as her husband Maple told the story, "She was going to beat the band, travelling so fast that some of the forks of the tedder came off and flew right off into the woods." *(Ilah (Westgate) Batley)*

***

By 1938, Fred Hurd had bought a piece of property just inside the Newport/Eaton Township Line off today's Route 210 beside the South River where he had started an abattoir. An abattoir is a place where an animal is slaughtered – usually a building equipped with a fenced-in yard and stalls, a hoisting mechanism, and a carving table. He had plenty of water from the adjacent river for flushing and cleaning the equipment. Fred's building was also equipped with an icehouse and a large walk-in cold room where the carcass was hung for several days prior to carving. This was the same location where Bill McCallum had built a smokehouse that he used for the curing of hams and bacon. Bill had left his trademark quart beer bottle nailed over the door. Fred had started out this business in butchering and peddling the meat around the district. His cousins Gifford Lawson Jr. and Lyle Rand worked with him during his startup earlier and during the latter part of the Great Depression.

By 1939 Lyle Rand worked part time for Fred Hurd delivering meat from his East Angus butcher shop. In 1940 Fred closed his butcher shop in favour of a store in the town of Sawyerville, Eaton Township, which was closer to home. At this point, Lyle continued working with him for a few months to set up his new shop.

"Dad named his new store Hurd's Meat Market and lived in an adjacent bachelor apartment. He was a wonderful dancer, and those dances were a major part of the social life of the time." (Judy (Hurd) (Jolliffe) Bernard)

***

Edmund[10] Lionel Hurd (1907-2001), son of Augustus[9] and Sarah Eliza (Hurd) Hurd, was born on the farm in Newport that his great-grandparents John B.[7] and Polly (Sawyer) Hurd had settled. In 1937 he acquired his surveyor's license and landed his first permanent job as a surveyor in Arntfield, Que. in the Abitibi-Témiscamingue region. He felt now was the time he could get married and be comfortable to support a family. In 1938 he married Eva Mary Wood (1914-1999) in Arntfield.[4, 31]

Lyle Rand in front of Hurd's Meat Market, opening up for the day (courtesy of Carol Rand)

Mary had been living in Bulwer in 1938 with her parents, Norris Ramsden and Eva Millicent (Wilkinson) Wood. Mary's grandfather had owned the Wilkinson Bros. Photographic Studio in Cookshire. Lionel and Mary had two sons: James Norman, born in 1939; and Frederick Edmund[11], born in 1940.

By 1939 the radio was the people of Newport's lifeline to learning what was happening all over the world. CBC would broadcast a twelve o'clock noon series of beeps for the farmers to adjust their windup clocks to the correct time.

Lionel Hurd and Mary Wood, 1938 (Hurd family collection)

Farmers in Newport would always try to come in from the fields by noon for dinner and to tune in for world news. Of particular interest were events happening in Europe – distinct reminders of an earlier time when so many of the older farmers had fought battles in those very lands – and they did not like what they were hearing. In the evenings, the radio provided an uplift with shows like "Amos 'n' Andy," and "Our Miss Brooks" which were favourite comedy entertainment for the family.

***

The winter of 1939 was particularly cold. Marshall N. W. Rand and his son Clinton were busy logging most days. Clinton and his team of horses hauled a load of logs every day down to Sawyerville to Staggs Mill. Here it was processed into staves for making barrels, a significant business during this era. Some of the wood destined for the mill that did not meet specifications was set aside for their own use as firewood. In early February, Clinton went down to Willis Leggett's and picked up a "saw rig." This was a portable circular saw on a sled, powered by an old Ford Model T engine equipped with a belt and pully that ran the saw blade. The operator would roll the logs with a "cant dog" onto a wooden tray and lever the tray forward into the saw, shifting the tray sideways with each block. Once Marshall and Clinton had the saw rig in place they hired a couple of wood sawers (Roland and Emile Dube) to cut the logs into blocks for firewood. It took them 2½ days – 16 hours of sawing – to complete the job, which gives one an idea of how much wood was cut for winter burning. The cost for the two men at that time was $16.00 for the job.[31, 46]

Marshie and Clinton Rand would still have to hand-split the blocks before spring as the wood splits easier when frozen. The wood would then need to be piled to cure for the following winter's burning. Usually they took turns, splitting a few blocks each day through February and March until completed, usually refilling the woodshed after sugaring season and just before planting season. These types of jobs all had a sequence to them simply because everything was seasonal on a farm, and if certain tasks were not completed there would be little time to catch up later. Other jobs would have priorities that could not be delayed. Most farm children were used to this kind of living and carried this sense of urgency or "getting things done" mentality throughout their lives. This was also one of the reasons farm children were usually hired quickly if they moved to urban centres, because they took initiative and anticipated what needed to be done. This was also a reason they generally did not do well in a factory workplace setting.[46]

Marshall and Edith went to work building a new barn sometime after the original "Hurd" barn had been struck by lightning and burned down in 1938.[46]

In 1939, when Marshall was tearing down the old burned-out barn, he lost his life from a falling beam. "The most memorable event that happened in Newport often spoken about by both of my parents was the tragic accidental death of Dad's father, Marshall Newell Wesley Rand, on July 18, 1939. He was a month away from his 51st birthday. Dad (Lyle Rand) was 24 years old and was working in Sawyerville for his cousin Fred at Hurd's Meat Market when he got a call to come home. My mother (Fay Parsons), who was 19 years old and still dating my dad, happened to be visiting Edith and Marshall that day. She was helping Edith to wallpaper a bedroom. Dad's brother, Clinton, and Billy Hall were at the farm helping Marshall tear down the old barn that day." Lyle was already 24 years old and was not living at home in Maple Leaf full-time although he was there often to help. Clinton was 19 at the time and had been working with his father most of the time. Hilda was only 14 years old.[46] *(quote: Carol Rand)*

"Three years before their marriage, my father, Lyle, and his girlfriend, Fay Parsons, spent most weekends at the farm from early 1939 helping Edith with the many household chores. At this time, Fay was working in Sawyerville for various families (Gertie Winslow, Volney Hurley) and lived with those families during the week. Sometimes she was home with her family in Knicky Knocky too. In 1941 to 1942, Fay worked for folks in Lennoxville (Mrs. Cass, McJurys) and she stayed in their homes during the week." *(Carol Rand)*

In February 1941, *"Lyle and Clinton butchered four pigs and sold them to Fred Hurd. They went to a dance that night at Randboro with Donnie Morrow, Donnie stayed the night with them after the dance."* [46]

"When Marshall died, Edith continued to run the farm until the Osgoods foreclosed. (Edith wrote annual diaries from 1922 to 1968)." Her diaries indicate that there was much help from many in the community including her brother Frank, as well as her sons Lyle and Clinton.[46] *(quote: Carol Rand)*

"This [photo below] is the house where my grandparents, Marshall and Edith lived, and where their children grew up. The picture was taken the day of Marshall's auction." *(Carol Rand)*

It was in June 1941 when *"the valuators were here, Mr. Edmund Bowker, Mr. G. Noonan and Mr. Stanley McVetty. Valentine and Laura Swail came up and spent the day with me and later Reg and Violet came up and spent the night."* [46] *(Edith (Morrison) Rand)*

"Mr. Osgood and Gertrude 'Gerty' held the mortgage on the property. Sometime in April 1941, Mr. Osgood and Gerty paid Edith a visit and again later in April the Osgoods paid her another visit. On April 27, 1941, her diary states *"We decided to have a sale"* which followed on May 6, 1941. "On Thursday, May 13, 1941, Dad and Edith went to Cookshire with Mr. Osgood and Gertrude. I'm assuming that was to a notary to arrange the foreclosure of the property." *(Carol Rand)*

Marshall and Edith Rand home, the original home Haskell and Eliza (McCurdy) Hurd build with Austin Rand's help (courtesy of Carol Rand)

Auction day was Tuesday, May 6, 1941. In the ad "1941" is written in ink in Edith's handwriting.

"At the end of June there was a neighbourhood farewell party," Edith wrote. On July 1, 1941, *"We left our Maple Leaf home."* Edith and Hilda moved to Sawyerville to a house she rented.

The house in Sawyerville was across the street from the United Church, a bit to the east. For a week in August of that same year, Edith and Hilda went to Montreal and Ormstown to visit relatives. In early August, Clinton went out

Marshall Rand estate auction (courtesy of Carol Rand)

west on one of the farm labour excursions that were still operating by CPR to get away for a while. This was an opportunity to make some good wages for a short period of harvesting work. Clinton returned at the end of September and began work at the Screen Plate factory in Lennoxville.[46]

And so, none of Edith's family were living in Maple Leaf after July 1941, except for her brother Frank and Mabel Morrison, who were still living on their old homestead on the lower section of Morrison Road. By the summer of 1942, Hilda (Rand) was finished school and got a job in Lennoxville.[46]

Author's note: The sudden death of Marshall Rand marked the end of the Rand family name in Newport for a few years, with most of the Rand families having moved elsewhere as they grew up, married, and sought opportunities elsewhere. The Depression left its mark on most of the younger generations; one took any job just to survive for another day. There was the lure of the military – if you were healthy, the forces were taking on whomever wished to volunteer.

Edith (Morrison) Rand died in September 1968. She was 79. Her last diary entry was on August 13 of that year: *"Monday, very cool, Frank's birthday, 74 years."*

***

In 1939, Bertha "Evelyn"[10] Hurd, daughter of Alonzo George[9] Hurd, who was born in Newport in 1916, married Lloyd Robert[2] French, son of Robert[1] F. French of Island Brook. The family moved to Sawyerville where they raised their three children: Eric George Robert[3], Barbara Ann and Susan J.

Author's note: The second French family of Newport initiated a third Hurd family connection with the marriage of a Hurd daughter, who was a direct descendant of Col. Edmund[5] Heard.

Evelyn French became a schoolteacher and taught at Sawyerville Consolidated School for many years. Many of our senior readers from the region would remember Evelyn well and were probably taught by her in various grades. Lloyd French worked for a time along with Jack Garneau Sr. at the Sawyerville Manufacturing Company, later serving as Mayor of Sawyerville in Eaton Township for several terms. Lloyd was in the lumbering contract business for many years, logging the Connecticut Lakes area of the Republic of Indian Stream near Pittsburg, N.H. Truck after truck crossed the border at Chartierville, hauling huge loads through Newport westward to the mills in Sawyerville and Cookshire.

When Alonzo Hurd died suddenly in 1941, his son George, age 29 at the time, who had graduated from Queen's University in 1934 and had been involved in the funeral and other businesses, took over the operation of the manufacturing part of the operation. "My father (Lloyd R. French) and Jack Garneau Sr. operated the sawmill part of the business for many years." George's brother, Eric, who was only 21 at the time of his father's death, joined the RCAF in 1942 and served in World War II. After the war Eric returned to Sawyerville and worked with his brother, George, for a few years before moving to Ontario with his family.[4, 31] *(quote: Eric G. R. French)*

***

Ingenuity at its best *(Eastern Townships Roots Facebook page)*

Chapter 15   The Winds of War (1925–1945)

By 1939, Europe was being threatened by both Germany and Italy; the powers of Germany, Italy and now Japan were posing a threat to world peace. Canada declared war against Germany in support of Great Britain on September 10, 1939, and began to raise an armed force of nearly four million men and women. By 1941, the "Axis powers" had captured virtually all of Europe and more of Southeast Asia and China.[3]

Author's note: Many Newport residents signed up for service in World War II. This chapter will describe the lives of those who remained in Newport and how the war affected lives on both the home front and abroad.

Many men and women from the Eastern Townships volunteered for active service in World War II. Some names a reader may recognize as descendants from the original settlers in Newport. They were Arthur Alden, Kenneth Bowker, Wallace Boyd, Norman Burns, Auvern Dawson, Stanley Dawson, Irene Desruisseaux, Léon Desruisseaux, Arthur French, Charles French, James Hall, William Hall, Bruce Hunt, Arthur Hurd, Eric Hurd, Lionel Hurd, Noel Kingsley, Lorne Latimer, Howard Loveland, Colin McCallum, Leslie McCallum, Chester Painter, Thomas Painter, Emerson Parker, Lyle Rand, Harold Sherman, Everett Speck, Reginald Statton, Walter Statton and Clifford Westgate.

Lionel Hurd, already associated with the 7/11th Hussars, formally enlisted in late 1939, followed by Arthur Alden and Arthur's cousin Eric Olson, from Bury Township, in 1940.[3]

Author's note: Lucy Ann Alden, a daughter of Augustus and Elizabeth Jane (Mills) and Fred Oliver Alden, were siblings. Lucy had married Herman T. Olson; her brother Fred had married Pearl Holbrook; each couple had sons that were to become prisoners of war ("POWs") after the battle of Hong Kong in the Pacific Rim.

***

Arthur Haskell[10] Hurd (1917-2000) was the third son of Augustus[9] and Sarah Eliza (Hurd) Hurd. In 1941 Arthur married Helen Alberta Tannahill (1919-2004), the daughter of Edward "Eddie" and Ester R. (Speck) Tannahill. Helen had left Newport when she was 16 and moved briefly to Montreal to train as a nurse and then moved to Toronto. "The Tannahill story began in 18th century Glasgow when an abandoned baby was found on a hillside behind the Tannery. The two notables in the family are a Scottish poet that has a brogue so thick a chainsaw cannot cut it. Arthur was in training at Camp Borden, Que., when Mother and he courted."[3, 4] *(quote: Malcolm Hurd, son)*

Arthur Hurd and Helen Tannahill

An excerpt from Edith (Morrison) Rand's diary: *"Saturday, November 22, on a beautiful sunny but cold day, Arthur and Helen Tannahill's Wedding Day. Lyle, Hilda, and I were invited up to the wedding dinner at Eddy and Ester [Speck] Tannahill's. Clinton came home from work and Fay came home from Majurys for good."*[46]

***

Author's note: Lots 2, 3, 5, 6, 7 and 9 of Range 11 of the Parker Hill region, Newport, were once part of the 1200-acre parcel of original land lots that were granted and assigned by Colonel Edmund[5] Heard to his son Captain Samuel[6] Heard. Nathanial Beaman Jr. had been assigned Lot 4 on Parker Hill. Samuel[6] and his wife Miriam Heard became one of the first homesteader families on Parker Hill in 1797. Later these original lots were severed to more-manageable farm acreages, making room for additional early homesteaders. These included the Parker, Montgomery, McCallum and Jones families. The Speck, Desruisseaux, Tetreault and Statton families were to follow.

When Charlie and Gertrude "Gerty" Montgomery married they had purchased the little store in Randboro from Samuel Heard, who was 69 years old at the time. They loved children and made sure there was a large assortment of candies and children's books on the store shelves that the children would browse through. They had no children of their own. They also purchased the land across the road, the site where Charlie Stone had his mill that had been destroyed earlier. He and Gerty ran a small hobby farm. Charlie had purchased the Parker Hill schoolhouse and converted it into a small barn.

Heading up Parker Hill Road, circa 1940s (Newport Homecoming 1802-1996)

Allen and his wife Mary (Law) Parker's farm was on Parker Hill Road, at the top of the hill on the left when approaching from Randboro. It bordered on the bottom of the original settlement of Joseph and Mary Parker (the farm that Charlie McCallum had traded with John Jones earlier). Allen and Mary raised four children: daughters Ruby, Pansy and Gladys, and son Clayton. The children would have all grown up as part of the community of Parker Hill and Randboro, perhaps starting their early school years at the Parker Hill schoolhouse and later moving to the new regional school in Sawyerville. Ruby married Gerald Alden, Pansy married Clayton Lowry, Gladys married Bert Hill, and Clayton married Fern Cook.

The photo above is a view up Parker Hill Road from Randboro, just after the bridge crossing the South River. Clifford "Tiffy" and Verlie Morrison's house is on the right; Allen Parker's house is on the left at the top of the hill. Harold Sutton's house is out in the open at the left.

Bill and Ilah Parker lived on a farm on the next corner of Statton Road. Their only son, Emerson, who had served in World War II, died just after the war.

George and his sister Ester Speck had grown up next to the original farm of Joseph and Mary Jane Parker further up Parker Hill at the crossroad of Statton Road. When George and his wife Elva Speck took over the farm, they raised their nine children there. His sister Ester married Eddy Tannahill; they purchased a farm on Grove Hill Road.

It was in 1941 when Clement "Clem" and Rose Tetreault and family moved from Ste. Edwidge and bought the old Samuel Heard farm on Parker Hill next to the Parker, Desruisseaux and soon to be Statton families. Clem and Rose raised four sons – Robert, Gerald "Gerry," Leander and Rene – as well as four daughters – Irene, Aline, Elaine and Estelle – on the farm. The family became part of the Parker Hill community, sharing their help along with their neighbours in bringing up large families and making sure there was enough food on the table. By 1951 their eldest son, Robert, age 14 at the time, began to work for many of the farmers in the immediate area, including the Bill Hall and Gardy Rand families whose farms bordered on the Auckland/Newport township line just south of Parker Hill. *(courtesy of Robert Tetreault)*

Albert and Hattie Desruisseaux raised a son, Léon, and two daughters, Irene and Lillian, in Eaton Township before moving to a farm on Parker Hill that he had purchased from Allan Parker. Their son, Léon Desruisseaux, met and married Mini Statton just after the war. They raised a daughter, Betty, and two sons, Floyd and Norman. They farmed for several years immediately after the war on Parker Hill adjacent to the Statton farm. Leon was an early school bus driver in Newport in the 1950s, later retiring to Sawyerville where he and Mini operated a small hobby farm.

***

Bernardin and Rachelle (Cliche) Théroux and family bought the original farm of Hannah Elvira (Rand) and William H. McCurdy, Lot 9 of Range 11, from John and Nellie Jones, circa 1939. Joining the Maple Leaf community of farmers, they operated the farm for several years into the late 1950s. They raised three boys and four girls on this farm during the mid-1940s and into the early 1950s. Bernardin bought a threshing machine and a Cockshutt tractor equipped with a General Motors four-cylinder engine. He hired himself out with his tractor and threshing machine around the local countryside in the same way as our ancestors had in the years past. The era had ended the old horse treadmill operations with the introduction of motor-driven equipment. An equipment-driven economy would now change the face of farming in Newport. *(Robert Tetreault)*

***

Part of Lyle Rand's career working for Hurd's Meat Market was delivering meats to the surrounding regions, which included both Eaton and Bury townships. Lyle had devised certain runs on certain days and the farmers' wives and children grew to expect and look forward to the meat truck's arrival. Even in this era, housewives did not get away from the farm often, so everyone flocked to the truck when it arrived. Delivering meat was Fred Hurd's innovative idea when he started his business and undercut the existing butchers, who were overcharging on the sale of meat and underpaying on the purchase of produce from the local farmers. Lyle could home-deliver meat, chickens, bacon, sausage and other meat products for a lower price than customers would pay in local stores, so business was brisk.[21]

Lyle Rand and Fay Parsons heading out on their honeymoon (courtesy of Carol Rand)

Lyle Ashley Rand (1914-2001), the son of Marshall[2] Newell Wesley and Edith (Morrison), married Fay Parsons in early 1942. "Lyle knew that he would sign up to serve in the army sometime in the fall, so he and Fay did not get a place of their own. They moved in temporarily with Edith and her daughter, Hilda, in Sawyerville. Later, that fall, when Lyle was stationed in Quebec City, Fay was able to join him there. She also joined him in Mont-Joli where they had two children, Royce Marshall, born in 1943, and Carol Edna, born in 1945. Royce and Carol lived in Mont-Joli as babies and they also stayed at the Parsons home in Knicky Knocky." *(Carol Rand)*

***

Author's note: During this time, Renford and Elizabeth (McCormack) Morrow's four older children were still working on the farm. However, entering their teen years and feeling pretty much grown up, the eldest, Donnie, started to contemplate where his own life might lead him. Their youngest daughter, Donna, would soon begin school in Sawyerville.

Donnie Morrow (1924-1980) married Doreen (Aulis) Stickles. They bought the Gardner "Gardy and Lily" Rand farm in Auckland Township at the foot of Morrison Road and the junction of the Auckland town line. They raised Doreen's three sons, Frank, Gordon and Richard, and a daughter, Sandra, and raised their own daughter, Dawn, together on this farm.

Renford and Elizabeth Morrow's eldest daughter, Jean Morrow, married Osmond "Snap" Aulis, a brother to Doreen. Myrlin Morrow married Irene Kerr from Island Brook. The youngest son, Waymond, married Elaine Coates; the youngest daughter, Donna, married Thead Hodge from Eaton Township. These families all relocated elsewhere in the Townships. *(Donna (Morrow) Hodge)*

***

Frederick Karl Hurd (1910-1984), second son of Augustus[9] and Sarah Eliza (Hurd) Hurd, was born on the farm in Newport. In 1942 he married Florence Stoddard (1910-1971). They had four children, two sons and two daughters: Judith Carol (born 1943), John Allan (born 1945), Peter Donald (born 1949) and Elizabeth Jean (born 1951).[4]

Frederick Hurd and Florence Stoddard

After they married, Frederick and Florence moved to an apartment over his "Hurd's Meat Market" shop. At age 32, his butcher business was well established. "His reputation for hunting was also well known and one weekend he took the sports editor (pen name Isaac Hunter) of the Montreal Gazette out hunting. He and Dad hunted along with other sports figures from the Montreal Canadiens and the Montreal Alouettes. I remember him saying that they always bought his bacon." *(Peter Hurd, son)*

"Dad always spoke with respect for the aboriginal people, who at different times were his guides for fishing trips. He took my mother on one of those trips during their honeymoon. He was given different types of baskets, including fish baskets, made for him by aboriginal people. Later, one of these baskets was used to carry me on his back going places on these sporting expeditions." *(Judy (Hurd) Bernard, daughter)*

The following story says a lot about how this generation presented their friends in the best possible light in spite of very unfortunate circumstances, and how they enjoyed the sport of hunting, the love of the woods and the taste of venison that younger generations to come will typically never experience:

> Fred was at a hunting camp with his good friend Earl, Earl's son-in-law and a few other friends as well. They were all experienced deer hunters except for Earl's son-in-law. Early in the morning they planned the day's deer hunt and everyone was supposed go in different directions so they would be alone in their own section of the woods. Earl's son-in-law was wearing a brown jacket, which Fred did not think was a good idea as it could be mistaken for a deer. The son-in-law got lost and ended up in Earl's section of the woods. Unknown to Earl, the son-in-law was a few hundred feet away from him when he decided to blow his nose with a white handkerchief. At this point, Earl was sure he was shooting at a deer through the thick brush. Unfortunately, a horrible accident occurred when Earl shot his own son-in-law. When Dad tells the story, he says, "On one hand Earl shouldn't have shot him, but on the other hand, the son-in-law shouldn't have been where he was. So, I guess Dad felt there was equal responsibility for what happened . . . quite a tragedy. *(Peter Hurd)*

> Dad saw "getting lost in the woods wearing a brown jacket in deer season as almost asking to get shot." Dad was sure that the son-in-law probably couldn't hit the broadside of a barn even if it were right in front of him (as the expression goes) and so, in his mind, he just shouldn't have even been there. The son-in-law was clearly not experienced in the woods and did not realize the danger he was causing for himself or others by wearing the brown jacket and then taking out a white handkerchief and giving it a shake before blowing his nose. I don't know if you ever heard a deer snort, but that is the sort of sound they make when alarmed. So, Earl, his father-in-law, must have thought everything fit together and since he thought that he was alone in this area of the woods, that sound and the white flash of his handkerchief had to be a deer. *(Peter Hurd)*

***

This was a time, i.e., the beginning of the Second World War, when once again our ancestors' young sons headed to enlist, for some just to have a job. To many, this was their chance to get out to see the world, the circumstances not dissimilar to what it was like before World War I. During this time (1940-41) penicillin, the world's first antibiotic, was developed. This was also when unemployment insurance was introduced in Canada.[48]

The introduction of a universal price freeze on food in December of 1941 was perhaps the most important factor brought about by the start of this war. It would change the way Canadians in general would shop, cook, and eat food on the home front. This was followed by the staged introduction of coupon rationing for sugar in July of 1942, tea and coffee in August, butter in December, and meat in March of the following year. These controls on food purchases came shortly on the heels of months of periodic food shortages and a precipitous spike in food prices. Price and rent controls, it was argued, would ensure that Canadians could continue to afford necessities like food, fuel and shelter, while rationing promised all Canadians a fair share of scarce necessities.

***

Eric James[10] Hurd, the youngest son of Alonzo George[9] and Evelyn "Eva" (Robinson) Hurd of Newport, was born in 1920. He enlisted with a Canadian Forestry Battalion and went to England in 1941. In early 1942 he enlisted with the R.A.F. in England, graduating as a sergeant observer with the R.A.F. overseas. He had met Bernice "Bernie" Maureen Baker during the war and they married in 1943. They raised five children – three sons and two daughters. Their first child, Gillian Maureen, was born in Torquay, Devon, England in 1944. James Rodney (born 1946) and Keith William (born 1951) were both born in Sawyerville, Eaton Township; Deborah Frances (born 1956) and Thomas Eric (born 1957) were born in Toronto.

Eric Hurd and Bernie Baker (courtesy of Gillian (Hurd) Anderson)

***

Author's note: Eric Hurd's father, Alonzo, and family had moved to Sawyerville when he had bought and began operating the mills. When Alonzo Hurd died in 1941, his wife Evelyn "Eva" and their eldest son, George, who was 29 years old, took on the task of managing the manufacturing entity. Lloyd French (Eric's brother-in-law) and Jack Garneau Sr. joined them in managing and operating the sawmill part of the business for several years.

The second week of June 1942 was unbearably hot and started to rain. The rains became increasingly torrential for three days. On Monday June 15 the dam and the covered bridge in Sawyerville washed out around 4:30 a.m.

Water is terrible everywhere, roads impassable, thousands of dollars of damage. Many could not get to work, and the children could not get to school. Some of the children had to board in Town in order to finish their final exams. Those who normally travelled on Flanders Road from the North River area had to detour down Grove Hill Road through Randboro to get to Sawyerville. Henry Parker's funeral is postponed until tomorrow. [46] *(Edith (Morrison) Rand)*

After the flood that took out the covered bridge over the South River in Sawyerville, 1942 (*Sherbrooke Record*)

The same flood washed out the bridge and Levi Lyon's clapboard mill in Island Brook. The Dawson brothers of Island Brook were contracted to build new cement bridges in both Island Brook and Sawyerville. After a year without these two bridges, the work was completed by the spring of 1943.

***

The Second World War era, 1939-1945:

Author's note: As this is a story of lives lived, I will not delve into the specifics of the war; however, I will discuss how the war affected the people of this region. More importantly, it is my intention to disclose how the lives of those who were imprisoned as POWs for nearly four years during Pacific War in Hong Kong managed to simply survive the inhumane POW camps, and how those who survived continued to suffer for many years after they finally returned home. Many were men from this part of the Townships who were caught up in a horrific tragedy that was playing out in the Pacific arena while the battles in Europe raged on. Some of those listed below from Newport and surrounding townships were to experience a different kind of battle; the battle for simple survival against a foreign culture that was completely void of compassion. History expounds on so much data relating to those who died in the wars, including Services of Remembrance, but not so much about those who survived the wars, wounded and battle-scarred. Their stories of how they lived afterwards is equally as important to be heard. The following references to the Pacific War are based on Heard/Hurd military documents and diaries.

Their World War II experience would not only change their lives forever, but would also change the lives of their families, and so this is what happened to them after they were captured. This is an accounting of what these Hong Kong veterans were to suffer through, along with those who survived to come home who could never forget their experience; the insurmountable losses of their comrades, their own suffering and that of their wounded compatriots. They did come to realize, over time, that they could and would hang on to their dignity. Their determination to live was what got many of them through. And so begins the story of those who survived behind the wire for 3½ years of absolute terror in Hong Kong and Japan.

Those who signed up for duty with the Royal Rifles of Canada (RRC) included Arthur Alden, Dr. Stanley M. Banfill, brothers Austin and Eric Batley, Rene Bedard, Ernie Bennett, Wells Bishop, Arnold Brazel, Ozzy Clark, Jim Coleman, Alfred Davidson, brothers Elmer and Everett Dennison, George Everett, Bill Harlow, brothers Cameron and Argyle Harrison, Lionel Hurd, Noel Kingsley, Lorne Latimer, Bill Lobdell, Tom MacAulay, Russell Noble, Eric Olson, William Parker, Edward Philips, William Pope, brothers Fred and Walter Royal, Cliff Royer, Leslie Shore, Colin Standish, brothers Leslie and Franklin Stickles, Ray Stoddard, Renwick Thompson and Alfred Wonnacott, to name just a few. Many of these men, whose ancestral families were all part of the original settling of the Eastern Townships, would all have known each other or would have had a general knowledge of both their families and their ancestors.

***

When war broke out in 1939, Sherbrooke's 7/11th Hussars were professionally qualified but did not mobilize, largely for political reasons. The Hussars were a "French-speaking" regiment, whereas the Royal Rifles of Canada, stationed in Quebec City, was an old "English-speaking" regiment. (This French-English division dates to when Sir Guy Carleton was Governor of Quebec and Governor General of British North America in the late 1700s.) "The Royal Rifles claim that this was their ancestral English-speaking unit which fought during 1812 against the Americans."[3]

The "military of the day" wanted an English-speaking unit, probably a throwback to colonial days. The 7/11th Hussars remained as a "reserve" force, however when the Royal Rifles of Canada mobilized sometime in early 1940 and recruitment began, many in the reserve force stood ready and willing to serve.

Capt. E. Lionel Hurd, Royal Rifles of Canada (E. L. Hurd military historical archives and diary, 1941-1945)

At this time, Lionel Hurd had remained on duty as a captain in rank with the 7/11th Hussars at headquarters staff in Military District No. 5, an internment camp for German POWs in Sherbrooke. The prisoners were mostly unfortunate Jewish German people who had been interned in England because they had German citizenship.

A large contingent from the Eastern Townships enlisted with the Royal Rifles of Canada. Many of them are named above; 14 were officers and about 300 were other ranks. There were also 109 from Ontario and approximately 100 from the Bay of Chaleur, the Gaspe coast and regions of northern New Brunswick. The unit was largely English-speaking, but many French Canadians who spoke English volunteered because they preferred to be with the Royal Rifles. Though their names were of French origin (many from the island of Jersey off the coast of France), they were completely bilingual. To quote my father, "We thought it strange that since the Royal Rifles was a Quebec City unit, there weren't that many who actually came from Quebec City itself." *(Capt. E. L. Hurd)*

When the Royal Rifles mobilized, Lionel Hurd and Arthur Alden from Newport, along with many other young men listed above that he knew from the Townships, had attended Camp Valcartier, northwest of Quebec City, for a period of training. Many of these men soon found themselves on trains heading to Newfoundland. They thought they would probably be in Europe by year-end. Some of these men, however, would be going elsewhere, travelling back west through Canada and beyond, across the Pacific Ocean.

Edmund Lionel Hurd, born in Maple Leaf, Newport, the son of Augustus[9] and Sarah Hurd, transferred to the Royal Rifles in the fall of 1940. He continued his training in both Valcartier, Que., and Sussex, N.B., and then joined others from the Townships on their way to Newfoundland in early spring 1941. The Royal Rifles had too many captains in rank, so Lionel dropped from captain to lieutenant to be in the regiment. In six months he had re-earned his rank of captain, taking on the responsibility of battalion quartermaster, effective once they were to arrive in Hong Kong. The quartermaster in Ottawa was responsible for the assembly of all military personnel, equipment, medical supplies and food scheduled to be sent ahead of or with the men to Battalion Headquarters in Hong Kong. Lionel felt the position carried with it an exceedingly difficult and heavy responsibility because in his words, "You are responsible for everything, from every bit of food to every piece of equipment that you draw and responsible for the accounting of it all." He would be more than disappointed later to find out that a major part of the military equipment destined for Hong Kong had been shipped late from Vancouver and was diverted to Singapore.

Capt. E. L. Hurd with sons Freddy (the author, in arms) and Jimmy (in carriage), June 1941 (Hurd family collection)

"The strange thing was," he commented in Hong Kong as quartermaster, "you were supposed to be behind the lines, organizing the equipment, supplies and food to the front lines of battle, but we were all right in the front line. That was one of the first places the Japanese bombed . . . all the supply depots and barracks." *(Capt. E. L. Hurd)*

The Canadians were the second line of defence on Hong Kong Island. Brigade Headquarters (HQ) were in Kowloon on the mainland of Hong Kong Peninsula. The sparse equipment that had been shipped with them was all they had. The ships following them to Hong Kong with all the munitions, armoured tanks, troop carriers and large ordnance were late in arriving and diverted to Singapore when Hong Kong was attacked. They had no artillery and no transport equipment to move either the men or the small amount of supplies they did have. They had to confiscate civilian trucks, three-wheeled little pickup trucks to haul what little they had for equipment.

Brigade HQ was forced to move from Kowloon, first to Hong Kong Island, at West Fort, Lei U Mun, where Major Wells Bishop's Royal Rifles C Company, Sgt. Robert Clayton and their men faced the Royal Rifles' first battle with the Japanese. Brigade HQ again was forced to move south to Tai Tam Bay, with Lt. Col. W. Home, Major J. H. Price. Royal Rifles A Company under Major Young was positioned at Repulse Bay; B Company, under Capt. E. Dennison, was positioned at Stone Hill; D Company, under Major M. Parker, was positioned at Shek O Wan, a peninsula parallel to Stanley Peninsula.

Brigade Headquarters, along with all the other battalions, were on constant move until they were pushed to the south of Hong Kong Island on Stanley Peninsula, where they held on for two to three days. On December 19, Argyle Harrison of Bury met death by a Japanese firing squad. Major Tom MacAulay (wounded) and Captain E. L. Hurd were left to stand their ground with their men at Stanley Fort at the end of the Peninsula for their last battle. This group of "Townshippers," which included A, B, C and D Companies, were still fighting after the surrender of Hong Kong had been declared. They had not received the message until eventually, on Christmas Day, some British and Japanese got through to tell them.

Lionel Hurd, along with Arthur Alden from Newport and Eric Olson (Arthur's cousin), Wells Bishop, Colin Standish, Ray Stoddard, Eric Batley and many others who had joined the Royal Rifles from the Townships, fought to the end in Stanley Village, the last stronghold in Hong Kong. They were taken as prisoners of war (POWs) on Christmas Day 1941. Some of them, including Lionel Hurd and Arthur Alden from Newport survived to return home in late 1945.

The following is quoted from Capt. E. L. Hurd's records of a conversation between him and a Japanese officer:

- A Japanese officer who spoke English asked Capt. Hurd who they were. His reply: "Canadians."
- The officer asked him many questions about Canadians. "Why are you fighting this battle?"
- Capt. Hurd noted, "They didn't know much about us. They knew we were not Americans; they knew we were not British; but they were not just quite clear who we were."
- The Japanese officer remarked that . . . "as soon as we faced off with the troops on the island, we had a tougher time than we did with the others on the mainland." *(Capt. E. L. Hurd)*

Arthur Alden, born in 1911 and raised in Island Brook, Newport, was the son of Fred and Pearl (Holbrook) Alden. "He fought in the battle of Hong Kong, was taken prisoner of war in Hong Kong, in Stanley Village, and survived to come home in 1945."[32] *(submitted by Arthur's sister, the late Mabel Alden, wife of Doug Mackay, living in Sawyerville)*

From Stanley Village, the surviving Royal Rifles of Canada, including the wounded, were marched as POWs to the camp known as North Point, at the northern part of Hong Kong Island across the bay from the city of Kowloon. "Looking across the bay, we could see food markets and deliveries taking place, while we were starving behind electrically charged fences in squalor and dying of malnutrition and diseases, both food and medical supplies, all readily available such a short distance away." *(Capt. E. L. Hurd)*

This was now to be their lives lived as POWs behind the wire for three years and eight months of hell, from December 1941 to August 1945. Both the Canadians who were still living and those who were wounded, along with the Allied Commonwealth military forces captured in Hong Kong, were all POWs under the Imperial Japanese Army. Another 267 Canadian soldiers were to die of starvation, beatings and disease in Japanese prison camps during their internment. At this point, over 1,600 Allied men had been killed, 1,700 wounded and many more missing in action. Of the 2,000 Canadians, 290 soldiers were killed and 493 wounded with others missing in action.[3]

> *Author's note: The following is an accounting of what all these Hong Kong veterans were to suffer through and what those who survived to come home who could never forget: the insurmountable losses of their comrades, their own suffering and that of their wounded compatriots. They did come to realize over time that they would hang on to their dignity, and their determination to live was what got many of them through. And so begins the story of those who survived.*

North Point Camp:[3]

North Point Camp, located on Hong Kong Island, was an abandoned refugee camp alongside horse stables, all of which had been ransacked during the battle. Lionel kept a diary which he kept buried each day. "To be caught with a diary meant instant death by firing squad." When they were liberated, he was able to retrieve the notes he had scribbled on any scraps of paper that he was able to find at the time. Following are excerpts from that diary:

"There were dead horses all over and nothing but debris covered concrete floors with little in the way of shelter provided. The men were herded into this camp where both able-bodied and wounded prisoners were to spend the next nine months. Officers and those men who were able, under constant guard, were sent out to search for cots, bedding, cooking utensils or anything that they could muster that would make their lives more tolerable. There was no running water, the floors were filthy, bug infested, and disease spread rapidly among the wounded with no medical help. They survived on a meager ration of rice laced through with maggots and rat droppings along with anything that they were able to scrounge when out on these search parties. This camp held predominately Canadian POWs until the Japanese transferred the Officers to the Argyle camp and their men to Shamshuipo camp after about nine months."

Many of the letters written by their loved ones were received one year later, if at all. Some letters were not received until the POWs were released in 1945. Their loved ones were kept mostly in the dark, frantically trying to find some snippet of information as to the whereabouts of their sons or for some word as to whether they were even alive. Many did not receive any letters until two or three years later.

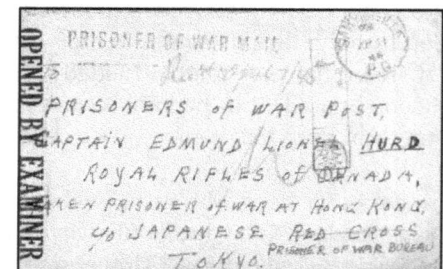

Envelope of letter to POW Capt. Lionel Hurd postmarked April 11, 1944; marked received April 7, 1945

Argyle Street Officers camp:[3]

During the 1941-45 Japanese occupation, the camp originally erected in 1939 by the Hong Kong government as temporary quarters for refugee Chinese soldiers in the Sino-Japanese War was used for officers for a period of a year and a half.

"The Japanese, ever vigilant and constantly apprehensive about the possibility of escape, surrounded the camp with triple rows of electrically charged barbed wire fences. Also surrounding the camp were floodlights and sentry towers. All the bunks, stools, shelves, and utensils were gradually fashioned by the prisoners from scraps that they scrounged and those brought back from work details for the Japanese outside the camp. They picked up gunny sacks, nails, barbed wire, bits of planks, asbestos sheeting; whatever they could find. They would then make things they needed, from cooking utensils to an operating table, and their tools were just scraps of glass or saws made from old knife blades. Sometimes these home-made tools were confiscated, and the prisoners punished." *(Capt. E. L. Hurd)*

"Many of the activities undertaken by the prisoners depended entirely on the mood of the Japanese soldier on duty. The captors were unpredictable, and nothing could be taken for granted." *(Capt. E. L. Hurd)*

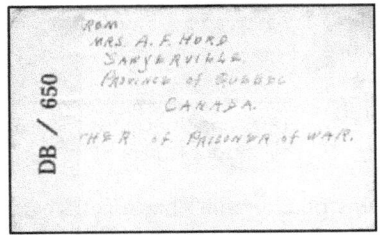

Envelope of letter mailed in 1944 by Lionel's mother, Sarah.

Lionel had received only one letter from his family, in 1943, and none further until April 1945, when the Japanese allowed some letters through their censorship. News of the death of Argyle Harrison, shot by a Japanese firing squad, did not reach his parents in Bury Township until January 1943, and by November 1943 they were to learn of the September death of their other son, Cameron, in the shipyards of Yokohama.

The POWs had virtually no communication from the outside world for almost four years. Every letter was censored, as indicated on the envelope. Many of the families were constantly sending letters via the Red Cross with very few responses, and so for almost four years the families on the home front, with great anxiety, travelled to their mailboxes hoping for even one letter that might allow them some comfort of just knowing if their loved ones were in fact still alive.

"The living quarters were so cramped that one of the two captured doctors, Dr. Stanley Martin Banfill of Cookshire, encouraged us to walk outside whenever it was allowed. But the fear of escape made the Japanese reduce the exercise area by increasing the distance that we had to stay away from the charged barbed wire. The distance kept on changing, and the penalty for overstepping the line was brutal physical punishment." *(Capt. E. L. Hurd)*

Author's note: The second captured doctor, Dr. Jonathon Reid, was shipped to Japan in 1943 from Camp Shamshuipo on one of the unmarked Japanese ships with many more men destined as slaves to work in the shipyards of Yokohama.

***

William "Billy" John Graham, the only son of John "Irvin" and Ruth Lillian Graham, married Roberta Beryl Richardson in 1943. Roberta was born in Waterville, Que. Billy and Roberta lived on the farm that Billy's parents had settled on Grove Hill Road, just north of the village of Randboro. Billy's parents had bought this farm from George Coates circa 1900. The farm had been subdivided into smaller parcels from the original 200-acre original farm of Artemas[6] and Louisa Rand. *"It was on Saturday, June 26, 1943, a showery day, that Billy Graham and Roberta Richardson were married, and we all went up to the church to see the wedding. Ronald Ward and Ardice Wheeler stood up with them, such a pretty wedding."*[46] *(Edith (Morrison) Rand diary)*

Billy and Roberta raised three daughters and a son: Carolyn Ruth (born 1944), Aubrey Donald (born 1945), Gladys Roberta (born 1947) and Linda Gertrude (born 1954). They operated a mixed farm of cattle as well as a campground on the lower part of the property adjacent to the South River and today's Route 210. The campground was situated just past the river's gorge where the original mill was located circa 1810 and operated into the mid-1800s. "It was a small farm with a few milking cows and one or two beef animals, a couple of workhorses and some hens and roosters.

Our dad also worked five days a week in Sherbrooke. Later we got a tractor but hired out planting and fertilizing the land. We had a good life with lots of hard work and fun, swimming in the river below in the summer and skating on it some winters. We made our own fun." *(Carolyn (Graham) Grapes)*

***

By now, many residents were driving their cars, taking a bus, or catching a train to travel outside of Newport to other villages and towns. They were travelling now to shop, to visit, and to attend Saturday night dances. Places like Bulwer, Eaton Corner, Birchton, Cookshire, Bury, Scotstown, East Angus and Sherbrooke did not seem so far away with better roads and these new means of getting around quickly. And so, the communities of Randboro, Maple Leaf, New Mexico, Lawrence Colony, Island Brook and Learned Plain were now extended to a much broader range in the Townships. Many of our Newport inhabitants were now becoming part of these other communities, going to their church suppers and visiting with folks who had moved from Newport to these settlements.

Many of the farms had built silos and were now harvesting "field" corn on their farms. Some farmers were switching to more specialized farming, rather than mixed farming, and these silos provided the means to feed the growing number of animals such as pigs. During this era, farmers were using new technology in farming, and with more modernized farming equipment were able to accommodate large milking, beef, poultry and pig farms. Field corn became a preferred crop because of how it could be stored in these silos.

1890 and 2000 silos (photo by Sandra Hurd)

***

The radio was still the best forum for up-to-date news, and everyone listened to Winston Churchill's broadcasts from England and Franklin D. Roosevelt's from the U.S. Victory Bonds were being sold all over the countryside to anyone who wanted to support Canada's war efforts. The communities in Newport held many church suppers, the proceeds going to support families who had already lost fathers and sons overseas in Europe.

***

On the afternoon of a very cold day in January 1942, families in Newport were huddled around their radios listening to an address by President Roosevelt. The United States was still reeling after the attack and total destruction of their naval base in Pearl Harbor by the Japanese only three weeks earlier, on Christmas Day. The President was addressing the nation on the consequences of the German, Italian and Japanese declarations of war on the U.S., the Japanese attack on Pearl Harbor and the Japanese occupations around the Pacific Rim. The sleeping giant had been awakened and was about to unleash its might – drafting and remobilizing its entire European and Pacific fleets of navy, air force and military ground forces from an active force of about 2.2 million in December 1941 to over 30 million by the end of 1942.[6]

***

In the fall of 1942, Lyle Rand volunteered for service in World War II. He served in Quebec City and Mont-Joli for the Royal Canadian Army Service Corps until 1946, coming home on leave for a week at a time. After the war he returned to work in Sawyerville at Hurd's Meat Market. Lyle continued working there through the 1950s and early '60s.

***

Arthur Hurd, the third son of Gussie and Sadie, served in the Canadian Armed Forces in World War II from 1940 to 1945. He was shipped overseas in 1942, serving with the Royal Canadian Air Force until the war ended. After the war he and Helen (Tannahill) briefly lived in Red Rock, Ont., next to Port Arthur (now Thunder Bay) where their

Lyle Rand (courtesy of Carol Rand)

RCAF Sgt. Arthur Hurd in England, 1945 (Hurd family collection)

first son, Malcolm Edward, was born in 1947. "Father suffered an industrial accident that severed his left foot. We moved back to Sawyerville (I was baptized there) for some months before coming West." They moved to Vancouver in 1950 where their second son, Graeme Haskell (1953-1984), was born. *(ref. and quote: Malcolm Hurd)*

"Lionel and Fred were considerably older than Arthur so there were no childhood memories of shared experiences that Father related to me. Father only made one trip back to the Townships in about 1959 and never returned. Mother made several trips back to support Aunt Nettie and Uncle Harold Locke." *(Malcom Hurd)*

Arthur spent a lot of his time, both in his early years and during his teens, with Clinton Rand, working with him on the farm, together hauling lumber down to the mills.

"It was on June 15, 1943, almost a year to the day, when another heavy rainstorm hit Newport, terrible storm at night, torrential rain, thunder and lightning, terrible damage done during the night. The water took out Roy Lake's Mill on the North River, the dam, and the bridge as well." This would have been at the corner of Newport and Eaton townships on today's Route 210 (the main road from Cookshire to Island Brook). The original covered bridge crossing the South River on Route 210 from Newport to Auckland at Willis Leggett's farm was also lost in that storm. The reconstructed *"part of the dam in Sawyerville along with part of the original Sawyers Grist Mill was also lost."* Once again the roads were virtually impassable. *"The destruction is awful"* [46] *(Edith (Morrison) Rand diary)*

The west bank of South River past the bridge in Sawyerville showing the flood devastation, 1942 *(Sherbrook Record)*

This flood left the gristmill building still standing but completely inoperable; that part of the business ended in 1943. The covered bridge was replaced with a cement one by the fall of 1943, however the dam was never rebuilt.

***

Meanwhile, back on the home front, Clinton, the second son of Marshall Newell W. and Edith (Morrison) Rand, married Doreen McCormick from Bury in 1943. Doreen was the daughter of Bill and Lila McCormick who lived in Bury Township. They raised three sons and two daughters. Clinton worked for Screen Plate in Lennoxville when their first son, Bob Marshall, was born in 1944. Clinton had saved his money from his harvesting excursion to the Prairies a couple of years prior and from working at Screen Plate, so they were able to purchase a farm on Hardwood Flat Road in Bury, just above Newport Township. Here their first daughter, Ruby, was born in 1945. Clinton had always loved farming and knew that if the opportunity arose he would have to get back to farming – he knew he was just not cut out for factory work. It was also important to note that, in times of war, governments were encouraging farmers' sons to work the farms to provide food to ship overseas.

Later that month in 1942, the Maple Leaf community of families – Nugent, Austin, Hurd, Cable, Loveland, Willard, Leggett and Rand – attended the funeral of Laura (Hurd) Swail (Lionel's aunt). The pallbearers were Archie Jones, Lawrence Mackay, Carl Bailey, Lloyd French, Ernest Middlemiss, and Charlie Montgomery. Edith (Morrison) Rand served freshly baked donuts accompanied with tea and coffee. The very next day Rev. Wilson's son was killed in a plane crash overseas and Melva (Jones) Williams' baby died.[46]

Clinton Rand and Doreen McCormick wedding (courtesy of Ruby (Rand) Pehlemann)

In 1943 Lyle and Fay Rand christened their baby boy, Royce Marshall; Fred and Florence Hurd stood in as his godparents.

***

Author's note: Grant and Harriet "Hattie" Nugent had migrated from Maple Grove (Thetford region) with their four children Hubert, Muriel, Harris and Doris Eva (who was 11 or 12 at the time) and purchased a farm in the northwestern Flanders region of Newport circa 1928-29. Their fifth child, Robert "Bobby," was born on their farm in Flanders. Doris later established a Nugent connection with the Heard/Hurd family of Newport.

The Nugent farm was located on Flanders Road in the central-western area of Newport. Hubert married Marion Lake; Muriel married Clifford Westgate then Norman Winslow; Harris married Gloria Coates from Bury; Doris married George Hurd from Sawyerville; and Bobby married Truth Hamilton from Sawyerville. *(Terry Winslow, Norman and Muriel's son)*

Grant had originally bred milking Shorthorn cattle, however, over time they changed over to breeding Holsteins, built a large dairy herd, and became part of the Quebec milk quota system. When Grant and Hattie retired in the early 1960s, the farm was quite successful and was passed on to their son Harris.

When Harris took over the family farm he created a family corporation. Over the next several decades he acquired several adjacent farms and expanded the corporation's holdings to around 700 acres. Harris and Gloria raised two boys, Danny and Kim, who would both stay and farm along with the family. Danny Nugent served his community as councillor for Newport circa 1995 as other family members had done before him.

***

The French families served their community in many capacities over the years. Archie French served for 15 years as chairman of the local school board and several years as representative of the new Compton County Protestant School Board. His son, Kenneth, and daughter-in-law Joyce were presented with a plaque for 15 years of service as school janitors for Island Brook School. Abel, a son of John and Emma, married Alma Patton and they raised five children in Newport. One of their sons, Aubrey, stayed on the original farm where he and his wife Blanche (Dempsey) raised their daughter Brenda.

Clinton Desmond French, the third son of James H. and Hannah (Harvey), married Marjorie Berwick and raised their family of three daughters, Linda, Mary Ellen and Wendy, and a son, Jeffrey, on Lot 1 of Range 6. Clinton French had taken over his grandfather Robert Foster French's farm. Clinton and Marjory carried on his parents' and grandparents' tradition of beef farming, raising a herd of purebred Ayrshires in the late 1950s to early '60s, the herd growing with each generation. They harvested several acres of oats each year that they placed in a granary, taking out a portion to grind into meal for the cattle to supplement their diet of hay in the winter months. "I remember Clinton had built a granary on stilts to ward off the rodents." *(Eric R. French)*

Linda (French) Oliveras remembers when the family had a flock of "banty" chickens. These are essentially small chickens similar in size to Cornish hens. The roosters would terrorize her younger sister, Ellen, and so she always took a wide berth around them when walking.

James "Jim" (the eldest son of Robert and Mary Ellen) and Hannah French lived their entire lives on the farm in Newport. Hannah died of complications from the Asiatic flu in 1957 and James died in 1987. Their son William Victor took over the farm.

Authors note: The heritage of James[3] Henry and Hannah Mary (Harvey) French, the descendants of William[1] V. and Elizabeth (McGee) French as well as the descendants of William's brother John and his wife Emma (Parsons) will be covered in the family's latter three generations.

***

Author's note: The following documentation has been submitted by Gillian Maureen (Hurd) Anderson, Eric James Hurd's daughter.

Meanwhile, on the European front the battles raged on. *The [Montreal] Gazette* reported on May 24, 1944, that "P/O Eric Hurd RCAF (C/18877) was awarded the DFC [Distinguished Flying Cross] for service with 408 Squadron." Eric was the youngest son of Alonzo and his wife Eva Hurd of Newport. He was born in Sawyerville in 1920, enlisted in London, England, on March 27, 1942, and was commissioned in 1943.

There was no citation to Eric's DFC as such, other than *"completed . . . many successful operations against the enemy in which [he has] displayed high skill, fortitude and devotion to duty."* The recommendation for his award, however, states that *"Pilot Officer Hurd has nearly completed his first tour of operations. As a navigator he has been responsible for directing his aircraft on many occasions to very distant targets in enemy territory, including over eleven trips to Berlin. He has at all times displayed great keenness and devotion to duty."* (Minister of National Defense for Air, signed by Charles J. Power, Ottawa, June 1944)

RCAF P/O Eric Hurd receiving his DFC award, 1940

Every operational flight created the jitters.

> The pilot, John Douglas Harvey "received a gold watch for the highest number of Ops flown to Berlin" out of all pilots in 408. No wonder there were jitters before going up, Berlin being the worst target in a service with a 60 percent casualty rate, the highest of any branch of service of any western allied military. Of the 125,000 aircrew that flew with Bomber Command, close to 56,000 were killed; add in those who were wounded, became POWs, or were labeled L.M.F. and grounded. The odds on completing an operational tour of 30 missions for newly assigned crews was close to 1 in 3. If one were to look at the number of ops these men flew on, it would give a pretty good idea of how little rest these crews got. It was apparently rare for British and American crews to fly ops on consecutive days, yet there's a few times that apparently happened to the S-Sugar crew in late July 1943 to Essen and Hamburg (one of the most controversial series of raids), and again to Berlin on the 27, 28, 30 of January in 1944.

> On the night of October 7-8, 1943, this aircraft was one of 343 Lancaster aircrafts on route to bomb Stuttgart; it was also the first 408 Squadron operational flights since the squadron converted to flying the Lancaster type. The Lancaster DS724 took off from Linton-on-Ouse at 20.59 hrs. and soon after the flying controls jammed. With some difficulty the pilot managed to climb the aircraft to 5000 feet where the crew abandoned it, it crashed soon after with a full bomb load on board close to Manor Farm, Spaunton at 21.08 hrs. On impact it exploded causing a massive blast and carrying a full bombload, the explosion was heard for many miles. The crash is noted in a Scarborough's ARP war diary so one assumes it was heard at least 20 miles away. Sadly, there was one fatality involved, the farmer at Manor Farm, Mr. George Strickland. He was about to come out of his house when he was killed as the blast blew the heavy farm door in on him. It is likely that he heard the initial crash and had then gone towards the door to see what had happened. In some cases, some of the bombs would explode moments later and this may have been the case here. *(Jonathan Hurd, son of Rodney Hurd, grandson of Eric Hurd)*

Lancaster bomber

Pilot Officer Eric Hurd had to bail out with other members of a "Goose" Squadron crew when their heavy Lancaster bomber turned temperamental and had to be abandoned. The plane had just taken off for Stuttgart, Germany, when the skipper found his controls wholly useless. Flt. Sgt. Doug Harvey recalled, "I had just gotten the wheels up when the kite started to drift to port, but we managed to make five thousand feet." Navigator Sgt. Hurd recalled, "We were climbing at the start and couldn't seem to stop. I guess Doug decided it just wasn't the right time to get to heaven. It was a nice trip down although the landing was somewhat abrupt. It was a wonderful feeling to see the chute opening up, though." *(Sherbrooke Record, 1943)*

"Of the crew on board DS724, all but one landed safely within a few miles of the crash location, stretching back towards Pockley [North Yorkshire, England], however, one of the crew had sustained slight injuries in a bad landing but recovered." *(Jonathan Hurd)*

There is a list of all the operational flights Eric Hurd had taken part in up to the DFC recommendation being made as "Navigator Sgt. Eric James Hurd RCAF (C/18877), of Sawyerville, Que., Canada." As a result, almost certainly many of the following crew flew with him during these flights: Pilot, F/Sgt. John Douglas Harvey RCAF (R/141147), of Toronto; Flight Engineer Sgt. H. .J Branton RAF; possibly Henry John Branton (1604002); Bomb Aimer – F/O Stephen William Dempsey RCAF (J/21039), of Oshawa, Ont.; Wireless Operator/Air Gunner P/O George Ernest Ray Butchart RCAF (J/18341) (a.k.a. "Slick" or "Rae"); Mid-upper Gunner Sgt. Stanley Enos Campbell RCAF (R/160645), of Drumheller, Alta., who had broken ribs and a dislocated shoulder; and Rear Gunner Sgt. K. L. Davison RCAF.

"I always liked the one about [Bernie's] mother never pouring him more than two inches of tea, so he wouldn't be embarrassed if his hands shook and the tea spilt – I haven't read the book *Boys, Bombs and Brussels Sprouts* in a long time, but I think I recall there's an anecdote where the crew tease him good-naturedly because he had trouble drawing a straight line on a piece of paper before an op, which sounds familiar to Grandma's account." *(Jonathan Hurd)*

***

Meanwhile, on the other side of the globe, in May 1944, the Canadian officers who were POWs in Hong Kong were moved from the Argyle Street camp to the Shamshuipo camp in Hong Kong. However, they were still segregated from the rest of the internees. They recognized their men from afar but were under strict orders from the Japanese Commandant that they were not allowed to converse or mix. "Bedbugs infested both camps. They were everywhere and drove the prisoners to distraction. They were in the bunks, the stools, the chairs and clothing and there was no way to eradicate them. Hot water was not permitted, nor were insecticides. The only remedy was to accept them."[3]

My father, Lionel Hurd, also had a letter addressed to Mrs. T. MacAulay in his files, dated December 13, 1943, unsigned and leaving us to question who the author might be. The letter gave a first-hand description of the realities of hospital life in Hong Kong, specifically speaking to the condition of Mrs. MacAulay's husband, Major Tom MacAulay with the Royal Rifles. He had been severely wounded but recovered well enough to be sent to back to POW Camp Sham Sui Po early in 1944. According to my father's diary, March 1944 was when Tom was put in charge of the canteen. An excerpt from the letter:

> *He (Major MacAulay) along with a few others are waiting for bone-grafting to be done. Equipment and other things are necessary at Bowen Road (Hospital) and they do not have it, so it is a case of marking time. Difficulty in finding wood to keep the place warm. Sometimes Major MacAulay would come up to help with an axe to smash them for us with his one arm, and you would hear me yelling "Do be careful . . . mind that axe." Your husband never forgot his men. We had a lot of Canadians who went through hell alright.*

Lionel's parents Sarah and Gussie Hurd still had received no word as to what had happened to their son. The only news they had was an indication through the Red Cross that there were many men held in POW camps, many of whom had been moved to the island of Japan. Sarah had written a letter in the spring of 1942, addressed through the General Post Office in Ottawa rather than the Red Cross, in a concerted effort to get a letter through to Hong Kong. Sarah's letter mentioned that "*Freddie [is] nearly two years old. He has grown such a lot.*" This was the first letter received by Lionel – on April 5, 1943, exactly one year after being mailed.[3]

Unlike the Argyle Street Camp, which was in the middle of a semi-residential part of Kowloon, the Shamshuipo camp was located on the western side of Kowloon Peninsula, right on the water's edge on a cliff overlooking the harbour. This camp had been the British Military Headquarters, equipped with the absolute best in living quarters prior to the

Japanese attack on Hong Kong. Arthur Alden and many others from the surrounding townships had been transferred to this camp from the North Point Camp where mostly Canadians had been interned right after the battle.

When prisoners first arrived in the Shamshuipo camp, the huts were mere shells, stripped of everything and in complete squalor. There were missing doors and windows and the concrete floors were bare and filthy. There were no beds or bunks or blankets— nothing was provided. The prisoners had to sit and sleep on the concrete floors. In the first days of captivity, they had the food they had brought with them, whatever they could carry, and they were able to barter or to buy basic necessities such as a cup or some cooking utensils from the local Chinese through the barbed wire. Ill-clothed, tired and starved, officers returning after a day's work detail were humiliated by the Japanese when, outside the camp, they were ordered to salute Japanese officers and army privates as well.

Though everything was available in a city like Hong Kong, the Japanese provided nothing for the hundreds of men in their captivity and reduced them to an almost primitive existence.

Letter from Sarah Hurd to POW son Capt. Lionel Hurd

The prisoners had to be inventive and skilled, with no tools to speak of, to make the most basic things such as washstands made from rusty pieces of corrugated galvanized iron. Over 500 men used these tubs to do laundry in cold water with no soap. Some of these same homemade tubs were also used to cook food.

The only garment distributed to the prisoners was called a "pandochi," a type of cloth diaper. Prisoners wore these to save their shorts or trousers for the obligatory twice-daily muster and at times when the Japanese insisted upon proper dress code. The men's good clothes were threadbare; they were darned and patched over several times. For footwear, the Japanese provided clogs. Some men wore them and repaired them with scrap materials; others preferred by necessity to go barefoot because the clog straps rubbed and grated the skin, causing sores that without medication or bandages had to be avoided.

The Japanese counted the prisoners twice-daily and often several times at night. Day musters were held rain or shine and the Japanese insisted on proper dress. After several prisoners escaped from the camp, the Japanese increased security measures by making the prisoners take turns during the hours of darkness to account for everyone in each hut. There was a time they demanded a report as often as 10 times a night, making prisoners responsible for their own group of friends, which served to exhaust them even more.

After a successful escape, collective punishment was applied. They caught the four escapees, called everyone to the parade square and executed them on the spot, so all could see. The already-meager rations were cut, and the guards were ordered to physically assault the internees. After months of being terrorized and being brought to near starvation, the results were such that even the Japanese authorities became concerned and cancelled certain restrictions. Some Japanese displayed vicious brutality, and their tempers were mercurial. They would often use the butt ends of their rifles to inflict blows. The severity of some of these beatings would require hospitalization. A Japanese-Canadian that the POWs called the "Kamloops Kid" was especially vicious.

> *Author's note: When the Canadian soldiers arrived in Hong Kong, they patronized a barber at the Peninsula Hotel. Only later, as POWs, did they discover he was the "Kamloops Kid," a Japanese and not Chinese citizen as they had assumed. One can only imagine how much information the barber gleaned from his unsuspecting clients.*

For nearly four years, the prisoners existed on exceedingly small portions of white rice, often rotten, dirty and infested with bugs, which they cooked themselves. The rice was occasionally accompanied by poor-quality "bok-choy" or rotting turnip, or generally the refuse from outside vegetable markets. The Japanese supply corporal sent in whatever he wished. A few of the luckier prisoners in Shamshuipo managed to establish little garden plots and grow a few vegetables for their kitchens.

Initially, no senior Japanese officer would concern himself with the food supply for the prisoners until pellagra and beriberi, with their attendant physical degeneration, swept through the camp. The near-starvation diet resulted in a high death toll and caused the Japanese some alarm. It was then that small supplementary supplies of peanut oil, fish and flour appeared for a short time. "The men believed that this sudden expression of generosity was perhaps an indication the 'Japs' might be losing the war." *(Capt. E. L. Hurd)*

Of the Red Cross parcels sent to the prisoners, only a few were ever received. In fact, in 44 months of captivity, no one received more than seven food packages. All mail was censored; there was no flow of personal communication. Ultimately, mail was received two years or longer from the posted dates, some received after the war ended. Families did not even know whether their loves ones were dead, wounded or alive, and knew nothing of their whereabouts other than what the media provided, i.e., that POWs had been taken.

Major Wells Bishop, Captain Lionel Hurd and the remaining officers were interned in all three camps from December 25, 1941, to late August 1945. Those who had been wounded and had recuperated in hospital were sent back to the prison camps to take their place among the others, continuing to survive on a starvation diet and expected to work alongside their comrades. It was from the Shamshuipo camp that the POWs were systematically shipped via the "Hell Ships" to Japan to work as slaves in the factories and mines, as they needed men to replace those who had died there. Many of these unmarked ships were inadvertently torpedoed by the Allies en route, causing many more POW deaths.

May 9, 1945, a note in Lionel Hurd's diary: "Freddy's birthday today, I don't know if I will ever see him again."

The Japanese had their counterpart to the "Nazi Gestapo," i.e., skilled torturers known as the "Kempeitai." One of their favourite tortures was to force fistfuls of rice down a POW's throat, insert a water hose down their throats until their bellies swelled and then mercilessly jump on their stomachs.

The Japanese also operated death factories, commissioned by an outfit referred to as Unit 731, during their occupation. Unlike the Germans who apologized for the Holocaust, the Japanese government has not really acknowledged their own war crimes and most assuredly not those of Unit 731.

The Japanese military had factories and laboratories all over the Asia-Pacific Rim, no different than the Germans, and were responsible for Japan's biological warfare efforts. They experimented on POWs by subjecting them to every virus known to mankind. They engineered bubonic plague, typhus, and anthrax outbreaks in several Chinese cities. Another trick was that they would contaminate a town or city's drinking water supply, making everyone sick prior to an attack.

They would hang POWs upside down by their feet on tripods positioned over the latrines; the stench unbearable, just to see how long it would take them to die.[3]

The world learned that the Japanese surrendered on August 14, 1945, officially announced by Emperor Hirohito on August 15. The Union Jack was raised over Camp Shamshuipo on August 18, the POWs hearing the news of the surrender on hidden radios in the camp. However, the Japanese camp administration continued to withhold the news from the POWs. Interestingly, 15 days would pass from the official announcement by the Emperor before the Japanese actually left Hong Kong.

This was another tenuous time for the POWs as they were acutely aware of orders to the Japanese military that all POWs were to be killed upon any surrender. One day the Japanese donned civilian clothes and simply walked away, melding in with the Chinese so they would not be detected as easily. The image on the page opposite is of the first

South China Morning Post, Aug. 31, 1945 (Hurd family military collection)

issue of the South China Morning Post on August 31, 1945, after a hiatus of over three years. The paper was produced under great difficulty because the Japanese were still occupying the newspaper offices up until the day before. The Japanese had used the facilities to print their own paper during the occupation. This issue was regarded as an emergency issue for the purpose of acquainting the public with what was happening.[3]

This issue was distributed by Capt. E. L. Hurd of the Royal Rifles of Canada. In his handwriting, there was a note on the upper right corner, "Please return to Capt. E. L. Hurd, RRC, Shamshuipo Camp."[3]

Author's note: This was the life these POWs from the Eastern Townships lived during this period. They survived the battle of Hong Kong but then endured horrendous atrocities for almost four years in the custody of the Japanese Military. What has been written here is what life was like for all of these men as prisoners of war. For the wounded and many others who were sent to be slaves in Japan, their lives lived during internment was even worse. When the POWs were found, the Allies witnessed long rows of shocked, bulging eyes peering curiously, belonging to men who truly were half dead. Many limped when they walked, their heads perched loosely atop wrinkled pencils of necks, their ribs countable, clavicles protruded, uniforms worn thin, pants and shorts roughly sewn together and even some uniforms dissolved into dingy gauze.

My father found it hard to accept that, as he had just about lost all will to live, he was free and going home. He was one of the few prisoners still capable of making his way unaided, perhaps because he was an officer or perhaps, like some of the others from the Eastern Townships, he was used to hardship and hard labour while farming and lumbering. He felt that as officers they were indeed treated somewhat better; nonetheless, some were in such bad shape they had to be carried out of the camps.

Excerpts from Lionel Hurd's letters received at home, after his release in late August 1945 from POW camp in Hong Kong:

1. Aug. 31, letter to Father and Mother: "Just released. I have had no news from anyone for over a year. Your letter of August 1944 the last. I am starting to gain some weight with better food."

2. Sept. 5, letter to his sister-in-law Helen (Tannahill) Hurd: "Please excuse my pencil writing as I sold my watch, pen, and other personal belongings to get a bit of better food in the prison camp."

3. Sept. 6, letter to Father and Mother: "We are still in HK. The Empress of Australia is in the Harbour. The rounding up of the Japs gives us a lot of satisfaction and they will be put in our old Shamshuipo prison camp. They look very depressed and have lost 'plenty of face' now."

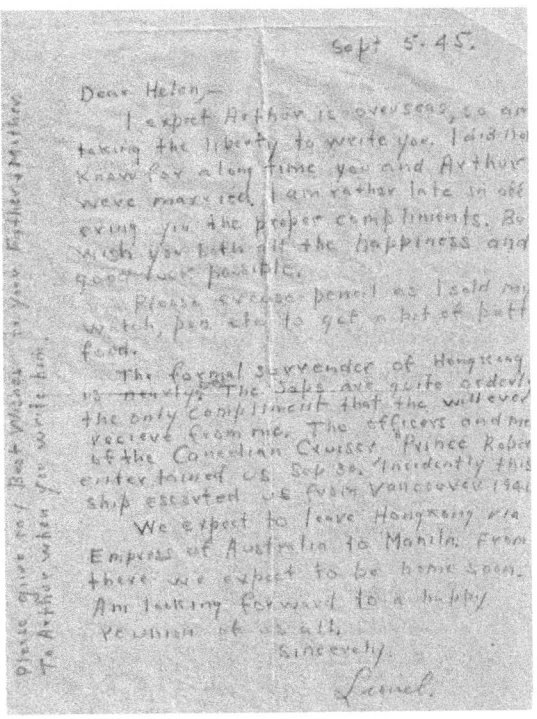

Letter from Lionel Hurd to sister-in-law Helen (Tannahill) Hurd

4. Sept. 19, letter to Father and Mother: "I have often thought about my old home and good father and mother I had. I hope I have been and can still be a grateful son. I am so far behind in all the news of my friends etc. It took as long as two years to get a letter through and most of them the Japs never bothered with. They sometimes just dumped them in a trash bin and burned them in front of us."

5. Sept. 23, letter to Mary: "This prison life has made me feel that I want to be away from all discipline and the men I have been with for so long. We will go somewhere where we are together by ourselves."

6. Oct. 1, letter to Father and Mother: "On the way home. I am with Wells Bishop and Bill Harlow on the Empress of Australia ship, the only two from the Townships that you would know. We have stopped in Manila, which is in shambles as everywhere the Japanese go, they rob and loot. I will have hundreds of questions to ask. I do not think I have changed much from what I see in the mirror, the first time after three-and one-half years. Most of the POWs as well as myself suffer from loss of memory in many ways, very annoying. The whole ordeal is appearing to me now like a bad dream."

7. Oct. 3, letter to Jimmy and Freddy: "We are Boarding the U.S.S. Gosper to Pearl Harbor, from there to Vancouver. Will be home soon and so anxious to see how much you have grown."

Upon arrival in Vancouver in early October, the Canadian POWs had to undergo medical examination and treatment before they were finally released to go home. Lionel had essentially been away from home since when he had signed up with the Royal Rifles in the spring of 1941. The men were generally annoyed that they had been separated on different ships coming home and so they did not know who had survived and who had not. Lionel took the train from Vancouver to Toronto to Quebec City, and then back to Sherbrooke on the Quebec Central Railway, a long journey indeed.

***

Arthur and Nora (Parsons) owned a farm just up the road off today's Route 210 on the west side of the road to North River and were a source of great support for Sadie and Gussie during the war years.[31]

L-R: Dorothy Loveland, age 13; the author, Lionel's son Freddie on his 5th birthday; Lionel's mother, Sarah Hurd; Dorothy's mother, Nora Loveland; early 1945

Arthur Lowry used to visit once a week. He walked down from Cora Austin's farm where he boarded, located just beyond Arthur and Nora's place. He worked as a farm hand in the summers. Sarah had a chair strategically placed just inside the kitchen door expressly for Arthur to sit on. Sarah soon learned that Arthur never took his boots off when he dropped by, he just swaggered in and took a seat at the kitchen table, and so that was why Sarah had that chair positioned right at the door. Arthur also had a hearing problem derived from the many years of working with lumbering equipment, his voice vibrating throughout the building. Gussie always knew when Arthur had arrived as he could hear him all the way down to the barn.

Author's note: When I was only 6 or 7 years old, visiting my grandmother, I remember this man sitting on that chair, his voice bellowing. I always wondered where he came from, because he would just suddenly appear. I also remember my grandmother saying, "Don't let the door hit you on the way out" – which I found rather odd since the door opened inward.

***

George[2] Robinson[10] Hurd, first son of Alonzo, was born in Newport in 1913 and graduated from Queen's University in 1934. He managed and operated the Sawyerville Manufacturing Company with his mother Eva for many years. In 1945 George married Doris Eva Nugent, who was born at Maple Grove in the Thetford region. George and his family lived in Sawyerville and raised their three children: Allan Grantborn (born 1947), Cynthia Doris (born 1950) and Deanna Evelyn (born 1953).

> *Author's note: Doris was the daughter of Grant J. and Harriet "Hattie" E. (Williamson) Nugent, who were living in Maple Grove near Thetford Mines at the time. They had five children: Hubert, Muriel, Harris, Doris, and Robert. They had moved to Newport and purchased a farm in the Island Brook region.*

***

On Saturday, September 22, 1945, Edith (Morrison) Rand of Newport, made a note in her diary that *"Arnold Brazel arrived home from Hong Kong."* On Monday, October 29, 1945, Edith also made a note *"Lionel Hurd and Mary called on me this afternoon. Lionel has just been home a week after been liberated from Hong Kong where he was a prisoner of war since Xmas, 1941."* (Rand family diaries, courtesy of Carol Rand)

Now, this was to be Lionel Hurd's life. Anxious to get home, he would soon learn that it was not uncommon for many of these men both from the European and Pacific fronts to come home to empty nests. Many of the wives had to find ways to support themselves and their families. There were those who had no idea whether their husbands had survived the battles and if so, had they survived the POW camps of Hong Kong. Communication was virtually nonexistent from this part of the world during their four years in captivity.

Lionel came back to a different world than he had left some five years prior. For him it was almost as though time had shifted forward. He realized that his memories were of a "time" that had in reality "stood still" only in his mind. Many of his friends had moved away, some had served in the European war, and some he would never see again. Others he had known so well in the community were married, working, raising their families, and prospering. He only remembered his two boys as babies and now they suddenly appeared as little people with minds of their own. He realized then that he had missed so much in his life. He would soon learn that he was to start all over again, even in his marriage.

The soldiers returning from the European conflict were returning victorious, while Lionel felt the Hong Kong soldiers had failed simply because they had all been captured. This feeling of failure was not only his own but was felt by all his Hong Kong comrades, and it took many years for them to come to grips with this stigma.

Lionel's mother Sarah was on crutches – she had fallen and broken her hip, didn't go to a doctor to get it fixed and so was struggling but still intent in looking after her hens. His parents were still living on the old farm; however, his father Gussie was looking much frailer now and had retired – the farming finally too hard for him to continue.

Lionel's aunt, Laura Swail, had passed on in 1942, the funeral held in the Randboro church. Renford and Elizabeth Morrow's children, that he had known in the Maple Leaf community, were so much older. Donnie and Jean Morrow were now grown up and dating, both Lyle and Clinton Rand had also grown up, had married and had children and were living their lives. Lyle was working for Lionel's brother, Fred, at his meat market. Clinton and Doreen had bought a farm on Hardwood Flat Road in Bury Township and were raising two children. They were all younger than him, and it did not escape his notice that they were well-settled and prospering. Time had stood still for Lionel but not for the people he had been connected to prior to the war.

His brother, Fred, had a thriving butcher business, had married in 1942 and they already had a daughter, Judy. His youngest brother, Arthur, had also married in 1941, served with the Canadian Armed Forces in England, had moved to Red Rock, Ont., lost his foot in a mill accident and was walking with a specially fitted boot. His favourite uncle, Joe Riddell, had died just a few weeks before he arrived home, and so he had only the memories of when he had worked with Joe so many years ago.

While Lionel was away the floods of 1942 and 1943 had burst the large dam in Sawyerville and the large lake upriver that had run all the way up to Munns farm in Newport was drained. The covered bridge crossing the South River at the mill was also gone, replaced by a new cement bridge. His fond memories of skating in the winter with his school friends and later as a young man were to remain as mere memories.

Lionel's experiences that took place in a different part of the world during the Pacific War had caused him to reflect on his place of birth, his rich ancestry, his family and his friends who stood by him. These were all factors that he considered carefully and were instrumental in his making the decision that he would take his place along with his ancestors and stay in Newport to start a new life farming the land he knew so well.

Lionel's uncle and aunt, Joe and Jessie (Hurd) Riddle, had bought the original Heard/Hurd settlement farm (lineage: Col. Edmund[5], Luke[7], George[8], Alonzo[9]), commonly known as the old Luke Heard farm in a bankruptcy sale in 1932. Joe and Jessie rented the farm to the Kingsley family for many years, the farm becoming generally known then as the Kingsley farm. When World War II broke out and Lionel was captured in Hong Kong, they had made a vow that if he were to return alive, he could have the farm. Joe died in late August of 1945, just before the news of the Hong Kong POW release.

The new bridge at Sawyerville, 1943: Flanders Road going south onto Main Street (*Sherbrooke Record*)

> *Author's note: My father decided to live on the family farm because of his health; he just wanted to be outside and free and so he set about in 1946 to prepare the original homestead of his ancestors as his own homestead. He continued operating the old Luke Hurd farm (as it was still known in Newport) from 1946 to 1972. This too is part of our heritage.*

The British Empire had remained dominant in the world until 1945. The aftermath of the Second World War left Europe and Britain in ruins. Insolvency and a rising anti-colonial movement caused the British government to adopt a policy of disengagement from its colonies.

In the post-Second World War era, we have two separate countries, Canada and the United States, with common roots and in many ways, alike. The two countries, however, have been shaped by different histories, different geographies, different climates and different needs. Americans are in general more individualistic, more dedicated to protecting their personal liberties and more suspicious of governments. Canadians, on the other hand, have more trust that their governments are looking out for their best interests and thus are prepared to allow personal liberties to be limited in the interests of our communal need to protect our collective well-being. Women who had become much more diversified during the war years, who also had the opportunity to participate in every aspect of life, became more vocal in expressing to their husbands that war should be treated as a last resort to ensure that their own children have a chance to live free. After the war ended in 1945, the Family Allowance program was established in Canada – just in time for the upcoming baby boom of the mid-1940s to late '50s.

***

> *Author's note: Brothers Herbert and Robert Statton had been born in the Island Brook region of Newport. Herbert married Oscar Painter's widow, Gertrude "Gertie" (Labree) Painter, and they continued farming in Island Brook. Gertie had two sons from her first marriage, Lindsay and Gleason. Robert Statton married Harriet Latty; they had a son, Walter, who after the war settled on a farm on Parker Hill.*

Just after his service in World War II, Walter Statton purchased the farm next door and just east of the Desruisseaux farm and married Lillian Desruisseaux. They raised their family of four sons and three daughters on a farm adjacent to the families of Desruisseaux and Tetreault. Eugene married Anita Cormier; Lionel married Ruby Sayers; Chester died at 35; June married Donald McCormick; Lydia married Douglas Judge; Walter Jr. married Ruth Cote; and Judy married Keith Smith. The children all grew up on the Parker Hill farm; all left Newport as they were married, except for June; she and her husband Donald bought a farm just east of Randboro. Walter's uncle, Herbert Statton's son, is still farming in the Island Brook region, and so there are still Statton families who are associated with Newport Township today. *(courtesy of Lydia (Statton) Judge)*

And so, the Parker, McCallum, Speck, Tetreault, Desruisseaux and Statton families were all neighbours on Parker Hill farms. Both their ancestors and their descendants would have had a sentimental association with the Parker Hill community, all part of Newport Township's rich history.

***

Austin Bowker

When Austin Bowker's stepmother died in April 1929, Austin and his wife Ruth (Gilman) took over the old homestead. His father Herbert lived with them until his death in 1950. Austin and Ruth built a large dairy herd and were now taking part in the Quebec milk quota system. The basic idea behind the quota system is supply management designed to manage production so that supply is in balance with demand, and the farm gate price enables farmers to cover their costs of production, including a return on labour and capital. Each farm owns a number of shares in the market (a quota) and is required to increase or decrease production according to consumer demand. Because production is in sync with demand, overproduction is avoided; this enables farmers to earn a predictable and stable revenue directly from the market. They could now sell a farm which would include this milk quota, almost a business guarantee for the purchaser. In 1941, Austin and Ruth's big dairy barn burned down. Austin and a crew of men harvested lumber from the farm that winter, had it milled and a new barn built in the summer of 1942. Their family continued to operate the farm well into their next generation.

Austin Bowker served as mayor of Newport from 1943 to 1950, followed by Thomas Burns Jr. who was elected in 1951.

Chapter 16   Post-war Newport (1945–1950)

After the war Eric Hurd partnered with his brother, George, to operate the Sawyerville Manufacturing Company for a few years before moving with his family to Toronto. Eric and Bernice "Bernie" Hurd raised their family of five children in Toronto: Gillian (Anderson), Rodney, Keith, Debbie (Deller) and Thomas. Eric worked at the Premier Door factory for many years. Eric died in 1988; Bernie died in 2016. Both are buried in Maple Leaf Cemetery where all his ancestors are interred.[4]

***

Electricity was being introduced in Newport; poles being erected by Southern Canada Power and most of the countryside was now going to enjoy electrical power. This began the transformation of Newport into a more modern mode. By 1947, post-World War II immigrants from Europe, including Italian, Swiss and Germans were using English as their second language. Chinese women were permitted to immigrate for the first time, thus allowing Chinese immigration to grow. The Quebec Radio Farm Forum was established in the Eastern Townships to educate rural people about farming advancements and issues.[48]

By 1950 the first computers were coming into existence in the large banks and commercial businesses. Education was key, schooling was improved and students began to flock to colleges and universities. Entrepreneurs were flourishing and salesmen were once again peddling their wares over the countryside. This era was to become an idealistic time of peace and prosperity and for the younger population, a time when jobs were available, one just had to decide which career one might choose to pursue.

Herman Stevenson (William Stevenson and Matilda Hurd's son) continued working the farm in Learned Plain throughout this period. Herman was the school commissioner and continued to be an organizer for the "Patrons of Industry." He was a prominent officer of the I.O.F. Herman was also tasked with the responsibility of finding ways to get students from the rural areas of Newport to the "consolidated schools" in both Cookshire and Sawyerville.[32]

After the war ended in 1945, motorized vehicles became more available. Surplus army equipment was available everywhere and communities in the Eastern Townships were eager to buy up as many as they could afford of the four-wheel drive jeeps, specifically four-wheel drive army trucks for use in the more rural areas.[40]

Municipalities were quick to purchase these trucks for school buses and snowplows. These old army buses and trucks came into use for spring and fall conveyance for the students in Newport and surrounding regions. From these early school buses and army surplus vehicles evolved the school buses of the modern era.[40]

Doug Mackay

Doug Mackay (pictured) owned the Texaco gas station and Mackay's Garage in Sawyerville. He also drove the school bus for many years, from the 1940s through to the late the 1950s, from the army trucks to modern-day school buses, including the Bombardier snowmobiles. His wife, Mabel, was a sister of Arthur Alden who survived to return home from his ordeal as a Hong Kong POW.

By 1947-48, grades 9 and 10 pupils of the Island Brook school were now being transported by school bus to Cookshire High School. Local bus drivers were Maple Westgate, Arnold Alden and Tom Parsons. Maple drove the bus for more than 20 years, including snowmobile buses for two winters. One of those winters included the year of the largest snowstorm of the 20th century, in March 1947. The roadbeds had not been built up over the years, so they were essentially lower

Hand shovelling the road to free a buried car, 1947 (Sunderland & District Historical Society)

All three snowmobile buses lined up after school. The arrow points to the author, who notes "My school travel days in the big snowmobiles is a memory I will never forget."

than the farmlands beside them, many with trees and bushes lining the roadsides. March storms were usually associated with blowing winds, so these roads became virtually impassable. The poor road conditions in winter was one of reasons school boards purchased Bombardier snowmobiles for use as buses to transport the children to school, and municipalities purchased four-wheel drive army vehicles for buses and plows.

Most of the early snowmobile school buses will be remembered by all who travelled from Newport and Eaton townships to the consolidated schools in Sawyerville and Cookshire. The roads were sometimes impossible to plow when the snow drifted in to be level with the higher roadsides and accumulating snowbanks. These "school buses" would even have to leave the roadways to travel across the fields to pick up children for school.

The "Bombardiers," as they were commonly known, were also used by doctors, rural mailmen, taxi services, winter fishermen and even in the logging industry. This was the forerunner of the Ski-Doo, which became a personal carrier for sport. During the war years of 1939-45 they had been shipped overseas to be used by the military.

Our school in Sawyerville had three of these snowmobiles, powered by Chevrolet 6 and Ford V/8 engines, operating with a three-speed transmission. There were two snow skis on the front to steer with, much like a car, and two hand brakes on either side of the driver, who sat in the middle of the vehicle. These hand brakes were used to quickly brake one side or the other to help steer, so the vehicle could make a U-turn relatively quickly and easily, even though it did operate with a regular car steering wheel. Traction was via two track assemblies which provided both flotation over the snow but also the traction to move forward. There was a reverse gear; however, moving backwards was not an easy task so the driver would anticipate where he needed to be without having to back the vehicle up. The drive train was reversed compared to a car or truck, in that the engine was at the rear of the vehicle; the drive unit ran under the passenger seating area to sprockets driving the traction lags. The hood was reversed so that when running it was set partially open at the back end so the wind from operation kept the engines cool. The body was made entirely of plywood with porthole windows along each side. Two doors with windows that opened were situated to the right and left of the driver with an additional two seats, making the front driver's zone a three-seat cab. Children sat in the back on benches down each side and across the rear, with a straddle bench down the middle. Non-opening porthole windows ran down each side of the vehicle.

Clifford "Tiffy" Morrison also drove the school bus for many years specifically in Newport on the Randboro/Maple Leaf route and the North River/Flanders Road route. He worked for Tommy French who owned a garage beside the school where Tiffy parked and repaired the bus. Tiffy married Verlie Laroche (the daughter of Claude and Marion). Tiffy and Verlie lived in Randboro where they raised a son, Sidney, and a daughter, Cheryl.

Tiffy was driving an average of four hours each day as part of his workday. Each of the three drivers for the school had two route runs, so the routes would switch half-way through the school year when the early pickup would switch to the late pickup. Of course, as children we liked the later run because we did not have to get up as early and we could play in the schoolyard after school for an hour.

***

Lionel Hurd divorced his wife Mary in early 1947, and married his second wife, Margaret Irene Matthew (1909-1980), in late 1947. Irene was the eldest daughter of George and Mary "Mamie" (Ord) Matthew. Irene had graduated in 1931 with an R.N. degree from Jeffrey Hale Training School for Nurses in Quebec City and began her nursing career in the Jeffrey Hale Hospital that same year. She had volunteered for service in the war effort in 1941, joining the Royal Canadian Army Medical Corp. She was dispatched to the South African Nursing Service in Cape Town, South Africa, and served as assistant matron from late 1941 to 1945. She retired from the service with the rank of captain, returning to work at the Jeffrey Hale Hospital until she married in 1947. She and Lionel had no children.

Irene Matthew

Gussie Hurd and horse Dinah raking hay; his grandchildren Jim and Fred (the author) on tractor, 1947

In June 1947, Lionel bought a 1945 Ford tractor with an attachable mower. Gussie had given him his hay rake and tedder, driving over in his Model A Ford from time to time to help. Gussie delighted in raking with his old horse, Dinah, a horse he had also given Lionel.

In 1949 Lionel bought a second-hand 1932 Chevrolet Coupe single-bench-seat automobile with an open air "rumble seat" that flipped out at the back. Since there was no back seat or trunk, he removed the rumble seat and replaced it with a box to resemble a small truck so he could haul stuff.

Lionel and Irene brought Lionel's youngest son, Fred (Frederick Edmund[10], the author), from Montreal to live with them during the Christmas holidays in 1947. Fred had been living with his mother Mary (Wood), his stepfather Jim Armstrong, and brother, Jim Hurd, in Montreal throughout the war years.

Author's note: I have a vague memory of seeing my father coming off a train in October 1945. I met my dad twice, later in the summers of 1946-47 at my grandparents' (Sarah and Gussie Hurd's) farm in Maple Leaf. Jim and I had stayed with my grandparents a few times from an early age and so I did know them. For me, the war had essentially robbed me of any association or memory of my father up to this time. Essentially, I suddenly went to live with people I did not know; starting school in Sawyerville on January 2, 1947, with other children I also did not know and separated from my brother and mother.

Lionel and Irene moved into the old farmhouse in early 1947 remodelled it. Throughout the renovation they maintained the basic integrity of the original cabin, merely reorganizing the inside somewhat. The original structure and framework remain intact at the time of writing. They did, however, modernize the interior somewhat. In the kitchen they removed the "water box" that had served as the household refrigerator. It was a simple cedar box, 36 x 48 inches, through which cold spring water ran continuously so it never froze in winter. The water came from a spring at a higher elevation and was piped through cedar logs fashioned into water pipes. The logs were augured through the centre and nested into the end of each other with a

The original Col. Edmund Hurd home after Lionel and Irene renovated and added a woodshed, 1948

pointed end and a concaved end that produced a continuous pipe. They created a new kitchen and installed an upstairs bathroom over the kitchen. Lionel created the first two rooms (bathroom and bedroom) upstairs on the south side of the house in what had been one large room for sleeping quarters. They changed the staircase from the centre of the large loft room on the north side to run up between the addition to the original house and the kitchen and over the cellar staircase. In 1948, he hired Charlie Montgomery to close in the other half of the upstairs loft, dividing it into two bedrooms, so there were three bedrooms and a bathroom including part of the original loft built by Col. Edmund[5] Heard. They installed a steel pipe to provide cold water to the bathroom upstairs.

Author's note: My father was frugal with everything he did, repairing, reconstructing, and painting. The only paint he used was for the front and one side of the house where he had clapboarded. The backsides were and remain to this day the original shingles installed by Luke Heard, circa 1840. My dad's motto was "If it works, why change it?"

After the war many Europeans emigrated to the U.S. and Canada seeking new opportunities. Both Dutch and Danish immigrants were able to fast-track their applications to settle in Canada if they applied to work on farms for a two-year indenture program to learn the language. This facilitated immigration for both Dutch and Danish families who were fleeing their homelands that had been decimated by the war. Lionel and Irene took in a young Dutchman, Teddy Miltenberg, who was just 21, placed with us to learn English before he was to move on. Unfortunately, just prior to his arrival, Teddy contracted rheumatic fever. As a nurse, Irene took care of him for most of a year. Once Teddy was well, he insisted he would help Dad for another year in exchange for the excellent nursing care he had received from Irene. Teddy was a huge help in taking down the old barns and helping Lionel get back on his feet again. The old barns had to be either torn down or reconstructed; this took an enormous amount of work that was in addition to the normal farming tasks required to operate and grow the farm.

The author with pal Lassie, in the spring of 1948, the first year living on the farm. The barns in the foreground were taken down, leaving a large and the smaller barn on the left.

Over the next three years, Lionel tore down two barns; another was moved adjacent to a brook below the sugar bush. This building became their "maple sugar camp." In later years, Lionel expanded the stables of two barns then built an addition between two existing barns to make them into one. He made the forms and poured the cement by himself; the only new lumber he used was for the roof on the addition between the two barns. He prided himself in reusing everything, always removing the nails from old barn wood and reusing the boards.

Author's note: When he had decided to join two barns with an addition, he harvested some lumber and had it milled in Sawyerville to use for the roof trusses. He ran the farm as one would operate a business, keeping immaculate records on everything. Nothing was used without first being assessed as to its value; was it absolutely necessary and if not, then instructions were that one cannot just use it for any old purpose. Everything was to be accounted for. I believe he ran the farm in this manner because he had trained for and really wanted to be a businessman – not a farmer.

The sugar camp was equipped with an evaporator with a "Monroe arch" for boiling the sap. The arch was purchased second-hand, built in Coaticook, Que., by a well-known manufacturer of these cast iron fire jackets so he knew it had longevity. He had another smaller evaporator to facilitate the final and delicate process of making the syrup. These evaporators were designed with a corrugated bottom so that the fluid being boiled had maximum heat from the fire below, essentially through a ribbed bottom, rather than a flat bottom. Because the sugar camp was situated in a bit of valley, the sap was gravity-fed through a pipe from a tank across the brook adjacent to the sugarbush.

Electricity came to the farm in 1951-52. Lionel built the chimney on the south outside wall for a combination wood/electric kitchen stove. The inside water pipes were installed on the surface of the kitchen walls up to the bathroom directly above, which now included a hot water line to the tub. Until electricity was available, Lionel and Irene had been using the original circa 1850s wood stove which had replaced the hearth in the centre of the house. In the mid-1950s, he installed a used wood furnace in the basement. Before electricity was installed, Irene had to wash clothes the old-fashioned way, in a washtub with a wringer on top. She was delighted to have a regular electric wringer washing machine, located in the shed at the side of the house. In winter, the washing machine had to be moved into the kitchen and rolled over to the kitchen sink to be drained, but was still a huge improvement. Every Monday was washday; in the summer she hung the laundry outside in the front porch to dry; in the winter it was around the wood stove in the hall.

> *Author's note: I cannot imagine how Irene must have felt coming from Sawyerville, having worked in Quebec City and South Africa, which had electricity, to live at a farm that was essentially still ensconced in the "olden times." Irene must have felt she had just stepped backwards into a time warp. Oddly for me, having come from Montreal, I don't remember anything particularly different other than there were no lights and it seemed to take forever to get enough hot water for a bath. My recollection was that we seemed to emerge from everything being done as they did in the previous generation to suddenly becoming modern when the electricity arrived, and from there progression was rapid. When electricity came and replaced my lantern, I was amazed to see all four corners of my room at once.*

Lionel and Irene first started with a mixed farm of Shorthorn cattle and a few pigs. They lost most of this herd of cattle to "blackleg," an infectious disease similar to the "foot-and-mouth disease" that hit Western Canada in later years. They then started a herd of Hereford cattle, purchasing a purebred Hereford bull they named "Westley" from the Nichols farm in Lennoxville. He was huge, over 1900 pounds, but very gentle. Over the years they built up a significant herd to the point where Lionel had to start expanding the barns again to accommodate the additional cattle. He built and cemented in all the expanded pens and stalls until all the space beneath the two original barns, including the extension, had been made into pens. In the spring, Lionel and Fred herded the cattle on the road as far as the Tenth Line Road, where Lionel had rented pasturage for several summers. For a while they also used part of a 200-acre lot at the backside of his father Gussie's farm for pasturing, before Gussie and Sarah sold their farm to Clement Tetreault and family in 1951. It was at this time that Robert Tetreault, who was 16 years old, came to work for Lionel during key harvesting times from spring to fall. Robert worked for five years before he moved on, married and started his own life.

Lionel's son Fred trained his dog Lassie, a first-class sheepdog, to herd the cattle. Lionel would drive ahead of the cattle to block a side road, and Lassie would run up both sides of the herd making sure they didn't wander or go into a driveway. Fred brought up the rear, a long walk for a 9- to 12-year-old boy.

When Lionel needed new logging sleds he went out into the woods and found a couple of trees with exactly the right curvatures in the root system. He selected four of these root curvatures, and rough-cut them to size. Charlie Montgomery took these runners and, using the steel from his old sleds, built Lionel a full set of logging sleds. The following winter Lionel and his son Fred harvested a 200-acre woodlot owned by Gussie and Sarah. This lot was at the back of the first farm that Joe and Jessie (Hurd) Riddle had owned in Newport, just north of Maple Leaf Cemetery on Lot 8 of Range 9. Lionel and Fred worked for several winters cutting the large grove of huge, virgin 70-80-foot-tall beech trees and hauling out the logs. Lionel essentially worked alone in this woodlot during the week (while Fred was in school), cutting then pulling the logs with the horses into piles so they could be loaded onto the sleds. On the weekends Lionel and Fred would haul the logs out to the roadside for shipping to the mills.

Farming in this era was no different than in earlier years. Farmers cut hardwood trees, saving some wood for burning; they made maple syrup; they planted and harvested turnips, potatoes, soybeans, red clover, corn, and other sileage crops, as well as oats and barley; and raised their livestock. The old horse-drawn equipment – including mowers, tedders, rakes and wagons – were modified to be pulled by a tractor. As with most farmers, Lionel and Fred harvested something all year long, took care of their livestock – all activities that kept a farmer tied to the homestead. Vacations were not ever a part of the equation, so work became part of a farmer's natural being. Even in retirement most farmers never really retired as they are always there for their children and neighbours if needed.

Author's note: Having had this experience, in my view, I believe farming becomes part of one's genetic makeup built on trust in others and in themselves. Along with their logic in how things are done, I believe this code of ethics always stays with them as a natural part of their instinct and culture.

Lionel never forgot his army buddies and spent a lot of time on their behalf making sure they received the care and treatment they deserved. He was liked by his men and that was all he needed to survive his own mental issues. He was the driving force behind the publication of the book *The Royal Rifles of Canada in Hong Kong, 1941-1945*, written by Grant Garneau as his master's thesis. He served active terms as regional president then national president of the Hong Kong Veterans Association of Canada. The Hong Kong Veterans Commemorative Association (HKVCA; www.hkvca.ca) continues to honour and support those veterans who are still alive and their families.

L-R: Jim Lowry, Mamie Matthew, Irene Matthew and Blanche Hunt having a conversation, likely about the garden

Irene continued looking after Cora Austin, Eliza Hurd, and many others in the community when they needed medical assistance over many years. She loved gardening and always referred to others who had large flower gardens as having "beautiful grounds." Irene was very proud of her vegetable garden, and she worked hard at it, harvesting the very best of carrots, potatoes, corn, peas, beans, and squash. She also planted strawberries and raspberries. Any spare time was devoted to weeding the garden. If someone came to visit you can be sure they would be taken to the garden as part of the visit. Irene always made donuts on Fridays, which Lionel savoured with a touch of maple syrup every night before bed – something he dreamed about so often during his long nights in captivity.

Lionel and Irene's retirement marked the end of over 200 years of this ancestral homestead being lived in by the Heard/Hurd families. A plaque was placed in this original Colonel Edmund[5] Heard homestead that he had built in 1793-94. It was now listed and recognized as an historical home in Newport.

Author's note: Irene was a wonderful stepmother who helped me through my early years of trauma after being separated from my brother and the only parents I had known. Irene's mother, Mamie Matthew, and her siblings Ruthie, Kathleen and Lincoln, Kathleen's husband Lawrence Mackay and Lincoln's wife Sybil were instrumental in making me feel that I belonged to their family as well.

***

Author's note: The Westgate family story has been graciously provided by Ilah (Westgate) Batley. Excerpts from this story provide another excellent snapshot of lives lived in Newport through the different eras.

Maple Westgate, who lived in the Island Brook region of Newport, bought his first tractor in 1948, a two-cylinder John Deere. As with most farmers during this time frame, money just after the war was still tight and many could not afford to buy the tractor equipment that was flooding the market. However, farmers were resourceful enough to begin the transition from horse-drawn equipment to tractor-driven. They did this by cutting off the long drawing poles, making them shorter and attaching a clevis or steel bracket with a pin that could be connected to the tractor drawbar. Maple began by converting the mowing machine first. It was one of his daughters, Ilah, whose job was to ride on the mower to manually lift the cutter bar, up and down at the end of each row. Rabbits were abundant in these fields of clover, their burrows found throughout in this great smorgasbord of food. This was an exciting time for Ilah. When she saw a rabbit, she would signal Maple, who would stop the tractor. Ilah would then jump off with great delight to catch the rabbit. The rabbits were not able to hop very well in the thick clover, as the clover vines would catch in their legs. Once caught, she would take them over to the woods, petting them tenderly and probably reluctantly setting them free.

When pulled by a horse team, the mower had a seat for the operator to sit on while driving the horses, and the mechanism for lifting the cutter bar was right there beside him, within easy grasp. This was not the case when seated on the tractor. As in many of these machine transitions from horse- to tractor-drawn, there were drawbacks like these that had to also be compensated for. The younger children delighted to be able to ride these pieces of equipment now all over the fields, operating the levers on the equipment, perhaps imaging themselves as grown-up people operating hugely complex pieces of heavy equipment. Imagination for the children was a very real thing and made for a lot of fun in their lives.

***

A medical doctor was especially important to the well-being of many people living any of in these rural communities in Newport. Dr. Curtis Lowry, (BA, MA, MD, Doctor of Civil Law; 1918-2019) was "one of a kind," serving several communities for 55 years. "Dr. Lowry was an icon. He was my family doctor from the time I was born until I left home at the age of 18 and he continued long after that." *(Doug Bowker,* The [Sherbrooke] Record, *2019)*

"One could talk to almost anyone in Sawyerville or the surrounding communities and each would have their own story of how the doctor changed their life. He made house calls all around the area for decades and decades, long after no other doctor was doing it." *(Doug Bowker, Executive Director of Grace Village Retirement Home and former patient)*

> *Author's note: I remember Dr. Lowry came to my father's home when he was in his late eighties to check on my father's breathing difficulty. He pulled out his stethoscope, listened and stated that my father's lungs were clear. Dr. Lowry himself was as deaf as a doornail, as was my father, so the conversation between the two was rather hilarious, and we wondered just how much Dr. Lowry could hear as to how his lungs were functioning. His passion to help others was evident throughout the communities and never changed throughout his life; he could be counted on to be at one's side.*
>
> *I remember in the early 1950s, Dr. Lowry had his own snowmobile, built very similar to our school buses but a bit smaller in both length and width, which he used in the winter months for any emergency call in the countryside, especially for births in the farmlands. When I was a boy, Dr. Lowry and Irene saved my life when he rushed to our home with an EpiPen after I was stung by a bee.*

Dr. S. J. Bennett, another doctor who had a practice in Cookshire, would more often than not be called upon to a household in need, serving in the communities of Learned Plain, Island Brook, Knicky Knocky and New Mexico. One stormy winter night, the doctor was called upon to deliver a baby in the Lawrence Colony region. The road was passable only as far as Island Brook. Always ready to help, Maple Westgate was there to take the doctor by horse and sleigh the five or seven miles to the waiting family. Ilah said, "He spent many nights waiting in the stable with his horses to take the good doctor back home." *(Ilah (Westgate) Batley)*

***

Another French/Hurd family connection:

Robert "Rob" and Mary (Lebourveau) French's son, Lloyd Robert French, was born on the farm in Island Brook. He married Bertha Evelyn Hurd in 1939; she was born on the farm in Maple Leaf, Newport, the daughter of Alonzo G. and Evelyn Hurd. They raised three children: Eric G. R., Barbara Ann, and Susan J. They lived in Sawyerville while Lloyd operated logging operations both in Emberton Woods Township and the Republic of Indian Stream area, near Pittsburg, N.H., importing hardwood logs through Newport to the mills in Sawyerville. Evelyn taught school for many years in the new consolidated school in Sawyerville. Most of the children growing up in her era would remember her well as a great teacher.[4]

***

The next generation of the Bowker families *(Florence (Bowker) McVetty family history)*:

Gordon Lewis Bowker (Austin's son) was born in 1925 and married Audrey Mabel Aldous in 1954. They raised five children, three sons and two daughters: Douglas Gordon (born 1955), Joanne Mildred (RN) (born 19560, Steven

James (born 1957), Nancy Jane (RN) (born 1962) and Jeffrey Grant (born 1964). They continued living on the original lots assigned to their ancestors, Jonathon and Solomon Bowker, in 1799.

It was at this time that diapers were available in Newport. Clothes washers had become more automated, equipped with electric wringers (no more cranking these by hand) and an automatic pump to drain out the dirty water. As soon as Gordon and Audrey's first son, Douglas Gordon, arrived, Audrey was looking at the Eaton's catalogue, pricing a new washer. When electricity was installed in late 1952 and early 1953, Audrey's first purchase was a new washing machine. Audrey still hung the wash out on a clothesline, but laundry was a far easier chore than it had been for her parents' generation. Diapers would be a boon for these younger homemakers; however, with a new washer, the expense of buying diapers would not warrant using these just yet in the country setting of Newport. They would continue, as their ancestors did, to use the old flannel-style sheets they cut up and sewed into diapers simply because they could re-purpose these at no extra cost.

***

Arthur McVetty (James A. McVetty's son) and his wife Ruby (Hearn) bought the farm in the Maple Leaf region of Newport from John William Planche, the eldest son of Willy and Jennette (Heard) Planche. Arthur and Ruby raised four children there: Jimmy, Malcolm "Mac," Dorothy, and Mabel. They farmed a herd of Shorthorn cattle and pigs, while Ruby raised a large flock of turkeys. The McVetty family had previously lived in High Forest, a farming community in Eaton Township, where their children were all born. Arthur's parents originally resided in the Learned Plain region of Newport before moving to High Forest. The children had all attended school in a small schoolhouse in High Forest. After moving to the farm in Newport they attended school in Sawyerville.

> *Author's note: This is the same farm that William[5] and Thirza Heard had settled in 1799. The William and Jenette (Hurd) Planche family followed after William[5] died, when his wife Thirza went to live with her son, Jeremiah "Jerry" in Barnston. William Planche was a son of JP and Elizabeth; he had married Jenette Heard, the granddaughter of Captain Edmund[6] Heard.*

Arthur McVetty had purchased a large horse-drawn seeder which allowed for seeding and fertilizing at the same time in a swath over eight feet wide. This new machine could seed different grains of seed such as corn, buckwheat, barley, oats, timothy and clover. The seeder could be adjusted to sow corn in wider rows by simply shutting off every second leader, a much more efficient way of seeding than the single-row seeders that had been used up to this time. The unit had a hopper for the grains and a separate hopper for fertilizer so both could be laid down at the same time. Arthur shared his new equipment with other farmers in the community as our forefathers had done before him. Later in the 1950s, Arthur also purchased a threshing machine which he operated with his Farmall tractor, taking the equipment from farm to farm around the communities at harvesting time. The farmers would move on in turn to the next farm to help with the threshing as their own farm was completed. This was community sharing at its best as no one farmer had to pay for help. The only cost for each farmer was the time used with the thresher which was how Arthur would pay himself back for the equipment cost. This made good business sense as he had the use of the tractor all year-round which was essentially paid for by the threshing operation.

> *Author's note: The Farmall line of tractors continued to be a leading brand of all-purpose tractors. Its bright red colour was a distinctive badge in the 1950s.*

In the mid-1950s, Malcolm "Mac" McVetty decided to hold a "turkey shoot" at the farm. This was another way of selling turkeys by simply inviting people to come and try their luck at target shooting at a cost of so much a shot. A bullseye meant the shooter won a turkey. One had to be a good shot (of course, everyone thought they were the best shooter) and so much more money was collected in relation to the number of turkeys that were actually won. Mac set the targets up along their driveway which was quite long and clear on both sides. The targets were set up in a row at the bottom of a rolling hillside facing Lionel Hurd's farm on the other side. People could park their cars in the field beside the driveway opposite the shooting gallery. When the shooting began on this opening day, Irene Hurd was sitting on the porch and Freddy Hurd happened to be walking up to the barn. A bullet hit the porch roof, surprising us as we knew about the turkey shoot, but did not know that the targets were facing our farm. Freddy immediately headed into the direct line of fire, thinking of course that the first shot must have been a stray bullet. The shooting had just stopped for the next round when Freddy's head peeked over the hill. It was at that time that

Freddy realized that the targets were right in front of him and so he doubled back home, approaching the farm from the main road running down their lane to tell Mac that the bullets were hitting Lionel and Irene's roof. The shooting stopped immediately and Mac had to postpone the shoot to another week in order to reposition his targets. Lionel naturally was not impressed and took a rather dim view of Mac's enterprise.

James "Jimmy" Arthur McVetty married Florence Verna Bowker, daughter of Austin Stevens and Ruth Ethel Bowker (the Bowker family of Newport). Since Jimmy was working in East Angus, they left Newport to live in Sawyerville. Malcolm McVetty married Mabel Fraser in 1960, daughter of Ken and Susie Fraser, proprietors of the famous Dew Drop Inn in Cookshire. Mabel, Arthur and Ruby's youngest daughter, married William "Billy" Hall, whose family lived on the Auckland town line south of Parker Hill.

The Hall farm was on the 11th Range above Parker Hill in what was actually Auckland Township. Their ancestors were Loyalists and settled there circa 1800. Besides John, William, and Mary Barnet, three Hall children had received land grants in Auckland/Clifton Township: Isaac Livingston Hall, Mary Catherine Christy Hall and Ann Blake Hall. These were Billy Hall's direct ancestors. *(The Loyalists of Quebec 1774-1825: A Forgotten History, p. 28)*

***

Arthur and Nora Loveland's eldest son, Howard, left the farm searching for a different life in another township where he married and settled. Their daughter Dorothy trained as a nurse, moved to Montreal where she married and raised her family. Their youngest son, Herbert, attended school in Sawyerville and stayed in Newport working with his father until Herbert and Dorothy "Dot" McVetty decided it was time to marry and start their own lives. Dot lived just down the road on the next farm. They raised two boys, Raymond and Barry, on the original homestead of William[1] and Eliza (Beaman) Loveland. They raised Shorthorn cattle on this farm for many years before buying and moving to the McVetty farm when Dorothy's parents retired. To the south on today's Route 210, was Gussie and Sarah Hurd, as well as Herbert's friends, Clinton and Lyle Rand, who were close by at the corner of Morrison Road.

Author's note: The original William[2] Loveland farm was located next door to Herbert's parents, Arthur and Nora, which was the original farm of Charles and Charlotte Loveland. William[2] and Eliza's eldest son, Victor[1], had died at 23 in a farm accident, and William[3] died at age 35. After William[2] Loveland died in 1899, Eliza had stayed on the farm with her son William[3]. When he died in 1902, the property was sold and owned for short periods of time by several families, including the Albert Riddell family. The property was later owned by Herman and Mildred (Loveland) Lowry, Eliza's granddaughter, before Herbert and Dot bought it.

Herbert and Clinton Rand continued to be great friends. As their children were growing up, they helped each other out at harvest time when an extra pair of hands was needed. Herbert and Dot went to dances with Clinton and Doreen in Island Brook, at Charlie Montgomery's Hall in Randboro, and at the IOOF Hall in Sawyerville.

***

Author's note: After the untimely death of Marshall Newell Wesley Rand in 1939, the family moved to other parts of the township. The old Heard/Hurd family homestead that Marshall had purchased and raised his three children on had been sold. His father, uncles and other members of the Rand families, who had contributed so much towards the growth of Newport, were now past history. That history was to be revived with the arrival of a Rand descendant in Newport. The following excerpts were graciously provided by Ruby (Rand) Pehlemann, Clinton and Doreen's daughter.

The original Willard Stedman and Sarah (McCurdy) homestead in Maple Leaf, where Clinton and Doreen Rand raised their family

In 1947, Clinton and Doreen Rand moved from their farm in Hardwood Flat in Bury Township back to Newport where they bought Lot 11 of Range 11, designated in 1799 as part of the original land grants in Maple Leaf. They raised five children on this homestead, three sons and two daughters. This was a land lot that had been set as common ground for exchange if local roads, carved through other lots, were taking too much of a landowner's property.

Since the lot was free from any encumbrance and no parts of it had been taken in exchange, the lot had become available for sale.

Augustus[8] Hurd's father-in-law, John[1] Paul Planche, had originally purchased a divided part of Lot 11 on the south end from Augustus Hurd, who had been lumbering the lot with Marshall Rand as part of their lumbering operations. He purchased the lot mainly for the river frontage as he was contemplating building a mill there. He had also purchased a partial lot on the other side of South River in Auckland Township from Augustus for this same purpose circa 1860, when he and his son John Paul[2] had started a mill site there. "The Auckland site was better known in later years when the mill reopened circa 1931 as Lester Wooten's Mills."[46]

This separated parcel of land was restored back to the full lot when it was purchased from JP Planche Sr. in 1885 by Willard Stedman and Sarah (McCurdy) Rand. They had purchased the north end of the lot from Augustus Hurd and continued clearing the land for farming. Their only son, Scott left the farm after he married Beatrice Boyd, (Wallace Boyd's sister), moved first to the Maritimes and then to Western Canada. When Willard died in 1915, Sarah was distraught by this loss but carried on farming for a couple of years after his death. Sarah was so lonesome and missed Willard so much that she decided to move out west where Scott and his family lived. Sarah sold the farm to Renford Morrow, just after he had returned from the Great War in 1919. After the tragic death of his neighbour Marshall Rand, the Osgoods had foreclosed on the mortgage and Edith Rand's farm went up for auction in 1941. Renford and Elizabeth Morrow had bought a portion of the original Haskell Heard Lot 10 after Renford had returned from the war. Edith's farm was taken over by Mr. Osgood and his daughter Gertrude "Gerty."[4, 31] *(Carol Rand)*

> *Author's note: Renford Morrow was one of the six sons of William and Hattie (Cable) Morrow who had been raised in Newport's Island Brook region. Hattie had been raised on a farm just adjacent to the covered bridge crossing South River in Auckland Township.*

Until now, this community of farms from lots 6 to 13 had all belonged to the Heard/Hurd/Planche/Willard/Rand families since the first settlers had arrived and the lots had been assigned in 1799. The next farm towards the east on Lot 12 had been the farm owned by Willard Rand's brother Newell Clement and Laura McCurdy. Newell's father Marshall S. and Mary Maria (Hurd) had owned the next farm to the east on Lot 13, just before the Auckland covered bridge. Charlie Cable and his wife Abigail (Hurd) and their family had lived on the other side of the covered bridge in Auckland Township as did the Leggetts, Elijah and Mary Elizabeth (Hurd), who were all interconnected families that have been a part of the heritage throughout this story.[31]

Clinton Rand was born and grew up on the old Edmund[8] Haskell Hurd and Eliza (McCurdy) homestead, which had been purchased circa 1920 by his parents, Marshall W. and Edith (Morrison) Rand. Having always been friends growing up in Newport, they had helped each other with the farm work in their younger days. And now, Clinton was home again in Maple Leaf where he had grown up, happy to be near his friend Herbert and Dorothy "Dot" (McVetty) Loveland. They could help each other out once again while their own children were still young. Their second son, Richard "Ricky," joined the family in 1948.[4, 31]

Clinton Rand with his pride and joy, work horses Bob and Dick (courtesy of Ruby (Rand) Pehlemann)

Clinton started out with two "big black Percheron" workhorses, Bob and Dick. "One day Dad had harnessed and hitched these guys up to the wagon and looked around to make sure the children were out of harm's way. I was quite enjoying myself, standing on the pole between the horses and it took Dad a bit of searching before he noticed where I was. The horses were standing ever so quiet, to not frighten me, as horses sometimes will do. Clearly, I got a lecture on safety that day!" *(Ruby (Rand) Pehlemann)*

Haying was hard work in those days so when Clinton bought a "hayloader" in the early 1950s it was a welcome piece of equipment. He was so proud of that machine because it was

Rand family photo, L-R: Jimmy the family dog, Bobby, father Clinton, Ruby, Ricky (standing at the back), Dale, mother Doreen, Trudy (in Doreen's arms) (courtesy of Ruby (Rand) Pehlemann)

his first automated piece of equipment for their farm. His hard work in building up the farm was starting to show enough profit so he could now afford it. He no longer had to pitch the hay up onto the wagon, so that back-breaking job was now a thing of the past.

In August 1951 Dale was born. A year later, in August 1952, their second daughter, Trudy, completed their family.

Clinton and Doreen Rand chose to build on a dairy farm business, which meant an early morning start every day to make sure the "milk stand" by the road was filled each morning in time for the milk truck. The milk was being delivered to the Carnation Plant in Sherbrooke. "As children, we would run to the stand because we always enjoyed watching Lucas Gilbert piling up the cans each morning and listening to his stories. One day Rick was allowed to go with him on the truck to Sherbrooke, a really big deal for a young farm kid." *(Ruby (Rand) Pehlemann)*

Doreen and Clinton Rand (courtesy of Ruby (Rand) Pehlemann)

Clinton and Doreen bought their first tractor, an International Farmall A, later in the 1950s; a welcome addition having another set of now (mechanical) horses to work the farm. Bobby was of an age where he would learn to drive the tractor, relieving Clinton of much of the workload. Clinton was good at building and patching up the farm equipment along with the daily chores of milking and looking after the buildings and all the fences. "House chores, not so much, although he could do a tasty peanut butter sandwich" and so Doreen was well entrenched with the running of the household. With five children, doing laundry, making beds, cooking meals, and looking after the children's needs, it took all her efforts in her younger years, but in later years Doreen was out tending her chicken coop and pretty much always helping with the farm chores as well. *(Ruby (Rand) Pehlemann)*

"The family was fortunate to have a pair of "bobsleds" and as we lived on the top of a hill, those sleds were well used all winter long. There were no such thing as salted roads during this era, so the hills on the roads made excellent sledding." Bobsleds were essentially two sled runners joined with a long wide board; the back runners hooked to the front runners with a crisscross of ropes which allowed the back runners to turn in conjunction with the front runners. Once a driver was decided upon, the children all sat in a row behind the driver, the board holding as many as five or six children. "These rides were fast and probably would be considered dangerous by today's standards, with no helmets, no supervision, but such fun for everyone. In this era, older children always looked after the safety of their younger siblings, but never hampered their penchant for having fun. Sliding down was a hoot, but pulling the sleds back up . . . well, that was another story." *(Ruby (Rand) Pehlemann)*

Once at the bottom, sometimes, if the children were lucky, a car might come by and they would hook the rope on the "bumperettes" and get another ride back up the hill on their sleds. Of course, the person on the front of the sled got peppered with snow from the car tires, so when they unhooked at the top of the hill, their face and the front of their jackets were covered in snow. Dangerous, probably; but nevertheless, a fun event of the past that children would never experience in today's world. Most cars in the 1950s had these chrome bumperettes attached to the bumpers, really for no reason other than cosmetics.

"On Sunday afternoons, all the kids, both French and English, would gather and enjoy this afternoon activity, just like a big party. Doreen provided hot chocolate for all at the end of the day. Their dog, Jimmy, would be running as fast as he could following them down the hill and then back up again; after all, he was a part of the family." *(Ruby (Rand) Pehlemann)*

Author's note: Regardless of which language was being spoken at home, either French or English, it was never an issue. The children and families blended together as one and often used either the French or English word or expression that came to mind first when speaking with friends such as the Theroux, Vaillancourt, Charpentier or Tetreault families. This is how we learned each other's languages.

"Our grandfather, Marshall, had hired Napoleon Albert, the blacksmith in Randboro, to build bobsleds for Lyle and Clinton when they were young boys. Now our family was using these same sleds at sliding parties on Clinton's Hill."[46] *(Carol Rand)*

Clinton purchased his first binder circa the late 1950s. This piece of equipment allowed him and his eldest son, Bobby, to plant almost double the crop plus they were able to harvest his barley and oats far quicker than they had in the past. Having more grain to feed the cattle meant the family could increase their herd of milking cows and sell more milk. Clinton could also pay back the equipment by hiring himself out with the binder as his ancestors did before him with their new equipment.

Clinton Rand operating the binder, circa 1950 (courtesy of Ruby (Rand) Pehlemann)

Hilda Rand (courtesy of Carol Rand)

Hilda Margaret Rand (1925-2010), daughter of Marshall and Edith, married Ernest "Ernie" Berwick (1911-1979) in 1943 in Sawyerville and raised five children: Barry Marshall (born 1946), Norman (born 1949), Steven (born 1953) and twin girls Brenda and Bonnie (born 1950).

Ernie worked for the Town of Sawyerville for many years. Even though these children were brought up in Sawyerville, they would as others, inherit a common treasure, a genuine link to their past generations who settled this land. Hilda and Phyllis Morrison were constant companions as they were growing up living on adjacent farms and they remained great friends throughout their later lives.

Author's note: Phyllis (Morrison) married Gordon Dempsey and they lived in Sawyerville next to the United Church manse, where they raised their daughter Donna, who married one of the Lister boys from Island Brook. One of their sons, Michael Lister, is the current owner of the farm on Tannahill Road, where the old Maple Leaf schoolhouse is now located.

***

Denis Palmer was born in Montreal in 1948, studied architecture at McGill University and earned his bachelor's degree in 1974. Since 1979, he has lived in Randboro near the village of Sawyerville where he met his wife, Judy. They have a daughter, Kaila. During this time, he has created drawings and watercolour paintings of the people and places along with local events in Newport and surrounding communities. For 25 years, he has also taught drawing and the difficult art of watercolour painting to both the older and younger generations in the surrounding districts. His paintings have been used as backgrounds for several books written of the area, such as *Homage* and *Even the Owl Is Not Heard*, the latter referenced in this book.

***

Author's note: This chapter has brought forth many new names associated with Newport, some interchanged in marriage with our original settlers, along with others who have moved to Newport to raise their families, and still others who have been closely associated with many of our ancestors.

Family, like branches on a tree, all grow in different directions, yet our roots remain as one.

We often hear the question "What's in a name?" It may sound senseless, but we know that names have had their part in our country's history. Some of the names such as Batley, Bowker, Burns, French (Thomas), Lister, Nugent, Parker, Spaulding, Stanley, and Westgate still remain with us. We often ask, what is family history? Family history is often difficult to write about, to search for, and so this story about family lives lived will have taken a reader back over 320 years, painting a picture of their lives to give us just a glimpse of our families' past. A series of articles compiled in book form, as they appeared from 1951 and on, published in the Sherbrook Daily Record, has been a valuable source of material for writing this book.[24] *(Bertha W. Price,* Glimpses into the Past*)*

The names Bailey, Baker, Beaton, Boutin, Boyd, Cable, Cairns, Cook, Darker, Dawson, Desruisseaux, Dube, Evans Ewing, Fisk, Fraser, French, Goodenough, Grapes, Hall, Harvey, Heard, Hunt, Hurd, Jones, Kerr, King, Kingsley, LaFleur, Latimer, Lebourveau, McCallum, McCloud, McGee, McVetty, Montgomery, Morrison, Morrow, Munn, Nugent, Painter, Parker, Parsons, Rand, Richardson, Rutherford, Sherman, Speck, Statton, Stevenson, Stoddard, Sunbury, Swail, Tannahill, Todd, Vibert, Watson, Williams, and Wood, and many more found in the communities of Knicky Knocky, Flanders, Island Brook, New Mexico, St. Lawrence Colony, Maple Leaf and Randboro, still remain with us as descendants and have had their part in the history of building a township.

***

There is an "Eastern Townships Roots" Facebook page where people were asked to describe the Eastern Townships. We felt it important to reference this material because it "says it all."

> . . . A place of peace and tranquility! Tight families, supportive communities filled with good people. A place anyone would love to live. *(June Gerrie)*

> . . . A place I still call home and visit as often as I can. The prettiest part of our Province of Quebec. *(Joyce Marineau)*

> . . . When you say "home" it gives a visual impression that there was a place that they settled into easily. Reading extensively about who came to the area and cleared the forest in order to plant crops that could be harvested and roads that had to be built to get around, it seems it only became "home" after much toil and sacrifice. The railroads weaving through the areas was a critical piece of the puzzle to transport goods to the areas it was required. Prior to the RR's, it was the rivers and rudimentary roads that took days to go as far as we can drive in half an hour today. In my opinion, we should never forget our ancestors who broke the lands we glide past in comfort today and appreciate their strife to make something useful to the human race. *(Samantha Bliss from Charles Neville Ross)*

Chapter 17   The Idyllic Years (1950–1960)

The 1950s era brought prosperity; people were able to afford the new kitchen gadgets like blenders and toasters. We were introduced to store-bought items such as Shredded Wheat, Kellogg's Corn Flakes, and Wonder Bread. A pound of butter cost 40 cents, sugar was 45 cents for a 5-pound bag, and a loaf of bread could be purchased for 17 cents. Cosmetic companies flourished and salespersons went door-to-door representing Avon and Mary Kay.[35]

Workers' lives were revolutionized with new automatic equipment coming into the factories. Service industries began to flourish as people had more cash and time on their hands. "Fast food" made its debut; rock 'n' roll music began to hit the charts; and drive-in restaurants were introduced, where young girls delivered hamburgers and French fries, placing the food tray on your car door window. Cars were marketed in two-tone paint colours; the new models were kept under wraps until November of each year when revealed with great fanfare at the dealerships.

Life in Newport Township continued much as it always had; farmers and their communities supported each other and their churches. Pies, strawberries and chicken were the staples for their fund-raising suppers. The children continued to grow up learning how to build things, care for livestock, build fires, produce maple syrup, cut wood, sharpen blades and axes, operate ever-larger pieces of farm equipment, repair things, and in general continue to be resourceful and make do with what they had. Children learned respect for those in authority, their families and to those of their communities, an unrestrained commitment and compassion for taking care of the people they loved. The environment in the rural communities allowed these children the opportunity to be imaginative and creative. They learned to share and possessed a team spirit both in sports and in work, simply because that was the way it had always been.

The Burns family of Newport:

Thomas Burns 1951

Thomas Burns

Thomas Burns Jr. served as mayor of Newport for seven years beginning in 1951. He also served for 24 years as school commissioner and chairman of the local school board.

Thomas married Glenna Watson and they raised four children – Robert, Douglas, Margaret and Malcolm – on an original family farm settled by the Byrnes/Burns family in Island Brook, Newport Township. Douglas moved from Newport after graduation for a career in the banking sector.

Malcolm Burns and his wife Diane (Letourneau) continued operating the original family farm on today's Route 212 in the Island Brook region of Newport Township. They raised two daughters and a son, Johnathon. They had a very special heirloom black kettle at his sugar camp where he carried on the tradition his father, Thomas Burns, had started: doing a sugaring-off for anyone who came to his camp to visit in springtime. The only visible remaining trace of this practice of boiling in these old kettles are pieces of iron railway tracks which were used as the base to support the large black kettle which was placed over the fire. Malcolm and Jonathon are still running the farm in Island Brook.[32]

One of Malcolm and Jonathon's cousins, Neil Burns, with his wife Marlene (Cairns) and sons Matthew and Cameron, continue to farm today on an original homestead of Byrnes/Burns families in Island Brook, the family following the six generations that had lived in Newport. At the time of writing, Neil and Marlene continue to take care of the Island Brook Cemetery which is still functioning. The original Methodist/United Church that had been in located in front of the cemetery was closed and torn down in recent years.

In the early 1900s, there were more than 30 farms operating in the Island Brook Road area, but by 1993 there were only three dairy herds – belonging to Malcom Burns, Neil Burns and Earl Stanley – and two beef herds, belonging to Bruce and Ilah (Westgate) Batley and Earle Dawson. There had been 10 sugar bushes in operation along this same stretch of today's Route 212, but by 1993 there were only two, operated by Malcolm Burns and Earl Stanley. By the late 1950s, a new method of collecting sap was appearing in some local areas. This system of plastic piping began to replace sap buckets in the sugar bushes, decreasing the labour-intensive work of earlier generations.[32]

The author (left) consulting with Robert Burns (photo by Sandra Hurd)

Thomas Burns Jr.'s eldest son, Robert, married Marie Ori and opted for a career in local real estate – a 45-year-long career, from 1963 to 2008. They raised two children, a son Andrew and a daughter Cathy; both moved away after graduating. He is still living in Island Brook and enjoying life in his nineties at the time of writing. Robert has become the historian of his day, able to recount many of the stories emanating for the many early settlers in the region and has been a valued mentor and advisor during the research for this book.

***

Lewis Farnsworth may have held the office of secretary treasurer of Newport for the longest term on record. He was also secretary of the Island Brook School Board until it closed in 1969. He was considered a genius in mathematics and had a tremendous memory. Until the late 1970s, the municipality carried its own fire insurance called The Mutual Fire Insurance of the Township of Newport. On the day your policy might expire, if Lewis could not reach you by telephone, he would come to your home and let you know, in his gentlemanly manner, that your fire insurance was due, checking the safety of your wood stove and pipes while he was there.

***

In 1952, the first Canadian television programs were broadcast, and everyone flocked to watch the Ed Sullivan Show on television out of New York. Surging demand for TV's spurred mass production. Electricity was becoming increasingly available in rural areas, though Newport would still wait a few more years until electricity was universally available by the end of the decade. In 1955 polio vaccine was developed, pre-made "diapers" had arrived, washers become more automated, and the baby boom was upon us. There was a spending boom as never before, with idealistic lifestyles. "Push buttons" were developed for use in every part of our lives.

***

In 1956 the Quebec Farmers' Association was started. Modernization proceeded quickly, from automated equipment for milking cows in the barns, to kitchens containing electric refrigerators, stoves and washing machines – all changing much of the everyday chores and drudgery.[48]

The Hurd family of Newport:

In 1956 Lionel Hurd bought a new tractor, a large International with torque converter, from his long-time Hong Kong veteran buddy Colin Standish. He also bought a McKee harvester with a special wagon that attached to the harvester to do the haying. The harvester picked up the raked hay, processing and blowing it into a fully enclosed wagon. To unload the hay, the back of the wagon moved forward on a track as the hay was forked back into the harvester from the back end but internally switched to connect to a large piping system, which blew the hay into the barn. While most farmers were now buying balers, in Lionel's view, the hay was much softer on the cattle's mouths with this system.

The author harvesting silage with the McKee harvester, 1958

The day the equipment came to the farm, he assigned his son Fred the task of the complete operation and maintenance of this new equipment. That included responsibility for the upkeep of the tractor, harvester and wagon. Lionel was comfortable with his smaller 1945 Ford tractor and operating the equipment that came with it, simply because he was used to it. Lionel always felt more comfortable with his beloved horses than any piece of equipment.

Author's note: He drove his car much like his father (Gussie) before him, steering it as if he were pulling the reins on a horse . . . kind of jerky, and he really did not much care what the car looked like, as long as it ran.

After his son Fred left the farm in 1961, Lionel and Irene ran it for a couple of years, then decided to begin the retirement process and moved to Sawyerville. Lionel continued to run the farm from Sawyerville for another couple of years, continuing to cut his firewood and hauling it from the farm. He sold the farmland first; and later severed the house and five acres to sell separately, keeping the maple sugar bush.

Author's note: I believe my dad found it hard to sell the homestead that his ancestors had worked so hard to acquire. The farm represented his ancestral legacy, the last to be owned by a Heard/Hurd or ancestor in Newport Township, and it would have been hard for him to give that up. I believe he kept the sugar bush simply to be able to say that he still owned a piece of land that was originally settled by his ancestors.

Lionel Hurd and Kay Ward, circa 1993

Lionel retired in Sawyerville with Irene after they sold the original Heard/Hurd farm in Newport in 1965. Irene died in 1980. During the following 10 years he worked on the family history, sorting and assembling the hundreds of documents and letters he had inherited from his ancestors. He also worked for his friend Colin Standish in spraying operations in Quebec and Ontario.

In 1992, Edmund[10] Lionel Hurd married his third wife, Kathleen "Kay" Anna (Ward) Harding. Kay, born in 1922, was the daughter of William Wendell and Irene Coad (Gillbard) Ward.

In 1993, Lionel met with and invited Edward Hanson, a genealogist and lecturer in the Department of History at Northeastern University in Boston and a Heard/Hurd descendant, to attend a Hurd reunion that our family was organizing at Bishop's University in Lennoxville. Over 300 descendants attended this event. Ed had compiled the Heard/Hurd family history and this event allowed him to complete the genealogy on the Canadian side of the border. Lionel was proud of his ancestry and encouraged his family members to continue the family connections and to always treasure our history. He had always recognized that to have a history was a privilege; there are millions in this world who have no idea where they came from.

Lionel lived a full life until his death in February 2001, one day before his 94th birthday. I am immensely proud and thankful to have been able to know him along with many of his friends and comrades who survived the POW camps. His third wife, Kay, at the time of writing (April 2021) is living at the Wales Home in Richmond, Que., and is 99 years old.

For some reason, Lionel had survived not only the Battle of Hong Kong but also the brutality of the POW camps where he had been kept prisoner for nearly four years. I share his thoughts so others will have a better understanding of what can happen to a society, to a country and to the men, women and children who enjoy freedom today.

My father often commented that he hated how he had changed – hated what he had been forced to witness. Some of his comrades died before they could get home. "It was just another death" . . . he had seen so many. I remember his comment to me many times that he "had nothing against the Japanese people, just their military." He talked to me about his experience only in his later years, and now as I look back I have come to realize that perhaps he did not say much for the same reason most men who have seen combat just kept silent. "The totality of it was simply too painful for words." *(Capt. E. L. Hurd)*

Capt. E. L. Hurd

Author's note: As a young boy, I could not relate to how he must have been feeling. When I finally met my father, I was 5 years old, and I vaguely remember someone saying to me, "There is your father" as he disembarked from a train with others returning from the war. I was not to have known that day that I would be in the same school with others who never got to meet their fathers that day. I also now know that the reason he went out in the middle of the night, many times, was to help fellow Hong Kong veterans cope with illness and the mental instability that they suffered post-war. To have been able to have the honour of being able to call him "Dad" was indeed a privilege.

***

The Loveland/McVetty family of Newport:

Herbert and Dorothy "Dot" (McVetty) had bought the farm from her parents, Arthur and Ruby McVetty, and moved there from farming on the original William Loveland farm just up the road. Their two sons, Raymond and Barry, were just starting their teenage years and the family continued operating a mixed farm of Shorthorn cattle. The family prospered by expanding their livestock on the additional acreage of their new farm. After graduation and then marriage, both Raymond and Barry left the farm. After selling the farm, Herbert and Dot retired in Eaton Township. Marie-Antoine Roy, who owns the Loveland farm today, amalgamated with the original Col. Edmund[5] Heard/Luke/Alonzo/Lionel Hurd farm in 1964 and the combined farms are now considered to be one of the largest sheep farms in Quebec. His son, Marc-Antoine, has recently taken over the farm.

The Bowker families of Newport: *(Herbert (Bert) Drouin; Bowker family history)*

Gordon and Audrey Bowker's son, Jeffrey Grant Bowker, married Carolyn McBurney 1987 at the Baptist church in Sawyerville. They continued to live and operate the farm on the original Bowker homestead on North River Road, lots 3 and 4 of Range 7. They renovated the house, restocked the farm and are currently leasing part of the adjacent farm. They have three children: James Patrick (born 1992), Timothy Ryan (born 1993) and Joshua Scott (born 1998). Jeffrey's parents Gordon and Audrey Bowker moved to the adjacent property, formerly owned by George and Agnes Buck, on Lot 5 of Range 7.

> *Author's note: I remember my good friend, Bill Buck, and his sisters Linda, Phillis, Marilyn and Jennifer, who all grew up on that farm.*

Wesley H. G. and his wife Hope Lillian (Gill) Bowker took over the farm owned by his parents Edmund and Naomi (Gilman). They remodelled the original farmhouse on Flanders Road so his parents could continue to live there. The farm was eventually sold to a Nugent family member.

***

The Rand families of Newport:

Author's note: The Rand family historical information and excerpts have been graciously provided courtesy of Carol Rand and Ruby (Rand) Pehlemann.

In later years, Clinton Rand enjoyed driving the children to school in a minibus and listening to their stories. After retiring from the farm, he and Doreen worked together for Canada Post delivering mail to the area. They celebrated their 50th wedding anniversary on July 24, 1993. After retiring, they lived in Sawyerville. Clinton and Doreen were the last of the Rand families to live in Newport; their children all moved to different parts of the Eastern Townships and beyond. Robert moved to Tillsonburg, Ont. Ruby married Bruce Pehlemann and they raised their family in Bury Township. Rickey moved to Brampton, Ont., where he raised his family. Trudy married Alvin Doherty; they raised their family in Lennoxville, Que. Dale moved to Western Canada, married there and raised his family; however, he passed away at a young age.

Clinton and Doreen Rand 50th wedding anniversary

Lyle Rand (Clinton's brother) and wife Fay raised their four children in Sawyerville. Royce and Carol had been born during the war. James Argyle was born in 1951 and Sylvia Margaret in 1952, both in Sawyerville. The family moved to Milby, Que., in 1962 and later to Huntingville, Que., where Lyle accepted an offer to work as a butcher in Clifford Hunting's IGA store in the village. They later retired to Lennoxville where they lived their remaining years. Royce and his wife, Sharon (Moore), are still very active in the community and the Eaton Corner Museum.

"When I was growing up my mom was a seamstress, sewing everything from lingerie to wedding gowns. She decorated wedding cakes from the early 1950s to 2003. From 1964 to 1968, Mom worked as a pastry cook at Fred Loach's Lunch in Lennoxville. She recorded all the pies she baked in a little book; the total: 15,619." *(Carol Rand)*

Author's note: Lyle and Fay's second son, James, whose middle name was Argyle, was named after Argyle Harrison, cousin of Fay Rand (Parsons), who was executed by the Japanese in Hong Kong in December 1941. Their children all lived outside of Newport, two of whom moved to Ontario. (Carol Rand)

Carol Rand is a lifelong reader with a special interest in history. She spent her early years in Sawyerville with her parents, Lyle and Fay, and siblings Royce, Jim, and Sylvia. Nearby Randboro was often a destination for family visits to the township founded, built and farmed by their pioneer ancestors Rand, McCurdy, Hurd, Morrison, Parsons, Ellis, Lefebvre and more. Carol earned a teachers' diploma from Macdonald College at McGill University and a B.A. from Trent University. She lives in Peterborough near her daughters and sons-in-law, Pamela Forgrave and Doug Hamilton, and Shelley Forgrave and Bob Rivers, and her grandchildren Lowell, Makeda, Aiden and Brody.

***

Richard and Vivian Mackay came to Randboro from Cookshire, Eaton Township, where they had farmed and sold milk produced on their farm. The Mackay family of Randboro consisted of Richard and Vivian and their only son, David. They bought and took over the store from Charlie and Gerty Montgomery, circa 1956 or '57. "I know they were there in 1958 when my mother died because Cousin Merle [Colin McCallum's daughter] and I were sent to a bedroom over Mackay's store." Charlie and Gerty continued living in Randboro, operating a small hobby farm across the street from the store on the original Charlie Stone mill property. "In 1959 Richard Mackay's sister, Olive, and her husband Mark Porter, moved from Bishopton to the house directly across the road from us. I called it the Lafleur house because I had grown up with Charlie and Grace Lafleur living there. My dad [Leslie] was actually born in that house." *(Diana (McCallum) Langworth)*

Mackay's store, Randboro (Eastern Townships Roots)

"As young teenagers in the 1950s when the post-war economic boom saw most families owning a car and taking to the roads for a vacation, we would compete during summer's touring season to see how many different licence plates we could tally: Ontario, Nova Scotia, New Brunswick, Connecticut, New Hampshire, New York, Maine, Vermont, and Rhode Island. Several boldly framed license plates in plate holders declared 'Give Me Liberty or Give Me Death.' Even before checking if the vehicle had come from New Jersey or Maryland, we knew it was from good ole' U.S.A." *(David Mackay)*

***

The McCallum families of Newport:

Leslie McCallum married Joyce Elizabeth Richardson, whose family was living in Eaton Township. They raised their two daughters, Audrey and Diana, in Randboro in the original Ephriam and Hamilton Cable home. At the back of their home was a spring and brook in which the water flowed constantly. Leslie had a particular interest in providing water for the horses as they passed through town, so he got a stave barrel, cut it in half, and set it up with a water pipe from the spring, allowing water to run into and out of the barrel. Summer or winter, horses passing through would always stop for a drink from his barrel. A few years later Leslie added a tap so people could also get a drink or fill up their bottles with first-class spring-fed drinking water.

> This was my dad's favourite summer occupation . . . keeping the water pumping for those who stopped to drink. As a kid growing up in Randboro, the water ran continuously from a spring in the maple bush in our pasture to a large iron tub. This was for watering the horses as they travelled from Maple Leaf and beyond to Sawyerville. *(Diana (McCallum) Langworth)*

The house where Audrey and Diana lived with their parents in the 1950s was next to their grandparents, Charlie and Lottie McCallum.

> When Royce and I were very young we went with Mom and Dad to visit Gardner "Gardy" W. Rand and his wife Lily Parker. They lived with Leslie, Joyce, Audrey, and Diana in their home in their old age. Lottie and Lily were twins and lived side-by-side in their retirement years. Lottie and Lily celebrated their 80th birthday together in the original home that had been owned by Austin and Flora Rand, Stillman and Celestia Rand and finally Charlie and Lottie McCallum. I was there! So was all our family, including Sylvia, who was very young. *(Carol Rand)*

Audrey and Diana spent many hours on hot summer days in the swimming hole in the South River below Harold Sutton's farm:

> The swimming hole in Randboro was where I learned to swim and spent hours in that small swimming area and learned to dive from the top of a boulder which gave a 6-foot above water height to a water depth of about 6 feet, so it was important to recoup your dive quickly. There were days when that swimming hole would have 10-15 swimmers in it, mostly from Sawyerville. I used to have a picture taken there where Bruce Bennett, Peter Mogensen, Perry Williams and several others were in the water. Dad was keeping the books and did various other office jobs at Hurd's sawmill in Sawyerville, so I had met Gillian Hurd and her brother Rodney. Gillian and I were best friends in grades 1 and 2. We kept in touch letter-writing for several years after she moved to Toronto. I saw her at the Sawyerville High School Reunion but time erases connections. *(Diana (McCallum) Langworth)*

Both Audrey and Diana McCallum moved away from Randboro after they were married.

Leslie McCallum's older brother, Ernie, had moved to Ottawa and married Mary Renfrew. Their six children were all born there. Ernie bought his father Charlie and Lottie's house in Randboro around 1965 (this was the original home of Austin and Flora, then later Stillman and Celeste Rand) and moved his family there. Charlie and Lottie had sold their farm on Parker Hill and had bought the home after Flora Rand married Newell Rand and went to live in Maple Leaf on his farm. Ernie and Mary looked after his parents for several years. The four younger children spent some of their school years in Randboro. Eventually the whole family moved to Toronto.

> *Author's note: It was when Ernie returned to Randboro that he wrote his book,* Autobiographical Recollections. *His ideology was to study the past to plan the future. His journal of recollections was instrumental in my ability to capture many interesting facts of life in Randboro circa the early 1900s. His hand-drawn maps of both Randboro and Parker Hill give us an excellent snapshot as to who lived where and was of great help in laying out sequences of events. Luvia (Leggett) McCallum, a stepdaughter of Charlie McCallum, moved back to live with her parents in Randboro after her husband, George, had died at a young age. George McCallum was a cousin of Charlie.*

***

The French families of Newport:

> In August 1995 while my brother Jeffrey French was farming the homestead, and my father Clinton D. French still owned the farm, there was a hundred-year flood. The house sustained considerable water damage as the water levels rose up to the first floor. The house was uninhabitable as Jeffrey had a young

family at the time. My dad, Clinton, bought a house in Sawyerville for Jeffrey and his family to live in. They continued to farm the land until February 2006 when the property was sold to Marc Blais and his wife Johanne Theriault. Marc and Johanne built a new home on the hill across the road from the huge rock on Aubrey and Blanche French's place. *(Linda (French) Oliveras)*

French Valley Farm (courtesy of Wendy French)

"[The photo opposite] is an aerial photo of the homestead I grew up on. It was called French Valley Farm and was owned by my great-grandfather Robert French before it passed to my father, Clinton D. French. It is situated on Flanders Road by the North Branch of the Eaton River." *(Wendy French)*

The William V. French farm (by the bridge, pictured opposite), and the John William French farm (where the huge rock is) were across the meadow from each other. The farm across the river belonged to the Bowker family. Clinton rented it from them. The third French farm in Newport was located further north and east; it was the original Millar farm on Lot 8 of Range 5 and was farmed by the James H. and Hannah M. French family.

John and Emma (Parsons) French of Newport raised several children, one of whom was their son Abel "Abe," who married Alma Patton. Abe and Alma also had several children, one of whom was Aubrey French, who married Blanche Dempsey. Their daughter, Brenda, married Ross Thomas and have two children, Megan and Aaron. They are the only French family still farming on an ancestral farm property in Newport.

I had a young friend who used to come and play here in the 1950s. He was so afraid the rock would roll down that he would not play near the pond below the rock. The rock appears to be just sitting there, not really underground. We climbed it many times. *(Brenda (French) Thomas)*

As children we were fascinated by this rock. I often thought of it as a giant baby bassinet. We had its baby brother on the hillside behind our barn; small in comparison. *(Wendy French)*

There is another rock, only smaller, on the hill behind the barn that once belonged to William, then Robert F. and lastly by my father Clinton. Indeed, there was an Indian encampment. The field on the left side of the bridge looking up the hill towards the Nugent homestead was where they had their tepees and tanned their hides. On the right side of the road going up the

The big rock, a glacial erratic estimated to weigh 100,000 tons, on the French farm stands today as it has since the Ice Age (photo by Sandra Hurd, 2019)

hill towards the Nugent homestead at the top of the first knoll is where the Indian graveyard is. When I was a child, before my great-grandfather Robert F. French passed away in 1961, archaeologists came and dug several square holes looking for artifacts. I remember being told they had found evidence of a graveyard there but I don't remember being told what exactly they had found. I remember going over there with my dad and him showing me where the soil changed colours on the sides of the dug holes. Dad told me it was most likely evidence of what the bodies had been wrapped in. *(Linda (French) Oliveras)*

As published in the *Sherbrooke Record*, an unfortunate accident took place in Island Brook in January 2000. Police in Quebec's Eastern Townships were investigating the death of an Island Brook man who was hit by a snowplow early Sunday morning. Kenneth French, 76, had been walking on highway 212 when he was struck from behind. The snowplow operator ran to a nearby restaurant for help. It was dark at the time of the accident, there was drifting snow, and it appears that Kenneth had been walking in the middle of the lane. No charges were laid as it was deemed an accident. It was very unfortunate as that meant that his only son, Sydney, could not remain in the only home he knew. He moved to the Wales Home in Richmond, Que., where he passed away in 2014.

Monique and Marie Paul Boutin's restaurant, where the snowplow operator ran to, has been a landmark and has served the community since 1992. The restaurant served up great meals for many local patrons and was a welcome stop for the many travellers heading to the U.S. through the village of La Patrie. From any seat one enjoyed a spectacular view of the landscape; often deer could be seen feeding down the valley.

***

The Nugent families of Newport. A Nugent Heard/Hurd family connection *(ref.: Terry Winslow)*:

> *Author's note: Grant Nugent and his wife Hattie had five children: Hubert, Muriel, Harris, Doris and Bobby. After the children married, Harris was the only one of the children who remained and raised his family in Newport.* (Truth Nugent)

Grant and Hattie Nugent's eldest son, Hubert, and his wife Marion (Lake), had two daughters, Cheryl and Mary, both of whom still live in the Eastern Townships. Muriel married Clifford Westgate; they had two daughters, Marilyn and Helen, who both moved to Ontario. A son, Terry, from Muriel's second marriage to Norman Winslow, still resides in the region. Their second daughter, Doris, and her husband George Hurd (Alonzo's son) had two daughters, Cynthia and Deanna; both reside in Nova Scotia. Doris and George Hurd also had a son, Allan, who lives with his wife on Vancouver Island, B.C. Their youngest son, Bobby, and his wife Truth (Hamilton) raised four daughters and a son in Ontario, where they still live. Bobby and Truth's family are Laurie, Paula, Rosemary, Jennifer, and a son, Chris, who passed away several years ago.

Grant and Hattie Nugent's second son, Harris, married Gloria Coates. They raised their two sons, Danny and Kim, on the family farm. Gloria predeceased Harris, and after Harris passed away the two sons took over the family corporate farm. Danny married Donna Taylor from Birchton, and they had two children. His brother Kim married Sharon Burton from Compton and they have three children. Kim continues to farm with his son, Corry, and they recently started a large flock of sheep. "Just recently, sadly and tragically, Danny died. Kim, who is 58, now owns the farm. His son, Corry, is apparently living there raising sheep. A new venture indeed . . . Good for him! So, it's still a Nugent farm. Hopefully Corry can keep it that way. He is the only one of his generation who can officially use that surname." *(Truth Nugent)*

***

The Westgate families of Newport
(Ilah (Westgate) Batley):

Maple Westgate had a severe stroke in 1967 and never regained his body strength, making him unable to continue doing the things he was used to doing. During his long hospitalization and recovery, his wife Verna kept on milking the cows, and with the help of a hired hand kept the farm going. The eight-gallon milk cans were hauled each day to the roadside, placed on the special high milk stand, to be picked up and transported to Carnation Milk Company in Sherbrooke. Note the signpost with an illustration of Maple Westgate and the school bus he operated for more than 20 years.

Newport Township welcome sign, featuring Maple Westgate and his school bus (courtesy of the artist, Denis Palmer)

In 1967, Verna's father, William Painter, was unfortunately killed in a car accident in Bury, Que. Verna inherited her parents' farm which was just across the road from Maple and Verna's farm. They realized the milk farm chores were too much for them to handle, so they sold their dairy farm business to Bruce and Ilah Batley and moved across the road to the now-vacant Painter farm and began to build a beef farm operation. This made things easier for a while, until Maple died in 1982 at the age of 77.

Verna lived on in the home of her birth, was active in ping-pong and cross-country skiing with her grandchildren, and was a sharp card player. She loved to play 500 or cribbage. She drove her own car until she was 103 years old. When she was refused her driving license at age 100, she said she felt like a "bird in a cage." She apparently pestered the officials for four months until they re-issued her driver's license. At 104 Verna moved to a seniors' home where she, moving around with a walker, carried a cribbage board and a deck of cards, trying to find someone who would play cards with her. Her reply to anyone who said they didn't know how to play the game was that it was "never too late to learn." On July 17, 2016, at 108, years old she just faded away, leaving fond memories for her family and friends.

Maple and Verna raised five children, a son and four daughters:

Mailin Westgate with his parents Verna and Maple (courtesy of Ilah (Westgate) Batley)

Mailin Painter Westgate (1929-2016) married Mavis Clark and they farmed with his father Maple for a few years. The farm was too small to support two families and with Mavis having asthma, farming was not to be, so they moved to Kingston, Ont., where they raised their four children. Mailin worked as a carpenter and Mavis worked as a librarian.

Patricia Westgate (1931-2011) married first Frazer McCloud then Norman Smith. Pat taught school in Milan, Que. She and Norman later moved to Drummondville, Que., where they raised her and Frazer's two children, Catherine (born 1951) and Robert (1955-2010).

Norma Westgate (born 1935) married John Gill and lived in Cookshire where they raised four children. Norma loves horses and was an avid horsewoman when growing up on the farm.

Ilah Westgate (born 1945) married Bruce Batley. They lived in Montreal for a period, where Bruce was a mechanic for CPR and Ilah worked for Clough Chemical Co. In 1969 they moved back to Island Brook and bought the old homestead farm from Ilah's parents, Maple and Verna. Bruce and Ilah raised their three daughters, Tracy (born 1967), Christine (born 1971), and Ginger (born 1972) on the original Westgate farm. Bruce and Ilah retired; they are still living on the farm near Island Brook and are still active in community affairs in Newport at the time of writing.

Linda Westgate (born 1948), the youngest of Maple and Verna's five children, married Leslie MacLeod. They live in Island Brook on Alden Road. Leslie was a customs officer for Canada Customs. Linda was a nurse working in the emergency room at Sherbrooke Hospital until she retired. They continue to live in Newport. Their son Angus (born 1971) owns his grandmother Verna's farm, the old Westgate/Painter farm on Route 212 in Island Brook.

Farm life kept everyone busy, and not unlike farm life in the past, as soon as the children were of helping age, they did just that. Ilah (Westgate) Batley recalls:

> Even on a hot summer day we would not fail to take our faithful dog "Rinky" up to the pasture to bring the cows back to the barn for milking. Rinky, short for our version of Rin Tin Tin (the infamous 124-episode TV show for children) was trained to criss-cross back and forth, herding the cattle with us, running as fast as our little legs would carry us, right to the gates of the barn. As children, we would get so excited when there were calves to be fed milk from a pail because, of course, the calves would bump the pail when it was almost empty, splashing the milk all over them. Cats and more cats – there were always barn cats and beautiful kittens for all of us to play with. Of course, we girls would wrap them up in doll blankets and make houses in the hay loft. Linda and Ilah would ask big brother Mailin to identify if the cats were boys or girls. He finally told us to shake them and if they rattled, then they are boys.

Maple had a pond built; it was spring-fed and so the water was cold. It always provided a fresh and cold supply of water for the cattle, even in times of drought. He made a raft out of two barrels, and we spent hours paddling around on this raft. There were frog eggs and then tadpoles and, in the spring, we could hear the frogs singing, with a croak here and burp there, sounding just like a choir. One day Verna was looking for her colander; of course we had to admit we had it at the pond – the perfect tool for catching tadpoles and small frogs.

On hot summer days we all headed to the North River or the Island Brook creek for afternoon swims at our favourite swimming holes. There were always other children there and so our parents had a chance to catch up on the community gossip as well. Verna always took great delight in packing a picnic lunch for us all, and so we had a chance to trade goodies, always satisfying ourselves that we made the best deal.

Maple had a Clydesdale mare we called Lassie that he enjoyed exhibiting each fall at the Cookshire Fair. Linda and Ilah competed at the fair with their saddle horses; Linda, who belonged to the 4-H Club, showed her calf in the competitions as well.[32]

The Island Brook community was always an active group, working together on potluck church suppers held at private homes to raise money for community services. Hazel and Franklin Kerr, Jean and Earl Dawson, and Hazel and Hollis Burns had large homes where people would gather for these home-cooked meals. These scrumptious suppers soon became social events, a fun time for everyone after a hard week's work in the woods in winter or in the fields in summer.

During this era in Newport baths were still rather strenuous events. Water was piped from a well or spring, usually through the barn first and then to the house, to a hand pump located on the kitchen sink. For hot water a pipe ran through a "heat jacket" (a cast iron manifold welded right into the kitchen stove fire box), and connected to a reservoir, situated alongside the stove. Of course the stove had to be lit in summer to heat the water, so usually a summer bath would follow soon after supper was cooked and eaten. In winter, the stove was pretty much always hot, so baths could be taken at any time. The water was carried to a 3-foot metal tub in a small room just off the kitchen. The hot water reservoir was small so there could be only one bath per evening. Verna used to make her own lye soap; a rather harsh soap that left no room for bacteria. In the winter, since these old houses weren't insulated, the air was cold and one did not spend time lounging in the tub. After bathing the water had to be "pailed" out, the tub cleaned, and the water dumped outside.

***

The Graham family of Newport: *(Carolyn (Graham) Grapes)*

Billy Graham, the only surviving sibling of John "Irvin" Graham and his wife Lillian, worked in Sherbrooke and operated their 50-acre farm more as a hobby farm with his family. Irvin died in 1965; Lilian died a year later, in 1966; both are buried in Maple leaf Cemetery.

The Graham family operated a campground for many years at the foot of Grove Hill in Randboro on a part of their farm. This site was next to where the original gristmill was established circa 1810 by the Rand and Beaman families. Billy Graham was an ardent musician and singer, played his guitar at many local events, dances, and fundraisers. He died at a dance at the Church Hall in Bulwer in March 2000, doing what he loved best. At the end of his set, he sat down on a chair on the stage to rest and simply faded away as the dancing continued. Most of the dancers thought he had just fallen asleep. His son Aubrey carried on his father's musical tradition. A musician in his own right, Aubrey moved to the Ottawa Valley, Ont. He and his wife, Anne Sundborg, invited many former Townshippers, along with local Ottawa Valley musicians, to play every year at his property. This private party was attended as almost a reunion of fellow classmates and folks from Newport for many years. His sisters, Carolyn (Graham) Grapes, Linda (Graham) Fisk and Gladys (Graham) Fisk were part of the committee formed by Florence (Bowker) McVetty in 1994 to organize the Sawyerville School reunion.

***

Bill Parkinson was a bachelor living on Parker Hill circa the 1950s. Apparently he never took a bath and was so lazy he had started to burn pieces of his house as firewood to keep his house warm in the winter. The story is told that he became very ill, so his sister in Randboro picked him up, and took him to her home; gave him a bath, fed him and put him to bed. He died during the night, but, as she was to have said, he was clean for his burial.

Author's note: I remember travelling past Bill Parkinson's place on the Parker Hill Road in the school bus when we noticed Bill had begun removing the posts from his veranda to burn as firewood. He simply shoved them into his pot-bellied stove; as the post burned, he would keep pushing it into the fire. Each day as we passed by, we would ask Tiffy to slow down so we could see how many posts were left, expecting one day to see the veranda collapse – which it finally did.

***

Wells Bishop

Wells A. Bishop grew up in Bishopton in Dudswell Township. He served in World War I at age 15. He was wounded at the Battle of Vimy Ridge, strafed by a German aircraft, *the bullets went right through his back, but touched no vital organs.* Wells survived and was awarded the Distinguished Service Order (DSO) medal. He returned to his hometown of Bishopton. Wells volunteered with the Royal Rifles in World War II, served in the Battle of Hong Kong, and was held as a POW from Christmas 1941 to 1945. He returned home after the war and purchased and operated two farms on the North River in Newport. He also operated a hunting lodge on his farm, the North River Fish and Game Club, and served for several years as the game warden for Newport. He installed a small landing strip in one of his fields so members of the Club could fly in on the summer weekends.

Wells Bishop was elected mayor of Newport Township in 1959 and served a term of four years. He was Commanding Officer for the Bury Armories, overseeing recruiting. For several years he held military training exercises on his other farm. The recruits came from far and wide for the privilege of training each year for two weeks at the farm under the full direction of Major Bishop. One of the farmhouses was set up with bunks for the troopers to sleep in and full kitchens to feed the men. The barns housed armoured troop carriers, tanks, jeeps, and all types of surplus equipment to support a full battalion of men in carrying out real live military exercises. They used blanks instead of any live ammo; this allowed the trainees to learn to load and shoot. These military training exercises were carried out over his entire 400 acres of property.

Somehow Wells managed to operate his farm as a ranch-style operation, doing all the things farmers have to do to live. He was a man loved by men and women of all ages, and there were no exceptions.

***

The original home of Augustus and Eliza (Planche) Hurd, then their son Gussie and Eliza (Hurd) Hurd, now Tetreault family home (photo by Sandra Hurd)

The Tetreault family of Newport: *(ref.: Robert Tetreault)*

The Tetreault family of Parker Hill bought Gussie and Sarah Hurd's farm on the 9th Range in 1951 and continued to live there throughout the 1950s into the 1980s. They were now living on the original John B.[7] and Polly (Sawyer) Heard farm, so the Tetreault family essentially had lived on two Heard farms that were part of the original land grants arranged by Colonel Edmund[5] Heard. Gerald "Gerry," the second-oldest son, took over the farm, fixed up the house, built a new barn, expanded the livestock and operated it until he and his wife retired in the late 1980s. His brother Rene Tetreault served the community as a councillor in 1995.

***

Denis Palmer, a local artist living in Randboro, designed, painted and installed "Newport 1801" signs in each corner of the township: one on Route 210, just east of Sawyerville; one on Parker Hill near the Auckland town line on Range 11; one on Route 210 east of Chartierville near the Auckland and Ditton township borders; and one on Route 212 east of Island Brook at the Ditton border. Denis has painted many depictions of "lives lived" in the Townships from the time he first chose Newport as his permanent residence in 1979.

***

The Willard family of Newport:

The home of John B.[9] and Emma (Austin) Hurd became known as the Willard homestead when their daughter Flora (1872-1943) married Clark Stewart Willard (the son of Lockhart Longley). They raised five children on the farm; all moved to various regions of the U.S. as they married. Flora rented the farm out for a few years after she left to live her final years in the U.S. with her children. The farm was sold when she died in 1943.

This was a time when serving your country was a privilege, and to live in this country was an even bigger privilege. Our ancestors' lives were governed by the Bible, good judgement and common sense. They were taught to know the difference between right and wrong and to stand up and take responsibility for their actions. Anyone who has grown up here has no doubt felt and continues to feel connected to Newport. It was a culture that was special. Time can be a greedy thing . . . sometimes it steals all the details for itself and so hopefully a reader will have had some details filled in with the revelations of "lives lived."

"Welcome to Newport" sign on Route 210 east of Sawyerville (courtesy of the artist, Denis Palmer)

The original John B. and Emma (Austin) homestead beside John's parents Augustus and Eliza (Planche) Hurd. John and Emma's daughter Flora, who married Clark Willard, inherited the farm which became the Willard homestead (photo by Sandra Hurd)

> *Author's note: The story of Newport Township is typical of many of the other townships, and I hope the use of this history may become an influencer in bringing history to life on paper, an important tool for generations to come.*

***

The last covered bridge in Newport Township:

This bridge (pictured opposite) is equipped with "ships knees," visible if one takes a peek inside, and looks up to the roof joists. Ships knees were a key support mechanism keeping these buildings intact through the many years of service. Because the infrastructure of these old bridges was made of wood, the roofs were designed for the protection of the lower infrastructure. This bridge (see photo on next page) is located on McDermott Road, southwest of Island Brook off Route 212, straddling Lot 1 of Range 5, over the North River, about 200 feet from the Newport/Eaton township line.

***

The province of Quebec started as a French colony, changing to an English/French colony when the region was renamed Lower Canada. Both the French and English, along with an influx of newer immigrants from many countries including those of Scottish, Irish, Italian and German descent, became a society with a multilinguistic culture. They all lived and thrived together as one populace. This society was indeed one of envy the world over. A collection of different people with different backgrounds, including different religions, proved itself to be a successful society in which peoples of all races could not only survive but prosper together as one. The uprising of 1837 was to be the one event which triggered a French/English Canadian nationalism, when for the first time both French and English civilians joined together in opposition to the British colonial administration.

McDermott covered bridge (unknown Internet source)

Over time, the French peoples and language began to grow exponentially with larger families, and the province began to shift to more of a French/English province. Both peoples and their languages continued to prosper together until 1974, when the Official Language Act (Bill 22) was enacted. Many English-speaking residents had married into French-speaking families as well as French to English, over many years and so bilingualism had flourished in the province. Not unlike European societies, there were no language barriers, creating a society able to communicate and conduct business, with a distinct competitive advantage on the world stage. However, with the enactment of the Official Language Act, this advantage began to unravel. And so, during the 1970s, there began years of exodus of English-speaking workers and businesspeople, often but not exclusively unilingual, which coincided with the economic boom of Toronto and continued across the western provinces. This boon to other parts of Canada continued its acceleration over the next decade. More than 300,000 English-speaking Quebecers left the province.

For the most part, the inhabitants in Newport and the surrounding communities, where the culture still remains with the same shared value of bygone days, both French- and English-speaking families continue to embrace bilingualism and continue to help each other to survive. However, this too may change over the next few decades.

"Of all our national assets, archives are the most precious, they are the gifts of one generation to another, and the extent of our care of them marks the extent of our civilization." *(Sir Arthur Doughty, "Dominion Archivist and Keeper of the Records," 1904-1935)*

Island Brook, Then & Now
by Manlius Holbrook

So now to all strangers who may happen this way, to guard you from danger, please heed what I say.
Then give strict attention as I show you around. Mind all may mention, about things in this Town.
If you face towards the East, pass St. Valentine's door, the first man you meet is a very great bore.
Turn square to the South and pass the Westgate, don't open your mouth, nor stop to debate.
Dangerous Woods to pass by and Carnical ones too, and Riddles to spy before you get through.
Now return to the Borough, then turn to the North, now wait on the Morrow on the St. Lawrence set forth.
Now, to learn all the news just call on St. John, pay the rent on your pews, then prepare to move on.
There is danger ahead look out for the Carr's. If you are not dead yet with no serious scars,
Look out for the Kerr's that may stand in the street. Go on to the Painter with twelve toes on his feet.
Now return to the village and turn down the road. If you admire good tillage just call on R. Todd.
Now put on your helmet you have Burns to pass, a Millar to grind you and a charming little lass.
No night on this street, but one endless day. If sore thumbs you should meet have nothing to say.
Look out for the Seale, that wears a coon coat. He will do a good deal to capture your vote.
We have a Lyon that saws shingle, A Kidd that drives team, a man that lives single.
Our Carr's go without steam, our Camel had departed to Cookshire's fair clime,
The whole Brook just started to compose a short rhyme.

–Manlius Holbrook, Sergeant Major, U.S.S.S.
circa 1900

Dedicated to the Memories of the Pioneers
by Ray "Sliver" and Molly Griffin

On Clifton's lofty heights and Newport's lane, lies Auckland on the shady side with pine trees.
To the state of Maine, with axe and saw those woods did ring,
This makes me think of Mitchell King,
A man who knew most every tree, and so did Russell Sunbury.
As hunters I have heard tell, many bears, deer, and wolf as well,
Before their Snyder rifle fell.
At Maple Leaf, God's acre there, rest ye in peace all mortal care.
To dust returns, as Burns once told, was not spoken of the soul.
A church once stood at Maple Leaf, where pioneers once sought relief.
From toil and care in reverence come, Praise God on high, "Thy will be done."
The parson, with his chosen words, met Leggetts, Cables, Rands and Hurds.
With ox teams they plowed those meadows low,
Bow-hoist, Buck-gee star, whoa, was just about the only word,
Down through the glen that could be heard.
At Randboro the water mill washed down the stream to Sawyerville,
Where once Captain Sawyer, with well-earned fame
Was monarch of that fair domain.
The freckled youngster, with line and hook,
Brought speckled trout from Sawyer Brook.
Where village cows have often fed, now on concrete paths we tread.
Oh! Things have changed yet lingers still, a memory of Jim Cromwell's mill,
Where men toil hard, their home to build, 1757-1837
Now down the streets the motors scoot, and lots of barrel staves to boot.

– Ray "Sliver" and Molly Griffin,
Sawyerville, Eaton Township, circa 1950

Captain Josiah Sawyer statue in its initial location in Sawyerville

Chapter 18   Reflections (1947–1961)

After I had started writing this book, Sandra and I were fortunate enough to locate the current owners, Anne Fortier, her husband Felix-Antoine Rhéaume-Gonzalez and their son Ulysse Fortier-Gonzalez, who work currently in the Boston area (the same stomping grounds as our ancestors) and arrange to stay for a week at the old original Heard homestead farmhouse. The kinship I suddenly felt for the old land surprised me. Sixty years ago, when I lived on these lands, I made a choice to move away. Now, the decision to learn more about that history and to initiate the effort to write this book was a choice that landed me right back on this soil, and I felt a certain comfort about it. I sensed the presence of our ancestors everywhere I went . . . this had been their home where

The author's ancestral home in Maple Leaf (photo by Sandra Hurd)

their blood, sweat and tears had shaped theirs and ultimately our lives. I wanted to learn just what role my ancestor Colonel Edmund[5] Heard had played in settling Newport Township. I wanted to know what it was all about; what had influenced its unique culture. Col. Edmund knew that he liked what he saw, and he knew immediately that this is where he wanted to return with his family to establish a settlement on the land.

Who we are today is inextricably woven throughout our lives with memories of who we were yesterday, and the days before that – all threads in the same complicated tapestry. The foods we've developed a taste for, the multiple skills we've mastered or failed at, the movies we've enjoyed, the music we have danced to, what we admire and what we don't, are all part of who we are. And so, it is our memories that define us; without them, we have no identity.

Firsthand accounts from parents and grandparents have added immensely to my understanding of the early days of lives lived in the 19th century. As I write today, a heavy wet snow is blowing across the windows, the temperature outside is minus 20 degrees, and I am thinking of those pioneers. When our ancestors faced this kind of weather, they had a lot more to do than turn up the thermostat or flip on the light switch at sundown!

I share my memories of growing up in Newport with you so that, perhaps, it might inspire you to share your own memories with your grandchildren and loved ones. One day they may cherish your thoughts and perhaps share them with their children in the years ahead.

I have only a very vague memory of when I was around 5 years old. I believe younger generations today will remember things at a much earlier age because they see themselves often now in colour photographs and videos taken often while they were young. In my young days when a picture was taken using a film of 12 images, it was in black and white (no colour then). The film of "negatives" had to be taken or mailed to a photo studio to be developed and once you got it back, around two weeks later, you got to see the pictures. Out of the 12 pictures, perhaps only a couple would be good enough to keep and put into an album which would be reviewed on occasion.

I remember painting our old rusty hay rake – red with yellow wheels and black trim. I was so proud of it that I took a picture. When I got the pictures back, disappointment was an understatement because, the photos were in black and white, not colour, just different shades of grey. Just another of many learning experiences for a young kid.

I did not even know my father, who had been a POW in the Pacific during the Second World War. I had been a baby when he left and had met him only when he came back from the war when I was 5 years old. I had been living with my mother, brother and stepfather in the city of Montreal where streetcars, electricity, buses and cars, and people were everywhere – some good memories, some not. I went to live with my father when I was 7 years old and that is how I ended up living on the ancestral farm in Newport.

I remember when my brother, Jim, and I would be put on a train by my mother in Montreal, the conductor instructed to watch for us and make sure he put us off the train in a place called Bulwer. Here was where my maternal grandparents, Norris and Eva (Wilkinson) Wood, lived on a farm, just up a long hill from the train tracks in Bulwer. I remember a little store on the other side of the tracks where mail was placed in little slots on a wall. A big mail bag had been dropped off on the boardwalk when the train stopped. Someone in that store, a Mr. Rodgers, used to sometimes give us an ice cream cone and we believed he was really special. I remember a barber's chair in the corner by the window and a small round table full of newspapers.

Jimmy and Freddy (the author) Hurd at the pond at their Wood grandparents' farm in Bulwer, 1946

Jim and I seemed to spend a bit of time there during the summers at an early age and I remember a meat truck that would pull into the village occasionally. A man named Lyle would cut up meat that Grandmother would select from the back of his truck.

My grandparents had a pond on their farm that everyone would come to; it was quite a walk through a pasture behind the barn. I remember the Parker boys coming to swim there. My family seemed to have a picnic there every Sunday and we always had such fun. Grandfather loved children and he was always building something for us and playing along as if he were our age.

I started Grade 1 in Montreal in 1946; Jim was in Grade 2. We lived on the sixth floor in a flat, our backyard was an iron fire escape, looking down into a small yard surrounded with the backside of buildings on all four sides. The school was on the other side of a huge yard of railway tracks and, of course, I remember this vividly. We had to walk from our street to a connecting main street with streetcars, then walk a few blocks where we entered the darkest and scariest part of the trip. We had to enter this tunnel under a bridge where the "boogeymen" were hanging out. They would grab at our feet as we were running through and call out all sorts of things; and run we did as fast as our little legs would go.

Since we could not seem to convince my mother that we just did not want to go to school, we decided there was a better way to go. We simply climbed this huge fence each day, running for our lives across the tracks, looking both ways and dodging the trains. I remember it was not long before some men were also chasing after us every day, trying to catch the "little buggers" (as they called us) on the tracks, so we had to change our course each day, planning our escape. After a while this became a game for us; I remember Jim and I being quite proud of our efforts at not being caught; it was still much more favorable than the boogeymen route. Apparently the school became aware, and we were severely punished and so it was back to dodging the men in the tunnel. These people haunted me for a long time, and it was only years later, when I moved to Toronto, that I finally realized that they were likely the homeless and perhaps winos sleeping around the pillars in the tunnel.

I remember visiting my paternal grandparents, Gussie and Sadie Hurd, on their farm one winter, perhaps at Christmas. I have no idea how I got there. I remember looking out the window at horses pulling a long box on a sled with a small chimney pipe sticking out the back. My grandmother told me it was the school bus taking the kids to school in Sawyerville, the small town about 10 miles (no kilometers then) away. The sled, with the long box on top, was heated by a small wood-burning stove inside, pulled by horses over a rolled snow road. She told me they used horses to pull exceptionally large rollers over the snow to pack down the road so the horses could walk or trot on top of the packed snow. I remember her telling me that people used sleighs to get around instead of cars and that very few people had cars, but everyone had horses here.

Jim and I must have spent part of a summer there in 1946-47, as I remember Grandfather (Gussie) raking the hay with his horse Dinah. This was when I met my father and Uncle Arthur. I remember my Uncle Arthur because he had lost a foot in a logging accident and showed me how he had to wear this long, big boot with a hundred laces up the front to be able to walk. I thought he must have lost his foot in the war. I also met my Aunt Jessie (Riddell) and many other families that seemed to visit my grandparents that summer.

Jim and I went to Sawyerville a few times in my grandfather's Model A Ford, and we stood in the back holding on to the back of the front seats with our fingers in the crease. We soon learned that you had to get your fingers out of that crease when he started the car, because he pushed back so hard that our fingers would be pinched in that crease. We also learned quickly that if our fingers were stuck in the crease, it would be best not to complain because we should not have had them there in the first place. My grandfather was very adamant about that. To start the car, the driver had to use his foot to push down on the starter button, hence the push back on the seat. I also remember when Grampa could not find the keys and we were told "the devils imps must have played with them."

I met my Uncle Fred Hurd for the first time and was utterly confused because he was driving the same meat truck I remembered seeing while it delivered meat to my grandparents (the Wood family) in Bulwer, except the drivers were different. Uncle Fred appeared to be driving in this area; not Lyle (Rand) who had done the deliveries in Bulwer.

For me, Bulwer could have been anywhere in Canada at that time; I had no idea that these two places (where my two sets of grandparents lived) were even possibly close to each other. One place needed a train and the other a car to get to and that is all I knew.

Jim and I spent Christmas 1947 at our grandparents' house in Bulwer, which I remember very well. We received a Lionel train set which was all set up on the living room floor, with a station and all the little baggage cars and little metal cars and trucks. A couple of days later I found myself at the farmhouse in Newport with Dad and stepmother, Irene. When it was time to go back to school, Jim was gone, and I found myself starting Grade 2 in Sawyerville. My teacher was Miss Riddle, and simply from her last name, I concluded she must have something to do with my new Aunt Jessie Riddle, so I felt comfortable. This was my introduction to what became my new home as I was not able to go back to my grandparents in Bulwer nor to see my mother and brother in Montreal for several years.

I remember that first year Irene stored milk and meat that needed to be kept cold in large Mason jars placed in a tub in the kitchen that had water running through it continuously. She kept ice cream buried in the snowbank behind the woodshed in a large round cardboard carton. I had never seen ice cream stored this way before, and it was so exciting when Irene would ask me to dig up the ice cream, which of course I buried in different spots so only I would know where it was. People in towns and cities had the modern conveniences. People living in the rural areas in Newport, where I was now growing up, did not. We were still using older machinery and appliances, but they worked.

Our lights were lanterns and kerosene lamps. We had one special "Coleman gas" lantern with two cloth filaments which had to be replaced from time to time. You had to pump the gas occasionally to keep the pressure up or the light would begin to dim. This style of lantern was the safest to take where there was hay and so we took that one to the barn to use when we were doing the chores after supper. Because this one was also the brightest, we used it in the kitchen so we could see better to eat. I remember at night you could not see into the corners of a room, so you can imagine my excitement when we got electricity, just like in town.

I was in Grade 6, around 11 years old, when the hydro was hooked up. They had installed one light bulb in the centre of each room. I could do my homework at night after dark and still see all four corners of the room at once! That one light bulb in the centre of the ceiling flooded the room with light, just like I had remembered it in Montreal. Working in the barns with lights in the stables was a real treat, after having to use the Coleman lanterns. With electricity, we could now have a fridge and electric stove and an electric radio. Sometimes Irene and I would sit and listen to stories being told on our new electric floor-model radio – and you could listen to music, too. "Our Miss Brooks" was a favourite of Irene's. I especially liked hearing the hockey broadcasts on Saturday nights and went to sleep listening to the Wheeling, W.V., Saturday night country music jamboree on my little desktop radio my Aunt Jessie had given me.

Dad would never miss the CBC news at 12 noon sharp. We would have to be sitting down when the radio started off with beeping and then one long beep, signifying noon. Everyone would set their watches and clocks to that signal. That was when we had dinner and Irene and I had to be absolutely silent while the news was on. I soon learned that whatever you put on your plate in our house had to be eaten. There was absolutely no leeway – even if you did not like it, you ate it. I learned early to advise my friends who came for any meal to take only what you will eat. Over time I came to understand the reason why. My dad's experience as a starving POW was evidence enough to see his reason for being so strict about eating.

In the winter we went everywhere by sled or sleigh, covered with old buffalo hides (that were moth-eaten and full of hay dust) to keep us warm. Sometimes when it was really cold, Irene heated up special smooth rocks on the stove and covered them with cloth; we would use them to keep our feet warm for "a short time." The first couple of winters I remember we had an old army jeep with four-wheel drive, but if there was a heater, I certainly never felt it sitting on the back bench. Later my dad bought a 1932 two-door Chevrolet coupe that had a box on the back where I would sit if it were not raining, otherwise I had to sit between Irene and Dad, the stick shift between my legs. Of course I loved sitting outside in the box where I could pretend to be a sniper on the end of a tank with a wooden gun I had made.

When I began school in the winter of 1947, they had big snowmobiles equipped with Ford V/8-cylinder engines that would hold about 20 children, all closed in, that would run on the roads and through the fields to pick us up. I rode in this "unique" school bus every morning and afternoon in the late 1940s and early 1950s, along with the many neighbouring boys and girls going to school. The front had three seats; the driver sat in the centre. I was lucky because I was the first to be picked up so Tiffy Morrison, the driver, allowed me to sit in one of the front side seats. That meant I had to get out at each stop to let other kids into the back. I learned to operate this vehicle because I got to watch everything the driver did, day after day. I learned very early that you can learn so much by just watching how people do things. Regular school buses took us to school in spring and fall.

Dutchman Teddy

There was a Dutchman, Teddy, who lived with us for a couple of years. He and I became great friends during this time when he was learning English. Teddy seemed more interested in my homework than I was, so he and I would read my textbooks together. He went home to Holland after the first year for a short visit and when he came back, he brought me a pair of wooden shoes. They were the most uncomfortable shoes I had ever put on and I couldn't believe how he ever survived wearing his, which he did every day when he worked in the barn.

From that time onward, changes came rapidly in my life; we became modern, with a car too, and with tractors and equipment that made both living and farming much easier. I believe I was lucky to have lived in these two worlds. I experienced both the olden ways of living and yet was quickly marched into the modern world.

Jim on the wagon and Fred (the author) on the tractor on the farm in Maple Leaf, 1947

I learned by watching and quietly positioned myself so I was always able to see how things were done. This was what interested me – how things worked. Perhaps this came from my dad's incessant reminders to "pay attention" and this I did with everything happening on or around the farm. I didn't pay attention in the classroom so much, because for me it was boring. I always tried to sit at the back of the class so I would be less visible, my mind active in building a car, or creating something new, or trying to imagine how I would devise an easier way of doing something. Nobody taught me how to drive the tractor, make cement or build a building; my learning habits best suited to simply watching. One day Dad asked me to bring the tractor over and so I jumped on and did just that. I was 8 years old and had to slide off the seat to reach the clutch to shift the gears or to brake.

I remember when we got our first telephone. We had a "party line" so if you wanted to call someone, you had to pick up the receiver and listen first to see if anyone was on the line. Of course there was no dial; you had to crank a lever, like a wind-up toy, which would ring on the phone as well as to someone you may want to speak to. So, you would crank one long crank for the operator and when she answered, ask her to connect you with whomever you wanted to speak to. If I wanted to speak to my grandmother, then I would crank two shorts and two long cranks, and she would answer. Sometimes when you picked up the receiver to phone someone, people might be talking (they were "on the line"), so you were supposed to hang up. However, as a kid, I might listen in to other people talking. You had to be careful not to breathe or make any kind of noise or they would hear you and tell you to get off the line. I really wanted to know how this thing worked and when I asked my dad, he would always say, "What do you want to know for? It works, doesn't it!" I resigned myself to think that perhaps he didn't know either.

I loved going to school to be with all my friends. Sometimes I would stay in town overnight, on Cub Scout nights, with my Great-aunt Jessie whom I loved very much. She did not have any children so she loved hearing my school stories, and I loved to tell stories. She especially loved to see me eat because I loved food, so I always made a big deal about how much I loved her food – and, of course, the milk and donuts before bed was a real treat. Her house was huge, with square ceilings even in the bedrooms which I thought was really modern because our house at the farm had slanted ceilings . . . and there was hot water – as much as you wanted – with lots of pressure, and a shower too. These were all new experiences for me as I was growing up. Armand McBurney was the best Cub/Scoutmaster ever; I remember his family very well as they made me feel I was a part of the community and that this was home for me now.

Sometimes my friends – Terry Lowry, Bruce Noble, Bobby Cairns, and later Billy Buck, Larry Buck, Norman Desruisseaux and Gordy Hodge – would come and stay with me on some weekends. We did not need toys; we made our own fun, dreaming up so many escapades; tasking ourselves to build huts, bunkers, bridges, wagons, sleds, wooden guns, and anything we could "invent." I remember on Sundays when Dad and Irene went to town, we would pretend to be ranchers in Montana, letting the calves out and then as ranchers we would lasso them with great anticipation and always, of course, alluding to our own great skills.

I remember convincing a couple of the boys to pee on the electric fence knowing the town kids would not know that when the little box clicked it was definitely time to withdraw quickly. Looking back now I might wonder if they were lucky if they had any children at all.

L-R: Friends Terry Lowry, Bruce Noble, Fred Hurd (the author) and Bobby Cairns at Fred's birthday, spring 1949

At an early age I met Rodney Hillman at John and Nellie Jones's farm at the top of our road just past the sugar bush. Rod and I made tunnels in the haymows under the beams, spending hours travelling to little rooms we made in the hay. These were our forts, our imagination creating all sorts of scenarios one might experience in the movies. Rod, being the joker he was, convinced me I should torpedo the replica Queen Mary boat I had so carefully built to float on our pond; the boat was connected with two strings so it would sit in the middle of the pond. I had even filled it with stones so it would float deep in the water. Testing our skills at skipping flat rocks towards the boat, it was not too long before one connected, and just like a torpedo, the ship went down exactly like a real liner would. Naturally Rod thought it was his torpedo that had made the direct hit and was enormously proud of his skill in doing so.

I had built a little replica barn for my pretend farm which eventually, as I grew older, had fallen into disrepair. We thought a real fire would be appropriate for its finale. Having an acute awareness of the damage fires could cause, we took the barn way out into the pasture and placed it on an exceptionally long and wide bedrock ledge. Wanting to see for ourselves how green hay can become combustible, we placed a small can of gasoline in the haymow of this little barn, packing it tight with hay we had brought with us. We wanted to see first-hand how these things worked; in our view, a sort of science lesson. And so, the match was struck! The explosion was quite dramatic! Did we have water? Nooo . . . but all went well because the rock ledge was large and no fire went beyond. However, the black soot left on the rock face was quite noticeable and did not miss the attention of my dad after being alerted by our neighbour Herbert Loveland. (He must have seen the smoke over the ridge from his farm and paid a visit after we were gone.) I was grounded for two weeks and Rod, my co-conspirator, was not allowed to visit me. I was annoyed that he could still go anywhere else he wanted to, so I felt that he was not grounded at all.

"Cowboy Fred" (the author) on Dinah, 1950; note our old car, a 1932 Chev with a rumble seat

My memories of growing up on the farm are of wonderful fun-filled times, whether I was alone or with my friends who came often to visit. Irene was great at having all these kids around and always made everyone feel welcome. I was creative and was always dreaming up something to build or create that would make our jobs easier. Dad was a strict, military-style father, but he gave me one big chance at life. He always said to me, "Try it, if you don't take a risk, you won't learn anything." Maybe because he had had no real childhood, he knew only how to work, and provided I was prepared to work, he gave me freedom to make my own decisions with whatever I chose to build or do as long as "it did not cost him anything."

I remember when Robert Tetreault came to work for us during the sugaring and harvesting seasons. He was 16 that first year and became my pal throughout the five years he worked with us on the farm. We played hours of hockey with little hockey sticks I had made and using a disk from a Crokinole game as a puck. I remember when he bought his first accordion and learned to play it. I was so impressed that Robert could yodel. I wanted him to teach me, but he told me "It just comes," so keep trying. So try I did, when operating the tractor in the fields where I hoped no one could hear me. I learned a lot from Robert during these years. When we were invited to his wedding, I was so excited that I was invited too, and of course they had country music, which I loved, and I was just learning to dance.

I could join the Cubs, the Scouts, or the Army reserves but if I wanted to play hockey or join in any sport, then no, my dad would not pay for the equipment or even drive me there. For my dad, that would be considered playing and there was no time for that. That was just his way, simple as that, and I accepted it, as it was to be.

My life was also one of work, but I was creative in the way I approached it. I was dreamer, always pretending and making whatever chore it was, fun to do. The manure fork became an automated piece of equipment, the shovel an integral part of a large construction machine. I learned to build and repair things. I loved animals and would create things to make the animals more comfortable. When I had friends up, we all became pretend people, becoming daredevils and performing great acts of bravery. Brooks become great rivers; ponds were lakes and seas to conquer; buildings became huge and complex cities. Damming up of the brook in springtime, watching the dams collapse with too much water, all became lessons in engineering. Our exploration of the meadows could turn us into great jungle explorers. The war escapades and the gun battles, all were planned and executed on the banks of the old gravel pit down in the meadow, even the old barn could become a subject of attack. We made wooden guns and threw rock grenades. The farm was my playground, the equipment became my toys, always handled with respect. Tools were to make things and the animals were to look after – memories I cherish to this day. My dad gave me freedom to do what I wanted to do; however, he also taught me that it came with consequences, so make wise choices. Perhaps his years in captivity dictated his desire to be free himself, to do what he wanted. It appeared he wanted to pass that on to me.

One day Uncle Fred asked my dad if he could dig some ponds on our farm as he was in the process of raising brook trout. Dad thought he was nuts; however, he could do it provided they were dug alongside the road in an area that was wet and unusable anyway. There were two additional caveats. Since he would be hiring a bulldozer and operator to dig the ponds, he was to complete our driveway so that the hill up to the house was less steep, and pull one of the old barns Dad was planning to tear down closer to the sugar bush so he could remake it into a sugar camp.

My uncle Fred had constructed a series of troughs in his basement, with a continuous flow of water at a specific temperature, complete with sand for spawning fish eggs. He monitored the water temperature daily and sure enough, the eggs hatched into about 10,000 tiny fry speckled trout. He fed them with ground beef from his meat market, and by the spring of 1952 they were ready to be placed into a pond. I had thought my Aunt Flo had to be pretty laid-back to have entertained any notion of having of 10,000 fish swimming in her basement.

Uncle Fred built three ponds on our farm, designed in such a way that he could open a fish gate and release the fish to the next pond as they grew larger. It became pretty exciting for me as I experienced a fish farm operation on our own farm, and he gave me the job of feeding them daily with the ground beef he provided. The deal for me in payment for my time was that once they became big enough to fish, I would have exclusive fishing rights on the lower pond. It was not long before they grew to about four inches in length when we transferred the first batch to the second pond, while Uncle Fred replaced them with another batch of "fingerlings" in the first pond.

Once the first batch of speckled trout became about six inches long, I was instructed to open the gates and release them into the third pond. At one point he had in excess of 30,000 fish in all three ponds, and by the fourth year, the lower pond was beginning to show fish about 12-14 inches in length. I was really liking the idea of this fish farming! Now I must mention that my Uncle Fred was an ardent fisherman as well as a hunter and everyone from far and wide knew it. After a while I noticed that when he went on his fishing trips, if he did not fare well, he would drop by to fill his baskets with fish from our ponds. I suspected that fish stories abounded around the region as to how Fred seemed to find the best fishing holes which he of course always kept secret. I would suggest that my cousins could pretty well count on my uncle always coming home with a full catch while others seemed to waste their time. His fishing prowess did not escape Wallace Boyd's attention. He and Lizzie lived across the road from our driveway, and when they would see my uncle drive in after a fishing day, Wallace would say to Lizzie, "I'll bet you a dollar to donuts Fred has had a bad fishing day."

These ponds gave me an opportunity to raise a flock of ducks, imagining in my mind that someday I might somehow compete with the famed Brome Lake duck farms, providing plump ducks to the restaurants, perhaps even a few fish as a bonus. After all, I thought ponds were not complete without ducks to keep the ponds clean of debris and especially blood suckers. A heavy rain one day prompted my flock of ducks to suddenly move themselves to the lawn, working their beaks in the grass. That was the day I was told that my job was to mow the lawns every week from now on. There was to be no duck poop, no different than chicken poop as far as my father was concerned, and he was not about to have it collecting on his boots, "thank you very much!"

By the fourth year the fish in the lower pond began spawning themselves, going up the spring-fed brook by the hundreds. We had an old cat that was toothless, but she knew how to fish, and it was not long before she discovered this phenomenon in the brook. From then on, we could expect fish for breakfast pretty much every day. She would suddenly arrive and drop the fish, still flipping, on the doorstep to the kitchen. She would repeat this until we felt we had enough for a good feed, and we would cut one up for her after which she would stop for the day. Unfortunately for me, or perhaps fortunate for Uncle Fred, the cat died the following year, so I took over my rightful task of fishing. I delighted in asking Irene if she would like fish for dinner. I would head down to the pond and, being creative, I made up the line with a series of six hooks. One cast, six fish, a great battle, and I had my catch for dinner in less than five minutes.

During my teen years I planned and hosted the Boy Scout camps in our meadow. Armand McBurney was the Scoutmaster, and he was the best. He would come every evening and examine the camp setup, the cooking arrangements and all we had built, the ropes we had tied – of course with proper knots – and the dam we had built on the river. At the end of camp week at our final nightly bonfire he awarded the earned badges. Our Scout camps were lively affairs and apparently the Scouts who attended never forgot them. I still get stories from Rodney Hurd that my bacon and eggs breakfast was the best. He said this was the first time he had experienced "deep fried" bacon, several pounds of bacon literally floating in the grease, and the eggs done the same way. Food for me was always the most important element in keeping the Scouts happy with what was being asked of them to do. We literally ran an "army" camp environment that they all loved.

I remember when we were still farming with horses and the small 1945 Ford tractor, still using basic hand-operated implements for the first few years. After hydro was expanded into the farming regions in 1952-54, Dad bought a 1956 International tractor that started the conversion to modern farm equipment, and the rest is history. The day he brought the tractor to the farm, Dad told me I was to operate it, maintain it and keep track of every expense to do with it, including the new "McKee harvester" and special hay wagon he had bought that was part of the haying equipment. When he bought a pail of grease in the spring, I was instructed I had to make that last for the year; so, one squirt per fitting, not two! Everything on the farm was to be accounted for, always! I learned from this experience, and perhaps it was Dad's way of teaching me how to run a business. I can assuredly say his style of "strict army freedom" also served me well throughout my own career over the years. My dad would often say, "If you cannot think on your feet, then you are not going to be worth much to anybody, so snap to it!"

I introduced my dog, Lassie, to riding on the tractor seat with me while we raked and loaded hay, ploughed, harrowed, logged, sugared, hayed, harvested, and even through threshing season. I trained her to herd cattle and to look after the cattle, horses and pigs, herding them in the right direction. All these jobs became great adventures for me in real time and I loved it.

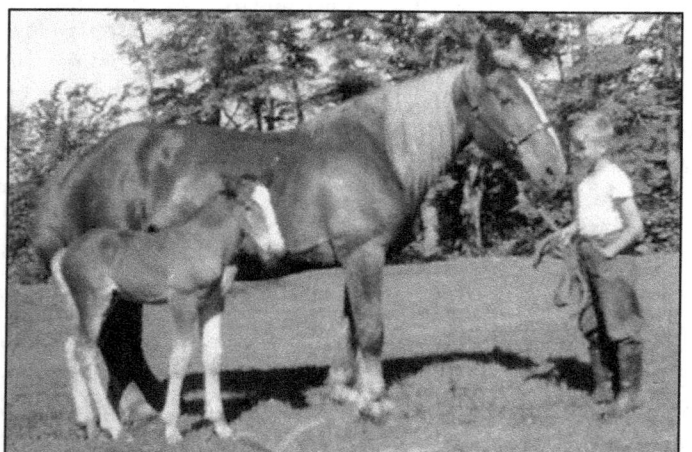

The author with new colt, Yankee and mother Dolly, 1950

I learned to ride bareback on my grandfather Gussie's old black mare, Dinah, and then on our Belgium workhorse, Yankee, that Dad raised from a colt. She was my Roy Rogers horse Trigger and I rode her everywhere on the farm. I learned to embrace change and thrive with it. "So many things to learn, so many discoveries to encounter; so many dreams to look forward to." I genuinely loved the farm life.

For winter fun, I built little plows that I attached to homemade sleds and pushed these, around clearing a path to the barns for my father. I remember waking up in the middle of the night, the wind blowing during a huge snowstorm and so for realism, I felt it absolutely necessary to bundle up and go out to plow, just as the grownups would have done. Irene was taken aback that I would just go out like that and, of course, my dad took a dim view of that idea, probably thinking "this too will pass."

This same winter Rodney Hillman was visiting his grandparents, John and Nellie Jones, who lived on the farm beside Wallace and Lizzie Boyd, across the road from our sugar camp. Over the winter, a huge drift of snow had accumulated between the barn and the Jones's house. Clearly, it became the perfect place for Rod and me to build a snow house. We dug way down in the snow, making a room. Then, to make things real, we commenced a tunnel into another room where we excavated the snow, and yet another tunnel out the other side. It involved a lot of work but was loads of fun because his sister, Judy, could never find us, so we were really happy with our progress. As the story goes, apparently one day in late March Nellie happened to be looking out her kitchen window, looking to see if John was heading out of the barn for breakfast after the morning chores. There he was, carrying two pails of milk, walking up the path when all of a sudden he disappeared – the two pails were sitting on each side of the path, but John was gone! Nellie could not believe her eyes . . . where did he go? John was always a practical joker himself, so Nellie was beside herself as to how he did it. John apparently appeared out of the side of the snowbank, picked up the two pails, and never disclosed to Nellie that he had fallen right through the snowbank to the room below that Rodney and I had cut out of the snowbank earlier that winter. Nellie always thought it was trick of John's until Rodney heard the story and knew immediately what had happened. Rodney, however, kept John's secret and never told his grandmother how his grandfather had disappeared that day. I would hazard a guess that we were lucky that John didn't break a leg when he fell through into the room below. John was always a good sport, though, and would always take our side on any adventure Rod and I might conjure up.

Noon hour at school was another experience for us kids who travelled by bus because we were not allowed to leave the school grounds at noon; only the in-town students were able to go home. Spring and fall would find us all out in the back field playing soccer, as we called it, some of the girls on the swings and teeter-totters, others with us in the game. There was an especially great wooden wheel thing (I don't remember what it was called) we would jump on after running along-side to get it spinning. It was like a merry-go-round, close to the ground with pipe bars to hang on to as it rotated. Much too dangerous for today's playgrounds. In our day there were no rules, no structure, no coach, just a general free-for-all. The town students envied us and would try to sneak in, just as much as we envied them that they could go to the restaurant and stores during this noon break. During the winter, however, we were the lucky ones, as we did not have to walk home in the cold for lunch. Instead so we listened to music and the girls taught us to dance. Audrey McCallum was great at playing the piano, so in grades 5 and 6 we learned how to rock 'n' roll and dance the two-step to country music.

"I remember all thru' the winter months for about two years, 1953-54, if someone was not on the piano then we played records every noon hour, and the girls taught the boys to dance in the Grade 5 classroom. We, of course hoped that it had some impact on how the guys danced. One day, in the spring of 1954, some of the students had been looking out the window upstairs toward the street and noticed a brown object hanging from the flagpole directly below the flag. It was pointed out to the teacher, who notified the principal, who in turn went investigating. The object turned out to be the suit jacket of the teacher, Miss Ursula Bozer, put there by the Pike twins. Last seen, the Pike boys were headed for the principal's office." *(Edna (Mogenson) Lowry)*

As was the custom among farmers, when a son turned 12 years old he was given a cow so he could begin starting his own herd of livestock. The idea was that when the son turned 21, he would already have a significant herd of his own. I was so proud of my first bull Hereford calf and cared for him with "extra" everything. He was groomed constantly and would one day be a show winner, as far as I was concerned. In my mind I was on the way to becoming a rancher and I would need to learn how to protect my herd. I studied every kind of disease that might affect my herd of two, which feed would produce the best meat, what markings would produce a show animal, all things that preoccupied my mind while I was sitting in a classroom trying to concentrate on the most boring books one could imagine.

My first purebred Hereford bull calf, sired by Wesley, our new Hereford bull

I remember watching the first NHL hockey game that was televised, on October 11, 1952. Our neighbours, Wallace and Lizzie Boyd, were one of the first families in Maple Leaf to buy a television, and I was invited to their house to watch the Montreal Canadiens take on the Toronto Maple Leafs. The picture was so snowy that we could not see the puck at any time throughout the game. Wallace would go up into his shed loft and crank the antenna, calling to us to see if the picture was any clearer. Of course, the minute he took his hands off the crank, the picture would fade again. Wallace spent most of the game up in the attic trying to adjust the antenna. While Wallace was up working the antenna, Lizzie would fix up bowls of ice cream and put out cookies, which got my immediate attention, so forget the game, Wallace! These television evenings were a great time for me during the early 1950s, carefully deciding on the best evenings that my favourite shows would be on so as not to wear out my welcome.

The photograph on the following page, taken in the early 1950s, shows an idealist life as I looked forward each year to a visit from the Lawson family from Maryland in the U.S. Terry and Mary (Hurd) Lawson were two of my favourite cousins; their visits were probably not dissimilar to the visits of her parents and their parents before them when they came to visit our ancestors in past years. My grandfather Gussie's old horse, Dinah, that I am lying on in the picture, was my cohort, "my bicycle" and my transportation everywhere. Dinah played an important role with the other horses in the many wild west escapades we conducted in the barnyard and down in the meadow with many of my school chums on Sundays.

L-R: horses Jackie and Yankee; cousins Terry and Mary Lawson; the author lying on Dinah

As I entered my early teens, I soon came to realize that I loved building and fixing things and the car was no exception. We now had a 1949 torpedo-back Chevrolet that was dented and rusting. I had watched Clifford "Tiffy" Morrison repairing and doing bodywork in Tommy French's garage in Sawyerville. I spent most of my lunch hours, whenever I could, in that garage, right beside the school. Tiffy gave me body filler, so I went to work on Dad's car, attempting to emulate what I saw Tiffy do. The rocker panel was completely rusted out, so I fitted in a two-by-four of wood and plastered body filler everywhere. I learned quickly that this body filler had to be sanded and not having a power sander meant hours of hand sanding, which taught me to be much more careful on the amount of body filler to use. Dad was not impressed, however, so Tiffy helped me out with a final sanding and painting, which I had to pay for, of course. It took me a long time to pay my dad back from my allowance of $5 a week. I grew to love cars, however, and imagined that when I would have one of my own I would customize it just like the Barris Brothers in California did. I was not to know at that time that I would embark on a career in the automotive industry, which would take me all over the world. Years later I got to meet the famous Bob Barris in California at a car rally where he had on display the Batmobile he had built for the TV show.

During my last few years at school I was the only one wearing "desert boots." These suede leather shoes were not available to purchase locally; my mother had sent them to me from Toronto. I had worn them to the point of replacement so she sent me another pair. I decided one day to dye the old shoes blue ("Elvis's blue suede shoes") using Irene's food dye. I did not know that when it rained, the blue dye "spotted" and kind of disappeared. Barry Berwick, however, really wanted these boots, so I made a deal for a banty rooster and three banty hens which he offered in trade. Understanding my dad's dislike for chickens of any sort, I knew they would likely have short lives. I smuggled them home in a burlap bag in the trunk of the car and put them in the barn with the ducks while I made a deal with Irene to perhaps cook them for dinner one day . . . soon! Their lives were to be shorter than I had anticipated. The discovery took place the very next morning when my dad opened the barn door and the sunshine permeated the dark stable. The rooster decided it was appropriate to announce the dawn of a new day and "crowed." Things became tense in the barn until I mentioned I was planning a surprise dinner of fresh chicken for Irene. Irene, always a good sport, was prepared to cook them immediately and so I was proud to announce to my dad that we would be having four succulent roasted chickens for dinner. What Barry neglected to tell me was that these birds were probably as old as he was. We sat down for dinner in anticipation, however they were so tough that we could not eat them, and my dad just looked at me . . . he didn't need to say anything . . . I just knew what he was thinking, that he was glad we hadn't wasted any grain to fatten them up.

Col. Wells Bishop (Hurd military archives)

At 16 I joined the reserve army. This was a positive move in my dad's view, but for me it was a way to pay Tiffy for the car work. I ended up really enjoying this venture and remember the best part of this experience was the week-long exercises at Colonel Wells Bishop's farm at North River. Another amazing thing about Wells was how he found the time to arrange the most complex training maneuvers around his farm that one could even imagine. I remember many other first trainees coming from all over the province, staying at the farm which was equipped with hundreds of bunks and a large cookhouse. He had a small airstrip in one of the fields where people flew in from Sherbrooke to participate in the fish and game club which he also operated, and so this airstrip became part of the army operations. There were army tanks, personnel carriers, jeeps, and wireless equipment to work with.

The week-long learning process was both immense and intense. Col. Bishop arranged us into several platoons, each assigned to carry out specific instructions and maneuvers. We had two days of intense instructional teaching at the barracks, each platoon being assigned certain target routes, and all to leave the base in different directions and at different times. We had assigned captains, lieutenants, corporals and platoon leaders complementing the riflemen. This was survival at its best; we were loaded down with perhaps a hundred pounds of equipment, knapsacks with food for three to four days, rifles, binoculars, gunny sacks – all the normal fare of a live-war exercise. Big four-wheel army trucks carried tents and other equipment for staying overnight, some trucks carrying the platoons as well.

This exercise was not running around in the fields, because if you were in a field, you were exposed and so the trails were through dense woods, going through bogs, crossing the river several times, and climbing up huge hills. This was all part of the training and so each platoon had to make decisions as to how they might get across a bog or around a hill, all a part of making the right decisions.

Some of us were assigned forays in cognizance for covert operations and if we read the instructions and mapping incorrectly, we might find ourselves coming in the crosshairs of another platoon.

North River showing the huge gravel riverbank on Wells Bishop's farm where all simulated battles ended (photo by Sandra Hurd)

Towards the end of the week all platoons arrived at the same spot where the enemy was located, and the firing began – all aimed at a large bank of gravel some 60-70 feet high on the curve of the river. The tanks and guns were firing blanks, of course, but the noise was the same as the real thing.

The second year for me was the best, only in that I knew what the layout was going to be and so Col. Bishop assigned me as reconnaissance of operations in the little two-seater plane complete with army binoculars, where I was put in charge of reporting how platoon operations were playing out on the ground, who was getting lost and which platoons needed to change course for interception – all part of the operation. When the exercises ended on Sunday morning at the end of the week, a debriefing took place where we all had to give our accounts as to what mistakes were made and how we might improve.

This was an experience one never forgets, and especially for me, as I was fully engrossed, imagining I was taking part in a full-fledged war. When I was 18 I had the opportunity to go for training at the Army training camp in Farnham, Que., for a week. I anticipated some real training maneuvers, because this in my mind would be training with the "big boys." Wrong! We learned to march, polish our boots, clean our guns, make our beds just so, and muster at the crack of dawn for parade duty. The food was the only highlight of that trip, and I realized just how much Col. Bishop had put into his training sessions and contributed in his own way to the training of our troops. Like all the young recruits at his training camp, I respected and loved Col. Wells Bishop and am forever grateful for how he trained and treated his men, always with a firm hand but with absolute fairness and a positive attitude, and always with a twinkle in his eye. Apparently the training camp run by Col. Bishop was unauthorized by his superiors, and my own uncle, Brigadier John Wood, was dispatched to disband the operation as it was perceived that Wells had been using army equipment and government gas for the general operation of his farm. I admit I do remember using a jeep to pull the hay rake a few times and an army truck to haul some hay, but in my view we were getting the land cleared up in preparation for the coming week of training.

I remember one summer when my dad told me to take the McKee harvester to Wells's farm and help him finish his haying, simply because Wells was so busy he had fallen behind in getting it done. This is what neighbours and friends did in the countryside for each other. I also remember the Vaillancourt family coming to help us with our haying during a particularly wet summer when we were behind in our harvest.

During my last years on the farm, I came to realize that I loved farming, but I also loved building and enjoyed working on cars. I also realized that I needed to experience something different to find my own way in life. My dad never encouraged me to take over the farm. Perhaps he sensed we had such different views on how the farm should be run, or perhaps he just wanted me to experience opportunities elsewhere and see a different world. I was an opportunist, a dreamer who embraced change, who liked things to look nice; Dad never cared how something looked, so long as it worked. I came to realize, during the two years after completing high school when I worked with him, that the farm would never be an option for me – which deeply disappointed me.

In the fall of 1961 an opportunity presented itself: join my friends Charlie Twyman and Johnny Olsson, who were going to Toronto to find work with a Mr. Frank Jones (who had lived in Sawyerville). I jumped at the chance, ready to take on this new adventure. After a week of travelling beyond Toronto, visiting with other friends who had moved to Hamilton, both Charlie and Johnny decided to return home, but I had remembered my dad's words, "Try it." So, try it I would; I literally dumped myself unannounced at my mother's home in Toronto, bunking in with my brother Jim, determined to stay. My mother was rather taken aback; she was one who always had to plan things ahead, so my sudden arrival was not necessarily appropriate in her view, especially with no job. How was a farm boy going to find a job in Toronto? Missing the farm and the community in which I grew up was the largest hurdle I had to face, but I knew I would have to face it.

After a short stint working in retail to pay for my formal education in automotive service, I began a career in the automotive business as a service centre manager. I later graduated to wholesale, manufacturing, purchasing, and marketing, ending my career in senior executive positions in the corporate automotive field of business. These opportunities would not have been possible had I not had the experience of growing up in such a diverse atmosphere of trust, integrity, creativity, and general know-how, that I learned on the farm in Newport working with my dad and with many of our neighbours.

With each opportunity I never forgot my dad's words "just try it." These words alone gave me the impetus which propelled me towards many opportunities while conducting business throughout the world and have stuck with me for over 40 years. I was indeed fortunate to have had many people through the years who believed in me enough to entrust their futures with me in the development of new concepts that embraced change in the marketplace. I was fortunate that my career took me on journeys and adventures to many countries in the world; my job to source new business opportunities, from conceptual, to product, to systems and all while working in a corporate business environment which was where I wanted to be.

The road to North River via Maple Leaf, off Route 210, pictured here in 2019 but not much different from the 1950s (photo by Sandra Hurd)

My roots in Newport and the many inspiring people who lived there continue to inspire me, and I am forever grateful to have grown up there knowing that I would not have had the life I did were it not for my experiences of those days long ago.

My wife Sandra's family was also rooted in the Eastern Townships; our ancestors interconnected through settling the Townships. Our family and work cultures were very similar. Sandra's background allowed her to explore the corporate world in high profile roles where she interacted collegially with presidents and senior-level executives both in large corporate settings and in privately held companies. I also watched her make choices the way many women did in the 1960s, trying to reconcile her identity as an independent, ambitious professional, yet with a desire to mother our two daughters with the same level of care and attentiveness that her mother had given her and her siblings. Sandra took a leave from her professional career in the early years while our daughters were growing up, volunteering with school activities and field trips. Later, on her own terms, she rejoined the corporate world she loved. She enjoyed this opportunity to develop a strong network of colleagues. She also was able to weave into her schedules the flexibility she sought to devote herself to "family life." My career in the automotive field, with its long absences from home, made it challenging for her to decide whether or not to pursue opportunities that interested her but may have demanded too much time away from the girls. She was able to manage the push and pull of everyday life and, amidst it all, was able to join me on occasion for business travel to the U.S. and the Pacific Rim. She also offered to help me plan the Canada Night events in Las Vegas for the automotive trade shows, working with the companies I was involved in. Just when she thought she would retire, she just could not resist a contract to work with a principal at the University of Toronto – "just to diversify" her experience from corporate to education. Multi-tasking was an understatement. I feel fortunate to have a partner who generated and continues to generate such a significant impact and difference in our family lives; a role she handles with enthusiasm. We are also immensely proud of our two daughters individually; Wendy and Joanne who have each handled their own lives and careers with integrity and accomplishment. Joanne, along with our son-in-law, David Morris, have also given us the pleasure of two granddaughters, Vanessa and Dayna.

We were part of the first generation to experience the juggling of a two-parent working household while raising our children. I believe it would be fair to say that the farming families had been working this way for many decades, and for those families it was life as usual, but in urban environments this notion was only beginning to be the new normal in the 1960s and '70s.

We hope we are the last generation in this era that can remember our parents climbing out of the depression and that can perhaps vaguely remember the impact of a world at war – which rattled the structure of our daily lives for several years. We are hopefully the last to remember our parents telling us about the ration books for everything from gas to sugar to shoes to stoves. We remember them saving tin foil and pouring fat into tin cans; even waxed paper was saved from the cereal boxes. We remember grieving neighbours who never forgot their sons who died in World War II and did not come home while some of us saw our fathers come home from the war and begin to build their lives all over again. The ongoing skirmishes taking place around the globe are presenting similar circumstances to the next generations.

We are the last generation to spend childhood without television; instead, we listened to the radio and used our imaginations. With no TV until the 1950s, we spent our childhood playing outside. The lack of television in our early years meant we had little real understanding of what the world was like. We would sometimes be treated with movies at the IOOF Hall in Sawyerville, which gave us newsreels sandwiched between westerns and cartoons. Telephones were one to a house, hung on the wall in the kitchen (no one was concerned about privacy), and often with the circuit shared by several households (party lines). Typewriters were driven by pounding fingers, throwing back the carriage, carbon paper, and changing the ribbon.

Newspapers and magazines were written for adults and the news was broadcast on the radio in the evening. As we grew up, the country was exploding with growth. The radio network expanded from three stations to thousands. Our parents were suddenly free from the confines of the Great Depression and World War II, and they threw themselves into exploring opportunities they had never imagined. This was also a time when men stood up when a woman left the table and took off their hats when eating a meal and our mothers were still making donuts every week for us to dip into maple syrup.

The government gave returning veterans the means to get farm loans which fanned an agricultural boom. Pent-up demand for new products coupled with new instalment payment plans opened many factories for work. New highways brought jobs, mobility and more cars. The veterans joined civic clubs and became active in politics and ran to the other side of the car to open the car doors for the ladies.

We were not neglected; we did not wear watches or carry cellphones; we were not like any of today's all-consuming "helicopter" families. My friends who lived in town played outside until the streetlights came on, which indicated it was time to go home. We entered a world of overflowing plenty and opportunity; a world where we were welcomed, enjoyed ourselves and felt secure in our future although depression and poverty were deeply remembered just by the way we lived. Polio was still around and a crippler that we children all feared.

We came of age in the 1950s and 1960s when we looked forward to viewing the new models of cars, painted in two-tone colours, unveiled each November at the showrooms where everyone flocked. And later, when TV became the place to see them on the Ed Sullivan show broadcast out of New York. We are the last generation to experience an interlude when there were no perceived major threats to our homeland. The Second World War was long over, and the Cold War, terrorism, global warming, and perpetual economic insecurity would be yet to haunt life with unease. Only our generation can remember both a time of war and insecurity and yet experience a time when our world became secure and full of bright promise and plenty.

All of us who were a part of Newport Township history should consider ourselves privileged to have experienced our own "lives lived" in the Eastern Townships, a place steeped in an abundance of historical background; much of which has been kept and treasured by so many families. We can be proud of the rich heritage we have inherited.

One can become emotional when speaking of our youth simply because we become and feel always connected to places where we spent our young years growing up. For me, because of the war, it was only a short 14 years that I actually lived there, and yet it seemed like a lifetime. This our heritage. This is who we are.

Frederick Edmund [11] *Hurd*

Newport Township, looking toward Ditton Township and Megantic Mountains, 2019 (photo by Sandra Hurd)

Epilogue

To quote George Orwell: "The most effective way to destroy people is to obliterate their own understanding of their history." The reason for having written this book is to preserve a small piece of our English Canadian history. It is an effort to regain part of this history describing how these settlers lived their lives which might have become erased through time. In some instances, political and military issues needed to be included to support and drive the narrative.

Earlier I referred to a mystery surrounding the existence of a "hidden history" of Newport, 1791-1814. To my knowledge, the Heard/Hurd archives I had inherited, including *The Firfh Records of Newport Township of 1800*, had been kept hidden; they had not been shared, nor was their existence known by any other historical archives. These beliefs were also substantiated by further research drawn from information outlined in the book *History of Compton County* by L. S. Channell, published in 1896, that states there were "no official records known for the Township of Newport until 1841 when the Government established Municipal Councils."

Therefore, I found it somewhat of a mystery to discover that the existence of such records was referred to in the article "The fostering care of Government: Lord Dalhousie's 1821 Survey of the Eastern Townships," inferring that of all the townships, "Town minutes have been found only for Newport Township, and they end in 1814." *(Professor J. I. Little, "State and Society in Transition: The Politics of Institutional Reform in the Eastern Townships, 1838-1852," pp. 119-120, published in 1997)*

How was it, then, that Professor Jack Little was able to write about history that could only be substantiated by these ancestral records when it was my understanding that the documentation in question had been kept within our family archives and, to my knowledge, had not been publicly shared? How could Prof. Little have known about these records from 1792 to 1814 that had been kept hidden?

In a recent conversation with Prof. Little, he confirmed that he indeed had been invited to read the contents of Newport's first records on a visit with my father, Lionel Hurd, many years ago at the Compton County Museum when Jack was writing his book – hence his notation that these records actually did exist. No copy of the book was made, but Prof. Little was indeed able to substantiate the existence of the records and through his own research was able to make the statement in his book that "no other Township had kept Records except for the Township of Newport." Professor Little referred to the book in question as the *Minute Book of Newport*.

The following paragraphs are direct quotes or paraphrased excerpts from *"The fostering care of Government": Lord Dalhousie's 1821 Survey of the Eastern Townships* by Prof. J. I. Little, Department of History, Simon Fraser University, Burnaby, B.C.:

> Prior to 1829, when the Eastern Townships region of Lower Canada was finally granted its own electoral constituencies, petitions were virtually the only means of expressing popular will. Numerous petitions from the largely American settlers of the region, however, met with a deaf ear in the Legislative Assembly as French-speaking members did not want to facilitate English Protestant settlement in the colony. A survey, instigated by Governor-General Lord Dalhousie in 1821, provided opportunity for selected local spokesmen to express their views but the survey was never published. It does, however, offer additional insight into how and why this borderland between New England's northern boundary and Lower Canada's seigneurial zone remained a settlement whose social institutions were still underdeveloped nearly 30 years after it had first been opened to colonization. *(ref.: Prof. J. I. Little)*

> The unofficially recognized leader and associates system under which Crown land was initially granted beginning in 1792 had been designed to establish a basic economic infrastructure for each township – with the township "leader" and his financial backers being compensated with much of the land. The result, however, was that large tracts of land fell into the hands of absentee speculators with connections to the government.

The Yankee settlers had a resourceful and independent outlook that resisted outside interference and the centralization of authority, but they did petition the government for road subsidies that would provide access to external markets and they did demand institutions of local regulation and governance. When Lord Dalhousie was appointed Governor-in-Chief of British North America in 1820, in his Throne Speech he advocated reforms that would remove obstacles to these settlements; "careful not to alienate the French-Canadian majority in the Legislative Assembly, adding that he was aware that Lower Canada possesses in itself an abundant population to settle these waste lands as yet unconceded seigniorial territories." He recommended the construction of Catholic churches and access roads as other inducements to colonize the townships.

The French-speaking MLAs had turned a deaf ear to numerous petitions from the English-Protestant settlement in the colony, yet they were concerned that the St. Lawrence seigneuries were becoming overcrowded.

Colonel Edmund[5] Heard had originally applied as an Associate in the original application for the Township of Newport submitted by the Leader of this group, Stephen Williams of Danby, Vt. Williams, however, neglected to come forth on the claim and so it was petitioned directly by Col. Edmund[5] Heard as Leader in 1797. This first application by Williams may have been applied for simply as a speculator with no intention of settling the lands. Although the 1844 census recorded over 40% of the Eastern Townships settlers as non-proprietors, most of whom were doubtless squatters, there were no land riots in this region and this was why Col. Edmund[5] Heard was so insistent that his Associates, including his own family, settle on the granted properties. *(J. I. Little, The fostering care of Government)*

This explains why when the government of the day began a system of registration for their lands as detailed in the Newport Records, based on Massachusetts law, Col. Edmund[5] Heard initiated a meeting to address the subject and with Captain Samuel[6] Heard as Newport Clerk, they recorded as follows: Article 2, That each settler shall have sufficient voucher and taketh up any lot of land in said Township to have a Certificate and payment registered with the clerk, and such Certificate shall be allowed to be a sufficient security against any depredations committee by any other person. Signed by Samuel Heard, William Hudson, and John Lebourveau, Committee. Recorded from the meeting of September 1799, convened at the home of Asa Waters.

After Col. Edmund[5] Heard and his Associates had been issued grants and were self-governing, times were still uneasy while the settlers maintained the official records of settling their homesteads and building roads, bridges, a mill and a school. Prior to the War of 1812 with the newly formed United States of America, and with the government in Lower Canada still unstable, the settlers' livelihoods were becoming increasingly uncertain. They could see that the French were pressuring from the north, the Americans pressuring from the south, and the First Nations were choosing sides with one or the other, with events on both sides causing great concern. They still harboured many memories of their lives back in the New England Colonies when the winds of change began to occur with families choosing sides, and that once again they might perhaps find themselves sitting on the wrong side of the fence. One might wonder why *The Firfh Records of Newport Township of 1800* abruptly stopped in 1814. There is a reasonable amount of evidence to suggest that they stopped recording and hid these records so they would retain some documentation as to their legal rights to the lands in Newport they had worked so hard to obtain. Their memories were still vivid, their resolve still raw from the ravaging and burning of their homes and papers destroyed back in the New England Colonies. They had lost all they owned, their families destitute, some resorting to leading a clandestine existence to survive, as did Col. Edmund[5] Heard, able to hang on to their holdings for a while.

I could now verify that certain facts were generally known, such as the arrival of Col. Edmund[5] Heard with Capt. Josiah Sawyer, based on other references from adjoining townships. These specific additional references that were associated with work that had been done, were recorded later in the *History of Compton County*, by L. S. Channell in 1896, sources from other records pertaining to adjacent townships, and were not based on *The Firfh Records of Newport Township of 1800*. Activities such as the roads to and from Newport to Nicolet and portaging on the south shore to the Three Rivers crossing were common knowledge associated with the neighbouring townships. Without this documented *Firfh Records of Newport* substantiating a trove of raw historical information of associated facts of Newport's earliest settlers in handwritten prose, the specifics surrounding settlement of Newport would not have been known – hidden history indeed.

Epilogue

The last entry in the book was made by David Metcalf, Newport Clerk, dated September 12, 1814. The last page has a series of entries by David Metcalf noting his own family's births and deaths from 1801 to his daughter's death in October 1816, after which David Metcalf left Newport and returned to the United States. The Minute Book was left in the care of Capt. Edmund[6] Heard.

Col. Edmund[5] Heard died in February 1814. A year later, in May 1815, his son Capt. Samuel[6] Heard, former clerk of Newport, drowned. This left Col. Edmund[5] Heard's eldest son, Capt. Edmund[6] Heard, heir of the properties in Newport and custodian of the Associates' property registrations. The author suggests that the *Minute Book* references, and all the supporting documentation, letters and property references were kept by Edmund[6], simply because he too was witness to the loss of their lands and records in the New England Colonies. Being a military man and of similar character and background as his father, it would not have been unusual that Edmund[6] would have safeguarded these records. With the government in Lower Canada still unstable and a threat beginning to manifest from the Patriots to the south, these records may have been the only reference they would have to challenge ownership of the lands in Newport. The author suggests, based on hundreds of additional and subsequent documents in the Ancestral Heard/Hurd Collection, that this assumption is correct. With more government control and interference in the affairs of Newport, perhaps there was no longer a need for their own records to continue and so the entries to the *Minute Book* ceased in 1814, but recordings continued in their letters and other documents. The fact also remains that both men who had been driving forces to continue the process of "official minutes" were dead after 1814, and so no surprise that the minutes ended abruptly, as stated in a note to the author from Prof. Little. This explains the mystery of the hidden records of Newport.

The historical events and characters framing the story are true, including the hardships, anxieties, expectations, and fears; all documented history expressed by them in their records, diaries and personal letters. The author's references to the call to arms, skirmishes, and wars are indeed all part of the story but placed more as bookmarks in time, discussed more in the context of how they affected our ancestors' lives, rather than to focus on the events themselves.

There was indeed a nostalgic longing for these early settlers to hear from those who were still living in the New England states. Those they had left behind also had a genuine concern as to how the settlers were managing on their new land, the "waste lands of Lower Canada." The settlers' children were also developing their own lives on what they considered their own land, so they became part of the culture and the land itself lived within them.

My own familiarity with the geography of Newport helped to shape the storytelling as well. The many submissions from our extended family and other descendant families have greatly enhanced the contents. Without the documentation and immense amount of historical material my family had passed down over decades, the inspiration to write this story would/could perhaps never have happened.

In December 2019 I donated a copy of the 76-page document *Newport first Records, 1800* to the Municipality of Newport archives in Island Brook.

***

Following are the names of many Newport residents, from the first group of Associate settlers in the late 1700s to the mid-20th century, i.e., late 1950s and early 1960s, all of whom have left "footprints" into and within Newport Township. Most descendants of the early settlers are buried in Newport Township's Maple Leaf or Grove Hill cemeteries, or, in Eaton Township's Cookshire or Eaton cemeteries. Many are Heard/Hurd family descendants.

Three families of Hurds are direct descendants of both Colonel Edmund[5] Heard and Captain Josiah[4] Sawyer.
- They are Edmund[10] Lionel Hurd, Frederick Karl Hurd and Arthur Haskell Hurd. Their common ancestor is John Bennett[7] Hurd, who married Polly Sawyer, a granddaughter of Capt. Josiah[4] Sawyer.

The following families are direct descendants of Edmund[5], Edmund[4], Edmund[3], Edmund[2], and Luke[1] of Ipswich, Mass.[4]:
- Heard/Hurd families who moved to Newport, 1793-98: Edmund[5], William[5], Edmund[6], Samuel[6] and Hannah.[6]

- Those who were born and raised in Newport, 1806-1940: John B.[7], Tyler[7] W., Luke[7], Sarah[7], Samuel[7] A, Mary Maria[8], Lucy Minerva[8], Matilda Rosetta[8], Edmund Haskell[8], Abigail Susanna[8], Augustus[8], Catherine Jennete[8], Gratia A.[8], Lucy Gibson[8], Samuel[8] Newell, George Gibson[8], Frederick Augustine[8], Laura Abilgail[9], Mary Maria[9], Edith A.[9], Augustus Frederick[9], Alonzo George[9], Julia Lois[9], Kate Marie[9], Florence Agnes[9], Flora N.[10], Edmund[10] Lionel, Frederick[10] Karl, Arthur Haskell[10], George[10] Robinson, Bertha Evelyn[10], Eric James[10], and Frederick Edmund.[11] All are descendants of the Heard/Hurds of Ipswich, Mass., and Newport Township, Lower Canada.
- Hurd families who were born and/or raised in Eaton Township or elsewhere, 1943-1955: Judith Carol[11], John Allan[11], Peter Donald[11], Elizabeth Jean[11], Malcolm Edward[11], Allan Grant[11], Cynthia Doris[11], Deanna Evelyn[11], Gillian Maureen[11], James Rodney[11], Keith William[11], Deborah F.[11], and Thomas E.[11]. The "second" French families of Newport were Eric G. R., Barbara Ann, and Susan J.

Newport families who have forged an intimate connection to their land, passed it along to their children which continued for many generations:[4]
- Direct descendants of the Heard/Hurd families of Ipswich who settled in Newport, include surnames from the marriages of the female lineage of Newport's Heard/Hurd families: Alger, Anderson, Arnot, Bartlett, Beecher, Bennett, Berwick, Blair, Bowker, Brown, Cable, Chaddock, Clout, Clovis, Cooper, Deller, Doherty, Draper, Drew, Elias, Farnsworth, Flaws, Forgrave, French (two families), Frasier/Fraser, Gill, Goodenough, Hamilton, Hornby, Hunt, Hurd, Joliffe, Jones, Jordan, Kinghorn, Lafleur, Lawson, Leggett, Lepitre, Lindsay, Lothrop, McCurdy, Middlemiss, Mitchell, Morris, Nourse, Nugent, Pagot, Parker, Pehlemann, Planche, Prah, Rand, Richardson, Riddell, Rivers, Rugg, Rutherford, Sanaster, Seale, Stevenson, Swail, Tannahill, Willard, Wilford, Williams.

Many unrelated families were an integral part of and played an important role in the overall growth and development of Newport Township.
- These are families who settled and whose footprints are indelibly entrenched in Newport. They were/are: Alden, Austin, Bailey, Banks, Batley, Beaman, Bishop, Boutin, Bowen, Boyd, Buchanan, Buck, Burns, Buttemer, Byrnes, Cairns, Carr, Charpentier, Christie, Clark, Coates, Cote, Crawford, Cyr, Darker, Dawson, Dempsey, Desruisseaux, Dorman, Dougherty, Drolet, Drouin, Dunsmore, Dutton, Eastman, Ewing, Fallon, Faulkner, Fisher, Fortier, French[1], Gagne, George, Giroux, Goodenough, Graham, Grapes, Guertin, Hammond, Harbinson, Harvey, Head, Herrings, Hodge, Holbrook, Hudson, Jones, Kerr, Lake, Lapointe, Laroche, Latimer, Lawrence, Learned, Lebourveau, Leroux, Lowry, Lister, Lizotte, Lord, Loveland, Lyon, Malloy, Martin, Maynard, McCallum, McCloud, McCormack, McKeage, McLeod, McNab, McNaughton, McVetty, Metcalf, Millar, Mogensen, Montgomery, Morgan, Morrison, Munn, Neilson, Newman, Nugent, Painter, Parker, Parsons, Prince, Redman, Reeves, Rouleau, Rutherford, Scholes, Shaw, Spaulding, Speck, Stanley, Statton, Stevenson, Stone, Stronach, Sunbury, Sylvester, Taylor, Tetreault, Theroux, Thompson, Todd, Trombley, Vaillancourt, Warburton, Westgate, Weir, Wilford, Williams, Wood(s), and more.

The lives of those families included in this book are typical and representative of most of our ancestors' lives. There are many names that have not appeared in this story. One should not conclude that their lives and the lives of any of their ancestors were unimportant. They are every bit as entitled to be proud of their heritage in the building of Newport Township as any other.

Appendix: Genealogy Charts

Based on material graciously provided by the Rev. Edward Hanson whose thesis was "John Heard of Ipswich, Mass."

*Author's Note: All Heard/Hurd and family connections by marriage, those who were born in Newport and stayed in Newport are identified in **bold**. The families listed are in sequential order as they appear in the book; depending on their age some may appear in several chapters as they progressed through their lives lived. Lineage runs from Luke^1 Heard, Edmund^1, Edmund^2, Edmund^3, Edmund^4 and Colonel Edmund^5 Heard, first of the Heard settlers in Newport. Edmund^6 and Edmund^7 Heard were born in the New England states but raised in Newport.*

Lineage: Colonel Edmund^5 Heard   1743-1814

Married 1. Sarah Willington in 1765

1. Sarah 1766-1849 — Married J. Parmenter. Stayed in the U.S.
2. **Edmund^6 1768-1830** — **Married Lucy Bennett in Lancaster, Mass. Settled in Newport.**
3. Luke^6 1770-1808 — Married 1. Mary (Polly) Emmerton.
   Married 2. Hannah Hanover.

Edmund^6 Heard moved from Lancaster, Mass. to Holden, Mass., then to Newport.
Luke drowned in Kennebunk, Me., but had intended to move to Newport with his family.

Married 2. Elizabeth Andrews in 1772

4. **Samuel^6 1773-1815** — Married Miriam Gibbs. Settled in **Newport.**
5. Hannah 1775-1831 — Married William **Bernard.** Moved to the U.S.

Samuel^6 and his sister Hannah moved to Newport with their father Edmund^5. Samuel married in the U.S., returned to Newport, and settled with his family. Samuel^6 drowned at Brompton Falls, Lower Canada, in 1815.

***

Eaton Township first settler, Sawyer families

Lineage: Son of Captain Ephraim^3 Sawyer of Grand Isle, Vt.

Captain Josiah^4 Sawyer   1757-1837
Married Susanna Green, circa 1782-3

1. Peter Green 1783-1867 — Married Polly Hall in 1803. Settled in **Newport,** then Eaton.
2. Josiah^5 1786-1839 — Married Nancy Rice. Settled in Eaton Twp.
3. Susanna 1786-1861 — Married James **Lobdell.** Settled in Eaton Twp.
4. John 1788-1869 — Married Theodotia Laberee. Settled in Eaton Twp.
5. Polly 1792-1846 — Married Nathanial **Currier.** Settled in Eaton Twp.
6. Abigail 1795-1885 — Married Asa **Alger** in 1818. Settled in Eaton Twp.
7. Rufus^5 1798-1874 — Married Ruth Alger in 1823. Settled in Eaton Twp.

Note: Polly was the baby Susanna carried with her on horseback to Eaton Township.

***

"The accident of birth determines whether we are female or male, free or not free, Protestant, Jewish, Buddhist, Muslin or Atheist, imprisoned in a refugee camp, or Canadian. Wherever we find ourselves drawing first breath opens a lifetime tug of war between that fickle finger of fate and personal will." (J. Patrick Boyer, author, columnist, and former MP)

***

William Heard, first settler family of Newport, brother of Colonel Edmund⁵ Heard

William⁵ Heard   1755-1829

Married 1. Betsey Dix, born in 1783 in Holden, Mass. Died 1794.
Children born in the New England Colonies, U.S.

1.	Thomas 1784-1863	Married. Returned to the U.S.
2.	Eunice 1785-1866	Married Issac B. **Burnham**. Settled in Melbourne, L.C.
3.	William 1788-1850	Married. Returned to the U.S.
4.	Betsey 1789-1869	Married. Returned to the U.S.
5.	Nancy 1791-1855	Married Ezra **Brainerd**. Settled in Melbourne, L.C.
6.	Sally 1793-1877	Married. Resided in Melbourne, LC.

Married 2. Thirza Z. Williams in 1797 in Northumberland, N.H.
Children born in Newport, Lower Canada

7.	Wilder 1798-1829	*Unknown.*
8.	Zilpha 1801-1823	Died young.
9.	Edmund 1803-1868	Married Miss Spaulding. Settled in Barnston, L.C.
10.	Anna (twin) 1805-1828	Married Lyman **Jones**. Anna died young.
11.	Fanny (twin) 1805	Died in childbirth.
12.	Chester 1807-1888	Married Hannah Carr. Moved to North Hatley. Ordained.
13.	Jeremiah "Jerry" E. 1809-1871	Married Abigail Stearns. Settled in Barnston, L.C
14.	Stratira P. 1812-1892	Married Allen **Sweetland**. Moved to Wisconsin, U.S.
15.	Lois 1814-1901	Married George **James**. Moved to Bradford, Vt., U.S. Descendants: Chatfield, and Hastings.

***

Lineage: Colonel **Edmund⁵** Heard

Captain Edmund⁶ Heard   1768-1830

Married Lucy Bennett 1792. Three children died as infants
Children born in Lancaster, New England Colonies:

1.	Edmund⁷ 1795-1852	Married 1. Mary Willard. Married 2. Abigail Haskell. Lived in **Newport.**
2.	John Bennett⁷ 1797-1848	Married Polly Sawyer (*granddaughter of Captain Josiah⁵*). **Newport.**
3.	Lucy 1801-1869	Married George **Gibson**. Moved to Melbourne, L.C.
4.	Luke⁷ 1801-1873	Married Persis Hubbard. Lived in **Newport.**

Children born in Newport, Lower Canada:

5.	Sarah 1803-1865	Married Gardner **Bartlett**. Moved to Illinois, U.S.
6.	Tyler Wellington 1806-1877	Married Abigail S. French. Moved to Eaton. Abigail was John⁵ S. French's daughter.
7.	Betsey Eaton 1810-1828	Died young.
8.	Leander Curtis 1813-1814	Died in infancy.
9.	Samuel⁷ Andrews 1815-1877	Married Catherine Hubbard. Moved to Eaton.

***

Genealogy Charts

Captain Samuel[6] Heard   **1773-1815 Drowned at Brompton Falls, Lower Canada**

    Married Miriam Gibbs 1797. Three of their 8 children died in infancy.
1. Henry Herschel 1799-1860. Moved to Berlin, Mass.
2. Elizabeth Andrews 1803-1844. Married Nathanial **Cooper**. Moved to Saxonville, Mass.
3. *****Samuel[7] 1805-1887** Married Sophronia (surname unknown). Lived in **Newport**. They farmed the original homestead on Parker Hill, Newport Twp. Raised six children.
4. Robert Powers 1807-1860 Married Sarah Bunker. Moved to Wisconsin, U.S.
5. Miriam Gibbs 1815-1891 Married Thomas **Brown**. Moved to Eaton Township.

    It is said that Miriam married second a Rev. Chester Heard (her cousin William[5] Heard's son); and third a John McKnight.

***

Lineage: Captain Josiah[4] **Sawyer** Family of Eaton Township

Peter Green Sawyer[5]   **1783-1867**

    Note. Peter Green Sawyer moved from Eaton Township (Sawyerville) and lived in Newport Township. Both Peter and wife Mary are buried in Grove Hill Cemetery.

    Married Polly "Mary" Hall 1785.
1. Polly Sawyer[6] 1804-1879 Married John Bennett[7] **Heard** 1797-1848. Settled in **Newport**. John Bennett is a son of Captain Edmund[6] Heard.
2. Artemas 1809-1889 Married Betsey Sunbury. Stayed in Eaton Twp.
3. Emma 1817-1868 Married George **Picard**. Became a tanner in Eaton Twp.
4. Charles 1822-1907 Married Hannah Laberee. Her family Rufus and Olive came from Charleston, Vt. in 1798 and settled in Eaton Twp.
5. Jerome 1834-1919 Married Margaret Cairns. Her family Henry and Jane came from Ballylintagh, Ireland in 1835 and settled in East Clifton.

***

Lineage: Edmund[5], **Edmund**[6] Heard children and family of Newport.

Edmund[7] Heard   **1795-1852**

    Married 1. Mary Willard in 1818
1. Mary Maria 1819-1868 Married Marshall **Rand**. Lived in **Newport**.
2. Lucy Minerva 1824-1897 Married Lewis **Bowker**. Lived in **Newport**.
3. Matilda Rosetta 1827-1870 Married 1. Charles **Planche**. Lived in **Newport**.
   Married 2. William **Stevenson**. Lived in **Newport**.

    Married 2. Abigail Haskell in 1831
4. Edmund[8] Haskell 1836-1923 Married Eliza McCurdy. Lived in **Newport**.
5. Abigail Susanna 1839-1910 Married Charles **Cable**. Moved to Auckland.

***

Lineage: Edmund[5], **Edmund**[6] **Heard** children and family of Newport

John[7] **Bennett Heard**   1797-1848

    Married **Polly Sawyer** —3 children died young or in infancy.
1.	**Augustus**[8] **1821-1905**	Married Eliza **Planche**. Lived in **Newport**.
2.	Catherine Jennete 1825-1899	Married William G. **Planche**. Lived in **Newport**.
3.	Gratia 1829-1874	Married Edward **Planche**. Moved to Eaton Twp.
4.	Bartlett 1831-1851	Moved to Chicago. Died young. No children.
5.	Cyrus Alexander 1842-1919	Married Mary E. Langton. Moved to Eaton Twp. One child Nellie died young.
6.	Maria Lily 1843-1914	Married William C. **Wilford**. Moved to **Eaton**. No children.

***

Lineage: Edmund[5], **Edmund**[6] **Heard** children and family of Newport

Luke[7] **Heard**   1803-1873

    Married **Persis Hubbard**. Three children died in infancy.
1	Lucy Gibson 1830-1875	Married Charles D. **Chaddock**. Lived in **Newport**.
2.	Achsah Hubbard 1834-1897	Married Charles **Drew**. One daughter Alice.
3.	Samuel[8] Newell 1837-1906	Married Persis D. Williams, **Randboro (Randville)**. One daughter, Phineas, died young. Samuel[8], was postmaster.
4.	*George[8] Gibson 1838-1907	Married 1. **Mary L. Sawyer*** Married 2. Achsah A Hodge George and Mary settled on his father Luke's farm.
5.	Julia A. 1844-1864	Died at age 20.

*Mary Sawyer was the great-granddaughter of Captain Josiah Sawyer; another Hurd/Sawyer connection.

***

Lineage: Edmund[5], **Edmund**[6] **Heard** children, and family of Newport

Tyler Wellington Heard/Hurd   1806-1877   *First to change surname spelling.*

  Married Abigail Sage French   1812-1891
    Her father, John[5] Sage French, drowned at Brompton Falls with Capt. Samuel Heard.
  Children born in Newport. Five of their children died young or as infants.
1.	Sarah Malvina 1836-1898	Married William **Fraser (Frasier)**. Moved to Eaton Twp.
2.	John F. 1838-1852	Killed by Indian boy, gun discharge accident while hunting.
3.	Wellington F. 1843-1870	No further information.
4.	Theodore Augustus 1850-1928	Married Ellen A. Alden. Moved to Eaton Twp. Three children, two died young.

  Children born in **Eaton** Township:
6.	Frederick Augustine 1857-1950	Direct descendant of Edmund[5] Heard, founder of **Newport**.

    Married 1. Hattie Davis 1858-1892, 3 children. Hattie died at age 34 in childbirth.
1.	Harold M. b.1880	Married Edith Murdoch
2.	Kate Marie 1882-1950	Married in 1905, Lloyd Leslie **Planche** 1881-1939.
3.	Hattie Eva b. 1892	Married S. **Carmichael**.

    Married 2. Agnes A. Baker 1868-1949
4.	Florence Agnes Hurd	Married Charles M. **Kinghorn**, from California.

***

Lineage: Edmund[5], Edmund[6] Heard children and family of Newport

Samuel Andrews[7] Heard   **1815-1877**

Married **Catherine Nash Hubbard** (1816-1885)
1.	Edward Payson 1838-1899.	Moved to Newburyport, Mass.
2.	Ellen Corilla b.1840.	Married Henry C. **Rugg.** Moved to Stanstead.
3.	Lucy Jane 1845-1871.	No children.
4.	Laura Ann b.1848	No children.
5.	Samuel Augustine b.1850.	Married. Became a lawyer. Moved to Sherbrooke. Operated a practice there.

***

Lineage: Edmund[5], Edmund[6] Heard children and family of Newport.

Sarah Hurd   **1803-1865**

Married Gardner Bartlett 1831.   Three children: two sons and one daughter. Moved to U.S.

***

Lineage: Edmund[5], Samuel[6] Heard children and family of Newport. Six children.

Samuel[7] Heard 1805-1887, married Sophronia (surname unknown). Lived in **Newport.**
1.	Sarepta A.	1830-1884	Married Henry **Alger** (son of Asa and Abigail Sawyer).
2.	Samuel A	1831	
3.	Annet	1833	
4.	Elbs	1835	
5.	Elvira	1839	Schoolteacher in 1861. Single.
6.	Ann Maria	1835	

Author's note:* Sarepta A. Heard, a daughter of Samuel and Sophronia, married Henry Alger as her second husband in 1854. Henry was the son of Asa and Abigail Alger (Sawyer), daughter of Capt. Josiah and Susanna Sawyer, another Sawyer/Heard connection.

***

Heard/Hurd, Rand, Bowker, Cable, Planche & McCurdy Connections

Lineage: Edmund[5], Edmund[6], Edmund[7] Heard/Hurd/Mary Maria Heard/**Hurd**/Marshall **Rand** families of Newport
The Hurd/Rand Connection

Mary Maria Hurd (note name change**)   1819-1878**

Married **Marshall[7] Spring Rand, b. 1810.** Three children died in infancy or young.
  Marshall S. Rand, born the second son of Artemas[6] Dodge Rand and Louisa Spring Rand.
1.	Lucy Eleanor 1841-1874	No further information.
2.	Hannah Elvira 1848-1922	Married 1871 Howard **McCurdy.** One son, Marshall McCurdy.
3.	Newell Clement 1850-1922	Married first 1873 Laura **McCurdy.** Four children.
		Married second: his brother Austin's widow, Flora A. Rand
4.	Austin Spring 1852-1895	Married Flora Arrabella Rand. (his first cousin and daughter of Gardner[8] S. D. Rand). No children.
5.	Willard Stedman 1854-1915	Married 1878 Sarah **McCurdy.** Son, Scott[9] Rand born in 1881.
6.	Frederick George 1854-1875	Died at age 21.
7.	Gardner Wheeler Rand 1866	Married Lila Parker (twin sister of Lottie who married Charlie McCallum)

***

Lineage: Edmund[5], Edmund[6], **Edmund**[7] Heard/Hurd/Matilda R. Heard/Charles **Planche** families of Newport.

The first Heard/Planche connection

Matilda Rosetta Heard (*note name retained***)**   **1827-1870**

    Married first Charles **Planche 1823-1847**
    1.   Mary Elizabeth 1846-1939.   Married Elijah **Leggett.** Moved to Auckland Twp.
    Married second in 1851, William Stevenson
    2.   Lucy A Stevenson   Married Herman **Gates.** Moved to Eaton.
    3.   Sarah Stevenson   Married first: **Goodenough.** Moved to Hampton.
    4.   Edith Stevenson   Married T. **Studd.** Moved to the U.S.
    5.   **Herman A. Stevenson**   Lived in Learned Plain, **Newport.**

***

Lineage: Edmund[5], Edmund[6], **Edmund**[7] Heard/Hurd/Lucy M. Hurd /Lewis **Bowker** families of Newport.

The Hurd/Bowker Connection

Lyman James and Betsey (Merriam) Bowker resided in Lunenburg, Vt., where all five of their children were born. They immigrated to Newport in 1834 and lived on the North River Road in Newport Township. Lyman established the property where "Bowker families" still reside. Lewis was the second son of Lyman & Betsey.

Lucy Minerva Hurd (*note name change*) **1834-1897**

    Married Lewis **Bowker** 1845
    1.   Edmund Hurd 1849-1929   Married Lucy Ferguson. Moved to the U.S.
    2.   Lyman James 1853-1924   Married Clarinda Harvey. Moved to Eaton Twp.
    3.   **Herbert Rice 1857-1950**   Married Ormasinda Farnsworth. Lived in **Newport.**
    4.   **Luvia Amanda 1855-1884**   Married Artemas S. **Farnsworth.** Lived in **Learned Plain, Newport.**

***

Lineage: Edmund[5], Edmund[6], **Edmund**[7] Heard/**Hurd** children, and families of Newport.

The Hurd/McCurdy Connection

Edmund[8] **Haskell Hurd** (*note name change*) **1836-1923**

    Married first **Eliza McCurdy** in 1863   Eliza died in 1888.
    1.   **Laura Abigail 1865**   Married Valentine **Swail. Farmed in Newport.** Raised three children, one died young.
    2.   Mary Maria 1870 U.S.   Moved to Boston. Married Gifford **Lawson.** Resided in the
    3.   **Sarah Eliza 1875**   Married **Augustus**[9] **Hurd.** Lived on the John Bennett[7] and Polly (Sawyer) Heard farm in **Newport.** Raised three boys.
    4.   Jessie Minerva 1878   Married Joseph **Riddell.** Moved to Eaton Twp. No children.

    Married second: Adelene **Stevenson** 1892-1907.   No children.

Genealogy Charts

***

Lineage: Edmund[5], Edmund[6], **Edmund**[7] Heard/Hurd/Abigail S. **Hurd**/Charles **Cable** families of Newport.
The Hurd/Cable Connection

Abigail Susanna Hurd (*note name change*)   1839-1910

>   Married **Charles Cable**
>   1.   Flora May Cable 1865-1943   Married A. **LaFleur**. Moved to Auckland Twp.

***

Lineage: Edmund[5], Edmund[6], **John Bennett**[7] Heard Children of Newport.

John[7] **B.** Heard/**Hurd** children and family of Newport. **The second Hurd/Planche connection**

Augustus[8] **Hurd** (*note name change*) **1821-1905**

>   Married **Eliza Ann Planche** in 1847
>   1.   **John Bennett**[9] 1850-1907   Married Emma J. **Austin**. Lived in **Newport**.
>   One daughter, Flora, married Clark Willard.
>   2.   **Ella Jane** 1853-1926   Married Lorin[2] G. **Jones**. Lived in **Newport**. No children.
>   3.   Edith A. 1857-1920   Married Charles **Lindsey**. Moved to U.S. Two children.
>   4.   Ellen 1861-1953   Married Hazen **Beecher**. Moved to the U.S. No children.
>   5.   Eliza Mary 1863-1953   Married Henry S. **Nourse**. Moved to Coaticook. No children.
>   6.   **Augustus**[9] **Frederick 1866-1956**   Married second cousin, **Sarah Eliza Hurd** (daughter of
>   Edmund[8] Haskell Hurd). They lived on the John B[7] and Polly (Sawyer) Heard farm in **Newport**.

***

Lineage: Edmund[5], Edmund[6], **John B**[7] Heard/Hurd/**Catherine J. Heard/Planche** children and families of Newport.

The third Heard/Planche connection

Catherine Jennete ("Janet") Heard (*note no name change*)   1825-1899

>   Married **William George Planche** in 1842.
>   *Author's note: Lived and raised their family in Newport as farmers, moved to Massachusetts
>   briefly, and returned to live in Currie Hill. William died at 77 in Newport in 1888; Jennete died in
>   Bridgewater, Mass. in 1899 at her daughter Lucy (Lothrop)'s home.*
>
>   1.   John William 1843-1901.   Married Lenora Williams. Lived at Currie Hill. Three children:
>   **Eva** married Robert **Seale**, continued to live in **Newport**;
>   Frederick married Ellen A. **Frasier** of Eaton Twp.; and Florence
>   married Ernie **Taylor** of **Newport Twp.**
>   2.   Emma Elizabeth 1844   Married Willis **Jordan**. Lived at Jordan Hill, Eaton.
>   One child, Fred.
>   3.   Lucy Ann 1846-1916   Married Howard **Lothrop**. Moved to the U.S.
>   4.   Elva Jennette 1848   Married Eben **Lothrop**. Moved to the U.S.
>   5.   Charles Edward 1853-1924   Married Kate M. Sunbury (Cora Austin's sister). Moved to
>   NY. Adopted a son, Russell Planche (Cora's only nephew).
>   6.   **Henry B. 1853-1929**   Married 1. Jennie **Grant,** 2 children Roy and Leon.
>   Married 2. Matilda Smiley, 2 children, Ada, and Fred. Raised
>   the four children in **Randboro, Newport.**
>   7.   **Corilla** 1857-1924   Married William Stone (brother of Charlie Stone, Randboro
>   Mill operator). Also **lived in Randboro, Newport**. No children.

***

Lineage: Edmund[5], Edmund[6], **John B**[7] Heard/Hurd/**Gratia A Heard/Planche** family of **Newport**

The fourth Hurd/Planche connection

Gratia A. Hurd (note name change) **1829-1874**

    Married Edward **Planche** in 1855   Moved to Eaton Township.
    1.   Ada 1857   Married Alexander Ross in 1892. No children.
    2.   John Harold, 1865-1958   Married Charlotte McKay.

***

Lineage: Edmund[5], Edmund[6], **John B**[7] Heard/Hurd children and family of Newport.

Cyrus Alexander Hurd (note name change) **1842-1919**

    Married Mary Langdon   Moved to Eaton Township. One child.
    1.   Nellie 1866-1880   Died young

***

Lineage: Edmund[5], Edmund[6], **Luke**[7] Heard/Hurd/**Lucy G. Heard**/Charles D. **Chaddock** children and family of Newport.

Lucy Gibson[8] **Heard** (note no name change) **1830-1875**

    Married: Charles D. **Chaddock.**   First six children died young. Lived in **Newport.**
    1.   George C. 1866-1938.   Married Ida Blodgette. Three daughters: Miriam, Pearl, Ruth.

***

Lineage: Edmund[5], Edmund[6], **Luke**[7], Heard/Hurd/**Achsah H. Heard**/Charles **Drew's** children and family of Newport.

Achsah Hubbard Heard (note original name) **1834-1897**

    Married: Charles **Drew**   One daughter died at age 20.

***

Lineage: Edmund[5], Edmund[6], **Luke**[7], Heard /Hurd/**Samuel N. Heard** children and family of Newport.

Samuel[8] **Newell Heard** (note original name) **1837-1901**

    Married: Persis D Williams   One daughter, Phineas, died at age 21. Lived in **Newport.**

***

Genealogy Charts

Lineage: Edmund[5], Edmund[6], **Luke**[7] Heard/ Hurd/**George G. Hurd** children and family of Newport.

George[8] **Gibson Hurd** (note name change) 1838-1907

    Married 1. Mary Lorinda **Sawyer**   Died young at 37. No children.
    Married 2. Achsah Amelia **Hodge**

1.   **Alonzo George** 1882-1934.   Married Evelyn (Eva) F. Robinson. Lived in **Newport**. Moved to Sawyerville, Eaton.
2.   Julia Lois 1893-1976.   Married Lloyd **Hunt**. Moved to Sawyerville, Eaton.

***

Lineage: Edmund[5], Edmund[6], **Luke**[7] Heard/Hurd/**Edmund**[8], children and family of Newport

Edmund[8] **Haskell and Eliza (McCurdy) Hurd** family and children of Newport.

Laura Abigail Hurd 1865-1942
Married Valentine **Swail** 1863-1946   Married 1886, **lived in Newport**.
1.   Lawrence Hurd 1890-1965   Married Mildred McFee. Moved to Alberta.
2.   Evelyn Sarah Eliza 1893-1956   Married Rufus H. **Riddell.** Lived in Auckland, then Alberta.
3.   Emerson Henry 1901-1917   Died young.

Mary Maria Hurd 1870-1938
Married Gifford Hazel **Lawson** 1880-1954   Married in 1907. Moved to Alabama, U.S.
1.   Gifford Edmund Lawson 1880-1954

Sarah Eliza Hurd 1875-1961
Married Augustus[9] Frederick **Hurd** 1866-1956   Married in 1892, lived in **Newport**.
1.   **Edmund**[10] **Lionel** 1907-2001   Married 1. Mary Eva Wood of Bulwer.
                                               Married 2. Margaret "Irene" Mathew. Lived in **Newport**.
                                               Married 3. Kathleen "Kay" (Ward) Harding. **Newport.**
2.   Frederick Karl 1910-1984   Married Florence Stoddard. Moved to Sawyerville, Eaton.
3.   Arthur Haskell 1914-2000   Married Helen Tannahill of **Newport**. Moved to Port Arthur, Ont., then to Vancouver, B.C.

Jessie Minerva 1878-1957
Married 1902, Joseph **Riddell** 1873-1945.   No children. Lived in **Newport**. Moved to Eaton Twp.

***

Lineage: Edmund[5], Edmund[6], **Luke**[7], **George G**[8] Hurd family and children of Newport

Alonzo George[9] Hurd 1882-1941
Married Evelyn "Eva" Francis, **Robinson** 1884-1967
1.   George[10] Robinson 1913-1980   Married Doris Eva Nugent in 1945. One son, two daughters. Moved to Sawyerville, Eaton.
2.   Bertha Evelyn 1916-2003   Married Lloyd Robert **French of Newport**. One son, two daughters. Moved to Sawyerville, Eaton.
3.   Eric James 1920-1988   Married Bernice M. Baker in England. Three sons, two daughters. Moved to Toronto.

Julia Lois Hurd 1893-1976
Married Lloyd H. Hunt in 1918.   Resided in Sawyerville, Eaton.
1.   Bruce H., 1925   Married Charlotte Whitcomb. Moved to Buckingham, Que.
2.   Gordon G.   Married Jean Robinson. Moved to Chapidos, Que.

***

Lineage 1: Edmund^5, Edmund^6, **John B^7**, Augustus^8, Augustus^9 F. Hurd.
Lineage 2: Edmund^5, Edmund^6, **Edmund^7**, Edmund^8 H., Sarah Eliza^9 Hurd.

Augustus^9 Hurd and Sarah Eliza Hurd's children and families of Newport. Three sons.
Note: Augustus^8 F. Hurd married his **second Cousin** Sarah E. Hurd

*Author's note: These three families are descendants of both Col. Edmund Heard and Capt. Josiah Sawyer; the connections are in the seventh generation as bolded. **John B.**^{7} married Josiah's granddaughter, Polly^2 Sawyer.*

Edmund^{10} Lionel Hurd 1907-2001
Married first: 1939, Eva Mary Wood 1914-1999

1. James Norman 1939 (adopted) — Raised in Montreal and moved to Toronto. Married Evelyn **Lawrie** 1938-2007. Raised two sons David and Murray, and daughter, Lawrie. Second son, Murray Edmund 1968-1972, died at age four.
2. Frederick Edmund^{11} 1940 — **Raised in Newport**, moved to Ontario. Married Sandra Kathryn Blair b. 1943 (Planche and Hurd descent). Moved to Ontario. Raised two daughters: Wendy Kathryn and Joanne Michele.

Married second: 1947, Margaret Irene Matthew 1909-1980. No children.
Resided on the original **Colonel Edmund^5 Heard homestead in Newport**.

Married third: 1992, Kathleen Anna (Ward) Harding, b. 1922. No children.
At the time of writing (2021), Kathleen resides at the Wales Home in Richmond, Que.

Frederick Karl Hurd 1910-1984
Married: Florence Stoddard 1910-1984 — Moved to Sawyerville, Eaton. Four children.

1. Judith Carol 1943 — Married 1. Keith D. **Joliffe** in 1965. Moved to Montreal, raised two sons, Robert Donald and Stephen Andrew. Married 2. Jean-Marie **Bernard**, no children.
2. John Alan 1945 — Married Denise Vallee in 1970. Moved to Montreal. Raised a daughter, Caroline Amy, son Allen Peter Edmund
3. Peter Donald 1949 — Married Linda Taylor 1945-2013 Moved to Nova Scotia. No children. Married second: Ann Fogarty in 2016.
4. Elizabeth Jean 1951 — Married in 1968, Robert Leslie **Richardson.** Moved to Montreal, with a second residence in Eaton Township. Two daughters, Cynthia Leigh and Joanne Gail.

Arthur Haskell^9 Hurd 1917-2000
Married: Helen Alberta Tannahill of Newport 1919-2004.

Moved to Ontario, then to Vancouver, B.C. Two sons.

1. Malcolm Edward 1947 — Married Doris Ruth Dreger. One daughter, Kelsie.
2. Graeme Haskell^{10} 1953-1984 — Unmarried. No children.

***

Genealogy Charts

Lineage: Edmund[5], Edmund[6], **Luke**[7], George G[8], **Alonzo George**[9] Hurd children and family of Newport

George[10] Robinson Hurd   1913-1980
Married 1945, Doris Eva Nugent 1924-1968. Born at Maple Grove, moved to **Newport.** One son, two daughters. Resided in Sawyerville, Eaton Twp.

1.	Allan Grant 1947	Married 1. Marie Andree St. Amande. Daughter: Annie Pierre. Married 2. Gayle A. Chiykowski. Step-Dtrs: Laura and Dahlke. Married 3. Susan Elizabeth Wilson.
2.	Cynthia Doris 1950	Married Allen Gratian **Clovis.** Daughters: Tanya and Mykl.
3.	Deanna Evelyn 1953	Married David Arthur **Jones.** Daughters: Kylah and Robyn.

Bertha Evelyn Hurd 1916-2003
Married 1939, **Lloyd Robert**[2] **French** 1910-1998

Resident of **Newport.** One son, two daughters. Moved to Sawyerville, Eaton Twp.

1.	Eric George[11] Robert[3] 1942	Married James Arneauld
2.	Barbara Ann 1947	Married Harry Irving **Lawson.** Two daughters: Leanne and Angela
3.	Susan J. 1956	Married Hugh **Rutherford.** Two daughters: Shari and Krysten

Eric James Hurd 1920-1988
Married 1943 in England, Bernice Maureen Baker 1923-2016.

Two daughters, three sons. Moved first to Sawyerville, then to Toronto.

1.	Gillian Maureen 1944	Married James D. **Anderson.** Son Stephen; daughter Heather.
2.	James Rodney 1946	Married Janet Scott. Two sons: Andrew and Jonathan.
3.	Keith William 1951	Married Annie Po-Lin Mark. Two sons: Geoffrey and Michael.
4.	Deborah Frances 1956	Married Gary **Deller.** Son Bradley, daughter Sarah.
5.	Thomas Eric[2] 1957	Married Bronwyn Jones. Two sons: Eric[3] and Gavin.

***

Lineage 1: Edmund[5], Edmund[6], **John B**[7], Augustus[8], Augustus[9] F., **Edmund**[10] **L. Hurd**
Lineage 2: Edmund[5], Edmund[6], **Edmund**[7], Edmund[8] H., Sarah Eliza[9], **Edmund**[10] **L. Hurd**
Lineage 3: Edmund[5], Edmund[6], **Tyler**[7], Frederick[8], Kate Marie[9] (Hurd) Planche, **Laura**[10] **(Planche)** Blair

Frederick Edmund[11] Hurd, b. 1940
Married 1964: Sandra K. Blair, b. 1943, daughter of Charles Leidy Blair and Laura (Planche), a Hurd descendant.

1.	Wendy Kathryn b. 1965	Married J. Brooks. Divorced. No children. Lives in Ontario.
2.	Joanne Michele b. 1967	Married David Michael **Morris.** Daughter: Dayna Pauline Morris, b. 2010. Stepdaughter, Vanessa L. Morris, b.1995. Family lives in Ontario.

Author's note: Wendy, Joanne and Dayna are direct descendants of both Col. Edmund[5] Heard and Capt. Josiah[4] Sawyer.

***

Reference Materials

Footnotes:

1. Wikipedia: Eastern Townships — Internet
2. Early Military History Eastern Townships, unpublished, no date, 4pp. typewritten Lt. Colonel E. Dennison E.D.
3. Heard/Hurd Military History…..unpublished 1792 and up — Hurd Family Collection
4. "John Heard of Ipswich, Mass" 290 pp. & "The Ancestors and Descendants of Col. Edmund Heard of Newport Township" 48 pp. Author and Genealogy Professor Edward Hanson — Hurd Family Collection
5. The Loyal American Associators of Boston, Worcester County, "Mass Warnings 1737-1788" p. 310 Hurd family Collection
6. Maple Leaf Cemetery, donated by William Heard document — Hurd family Collection
7. Microfilm C2532 pp. 51115, 51121 & 51129 — Lower Canada Land Records
8. "Le Haut Francois Paper." Published Interview w/E. L. Hurd Aug 24, 1995 — Hurd family Collection
9. "Historical Facts." Samuel A Hurd, family records. Unpublished — Hurd Family Collection
10. Heard/Hurd family letters, Section One…Unpublished — Hurd Family collection
11. Heard/Hurd Records Heard Collection 1850 (vol. AA-1 Baker Lib. Harvard Univ.) (77 pp.) — Samuel A. Hurd
12. New England Historical and Genealogical Register — Fiche no 143[1989]: 220
13. Old Families of Salisbury and Amesbury, 382. — David Hoyt
14. Historic Ipswich Website & Town Records. — Historian Gordon Harris
15. Jacob Hurd & His Sons Silversmiths 1752, Hurd Family Collection, Published 1972 — Author Hollis French
16. History of Compton County 1896 — Publisher L. S. Channell
17. History of the Eastern Townships- Civil & Descriptive Published 1869 — Mrs. C. M. Day
18. Excerpts" Puritan Paths from Naumkeag to Piscataquis" Historic Ipswich (Published by Newbury Press 1963) Lawrence G Dodge & Alice C Dodge
19. Certificate signed by Col Edmund Heard[5] for Edmund Heard[6] as Sergeant — Hurd Family Collection
20. Newport First Records 1800 -1814 (76 pp.) Hand-written Unpublished — Hurd Family Collection
21. Heard/Hurd Family Letters Section Two — Hurd Family Collection
22. Notice of Smallpox, Posted in Newport Oct. 20, 1810 — Hurd Family Collection
23. Josiah Sawyer papers Typewritten document …Unpublished — Hurd Family Collection
24. Glimpses into The Past. (1872) Island Brook, Newport, Published 1951 — Bertha Weston Price
25. The Early Days of Eaton Vol. 1., printed/published 1980 — Waymer Laberee
26. Blood and Daring, How Canada fought the Civil War, published 2014 — John Boyko
27. Even the Owl is not Heard, Published in 2011, Surveyor David Thompsons 1834 Journals — Barbara Verity and Gilles Peloquin
28. Newport Township (1799 Lot applications overlayed on map) Conception Graphique 1995 — Rene Roy
29. The Loyalists of the Eastern Townships of Quebec, published as Centennial (1783-1983) 1984 ….Historical Sketches, Biographical Descriptions, Annals, Narratives, Verse. — Various Writers.
30. Massachusetts Justice. A collection of the laws of the Commonwealth of Massachusetts,1795-1802. Published Portland 1802 — Samuel Freeman, Esq.
31. Handwritten collection: Documents, IOU's, deeds, newspapers, Business letters — Hurd Family Collection
32. Island Brook: Then & Now unpublished typed booklet- Ruth (Burns) Morrow Revised Edition Geraldine (Morrow) Macaulay 1995
33. Knicky Knocky A story of Knicky Knocky Unpublished typed booklet No date… — Nina (Parsons) Rowell
34. Hon. John Henry Pope Eastern Townships Politician Thesis Unpublished typewritten booklet 1966. Author Waymer S. Laberee
35. The Canadian Housewife. An Alternate History… Published 2005 — Rosemary Neering

36.	The Imps and Bill McCallum the Glassman, 1993	Freeman Clowery
37.	History Old Trinity Lodge Lancaster Printed 1778, Past Master	Jonathan Smith
38.	Newport Field book (surveyor 1799) hand-written.	Christopher Bailey Leamington, Vt.
39.	The Witch of New Mexico Road Grant Myers (QAHN Article writer) & Hist. of Island Brook, Author Ruth Burns
40.	Sawyerville Reunion 1994 (Prepared by Committee) printed booklet	Chair. Florence (Bowker) McVetty
41.	Edmund H Haskell Hurd Diary and letters (1875 & 1905-1919) U. S. A	Terry and Mary-Hurd Lawson
42.	Past Life Tools	Andrew Hind
43.	A Treasury of Historical Articles, 228 pp. compiled by her daughter Nina (Parsons) Rowell. Mrs. George Parsons	
44.	Colebrook, N.H. 2019-20 Information & early maps	Kiwanis Club, Colebrook N.H.
45.	Illustrated Atlas of the Dominion of Canada, published 1881	H. Bilden & Co., Toronto, Can.
46.	Edith (Morrison) Rand diaries (personal archives 1922-1968)	Rand family historical collection, Carol Rand
47.	Autobiographical Recollections: Study the past to plan the future	Ernest C. McCallum
48.	Timeline-English-speaking Quebec	Heather Darch (QAHN)
49.	The U.E.L. A Chronicle of the Great Migration, Vol 13, 1914.	W. Stewart Wallace

Printed Primary Sources:

- *History of Compton County*, by L. S. Channell, 1896
- *History of the Eastern Townships*, by Catherine M. Day, 1869
- *Glimpses Into the Past*, by Bertha W. Price (born in Newport in 1872), circa 1923-1951
- *Jacob Hurd and His Sons Nathaniel & Benjamin*, by Hollis French (1868-1940), 1972
- *The Loyalists of the Eastern Townships of Quebec*, by Sir John Johnson Centennial Branch of UELAC, 1992
- *The Loyalists of Quebec 1774-1825: A Forgotten History*, by Heritage Branch of UELAC, 1989
- *Even the Owl is Not Heard: David Thompson's 1834 Journals in the Eastern Townships of Quebec*, by Barbara Verity and Gilles Peloquin, 2011
- *Quebec 1850-1950*, pictorial by Lionel Koffler, 2005
- *The Canadian Housewife: An Affectionate History*, by Rosemary Neering, 2005
- *Blood and Daring: How Canada Fought the American Civil War and Forged a Nation*, by John Boyko, 2013
- *"The fostering care of Government": Lord Dalhousie's 1821 Survey of the Eastern Townships*, research note by J. I. Little, 2010
- *State and Society in Transition: The Politics of Institutional Reform in the Eastern Townships, 1838-1852*, by J. I. Little, 1997

Printed Secondary Sources:

- *Historic Ipswich (1600-1800), A Walking Tour*, and *Brief History*, publications by Ipswich Chamber of Commerce
- *Hon. John Henry Pope, Eastern Townships politician,* M.A. thesis by Waymer S. Laberee, 1966
- *The Early Days of Eaton*, Vol. 1, by Waymer S. Laberee, 1980
- *Island Brook: Then and Now*, by Ruth Burns Morrow, revised edition by Geraldine Morrow Macaulay, 1995
- *Knicky Knocky 1836-1957* by Nina (Parsons) Rowell
- *Sawyerville Reunion 1994*, by Florence McVetty and committee
- *The Imps and Bill McCallum, the Glass Man*, by Freeman Clowery, 1993
- Kiwanis, Colebrook, N. Hampshire
- *Quebec Heritage News* magazines, QAHN, articles and authors as referenced
- Sketches of historical tools, by Andrew Hind
- *A Treasury of Historical Articles*, manuscript by Mrs. George Parsons, compiled by daughter Nina Rowell
- *Newport Homecoming, 1801-1996*, by community of Island Brook

Reference Materials

Newspapers:

- *The Globe*, 1867, original copy
- *Compton County Chronical*, 1893, original copy
- *Newburyport Daily News*, 1899
- *Sherbrooke Daily Record*, various dates

Other:

- *Newport Firfh Records, 1791-1816*, handwritten 76-page bound book of legal information
- Josiah Sawyer early papers, complied by E. L. Hurd
- Edward Hanson, Professor of History, Northwestern University; compiled an extensive 290-page document on the Heard/Hurd Genealogy, the family of his paternal grandmother
- Samuel A. Hurd, 77-page Heard/Hurd family manuscript, 1850. Heard/Hurd collection {Vol. AA-1} Letters- Baker Library, Harvard University
- Edith (Morrison) Rand, daily diaries from 1922 to 1968
- Autobiographical recollections (circa 1900-1925), Ernest McCallum
- Edmund Haskell Hurd, daily diary of 1875; a year in the life of a Newport farmer
- Capt. Edmund[10] Lionel Hurd, personal diary and letters, Hong Kong POW (1941-1945).

www.ingramcontent.com/pod-product-compliance
Lightning Source LLC
Chambersburg PA
CBHW081404080526
44589CB00016B/2476